Lecture Notes of the Institute for Computer Sciences, Social Informatics and Telecommunications Engineering

Editorial Board Members

Ozgur Akan, *Middle East Technical University, Ankara, Türkiye*
Paolo Bellavista, *University of Bologna, Bologna, Italy*
Jiannong Cao, *Hong Kong Polytechnic University, Hong Kong, China*
Geoffrey Coulson, *Lancaster University, Lancaster, UK*
Falko Dressler, *University of Erlangen, Erlangen, Germany*
Domenico Ferrari, *Università Cattolica Piacenza, Piacenza, Italy*
Mario Gerla, *UCLA, Los Angeles, USA*
Hisashi Kobayashi, *Princeton University, Princeton, USA*
Sergio Palazzo, *University of Catania, Catania, Italy*
Sartaj Sahni, *University of Florida, Gainesville, USA*
Xuemin Shen, *University of Waterloo, Waterloo, Canada*
Mircea Stan, *University of Virginia, Charlottesville, USA*
Xiaohua Jia, *City University of Hong Kong, Kowloon, Hong Kong*
Albert Y. Zomaya, *University of Sydney, Sydney, Australia*

The LNICST series publishes ICST's conferences, symposia and workshops.
LNICST reports state-of-the-art results in areas related to the scope of the Institute.
The type of material published includes

- Proceedings (published in time for the respective event)
- Other edited monographs (such as project reports or invited volumes)

LNICST topics span the following areas:

- General Computer Science
- E-Economy
- E-Medicine
- Knowledge Management
- Multimedia
- Operations, Management and Policy
- Social Informatics
- Systems

Francis C. M. Lau · Edmund Lai · Ivan W. H. Ho
Editors

Smart Grid and Innovative Frontiers in Telecommunications

Ninth EAI International Conference, SmartGift 2024
Hong Kong, China, December 9–10, 2024
Proceedings

Editors
Francis C. M. Lau
The Hong Kong Polytechnic University
Kowloon, Hong Kong

Edmund Lai
Auckland University of Technology
Auckland, New Zealand

Ivan W. H. Ho
The Hong Kong Polytechnic University
Kowloon, Hong Kong

ISSN 1867-8211 ISSN 1867-822X (electronic)
Lecture Notes of the Institute for Computer Sciences, Social Informatics
and Telecommunications Engineering
ISBN 978-3-031-96145-8 ISBN 978-3-031-96146-5 (eBook)
https://doi.org/10.1007/978-3-031-96146-5

© ICST Institute for Computer Sciences, Social Informatics and Telecommunications Engineering 2026

This work is subject to copyright. All rights are solely and exclusively licensed by the Publisher, whether the whole or part of the material is concerned, specifically the rights of translation, reprinting, reuse of illustrations, recitation, broadcasting, reproduction on microfilms or in any other physical way, and transmission or information storage and retrieval, electronic adaptation, computer software, or by similar or dissimilar methodology now known or hereafter developed.
The use of general descriptive names, registered names, trademarks, service marks, etc. in this publication does not imply, even in the absence of a specific statement, that such names are exempt from the relevant protective laws and regulations and therefore free for general use.
The publisher, the authors and the editors are safe to assume that the advice and information in this book are believed to be true and accurate at the date of publication. Neither the publisher nor the authors or the editors give a warranty, expressed or implied, with respect to the material contained herein or for any errors or omissions that may have been made. The publisher remains neutral with regard to jurisdictional claims in published maps and institutional affiliations.

This Springer imprint is published by the registered company Springer Nature Switzerland AG
The registered company address is: Gewerbestrasse 11, 6330 Cham, Switzerland

If disposing of this product, please recycle the paper.

Preface

We are delighted to introduce the proceedings of the ninth edition of the European Alliance for Innovation (EAI) International Conference on Smart Grid and Innovative Frontiers in Telecommunications (SmartGIFT 2024). This conference brought together researchers, developers and practitioners around the world to explore the forefront of smart grid and telecommunications technologies for smart cities.

The technical program of SmartGIFT 2024 consisted of 31 full papers, including 3 invited papers in oral presentation sessions at the main conference tracks. The conference tracks were: Track 1 – Smart Grid and Energy Systems; Track 2 – Vehicular Networks and Intelligent Transportation Systems; Track 3 – Communication Technologies I; Track 4 – Artificial Intelligence and Information Security; Track 5 – Communication Technologies II; and Track 6 – Autonomous and Electric Vehicles. Aside from the high-quality technical paper presentations, the technical program also featured two keynote speeches on "Joint Source-Channel Coding Systems based on Double-Protograph Low-Density Parity-Check Codes" presented by Francis C. M. Lau from The Hong Kong Polytechnic University, China, and "From Wireless Network Research to LLMind: Integrating Generative AI, IoT, and Human Intelligence for Superintelligent Systems" presented by Soung Chang Liew from The Chinese University of Hong Kong, China.

Coordination with the steering chairs, Victor C. M. Leung and Kun Yang, and member Peter H. J. Chong, was essential for the success of the conference. We sincerely appreciate their constant support and guidance. It was also a great pleasure to work with such an excellent organizing committee team for their hard work in organizing and supporting the conference. In particular, the Technical Program Committee, led by our TPC Co-Chairs, Francis C. M. Lau and Edmund Lai, completed the peer-review process of technical papers and made a high-quality technical program. We are also grateful to the Conference Manager, Veronika Kissova, for her support and to all the authors who submitted their papers to the SmartGIFT 2024 conference.

We strongly believe that SmartGIFT provides a good forum for all researchers, developers and practitioners to discuss all science and technology aspects that are relevant to smart grids and telecommunications. We also expect that future SmartGIFT conferences will be as successful and stimulating as indicated by the contributions presented in this volume.

Ivan W. H. Ho

Organization

Steering Committee

Peter H. J. Chong	Auckland University of Technology, New Zealand
Victor C. M. Leung	University of British Columbia, Canada
Kun Yang	University of Essex, UK

Organizing Committee

General Chairs

Ivan W. H. Ho	Hong Kong Polytechnic University, China
Ping Shum	Southern University of Science and Technology, China

Technical Program Chairs

Edmund Lai	Auckland University of Technology, New Zealand
Francis C. M. Lau	Hong Kong Polytechnic University, China
Saeed Rehman	Flinders University, Australia

Web Chair

Minglong Zhang	Mississippi State University, USA

Publicity and Social Media Chairs

Yuyi Mao	Hong Kong Polytechnic University, China
Kushan Sudheera	University of Ruhuna, Sri Lanka

Workshops Chair

William Liu	Unitec, New Zealand

Sponsorship and Exhibits Chair

Maode Ma — Qatar University, Qatar

Publications Chair

Duaa Zuhair Abduljabbar Al-Hamid — Auckland University of Technology, New Zealand

Local Chairs

Edward Cheung — Hong Kong Polytechnic University, China
Bishenghui Tao — Hong Kong Metropolitan University, China

Technical Program Committee

Siqi Bu	Hong Kong Polytechnic University, China
David Chan	Hong Kong Education University, China
Ben Cheng	Royal Melbourne Institute of Technology, Australia
Masoto Chiputa	Auckland University of Technology, New Zealand
Peter Chong	Auckland University of Technology, New Zealand
Kai Fung Chu	University of Cambridge, UK
Zhiguo Ding	University of Manchester, UK
Pejman Karegar	Auckland University of Technology, New Zealand
Bruce Leow	University of Technology Malaysia, Malaysia
Wei Lin	Hong Kong Polytechnic University, China
Liang Liu	Hong Kong Polytechnic University, China
Yuyi Mao	Hong Kong Polytechnic University, China
Josyl Reyes	University of Santo Tomas, Philippines
Zhengguo Sheng	University of Sussex, UK
Rui Song	Hong Kong Polytechnic University, China
Bishenghui Tao	Hong Kong Metropolitan University, China
Xinyu Wang	Harbin Institute of Technology, China
Yuhao Wang	Tsinghua University, China
Lingfu Xie	Ningbo University, China
Qingqing Ye	Hong Kong Polytechnic University, China
Shengli Zhang	Shenzhen University, China
Shuowen Zhang	Hong Kong Polytechnic University, China

Contents

Smart Grid and Energy Systems

Large Language Models in Smart Grid: Applications and Risks 3
  Jinze Li, Jinfeng Xu, Shuo Yang, and Edith C. H. Ngai

Mapping Optimal Space Simplification Analysis in Triple Phase Shift
Control of Dual Active Bridge Converters 20
  Wenjie Xu, Junwei Liu, Wenzheng Xu, Yixin Wang, and Taiming Chen

Modelling of a Vibration Based Kinetic Energy Harvester for Condition
Monitoring and Fault Prediction in HVDC Systems 34
  Qinwei He, Tian Lan, Chris van den Bos, Peng Li, and Richard Visee

Dual-Attention Fusion Transformer for Electricity Theft Detection
to Secure Smart Grids 47
  Cai Guo, Bishenghui Tao, and Hong-Ning Dai

Multi-objective Optimization of Energy Storage Capacity Using
Non-Dominated Sorting Artificial Cooperative Search and Composite
Weighted TOPSIS 60
  *Xiao Ye, Anping Li, Feng Mu, Xiaofeng Chen, Xiangjuan Meng,
  Shilei Li, Jingyao Yang, Liguo Yang, and Hongmei Li*

Vehicular Networks and ITS

Development of a Cost-Effective V2X Test-Bed to Study the Characteristics
of Vehicular Networks 73
  *Manoj Bandara Dissanayake, Shamika Lakshan Indrasiri,
  Hasini Prabodhika Dematawaarachchi,
  Kalupahana Liyanage Kushan Sudheera, and Peter Han Joo Chong*

Federated Learning-Based Channel Estimation in Vehicular Networks 90
  Cao Ding and Ivan Wang-Hei Ho

Deep Q-Network Based Intelligent Traffic Signal Control: Case Study
of a Large Single Intersection Using SUMO 108
  Wanshu Wang, Xutao Mei, Zheng Wang, Bo Yang, and Kimihiko Nakano

DCA-YOLO: Non-Prominent Feature Object Detection Using
the Dynamic Convolution Attention YOLO Model 117
   Yang Li, Xiaolong Yang, Yuekun Hei, and Xuting Duan

A Cross-Layer Congestion-Aware Routing Protocol for UAV-Aided
VANETs with Enhanced Line-of-Sight Communication 131
   *Prangya Priyadarshini, Lopamudra Hota, Arun Kumar,
and Peter Han Joo Chong*

Communication Technologies I

Pointing Errors Analysis for Inter-satellite MRR PNC System 147
   Hangfei Zhang, Audrey Christine Guo, Lu Lu, and Yanmei Jia

Hy-LiRF: Hybrid LiFi and WiFi Network Supporting Seamless Real-Time
Transmissions 161
   *Menghan Li, Runxin Zhang, Yuheng Zhang, Yongsheng Gong,
Jianhua He, and Lu Lu*

UAVs-Enabled Maritime Communications: Control Barrier Functions
for Physical Secure Systems 175
   *Zhitao Yu, Wake Shu, Xuanzhi Guo, Liang Mao, Guanchong Niu,
Man-On Pun, and Zhiming Cheng*

A Low-Complexity and High-Performance K-Best GFSK MSDD
with LLRs Outputs 187
   Jiajun Zhu and Francis C. M. Lau

Introduction of Direction of Arrival (DOA) Indoor and Outdoor Navigation
Based on Machine Learning 200
   Tong Liu and Wei Lin

Automatic Preamble Extraction System for LPWAN Signals 215
   Chun Ho Kong and Haibo Hu

AI and Information Security

An Automated Smart Contract Framework for NFT-Based Warranty
Management System with Account Abstraction 229
   *Sai Sambhab Chaini, Lopamudra Hota, Arun Kumar,
and Peter Han Joo Chong*

LTTS-GAN: A Long-Term Time Series Generative Adversarial Network 240
   Xiangyu Cui, Xianping Ma, Man-On Pun, and Zhimin Cheng

A Lightweight Encrypted JPEG Image Retrieval Model Based
on Self-attention Networks 258
    Yanfeng Chen, Jing Liang, and Peiya Li

Local-Channel Large Separable Kernel Attention 271
    Zengjie Deng, Tao Lei, and Haixia Cui

FLTP: A Fast and Low-Bandwidth Transaction Propagation Protocol
in Ethereum 282
    Deen Ma, Chonghe Zhao, Shengli Zhang, Taotao Wang, and Qing Yang

Communication Technologies II

Automated Topology Exploration and Design of Passive Microstrip Filters
Based on Grid-Like Topology 299
    Jingyun Bi and Xinyu Zhou

Physical Layer Security for Omni-DRIS Enhanced Visible Light
Communications 310
    Mengda Liu, Xinyan Xie, Defan Shen, Jianhua He, Yanmei Jia, and Lu Lu

A Hybrid Topological Heterostructure for Communication 324
    Xinyu Zhang, Yueyao Li, Sijie Li, and Menglin L. N. Chen

Zero-Shot Learning-Based Maritime Semantic Communication System 330
    *Lanxiang Hou, Jiayi Sun, Haoqi Liang, Liang Mao, Guanchong Niu,
Man-On Pun, and Zhiming Cheng*

Rate Optimization for Visible Light Communications Using Asymmetric
Bridged-T Pre-Equalizer 345
    Hewei Tian, Runxin Zhang, Jian Xiong, Jianhua He, and Lu Lu

Autonomous and Electric Vehicles

Mixed-Autonomy Traffic and Wireless Charging Problem for Autonomous
Electric Vehicles Using Reinforcement Learning 361
    Kai-Fung Chu, Yue Xie, Albert Y. S. Lam, and Fumiya Iida

A Review of Digital Twins for Electric Vehicles 373
    Yangyang Zhou and Chao Huang

Optimization of Orderly Charging Strategy of Electric Vehicles Based
on GWO Algorithm 385
    Shaokui Yan, Haili Ding, Fei Peng, Yuanfeng Zhou, and Ting Hu

Optimized Global Path Planning Based on Terrain Traversability Analysis by Plane Fitting Approach 402
Ruiqi Ren and Zheng Zhang

GMLO: Ground and Memory Optimized LiDAR Odometry 414
Kaiduo Fang and Rui Song

Author Index 435

Smart Grid and Energy Systems

Large Language Models in Smart Grid: Applications and Risks

Jinze Li, Jinfeng Xu, Shuo Yang, and Edith C. H. Ngai(✉)

The University of Hong Kong, Hong Kong, China
{lijinze-hku,jinfeng}@connect.hku.hk, chngai@eee.hku.hk

Abstract. The integration of Large Language Models (LLMs) in smart grid systems represents a transformative advancement in managing and securing critical energy infrastructures. By leveraging their ability to process and analyze vast datasets, LLMs can identify anomalies, enhance threat intelligence, and improve system management through natural language interfaces and automated report generation. We discuss the potential risks associated with the deployment of LLMs, including data privacy issues, security vulnerabilities, operational challenges, and ethical considerations. Through a comprehensive analysis, we aim to provide a balanced perspective on the capabilities and limitations of LLMs in smart grid, highlighting both their transformative potential and the imperative to address associated risks effectively.

Keywords: LLM · Smart Grid

1 Introduction

The convergence of artificial intelligence and energy infrastructure has ushered in a new era of possibilities for enhancing the efficiency, reliability, and security of smart grid [47]. At the forefront of this technological revolution are Large Language Models (LLMs), which have demonstrated remarkable capabilities across various domains [29,30].

Smart grid represent a significant evolution in electrical power systems, integrating advanced digital technologies to create a more responsive, efficient, and sustainable energy infrastructure [25]. These modernized grids incorporate two-way communication between utilities and consumers, real-time monitoring, and automated control systems to optimize power generation, distribution, and consumption. However, the increased connectivity and digitalization of the smart grid also introduce new vulnerabilities to cyber threats, making robust cybersecurity measures crucial for ensuring the integrity and reliability of these critical systems [21].

The smart grid ecosystem comprises several interconnected layers, including the physical infrastructure for power generation and distribution, a cyber-physical layer for control and measurement, and a cyber layer for data management and communication [26]. Each of these layers presents unique security challenges that must be addressed to maintain the overall resilience of the grid.

Digital substations, which play a pivotal role in smart grid operations, are particularly vulnerable to cyber attacks [14] due to their reliance on digital communication protocols and networked devices. The IEC 61850 standard, widely adopted for substation automation and protection, introduces sophisticated communication mechanisms such as Generic Object-Oriented Substation Events (GOOSE) [16] and Sampled Values (SV) messages. While these protocols enhance substation efficiency and flexibility, they also create potential attack vectors that malicious actors could exploit.

Traditional cybersecurity approaches for smart grid have relied on rule-based systems, signature detection, and machine learning models trained on historical data [3]. However, these methods often struggle to keep pace with the rapidly evolving threat landscape and the increasing sophistication of cyber attacks [14]. Moreover, the dynamic nature of smart grid operations, characterized by fluctuating power flows, intermittent renewable energy sources, and varying demand patterns, further complicates the task of distinguishing between normal operational anomalies and malicious activities.

In recent years, the field of artificial intelligence has witnessed remarkable advancements, particularly in the domain of natural language processing (NLP) [10]. Large Language Models, exemplified by OpenAI's GPT (Generative Pre-trained Transformer) [29] and Google's Gemini [30], have emerged as powerful tools capable of understanding and generating human-like text across a wide range of contexts. These models, trained on vast corpora of text data, have demonstrated an ability to capture complex patterns, infer relationships, and generalize knowledge to novel situations.

The potential of LLMs extends far beyond their initial applications in text generation and language understanding. Researchers and practitioners have begun to explore their capabilities in diverse fields, including cybersecurity [42]. The unique attributes of LLMs, such as their ability to process and analyze large volumes of unstructured data [20], interpret context, and adapt to new information without explicit retraining, make them particularly well-suited for addressing the cybersecurity challenges faced by smart grid.

The remainder of this paper is organized as follows. Section 2 provides an overview of smart grid systems. Section 3 explores the application of Large Language Models within smart grid operations, highlighting their various capabilities and potential use cases. Section 4 discusses the potential risks associated with integrating LLMs into smart grids Sect. 5 outlines future directions for research and development Finally, Sect. 6 presents concluding remarks on the integration of LLMs in smart grid systems.

2 Overview of Smart Grid

The Smart Grid represents a revolutionary advancement in electrical power systems, integrating modern technologies for more efficient and responsive infrastructure. It incorporates digital communications, automated control systems,

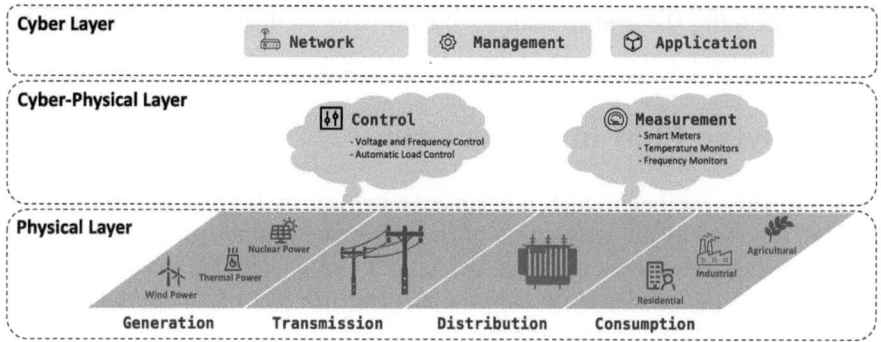

Fig. 1. Smart Grid Overview

and intelligent devices to enable real-time monitoring and management of electricity use and distribution. The Smart Grid evolved as a solution to modernize power systems, addressing critical challenges including growing electricity demands, the need for enhanced energy efficiency, seamless integration of renewable resources. It comprises three layers: Physical layers, Cyber-Physical layers, and Cyber layers, as shown in Fig. 1.

The Physical Layer forms the tangible foundation of the Smart Grid, encompassing the traditional power infrastructure that generates and delivers electricity to consumers. This layer consists of four key components: Power Generation, which harnesses energy from diverse sources; Power Transmission, which facilitates high-voltage electricity transportation across long distances; Power Distribution, which steps down voltage levels for local distribution networks; and Power Consumption, where end-users interact with the grid through smart meters and appliances. The Cyber-Physical Layer bridges the gap between physical infrastructure and digital systems, enabling real-time monitoring and control of grid operations. This crucial intermediate layer comprises two main sub-layers: Control, which manages grid components and maintains system stability; and Measurement, which collects and processes data throughout the grid infrastructure. The Cyber Layer represents the intelligent dimension of the Smart Grid, providing advanced computing and communication capabilities. This sophisticated layer includes three essential sub-layers: Network, which provides the communication infrastructure for data transmission; Management, which oversees and coordinates grid operations; and Application, which delivers software solutions and services for grid optimization and user interaction.

This three-layer architecture revolutionizes traditional power systems, transforming them into an intelligent, responsive network that underpins modern energy infrastructure. By seamlessly integrating diverse energy sources and facilitating bidirectional communication, the Smart Grid significantly enhances both operational efficiency and system reliability. This innovative approach marks a paradigm shift in the generation, distribution, and consumption of electrical energy, equipping the grid to address the evolving challenges and opportunities of the future.

3 Applying LLM in Smart Grid

In this section, we begin with a brief introduction to Large Language Models (LLMs), followed by an exploration of their diverse capabilities and applications within smart grid systems, as shown in Fig. 2. Through detailed case studies from current literature, we illustrate how the key features of LLMs can be effectively integrated into smart grid operations.

3.1 Overview of LLMs

Large Language Models (LLMs) represent a significant advancement in the field of natural language processing (NLP), characterized by their ability to generate, understand, and manipulate human language with remarkable proficiency. These models, which include well-known architectures such as OpenAI's GPT [29] series and Google's Gemini [30], are built on the foundation of deep learning techniques, particularly transformer architectures. The transformative impact of LLMs stems from their extensive training on vast datasets, enabling them to learn complex patterns, contextual nuances, and semantic relationships inherent in language. As a result, LLMs have found applications across a wide array of domains, including text summarization [17], translation [8], content generation [2], and even programming assistance [18].

The architecture of LLMs is primarily based on the transformer model [36]. This architecture employs mechanisms such as self-attention, which allows the model to weigh the importance of different words in a sentence relative to one another. This capability is crucial for understanding context and generating coherent responses. LLMs are typically pre-trained on large corpora of text data, where they learn to predict the next word in a sentence, and subsequently fine-tuned on specific tasks to enhance their performance. This two-step training process is pivotal, as it allows LLMs to leverage a broad understanding of language while also adapting to specialized applications.

3.2 Textual Analysis Capability

The textual analysis capability of a Large Language Model (LLM) refers to its ability to understand human text. LLMs can process large volumes of text, identifying patterns, themes, and key pieces of information. They are proficient in tasks such as sentiment analysis, summarization, topic extraction, and entity recognition. By leveraging their deep learning architecture and vast training datasets, LLMs can analyze text with nuanced understanding, capturing not only the literal meaning of words but also underlying contexts, tones, and relationships between concepts. This capability makes LLMs highly effective for tasks that require in-depth linguistic comprehension and manipulation of textual data.

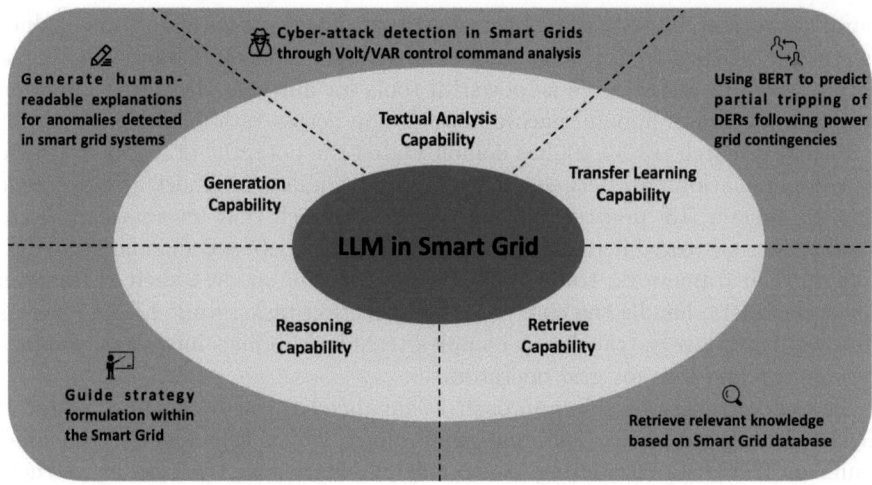

Fig. 2. Illustration of various capabilities of Large Language Models (LLMs) applied to SmartGrid systems, with corresponding examples for each capability.

Recent research has demonstrated the application of LLM capabilities in SmartGrid systems [31,43,45]. Notably, Selim [31] proposes an innovative approach using LLMs for cyber-attack detection in Smart Grids through Volt/VAR control command analysis. Their method converts numerical Volt/VAR commands into standardized text format (e.g., "Shift V1 left by 0.02 units"), validates the syntax, and processes them through a fine-tuned BERT or DistilBERT model. This specialized LLM analyzes command patterns and contextual relationships to identify potential security threats, automatically blocking suspicious commands and alerting human operators to prevent grid voltage stability disruptions.

The integration of LLMs in SmartGrid security represents a significant advancement in critical infrastructure protection. This approach offers several advantages over traditional rule-based systems, including improved adaptability to new attack patterns, better contextual understanding of command sequences, and reduced false positive rates. However, challenges remain in ensuring real-time performance, maintaining model accuracy over time, and addressing potential vulnerabilities in the LLM system itself. Future research directions may focus on developing more efficient model architectures, implementing robust validation mechanisms, and creating hybrid systems that combine LLM capabilities with conventional security measures.

3.3 Generation Capability

The generation capability of a Large Language Model (LLM) refers to its ability to produce coherent, contextually relevant, and human-like text based on a given prompt or input. Leveraging vast amounts of training data and sophisticated neural network architectures, LLMs can generate a wide range of outputs, including creative writing, technical explanations, dialogue, code, and more. This capability enables LLMs to serve as powerful tools for automated content creation, documentation, and human-machine interaction across various domains.

Recent research [13,39,40] has demonstrated the potential of LLMs to bridge the communication gap between machines and humans in smart grid systems. Notably, Rogaia [13] proposes an innovative approach that leverages LLMs to generate human-readable explanations for anomalies detected in smart grid systems. In their framework, traditional machine learning models, such as Random Forest classifiers, handle the core anomaly detection tasks, while LLMs serve as interpretability layers, translating complex technical findings into clear, comprehensible explanations for grid operators.

The effectiveness of this approach is enhanced through the integration of SHAP (SHapley Additive exPlanations) values, which help identify the most significant features contributing to anomaly classifications. By focusing on these key features, LLMs generate targeted, precise explanations that maintain technical accuracy while ensuring accessibility for human operators. This synthesis of traditional machine learning, explainable AI techniques, and LLM capabilities represents a significant advancement in smart grid operations, potentially reducing response times to anomalies and improving overall system reliability through enhanced operator understanding.

3.4 Reasoning Capability

Large Language Models (LLMs) exhibit remarkable reasoning capabilities, enabling them to perform a variety of cognitive tasks such as logical deduction, analogical reasoning, and problem-solving. Trained on extensive text datasets, these models can infer relationships, recognize patterns, and generate coherent responses based on given prompts. Their ability to understand and process natural language makes them versatile tools for numerous applications across different domains.

Several existing methods [7,24] have explored integrating LLMs into Smart Grid systems to leverage their advanced reasoning abilities. For instance, Chen [7] proposed utilizing the LLM's context-aware reasoning to guide strategy formulation within the Smart Grid. In this approach, the LLM first interprets natural language instructions from electric vehicle (EV) drivers regarding their charging preferences and requirements. These textual inputs are then processed by the LLM to generate a mathematically defined reward function, which directs multiple Dual Deep Deterministic Policy Gradient (D3PG) models to produce candidate dispatching strategies.

During the training process, the LLM continuously assesses whether the generated strategies align with the original driver instructions by constructing comprehensive prompts that incorporate task descriptions, user examples, episode results, and objective alignment queries. The LLM's outputs are then parsed into numerical values that serve as reward signals, further refining the dispatching strategies. This creates a closed-loop system where human preferences are effectively translated into operational power dispatching decisions through the guidance of the LLM. By integrating LLMs in this manner, Smart Grid systems can achieve more personalized and efficient energy management, aligning operational decisions with user needs.

3.5 Retrieve Capability

The retrieval capability of a Large Language Model (LLM) refers to its ability to access and utilize external knowledge sources, such as databases or search engines, to enhance its responses. This allows them to provide up-to-date, accurate, and more contextually relevant answers. By incorporating retrieval mechanisms, LLMs can overcome limitations in their training data, offering more specific and dynamic responses, particularly for tasks that require current information or specialized knowledge not included in the model's original training.

In the context of Smart Grid applications, Ni [27] proposes a comprehensive integration process for retrieval-augmented LLMs. The approach begins by preprocessing and vectorizing power dispatching domain documents—including dispatch rules, procedures, and equipment data—into a knowledge base using embedding models like BERT. The system employs both L2 and Jaccard similarity metrics to retrieve relevant knowledge when processing queries, which the LLM then combines with preset prompts and historical memory to generate informed responses. This integration enables the system to reason effectively about power dispatching contexts while maintaining technical accuracy.

The implementation of retrieval-augmented LLMs in Smart Grid systems represents a significant advancement in power grid management. This approach not only enhances the accuracy and reliability of automated responses but also ensures adaptability to evolving operational requirements. The system's ability to combine domain-specific knowledge with natural language processing capabilities makes it particularly valuable for training new operators, troubleshooting complex issues, and maintaining consistent operational standards across different scenarios.

3.6 Transfer Learning Capability

LLMs' transfer learning capabilities have proven valuable in smart grid applications. Thanks to their extensive pre-training, these models can be effectively adapted to specific domains using minimal task-specific data. This characteristic is particularly advantageous in smart grid scenarios, where acquiring large-scale training datasets can be challenging. The ability to leverage pre-trained knowledge significantly mitigates the common issue of data scarcity in smart grid applications [19, 22, 44, 46].

Zhao [44] demonstrates this by implementing BERT to predict partial tripping of Distributed Energy Resources (DERs) following power grid contingencies. The approach leverages BERT's pre-trained understanding of language patterns, acquired from extensive text corpora, and adapts it to power system applications through fine-tuning.

The system transforms power grid fault data into structured textual prompts (e.g., "A bus fault is detected at the bus location one with 0.12 s of fault duration time"). Using a modest dataset of just 7,765 power system scenarios—and maintaining effectiveness with as little as 10% of this data—the model is fine-tuned for the specific task. This transfer learning strategy enables the model to apply its pre-trained knowledge of sequence relationships and pattern recognition to DER tripping prediction.

The results are remarkable, with the model achieving 98–99% precision, recall, and F1-score. This performance significantly surpasses traditional machine learning approaches like XGBoost and MLPClassifier, particularly in scenarios with limited training data. The study exemplifies how transfer learning can overcome data scarcity challenges in power system applications while maintaining high accuracy.

4 Potional Risks

The integration of Large Language Models (LLMs) into smart grid systems, particularly for cybersecurity applications [42], presents a promising avenue for enhancing the resilience and efficiency of our critical energy infrastructure. However, as with any advanced technology, the deployment of LLMs in such a sensitive domain comes with significant risks and challenges that must be carefully considered and addressed. This section explores the potential risks associated with using LLMs in smart grid applications, focusing on privacy concerns [15], security vulnerabilities, operational challenges, and ethical considerations.

4.1 Data Privacy and Memorization Risks

One of the most significant concerns surrounding the use of LLMs in smart grid systems is the risk of data privacy breaches due to the models' tendency to memorize specific sequences from their training data [1,5,15,32].

LLMs are trained on vast amounts of data, and they have shown a remarkable ability to retain and reproduce specific information from their training sets [11]. In the context of smart grid, this could lead to the unintended disclosure of sensitive information such as personal consumer data, where LLMs might inadvertently reproduce individual energy consumption patterns, billing information, or other personal details that were part of their training data. Additionally, critical information about the grid's topology, vulnerabilities, or operational parameters could be leaked if the model reproduces memorized content. Furthermore, confidential information about energy management algorithms, trading strategies, or security protocols could be exposed.

The potential for LLMs to memorize and reproduce personal data raises significant concerns regarding compliance with data protection regulations such as the General Data Protection Regulation (GDPR) in Europe or the California Consumer Privacy Act (CCPA) in the United States [28]. Key issues include the right to be forgotten, as it becomes challenging to fully comply with an individual's right to have their data erased if personal data is memorized by an LLM.

Several approaches have been proposed to address the memorization issue [5] in LLMs. Differential privacy techniques add controlled noise to the training process to limit the model's ability to memorize specific data points, although this can potentially reduce the model's performance, especially in specialized domains like smart grid operations where precise information is crucial. Federated learning allows models to be trained on decentralized data without directly accessing the raw information. Regular model updates and retraining, which involve periodically updating the model with new, anonymized data, can help reduce the risk of outdated or sensitive information being retained; however, this process is resource-intensive and may introduce new vulnerabilities if not managed carefully.

4.2 Security Vulnerabilities and Adversarial Attacks

The deployment of LLMs in smart grid cybersecurity introduces new attack surfaces and potential vulnerabilities that malicious actors could exploit [9,38].

Adversaries may attempt to manipulate the LLM's behavior by injecting malicious data during the training or fine-tuning process [35]. In the context of smart grid, this could lead to false anomaly detection, where injected data causes the model to misclassify normal grid operations as anomalies, leading to unnecessary alarms or system shutdowns. Carefully crafted adversarial examples could train the model to overlook real threats, creating blind spots in the grid's defenses. Additionally, poisoned data could introduce biases in the model's outputs, potentially leading to unfair or discriminatory actions in grid management or energy allocation.

LLMs are highly sensitive to the way queries or prompts are formulated [34]. Carefully crafted prompts could trick the LLM into revealing sensitive information or executing unauthorized actions within the grid's control systems through command injection. Attackers might develop prompts that exploit the model's linguistic understanding to bypass security checks or anomaly detection mechanisms in evasion attacks. Furthermore, LLMs could be used to generate highly convincing phishing messages or social engineering scripts tailored to smart grid operators, augmenting social engineering efforts.

LLMs may produce unreliable or nonsensical outputs when faced with scenarios significantly different from their training data, which could be exploited to create confusion or false alarms in grid operations due to out-of-distribution vulnerabilities [6]. If the training data contains biases (e.g., in energy allocation or pricing), the LLM might amplify these, leading to unfair or discriminatory outcomes. Additionally, LLMs sometimes produce incorrect information with high confidence, which could lead to misguided decision-making in critical grid management tasks due to overconfidence in incorrect outputs.

4.3 Operational Challenges and Performance Limitations

While LLMs offer powerful capabilities, their deployment in smart grid systems presents several operational challenges that could impact the grid's reliability and efficiency.

LLMs are computationally intensive, requiring significant processing power and memory [33]. The time required to process complex queries through an LLM might be too long for real-time grid management tasks, potentially leading to delayed responses to critical events due to latency issues. The high computational demands of LLMs could ironically lead to increased energy consumption, potentially offsetting some of the efficiency gains they aim to provide in grid management. Furthermore, deploying and maintaining the necessary computing infrastructure for LLMs across a distributed smart grid system could be prohibitively expensive for many utilities, resulting in significant infrastructure costs.

Besides intensive computation, the "black box" nature of LLMs poses challenges in critical infrastructure applications like smart grid [12]. Many regulatory frameworks require explainable decision-making processes, which can be challenging to achieve with complex LLMs, potentially causing issues with regulatory compliance. When LLMs produce incorrect or unexpected outputs, tracing the root cause can be extremely difficult, potentially leading to prolonged troubleshooting and system downtime due to challenges in debugging and error tracing. The lack of clear explanations for LLM decisions might lead to resistance from human operators, potentially undermining the effectiveness of the system by affecting operator trust and adoption.

While LLMs excel at processing natural language, they may struggle with the highly specialized context of smart grid operations [37]. LLMs might misunderstand or incorrectly apply domain-specific terminology, leading to errors in grid management or security assessments due to misinterpretation of technical terms. They do not inherently understand the physical constraints and realities of power systems, potentially leading to impractical or dangerous suggestions due to a lack of physical world understanding. Additionally, the broad knowledge base of LLMs might lead to the application of irrelevant or inappropriate concepts to specific smart grid scenarios, resulting in over-generalization issues.

4.4 Ethical Considerations and Societal Impacts

The deployment of LLMs in critical infrastructure like smart grid raises important ethical questions and potential societal impacts that must be carefully considered [4,23]. Determining responsibility for decisions made or influenced by LLMs in smart grid management can be challenging, particularly in terms of legal liability when LLM-guided decisions lead to grid failures or security breaches. LLMs may face scenarios with ethical implications, such as balancing energy distribution during shortages, and ensuring these decisions align with societal values and ethical principles is crucial. Determining the appropriate level of human oversight and intervention in LLM-driven grid management is a critical ethical consideration [41]. The use of LLMs in smart grid applications could potentially exacerbate existing societal inequalities if they inherit or amplify biases present in their training data, leading to unfair distribution of energy resources or pricing structures. The sophisticated nature of LLM-driven smart grid systems might create a gap between communities with access to advanced grid management and those without, potentially leading to disparities in energy reliability and efficiency. LLM interfaces might pose challenges for individuals with disabilities or limited technological literacy, potentially excluding them from fully participating in smart grid benefits.

While smart grid aim to improve energy efficiency, the environmental impact of LLM deployment must be considered, as the energy-intensive nature of training and operating LLMs could contribute significantly to carbon emissions and increased electronic waste, potentially offsetting some of the environmental benefits of smart grid optimization and raising questions about priority setting in sustainability efforts.

5 Future Direction

5.1 Enhancing Security and Privacy in LLM-Powered Smart Grid

As the integration of Large Language Models (LLMs) in smart grid systems continues to evolve, future research and development efforts must prioritize addressing the critical issues of security and privacy. The potential for data leakage and privacy breaches due to the memorization capabilities of LLMs presents a significant challenge that requires innovative solutions. Future work should focus on developing advanced techniques for differential privacy that can effectively balance the need for data protection with the performance requirements of smart grid applications. This may involve creating new algorithms that can dynamically adjust the level of noise added to training data based on the sensitivity of the information and the specific use case within the smart grid ecosystem. Additionally, research into novel federated learning approaches tailored specifically for smart grid environments could prove invaluable. These methods would allow for the training of LLMs on decentralized data from various grid components and stakeholders without compromising individual privacy or exposing sensitive infrastructure details.

Another critical area for future development is the creation of robust defense mechanisms against adversarial attacks on LLM-powered smart grid systems. This will require a multi-faceted approach, combining advanced machine learning techniques with domain-specific knowledge of power systems and cybersecurity. Future research should explore the development of adaptive anomaly detection systems that can identify and mitigate sophisticated attacks, including those that exploit the linguistic capabilities of LLMs. This could involve creating ensemble models that combine LLMs with other AI techniques, such as graph neural networks and reinforcement learning, to provide a more comprehensive and resilient defense against evolving threats. Furthermore, significant effort should be directed towards improving the interpretability and explainability of LLM decisions in smart grid contexts. This is crucial not only for regulatory compliance but also for building trust among operators and stakeholders. Future work might involve developing specialized explanation techniques that can provide clear, actionable insights into LLM reasoning, particularly for critical decisions affecting grid stability and security.

5.2 Optimizing LLM Performance for Real-Time Smart Grid Operations

The operational challenges posed by the computational requirements of LLMs in smart grid applications necessitate focused research on optimizing these models for real-time performance. Future directions should explore the development of lightweight, specialized LLM architectures designed specifically for smart grid tasks. This could involve techniques such as model compression, knowledge distillation, and neural architecture search to create more efficient models that can operate within the latency constraints of grid management systems. Additionally, research into advanced hardware solutions, such as neuromorphic computing or quantum-inspired algorithms, could potentially offer significant improvements in processing speed and energy efficiency for LLM operations in smart grid environments.

To address the scalability and integration challenges, future work should focus on developing standardized frameworks and protocols for LLM deployment across distributed smart grid systems. This might involve creating modular LLM architectures that can be easily integrated with existing SCADA systems and IoT devices, allowing for seamless communication and coordination across the grid. Research into edge computing solutions for LLMs could also prove valuable, enabling more efficient processing of local grid data while reducing the burden on centralized systems. Furthermore, developing sophisticated version control and update mechanisms tailored for distributed LLM deployments in critical infrastructure will be essential. This could involve creating AI-driven systems that can automatically manage and orchestrate updates across multiple LLM instances while ensuring consistency and minimizing downtime.

5.3 Enhancing Domain Specificity and Contextual Understanding

To fully leverage the potential of LLMs in smart grid applications, future research must focus on enhancing these models' domain-specific knowledge and contextual understanding of power systems. This will require the development of specialized training datasets and fine-tuning techniques that can imbue LLMs with a deep understanding of power system physics, grid topology, and operational constraints. Future work might explore the creation of synthetic data generation techniques that can produce vast amounts of realistic smart grid data for training, including rare event scenarios and edge cases that are critical for grid reliability but difficult to capture in real-world data. Additionally, research into novel architectures that can effectively combine the linguistic capabilities of

LLMs with structured knowledge representations of power systems could lead to more accurate and reliable models for grid management and decision support.

Improving the contextual understanding of LLMs in smart grid applications will also require advancements in multi-modal learning techniques. Future research should explore ways to integrate various data types, including time-series sensor data, spatial information, and textual reports, into a unified LLM framework. This could involve developing new attention mechanisms or transformer architectures that can effectively process and correlate information across different modalities, providing a more comprehensive understanding of grid states and events. Furthermore, research into continual learning techniques for LLMs in smart grid contexts will be crucial for maintaining model performance in the face of evolving grid conditions and emerging technologies. This might include developing adaptive learning algorithms that can incrementally update LLM knowledge based on new operational data and changing grid dynamics, without compromising performance on existing tasks or falling victim to catastrophic forgetting.

5.4 Addressing Ethical Considerations and Societal Impacts

As LLMs become more deeply integrated into smart grid systems, future research and development efforts must prioritize addressing the ethical considerations and potential societal impacts of these technologies. This will require interdisciplinary collaboration between AI researchers, power system engineers, ethicists, policymakers, and social scientists to develop comprehensive frameworks for responsible AI deployment in critical infrastructure. Future work should focus on creating rigorous testing and auditing methodologies to identify and mitigate biases in LLM-driven grid management decisions, ensuring fair and equitable access to energy resources across diverse communities. This might involve developing new metrics and evaluation techniques that can assess the societal impact of LLM decisions in smart grid contexts, going beyond traditional performance measures to consider factors such as energy justice and long-term sustainability.

Research into creating transparent and accountable decision-making processes for LLM-powered smart grid systems will be crucial for building public trust and ensuring regulatory compliance. Future directions might include developing advanced explainable AI techniques tailored specifically for smart grid applications, allowing stakeholders to understand and scrutinize the reasoning behind critical grid management decisions. Additionally, work on creating adaptive human-AI collaboration frameworks for smart grid operations could help strike the right balance between leveraging LLM capabilities and maintaining appropriate human oversight. This might involve developing intelligent interfaces that can effectively communicate LLM insights to human operators, facilitating informed decision-making while allowing for human intervention when necessary.

To address the potential environmental impacts of LLM deployment in smart grid, future research should explore green AI techniques that can minimize the carbon footprint of these systems. This could involve developing energy-aware training algorithms, optimizing model architectures for energy efficiency, and creating intelligent scheduling systems that can balance LLM computational loads with available renewable energy resources. Furthermore, research into the long-term societal implications of widespread LLM adoption in energy systems will be essential. This might include studying the potential effects on employment in the energy sector, assessing the impact on consumer behavior and energy consumption patterns, and exploring ways to ensure that the benefits of LLM-powered smart grid are equitably distributed across society. By proactively addressing these ethical and societal considerations, future developments in LLM applications for smart grid can not only enhance technical performance but also contribute to a more sustainable, fair, and resilient energy future.

6 Conclusion

The potential of Large Language Models (LLMs) to revolutionize smart grid operations is profound, offering unprecedented capabilities in real-time data analysis, anomaly detection, and cybersecurity enhancements. However, these advancements come with significant challenges and risks that must be meticulously managed. Issues such as data privacy, model security vulnerabilities, and the ethical implications of automated decision-making systems pose critical concerns that need robust solutions. Additionally, the operational demands of integrating LLMs, such as computational resources and system interoperability, necessitate careful planning and substantial investment. As the smart grid landscape evolves, the strategic implementation of LLMs should focus on maximizing their benefits while mitigating risks through advanced security protocols, continuous model training, and adherence to ethical standards. This balanced approach will be crucial in harnessing the full potential of LLM technologies in smart grid applications, ensuring a secure, efficient, and equitable energy future.

References

1. Aditya, H., et al.: Evaluating privacy leakage and memorization attacks on large language models (llms) in generative ai applications. J. Softw. Eng. Appl. **17**(5), 421–447 (2024)
2. Agossah, A., Krupa, F., Da Silva, M.P., Le Callet, P.: Llm-based interaction for content generation: a case study on the perception of employees in an it department. In: Proceedings of the ACM International Conference on Interactive Media Experiences, pp. 237–241 (2023)
3. Ahsan, M., Nygard, K.E., Gomes, R., Chowdhury, M.M., Rifat, N., Connolly, J.F.: Cybersecurity threats and their mitigation approaches using machine learning–a review. J. Cybersecur. Priv. **2**(3), 527–555 (2022)
4. Beserra, M.: Smart grid systems code of ethics. In: Proceedings of the Wellington Faculty of Engineering Ethics and Sustainability Symposium (2022)

5. Biderman, S., et al.: Emergent and predictable memorization in large language models. Adv. Neural. Inf. Process. Syst. **36**, 28072–28090 (2024)
6. Chen, G.H., Chen, S., Liu, Z., Jiang, F., Wang, B.: Humans or LLMs as the judge? a study on judgement bias. In: Proceedings of the 2024 Conference on Empirical Methods in Natural Language Processing. Association for Computational Linguistics (2024)
7. Chen, X., Lu, X., Li, Q., Li, D., Zhu, F.: Integration of llm and human-ai coordination for power dispatching with connected electric vehicles under sagvns. IEEE Trans. Veh. Technol. **74**, 1992–2002 (2024)
8. Donthi, S., Spencer, M., Patel, O., Doh, J., Rodan, E.: Improving llm abilities in idiomatic translation. arXiv:2407.03518 (2024)
9. Fang, R., Bindu, R., Gupta, A., Kang, D.: Llm agents can autonomously exploit one-day vulnerabilities. arXiv (2024)
10. Feng, S.Y., et al.: A survey of data augmentation approaches for nlp. Association for Computational Linguistics(ACL) (2021)
11. Finlayson, M., Swayamdipta, S., Ren, X.: Logits of api-protected llms leak proprietary information. arXiv:2403.09539 (2024)
12. Fujiwara, K., Sasaki, M., Nakamura, A., Watanabe, N.: Measuring the interpretability and explainability of model decisions of five large language models. In: OSF (2024)
13. Gattal, R. LLM Based Approach for Anomaly Detection in Smart Grids. PhD thesis, Université de Echahid Cheikh Larbi Tébessi–Tébessa- (2024)
14. Guastalla, M., Li, Y., Hekmati, A., Krishnamachari, B.: Application of large language models to ddos attack detection. In: International Conference on Security and Privacy in Cyber-Physical Systems and Smart Vehicles, pp. 83–99. Springer, Heidelberg (2023). https://doi.org/10.1007/978-3-031-51630-6_6
15. Gupta, M., Akiri, C.K., Aryal, K., Parker, E., Praharaj, L.: Impact of generative ai in cybersecurity and privacy: from chatgpt to threatgpt. IEEE Access (2023)
16. Hussain, S., et al.: A novel hybrid methodology to secure goose messages against cyberattacks in smart grids. Sci. Rep. **13**(1), 1857 (2023)
17. Jin, H., Zhang, Y., Meng, D., Wang, J., Tan, J.: A comprehensive survey on process-oriented automatic text summarization with exploration of llm-based methods. arXiv:2403.02901 (2024)
18. Kazemitabaar, M., et al.: Codeaid: evaluating a classroom deployment of an llm-based programming assistant that balances student and educator needs. In: Proceedings of the CHI Conference on Human Factors in Computing Systems, pp. 1–20 (2024)
19. Khan, U.A., Khan, N.M., Zafar, M.H.: Resource efficient pv power forecasting: transductive transfer learning based hybrid deep learning model for smart grid in industry 5.0. Energy Convers. Manag. X **20**, 100486 (2023)
20. Li, B., Jiang, G., Li, N., Song, C.: Research on large-scale structured and unstructured data processing based on large language model (2024)
21. Li, J., Yang, Y., Sun, J.: Risks of practicing large language models in smart grid: threat modeling and validation. arXiv:2405.06237 (2024)
22. Li, Y., Mughees, M., Chen, Y., Li, Y.R.: The unseen ai disruptions for power grids: Llm-induced transients. arXiv:2409.11416 (2024)
23. Liyanage, U.P., Ranaweera, N.D.: Ethical considerations and potential risks in the deployment of large language models in diverse societal contexts. J. Comput. Social Dyn. **8**(11), 15–25 (2023)
24. Mongaillard, T., et al.: Large language models for power scheduling: a user-centric approach. arXiv:2407.00476 (2024)

25. Moreno Escobar, J.J., Morales Matamoros, O., Tejeida Padilla, R., Lina Reyes, I., Quintana Espinosa, H.: A comprehensive review on smart grids: challenges and opportunities. Sensors **21**(21), 6978 (2021)
26. Nafees, M.N., Saxena, N., Cardenas, A., Grijalva, S., Burnap, P.: Smart grid cyber-physical situational awareness of complex operational technology attacks: a review. ACM Comput. Surv. **55**(10), 1–36 (2023)
27. Ni, M., Zhang, J., Fu, C., Wang, J., Ning, X., Li, S.: Chatgrid: intelligent knowledge q&a for power dispatching control based on large language models and retrieval-augmented generation. In: 2024 IEEE 7th Information Technology, Networking, Electronic and Automation Control Conference (ITNEC), vol. 7, pp. 921–925. IEEE (2024)
28. Novelli, C., Casolari, F., Hacker, P., Spedicato, G., Floridi, L.: Generative ai in eu law: liability, privacy, intellectual property, and cybersecurity. SSRN (2024)
29. R OpenAI et al. Gpt-4 technical report. arXiv:2303.08774 (2023)
30. Reid, M., et al.: Gemini 1.5: Unlocking multimodal understanding across millions of tokens of context. arXiv:2403.05530 (2024)
31. Selim, A., Zhao, J., Yang, B.: Large language model for smart inverter cyber-attack detection via textual analysis of Volt/VAR commands. IEEE Trans. Smart Grid **15**, 6179–6182 (2024)
32. Staab, R., Vero, M., Balunović, M., Vechev, M.: Beyond memorization: violating privacy via inference with large language models. In: International Conference on Learning Representations (2024)
33. Stojkovic, J., Choukse, E., Zhang, C., Goiri, I., Torrellas, J.: Towards greener llms: bringing energy-efficiency to the forefront of llm inference. arXiv:2403.20306 (2024)
34. Suo, X.: Signed-prompt: a new approach to prevent prompt injection attacks against llm-integrated applications. arXiv:2401.07612 (2024)
35. Tete, S.B.: Threat modelling and risk analysis for large language model (llm)-powered applications. arXiv:2406.11007 (2024)
36. Vaswani, A.: Attention is all you need. Adv. Neural Inf. Process. Syst. (2017)
37. Wang, C., et al.: Survey on factuality in large language models: knowledge, retrieval and domain-specificity. arXiv:2310.07521 (2023)
38. Wang, J., et al.: Adversarial demonstration attacks on large language models. arXiv (2023)
39. Wen, X., Shen, Q., Zheng, W., Zhang, H.: Ai-driven solar energy generation and smart grid integration a holistic approach to enhancing renewable energy efficiency. Int. J. Innov. Res. Eng. Manag. **11**(4), 55–66 (2024)
40. Yang, Y., Li, C., Zhu, B., Zheng, W., Zhang, F., Li, Z.: Enhancing domain-specific text generation for power grid maintenance with p2ft. Sci. Rep. **14**(1), 26771 (2024)
41. Yao, S., et al.: React: synergizing reasoning and acting in language models. In: International Conference on Learning Representations (2023)
42. Zaboli, A., Choi, S.L., Song, T.J., Hong, J.: Chatgpt and other large language models for cybersecurity of smart grid applications. In: IEEE Power & Energy Society General Meeting (PESGM) (2024)
43. Zaboli, A., Choi, S.L., Song, T.J., Hong, J.: A novel generative ai-based framework for anomaly detection in multicast messages in smart grid communications. arXiv:2406.05472 (2024)
44. Zhao, T., Yogarathnam, A., Yue, M.: A large language model for determining partial tripping of distributed energy resources. IEEE Trans. Smart Grid **16**, 437–440 (2024)
45. Zhou, M., Li, F., Zhang, F., Zheng, J., Ma, Q.: Meta in-context learning: harnessing large language models for electrical data classification (2023)

46. Zhou, M., Li, F., Zhang, F., Zheng, J., Ma, Q.: Meta in-context learning: harnessing large language models for electrical data classification. Energies **16**(18), 6679 (2023)
47. Zibaeirad, A., Koleini, F., Bi, S., Hou, T., Wang, T.: A comprehensive survey on the security of smart grid: challenges, mitigations, and future research opportunities. arXiv:2407.07966 (2024)

Mapping Optimal Space Simplification Analysis in Triple Phase Shift Control of Dual Active Bridge Converters

Wenjie Xu[1]([✉]), Junwei Liu[1], Wenzheng Xu[2], Yixin Wang[2], and Taiming Chen[1]

[1] The Hong Kong Polytechnic University, Hong Kong, China
{joyboy.xu,junwei.jw.liu}@polyu.edu.hk,
24064008r@connect.polyu.hk
[2] The Beijing Jiaotong University, Beijing, China
{xuwenzheng,22291020}@bjtu.edu.cn

Abstract. Triple phase shift (TPS) is commonly utilized to enhance the efficiency of dual active bridge (DAB) DC/DC converters; however, the formulation of optimal phase-shift ratios poses a significant challenge given the versatility of the DAB converter in four distinct operational scenarios, each comprising five specific cases. Prior research has often sought the most effective local operation phase ratio set by analyzing parameters in every case, neglecting the importance of locating the global solution. Additionally, the expressions for circuit states such as peak or root-mean-square current value, and transmitted power in DAB fluctuate across different cases, further complicating the pursuit of global optimization. Consequently, it is crucial to examine the location of the optimal solution set when analyzing the optimal solution for a multi-case scenario. That is the pivotal task in this paper. A simulation is conducted to validate the case simplification analysis. The discussion space for general optimization is focused on cases 3 and 4, streamlining the analytical process and reducing the time required for comprehensive optimization.

Keywords: Dual Active Bridge DC/DC Converter · Tripple Phase Control

1 Introduction

DC microgrids are recognized for higher efficiency, superior current carrying capacity, and faster dynamic response compared to the conventional AC system [2]. They also provide a more natural interface with many types of renewable energy systems (RES) or energy storage systems (ESS) [1]. These advantages have contributed to the growing application of DC microgrid-type power architectures such as isolated bidirectional DC/DC converter (IBDC) which absolutely plays an important role. IBDCs can serve as essential blocks to interface of ESS like batteries and super capacitors and also can be integrated to operate solid-state transformer (SST) [3] architecture, which can facilitate the management of power flow between DC microgrid and upstream distribution network combing the electrical vehicle (EV) [4], photovoltaics (PV), wind turbine and so on [5].

The DC/DC stage predominantly adopts resonant topologies, with the Inductor-Inductor Capacitor (LLC) and Phase-Shifted full bridge configuration being common, but both lack bidirectional capability. Consequently, advanced topologies such as dual active bridge (DAB) and DAB operated in CLLC mode have gained attention. Table 1 sums up the DC/DC topologies mentioned before. In comparison to other topologies, the DAB topology stands out due to its unique advantages. The DAB converter has gradually become one of the most promising topologies and is widely used because of its advanced characteristics as follows.

- Auto-adjust bidirectional power flow, ideal for SSTs and ESSs in microgrids that often require fast changes in the power flow direction.
- Inherent zero-voltage switching (ZVS) capability, capable of achieving high efficiency with proper control.
- Wide voltage conversion gain range, which is essential to interface ESSs such as batteries, whose voltages can vary significantly r different states of charge.

Table 1. Pros and cons of isolated DC/DC converters.

	PSFB	LLC	DAB	DAB-CLLC
Power rating	Medium	Low	+ High	Medium
Power Flow	Unidirectional	Unidirectional	+ Bidirectional	+ Bidirectional
Turn ON loss	ZVS	ZVS	+ ZVS	+ ZVS
Turn OFF loss	High	Low (ZCS)	- High	+ Low (ZCS)
Total losses	Higher	Low	Medium	+ Low
Wide Voltage Gain	Yes	No	+ Yes	Limited range
Paralleling Modules	Easy	Intensive	+ Easy	Intensive

The single-phase DAB converter and the three-phase DAB (DAB-3) converter were originally proposed by de Doncker around the 1990s [4], and the topology and parameters the thesis defines are shown in Fig. 1. The core rule circuit follows to control the current of the leakage inductor by adjusting the phase shift angel such as single phase shift (SPS), which can achieve ZVS turn-on action of all switches at only the unity gain condition. ZVS fault will lose significant power in transmission; moreover, SPS control leads to high backflow power and current stress. Thus, more complex control methods like double phase shift (DPS), extended phase shift (EPS), and triple phase shift (TPS) are proposed to improve these drawbacks.

Over the past decade, there has been a significant effort toward dealing with the technical challenges for the efficiency optimization of the DAB converter with TPS control. However, the performance of the TPS control will vary under different combinations of variables. Thus, many optimal control strategies have been proposed in the literature for optimum combinations of the control goals, e.g. minimizing the peak or root-mean-square (RMS) values of the inductor current, reducing the backflow power losses.

Recent studies have made significant strides in enhancing the performance of TPS control. [6] proposed a unified optimal modulation strategy aiming to reduce the backflow power and thereby improve the efficiency, but numerous cases are considered with intensive calculation. [7] introduce a Quasi-Optimal modulation to minimize loss with global ZVS operation, despite its merits, this method involved repetitive works in selected four cases, namely, all of them actually bring burden in analysis and deduction because of three coupling values. Moreover, [8] put forward a modulation scheme with five degrees freedom modulation scheme to improve efficiency, analyzing nine modes to obtain the global minimum peak-to-peak solutions, but finally found a ZVS operation failure in light loss so further expanded cases are done. A novel work in [8] uses the neural network particle swarm optimization to automatically reduce the unsatisfactory performance and low accuracy, yet also lacks explainability in terms of math or engineering. [9] firstly simplify the operation condition and control cases and then obtain the optimal control the method is clear and easy but does not compare the power range just focuses on the current stress only. The graphic simplification is used to support its claims which makes the conclusions less conclusive. All studies proposed have various optimal modulation strategies but they overlook the necessity of case simplification which would decrease the implementation cost of TPS modulation to some extent, and may even render them practical.

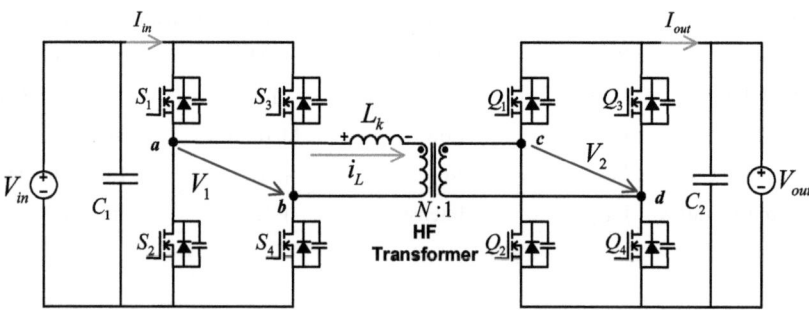

Fig. 1. Basic DAB converter topology and parameters

The research of TPS focuses on the unified global optimization cases analysis, the first work is related to the case selection. The operating cases of TPS control are 12 cases and then simplified to 5 cases [10]. With different operating modes and three degrees of freedom, it is challenging to obtain the global optimal parameters in 5 kinds of cases where the variables are complexly coupled. So, some researchers don't consider the case selection before optimal analysis or considering all the cases. The process is not necessarily to guarantee global optimization without waste of resources. This paper focuses on the case comparison to simplify the analysis procedure, organized as follows: Sect. 2 is a fundamental analysis of DAB in TPS control, apart from some necessary parameters' definition, current stress, and output power calculation is conducted. Section 3 introduces two ways to simplify the different cases in TPS control to only two cases in which you need analysis. Section 4 gives a simulation model to verify theoretical analysis before and final Sect. 5 finally concludes this paper.

2 Fundamental Rule of Triple Phase Shift Control

TPS control proposes that an intuitive way to suppress the backflow power and achieve the soft-switching operation in any operating power cases is to adjust the duty ratios of V_{ab} and V_{cd}, in other words, add two duty ratios to adjust the voltages amplitude of the primary and secondary sides. The phase shift angle can be adjusted further to reduce the reactive power and how to choose proper values of D_1, D_2, D_3 to minimize the backflow power and achieve soft-switching in a rated power is an active topic of research on DAB converter.

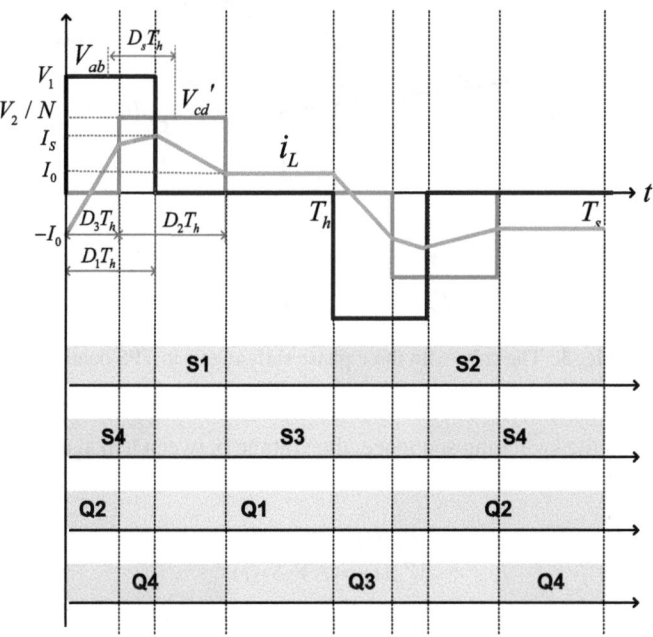

Fig. 2. Typical wave of triple phase shift control mode in DAB converter.

The topology and general operating waveforms of DAB with TPS control are shown in Fig. 2, where. T_h is half of the switching period T_s, D_s is the phase shift value between the primary and secondary:

$$D_s = (D_2 - D_1)/2 + D_3 \tag{1}$$

Although this kind of indirect definition method introduces certain difficulties in the region and plotting within the cube space, the solution form of the circuit parameters is more concise, which aids our optimization deduction analysis. Our cube space is tilted by 0.5-unit length, The three free phase shift $X = [D_1, D_2, D_3]$ is defined as shown in Fig. 3, and the power flow direction, i.e., the boundary where $D_s = 0$, is *ANCQ*/ Their Cartesian coordinates are $A(0,0, 0), N(1,0, 0.5), C(1,1, 0), Q'(0,1, -0.5)$ respectively. The boundary plane *MB*/*PD* in forward mode is defined with $D_s = 0.5$. The backward mode is in the same manner. The path of monotonic increase of D_f is the straight line is B//D/.

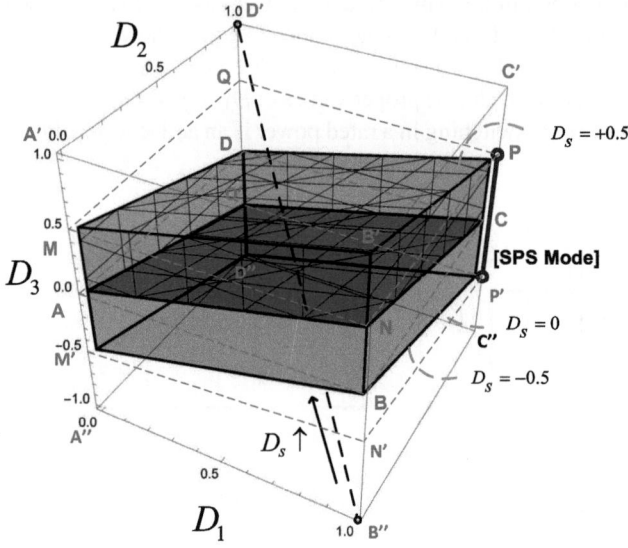

Fig. 3. The cube with three phase shift angels in TPS control

According to the switching sequence, the voltage between leakage inductor V_{ab} and $V_{cd'}$ are given by:

$$V_{ab}(t) = V_1 S_1(t) \\ V'_{cd}(t) = NV_2 S_2(t) \qquad (2)$$

where the switching functions for the two bridges are:

$$S_1(t) = \begin{cases} 1 & 0 \leq t < D_1 T_s \\ 0 & D_1 T_h \leq t < T_h \text{ or } (1+D_1)T_h \leq t \leq T_s \\ -1 & T_s \leq t < (1+D_1)T_h \end{cases} \qquad (3)$$

$$S_2(t) = \begin{cases} 1 & D_3 T_h \leq t < (D_2 + D_3)T_s \\ 0 & 0 \leq t < D_3 T_h \\ & \text{or } (D_2 + D_3)T_h \leq t \leq (1+D_3)T_h \\ & \text{or } (1+D_2+D_3)T_h \leq t \leq T_s \\ -1 & (1+D_3)T_h \leq t < (1+D_2+D_3)T_h \end{cases} \qquad (4)$$

Combining (2), (3), (4), the inductor voltage can be expressed in Fourier series as:

$$V_{ab}(t) = \sum_{k=1,3,5,\ldots}^{+\infty} \frac{4V_1 \sin\alpha \cos(k\omega_s t - \alpha)}{k\pi} \qquad (5)$$

$$V_{cd}(t) = \sum_{k=1,3,5,\ldots}^{+\infty} \frac{4NV_2 \sin\beta \cos(k\omega_s t - \alpha - \gamma)}{k\pi} \quad (6)$$

where $\omega_s = 2\pi/T_s$, $\alpha = kD_1\pi/2$, $\beta = kD_2\pi/2$ and $\gamma = kD_s\pi/2$. The ouput voltage are connected by the series leakage inductance. Thus, the inductor current and average transmission power with TPS control is obtained as:

$$i_L(t) = \sum_{k=1,3,5,\ldots}^{+\infty} \frac{2V_1}{k^2\pi^2 f_s L_s} \sin\alpha \sin(k\omega_s t - \alpha) - d\sin\beta \sin(k\omega_s t - \gamma) \quad (7)$$

$$P = \sum_{k=1,3,5,\ldots}^{+\infty} \frac{4dV_1^2}{(k\pi)^3 f_s L_s} \sin\alpha \sin\beta \sin\gamma \quad (8)$$

where d is defined as NV_2/V_1, symbol for voltage conversion. It can be deduced form (8) that power has the sinusoidal characteristic as D_s changes. Similar to the conventional operation, also the sign of D_s control the power flow direction.

Based on the findings in [10], D_s operates in two distinct ranges. Within the range of 0 to 1/2, it exhibits lower current stress while maintaining the same power output range (as the sine function is symmetric about $x = \pi/2$.) Therefore, D_s is defined within the interval [0,1/2], offering full power output and better performance.

Depending on transmitted power flow direction and voltage gain d, a DAB can operate in the four different scenarios: forward/buck ($P > 0, d < 1$), forward/boost ($P > 0, d > 1$), backward/buck ($P < 0, d < 1$), backward/boost ($P < 0, d > 1$). Considering the forward/buck cases, it can easily construct other three scenarios with the following equivalent transfer function as shown in (10).

$$\begin{cases} d' = 1/d \\ V'_{ab} = V_{cd} \\ V'_{cd} = V_{ab} \\ D'_1 = D_2 \\ D'_2 = D_1 \\ D'_3 = D_2 + D_3 - D_1 \end{cases} \quad (9)$$

TPS control has three degrees of freedom, so the discussion range is a cube as shown in Fig. 3. The primary and secondary bridge is mirror-symmetrical to each other. Therefore, only one power case is enough to obtain the optimal goal in four different scenarios, in this thesis, forward/buck is used to discuss.

3 Simplification of Different Cases in TPS Control

The operating cases of TPS control are 12 cases and then simplified to 5 cases mentioned before. Depending on the rising edge and falling edge of V_{ab} and V_{cd}, there are only five possible switching cases in the meshed cube as shown in Fig. 4. Different cases are different parts of the cube, 5 parts can be constructed all components of the cases in TPS control.

Before simplification proceeding, it is necessary to choose a proper indicator to compare the different cases, the current stress is most reasonable with an easy and direct curve view. Also, the power range is considered first while the ZVS operation is not since soft switching does not significantly impact the power range or current stress, its sequence order can be modified without any difference. Therefore, soft-switching operations were not considered in this paper.

Firstly, to analyze the power range in TPS control, usually, the parameters in SPS control mode are per-unit base value, namely, power base is equal to $P_b = V_1^2/(2\pi f_s L_s)$ and current base is equal to $I_b = V_1/(2\pi f_s L_s)$. The maximum power that can be transmitted in TPS control mode is $8/\pi^2$.

According to (9), the power output in different cases and the full operation range are plotted in Fig. 5, and the color of the cube is used to stand for the per-unit power. Some scholars calculate the power output by computing the integral form of the voltage and current at the input or output, which might be more accurate but holds little significance since the results are nearly identical. In Mathematica, it is very easy to perform the aforementioned two operations, and the resulting graphs are almost the same. It can be seen in Fig. 5(a) that the power is basically positively correlated with D_1, D_2 and D_3. The high power condition is concentrated near point P, while low power condition is concentrated near point A. This is a very natural result, aligning with intuition. Simultaneous, case 3 and case 4 can cover the entire power range. In addition to mathematical proof, this can also be intuitively observed from the graph in Fig. 5(d)(e). It can also be seen from the definition that the union of the regions of case 3 and case 4 is $D_2 + D_3 > D_1$, which covers the defined regions of DPS, EPS, and SPS. This is also our simplified TPS optimization space. The mathematical deduction firstly proves case 3 and case 4 have the wider power range and then the lower current stress. So, the 5 cases are simplified to 2 cases.

3.1 Mathematical Simplification

This section demonstrates the output power and current deduction in case 3 firstly, and then compares some cases to verify that case 3 and case 4 have higher output power and lower current stress. Figure 2 depicts the representative waveforms for V_{ab}, V_{cd} and i_L. The current at initial value is $-I_0$, current stress is I_s. With the symmetrical operation, i_L changes from $-I_0$ to I_0 over half a switching cycle:

$$-I_0 + \frac{1}{L}(V_1 D_1 - V_2 D_2) = I_0 \tag{10}$$

The per-unit current stress I_s can be calculated as:

$$I_s = (1 - 2d)D_1 + dD_2 + 2dD_3 \tag{11}$$

Then all the current values at any instant can be expressed with phase angle and voltage conversion. The output power also can be calculated as:

$$P_n = \frac{1}{T_h}\frac{1}{P_b}\int_0^{T_h}(v_{ab} \cdot i_L)dt = \frac{V_1}{T_h}\int_0^{D_1 T_h} i_L dt = (D_1 D_2 + 2D_1 D_3 - D_1^2 - D_3^2) \tag{12}$$

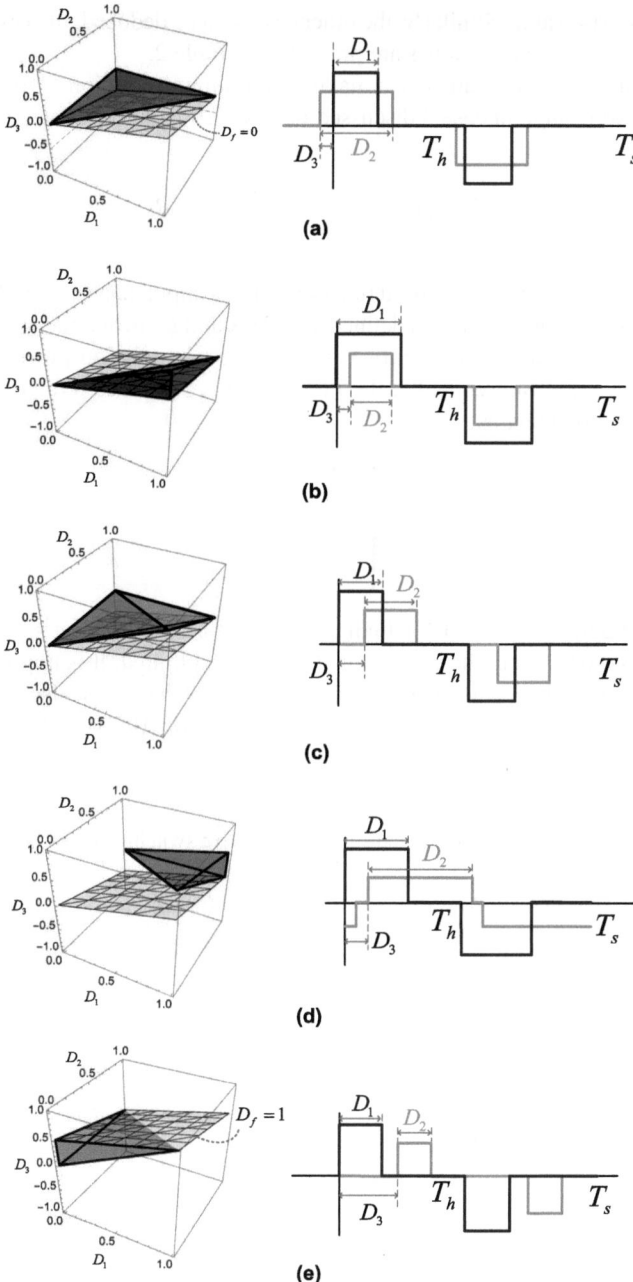

Fig. 4. Five cases in forward/buck scenarios ($D_s > 0, d < 1$). (a) Case#1 $D_3 \leq 0 \& D_2 - D_3 \geq D_1$ (b) Case#2 $0 \leq D_3 \leq D_1 \& D_2 + D_3 \leq D_1$ (c) Case#3 $0 \leq D_3 \leq D_1 \& D_1 \leq D_2 + D_3 \leq 1$ (d) Case#4 $0 \leq D_3 \leq D_1 \& 1 \leq D_2 + D_3$ (e) Case#5 $D_3 \geq D_1$.

where P_b is the base value. Similarly, the other cases can be deduced, the key parameters like power and current stress values are presented in Table 2.

The Lagrange approach satisfied at maximum/minimum solution of the constrained region. The power range in case 3 discussed in this section is formulated into standard form:

$$L(X, \lambda_i) = F_n(X) + \sum_{i=1,2,3,\ldots} \lambda_i B_i \tag{13}$$

where L is the Lagrangian, F is focused function with the input matrix $X = [D_1, D_2, D_3]$. In this case, F is the power function defined as (12). λ and B are defined as the Lagrange Multipliers Method (LLM). Substituting the average transmission power and limited condition in any case. Subsequently, the Lagrangian is constructed, and then extrema can be found by operating as:

$$\begin{cases} \dfrac{\partial L}{\partial X} = 0 \\ \dfrac{\partial L}{\partial \lambda_i} = 0 \end{cases} \tag{14}$$

Since the Lagrange method for finding extrema is a very common approach, the detailed process for solving the extrema in each case is omitted. It is important to note, however, that this method is not exhaustive, so boundary values must also be considered. For example, some boundary sets like $X = [1, 0.5, 0.5]$ or $[0.5, 0.5, 0.5]$ in the case 3 need to be considered to judge the maximum power.

Table 2. Expressions of the power and stress for effective switching cases in TPS control

Switch Cases	Transmission Power	Current Stress
Case 1	$dD_1 D_s$	$0.5\pi((1-2d)D_1 + dD_2 + 2dD_3)$
Case 2	$dD_2 D_s$	$0.5\pi(D_1 - dD_2)$
Case 3	$\frac{d\pi}{8}(D_1 D_2 - D_1^2 - D_2^2 + 2D_1 D_3)$	$0.5\pi((1-2d)D_1 + dD_2 + 2dD_3)$
Case 4	$\frac{d\pi}{4}(\frac{D_2-D_1}{2} + D_3)(1 - (\frac{D_2-D_1}{2} + D_3))$	$0.5\pi((1-2d)D_1 + dD_2 + 2dD_3)$
Case 5	$\frac{d\pi}{2} D_1 D_2$	$0.5\pi(D_1 + dD_2)$

Finally, the power range is used to simplify the optimal cases before applying the LLM method. Case 4 has full power ability, its peak output occurs at $X = [1, 1, 0.5]$, namely in SPS mode. And tase 3 can transmit 0.25 rated power when $X = [1/2, 1/2, 1/2]$. This combination has full range ability because its maximum value is larger than others ($Max.P_{n,1,2,5} = 0.125$). Also, light load is easy to obtain by setting $D_1 = D_2 \& D_3 = 0$. Since the derivate of peak current over the duty shift is larger than zero, the current in case 3 is less than case 4 with a smaller value of D_2, D_3. So, the case 3 is retaining to find optimal lowest current stress.

$$\frac{\partial I_{s,3/4}}{\partial D_2} = d > 0$$
$$\frac{\partial I_{s,3/4}}{\partial D_3} = 2d > 0 \qquad (15)$$

In addition, the current stress of case 2 is clearly larger than that of case 5. The only unclear magnitude relation is located in case 2 and case 3/4. The difference between is less than zero: with $D_2 + D_3 \leq D_1$ condition in case 2.

$$I_{s,2} - I_{s,3} = \frac{\pi}{2}d(D_2 + D_3 - D_1) < 0 \qquad (16)$$

In summary, Case 3 and Case 4 not only cover the full range of power output but also exhibit superior performance. Lower current stress means smaller RMS values and lower circulating power, indicating that in these two modes, the converter operates with higher efficiency. Therefore, the global optimal solution lies in Case 3/4.

3.2 Graphical Simplification

This section will prove that case 1,2,5 can be optimized to case 3 based on a graphical method. Take case 1 as an example first. As shown in Fig. 6., for any operating point in Mode 1, shrink of V_{cd} at the rising and falling edges with a period $D_3 T_h$ can let the DAB operate in case 3, this transformation maintains the same active power in the converter and decreases the reactive power which is the gray area. Meanwhile, the backflow power and RMS value of the inductor are exactly reduced. So there always exists a better point in case 3 for case 1 with the same power output but lower loss.

A comparable equivalence procedure can also be devised for case 2/5, as illustrated in Fig. 7 and Fig. 8. In case 2, reducing the width of primary wave width can lead to a decrease in the peak value of the current passing through the inductor while keeping the output active power unchanged. This occurs because the area of the secondary voltage and current remains consistent with the previous state. Similarly, by narrowing the width of the phase shift angle between the primary and secondary sides, an analogous equivalence can be observed in case 5.

Hence, the unique condition presented in case 3 offers superior circumstances characterized by lower peak values, specifically lower current stress and backflow power. Consequently, it is sufficient to analyze only case 3 and case 4 to pinpoint the global maximum efficiency solution for TPS control optimization.

4 Simulation Study

To substantiate the effectiveness of the proposed simplification method of TPS control optimization, the experimental prototype of DAB converter has been designed on PLECS and topology parameters is given in Table 3.

Converter power output is 0.2 per-unit for the test, the typical wave of case 1/2/3/5 in forward/buck mode is presented in Fig. 9. Given that case 4 encompasses a broader

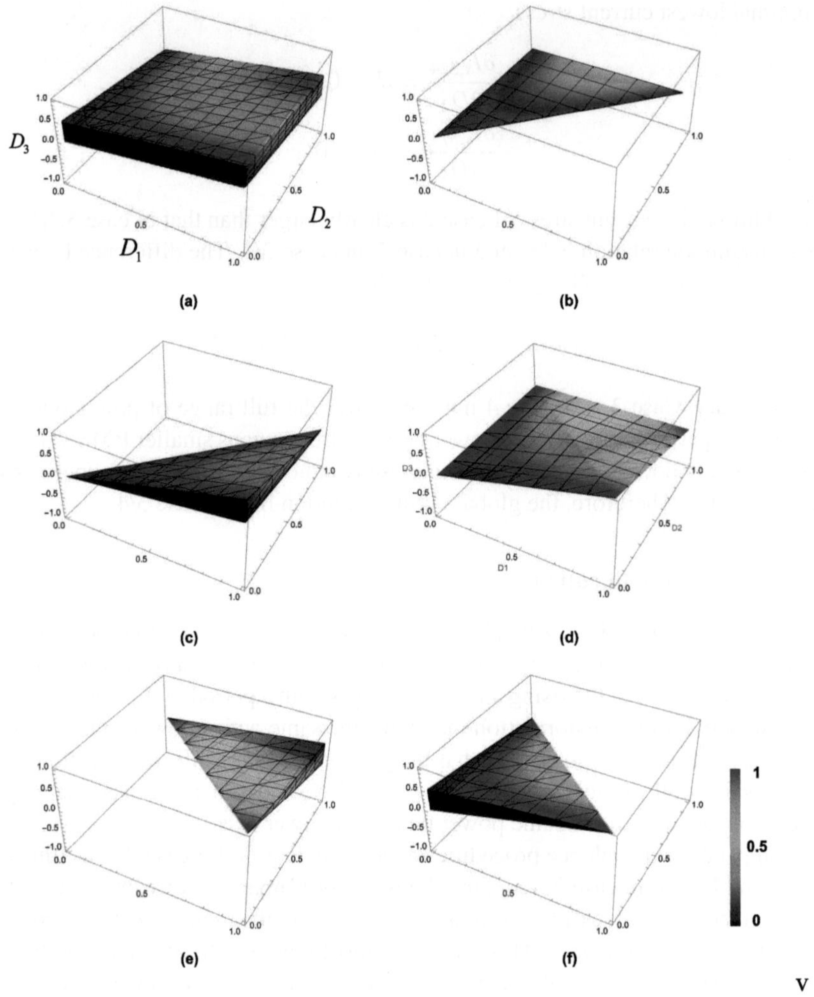

30   W. Xu et al.

Fig. 5. Power range of 5 cases in TPS control mode. (a) full range (b) case1 (c) case2 (d) case3 (e) case4 (f) case5.

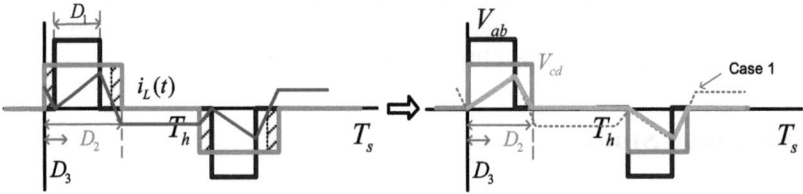

Fig. 6. Equivalence of Case 1 to Case 3

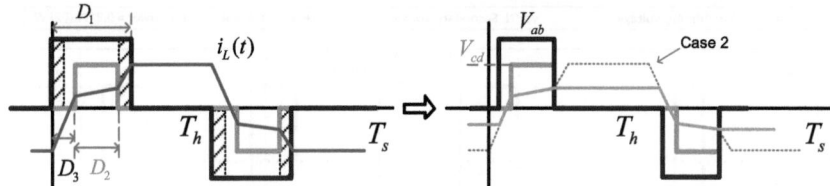

Fig. 7. Equivalence of Case 2 to Case 3

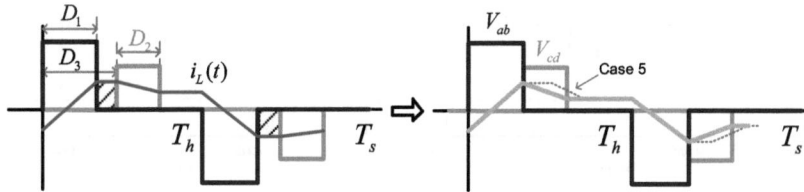

Fig. 8. Equivalence of Case 5 to Case 3

Table 3. Parameters of DAB DC/DC converters.

Parameter	Specifications	Parameter	Specifications
Input/Output Voltage	400/750 V	Transformer Ratio	1:2
Output Power	10 kW	Leakage Inductance	10 μH
Switching Frequency	100 kHz	Capacitor	100 μF

power range compared to the other cases and the four scenarios mode can be equal to others with transfer function (9), further consideration is deemed unnecessary.

It is indicated that case 3 exhibits the smallest peak values, suggesting that the global optimization is most effectively achieved under case 3 during light load conditions. This finding underscores the potential of the TPS control optimization simplification method in enhancing converter performance, particularly at light load while case 4 for full load.

Since soft switching does not significantly impact the power range or current stress, its analysis order is not critical in the optimization process, even though it is a key factor affecting efficiency. Therefore, soft-switching operations were not considered in the simulation verification in this paper.

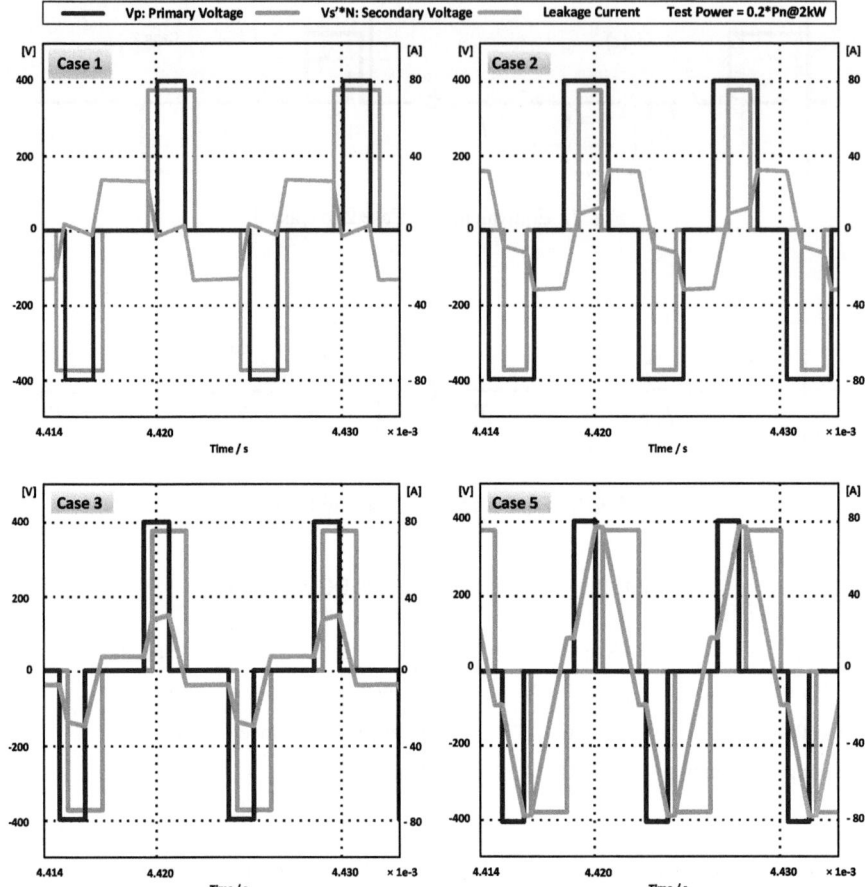

Fig. 9. The simulation verification results in forward/buck operation

5 Conclusion

This paper offers a streamlined approach to determining the optimal phase shift ratios. It employs both mathematical and graphical methods to enhance clarity and understanding. This paper firstly states the fundamental rule of DAB in TPS control mode. Based on the phase ratio space, the power range and current stress are plotted and analyzed. Finally, it was ultimately demonstrated, in a sufficient and necessary manner, that TPS optimization only requires searching within Case 3 and Case 4. These specific cases are not only capable of providing a full range of rated power output but also achieve this while minimizing current stress, thereby enhancing overall efficiency.

References

1. Qin, Y., et al.: Toward flexibility of user side in China: virtual power plant (VPP) and vehicle-to-grid (V2G) interaction. eTransportation **18**, 100291, October 2023. https://doi.org/10.1016/j.etran.2023.100291
2. Xu, Q., Vafamand, N., Chen, L., Dragičević, T., Xie, L., Blaabjerg, F.: Review on advanced control technologies for bidirectional DC/DC converters in DC microgrids. IEEE J. Emerg. Sel. Topics Power Electron. **9**(2), 1205–1221 (2021). https://doi.org/10.1109/JESTPE.2020.2978064
3. Zhao, T., Chen, D.: Active power backflow control strategy for cascaded photovoltaic solid-state transformer during low-voltage ride through. IEEE Trans. Ind. Electron. **69**(1), 440–451 (2022). https://doi.org/10.1109/TIE.2021.3051592
4. Kisacikoglu, M.C., Kesler, M., Tolbert, L.M.: Single-phase on-board bidirectional PEV charger for V2G reactive power operation. IEEE Trans. Smart Grid **6**(2), 767–775 (2015). https://doi.org/10.1109/TSG.2014.2360685
5. Fan, Z., Fan, B., Liu, W.: Distributed control of DC microgrids for optimal coordination of conventional and renewable generators. IEEE Trans. Smart Grid **12**(6), 4607–4615 (2021). https://doi.org/10.1109/TSG.2021.3094878
6. Li, S., Yuan, X., Wang, Z., Wang, K., Zhang, Y., Wu, X.: A unified optimal modulation strategy for DAB converters to tradeoff the backflow power reduction and All ZVS in the full operating range. IEEE J. Emerg. Sel. Topics Power Electron. **11**(6), 5701–5723 (2023). https://doi.org/10.1109/JESTPE.2023.3312298
7. Yu, H., et al.: Globally unified ZVS and quasi-optimal minimum conduction loss modulation of DAB converters. IEEE Trans. Transport. Electrific. **8**(3), 3989–4000 (2022). https://doi.org/10.1109/TTE.2021.3131192
8. Mou, D., Luo, Q., Li, J., Wei, Y., Sun, P.: Five-degree-of-freedom modulation scheme for dual active bridge DC–DC converter. IEEE Trans. Power Electron. **36**(9), 10584–10601 (2021). https://doi.org/10.1109/TPEL.2021.3056800
9. Shao, S., Jiang, M., Ye, W., Li, Y., Zhang, J., Sheng, K.: Optimal phase-shift control to minimize reactive power for a dual active bridge DC–DC converter. IEEE Trans. Power Electron. **34**(10), 10193–10205 (2019). https://doi.org/10.1109/TPEL.2018.2890292
10. Huang, J., Wang, Y., Li, Z., Lei, W.: Unified triple-phase-shift control to minimize current stress and achieve full soft-switching of isolated bidirectional DC–DC converter. IEEE Trans. Ind. Electron. **63**(7), 4169–4179 (2016). https://doi.org/10.1109/TIE.2016.2543182

Modelling of a Vibration Based Kinetic Energy Harvester for Condition Monitoring and Fault Prediction in HVDC Systems

Qinwei He[1]($\boxtimes$), Tian Lan[1], Chris van den Bos[3], Peng Li[2], and Richard Visee[3]

[1] Global Energy Interconnection Research Institute Europe GmbH, Kantstr. 162, 10623 Berlin, Germany
{qinwei.he,tian.lan}@geiri.eu
[2] State Grid Jibei Electric Power Co., Ltd., EHV Power Transmission Company, Beijing 102488, China
[3] Systematic Design B.V., Elektronicaweg 20, 2628 XG Delft, Netherlands
{c.vdbos,r.visee}@systematic.nl

Abstract. High-voltage direct current (HVDC) system plays a pivotal role in model power systems. The system's condition monitoring and fault prediction are also receiving more attention, facilitated by the development of the Internet of Things (IoT) and sensor technology. Ideally, sensors used in HVDC systems should be battery-free and maintenance-free. To realize this, vibration energy harvesters can be a solution. In this work, we proposed an electric model for a vibration harvester that can be used to harvest the vibration energy in the HVDC converter valve. The advantage of this model lies in its simplicity and the easy availability of its parameters. We first verify the proposed model by comparing the simulation results with the expected performance given in the datasheet of the vibration harvester. Furthermore, by using the vibration data in the field, we compare the simulation results from the proposed model with the actual experiment measurements of the vibration harvester. The results validate the effectiveness and accuracy of our model, and demonstrate the feasibility of using vibration harvesters to power sensors for HVDC converter valves.

Keywords: Energy Harvester · Vibration · HVDC

1 Introduction

In recent years, high-voltage direct current (HVDC) transmission technology has made significant progress, primarily due to its superior performance in long-distance low-loss transmission, high transmission capacity, and relatively lower cost than alternating current (AC) transmission in the same distance. Additionally, HVDC technology has greatly enhanced the accessibility of renewable energy sources, including solar energy, onshore and offshore wind farms, and hydropower. As a result, the importance of HVDC technology in future power systems is expected to increase significantly.

The HVDC converter valve is a vital part of HVDC systems, enabling the conversion of electrical power from alternating current (AC) to direct current (DC) and vice versa. Hence, the condition monitoring and fault prediction of the converter valves become critical to ensure the reliability and operational safety of the HVDC systems [4,14,15]. The advancements in the Internet of Things (IoT) and sensor technologies have already built the fundamentals for this [2,3,7,12]. However, in order to be effectively and safely deployed in the HVDC converter valve, sensors must ideally be maintenance-free and battery-free. In particular, batteries can pose additional safety hazards.

Energy harvesting presents a promising solution. This technology enables the collection of ambient energy from many sources such as solar, thermal, mechanical vibrations, etc., converting it into electrical power for electronic devices and sensors. It has been shown that there exists heat and vibration during the normal operation of the HVDC converter valve [9,11]. More importantly, according to analysis and research, the frequency and magnitude of these vibrations are very suitable for use by vibration energy harvesters [5,6]. Consequently, it is imperative to rapidly assess the potential energy yield from vibrations to ensure efficient energy harvesting design and optimization. Intuitively, the most effective way to evaluate it is through theoretical models.

In the literature, there are many theoretical models for vibration energy harvesters [8,10,13], which can characterize them more accurately. However, most of them are too sophisticated and complex, which are not suitable for rapid applications in engineering. A simple model that can effectively evaluate the vibration output power has not yet been proposed and verified. The objective of this work is to address this specific issue.

Our main contributions in this work are summarized as follows

- We propose a simple electrical model for electromagnetic based vibration harvesters. In particular, the parameters in the model can be easily achieved from the datasheet and by simple experiment measurement.
- We validate the effectiveness and the accuracy of the proposed model by comparing the results from simulations, datasheet, and experiment measurements.
- We show that the vibration harvester can generate sufficient energy to power IoT sensors at various positions in the HVDC converter valve.

The rest of the paper is organized as follows. Section 2 introduces the HVDC converter valve and its working environment. Section 3 provides information related to vibration harvesters and proposes an electric model for the harvester that can be used on HVDC converters. Afterwards, the proposed model is evaluated and validated in Sect. 4 by simulations and experiments. And finally, we conclude this work in Sect. 5.

2 HVDC Converter Operating Environment

HVDC converter valves play a crucial role in modern electrical power systems, facilitating the efficient transmission of electricity over long distances. Usually, the converter valve is installed in a specialized facility called converter hall to ensure safe operation. Depending on the types of the convert valve and engineering design, the structure of the converter hall varies. In this work, we mainly consider the thyristor based line-commutated converter (LCC) valve as it has been applied in many HVDC projects.

Fig. 1. An example converter hall for LCC valve [7].

An example converter hall for LCC valve A5000 is given in Fig. 1. There are six converter towers in the hall, which contain the most critical components. Typically, each tower has six layers, i.e., the top and bottom metal cap layers and four converter module layers. Each converter module layer consist of two identical modules as shown in Fig. 2. The valve module comprises thyristors, reactors, damping circuits, cooling pipes, etc., which makes it complicated in structure and requires many monitoring quantities.

Consequently, to assess the condition of these components, monitoring sensors must be deployed. From an engineering implementation perspective, wireless sensors are an easier option. Moreover, with the continuous development in semiconductor technology, wireless communication, and advanced materials, the average power consumption of wireless sensors has significantly decreased, reaching as low as just a few tens of microwatts. However, most wireless sensors on the market are battery powered, which are not suitable for applications in HVDC converter valve environments. On one hand, batteries carry a risk of explosion, especially in ultra-high voltage environments where ensuring their safety is even more difficult. On the other hand, the wireless sensors cannot be maintenance-free when using the battery. As the power-off maintenance time of the converter valve is extremely limited, replacing batteries will cause an additional burden

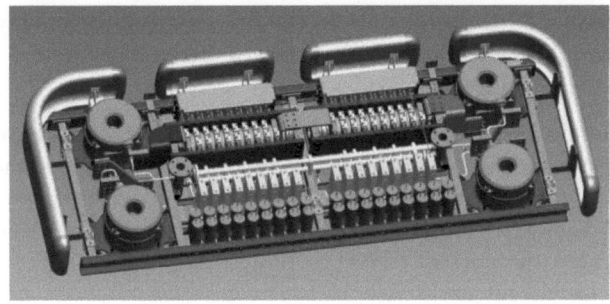

Fig. 2. A5000 LCC module [15].

on operation and maintenance work. To target this issue, we should utilize the energy that generated by the converter during its normal operation to power the wireless sensor. Therefore, finding effective and appropriate energy harvesting technologies for HVDC converters becomes crucial.

There are different types of energy sources, such as solar, magneto-electric, thermal, etc., that can be used for energy harvesting. However, when the converter valve is operating, there is no lighting in the hall. Moreover, considering the multi-layer structure of the converter tower, there will definitely be shading. Even if there is lighting, the light cannot cover every position of each converter module. Thus, solar is out of the option. The LCC valve can generate massive electromagnetic energy during its operation. However, this energy only exists where large currents flow, and will vary depending on the magnitude of the current. Similarly, for thermal energy, only some parts (e.g., the heat sink of a thyristor) of the converter module have high temperatures that can be exploited by thermoelectric generators (TEGs). Hence, we also need other energy source to cover the whole HVDC module.

Vibration is considered a favourable energy source that can serve as an optimal solution. First, when the converter valve is working, vibration will also be generated in the position where magneto-electric and thermal energy are unavailable. Second, since the mains frequency of the power system is 50 Hz, the vibration of the HVDC converter is also induced by this frequency, which happens to be an appropriate working frequency for the vibration energy harvester. Finally, the change of the operating current and voltage of the converter valve will not cause a large change in the vibration at 50 Hz [6].

Therefore, how to utilize the vibration harvesters to obtain the energy efficiently and effectively in the HVDC converter valve, and evaluate their performance is of great significance.

3 Vibration Harvesters

3.1 Vibration Harvester Types

The vibration harvester is a kind of transducer, which is responsible for converting ambient mechanical vibrations into usable electrical energy. Three primary technologies have gained prominence in the field of vibration energy harvesting: electromagnetic, piezoelectric, and electrostatic-based harvesters.

Electromagnetic Harvesters. This type of harvester follows Faraday's law of electromagnetic induction, where a relative motion between a coil and a magnetic field induces an electrical current in the coil. Typically, these devices consist of a permanent magnet, a coil, and an elastic structure (such as a spring). As the harvester vibrates, the magnet or coil oscillates within the elastic system, which generates an electric current.

Electromagnetic-based harvesters can offer several notable advantages. First, they are considered to be the most mature and developed technique. Typically, these harvesters rely on solid-state components (like magnets and coils), which allow for a long operational lifespan with minimal maintenance. In addition, the principle of electro-magnetic induction is well-understood, which facilitates the relatively simple and robust design of these harvesters. Secondly, this kind of harvester can work effectively at low vibration frequencies.

The main disadvantages of this kind of harvester are the difficulty in miniaturization due to the use of large coils or magnets and the potential interference of strong magnetic fields on the electronic components.

Piezoelectric Harvesters. This kind of harvester harnesses the piezoelectric effect, a phenomenon observed in certain materials, such as quartz crystals and specialized ceramics. When subjected to mechanical stress or vibrations, these materials generate an electrical charge proportional to the applied force.

Typically, thin piezoelectric membranes are employed in energy harvesters, allowing for a compact and miniaturized design. This compatibility facilitates easier integration with Micro-Electro-Mechanical Systems (MEMS) technology, which is why most MEMS vibration harvesters are based on piezoelectric principles. Another ad-vantage of the piezoelectric harvesters is their immunity to external and internal electromagnetic waves, making them more adaptable to the working environment in power systems.

On the other hand, piezoelectric harvesters have some drawbacks. First of all, piezoelectric devices can experience material fatigue over time, which can diminish the performance and lifespan of the harvester. Furthermore, these devices exhibit sensitivity to environmental conditions, such as temperature and humidity, which reduces their stability and reliability. Additionally, the installation and calibration process can be complex, requiring precise mechanical design and configuration to ensure optimal performance. Lastly, the relatively high cost of high-performance piezoelectric mate-rials may increase the overall manufacturing expenses associated with these energy harvesting systems.

Electrostatic Harvesters. This kind of harvester can convert mechanical energy from vibrations into electrical energy through electrostatic induction. Usually, the system consists of variable capacitors, in which the relative motion between two plates can change the capacitance between two electrodes, thereby generating electrical energy.

Unlike electromagnetic based harvesters, external magnets or coils are not necessary for electrostatic harvesters, making them more easily scalable and suitable for miniaturization. Consequently, micro-electromechanical systems (MEMS) technology has also been applied in the design of these electrostatic harvesters. The main disadvantage of the electrostatic harvester is the need for external power sources to start the energy harvesting process, which reduces the efficiency of the system and limits its implementation in maintenance-free devices.

3.2 Modelling of Electromagnetic Harvester

According to the above introduction of vibration harvesters, electromagnetic-based harvesters are considered to be the most mature and cost-effective solution for energy harvesting in HVDC systems. Therefore, considering the mains vibration frequency in the HVDC converter, we only investigate the electromagnetic harvester with a working frequency of 50 Hz. The product Xidas VEG-50 is used in our analysis and experiments in the following.

An electromagnetic harvester is very similar in construction to an electrodynamic loudspeaker. Therefore, the loudspeaker model can be used as the basis for an electro-dynamic model of the harvester. Our derivation process is illustrated in Fig. 3.

First of all, the electro-dynamic model of a loudspeaker is provided in Fig. 3 (a), where R_e and R_m are resistors, L_e and L_m are inductors, and C_m is the capacitor. Through this circuit, the electrical input is converted to an output voltage which is proportional to the sound pressure level.

Intuitively, the input and output of this model can be swapped, which means we use the loudspeaker as an actuator ("microphone"), thus resulting in the model illustrated in Fig. 3 (b). The effect of external sound pressure is represented by the current source I_a, whose value is proportional to the sound wave acceleration. After passing through the model, the sound is transferred into an electrical output.

Consequently, refer to Fig. 3 (b), since L_e has a much smaller impedance than R_e in the frequency band of interest, it can be neglected to simplify the model. A load of the electromagnetic harvester is represented by a resistor R_L. The vibration acceleration source can be modelled as a voltage and converted to a current by a transconductance with gain k. Finally, we can achieve the model of an electromagnetic harvester as given in Fig. 3 (c). The transfer from the voltage on pin A to the voltage on node res in the s-domain can be written as,

$$\frac{V_{res}(s)}{V_A(s)} = k \frac{sL_m}{1 + s\frac{L_m}{R_{eq}} + s^2 L_m C_m}, \tag{1}$$

where the resistance R_{eq} can be achieved by

$$R_{eq} = R_m || (R_e + R_L) = \frac{R_m (R_e + R_L)}{R_m + R_e + R_L}. \tag{2}$$

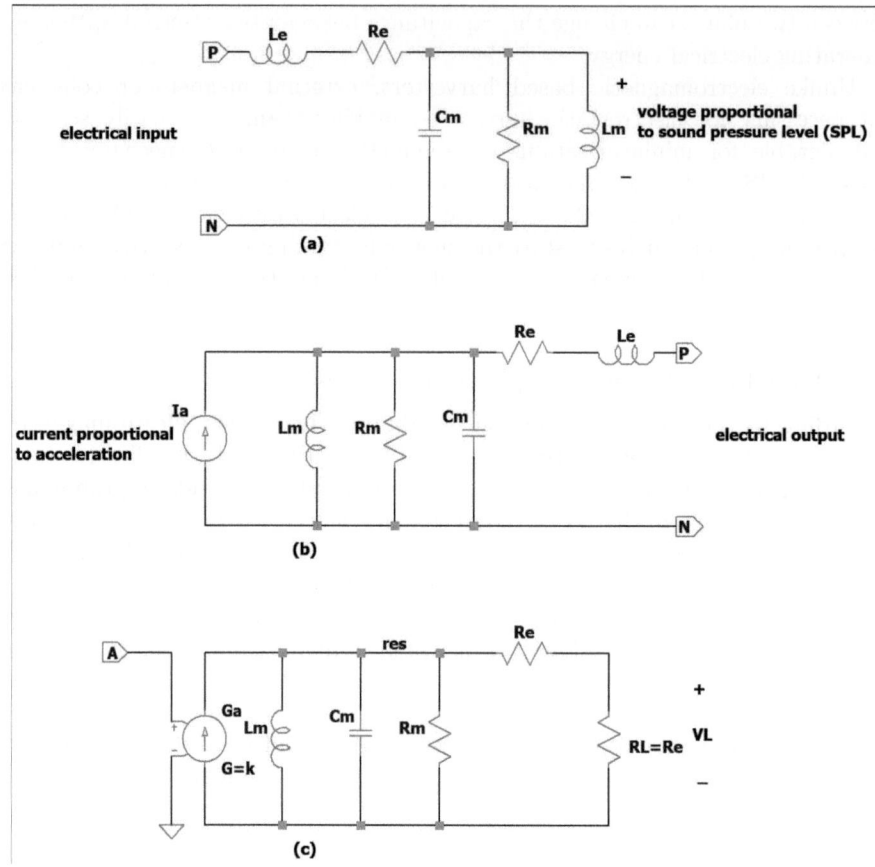

Fig. 3. Derivation process of the electromagnetic harvester model.

Equation (1) can be further written as

$$\frac{V_{res}(s)}{V_A(s)} = k \frac{sL_m}{1 + \frac{s}{\omega_n Q} + \left(\frac{s}{\omega_n}\right)^2}, \tag{3}$$

where $\omega_n = 2\pi f_n$ with f_n (approximately) equals to the resonance frequency, and $Q = f_n/B$ with B representing the -3 dB bandwidth of the transfer.

3.3 Parameters Calculation

In order to apply the derived model to the Xidas harvester, we must obtain the parameter of corresponding components.

For the resistor R_m, a straightforward calculation yields

$$R_m = R_L \left(\frac{V_{op}}{V_L} - 1\right) - R_e, \tag{4}$$

where V_L is the output voltage when the harvester is loaded with R_L and V_{op} denotes the output voltage when the harvester is unloaded under the same acceleration.

The L_m and C_m can be calculated by Eq. (5) and (6), respectively.

$$L_m = \frac{R_{eq}}{\omega_n Q} = \frac{R_{eq} B}{2\pi f_n^2}. \tag{5}$$

$$C_m = \frac{Q}{\omega_n R_{eq}} = \frac{1}{2\pi B R_{eq}}. \tag{6}$$

And the gain k can be obtained by

$$k = \frac{V_{op}}{R_m a_{op}}, \tag{7}$$

in which a_{op} is the acceleration (or amplitude in case of sinusoidal acceleration) at which V_{op} is determined.

When considering the utilized harvester Xidas VEG-50, some parameters for the above equations can be achieved from its datasheet, namely,

$$\begin{aligned} R_e &= 440 \ \Omega \\ L_e &= 24 \ \text{mH} \\ f_n &= 50 \ \text{Hz} \\ B &= 2.05 \ \text{Hz}. \end{aligned} \tag{8}$$

Moreover, the load in the datasheet is $R_L = R_e = 440 \ \Omega$, hence the root mean square (RMS) output voltage V_L at an acceleration of 0.2 g (also RMS value) can be calculated, which is

$$V_L = \sqrt{P_L R_e} = 1.483 \ \text{V}, \tag{9}$$

where P_L is the output power with a value of 5 mW given in the data sheet in this case.

On the other hand, the open circuit voltage is measured by an experiment which yields,

$$V_{op} = 15.83 \ \text{V}. \tag{10}$$

Therefore, by substituting these obtained values in (8), (9) and (10) into Eqs. (4) to (7), we can get the rest parameters for modelling this harvester, which is

$$\begin{aligned} L_m &= 93.58 \ \text{mH} \\ C_m &= 108.30 \ \mu\text{F} \\ R_m &= 3873 \ \Omega \\ k &= 0.0204 \ \text{S}. \end{aligned} \tag{11}$$

4 Model Validation

This section evaluates and validates the proposed model through two approaches. On the one hand, we compare the simulations with the results from the datasheet of the Xidas VEG-50. On the other hand, we conduct both simulations and experiments based on the real vibration measurement from the HVDC converter and analyze the simulated results and the real harvester performance.

4.1 Evaluation Based on Simulation and Datasheet

We first conducted the simulation of the output power versus frequency. The load R_L is set to 440 Ω, the acceleration is 0.5 g, and the vibration type is sinusoid with the frequency from 45 Hz to 55 Hz. The simulation result and the plot from the datasheet are illustrated in Fig. 4 in blue and red curves, respectively.

Obviously, the correspondence between them is reasonable, especially for the in-band frequency range from 49.5 Hz to 51.5 Hz (1 Hz bandwidth). The model predicts a slightly higher suppression of signals in high frequency ranges from 51 Hz to 55 Hz. On the contrary, for the lower frequency from 45 Hz to 49 Hz, the simulation provides a slightly higher output power. However, the energy at those out-of-band frequencies, after the attenuation, is negligible in any case.

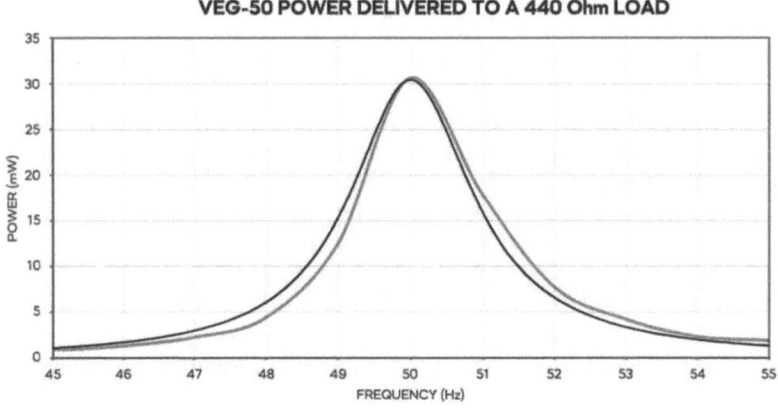

Fig. 4. Output power versus frequency at $a = 0.5$ g from the datasheet (red) and simulation (blue). (Color figure online)

It is also worth noting that the load resistance $R_L = 440\ \Omega$ in the above simulation is not optimum for power transfer. The optimal values is much higher. From the model in Fig. 3 (c), this can be seen as follows. At resonance, L_m and C_m can be omitted from the schematic. With an acceleration of 0.5 g, the simulated delivered power, as a function of the load resistance, is shown in Fig. 5.

It is interesting to see that the delivered power is a function of the load resistance but does not depend strongly on it. This means that the load resistance may be chosen somewhat other than optimum, for example to obtain a more convenient output voltage for the electronics in the sensor.

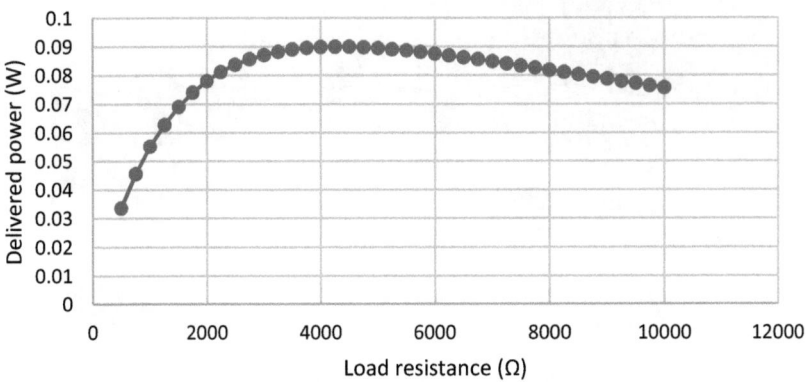

Fig. 5. Simulated delivered power versus load resistance, acceleration $a = 0.5$ g.

4.2 Evaluation Based on Simulation and Experiments

In this part, we use the real on-site vibration data for both simulations and experiments to further evaluate the performance of the model. The real vibration on the HVDC converter is not a simple sinusoid acceleration at a certain frequency. It is composed of the acceleration component at 50 Hz and its multiples, which can even be higher than 8 kHz. The power distribution of the real acceleration in the frequency domain varies according to their positions in the converter. More information and analysis for the vibration data can be found in [5,6].

In the experiment, a test bench is utilized to reproduce the recorded field vibration in our lab, which is shown in Fig. 6. This test bench comprises two components: a shaker system and a vibration controller. The shaker system features a permanent magnet shaker paired with a matching linear power amplifier, which produces vibrations based on commands from the controller. The controller utilizes data from a sensor attached to the shaker to create a feedback loop, allowing for precise control of the shaker's acceleration in line with the target vibration parameters. The Xidas VEG-50 vibration harvester is mounted at the top of the shaker, and its output is connected with a 4.31 kΩ load resistor. A multimeter is used to get the RMS voltage over this resistor.

Table 1 gives a summary of the both simulation and experiment results. We employ the field vibration data in the busbar, reactor and baseplate of the LCC valve. Each single experiment is performed 10 times and the measurement results are averaged. There are no significant and obvious measurement differences between the same experiments. The peak acceleration at 50 Hz for each

Fig. 6. Vibration test bench

position is included in the table to give an intuitive indication of the intensity of the vibration. Obviously, it can be seen from the table that the simulated voltage and power are very close to the measured ones. The maximum voltage difference is less than 4%. This verifies the effectiveness of the proposed harvester model. Moreover, we can notice that even when the acceleration is extremely small only 0.0278 g at 50 Hz in the baseplate, the harvester can still deliver over 100 μW power, which is sufficient for some IoT sensors designed for condition monitoring and fault prediction purposes, such as the one given in [1].

Table 1. The simulated and measured results

Location		Busbar		Reactor		Baseplate	
Acceleration at 50 Hz (mg)		35.6	74.4	137	147	27.8	42.8
RMS voltage (v)	simu.	1.04	2.07	3.83	4.14	0.78	1.19
	meas.	0.99	2.04	3.71	3.98	0.75	1.15
RMS power (mW)	simu.	0.25	0.99	3.40	3.98	0.14	0.33
	meas.	0.23	0.97	3.19	3.68	0.13	0.31

5 Conclusion

In this work, an electrical model for electromagnetic-based vibration harvesters is proposed. A commercial vibration harvester is modelled by given, calculated, and measured parameters. The validity and accuracy of the proposed model are verified by comparing the results of simulations, datasheets, and experimental measurements. More importantly, we demonstrate that sufficient energy can be produced to power the sensors from the vibration harvester during the HVDC converter valve operation.

In future work, we will first validate the proposed model with the vibration at different positions/components on the HVDC converter module. Afterwards, we will try to validate the model using other commercially available vibration harvesters.

Acknowledgement. This work is supported by the R&D project of State Grid Corporation of China (Research on the key technology of mathematical-physical fusion edge intelligent computing for the fault warning of main equipment of converter station, No. 5500-202358801A-3-9-HW).

References

1. Chen, M., et al.: A self-powered 3.26-μw70-m wireless temperature sensor node for power grid monitoring. IEEE Trans. Ind. Electron. **65**(11), 8956–8965 (2018)
2. Cui, Y., et al.: Development of a wireless sensor network for distributed measurement of total electric field under HVDC transmission lines. Int. J. Distrib. Sens. Netw. **10**(5), 850842 (2014)
3. Del Campo, G., Gomez, I., Sierra, S.C., Martinez, R., Santamaria, A.: Power distribution monitoring using LoRa: coverage analysis in suburban areas. In: International Conference on Embedded Wireless Systems and Networks, pp. 233–238 (2018)
4. Gao, C., et al.: Novel controllable-line-commutated converter for eliminating commutation failures of LCC-HVDC system. IEEE Trans. Power Delivery **38**(1), 255–267 (2023)
5. He, Q., Lan, T., Huang, H., Lan, Y., Wu, X.: A comparative study of vibration and energy harvesting in two types of HVDC converter modules. In: 2023 IEEE International Conferences on Internet of Things (iThings) and IEEE Green Computing & Communications (GreenCom) and IEEE Cyber. Physical & Social Computing (CPSCom) and IEEE Smart Data (SmartData) and IEEE Congress on Cybermatics (Cybermatics), Danzhou, China, pp. 300–304 (2023)
6. He, Q., Lan, T., Huang, H., Lan, Y., Wu, X.: The vibration analysis of HVDC converter module based on experiment under working conditions. In: 2023 IEEE 4th International Conference on Electrical Materials and Power Equipment (ICEMPE), Shanghai, China, pp. 1–4 (2023)
7. He, Q., Lan, Y., Liu, W., Liu, Y., Yang, H.: A comparison study of LPWAN technologies based on onsite measurements in a converter station hall. In: 2021 4th International Conference on Energy, Electrical and Power Engineering (CEEPE), Chongqing, China (2021)
8. Hudak, N.S., Amatucci, G.G.: Small-scale energy harvesting through thermoelectric, vibration, and radiofrequency power conversion. J. Appl. Phys. **103**(10), 101301 (2008)
9. Lan, T., He, Q., Lan, Y., Guo, T., Sun, Y.: Operational environment analysis of HVDC converter station for development of energy harvester: electromagnetic field and ambient power source. In: 2021 4th International Conference on Energy, Electrical and Power Engineering (CEEPE), Chongqing, China (2021)

10. Li, Y., Li, J., Yang, A., Zhang, Y., Jiang, B., Qiao, D.: Electromagnetic vibrational energy harvester with microfabricated springs and flexible coils. IEEE Trans. Ind. Electron. **68**(3), 2684–2693 (2021)
11. Rudolph, H., Lan, T., Strehl, K., He, Q., Lan, Y.: Simulating the efficiency of thermoelectrical generators for sensor nodes. In: 2019 4th IEEE Workshop on the Electronic Grid (eGRID), Xiamen, China, pp. 1–6 (2019)
12. Wang, Z., Zhai, M.: Research on application of LPWAN in state monitoring of distribution network. IOP Conf. Ser. Mater. Sci. Eng. **569**(3), 032049 (2019)
13. Wei, C., Jing, X.: A comprehensive review on vibration energy harvesting: modelling and realization. Renew. Sustain. Energy Rev. **74**, 1–18 (2017)
14. Yang, J., Gao, C., He, Z., He, D., Zhang, J.: Dynamic performance of controllable line-commutated converter (CLCC) in HVDC systems with weak sending end ac network. In: 2023 IEEE 6th International Electrical and Energy Conference (CIEEC), Hefei, China (2023)
15. Zha, K., Wei, X., Tang, G.: Research and Development of ±800 kV/4750 A UHVDC Valve. In: 2012 Second International Conference on Intelligent System Design and Engineering Application, Sanya, China (2012)

Dual-Attention Fusion Transformer for Electricity Theft Detection to Secure Smart Grids

Cai Guo[2], Bishenghui Tao[1(✉)], and Hong-Ning Dai[3]

[1] School of Science and Technology, Hong Kong Metropolitan University, Hong Kong, China
btao@hkmu.edu.hk
[2] School of Computer and Information Engineering, Hanshan Normal University, Chaozhou, China
c.guo@hstc.edu.cn
[3] Department of Computer Science, Hong Kong Baptist University, Hong Kong, China
henrydai@comp.hkbu.edu.hk

Abstract. In the context of escalating electricity demand and the critical challenge of electricity theft in smart grids, this paper presents a novel dual-attention fusion transformer model, termed DaFT, for improved electricity theft detection. By effectively integrating both horizontal and vertical attention mechanisms, our approach captures the multidimensional periodicity inherent in electricity consumption data, with a particular focus on weekly and day-specific patterns. Utilizing a comprehensive dataset from the State Grid Corporation of China, we rigorously analyze consumption behaviors to discriminate between legitimate users and electricity thieves. Experimental results reveal that DaFT outperforms state-of-the-art methods in terms of Mean Average Precision (MAP) and Area Under the Curve (AUC) metrics, achieving a MAP@100 of 0.988 and an AUC of 0.827 under optimal training conditions. Our results highlight the eligibility of the scheme to address the pressing issue of electricity theft, thereby contributing to the security and sustainability of smart grid systems. This work not only advances the field of electricity theft detection, but also opens avenues for applying similar methodologies to other time-series data analysis.

Keywords: Smart Grids · Transformer · Electricity Theft · Time-Series

1 Introduction

The concept of a smart grid has emerged as a groundbreaking advancement in energy management and distribution. As the electricity demand continues to

---

The work described in this paper was fully supported by Hong Kong Metropolitan University Research Grant (No. RD/2023/2.23).

rise, the need for an efficient and reliable power grid system has become increasingly urgent [11]. The traditional power grid infrastructure is no longer sufficient to meet the growing demands of modern society [14]. In response to these challenges, smart grid technology has been proposed as a trans-formative solution that integrates advanced communication, control, and monitoring capabilities into the existing electrical infrastructure. Smart grids are designed to enhance the efficiency, reliability, and sustainability of electricity generation, transmission, and distribution. By leveraging digital technologies such as sensors, advanced metering infrastructure (AMI), automation systems, and data analytics, smart grids facilitate real-time monitoring and management of electricity flow across the grid [18].

This interconnected system enables better prediction of energy consumption patterns, improved fault detection and response mechanisms, and in particular the detection of electricity theft [1]. Power theft is a particularly critical issue in many regions of the world. It poses a significant threat to utilities by undermining their revenue streams while imposing additional financial burdens on honest consumers who ultimately bear these costs through higher tariffs. It can take various forms, including illegal connections that bypass meter readings or tampering with meters, resulting in significant revenue losses for utilities that could potentially jeopardize their ability to maintain stable operations or invest in much-needed upgrades to modernize aging infrastructure.

Solving the problem of electricity theft has always been a difficult task, mainly due to technical limitations such as a lack of data collection/monitoring and a lack of methods to detect electricity theft. Existing methods for detecting electricity theft in smart grids, on the other hand, can be divided into two main types: hardware-based methods and data-driven methods. The former mainly rely on smart devices for smart grids, including but not limited to specially designed sensors, actuators and smart integrated systems. Data-driven approaches, on the other hand, mainly use machine learning methods to analyze and train the data collected by smart grids, where [10,21] used convolutional neural networks to study the grid data, and [15] further used deep neural networks, both of which elaborated on different perspectives of how using neural networks to train electricity consumption data can differentiate electricity theft from other behaviors. In addition, the work in [17] used graph attention networks to mine graph network relationships using correlations of electricity usage data, while research [2] adapts GoogLeNet architecture and work [9,13] are based on gated recurrent unit (GRU) to explore the direction of improving the results.

However, most of these methods have the following limitations: 1) Requiring complex expert domain knowledge or manually constructing the features; 2) Redundant method structure and high computational cost; 3) Low detection accuracy; and 4) Neglecting the multidimensional time periodicity of electricity consumption data.

To address the above limitations, we propose a dual-attention fusion transformer model that can efficiently and accurately detect electricity theft, ultimately ensuring that malicious users are detected while providing a safer smart grid energy environment. The contributions of this paper are summarised as follows:

1) Comprehensively analyzing electricity theft data and discovering the multi-dimensional periodicity of electricity consumption.
2) Proposing a transformer-based dual-attention fusion model (DaFT) that captures the two dimensions periodicity of electricity consumption data.
3) Conducting extensive experiments for comparison and demonstrating that our approach outperforms the other state-of-the-art baseline.

2 Problem Analysis

To investigate security solutions for smart grids, we undertake a thorough analysis of electricity theft, which is a nefarious practice characterized by anomalous patterns within electricity consumption data. The advent of smart grids facilitates the collection of high-resolution data, thereby laying the groundwork for data-driven methodologies aimed at detecting instances of electricity theft [3].

Our study employs a comprehensive examination of the extensively analyzed electricity consumption dataset from the State Grid Corporation of China (SGCC)[1], which encompasses daily consumption records spanning from January 1, 2014, to October 31, 2016. This dataset comprises information from over 42,000 customers, including 3,615 identified as electricity thieves, with the remainder categorized as regular consumers.

We first analyze the daily electricity consumption pattern of the users, as shown in Fig. 1. As an example, we selected 8 weeks of electricity consumption data from 1st January to 25th February 2014 for both ordinary users and electricity theft users. From Fig. 3, it is evident that the electricity consumption activities of ordinary users are smooth and regular, with small upward and downward fluctuations and few extreme values. On the other hand, the data of electricity theft user is more fluctuating, not regular and may have extreme or minimal values occasionally.

Therefore, we further hypothesize that the electricity consumption patterns of normal users may be related to the weekdays: working hours from Monday to Friday and weekend schedules may lead to periodicity in the electricity consuming activities. Specifically, if daily electricity consumption is considered as one data element, then each week is a sequence of seven elements. Moreover, the electricity consumption of a normal user should match the work cycle, indicating that the electricity consumption for each of the seven days of the week follows a similar pattern. For example, the electricity consumption of a household may be less on weekdays and more on weekends, whereas the electricity consumption of a workplace may be more on weekdays and less on weekends.

In order to better explore this weekly periodicity, we introduce the Pearson correlation coefficient $r_{x,y}$ to measure the correlation of weekly electricity

---

[1] State Grid Corporation of China http://www.sgcc.com.cn.

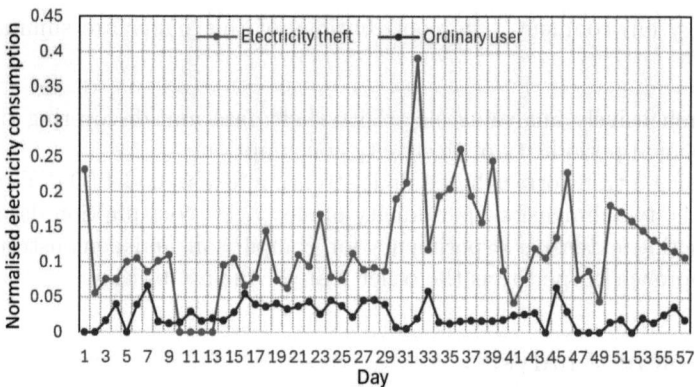

Fig. 1. Electricity consumption by day (8 weeks)

consumption as follows,

$$r_{x,y} = \frac{\sum_{i=1}^{n}(x_i - \bar{x})(y_i - \bar{y})}{\sqrt{\sum_{i=1}^{n}(x_i - \bar{x})^2 \sum_{i=1}^{n}(y_i - \bar{y})^2}}, \quad (1)$$

where x_i and y_i are the individual data of the week x and y, respectively, while $\bar{x}$ and $\bar{y}$ are the mean values of the data sequences of the week x and y. The Pearson correlation coefficient ranges from −1 to 1 and measures the strength and direction of the linear relationship between two weeks. Values between 0 and 1 indicate varying degrees of positive correlation, while values between 0 and −1 indicate varying degrees of negative correlation.

Figure 2 plots the correlation matrix heatmap. As shown in Fig. 2(a), the weekly electricity consumption data of an ordinary user shows more positive correlation, meaning that the weekly electricity consumption pattern of this user from Monday to Sunday is similar. Therefore, we introduce the *weekly periodicity* to measure this electricity usage pattern based on seven days of a week. In contrast, Fig. 2(b) is observed to be often negatively correlated or uncorrelated, presumably because electricity theft does not follow a fixed schedule and is not bound by weekdays. In other words, electricity theft users typically do not exhibit weekly periodicity.

On the other hand, in addition to the seven-day weekly periodicity, it is reasonable to assume that there is also a periodicity in the electricity use activity on specific days. As shown in Fig. 3, each row represents the electricity consumption activity from Monday to Sunday (represented by the same color) and each column represents the electricity consumption activity on the same day of each week (represented by the same graph). It has been stated in the existing works [21] that some common users have a peak electricity consumption period on every Wednesday. Therefore, taking Wednesday as an example, it is possible that there is a certain pattern in the red solid line box of Fig. 3.

In order to validate this conjecture, we separate the electricity consumption data from the global data for eight weeks on Wednesdays from ordinary users

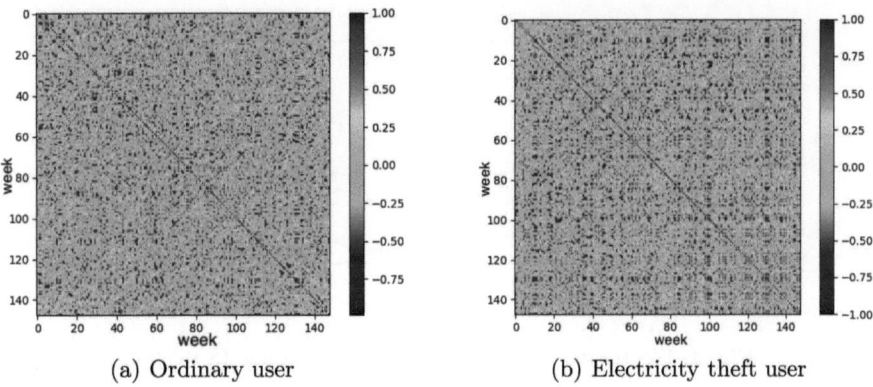

Fig. 2. Pearson correlation coefficient of 148 weeks for different users

	Mon	Tue	Wed	Thu	Fri	Sat	Sun
Week 1	△	■	●	◆	☆	✦	✹
Week 2	△	■	●	◆	☆	✦	✹
Week 3	△	■	●	◆	☆	✦	✹
Week 4	△	■	●	◆	☆	✦	✹

Fig. 3. Weekly periodicity (dotted box) and day-specific periodicity (solid box)

and electricity theft users respectively. The results in Fig. 4 indicate that the electricity consumption of the electricity theft users varies greatly every Wednesday, and the values show great fluctuations over the 8 weeks. On the other hand, ordinary users exhibit relatively stable values every Wednesday, namely *day-specific periodicity*.

Integrating the above clues and analyses, we find that there is a considerable difference between the electricity consumption pattern of ordinary users and that of electricity theft users. Firstly, the global data of electricity theft users exhibit large fluctuations, while ordinary users are more stable and regular. Secondly, the electricity consumption pattern of ordinary users is highly related to the seven-day working rhythm, which is called the weekly periodicity. In contrast, electricity theft users show less weekly periodicity. Further, we also indicate day-specific periodicity to account for the observation that the ordinary user will have similar electricity usage behavior on the same days of the week. It is reasonable to suppose that exploitation of the two periodicity can reveal insightful information about the time series of electricity consumption, and thus better distinguish electricity theft users.

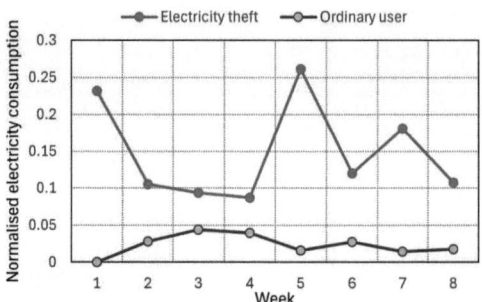

Fig. 4. Electricity consumption every Wednesday (8 weeks)

3 Our Approach

Transformer-based approaches [20] excel at handling time series data because they can capture long-range dependencies and context effectively through self-attention mechanisms. Therefore, we introduce parts of the structure in the Transformer to construct a more appropriate method for this topic. Figure 5 shows the overall architecture of the proposed Dual-attention Fusion Transformer (DaFT), which includes a parallel dual attention transformer block, a serial dual attention transformer block, a token fusion block, and a multilayer perceptron (MLP) block. Taking the SGCC dataset as an example, each customer contains 148 weeks of electricity consumption, so the input to DaFT is considered as a sequence of tokens of length 148, and each token in the sequence represents 7 days of electricity consumption. We first use a linear transform layer as an input embedding to embed a token from 7 dimensions to 128 dimensions, then add a learnable positional encoding to obtain embedding $\mathbf{X}$. Afterwards, $\mathbf{X}$ is taken as the input to both of the vertical attention and horizontal attention modules. The outputs $\mathbf{X_v}$ and $\mathbf{X_h}$ are fused using the token fusion block to produce $\mathbf{X_{vh}}$. Then $\mathbf{X_{vh}}$ is fed into the serial dual attention deformation block. Finally, we flatten the output of the serial dual attention transformer block and use the MLP block to output the final prediction. In the following, we present the detailed construction of the key components in DaFT.

3.1 Dual Attention Transformer Block

In DaFT, we propose a dual attention mechanism that contains both vertical and horizontal dimensions of attention to achieve a better comprehension of the two periodicities in a time series. In detail, the horizontal dimension self-attention focuses on global information, which is defined as:

$$\mathcal{A}_{\text{Horizontal}}(\mathbf{Q_h}, \mathbf{K_h}, \mathbf{V_h}) = \text{Softmax}[\mathbf{Q_h}\mathbf{K_h}^\top]\mathbf{V_h}, \quad (2)$$

where $\mathbf{Q_h} = \mathbf{X}^\top \mathbf{W}_\mathbf{h}^Q$, $\mathbf{K_h} = \mathbf{X}^\top \mathbf{W}_\mathbf{h}^K$ and $\mathbf{V_h} = \mathbf{X}^\top \mathbf{W}_\mathbf{h}^V$, meanwhile $\mathbf{W}$ denotes the projection weights of the attention head for $\mathbf{Q_h}, \mathbf{K_h}, \mathbf{V_h}$ [7].

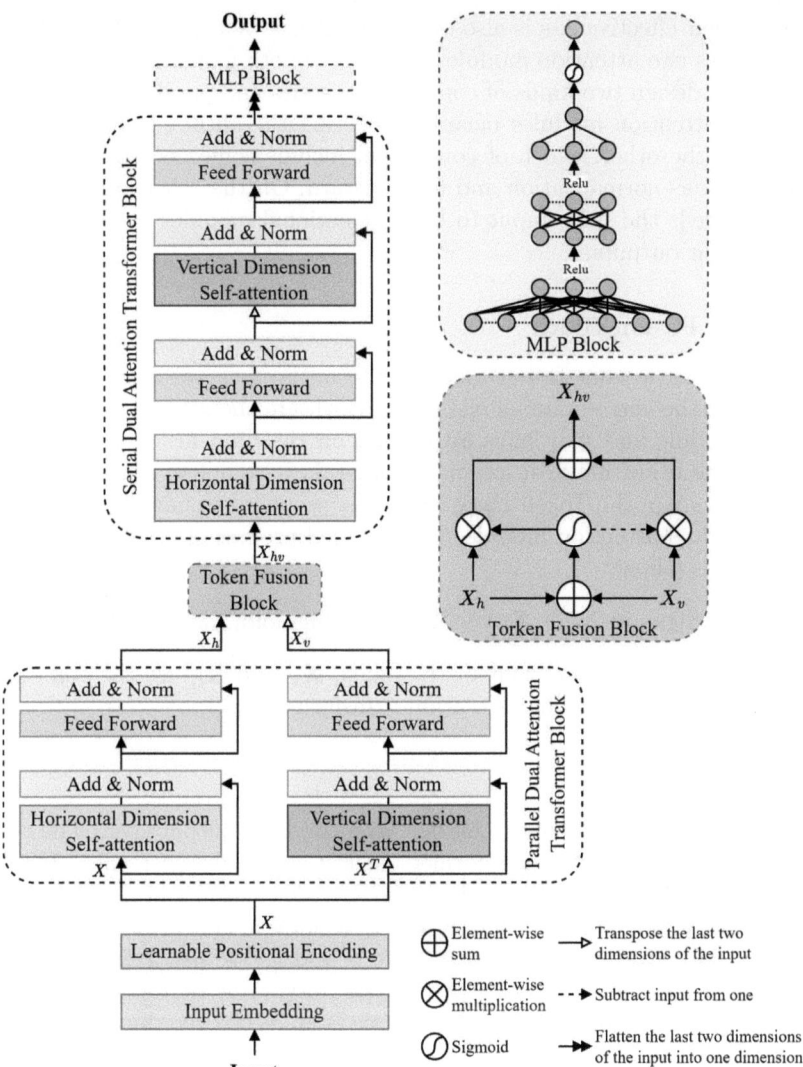

Fig. 5. Architecture of DaFT

Instead, vertical dimensional attention focuses on the processing of local features, which can be represented as:

$$\mathcal{A}_{\text{Vertical}}(\mathbf{Q_v}, \mathbf{K_v}, \mathbf{V_v}) = \text{Softmax}[\mathbf{Q_v}\mathbf{K_v}^\top]\mathbf{V_v}, \tag{3}$$

where $\mathbf{Q_v} = \mathbf{XW_v^Q}$, $\mathbf{K_v} = \mathbf{XW_v^K}$, $\mathbf{V_v} = \mathbf{XW_v^V}$ are weekly vertical level queries, keys and values. While using this hybrid dual-attention mechanism can undoubtedly capture the periodic characteristics of time-series data in a multi-dimensional context, such a combination of the two attentional mechanisms to maximize their effectiveness is also one of the issues we explore. A suitable connection allows two attention modules to preserve both global and local features. In DaFT, we design two kinds of connections: series and parallel. Series connection of two attention modules means connecting the output of one directly to the input of the other, which of course will include some necessary processing modules such as normalization and feed forward. On the other hand, a parallel connection feeds the same input to both attentional modules at the same time and fuses their outputs.

3.2 Token Fusion Block

In the attention feature fusion module, the initial features are fused by simply summing the corresponding elements, which are then taken as input to the attention module and may have an impact on the final fusion weights [5]. In DaFT, on the other hand, in order to maintain a complete perception of the input feature map, the Token Fusion Block is proposed to handle the output of the parallel dual attention module. The detailed process of token fusion can be represented as follows:

$$\mathbf{X_{vh}} = \text{Sigmoid}(\mathbf{X_v} + \mathbf{X_h}) \otimes \mathbf{X_v} + (1 - \text{Sigmoid}(\mathbf{X_v} + \mathbf{X_h})) \otimes \mathbf{X_h}, \quad (4)$$

where $\mathbf{X_{vh}}$ indicates the output of the block, $\mathbf{X_v}$ and $\mathbf{X_h}$ are the embeddings produced by the parallel dual attention transformer block.

3.3 MLP Block

The MLP module consists of two hidden layers and one output layer. The output of the serial dual attention transformer block is a high-dimensional (128×148) feature. So, we flatten it and use the linear transformation and the Relu activation function of hidden layers to reduce it to a suitable dimension (128). Finally, the output layer projects the feature into a scalar. We use a Sigmoid activation function to map this scalar to a probability value in the range of $[0, 1]$, representing the probability that the sample is an electricity thief.

3.4 Loss Function

Electricity theft detection can essentially be considered a binary classification problem,i.e., distinguishing whether the label is a normal customer or an electricity thief. Therefore, we use the binary cross entropy loss function as the loss function of DaFT,

$$\text{Loss}_{\text{DaFT}} = -\frac{1}{N} \sum_{i=1}^{N} \left[y_i \log \left(p(y_i) \right) + (1 - y_i) \log \left(1 - p(y_i) \right) \right], \quad (5)$$

where y_i is the label (we define 0 for normal customers and 1 for electricity thieves), expression $p(y_i)$ is the predicted probability of the electricity thief for the ith sample, and N is the total number of samples.

4 Experimental Evaluation

4.1 Experiment Settings

Performance Metrics. In order to evaluate the performance of the models, we adopt the following widely used metrics when comparing our method with other state-of-the-art benchmarks.

Mean Average Precision (MAP) [19] is a crucial metric for evaluating classification tasks. It combines precision and ranking, calculated as the mean of Average Precision (AP) scores across all queries:

$$\text{MAP}@\mathcal{N} = \frac{1}{r}\sum_{i=1}^{r}\frac{Y_{k_i}}{k_i}, \qquad (6)$$

where r in the number of electricity thieves in top $\mathcal{N}$ positions, Y_{k_i} indicates the number of correctly distinguished malicious users before the position k_i. Generally higher MAP values indicate better classification and ranking performance, and we consider MAP@100 and MAP@200 in this paper.

The Area Under Curve (AUC) [6] is another vital metric for assessing the performance of binary classification models. It quantifies the model's ability to distinguish between positive and negative classes across various threshold settings. The AUC is calculated as:

$$\text{AUC} = \frac{\sum_{i\in \text{theftClass}} \text{Rank}_i - \frac{M(1+M)}{2}}{M \times N}, \qquad (7)$$

where Rank_i is the rank value of user i, M denotes the amount of electricity theft users, with N being the amount of common users.

Training Details. The proposed DaFT and ablation models are implemented by the PyTorch 2.2 library. The critical components of the computer running the experiment are a processor, AMD Ryzen 9 7950X, a graphics card, NVIDIA GeForce RTX 4090, and two DDR5 32G memory. All models are trained with a batch size of 256 using the AdamW [12] optimizer with ten epochs. We set the learning rate constant at 1e–4 and weight decay at 1e–3.

4.2 Performance Comparison

In this section, we provide the experimental outcomes for the datasets analyzed in Sect. 2. Since some traditional methods, including Logistic Regression, Support Vector Machine and Random Forest, have been shown to perform relatively inferior to state-of-the-art methods [17,21], we select five outperforming approaches for comparison in the evaluation. In particular, we consider CNN [8], WDCNN [21], GCN [16], ARMAGCN [4] and DetectGAT [17] as baselines. For each method, we performed 50 trials for four different training ratios and calculated the average AUC and MAP values.

Table 1. Performance comparison of DaFT and other baselines

Groups	Metrics	Models					
		CNN	WDCNN	GCN	ARMAGCN	DetectGAT	DaFT
Group1	AUC	0.773	0.775	0.771	0.773	0.785	**0.808**
	MAP@100	0.930	0.933	0.940	0.944	0.961	**0.986**
	MAP@200	0.906	0.903	0.905	0.905	0.915	**0.966**
Group2	AUC	0.771	0.773	0.772	0.775	0.779	**0.813**
	MAP@100	0.939	0.937	0.947	0.944	0.965	**0.988**
	MAP@200	0.910	0.911	0.924	0.923	0.934	**0.967**
Group3	AUC	0.776	0.784	0.781	0.782	0.789	**0.824**
	MAP@100	0.967	0.955	0.955	0.958	0.981	**0.985**
	MAP@200	0.925	0.925	0.924	0.928	0.956	**0.960**
Group4	AUC	0.782	0.787	0.784	0.785	0.788	**0.827**
	MAP@100	0.947	0.965	0.954	0.955	0.978	**0.980**
	MAP@200	0.927	0.931	0.927	0.930	0.943	**0.950**

Table 1 provides a comparison of the performance of all the schemes mentioned and our DaFT, with groups 1 to 4, taking the different training ratios as 50%, 60%, 70% and 80%. The specific numbers of users in each group refer to the same distribution of work [17]. DaFT method performs experimentally better than other methods in terms of MAP@100, MAP@200 and AUC. It is worth noting that DaFT improves by 6% on MAP@200 and by more than 4% on AUC compared to other benchmark methods. In particular, DaFT achieves a MAP@100 of 0.988 at a training rate of 60% and an AUC of 0.827 at a training rate of 80%. This indicates that our method has superior accuracy and precision to better detect electricity theft users in the electricity system. Meanwhile, such enhancement comes from the fact that the horizontal and vertical dimensions of the dual attention blocks we use can profoundly acquire the weekly periodicity and the day-specific periodicity, to accurately capture the patterns of electricity consumption and therefore distinguish between different users.

4.3 Ablation Study

As previously described, the DaFT consists of Parallel dual attention transformer block, Token fusion block, Serial dual attention transformer block and MLP block. To show that each part of our designed architecture is necessary and reasonable, we set up ablation experiments to prove the significance of each module. The results of four experiments are reported in Table 2, including the original unadapted Transformer [20] (Transformer), two serial dual attention transformer modules connected in series (DaT), DaFT replaced the token fusion block with the simple addition (DaFT w/o TF), and our complete architecture DaFT.

Table 2. Results of ablation experiments

Groups	Metries	Models			
		Transformer	DaT	DaFT w/o TF	DaFT
Group1	AUC	0.805	0.801	0.807	**0.808**
	MAP@100	0.982	0.978	0.984	**0.986**
	MAP@200	0.962	0.959	0.963	**0.966**
Group2	AUC	0.811	0.807	0.812	**0.813**
	MAP@100	0.985	0.984	0.987	**0.988**
	MAP@200	0.962	0.962	0.965	**0.967**
Group3	AUC	0.818	0.820	0.823	**0.824**
	MAP@100	0.981	0.977	0.984	**0.985**
	MAP@200	0.955	0.952	0.956	**0.960**
Group4	AUC	0.820	0.823	0.824	**0.827**
	MAP@100	0.976	0.977	0.979	**0.980**
	MAP@200	0.946	0.945	0.947	**0.950**

From the results, we can conclude that both the introduction of dual attention and the token fusion mechanism contribute to the overall improvement of the model. It is also worth noting that by comparing Table 2 with Table 1, we can clearly see that Transformer-based methods are naturally suited to this type of time series processing, as they all outperform the existing baseline.

5 Conclusion

In this paper, we put forward a dual-attention fusion transformer (DaFT) approach for the detection of electricity theft in smart grids. In particular, the novel approach introduces two dimensional attention: horizontal dimension and vertical dimension to mine the weekly periodicity and day-specific periodicity of the electricity consumption. Furthermore, in order to enhance the integration of the outputs from each module, we also introduced the Token Fusion module to undertake the transfer between modules. We also designed the appropriate combination of topologies, combining series and parallel to maximize the benefits of the dual attention module. Through comparison with five of the best contemporary benchmark methods, we demonstrate the superiority of DaFT in terms of experimental performance. Last but not least, the ablation empirical results show the soundness of our architectural design. It is foreseeable that our method can be applied not only to smart grid datasets, but also to more time-series data in the smart energy industry to make further contributions.

References

1. Ahmed, M., et al.: Energy theft detection in smart grids: taxonomy, comparative analysis, challenges, and future research directions. IEEE/CAA J. Automatica Sinica **9**(4), 578–600 (2022)
2. Aldegheishem, A., Anwar, M., Javaid, N., Alrajeh, N., Shafiq, M., Ahmed, H.: Towards sustainable energy efficiency with intelligent electricity theft detection in smart grids emphasising enhanced neural networks. IEEE Access **9**, 25036–25061 (2021)
3. Arshad, A.: Cybersecurity issues in smart grids and future power systems. MDPI-Multidisc. Dig. Publ. Inst. (2023)
4. Bianchi, F.M., Grattarola, D., Livi, L., Alippi, C.: Graph neural networks with convolutional arma filters. IEEE Trans. Pattern Anal. Mach. Intell. **44**(7), 3496–3507 (2021)
5. Dai, Y., Gieseke, F., Oehmcke, S., Wu, Y., Barnard, K.: Attentional feature fusion. In: Proceedings of the IEEE/CVF Winter Conference on Applications of Computer Vision, pp. 3560–3569 (2021)
6. Davis, J., Goadrich, M.: The relationship between precision-recall and roc curves. In: Proceedings of the 23rd International Conference on Machine Learning, pp. 233–240 (2006)
7. Ding, M., Xiao, B., Codella, N., Luo, P., Wang, J., Yuan, L.: Davit: dual attention vision transformers. In: European Conference on Computer Vision, pp. 74–92. Springer, Heidelberg (2022). https://doi.org/10.1007/978-3-031-20053-3_5
8. Feng, X., et al.: A novel electricity theft detection scheme based on text convolutional neural networks. Energies **13**(21), 5758 (2020)
9. Gul, H., Javaid, N., Ullah, I., Qamar, A.M., Afzal, M.K., Joshi, G.P.: Detection of non-technical losses using sostlink and bidirectional gated recurrent unit to secure smart meters. Appl. Sci. **10**(9), 3151 (2020)
10. Hasan, M.N., Toma, R.N., Nahid, A.A., Islam, M.M., Kim, J.M.: Electricity theft detection in smart grid systems: a cnn-lstm based approach. Energies **12**(17), 3310 (2019)
11. Hasan, M.K., Habib, A.A., Shukur, Z., Ibrahim, F., Islam, S., Razzaque, M.A.: Review on cyber-physical and cyber-security system in smart grid: standards, protocols, constraints, and recommendations. J. Netw. Comput. Appl. **209**, 103540 (2023)
12. Ilya Loshchilov, F.H.: Decoupled weight decay regularization. In: International Conference on Learning Representations 2019 (2019)
13. Javaid, N., Qasim, U., Yahaya, A.S., Alkhammash, E.H., Hadjouni, M., et al.: Non-technical losses detection using autoencoder and bidirectional gated recurrent unit to secure smart grids. IEEE Access **10**, 56863–56875 (2022)
14. Khan, K.A., Quamar, M.M., Al-Qahtani, F.H., Asif, M., Alqahtani, M., Khalid, M.: Smart grid infrastructure and renewable energy deployment: a conceptual review of saudi arabia. Energ. Strat. Rev. **50**, 101247 (2023)
15. Lepolesa, L.J., Achari, S., Cheng, L.: Electricity theft detection in smart grids based on deep neural network. IEEE Access **10**, 39638–39655 (2022)
16. Liao, W., Yang, Z., Liu, K., Zhang, B., Chen, X., Song, R.: Electricity theft detection using euclidean and graph convolutional neural networks. IEEE Trans. Power Syst. **38**(4), 3514–3527 (2022)
17. Liao, W., et al.: Electricity theft detection using dynamic graph construction and graph attention network. IEEE Trans. Ind. Inf. (2023)

18. Mohassel, R.R., Fung, A.S., Mohammadi, F., Raahemifar, K.: A survey on advanced metering infrastructure and its application in smart grids. In: 2014 IEEE 27th Canadian Conference on Electrical and Computer Engineering (CCECE), pp. 1–8. IEEE (2014)
19. Turpin, A., Scholer, F.: User performance versus precision measures for simple search tasks. In: Proceedings of the 29th Annual International ACM SIGIR Conference on Research and Development in Information Retrieval, pp. 11–18 (2006)
20. Vaswani, A.: Attention is all you need. Adv. Neural Inf. Process. Syst. (2017)
21. Zheng, Z., Yang, Y., Niu, X., Dai, H.N., Zhou, Y.: Wide and deep convolutional neural networks for electricity-theft detection to secure smart grids. IEEE Trans. Ind. Inf. **14**(4), 1606–1615 (2017)

Multi-objective Optimization of Energy Storage Capacity Using Non-Dominated Sorting Artificial Cooperative Search and Composite Weighted TOPSIS

Xiao Ye[1], Anping Li[2], Feng Mu[1], Xiaofeng Chen[1], Xiangjuan Meng[1], Shilei Li[3], Jingyao Yang[3], Liguo Yang[3], and Hongmei Li[3](✉)

[1] China Energy Engineering Group Anhui Electric Power Design Institute Co., Ltd, Hefei 230601, China
[2] Huaihe Energy Power Group Co., Ltd., Huainan 232001, China
[3] School of Electrical Engineering and Automation, Hefei University of Technology, Hefei 230009, China
hongmei.li@hfut.edu.cn

Abstract. With the promotion and application of renewable energy sources such as wind and solar power, which effectively reduce carbon emissions, the intermittency and volatility of these renewable sources impact power quality and stability. Energy storage systems, with their rapid charge and discharge capabilities and ease of construction, can smooth out fluctuations in renewable energy output, reduce wind and solar curtailment, improve supply reliability, and support the achievement of carbon neutrality goals. Therefore, a multi-objective optimization scheme for energy storage capacity is proposed in this paper. For proposed scheme, a multi-objective optimization model for energy storage capacity under low-carbon constraints is first set up, then, the Non-Dominated Sorting Artificial Cooperative Search (NSACS) algorithm is integrated with Pareto evaluation to generate the Pareto front, moreover, the composite weighted technique for order preference by similarity to ideal solution (CW-TOPSIS) is proposed to determine the optimal solution on the Pareto front. At last, case studies demonstrate that the proposed scheme is able to automatically determine the optimal energy storage capacity effectively and achieve synergistic optimization of energy storage economic efficiency, reliability, and carbon reduction.

Keywords: Energy Storage Capacity · Multi-Objective Optimization · NSACS Algorithm · Pareto Evaluation · Composite Weighted TOPSIS

1 Introduction

The power grid connects electricity generation and consumption and serves as a central hub for carbon reduction in the power system. It must ensure large-scale development and efficient utilization of renewable energy while meeting the electricity demands of economic and social development [1]. With the large-scale application of renewable energy sources such as wind and solar power, carbon emissions have significantly decreased. However, the intermittency and volatility of wind and solar energy reduce power quality and affect electricity stability.

Energy storage features rapid charge and discharge capabilities and convenient construction, playing a crucial role in stabilizing renewable energy output on the generation side and reducing phenomena such as wind and solar curtailment. On the demand side, it performs multiple functions such as peak shaving and valley filling, and improving supply reliability [2]. Additionally, the rapid development of energy storage contributes to achieving "dual carbon" goals. Current research on optimizing energy storage capacity offers valuable insights. Gao, L. established a single-objective model considering constraints such as line loss and used an improved particle swarm optimization algorithm to optimize this model, obtaining configuration schemes for the energy storage system and operational costs for typical days in different seasons [3]. Feng analyzed the impact of demand response on storage optimization and achieved capacity optimization considering demand response [4]. In [5], a multi-objective optimization model for storage capacity was established to balance economic and reliability aspects, using annual investment costs and node voltage fluctuation improvement as indicators. Non-dominated sorting composite differential evolution was employed for model solving. Ding W et al. used the Harris-Hawk optimization algorithm to solve the multi-objective optimization model for storage capacity, reducing the average fluctuation of photovoltaic output [6]. In [7], a multi-objective optimization model for storage is developed considering carbon reduction benefits, and a relationship between reliability and economic indicators was established. In [8], the Artificial Cooperative Search (ACS) algorithm is applied to the load scheduling problem and compared with other metaheuristic algorithms. The results demonstrate that ACS effectively addresses key shortcomings of existing algorithms, such as sensitivity to initial control parameter values, high time complexity, and susceptibility to premature convergence. Its superior performance in high-dimensional multi-objective optimization problems is also validated.

Optimizing energy storage capacity, with a focus on both economic efficiency and reliability, is addressed as a multi-objective optimization problem. While non-dominated sorting optimization algorithms combined with Pareto evaluation are capable of obtaining Pareto front, however, direct determination of the optimal storage capacity on the Pareto front remains unattainable. To achieve synergistic optimization of energy storage economic efficiency, reliability, and carbon reduction, a multi-objective optimization scheme of energy storage capacity is proposed and the main contributions of the paper are shown as:

(1) A multi-objective optimization model for energy storage capacity is set up that includes a full lifecycle cost model, a full lifecycle carbon emission and carbon trading benefit model, a storage reliability model, and relevant constraints, based on the established model, the non-dominated sorting artificial cooperative search (NSACS) algorithm is integrated with Pareto evaluation to generate the Pareto front and realize the energy storage capacity multi-objective optimization without setting weight factors.

(2) A Composite Weighted TOPSIS is proposed to automatically determine the optimal energy storage capacity on the Pareto front, the problem of not being able to directly

determine the optimal solution from the Pareto front of multi-objective optimization has been successfully overcome.

2 Energy Storage Capacity Optimization Model with Carbon Reduction Considerations

2.1 Objective Function Design

Energy Storage Lifecycle Cost Model. The full lifecycle cost of energy storage (Life Cycle Cost, LCC), also known as total lifecycle cost, includes all costs from project planning, construction, and operation to decommissioning. Its Calculation Formula is:

$$f_1 = C_I + C_O + C_M + C_D \tag{1}$$

where f_1 is the lifecycle cost of the energy storage, C_I is the investment cost of the energy storage, C_O is the operational cost of the device, C_M refers to the replacement cost of the device and C_D signifies the disposal cost of the device.

The investment cost of the device also includes capacity costs and power costs, which can be expressed as:

$$C_I = \lambda_P P + \lambda_E E \tag{2}$$

where λ_P and λ_E are the unit power cost and unit capacity cost, respectively.

The operational costs of the device include the annual operating expenses for the energy storage power and capacity, which can be expressed as:

$$C_O = \sum_{n=1}^{N} \frac{\mu C_I}{(1+r)^n} \tag{3}$$

where μ and r are represent the operational cost coefficient and the discount rate, respectively.

The replacement cost of the device represents the cost of replacing the energy storage batteries after they have reached the end of their service life due to long-term operation. This can be expressed as:

$$C_M = \frac{\lambda_M E (1-\mu)^N}{(1+r)^N} \tag{4}$$

where λ_M and μ are the unit capacity replacement cost and the annual reduction rate in storage costs, respectively.

The disposal cost of the device represents the residual value and scrap costs of the energy storage system, which can be expressed as:

$$C_D = \frac{\delta C_I}{(1+r)^N} \tag{5}$$

where δ represents the residual value recovery rate.

Lifecycle Carbon Emissions and Carbon Trading Revenue Model for Energy Storage System. The total lifecycle carbon emissions of energy storage equipment include emissions from the production, construction, transportation, and virtual power plant operation of devices such as wind turbines and energy storage systems. The objective function is designed as:

$$f_2 = C_q + C_E \tag{6}$$

Carbon emissions costs for wind turbines and energy storage devices during production, construction, and transportation, calculated as follows:

$$C_q = \lambda_c P_m \tag{7}$$

$$P_m = \sum_{j=1}^{H} \left[(1+v_j)^{-t} o_{pi,j} m_{pi,j} + o_{bi,j} m_{bi,j} \right] + \sum_{j=1}^{I} o_{ti,j} m_{ti,j} \tag{8}$$

where λ_c is the carbon treatment price, P_m is the total carbon emissions during production, construction, and transportation, H is the number of material types used in the equipment, I is the number of fuel types required, $o_{pi,j}$ and $o_{bi,j}$ are the carbon emission intensities of the j-th material used during production and construction, respectively. $m_{pi,j}$ and $m_{bi,j}$ are the quantities of the j-th material used during production and construction, respectively. $o_{ti,j}$ and $m_{ti,j}$ are the carbon emission intensities and quantities of the j-th fuel used during transportation, respectively.

As a clean energy source, wind power projects can generate revenue through carbon emission trading by capitalizing on carbon reduction benefits. This compensation effectively represents the reimbursement from thermal power generation companies for the carbon reductions achieved by wind farms. The calculation formula is as follows:

$$C_E = r_s \sum_{t=1}^{T} \lambda_{ess} \left[\sum E(t) \cdot (1+v)^{-t} \right] \tag{9}$$

where r_s and λ_{ess} are the carbon trading unit price and the carbon emission quota per unit of electricity, respectively.

Energy Storage Reliability Model. To reduce the curtailment rate of wind energy and the load-side power deficit, a reliability model for energy storage equipment is established. The objective function of this model is designed as the sum of the wind energy curtailment penalty and the power deficit cost, with the following formulation:

$$f_3 = C_{qf} + C_{qe} \tag{10}$$

The wind energy curtailment penalty cost refers to the cost associated with the wasted wind energy that cannot be absorbed by the energy storage system due to its limited charging capacity once it reaches its maximum charge state. The calculation formula for this penalty cost is:

$$C_{qf} = \sum_{t=1}^{T} c_{qf} \cdot E_{qf} \cdot (1+v)^{-t} \tag{11}$$

where c_{qf} and E_{qf} are the curtailment penalty coefficient and the curtailed wind energy volume, respectively.

The power deficit cost refers to the loss incurred when the energy storage system, after discharging to its minimum charge state, is unable to meet the power demand or target due to insufficient capacity. The calculation formula for this cost is:

$$C_{qe} = \sum_{t=1}^{T} c_{qe} \cdot E_{qe} \cdot (1+v)^{-t} \quad (12)$$

where c_{qe} and E_{qe} are the power deficit cost coefficient and the volume of power deficit, respectively.

2.2 Constraints

In practical engineering applications, the rated power P_{BESS} and the rated capacity S_{BESS} of energy storage devices are set as optimization variables. To achieve a multi-objective optimization configuration for energy storage that balances economic efficiency, reliability, and carbon reduction, it is essential to reasonably set the constraints for wind power generation, energy storage, and power balance.

Wind Power Generation Constraint. The power constraint for wind turbine generation is:

$$PW_t^{\min} < PW_t < PW_t^{\max} \quad t \in T \quad (13)$$

where $PW_t^{\min}$ and $PW_t^{\max}$ are the minimum and rated power outputs of the wind turbines, respectively. PW_t is the real time power outputs of the wind turbines.

Electrochemical Energy Storage Constraint. The constraints that must be met for energy storage include state of charge constraints, energy storage capacity constraints, and power constraints for charging and discharging. The constraint condition of electrochemical energy storage is given as:

$$\begin{cases} SOC_t^{\min} \leq SOC_t \leq SOC_t^{\max} \\ S_{\min} \leq S_{BESS} \leq S_{\max} \\ P_{\min} \leq P_{BESS} \leq P_{\max} \end{cases} \quad (14)$$

where $SOC_t^{\min}$ and $SOC_t^{\max}$ are the minimum and maximum values of energy storage SOC, respectively. $S_{\min}$ and $S_{\max}$ are the upper and lower limits of the rated energy storage capacity, respectively. $P_{\min}$ and $P_{\max}$ are the upper and lower limits of the rated power, respectively.

Power Balance Constraint.

$$\sum_{i=1} P_{i,t}^{ess} + \sum_{i=1} P_{i,t}^{wt} + \sum_{i=1} P_{i,t}^{TH} = 0 \quad (15)$$

where $P_{i,t}^{ess}$, $P_{i,t}^{wt}$ and $P_{i,t}^{TH}$ are the charging and discharging power of energy storage, the wind power output, and the load power at time t, respectively.

3 Proposed Multi-objective Optimization Scheme of Energy Storage Capacity

To achieve a multi-objective synergistic optimization of energy storage capacity that contains energy storage economic efficiency, reliability, and carbon reduction, a multi-objective optimization scheme is proposed integrating NSACS algorithm, Pareto Evaluation, and CW-TOPSIS.

3.1 Generating Pareto Front Based on NSACS Algorithm and Pareto Evaluation

Artificial collaborative search algorithm is an advanced optimization algorithm that solves complex optimization problems by simulating the cooperation and information sharing mechanisms among multiple agents. For proposed scheme, the Pareto solution front is generated based on NSACS algorithm and Pareto evaluation, the implementation steps are shown as:

Step 1. Initialize the population and evaluate fitness.

Create the initial population for two super-individuals, A and B, as shown in Eq. (16). Then, compute the fitness of each individual in super-individuals A and B ($f_1(x)$, $f_2(x)$......$f_n(x)$). Use the non-dominated sorting principle to rank each individual in A and B and calculate the crowding distance (CD) for each individual. Finally, store each individual's fitness, rank, and CD in the super-individuals A and B.

$$A(i,j) = low_j + rand(up_j - low_j) \rightarrow y_{i,A} = fitnessA$$
$$B(i,j) = low_j + rand(up_j - low_j) \rightarrow y_{i,B} = fitnessB \quad (16)$$

Step 2. The selection between predator and prey.

Randomly select predator and prey among individuals A and B, as shown in Eq. (17):

$$if a < b|_{a,b \sim U(0,1)}$$
$$predator := A \rightarrow y_{predator} := y_A$$
$$prey := B \rightarrow y_{prey} := y_B \quad (17)$$
$$else$$
$$predator := B \rightarrow y_{predator} := y_B$$

Step 3. Offspring generation.

Utilize predator-prey interactions to generate new positions and directions, adjusted via a Wiener process. Predators determine cooperation probability based on crossover effectiveness. Compute offspring fitness, ranking, and CD, storing results separately. See Eqs. (18) and (19):

$$x = predator + R.(prey - predator)$$
$$R = 4 \times a.(b - c)|_{a,b,c \sim U(0,1)} \quad (18)$$

$$if a <= (P \times b)|_{a,b \sim U(0,1)}$$
$$x_{i,j} = stronger - predator_{i,j}$$
$$else \quad (19)$$
$$x_{i,j} = predator_{i,j}$$

Step 4. Elite selection.

Find the best population by combining predators and offspring, sort the combined population based on fitness and ranking and select the optimal individual.

Step 5. Generate the Pareto front using Pareto evaluation.

Repeat the above steps up to the maximum number of iterations to generate the Pareto front for multi-objective optimization of energy storage capacity.

3.2 Optimal Energy Storage Capacity Generation Based on Proposed Composite Weighted TOPSIS

For proposed scheme, based on the generated Pareto front, the optimal energy storage capacity can be automatically generated using proposed composite weighted TOPSIS, the specific implementation steps are:

Step 1. Process ω_1^T drawn from subjective weight and ω_2^T drawn from objective weight by linear combination to acquire combination weight ω^*:

$$\omega^* = \alpha_1 \omega_1^T + \alpha_2 \omega_2^T \tag{20}$$

Step 2. Use game theory concepts to find the Nash equilibrium points:

$$Min ||\omega^* - \omega_k||_2, k = 1, 2 \tag{21}$$

Step 3. According to the properties of matrix differentials, the optimal solution of Eq. (21) satisfies the following conditions:

$$\begin{bmatrix} \omega_1 \omega_1^T & \omega_1 \omega_2^T \\ \omega_2 \omega_1^T & \omega_2 \omega_2^T \end{bmatrix} \begin{bmatrix} \alpha_1 \\ \alpha_2 \end{bmatrix} = \begin{bmatrix} \omega_1 \omega_1^T \\ \omega_2 \omega_2^T \end{bmatrix} \tag{22}$$

Step 4. Obtain α_1^*, α_2^* After normalization and calculate the optimized combination weights:

$$\omega^* = \alpha_1^* \omega_1^T + \alpha_2^* \omega_2^T \tag{23}$$

Step 5. Evaluate the generated Pareto front using TOPSIS. Assume there are m objects and n evaluation criteria, we could construct the decision matrix and normalize and weight it to obtain the weighted decision matrix V:

$$V = \begin{bmatrix} \omega_1^* b_{11} & \omega_2^* b_{12} & \cdots & \omega_n^* b_{1n} \\ \omega_1^* b_{21} & \omega_2^* b_{21} & \cdots & \omega_n^* b_{2n} \\ \vdots & \vdots & \vdots & \vdots \\ \omega_1^* b_{m1} & \omega_2^* b_{m2} & \cdots & \omega_n^* b_{mn} \end{bmatrix} \tag{24}$$

Step 6. Determine the positive ideal solution and the negative ideal solution. Calculate the optimal and worst distances for each solution:

$$F^+ = \max_{1 \le i \le m} v_{ij} \tag{25}$$

$$F^- = \min_{1 \leq i \leq m} v_{ij} \tag{26}$$

$$d_j^+ = \sqrt{\sum_{i=1}^{m}(F_i^+ - F_{ij})^2} \tag{27}$$

$$d_j^- = \sqrt{\sum_{i=1}^{m}(F_i^- - F_{ij})^2} \tag{28}$$

Step 7. Calculate the comprehensive evaluation index C_i, and rank the solutions based on C_i to determine the optimal solution of the Pareto front:

$$C_i = d_i^- / (d_i^- + d_i^+) \tag{29}$$

The flowchart diagram for achieving optimal energy storage capacity based on the proposed scheme is shown in Fig. 1.

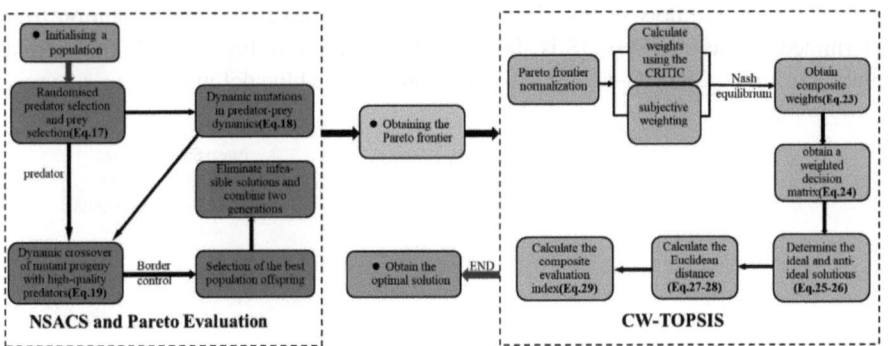

Fig. 1. The flowchart diagram of proposed scheme.

4 Case Study and Analysis

This paper uses a 250 MW wind farm in a certain region as a case study to implement the proposed scheme for optimizing energy storage capacity. The basic parameters are listed in Table 1.

The sampling period for the output power of the wind farm is 1 min, resulting in a total of 1,440 samples per day. By using the average of the correlated data at the same time across all days of the month, a simplified calculation of a typical day can be achieved, which is then used to obtain wind power data for each year within the lifespan of the wind farm.

To validate the effectiveness and superiority of the proposed scheme, the case study first uses NSACS and Pareto evaluation to generate the Pareto solution front. Subsequently, a comparative analysis is conducted on the two energy storage capacity configurations obtained using the traditional objective weighting (CRITIC)-TOPSIS method

Table 1. Basic parameters

Parameters	Value
Battery prices/(¥/kWh)	1085
Capacity maintenance cost/(¥/kWh)	10
Power maintenance cost/(¥/kWh)	90
feed-in tariff/(¥/kWh)	0.6
Carbon treatment price λ_c/(¥/kg)	0.0252
charge-discharge efficiency	0.95
SOC_t^{min}	0.2
SOC_t^{max}	0.8

and the proposed CW-TOPSIS method. The Pareto solution front generated for energy storage multi-objective optimization based on NSACS and Pareto evaluation is represented by the red dots in Fig. 2. The optimal solution of the Pareto solution front determined by the CW-TOPSIS is shown as the green dot in Fig. 2, while the optimal solution from the CRITIC-TOPSIS is represented by the blue dot in Fig. 2.

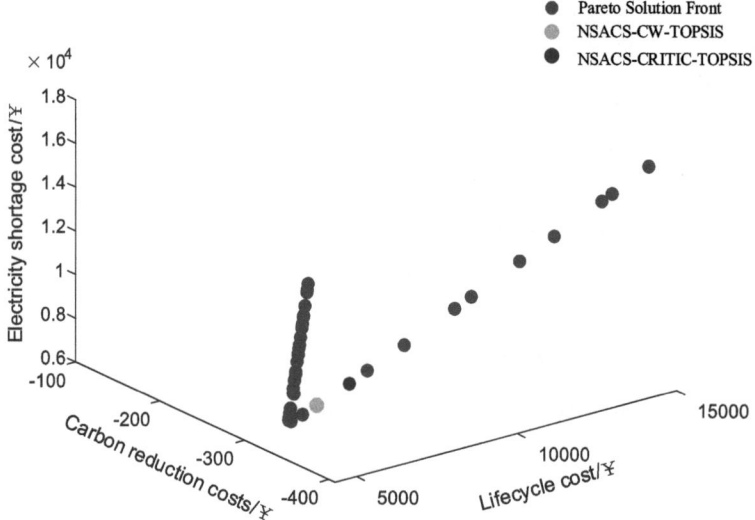

Fig. 2. The optimal solutions determined by different approaches.

For proposed scheme, based on the established multi-objective optimization model of energy storage capacity, the Pareto front is generated using NSACS algorithm and Pareto evaluation, there are a total of 88 solutions on the Pareto front, and then, the optimal solution for the Pareto front is automatically determined by proposed composite weighted TOPSIS or by CRITIC-TOPSIS and shown in Table 2.

Table 2. Optimal energy storage capacity under different schemes.

	NSACS-CW-TOPSIS	NSACS-CRITIC-TOPSIS
$S_{BESS}/MW \cdot h$	886.9	700.4
P_{BESS}/MW	192.6	227.1
$f_1/10^4$	5032.7	7473.2
$f_2/10^4$	−364.3	−380.2
$f_3/10^4$	8601.4	10863.0
$\sum f/10^4$	13260.8	17956.0

According to the proposed scheme, the optimal energy storage capacity is 886.9 kWh, the rated power is 192.6 kW, the total lifecycle cost is 50.237 million RMB, carbon trading revenue is 3.643 million RMB, and the penalties for load deficiencies and wind curtailment amount to 86.014 million RMB. Based on the 88 solutions on the Pareto front, the optimal solution determined by CRITIC-TOPSIS has higher lifecycle costs and load deficiency penalties compared with the proposed scheme. This demonstrates that the proposed scheme not only balances economic efficiency and reliability but also effectively reduces load deficiency rates and achieves carbon emission reduction goals.

5 Conclusion

The paper formulates a multi-objective optimization model for energy storage capacity, incorporating life-cycle costs, carbon emissions, carbon trading revenues, storage reliability, and relevant constraints, the non-dominated sorting artificial cooperative search (NSACS) algorithm is integrated with Pareto evaluation to generate the Pareto front and the energy storage capacity multi-objective optimization is achieved without the need to set weight factors, moreover, optimal storage capacity is subsequently determined using proposed composite weighted TOPSIS. The proposed scheme not only balances economic efficiency and reliability but also markedly reduces power shortage rates and enhances carbon reduction compared with the scheme based on NSACS algorithm, Pareto evaluation and CRITIC-TOPSIS, furthermore, the proposed scheme thus facilitates increased renewable energy integration and supports the attainment of Carbon Peaking and Carbon Neutrality objectives.

References

1. Xunkui, Z.: Development roadmap of new power system with new energy as the main body. Distrib. Energy **6**(06), 1–8 (2021)
2. Algarni, S., Tirth, V., Alqahtani, T., Alshehery, S., Kshirsagar, P.: Contribution of renewable energy sources to the environmental impacts and economic benefits for sustainable development. Sustain. Energy Technol. **56**(13), 103–111 (2023)

3. Gao, L., Xia, Y., Xiong, Y., Song, G., Xin, J.: Research on allocation of energy storage system in microgrid based on improved particle swarm optimization algorithm. In: Yang, Q., Li, Z., Luo, A. (eds.) The Proceedings of the 18th Annual Conference of China Electrotechnical Society. ACCES 2023. Lecture Notes in Electrical Engineering, vol. 1167. Springer, Singapore (2024). https://doi.org/10.1007/978-981-97-1064-5_77
4. Feng, H., Xu, H.D., Sun, F.F., et al.: An optimal allocation method of energy storage in the recipient grid taking into account the demand-side response capability. J. Zhejiang Elec. Power **42**(12), 107–116 (2023)
5. Zhao, W., Yuan, X.L., Zhou, Y.X., et al.: Capacity configuration method of a second-use battery energy storage system considering economic optimization within service life. Power Syst. Protect. Control **49**(12), 16–24 (2021)
6. Ding, W., Su, X.K., Liao, S.X., et al.: Optimization of photovoltaic energy storage capacity allocation based on Harris Hawk optimization algorithm. J. Elec. Des. Eng. **32**(01), 96–101 (2024)
7. Li, C.L.: Optimal allocation of energy storage capacity for photovoltaic microgrid based on discrete particle swarm algorithm. J. Electrotechnology **22**, 93–96 (2023)
8. Aghay Kaboli, S.H., Alqallaf, A.K.: Solving non-convex economic load dispatch problem via artificial cooperative search algorithm. Expert Syst. Appl. **128**, 14–27 (2019)

Vehicular Networks and ITS

Development of a Cost-Effective V2X Test-Bed to Study the Characteristics of Vehicular Networks

Manoj Bandara Dissanayake[1](✉), Shamika Lakshan Indrasiri[1], Hasini Prabodhika Dematawaarachchi[1], Kalupahana Liyanage Kushan Sudheera[1], and Peter Han Joo Chong[2]

[1] Department of Electrical and Information Engineering, University of Ruhuna, Matara, Sri Lanka
{eg183318,eg183342,eg183304}@engug.ruh.ac.lk, kushan@eie.ruh.ac.lk
[2] Department of Electrical and Electronic Engineering, Auckland University of Technology, Auckland, New Zealand
peter.chong@aut.ac.nz

Abstract. In recent years autonomous driving and efficient traffic management have become pivotal areas of focus, amplifying the research on Vehicle-to-Everything (V2X) communication technology. However, most research on V2X has relied heavily on computer simulations due to the scarcity and high costs of practical hardware test-beds, often failing to capture real-world complexities. This research presents a novel, low-cost V2X test-bed developed using commodity hardware components, offering a platform for studying V2X communication. The proposed test-bed, which integrates On-Board Units (OBUs) and Roadside Units (RSUs), demonstrates its ability to achieve latency and packet loss that meet relevant standards through extensive experiments under various V2V (Vehicle-to-Vehicle) and V2I (Vehicle-to-Infrastructure) scenarios.

Keywords: Vehicular Networks · Vehicular Ad-Hoc Networks · Latency · Packet loss · V2V · V2I · V2X Test-Beds

1 Introduction

The integration of autonomous driving technologies and Vehicle-to-Everything (V2X) communication has gained significant attention in recent years, mainly due to its potential to revolutionize road safety, traffic management, and overall mobility experiences. V2X communication facilitates real-time data exchange between vehicles, infrastructure, and other nodes in the transportation ecosystem by utilizing multiple communication types, including Vehicle-to-Vehicle (V2V), Vehicle-to-Infrastructure (V2I) [1]. This enables situational awareness, allowing vehicles to perceive their surroundings, which leads to safer and more efficient autonomous driving [2–4]. By leveraging V2X communication, numerous applications in V2V, and V2I can be implemented. Examples of V2V applications include forward collision detection, intersection collision detection, blind spot detection, and steep slope alerts. V2I applications include speed limit alerts, vehicle turn assistance, smart traffic light status alerts, and parking information notifications [5–7].

Despite the increasing popularity of V2X research, most of the research and development in this domain have relied on computer simulations [8]. Software-based simulators can be divided into three different categories, (a) Vehicular Mobility Generators, (b) Network Simulators, and (c) Integrated Simulators [8–11].

Vehicular Mobility Generators are used to generate realistic vehicular mobility traces which can be used as an input for network simulators. Examples are, SUMO (Simulation of Urban Mobility) [12], MOVE (MObility model generator for VEhicular networks) [13], VanetMobiSim [14], FreeSim [15], CityMob [16], etc. Many of these mobility generators, such as SUMO, can utilize real-world map data from OpenStreetMap to create more accurate and realistic urban environments for simulations [17]. Network Simulators can be used to test the performance of networking protocols. Using network simulators, researchers study how the network would behave under different conditions. Most widely used network simuators are, NS3 [18], OMNeT++ [19], OPNET [20]. Integrated simulators also known as VANET simulators [10], combine vehicular mobility generators and network simulators to provide a comprehensive simulation environment for studying VANETs by simulating both realistic vehicle movements and network communications in a single platform. Examples are, TraNS (Traffic and Network Simulation Environment) [21], GrooveNet [22], NCTUns Simulator [23], Veins [24].

Even though simulations offer valuable insights and provide controlled environments, they often fail to capture the complex dynamics of real-world scenarios. Factors such as environmental conditions, interference, and unpredictable human behaviour can significantly impact the performance and reliability of V2X systems, which emphasizes the need for practical, hardware-based test-beds. Yet, existing hardware-based V2X test-beds are often costly and primarily designed for industrial applications, making them inaccessible to most university-level academic researchers [25]. This accessibility barrier slows the progress of both theoretical and practical advancements in the field.

When considering examples of existing hardware-based V2X test-beds, several notable initiatives stand out. The *Connected Smart Mobility (COSMO)* [26] test-bed at Nanyang Technological University which comprises Dedicated Short-Range Communications (DSRC) On-Board Units (OBUs), Roadside Units (RSUs), hybrid (DSRC + Cellular) RSUs, and IP cameras, facilitates the development and testing of numerous V2V and V2I use cases based on DSRC technology. Similarly, Belgium's *Antwerp Smart Highway Test-bed* [27] which includes hardware that allows for the testing of Cooperative Intelligent Transport Systems (C-ITS) applications in open road scenarios, specifically on highways. Furthermore, *AstaZero* [28] is another V2X test-site, located near Gothenburg, Sweden. Its infrastructure includes diverse road scenarios, ranging from urban and rural settings to high-speed multi-lane highways, providing an ideal platform for evaluating vehicle dynamics and driver behaviour. The *simTD* [29] project primarily focuses on field operational tests on (public) roads for validation of V2X systems. Its infrastructure includes vehicles, RSUs, and infrastructural facilities for traffic and test management. Another approach is *Mcity* [30], driven by the University of Michigan, USA. It consists of more than sixteen acres of roads and traffic infrastructure including automated vehicles on public streets, roads, and highways. While these test-beds provide invaluable insights into V2X system performance under real-world conditions, their high cost makes them inaccessible to most university-level academic researchers.

To address this gap, this research presents the development and evaluation of a low-cost, hardware-based V2X test-bed specifically tailored for academic and research purposes. By leveraging commodity hardware components and adopting a modular design approach, the proposed test-bed offers a realistic and practical platform to study applications and characteristics of V2X technology.

There are two primary objectives in our research; The first one is to develop a cost-effective and resource-efficient test-bed that can be readily adopted in academic settings. The second one is to evaluate network performance in terms of latency and packet loss, which are critical factors for the reliable and efficient operation of V2X systems and to study the limitations and challenges in the proposed test-bed.

The remainder of the paper is organized as follows: Sect. 2 describes the system architecture of the communication setup and the methodology carried out throughout the research project. Section 3 provides an overview of the experiments conducted on the test-bed, the performance metrics and the obtained results. Finally, in Sect. 4, the conclusions and the future works have been discussed.

2 V2X Test-Bed

2.1 V2X Test-Bed Hardware Architecture

On Board Unit (OBU): The V2X test-bed utilizes two OBU devices. In an OBU, a Raspberry Pi 3 device acts as the central control unit, which is responsible for controlling sensors, executing algorithms, and managing critical functions. These functions include processing GPS and accelerometer data, handling Basic Safety Message (BSM) data, and displaying relevant information to the user. Figure 1a illustrates the hardware architecture of the proposed OBU device and Fig. 1b presents the physical setup.

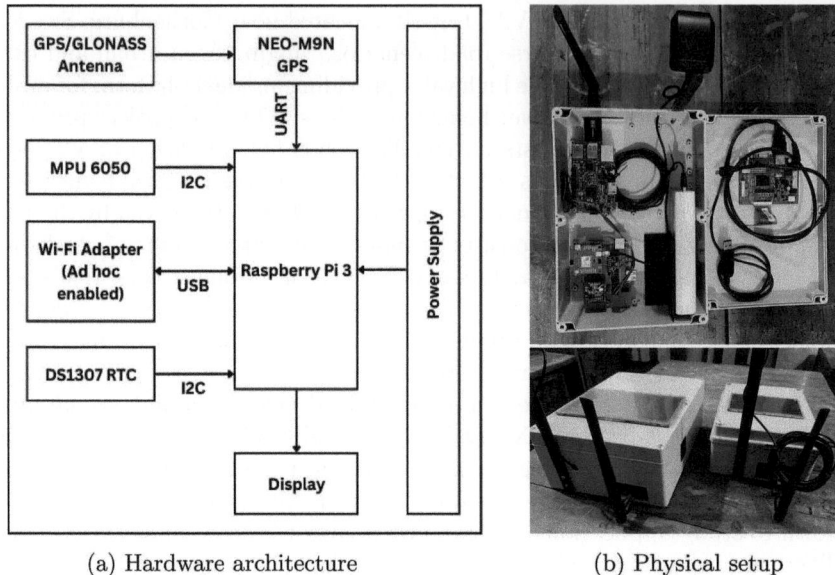

Fig. 1. Hardware architecture and physical setup of OBU

The OBU devices employ multiple sensors to gather essential data. For example, a SparkFun NEO-M9N GPS Breakout module is used to obtain longitude, latitude, and speed information. Additionally, an accelerometer is utilized to capture acceleration data. The GPS module communicates data to the Raspberry Pi via UART, while the accelerometer employs I2C communication for data transmission.

Upon receiving data from these sensors, the Raspberry Pi compiles the information into a BSM packet, which is broadcasted via the 2.4 GHz band of the Wi-Fi adapter at intervals of 100 milliseconds. This Wi-Fi adapter also receives BSM data packets broadcasted by other OBUs and RSUs within the same ad-hoc network. After receiving the BSM data packets, the Raspberry Pi extracts relevant information, including longitude, latitude, speed, and acceleration. These data are then processed through the algorithms presented in Fig. 5, enabling the determination of the relative positions of other OBUs and RSUs within the area. This positional information is subsequently utilized for critical operations, such as blind collision avoidance, and parking spot identification. Even though the 5.9 GHz DSRC band is usually used for BSM communication in V2X systems, we have employed the 2.4 GHz Wi-Fi band for BSM communication due to the significant cost reduction it offers.

Road Side Unit (RSU): The proposed V2X test-bed also incorporates an RSU, which also acts as a smart traffic light. The RSU is designed to explore V2I

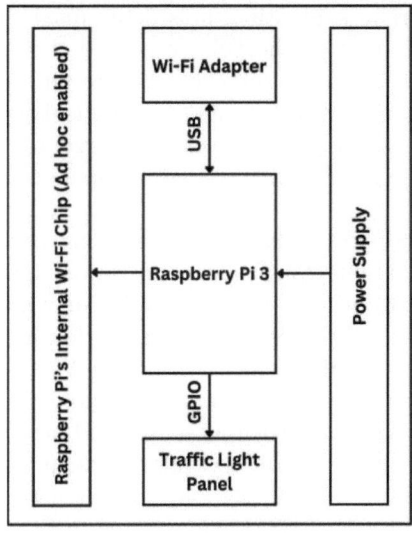 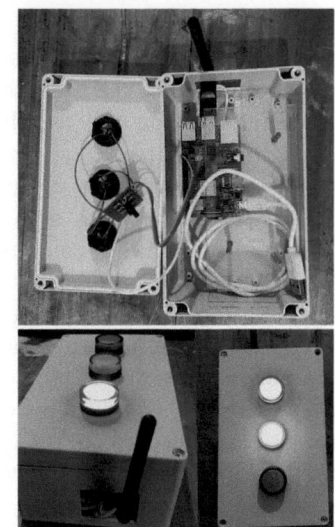

(a) Hardware architecture (b) Physical setup

Fig. 2. Hardware architecture and physical setup of OBU

communication, functioning as a fixed node within the V2X network. Figure 2a and Fig. 2b presents the hardware and physical setup, respectively.

In the RSU, the Raspberry Pi 3 device serves as the central processing unit. The Raspberry Pi's built-in Wi-Fi chip is utilized to establish an ad-hoc connection with the OBUs, enabling seamless V2X communication. Furthermore, an external Wi-Fi adapter is employed to connect the RSU to the Internet and cloud-based databases, enabling Internet of Vehicles (IoV) operations via real-time data updates and synchronization with the broader V2X network.

The RSU utilizes the cloud-based database to retrieve information about available parking spots within a 1 km radius. Through integration with MongoDB, the RSU conducts database queries to identify unoccupied parking spaces and broadcasts the coordinates of these available spots to nearby drivers through the ad-hoc network. This functionality addresses urban parking by guiding drivers to vacant spaces and facilitating effective traffic management.

2.2 V2X Test-Bed Software Framework

The software configuration for the V2X test-bed can be broadly divided into two main components: the OBU software and the RSU software.

OBU Software: The OBU software framework consists of three key elements: the design of the custom packet structure for the BSM, the implementation of the path prediction and collision avoidance algorithm, and the implementation of the OBU dashboard.

When considering the BSM, after careful evaluation, it is determined that certain details within the fundamental format of the BSM exceeded the specific requirements of the proposed V2X test-bed environment. As a result, non-essential information such as vehicle type, motion state, and optional fields were omitted from the packet structure. A custom packet format, tailored to the test-bed's requirements, is designed for the BSM, which is used to communicate between nodes in the V2X system.

The proposed BSM consists of a 28-byte packet structure. This packet includes essential data elements such as latitude, longitude, acceleration, speed, and timestamp. This approach helped to optimize the packet size and minimize additional overhead, ultimately enhancing the overall network performance. When packets are broadcasted utilizing the UDP protocol within the V2X network, a 42-byte header is appended to each BSM packet for routing and delivery purposes. The header consisted of essential details such as source and destination IP addresses, protocol type, packet length, and checksum. Consequently, the original 28-byte packet size expanded to 70 bytes (28 + 42) during network transmission. The basic structure of the proposed BSM is illustrated in Fig. 3.

Packet Header	Msg ID	Vehicle Info (Position, Speed, Acceleration, etc.)	Timestamp

Fig. 3. BSM packet structure

To achieve simultaneous transmission and reception of packets within the test-bed, multi-threading is used. Two separate threads were created for this purpose: one for transmitting packets at fixed intervals of 100 milliseconds (refer Fig. 5a) and another for receiving and unpacking incoming packets (refer Fig. 5b). These threads operated concurrently, ensuring efficient packet exchange.

In addition to the communication protocol implementation, the OBU software also incorporates a path prediction and collision avoidance algorithm. This algorithm processes the GPS data received from the OBU's sensors, as well as from the data packets broadcasted by neighbouring vehicles. By employing the algorithm in Fig. 5c, which uses the Kalman filter, the OBU is able to forecast the future positions of the vehicles, enabling the identification of potential collision scenarios. The anticipated trajectories of the vehicles are then used to identify potential collisions. If a potential collision is identified, the algorithm calculates the distance and time to the collision periodically at fixed intervals of 1 s and the data will be transmitted to the OBU dashboard, developed using Node-RED, to warn the driver.

Figure 4 illustrates an instance, where the collision detection algorithm identifies a potential collision between two vehicles by employing the Kalman filter to predict future trajectories of the two vehicles.

Furthermore, the dashboard also displays the available vacant parking spots on a map upon the request of the user, using the location (latitude and longitude) details of the parking spots that are extracted from the data packets received from the RSU.

RSU Software: The RSU software implementation mainly focuses on two primary functions: traffic light control and dissemination of parking availability.

Since the RSU also operates as a smart traffic light, the traffic light operation is managed by the Raspberry Pi 3 device through a predefined sequence of states: red, red-yellow, and green. Raspberry Pi's GPIO pins were utilized to control the lights. The status information of the traffic light is embedded and broadcasted through the BSM packets, which are then displayed on the OBU's dashboard in real time.

In addition to traffic light control, the RSU software also uses a cloud-based database to retrieve real-time information about available parking spots within a 1 km radius. Through the use of MongoDB, the RSU conducts database queries to identify unoccupied parking spaces and broadcasts the coordinates of these available spots via BSM packets, to nearby drivers. This functionality optimizes urban parking by guiding drivers to vacant spaces, contributing to congestion reduction and facilitating smoother traffic management. The RSU's software architecture is designed to execute these tasks concurrently through separate threads, enabling the unit to efficiently manage both traffic control and the dissemination of parking information.

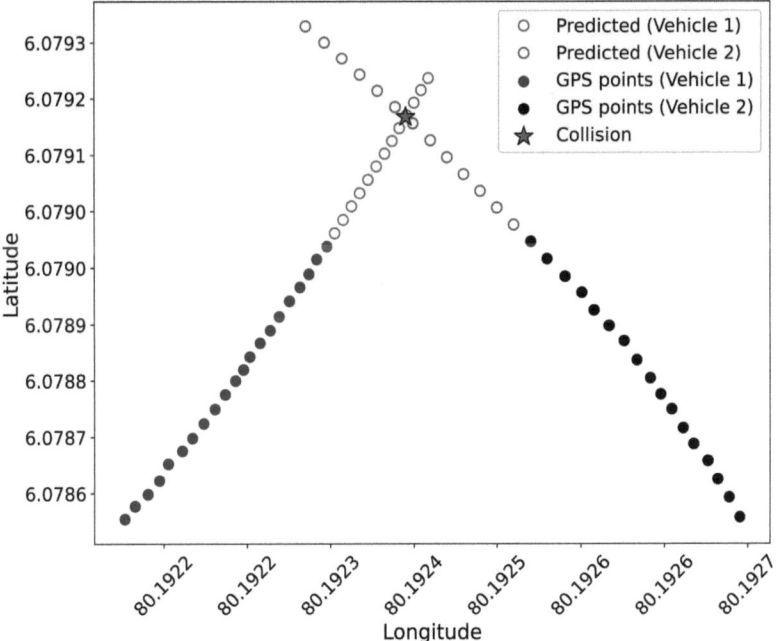

Fig. 4. Kalman path prediction and collision detection

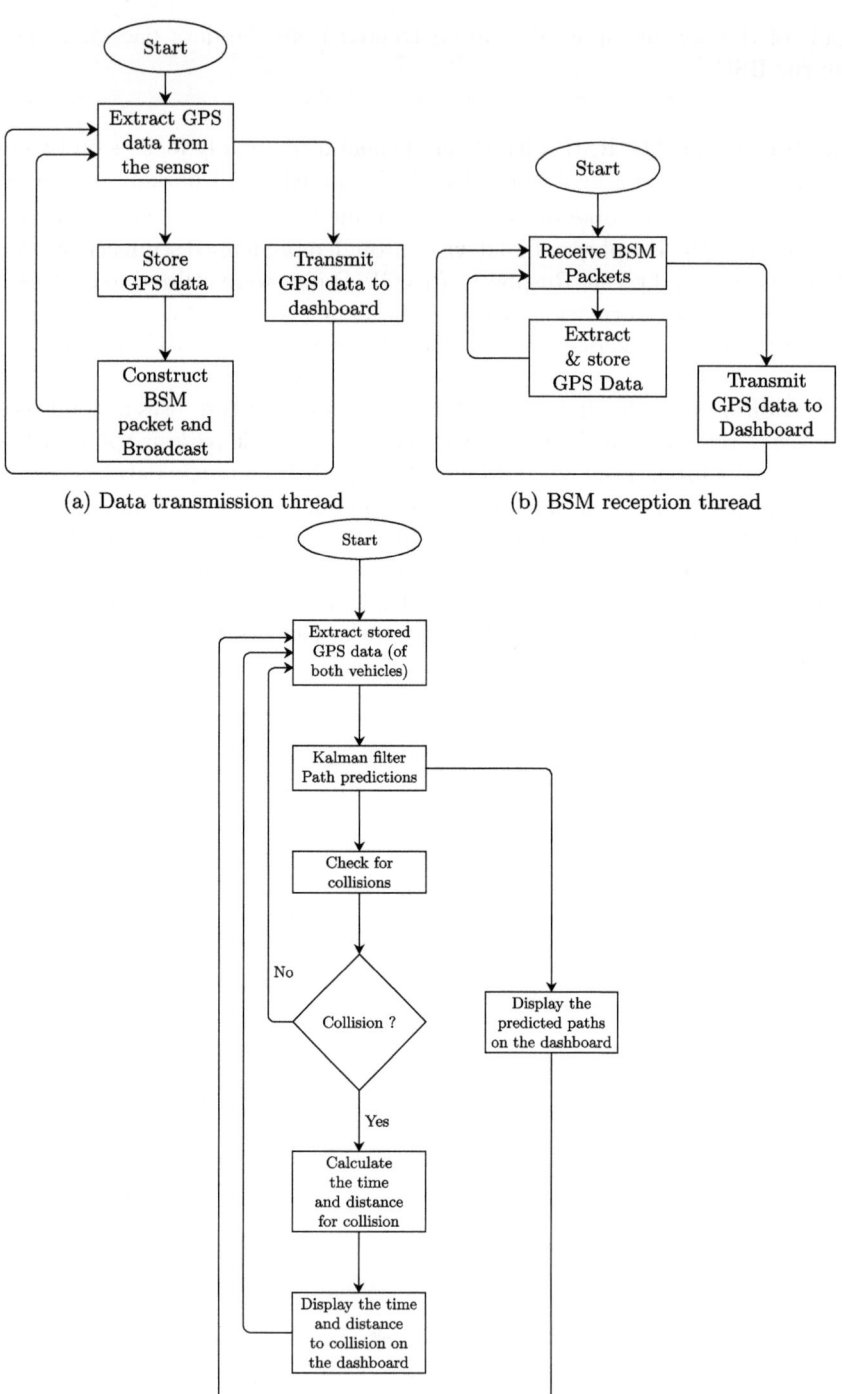

Fig. 5. Main threads in the OBU software architecture

By employing a modular and multi-threaded software design, OBU and RSU components of the V2X test-bed, work in tandem to provide a comprehensive and reliable platform for studying and evaluating various applications of V2X communication and its role in autonomous driving and intelligent transportation systems.

3 Performance Evaluation

3.1 Experimental Scenarios

To evaluate the performance of the V2X test-bed, latency and the packet loss characteristics of the test-bed were evaluated using two distinct scenarios: V2V communication and V2I communication. These experiments were conducted within the confines of the university premises.

V2V Communication Test Scenario: In the V2V test scenario, experiments were carried out to analyze the latency and packet loss characteristics using two vehicles in motion towards each other. The following settings were considered for the V2V experiments: *(i) Frequency Variation under Constant Speed*, and *(ii) Speed Variation under Constant Frequency*. The test location of this V2V communication test scenario is shown in Fig. 6.

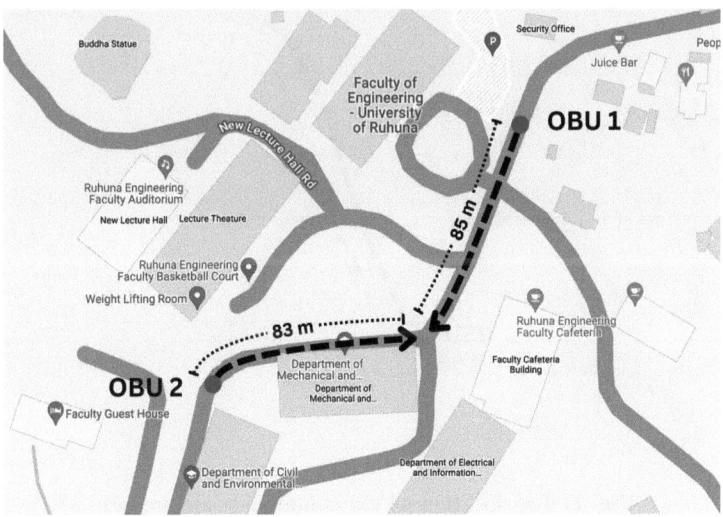

Fig. 6. Test location of V2V communication scenario

In the *Frequency Variation under Constant Speed* scenario, the vehicles maintained a consistent average speed of 20 km/h. Variations were introduced in the communication frequencies, as 1, 3, 5, 7, and 10 Hz. This setup allowed for a comprehensive examination of the impact of changing BSM broadcasting frequency on latency and packet drop in the V2V communication context.

For the *Speed Variation under Constant Frequency* scenario, a fixed BSM broadcasting frequency of 5 Hz was maintained, and the speeds of the vehicles were varied, with the average speeds set at 10, 15, 20, 25, and 30 km/h in both vehicles. The tests were conducted for each of these speed configurations. This configuration enabled an exhaustive exploration of how altering vehicle speeds, while keeping the BSM broadcasting frequency constant, influenced latency and packet drop within the V2V communication network.

V2I Communication Test Scenario: In the V2I test scenario, an in-depth analysis of latency and packet drop was conducted using a single vehicle interacting with the custom-built smart traffic light serving as the RSU. During this test case, the vehicle approached RSU, indicating movement towards the RSU. Similar to the V2V communication test scenario, two specific settings: *(i) Frequency Variation under Constant Speed* and *(ii) Speed Variation under Constant Frequency*, were considered for the V2I experiments. The test location for this V2I communication scenario is shown in Fig. 7.

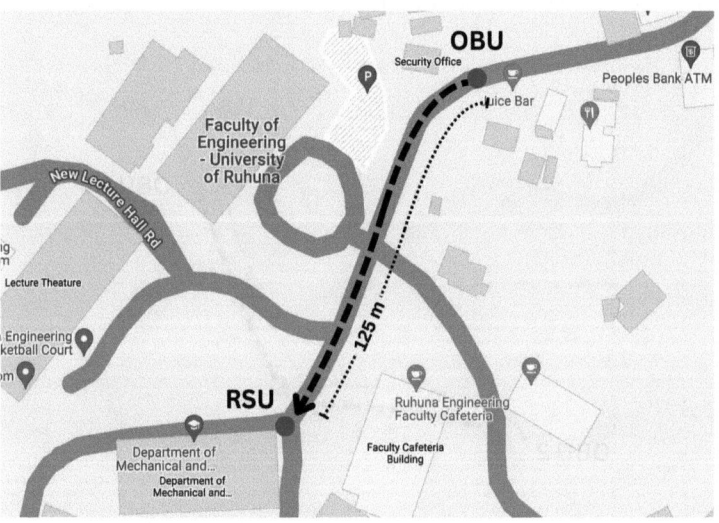

Fig. 7. Test location of V2I communication scenario

In the *Frequency Variation under Constant Speed* scenario, a consistent average speed of 15 km/h was maintained. The investigation involved introducing variations in BSM broadcasting frequency, which were set at 1, 3, 5, 7, and 10 Hz. Data were recorded for each frequency and conducted an assessment of the impact of frequency variation on latency and packet loss in the V2I communication context.

For the *Speed Variation under Constant Frequency* scenario, a fixed BSM broadcasting frequency of 5 Hz was maintained, and the vehicle's speeds were systematically adjusted, with the average speeds set at 5, 10, 15, 20, and 25 km/h. Data were recorded separately for each distinct speed, and an analysis of the influence of varying vehicle speeds on latency and packet loss in V2I communication was conducted.

3.2 Performance Metrics

After the completion of all test scenarios, a comprehensive analysis was conducted using the accumulated data. In the context of latency evaluation, we considered average end-to-end latency, which indicates the time a packet takes to reach the destination.

Packet Delivery Ratio (PDR) was calculated through the identification of delivered packets via their respective sequence numbers. By tracking the sequence numbers of the transmitted and received packets, it is possible to precisely quantify the number of packets that did not successfully reach their intended destinations. This method proved to be a straightforward and effective means of ascertaining PDR within the V2X test-bed.

The recorded data were comprehensively visualized through the generation of graphical representations. These graphical depictions provide a more intuitive understanding of the results. The graphs representing the data and their corresponding analytical key results are detailed in the Subsect. 3.3.

3.3 Result Analysis

The comprehensive evaluation of the performance of the proposed V2X test-bed, encompassing both V2V and V2I communication scenarios, has yielded valuable insights, in terms of packet loss and latency characteristics, under two specific test scenarios: *Frequency Variation under Constant Speed* and *Speed Variation under Constant Frequency*. The gathered data have been analyzed and presented through a series of graphical visualizations to facilitate a better understanding of the test-bed's characteristics.

Latency Analysis: The average latency values observed in the two test scenarios: *Frequency Variation under Constant Speed* and *Speed Variation under Constant Frequency*, for both V2V and V2I test cases are depicted in Fig. 8 and Fig. 9, respectively.

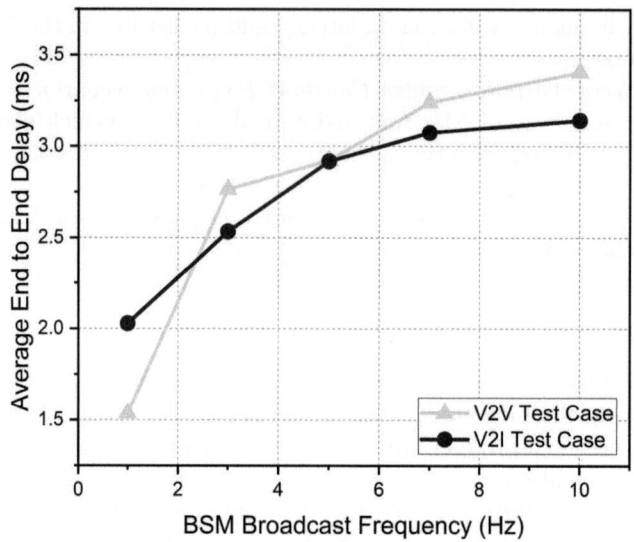

Fig. 8. Average latency for different BSM broadcast frequencies

As shown in Fig. 8, for both V2V and V2I test cases, the average latency values exhibit an increasing trend as the BSM broadcasting frequency is increased. This observation can be due to the increasing number of packets being transmitted per second, leading to packet congestion within the ad-hoc network. However,

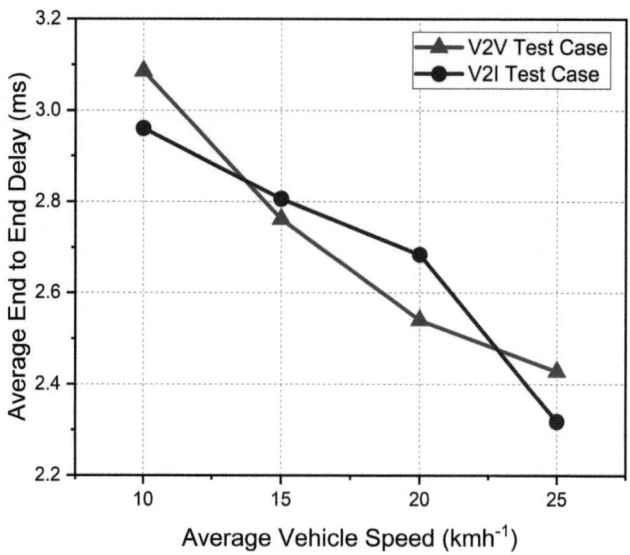

Fig. 9. Average latency for different speeds

it is noteworthy that the average latency remained at a reasonably low value of 3.4 ms, even at the highest tested frequency of 10 Hz. This finding underscores the proposed test-bed's ability to maintain low-latency communication, and meet the requirement for many V2X applications highlighted in [31] and [32].

Furthermore, Fig. 9 illustrates the relationship between vehicle speed and average latency, for both V2V and V2I test cases. It can be observed that there is an inverse relationship between the vehicle speed and average latency. The reason behind this behaviour lies in the enhancement of relative velocities, which contribute to the improved efficiency of packet transmission processes. Further, the drop in packets with increasing speeds (refer Fig. 11) may have resulted in easing the network congestion, and subsequently, the latency.

Packet Loss Analysis: PDR is calculated to analyze the packet loss in the two test scenarios: *Frequency Variation under Constant Speed* and *Speed Variation under Constant Frequency*, for both V2V and V2I test case and the results are graphically depicted in Fig. 10 and Fig. 11, respectively.

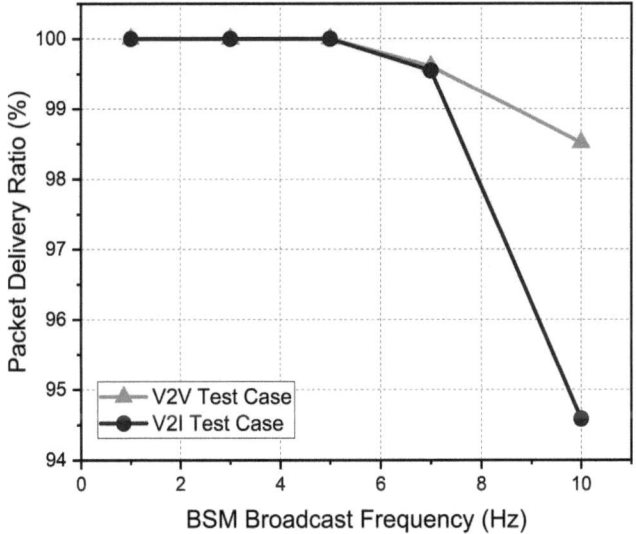

Fig. 10. PDR for different BSM broadcast frequencies

As shown in Fig. 10, no packet loss was observed for frequencies 1 Hz, 3 Hz and 5 Hz. However, a visible packet loss is present in frequencies 7 Hz and 10 Hz. This phenomenon is attributed to network congestion, wherein the increased packet traffic at higher frequencies may lead to packet drops and collisions. As illustrated in Fig. 11, a downward trend can be seen in the PDR values, corresponding to the increase in vehicle speeds. This phenomenon may occur due to link instability, which intensifies with higher velocities and leads to higher packet loss [33]. With higher mobility, the link lifetime (duration two vehicles stay in their transmission range) drops significantly, making the network unstable. This can be a leading factor for the increasing packet loss against increasing vehicle speed shown in Fig. 11.

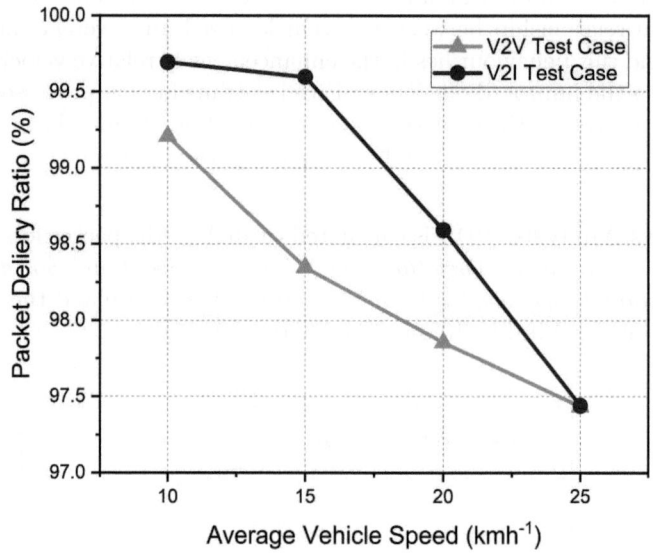

Fig. 11. PDR for different speeds

When analyzing overall results, it can be observed that as vehicle speed increases, PDR reduces in both V2X modes, but at the same time, latency reduces. It is possible that the drop in PDR may have been affected by the drop in latency, i.e., the packets that were delivered may have had a lower latency and the delayed packets may have been dropped.

4 Conclusion

In this work, we presented a cost effective V2X test-bed that can be effectively used in the academic setting to evaluate the performance of vehicular network applications and services under realistic network conditions. The proposed test-bed is able to successfully implement both V2V and V2I communication scenarios, maintain low latency across multiple transmission frequencies and vehicle speeds, and achieve acceptable PDRs under tested conditions, which demonstrate the reliability of the proposed low-cost V2X test-bed and its capability to support real-time V2X applications that require rapid data exchange.

For future work, we propose, expanding the test-bed to include more vehicles and RSUs to study scalability, implementing and testing additional V2X applications, investigating the system's performance under more challenging environmental conditions, conducting long-term reliability tests to assess the durability of the test-bed's hardware in vehicular environments.

References

1. Sudheera K.L.K., Ma, M., Chong, P.H.J.: Efficient flow instantiation via source routing in software defined vehicular networks. In: 2017 IEEE 86th Vehicular Technology Conference (VTC-Fall), pp. 1–5 (2017). https://doi.org/10.1109/VTCFall.2017.8288201
2. Zhou, H., Xu, W., Chen, J., Wang, W.: Evolutionary v2x technologies toward the internet of vehicles: challenges and opportunities. Proc. IEEE **108**(2), 308–323 (2020). https://doi.org/10.1109/JPROC.2019.2961937
3. Abboud, K., Omar, H.A., Zhuang, W.: Interworking of dsrc and cellular network technologies for v2x communications: a survey. IEEE Trans. Veh. Technol. **65**(12), 9457–9470 (2016). https://doi.org/10.1109/TVT.2016.2591558
4. Usman, M., et al.: A business and legislative perspective of v2x and mobility applications in 5G networks. IEEE Access **8**, 67426–67435 (2020). https://doi.org/10.1109/ACCESS.2020.2986129
5. Shuguang, L., Zhenxing, Y.: Architecture and key technologies of the v2x-based vehicle networking. In: 2019 IEEE 2nd International Conference on Electronics and Communication Engineering (ICECE), pp. 148–152 (2019). https://doi.org/10.1109/ICECE48499.2019.9058525
6. Kawser, M., Sajjad, S., Fahad, S., Ahmed, S., Rafi, H.: The perspective of vehicle-to-everything (v2x) communication towards 5g. IJCSNS Int. J. Comput. Sci. Netw. Secur. **19**, 146–155 (2019)
7. Lozano Domínguez, J.M., Mateo Sanguino, T.: Review on v2x, i2x, and p2x communications and their applications: a comprehensive analysis over time. Sensors **19**, 2756 (2019). https://doi.org/10.3390/s19122756
8. Ben Mussa, S.A., Manaf, M., Ghafoor, K.Z., Doukha, Z.: Simulation tools for vehicular ad hoc networks: a comparison study and future perspectives. In: 2015 International Conference on Wireless Networks and Mobile Communications (WINCOM), pp. 1–8 (2015). https://doi.org/10.1109/WINCOM.2015.7381319
9. Spaho, E., Barolli, L., Mino, G., Xhafa, F., Kolici, V.: Vanet simulators: a survey on mobility and routing protocols. In: 2011 International Conference on Broadband and Wireless Computing, Communication and Applications, pp. 1–10 (2011). https://doi.org/10.1109/BWCCA.2011.11
10. Martinez, F., Toh, C., Cano, J.C., Calafate, C., Manzoni, P.: A survey and comparative study of simulators for vehicular ad hoc networks (vanets). Wirel. Commun. Mob. Comput. **11**, 813–828 (2011). https://doi.org/10.1002/wcm.859
11. Kim, H., Kim, T., Kang, S., Yoon, C., Jung, J.: Design of v2x runtime emulation framework for evaluation of vehicle safety applications. In: 2014 4th IEEE International Conference on Network Infrastructure and Digital Content, pp. 262–268 (2014). https://doi.org/10.1109/ICNIDC.2014.7000306
12. Behrisch, M., Bieker-Walz, L., Erdmann, J., Krajzewicz, D.: Sumo – simulation of urban mobility: an overview, vol. 2011 (2011)

13. Karnadi, F., Mo, Z., Lan, K.C.: Rapid generation of realistic mobility models for vanet, pp. 2506–2511 (2007). https://doi.org/10.1109/WCNC.2007.467
14. Härri, J., Filali, F., Bonnet, C., Fiore, M.: Vanetmobisim: generating realistic mobility patterns for vanets. In: Proceedings of the 3rd International Workshop on Vehicular Ad Hoc Networks, VANET '06, pp. 96–97. Association for Computing Machinery, New York (2006). https://doi.org/10.1145/1161064.1161084
15. Miller, J., Horowitz, E.: Freesim - a free real-time freeway traffic simulator. In: 2007 IEEE Intelligent Transportation Systems Conference, pp. 18–23 (2007). https://doi.org/10.1109/ITSC.2007.4357627
16. Martinez, F.J., Cano, J.C., Calafate, C.T., Manzoni, P.: Citymob: a mobility model pattern generator for vanets. In: ICC Workshops - 2008 IEEE International Conference on Communications Workshops, pp. 370–374 (2008). https://doi.org/10.1109/ICCW.2008.76
17. Nawej, C., Owolawi, P., Walingo, T.: Design and simulation of vanets testbed using openstreetmap, sumo, and ns-2. In: 2021 IEEE 6th International Conference on Computer and Communication Systems (ICCCS), pp. 582–587 (2021). https://doi.org/10.1109/ICCCS52626.2021.9449197
18. Campanile, L., Gribaudo, M., Iacono, M., Marulli, F., Mastroianni, M.: Computer network simulation with ns-3: a systematic literature review. Electronics **9**, 272 (2020). https://doi.org/10.3390/electronics9020272
19. Varga, A., Hornig, R.: An overview of the omnet++ simulation environment. In: Proceedings of the 1st International Conference on Simulation Tools and Techniques for Communications, Networks and Systems & Workshops. Simutools '08, ICST (Institute for Computer Sciences, Social-Informatics and Telecommunications Engineering), Brussels, BEL (2008)
20. Chen, M., Miao, Y., Humar, I.: Introduction to OPNET Network Simulation, pp. 77–153 (2019). https://doi.org/10.1007/978-981-32-9170-6_2
21. Piórkowski, M., Raya, M., Lugo, A.L., Papadimitratos, P., Grossglauser, M., Hubaux, J.P.: Trans: realistic joint traffic and network simulator for vanets. SIGMOBILE Mob. Comput. Commun. Rev. **12**(1), 31–33 (2008). https://doi.org/10.1145/1374512.1374522
22. Mangharam, R., Weller, D., Rajkumar, R., Mudalige, P., Bai, F.: Groovenet: a hybrid simulator for vehicle-to-vehicle networks. In: 2006 Third Annual International Conference on Mobile and Ubiquitous Systems: Networking & Services, pp. 1–8 (2006). https://doi.org/10.1109/MOBIQ.2006.340441
23. Wang, S.Y., Lin, C.C.: Nctuns 6.0: a simulator for advanced wireless vehicular network research. In: 2010 IEEE 71st Vehicular Technology Conference, pp. 1–2 (2010). https://doi.org/10.1109/VETECS.2010.5494212
24. Sommer, C., Eckhoff, D., Brummer, A., Buse, D., Hagenauer, F., Joerer, S., Segata, M.: Veins: the open source vehicular network simulation framework, pp. 215–252 (2019). https://doi.org/10.1007/978-3-030-12842-5_6
25. MacHardy, Z., Khan, A., Obana, K., Iwashina, S.: V2x access technologies: regulation, research, and remaining challenges. IEEE Commun. Surv. Tutor. **20**(3), 1858–1877 (2018). https://doi.org/10.1109/COMST.2018.2808444
26. Nanyang Technological University, Centre for Information Sciences and Systems: Connected smart mobility cosmo. https://www.ntu.edu.sg/ciss/research-capabilities/research-programmes/cosmo. Accessed 15 July 2024
27. Hadiwardoyo, S.A., et al.: Smart highway: an interoperable V2X testbed for connected and autonomous mobility services in Belgium (2021)
28. Astazero. https://www.astazero.com/. Accessed 15 July 2024

29. Stübing, H., et al.: SIMTD: a car-to-x system architecture for field operational tests [topics in automotive networking]. IEEE Commun. Mag. **48**(5), 148–154 (2010). https://doi.org/10.1109/MCOM.2010.5458376
30. Mcity. https://mcity.umich.edu/. Accessed 17 July 2024
31. Mir, Z., Filali, F.: LTE and IEEE 802.11p for vehicular networking: a performance evaluation. EURASIP J. Wirel. Commun. Network. **2014**, 89 (2014). https://doi.org/10.1186/1687-1499-2014-89
32. Kanavos, A., Fragkos, D., Kaloxylos, A.: V2x communication over cellular networks: capabilities and challenges. Telecom **2**, 1–26 (2021). https://doi.org/10.3390/telecom2010001
33. Sudheera, K.L.K., Ma, M., Chong, P.H.J.: Link stability based hybrid routing protocol for software defined vehicular networks. In: 2018 IEEE International Conference on Communications (ICC), pp. 1–6 (2018). https://doi.org/10.1109/ICC.2018.8422399

Federated Learning-Based Channel Estimation in Vehicular Networks

Cao Ding and Ivan Wang-Hei Ho[✉]

Department of Electrical and Electronic Engineering, The Hong Kong Polytechnic
University, Hong Kong, China
caosnow.ding@connect.polyu.hk, ivanwh.ho@polyu.edu.hk

Abstract. Most studies on channel estimation make assumptions on statistical channel models, such as the Rayleigh fading model, but these assumptions are impractical. On one hand, the high-speed mobility of vehicles generates carrier frequency offset (CFO) and Doppler shift, which leads to inter-carrier interference (ICI). On the other hand, buildings in the connected vehicle environment cause propagation loss to the communication link, which is known as the urban canyon effect. To solve these issues, this paper exploits ray tracing technology to model the propagation loss and proposes a channel estimator based on federated learning and deep neural network (FL-DNN) techniques. The proposed FL-DNN estimator divides multiple geographical regions through K-D tree for local model training and uses trimmed mean averaging to aggregate the global model. Our results show that the channel estimation performance and data recovery accuracy of FL-DNN outperform traditional and learning-based channel estimators. Our results show that FL-DNN outperforms traditional and learning-based channel estimators by an average of 63.5% and 57.2% in channel estimation and data recovery accuracy, respectively.

Keywords: Federated Learning · Channel Estimation · Vehicular Networks

1 Introduction

Channel estimation plays an important role in vehicular networks, as it can estimate the wireless channel and recover the transmitted data symbols. The fast-moving vehicle nodes generate carrier frequency offsets (CFOs) and Doppler frequency shifts [1], which leads to inter-carrier interference (ICI). Accurate channel estimation is important for advanced communication techniques, such as non-orthogonal V2X communications [2]. However, existing channel estimation methods tend to assume static orthogonal frequency division multiplexing

---

I. W.-H. Ho—This work was supported in part by the Research Institute for Artificial Internet of Things (RIAIoT) (Project 1-CDJ5) and the Otto Poon Charitable Foundation Smart Cities Research Institute (Project Q-CDAS) at The Hong Kong Polytechnic University.

(OFDM) systems and do not consider the high-speed mobility of vehicles in the road network. In addition, vehicular channels are easily affected by surrounding obstacles or buildings, causing propagation losses in OFDM links, which is known as the urban canyon effect [3].

Existing channel estimators can be roughly divided into two categories. The first category is the traditional channel estimator based on pilot symbols and channel statistics, such as least square (LS) [4] and linear minimum mean square error (LMMSE) [5]. They perform channel estimation and data recovery on received data symbols by inserting specific pilot symbols. This type of channel estimator has many defects. The energy and bandwidth required for the transmission of data symbols will be severely depleted by the usage of a high number of pilot tones. The channel estimation accuracy of LS is relatively low, while the computational complexity of LMMSE is too large. Therefore, researchers have turned to the second category, machine learning-based channel estimators. Specifically, deep neural networks (DNN) and convolutional neural networks (CNN) are widely applied in channel estimation. Yang et al. developed an online DNN-based channel estimator for doubly selective fading channels [6], leveraging the learning and generalization capabilities of DNN. Cheng et al. introduced a ResNet-DNN based channel estimation and equalization scheme for filter bank multicarrier (FBMC) systems, replacing conventional modules with a Res-DNN model [7]. Since channel response matrices (CMR) can be recognized and processed as images, researchers proposed the a number of CNN-based channel estimators. Dong et al. introduced a spatial-frequency CNN (SF-CNN) based channel estimation method for millimeter wave (mmWave) massive multiple-input multiple-output (MIMO) systems [8], leveraging both spatial and frequency correlation. Pradhan et al. proposed a two-stage CNN-based channel estimation method for OFDM systems [9], utilizing pilot locations in the time and frequency domain. However, the above-mentioned works did not consider the urban canyon effect, but simply assumed some statistical channel models, such as the Rayleigh fading model.

To address the above issues, this paper proposes a channel estimator based on federated learning (FL) and DNN, which uses ray tracing technology to model the propagation loss model. The contributions of this paper are three-fold:

i. We propose a ray tracing technique to model the channel propagation fading model, which includes the reflection and refraction losses of buildings on signal propagation. In addition, the effects of building materials and conductivity on the loss are also considered.
ii. We propose a DNN-based channel estimator that can be used for local models training. The training of the local model not only considers the channel characteristics, but also the geographical locations of the transmitter and receiver and the losses of surrounding buildings.
iii. We propose to use trimmed mean averaging to aggregate the parameters of each local model and obtain the global channel model of the entire city. During the offline testing, the receiver can fetch the global model for channel estimation and data recovery.

The rest of the paper is as follows. Section 2 introduces the system model. Section 3 presents the federated learning-based channel estimation. Section 4 compares the numerical results with benchmark channel estimators. Finally, Sect. 5 gives conclusion of this work.

2 System Models

The 5G ray-tracing vehicular channels scenario is considered in this paper, as illustrated in Fig. 1, which includes vehicle-to-vehicle (V2V) communication and vehicle-to-infrastructure (V2I) communication.

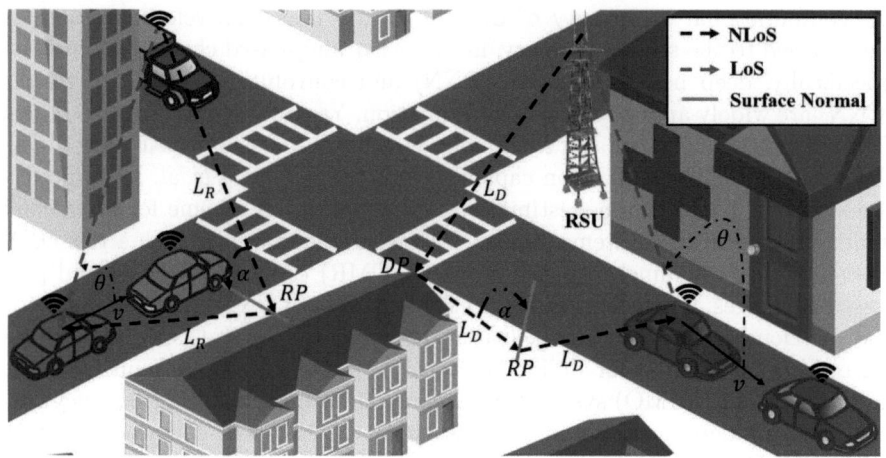

Fig. 1. 5G Ray-Tracing Vehicular Channels

2.1 5G Vehicular Channels

In the 5G vehicular channels, both the roadside unit (RSU) and the vehicle can transmit OFDM signals to the receiver through multipath propagation. As shown in Fig. 1, the multipath, which including Line-of-sight (LOS) and Non-LOS (NLOS) signals, experiences varying degrees of path loss and delay spread caused by the free space propagation model or the urban canyon effect. Assuming that the angle between the main propagation path and the driving direction of the receiver is θ, and the relative speed between the receiver and the transmitter is v, the complex channel gain for the m-th path can be described as

$$G_m(t) = \sqrt{\frac{P_m(t)}{R}} \sum_{r=1}^{R} e^{j\Phi_{m,r}} e^{j|v|\cos(\psi_{m,r}(t)-\theta)t}, \tag{1}$$

where $P_m(t)$ denotes the time-varying power, $\tau_m(t)$ is the delay spread for the m-th path, and $M(t)$ is the total number of propagation paths. R is the overall amount of ray components in one cluster. $\Phi_{m,r}$ represents the stochastic phase of the radio ray, which follows the uniform distribution of $[0, 2\pi]$. $\psi_{m,r}(t)$ is the angle of arrival (AOA) of the r-th ray component.

2.2 Ray-Tracing Propagation

Vehicle-to-everything (V2X) communications use radio rays to transmit signals, and ray tracing technology can effectively measure the path loss of obstacles (e.g., buildings) to the vehicular channel, so as to obtain more accurate received power, that is, the signal strength. Theoretical and empirical propagation models only hold true in situations that are similar to the modeling environment. However, these models typically cannot offer precise temporal or spatial information. The ray-tracing model, in contrast to these models, are tailored to the 3-D world and are thus suitable for situations such as urban areas.

In the ray-tracing model, a ray is defined as an independent radio signal transmission path, which propagates in a straight line through a homogeneous medium such as air, follows the principle of light reflection and diffraction, and carries limited energy. In the scenario shown in Fig. 1, the LoS link is blocked by buildings and the signal cannot reach the receiver. NLoS links can be reached through the reflection line L_R of the building surface and the diffraction line L_D of the building apex. The propagation matrix of the ray can be expressed as

$$P = \prod_i P_i, \tag{2}$$

where i is the number of reflection points. P_i and its initial value P_0 can be calculated as

$$P_i = \begin{bmatrix} s & p & k \end{bmatrix}_i \begin{bmatrix} R_V(\alpha) & 0 & 0 \\ 0 & R_H(\alpha) & 0 \\ 0 & 0 & 1 \end{bmatrix}_i \begin{bmatrix} s' & p' & k' \end{bmatrix}_i^{-1} \tag{3}$$

$$P_0 = \begin{bmatrix} 1 & 0 & 0 \\ 0 & 1 & 0 \\ 0 & 0 & 1 \end{bmatrix}, \tag{4}$$

where s, p, and k are the horizontal polarization direction, vertical polarization direction, and direction of the incident rays, respectively. s', p', and k' represent the same properties of the exiting rays. α is the incident angle of the ray. R_H and R_V are the Fresnel reflection coefficients for the horizontal and vertical polarizations, respectively. R_H and R_V can be calculated by

$$R_H(\alpha) = \frac{\cos(\alpha) - \sqrt{(\epsilon_r - \sin^2(\alpha))/\epsilon_r^2}}{\cos(\alpha) + \sqrt{(\epsilon_r - \sin^2(\alpha))/\epsilon_r^2}} \tag{5}$$

$$R_V(\alpha) = \frac{\cos(\alpha) - \sqrt{\epsilon_r - \sin^2(\alpha)}}{\cos(\alpha) + \sqrt{\epsilon_r - \sin^2(\alpha)}}, \tag{6}$$

where ϵ_r is the complex relative permittivity of the material. This work adopts The ITU-R P.2040-1 and ITU-R P.527 standards for setting ϵ_r, which can be expressed as

$$\epsilon_r = \epsilon'_r + j\epsilon''_r \tag{7}$$

$$\epsilon''_r = \frac{\sigma}{2\pi\epsilon_0 f'}, \tag{8}$$

where ϵ'_r is the relative permittivity of the building material, σ is the conductivity, ϵ_0 is the permittivity of free space, and f is the frequency of the radio ray. For distinct building materials, the permittivity and conductivity can be calculated as

$$\epsilon'_r = af^d \tag{9}$$

$$\sigma = cf^d, \tag{10}$$

where a, b, c, and d are constants determined by the building material. Table 1 summarizes the effect on permittivity and conductivity of common building materials in urban environments. The 2-by-2 polarization matrix can be expressed as

Table 1. Permittivity and Conductivity of Common Building Materials

Material	Frequency (GHz)	Real Part of Relative Permittivity		Conductivity (S/m)	
		a	b	c	d
Vacuum (air)	[0.001, 100]	1	0	0	0
Concrete	[1, 100]	5.31	0	0.0326	0.8095
Glass	[0.1, 100]	6.27	0	0.0043	1.1925
Wood	[0.001, 100]	1.99	0	0.0047	1.0718
Dry ground	[1, 10]	3	0	0.00015	2.52
Wet ground	[1, 10]	30	−0.4	0.15	1.30

$$R = \begin{bmatrix} H_{in} \cdot H_{Rx} & V_{in} \cdot H_{Rx} \\ H_{in} \cdot V_{Rx} & V_{in} \cdot V_{Rx} \end{bmatrix} \tag{11}$$

$$H_{in} = P \cdot (V_{Tx} \times k_{Tx}) \tag{12}$$

$$V_{in} = P \cdot V_{Tx}, \tag{13}$$

where Rx and Tx denotes the receiver and transmitter, respectively. H_{Rx} and V_{Rx} represent the directions of the horizontal and vertical polarizations for Rx, respectively. H_{in} and V_{in} represent the directions of the propagated horizontal and vertical polarizations for the incident ray, respectively. V_{Tx} denotes the direction of the nominal vertical polarization for the ray leaving Tx. k_{Tx} denotes the direction of the ray leaving Tx. To obtain the path loss, two 2-by-1 Jones polarization vectors are used to represent the normalized horizontal and vertical polarizations. When Tx and Rx are unpolarized, their values are

$$J_{Tx} = J_{Rx} = \frac{\sqrt{2}}{2}\begin{bmatrix}1\\1\end{bmatrix} \quad (14)$$

The reflection loss can be calculated as

$$L_{rf} = -20log_{10}|\boldsymbol{J_{Rx}}^{-1}\boldsymbol{RJ_{Tx}}| \quad (15)$$

For a first order signal diffraction, the diffraction loss can be calculated as

$$L_{df} = \boldsymbol{JV_{Rx}H_{df}JV_{Tx}}, \quad (16)$$

where $\boldsymbol{JV_{Rx}}$ and $\boldsymbol{JV_{Tx}}$ are polarization vectors (i.e., Jones vectors) for Rx and Tx, respectively. $\boldsymbol{H_{df}}$ is the diffraction matrix containing the diffraction coefficients for polarizations in ITU-R P.526 standard. In general, the ray-tracing propagation model accurately calculates building reflection and diffraction loss, which affect the quality of 5G vehicular channels.

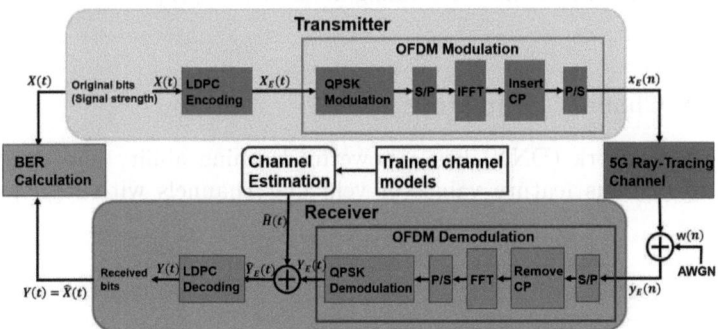

Fig. 2. OFDM Communication Link using Ray Tracing

2.3 OFDM Communication Link

The OFDM Communication Link using ray-tracing vehicular channels is shown in Fig. 2. In the initial stage, the transmitter performs channel coding on the original data $\boldsymbol{X(t)}$. Low-density parity-check code (LDPC) is a linear error correction code [10], that is, it can restore the original data in the case of partial byte errors, and can effectively reduce the bit-error-rate (BER) in the data recovery. After LDPC encoding, the encoded data $\boldsymbol{X_E(t)}$ performs the OFDM modulation process to convert the data from the time domain to the frequency domain (i.e., $\boldsymbol{x_E(n)}$) in preparation for transmission. During the wireless transmission, the function of the 5G ray-tracing channel can be expressed as

$$y_E(n) = h_{rt}(n) \times x_E(n) + \omega(n), \quad (17)$$

where $\boldsymbol{\omega}(n)$ is the additive white Gaussian noise (AWGN) under a certain signal-to-noise ratio (SNR). The receiver performs OFDM demodulation which contains the fast fourier transform (FFT) for converting the data from frequency domain to time domain (i.e., $\boldsymbol{Y_E}(t)$). Afterwards, together with the pre-trained channel estimator (i.e., $\boldsymbol{\hat{H}}(t)$), the data recovery process can be expressed as

$$\boldsymbol{\hat{Y}_E}(t) = \boldsymbol{\hat{H}}(t)\boldsymbol{Y_E}(t) + \boldsymbol{\Omega}(t), \tag{18}$$

where $\boldsymbol{\Omega}(t)$ is the noise in the time domain, through the FFT of AWGN. The LDPC-decoded data $\boldsymbol{Y}(t)$ is compared with the original data (i.e., $\boldsymbol{X}(t)$) for bit-error-rate (BER) calculation.

3 Federated Learning-Based Channel Estimation

In this section, we present the proposed federated learning and DNN-based channel estimation algorithm (FL-DNN) step by step. The general FL channel estimation process is shown in Fig. 3. The V2V and V2I communication data in 5G ray-tracing vehicular channels will be uploaded to local models as training and testing datasets. For local model training methods, we propose the DNN channel estimator.

3.1 DNN Channel Estimator

Deep neural network (DNN) has a powerful learning ability and can identify and classify various feature values of vehicular channels with high precision.

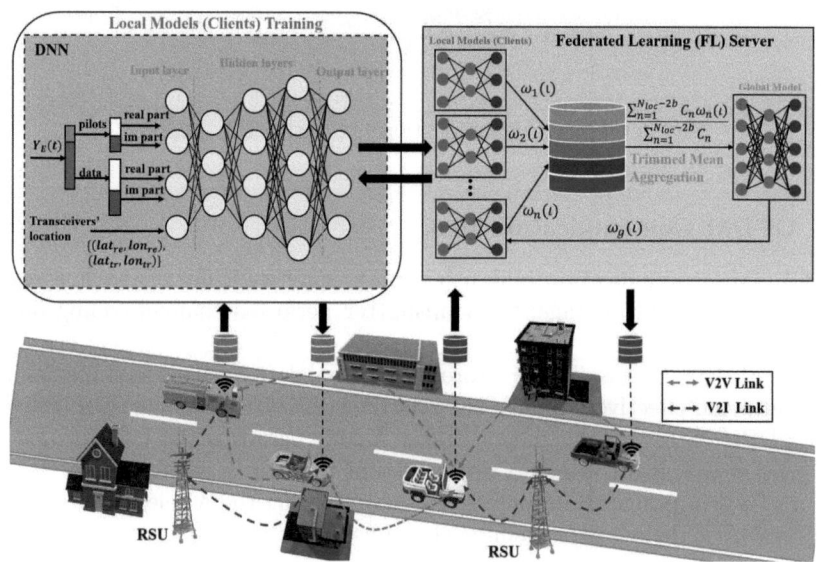

Fig. 3. Federated Learning Channel Estimation.

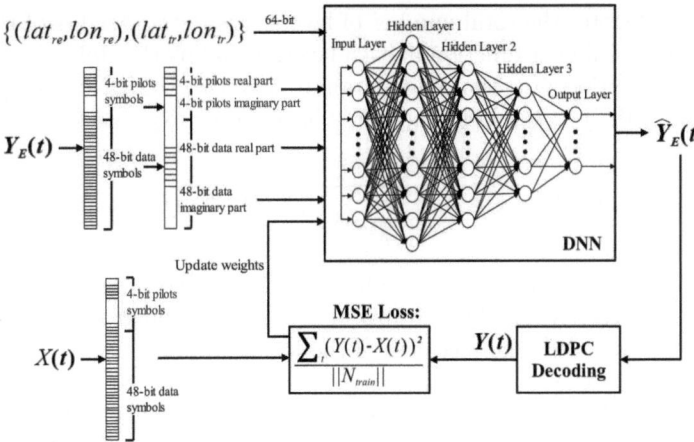

Fig. 4. The Training Process of the DNN Channel Estimator.

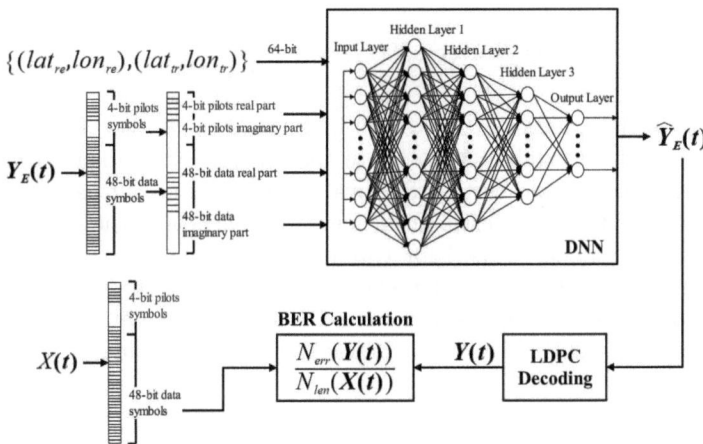

Fig. 5. The Test Process of the DNN Channel Estimator.

Therefore, DNN is selected as one of the methods to train local models. As shown in Fig. 4, the input to the DNN is the received symbol ($Y_E(t)$) and the original transmitted symbol ($X(t)$). They are composed of OFDM blocks, with a total 64 subcarrier, 11 guard band subcarrier, 1 null subcarrier, 4 pilot subcarrier, 48 data subcarrier. The output of the DNN is the estimated recovered data symbol ($\hat{Y}_E(t)$), which is obtained through cascaded nonlinear transformations performed by different layers in the DNN. The data recovery process of the DNN can be expressed as follows.

$$\hat{Y}_E(t) = f(Y_E(t), \varpi) \qquad (19)$$
$$= f^{(J_{DNN}-1)}(f^{(J_{DNN}-2)}(...f^{(1)}(Y_E(t)))), \qquad (20)$$

where J_{DNN} denotes the total number of layers, ϖ are the weights of the DNN. $f(\cdot)$ represents nonlinear function in each layer, including the ReLu function and the Sigmoid function. For the offline training process, the DNN use the mean square error (MSE) as the loss function, which can be expressed as follows.

$$MSE_{DNN} = \frac{1}{N_{tr}} \sum_{n=1}^{N_{tr}} \sum_{t=1}^{T} ||(\boldsymbol{Y}(t) - \boldsymbol{X}(t))^2||, \qquad (21)$$

where $\boldsymbol{Y}(t)$ is the recovered data symbol after LDPC decoding, N_{tr} is the size of the training set. After the training process, the estimated channel model ($\hat{\boldsymbol{H}}_{DNN}(t)$) is saved to the receivers of the local model.

For the offline testing process in Fig. 5, receivers will use the trained local channel model ($\hat{\boldsymbol{H}}_{DNN}(t)$) and the received symbols ($\boldsymbol{Y}_E(t)$) in the test dataset for data symbol recovery. The data symbols recovered by the DNN will be used to calculate the BER with the original transmitted data symbols after LDPC decoding. The BER is calculated as follows.

$$BER(\boldsymbol{Y}(t), \boldsymbol{X}(t)) = \frac{N_{err}(\boldsymbol{Y}(t))}{N_{len}(\boldsymbol{X}(t))}, \qquad (22)$$

where N_{err} is the number of error bits in $\boldsymbol{Y}(t)$, N_{len} is the bit length of the original transmitted symbol $\boldsymbol{X}(t)$. Note that the DNN channel estimator not only provide training and testing for local models in FL, but can also be used as an independent channel estimation method. When only the communication data of the local model is used for training, it is FL-DNN channel estimator. When trained using data from the whole vehicular network, it is a stand-alone DNN channel estimator. The stand-alone DNN channel estimator was selected as one of the benchmark algorithms in the section of performance evaluation.

3.2 Federated Learning-Based Global Model Aggregation

As illustrated in Fig. 3, the FL server first distributes the initialized global model parameters (i.e., $w_g(\iota)$) to each local model (client). Each local model uses local data for training and uploads the trained parameters (i.e., $w_n(\iota)$) to the FL server. In each FL iteration, local models experience K steps of gradient descent, which can be expressed as follows.

$$w_n(\iota) = w_g(\iota) - \eta_k \nabla \ell(w_n(\iota - 1)), \qquad (23)$$

where ι represents the number of FL iterations, $n = 1, ..., N_{loc}$ denotes the number of local models, and η_k denotes the learning rate of the k-th step of gradient descent. $\nabla \ell$ is the loss function of the local gradient descent, which is determined by the DNN training model:

$$\nabla \ell = MSE_{DNN}, \qquad (24)$$

The FL server aggregates and updates the global model (i.e., $\omega_g(\iota)$) with the trimmed mean averaging [11] of parameters from different local models, which can be expressed as follows.

$$\omega_g(\iota) = \frac{\sum_{n=1}^{N_{loc}-2b} C_n \omega_n(\iota)}{\sum_{n=1}^{N_{loc}-2b} C_n}, \tag{25}$$

where $b < \frac{N_{loc}}{2}$ is a constant, C_n is the contribution of the n-th local model to the whole traning dataset. Specifically, the FL server will eliminate the largest b parameters and the smallest b parameters, and then average the remaining parameters to obtain the global model parameters. The trimmed mean aggregation has been proven to be effective in preventing the fake local models from decreasing the accuracy of the global model averaging. After each iteration, the FL server again distributes the updated global model parameters to the local model for the next round of training. For the testing process, the receiver downloads the global model for channel estimation and data recovery instead of the local model.

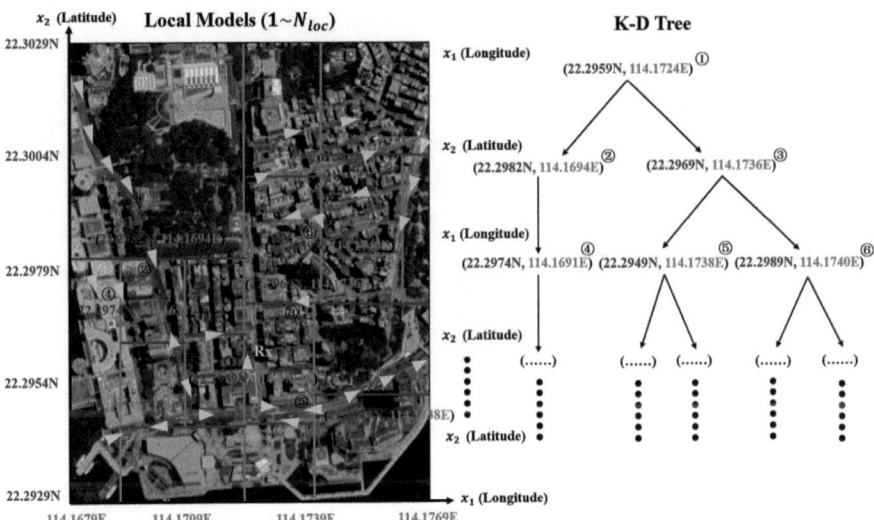

Fig. 6. KD-Tree-based Geographical Partitioning of Local Models.

3.3 KD-Tree-Based Geographical Partitioning of Local Models

Vehicular channel characteristics are highly dependent on geographical features such as terrain, urban structure (buildings), and even foliage [12]. Therefore, leveraging geographical information in FL training can lead to more precise channel estimation models that are tailored to specific regions. Our work proposes a geographical partitioning method based on KD-Tree (K-Dimensional Tree), as shown in Fig. 6.

First of all, we obtained the 3D spatial data of Tsim Sha Tsui (TST) area in Hong Kong from Lands Department, HKSAR. Secondly, random traffic flows of receivers (R_x) are generated in the TST area, and a KD-Tree (k=2) is constructed based on the latitude and longitude coordinates of the vehicles. As shown in the KD-Tree structure in Fig. 6, it selects the median of x_1 or x_2 coordinate as the root node each time and divides the area into two subsets. Finally, the TST area is divided into $N_{loc} = 16$ local models according to the longitude range $[22.29290, 22.3092]°N$ and the latitude range $[114.1679, 114.1769]°E$. When the transmitter (T_x) and receiver (R_x) of a communication process are located in two regions, such as N_1 and N_2, their communication data will be stored in the training datasets of N_1 and N_2. Therefore, irrelevant communication data will not appear in the training set of this local model, eliminating the impact of interference data in training. By partitioning the models by geographical location, local models training can significantly enhance the learning efficiency and model accuracy.

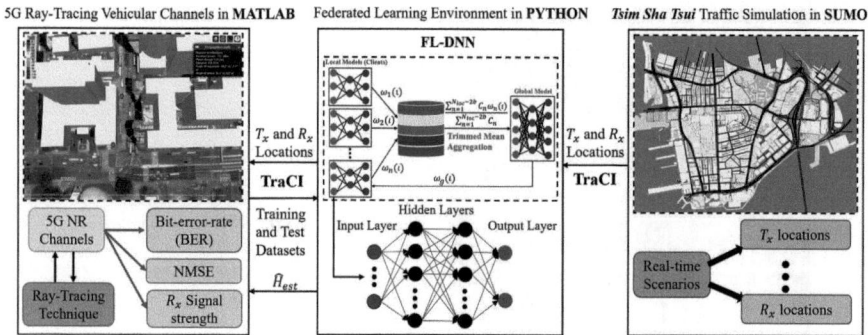

Fig. 7. The Simulation Framework.

4 Numerical Results and Performance Evaluation

This section compares numerical simulation results with several benchmarks to validate the performance of the proposed channel estimation algorithms. Figure 7 depicts the overall simulation framework, which consists of Python, SUMO, and MATLAB simulations. SUMO is implemented as a microscopic traffic simulator to generate a realistic Tsim Sha Tsui city model to derive the geographic locations of T_x and R_x vehicles in real time. MATLAB receives real-time locations through a TCP link over the traffic control interface (TraCI) and implements a 5G NR ray-tracing network to simulate the V2V and V2I communications. The developed method can be implemented in a digital twin platform for connected autonomous vehicles [13]. The FL, DNN training environments are implemented in Python, and their training and testing datasets are obtained from MATLAB in real time through the TraCI. Finally, the estimated channel and recovered data are compared with the groundtruth to evaluate various performances such as bit-error-rate (BER).

4.1 Simulation Parameters and Datasets

To fairly compare the performance of the proposed channel estimation algorithms with the benchmark algorithms, the initial parameters in the simulations remain consistent. As shown in Table 2, the simulation scene is a one-hour traffic in Tsim Sha Tsui, a central business district (CBD) in Hong Kong covering an area of 1.02 km^2. The traffic volume is 4,000 veh/h, which is relatively congested, and the speed limit on urban roads is 50 km/h. In addition, we also deployed five Base Station (BS) as RSU based on the BS locations provided by Hong Kong Telecommunications (HKT). Vehicles and BS are randomly selected as T_x and R_x for communication. We constructed the 5G NR channel with LDPC coding based on the dedicated short range communication (DSRC), in which the signal propagation model is ray tracing. The physical layer is IEEE 802.11p and the binary phase-shift keying (BPSK) is deployed for modulation. For the OFDM process, we set a total of 64 subcarriers, including 4 pilot subcarriers and 48 data subcarriers, with a subcarrier spacing of 312.5 KHz. The signal interference adopts AWGN, and the SNR level is superimposed at 5 dB, ranging from [0, 35] dB. The length of the cyclic prefix is set to 16 bits, while the symbol, data, and guard interval times are set to 4, 3.2, and 0.8 μs, respectively.

For the FL training, we used the Keras deep-learning framework based on the TensorFlow platform for DNN training and testing. The global model aggregates 16 local model parameters through the trimmed mean method. For the DNN structure, we applied a 5-layer fully connected network, including an input layer, 3 hidden layers, and an output layer. The number of neurons in each layer is 128, 256, 512, 256, and 48 respectively. The input layer and hidden layers both use the ReLu activation function, while the output layer uses the Sigmoid activation function to map the output to (0, 1). The training epoch, learning rate, and batch size are set to 10,000, 0.001, and 32, respectively. The other parameters can be referred to Table 2.

4.2 Channel Estimation Performance

Figure 8 compares the channel estimation performance of the proposed FL-DNN channel estimator with other benchmark estimators under different signal-to-noise ratios (SNR). We consider two types of benchmark estimators: one is the traditional channel estimator based on pilot signals or spatial information, such as LS [4], LMMSE [5], and the spectral temporal averaging (STA) [14] estimators. The other is channel estimators combined with machine learning, such as DNN, STA-DNN [14], CNN and SF-CNN [8] estimators. We reproduce these channel estimators and customize them in our system model. Normalized mean

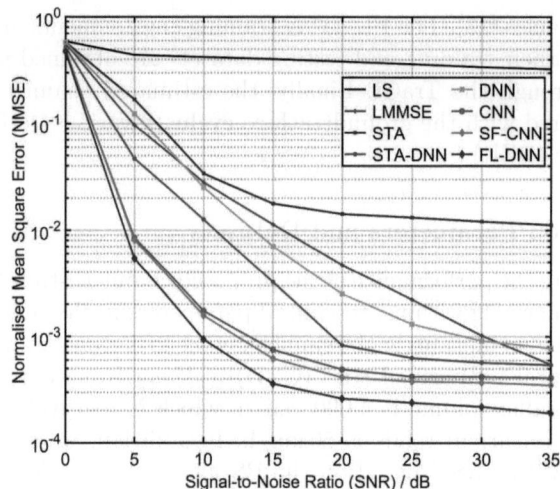

Fig. 8. Channel Estimation Performance Versus SNR.

square error (NMSE) is selected as the evaluation metric of channel estimation performance, which can be expressed mathematically as follows.

$$NMSE = \frac{\sum_{j=1}^{J}(H_{es}(j) - H_{th}(j))^2}{\sum_{j=1}^{J}(H_{th}(j))^2}, \qquad (26)$$

where $H_{es}(j)$ denotes the estimated channel matrix of the j-th channel in the testing dataset, and $H_{th}(j)$ denotes the theoretical transfer channel matrix. It can be seen from Fig. 8 that at each SNR level, the NMSE of FL-DNN outperforms other benchmark algorithms. Specifically, at SNR level of 25 dB, the NMSE of FL-DNN is 36.8%, 43.1%, 61.9%, 89.2%, 81.6%, 98.2%, and 99.8% lower than that of SF-CNN, CNN, STA-DNN, LMMSE, DNN, STA, and LS, respectively. However, at SNR level of 5 dB, the NMSE of FL-DNN is 33.4%, 36.4%, 88.5%, 94.4%, 95.7%, 96.8%, and 98.8% lower than that of SF-CNN, CNN, STA-DNN, LMMSE, DNN, STA, and LS, respectively. This means that as the SNR decreases, the NMSE of each channel estimator decreases significantly, while the NMSE difference between FL-DNN and other estimators is relatively stable. In addition, at most SNR levels, the NMSE performance of learning-based estimators are better than that of traditional estimators, and FL-DNN is the best among learning-based estimators. This is because FL-DNN is trained independently according to the communication characteristics of different geographical regions and aggregated into a global model. Such training accuracy is higher than that of separate DNN or CNN training.

Figure 9 shows the NMSE performance of the FL-DNN estimators at different numbers of FL iterations. It can be seen from the figure that at each SNR level, as the number of FL iterations increases, the NMSE of FL-DNN slowly decreases and tends to converge. In addition, when the SNR level is high, the FL-DNN

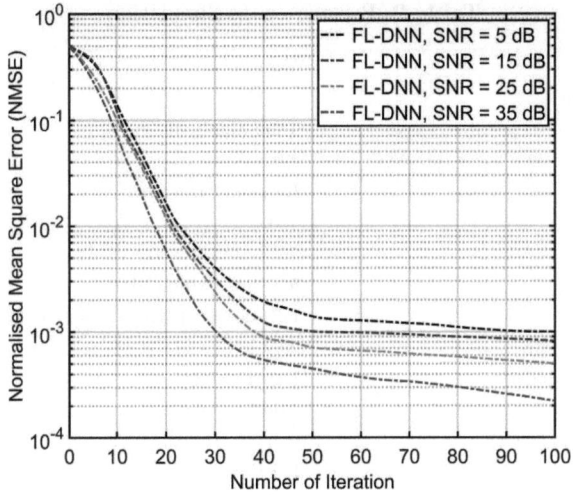

Fig. 9. Channel Estimation Performance Against Number of Iterations.

estimator has lower NMSE. This means that the number of iterations of FL-DNN does not need to be too large, as long as the NMSE is converged.

4.3 Data Recovery Performance

Figure 10 depicts the bit-error-rate (BER) performance of various channel estimators at different SNR levels. Since the LDPC coding is adopted, the BER can be reduced to an extremely low level (i.e., $10^{-7} \sim 10^{-6}$). We can see from the figure that the BER of each channel estimator decreases sharply with the increase of SNR, and the BER of the learning-based estimators tends to converge. FL-DNN has the best BER performance. Specifically, at SNR level of 5 dB, the BER of FL-DNN is 40.3%, 56.8%, 83.3%, 98.1%, 94.7%, 95.3% and 96.8% lower than that of SF-CNN, CNN, STA-DNN, LMMSE, DNN, STA and LS, respectively. When SNR rises to 25 dB, the BER of FL-DNN is 67.1%, 59.3%, 82.5%, 89.3%, 95.2%, 96.1% and 97.3% lower than that of SF-CNN, CNN, STA-DNN, LMMSE, DNN, STA and LS, respectively. This means that FL-DNN performs slightly greater than other estimators at high SNR levels.

4.4 Computational Complexity Performance

In this section, the computational complexity of various channel estimators is compared in Table 3. Since the time consumption of multiplication calculation is much longer than that of addition calculation, we only consider the number of multiplication calculations and its time complexity. It can be seen from Table 3 that the estimators from low to high in terms of time complexity are LS, STA, DNN, STA-DNN, FL-DNN, CNN/SF-CNN, and LMMSE. LS is the

Table 2. Parameters In Simulation

Parameter	Value	Unit
Simulation Duration	3600.00	s
3D City Model	Tsim Sha Tsui	N/A
Total Area	1.02	km^2
Mobility model	Random Trajectory	N/A
Traffic Conditions	4000	veh/h
Road Speed Limit	50	km/h
Vehicular Channel	5G New Radio (NR)	N/A
Channel Coding	Low-density parity-check code (LDPC)	N/A
Transmission Bandwidth	20	MHz
Signal Propagation Model	Ray Tracing	N/A
Signal Interference	Additive White Gaussian Noise (AWGN)	N/A
Signal-to-Noise Ratio (SNR)	0, 5, 10, 15, 20, 25, 30, 35	dB
Physical layer	IEEE 802.11p	N/A
Modulation and data rate	BPSK, 3	Mbps
Pilot, Data, and Total Subcarrier	4, 48, 64	N/A
Subcarrier Spacing	312.5	KHz
Length of Cyclic Prefix	16	bits
Symbol, Data, Guard Interval	4, 3.2, 0.8	μs
Transmission power P_t	20	mW
Communication Radius for vehicles	200	meter
Number of Base Station (BS)	5	meter
Communication Radius for BS	2000	meter
Packet Rate	10	packets/s
Federated Learning Platform	Keras TensorFlow	N/A
Number of Local Models N_{loc}	16	N/A
Number of Iteration	100	round
Global Model Aggregation Method	Trimmed Mean	N/A
Constant b in Trimmed Mean	3	N/A
Number of Neurons in DNN Layers	128, 256, 512, 256, 48	N/A
Train Epoch, Learning Rate, Batch Size for DNN	10,000, 0.001, 32	N/A
Training Set Size	20,000	symbols

simplest estimator, which divides the received symbols by the predefined pilot symbols. Since the predefined pilot symbols is BPSK modulated, $2N_{sub}$ divisions are required, where N_{sub} is the total number of subcarriers. All DNNs considered in this paper use 3 hidden layers, so the computational complexity is the transition of neurons in all layers, which can be expressed as $J_1 J_2 + J_2 J_3 + J_3 J_4 + J_1 J_4$, where J_1, J_2, J_3, J_4 denotes the number of neurons within the input layer, the first, second, and third hidden layer, respectively. FL-DNN uses trimmed mean averaging to aggregate the global model, so the amount of computation needs to be multiplied by the number of local models N_{loc}. The computational complexity of the CNN and SF-CNN estimators is the transition of N_{conv} convolutional layers, which can be expressed as $\sum_{l=1}^{N_{conv}} (D_x^l D_y^l W_x^l W_y^l F_{in}^l F_{out}^l)$. D_x^l, D_y^l denote

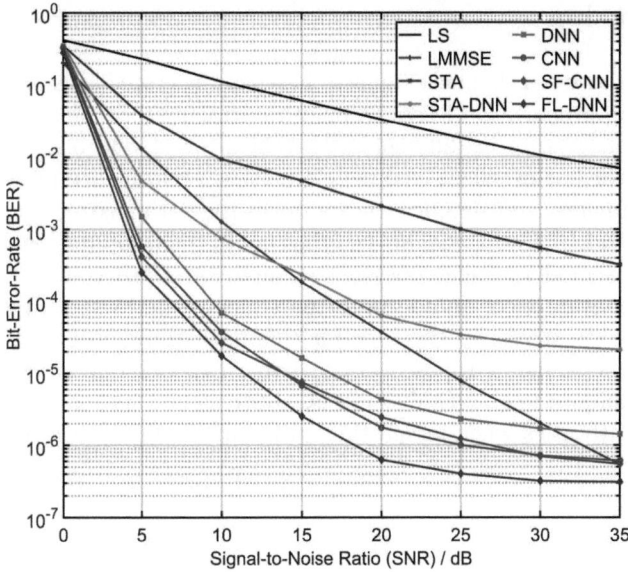

Fig. 10. Data Recovery Performance Versus SNR.

the column and row sizes of each feature map of the l-th convolutional layer, W_x^l, W_y^l denote the 2-dimension filter size, and F_{in}^l, F_{out}^l denote the number of input and output feature maps. LMMSE has the highest computational complexity because it uses singular value decomposition (SVD) for low-rank estimation, and obtaining the SVD of the channel autocovariance requires N_{sub}^3 multiplications.

In summary, the computational complexity of FL-DNN is lower than that of CNN, SF-CNN, and LMMSE, while the channel estimation performance is the best. It is a balanced estimator that trades off estimation performance and computational complexity.

Table 3. Computational Complexity Comparison

No.	Channel Estimator	Computational Complexity (Times of Multiplying Operations)	Time Complexity (From low to high)
1	LS	$2N_{sub}$	$O(2N_{sub})$
2	STA	$4N_{sub} + 2N_d$	$O(4N_{sub})$
3	DNN	$J_1 J_2 + J_2 J_3 + J_3 J_4 + J_1 J_4$	$O(J_1 J_2)$
4	STA-DNN	$82N_{sub} + 2N_d + J_1 J_2 + J_2 J_3 + J_3 J_4 + J_1 J_4$	$O(J_1 J_2)$
5	FL-DNN	$N_{loc}(J_1 J_2 + J_2 J_3 + J_3 J_4 + J_1 J_4)$	$O(N_{loc} J_1 J_2)$
6	CNN, SF-CNN	$\sum_{l=1}^{N_{conv}} (D_x^l D_y^l W_x^l W_y^l F_{in}^l F_{out}^l)$	$O(D_x^l D_y^l W_x^l W_y^l F_{in}^l F_{out}^l)$
7	LMMSE	N_{sub}^3	$O(N_{sub}^3)$

5 Conclusion

This paper proposes a channel estimator based on federated learning, which computes building propagation losses through ray tracing technology and can learn channel characteristics in different geographical areas. On one hand, the FL-DNN estimator has excellent channel estimation performance in vehicular network environments, and significantly improves the data recovery accuracy when combined with LDPC coding. On the other hand, the computational complexity of FL-DNN is moderate and does not occupy too much computing resources and energy consumption. In addition, the trained FL-DNN can provide offline testing, which greatly saves the time for channel estimation and data recovery. The FL-DNN estimator proposed in this paper can facilitate advanced communication techniques (e.g., NO-V2X) in 6G systems and have a profound impact on future smart cities when integrating with various digital twin platforms.

References

1. Wang, Z., Huang, J., Zhou, S., Wang, Z.: Iterative receiver processing for ofdm modulated physical-layer network coding in underwater acoustic channels. IEEE Trans. Commun. **61**(2), 541–553 (2013)
2. Situ, Z., Ho, I.W.-H., Xu, X., Guan, Y.L., Ding, C., et al.: Stochastic analysis of urban v2x communications: orthogonality versus non-orthogonality. ITU J. Fut. Evol. Technol. **3**(2), 19–33 (2022)
3. Acosta-Marum, G., Ingram, M.A.: Six time- and frequency- selective empirical channel models for vehicular wireless lans. IEEE Veh. Technol. Mag. **2**(4), 4–11 (2007)
4. Coleri, S., Ergen, M., Puri, A., Bahai, A.: Channel estimation techniques based on pilot arrangement in ofdm systems. IEEE Trans. Broadcast. **48**(3), 223–229 (2002)
5. Edfors, O., Sandell, M., van de Beek, J.-J., Wilson, S., Borjesson, P.: Ofdm channel estimation by singular value decomposition. IEEE Trans. Commun. **46**(7), 931–939 (1998)
6. Yang, Y., Gao, F., Ma, X., Zhang, S.: Deep learning-based channel estimation for doubly selective fading channels. IEEE Access **7**, 36579–36589 (2019)
7. Cheng, X., Liu, D., Zhu, Z., Shi, W., Li, Y.: A resnet-dnn based channel estimation and equalization scheme in fbmc/oqam systems. In: 2018 10th International Conference on Wireless Communications and Signal Processing (WCSP), pp. 1–5 (2018)
8. Dong, P., Zhang, H., Li, G.Y., Gaspar, I.S., NaderiAlizadeh, N.: Deep cnn-based channel estimation for mmwave massive mimo systems. IEEE J. Sel. Topics Signal Process. **13**(5), 989–1000 (2019)
9. Pradhan, A., Das, S., Dayalan, D.: A two-stage cnn based channel estimation for ofdm system. In: Advanced Communication Technologies and Signal Processing (ACTS) 2021, pp. 1–4 (2021)
10. Gallager, R.: Low-density parity-check codes. IRE Trans. Inf. Theory **8**(1), 21–28 (1962)
11. Nishimoto, K., Chiang, Y.-H., Lin, H., Ji, Y.: Fedatm: adaptive trimmed mean based federated learning against model poisoning attacks. In: 2023 IEEE 97th Vehicular Technology Conference (VTC2023-Spring), pp. 1–5 (2023)

12. Chen, Y., Ma, L., Ou, X., Liao, J.: Vehicular channel characterization in urban environment at 30 ghz considering overtaking and traffic flow. Wirel. Commun. Mob. Comput. **2021**, 1–11 (2021)
13. Ding, C., Ho, I.W.-H.: Digital-twin-enabled city-model-aware deep learning for dynamic channel estimation in urban vehicular environments. IEEE Trans. Green Commun. Network. **6**(3), 1604–1612 (2022)
14. Gizzini, A.K., Chafii, M., Nimr, A., Fettweis, G.: Deep learning based channel estimation schemes for IEEE 802.11p standard. IEEE Access **8**, 113751–113765 (2020)

Deep Q-Network Based Intelligent Traffic Signal Control: Case Study of a Large Single Intersection Using SUMO

Wanshu Wang[1(✉)], Xutao Mei[2], Zheng Wang[3], Bo Yang[4], and Kimihiko Nakano[1]

[1] Institute of Industrial Science, The University of Tokyo, Tokyo 153-8505, Japan
wangwans@iis.u-tokyo.ac.jp
[2] School of Civil Engineering, Harbin Institute of Technology, Harbin 150001, China
[3] Department of Computing Technologies, Swinburne University of Technology, Hawthorn 3122, VIC, Australia
[4] School of Computer Science and Systems Engineering, Kyushu Institute of Technology, Fukuoka 820-8502, Japan

Abstract. As urbanization continues to escalate, traffic congestion has emerged as a significant challenge in metropolitan areas. Existing traffic signal systems mainly rely on manually designed signal plans, which struggle to adapt to the dynamic and complex nature of modern traffic environments. This paper presents a theoretical introduction to an intelligent traffic signal control system based on Deep Q-networks (DQN) through a case study of a large single intersection. The DQN-TSC model is developed using the SUMO (Simulation of Urban MObility) platform. An agent for deep reinforcement learning (DRL) within the proposed model is designed by properly defining the state, action, and reward function. Through the appropriate parameter settings of the traffic model and reinforcement learning, simulation experiments are conducted in the SUMO environment. The comparative experimental results demonstrate that the proposed DQN-TSC model can effectively improve traffic efficiency at intersections, with significant improvements in evaluation metrics including total waiting time, average waiting time, and total number of stopped vehicles.

Keywords: Deep reinforcement learning · deep Q-network · traffic signal control · simulation of urban mobility (SUMO) · intelligent transportation system (ITS)

1 Introduction

As urbanization accelerates and the number of vehicles rapidly increases, traffic congestion has become a major challenge in metropolitan areas. At the same time, advancements in cameras, radar, and various V2X technologies have made real-time, precise traffic information sensing possible [1]. However, the traffic signal control (TSC) systems that are widely used today still heavily rely on manually designed signal plans. As a result, these systems are unable to dynamically sense the real-time information, and rarely adjust signal timing based on actual traffic conditions throughout the day [2]. On the other hand, deep reinforcement learning (DRL) systems, which can generate and execute different strategies based on the various information provided by the current environment and adjust these strategies in real-time according to environmental feedback, are seen as a highly promising solution to replace traditional systems and achieve vehicle-road connectivity [3]. Consequently, adaptive traffic signal control (ATSC) systems based on reinforcement learning (RL), and even DRL, have become one of the primary focuses of current research.

Deep Q-network (DQN), introduced by [4], represents a significant advancement in RL by integrating deep learning techniques to approximate the Q-value function. This approach utilizes deep neural networks (DNN) to handle complex, high-dimensional state spaces effectively, overcoming the limitations of traditional Q-learning. The key innovations such as experience replay, and fixed target networks stabilize the training process and address the instability issues commonly associated with Q-learning. DQN has demonstrated substantial potential in various domains, including ATSC [5–7]. Unlike conventional methods that rely on predefined rules and heuristics, DQN enables the autonomous learning of optimal control strategies through interaction with the environment. When applied to ATSC, DQN can continuously optimize signal timings based on real-time traffic conditions, thus enhancing traffic flow and mitigating congestion. This capability positions DQN as a powerful tool for developing adaptive traffic management systems that can efficiently respond to dynamic traffic patterns.

Previous studies on single intersections usually relied on road models with fewer lanes and a limited number of experimental vehicles. This paper aims to address traffic congestion in metropolitan areas, using a large four-way intersection model commonly found in urban environments as a case study to introduce an ATSC method based on Deep Q-Network (DQN). An integrated DQN-TSC model was developed, and its effectiveness was evaluated using metrics such as total waiting time, average waiting time, and total number of stops. Furthermore, the superiority of DQN-TSC was also verified through comparison with traditional fixed control and Q-learning control methods.

2 DQN-Based Adaptive Traffic Signal Control System

2.1 Deep Q-network

In the traditional Q-learning approach, the agent learns a policy that maximizes the cumulative reward by estimating the Q-values, which represent the expected future rewards for taking a particular action a. The Q-value is updated iteratively using the Bellman equation:

$$Q(s_t, a_t) \leftarrow Q(s_t, a_t) + \alpha \left[r + \gamma \max_{a_t} Q(s_{t+1}, a_{t+1}) - Q(s_t, a_t) \right] \quad (1)$$

where α is the learning rate, r is the immediate reward received after taking action a_t in state s_t, and γ is the discount factor representing the importance of future rewards. However, in the DQN architecture, a deep neural network (DNN), as depicted in Fig. 1, is utilized to approximate the Q-value function, allowing it to handle large or continuous state spaces. DNN typically comprises an input layer sized to match the state, multiple hidden layers that help in learning complex patterns, and an output layer corresponding to each potential action. The purpose of training the DQN is to minimize the difference between the predicted Q-value and the target Q-value obtained from Eq. (1). The loss function $L(\theta)$ is expressed as follows [8]:

$$L(\theta) = \mathbb{E}_{(s_t, a_t, r, s_{t+1}) \sim \mathcal{D}} \left[\left(r + \gamma \max_{a_t} Q(s_{t+1}, a_{t+1}; \theta^-) - Q(s_t, a_t; \theta) \right)^2 \right] \quad (2)$$

where θ and θ^- respectively represent the parameters of the Q-network and the parameters of the target network which are periodically updated to stabilize training. It is worth noting that $\mathcal{D}$ is the replay buffer that stores transitions (s_t, a_t, r, s_{t+1}) and samples mini-batches for training.

Figure 1 illustrates the application of a Deep Q-network (DQN) in ATSC using a SUMO simulation environment. The agent observes the current traffic state and uses DNN to select optimal actions, aiming to minimize traffic congestion. The environment responds to the agent's actions, providing feedback in the form of rewards, which guide the learning process.

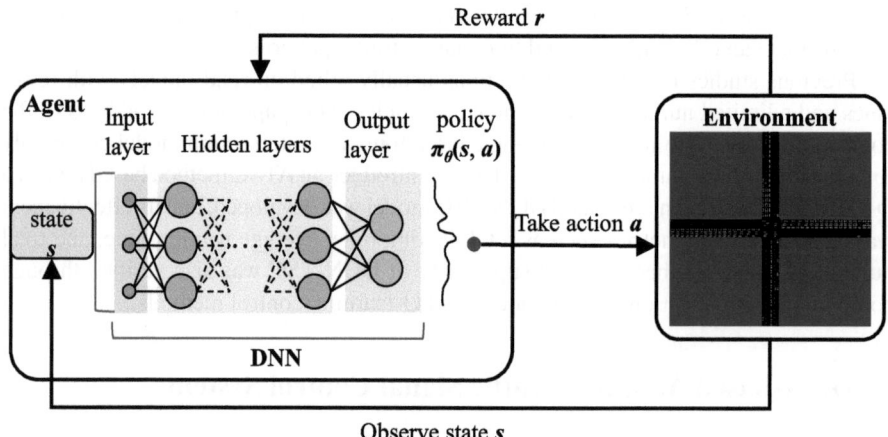

Fig. 1. Conceptual diagram of the DQN-based ATSC.

2.2 Agent Design

State Space.
The definition of state space can strongly influence the behavior and performance of an agent. At each time step t, the designed agent observes a state s_t which partially encapsulates comprehensive information about the traffic signal's current status and the conditions of the associated lanes. The state vector s in this study is defined by

$$s = [\mathbf{p}, m, d, q] \quad (3)$$

p denotes a one-hot encoded vector representing the current active green phase. Assuming there are N green phases for the traffic signal, **p** can be defined as $\mathbf{p} = [p_1, p_2, \ldots, p_i, \ldots, p_N]$. Note that $p_i = 1$ if the current green phase is i, otherwise $p_i = 0$. The binary indicator m signifies whether the minimum green time for the current phase has elapsed. Specifically, $m = 0$ if the time in the current phase is less than the sum of the minimum green phase and yellow time, otherwise $m = 1$. Let L stand for the number of lanes, and then $\mathbf{d} = [d_1, d_2, \ldots, d_L]$ is a vector capturing the density of vehicles in each lane, calculated as the ratio of the number of vehicles to the lane's total capacity. $\mathbf{q} = [q_1, q_2, \ldots, q_L]$ represents the queue length in each lane, defined as the proportion of stopped vehicles relative to the lane's capacity.

Action Space.
In the proposed DQN-TSC framework, the action space consists of the set of all possible green phases that the agent can select. The action space is discrete, with each action corresponding to the selection of one of these phases, thereby controlling which lanes are given the green light. Specifically, the case studied in this paper involves a large 4-way intersection, where each arm has 4 lanes approaching the intersection and 4 lanes leaving the intersection. Each arm has 5 traffic movement directions: the rightmost lane allows vehicles to either turn right or go straight, the two middle lanes are dedicated to straight movement, and the leftmost lane is for left turns only, as shown in Fig. 2(a). For ease of description, all 20 movement directions in Fig. 2(a) are sequentially numbered from 1 to 20. It is worth noting that in the SUMO simulation environment, "G" represents that the lane allows vehicles to pass with priority, "y" indicates a yellow light, and "r" means the lane is closed to traffic. The green phase configurations that the agent can choose in this study define 4 discrete actions, as shown in Fig. 2(b). Therefore, the detailed information about the traffic signal phase for each movement direction corresponding to each action is provided in Table 1. It should be mentioned that before transitioning from one action (green phase) to another, the previous phase needs to be set to yellow. For the sake of traffic safety, the yellow phase time in this case study is set to 4 s.

Reward Function.
The reward function is a critical component of a DRL-based ATSC, as it defines the objective that the agent seeks to optimize [9]. This means that a well-designed reward function can play a crucial role in improving traffic flow efficiency. Since the goal of this study is to minimize traffic congestion and reduce vehicle waiting times, the cumulative vehicle waiting time D_t is selected as an important metric, defined as follows:

$$D_t = \sum_{i=1}^{n} d_i(t) \tag{4}$$

where $d_i(t)$ represents the waiting time of the i-th vehicle at time t. Furthermore, the change in cumulative waiting time, i.e., the change in cumulative vehicle delay time, is designed as the reward function, expressed as follows:

$$R_t = D_{t-1} - D_t \tag{5}$$

This formulation aims to reward the agent for actions that decrease overall vehicle delay, thus promoting more efficient traffic flow.

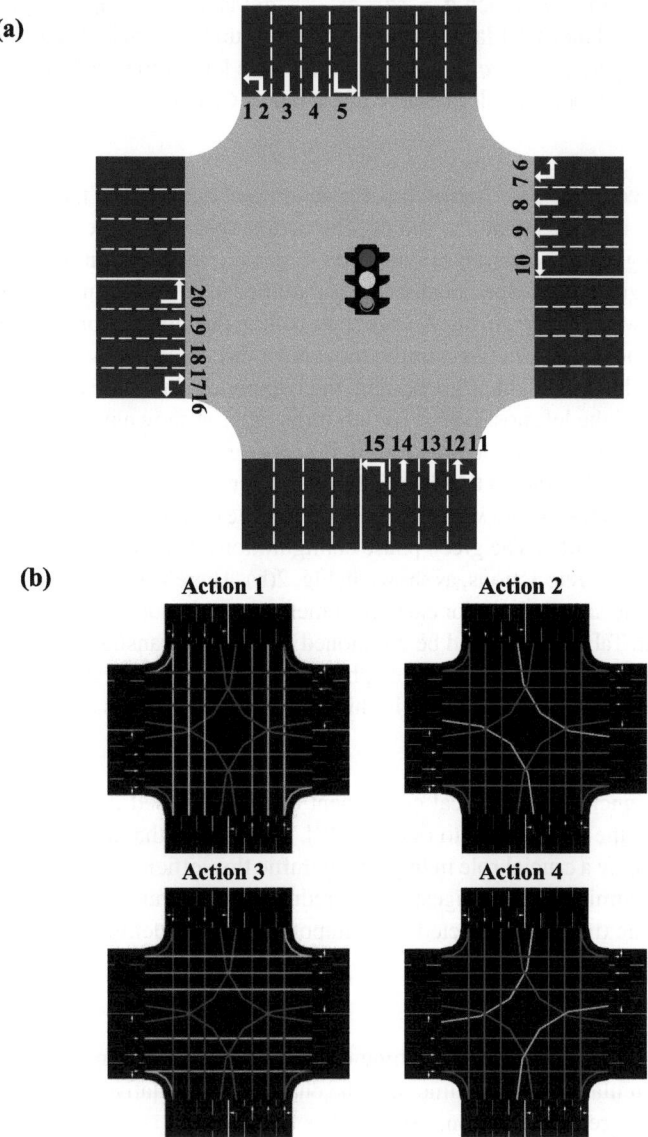

Fig. 2. (a) Movement direction number of the large single intersection, and (b) Traffic signal phases for each action.

Table 1. Detailed information for each action corresponding to the traffic signal in Fig. 2(b)

Action No.	Traffic signal phase corresponding to the order of movement direction (from 1 to 20)
1	GGGGrrrrrrGGGGrrrrrr
2	rrrrGrrrrrrrrrGrrrrr
3	rrrrrGGGGrrrrrrGGGGr
4	rrrrrrrrrGrrrrrrrrrG

3 Experiments

3.1 Simulation Environment

As mentioned multiple times before, this study is based on simulations conducted using SUMO (Simulation of Urban MObility), an open-source traffic simulation software designed to handle large road networks and simulate the movement of vehicles and pedestrians. In the SUMO environment, TraCI (Traffic Control Interface) is used to retrieve statistical data corresponding to the simulated objects and manipulate their behavior during training. The scenario investigated in this case study is a large single intersection (see Fig. 2), which has been described in detail in Sect. 2.2. The simulation time for each experiment in the SUMO environment is set to 6000 s, and the vehicle flow is set at 2,400 vehicles per hour, with 75% of the vehicles randomly choosing to go straight, and the remaining vehicles choosing to turn right or left. To optimize traffic flow, the green light duration needs to be dynamically adjusted. Hence, in this case, the minimum and maximum green times are set to 5 and 60 s, respectively. Furthermore, for the training of the DQN-TSC framework, we selected the multilayer perceptron as the policy network and set the learning rate to 0.0001. The size of the experience replay buffer was set to 50,000.

3.2 Comparative Performance Analysis

In this case study, total waiting time, average waiting time, and total number of stopped vehicles are chosen as evaluation metrics for the proposed DQN-TSC framework, as shown in Figs. 3, 4 and 5. To highlight the superior performance of the proposed framework, experimental results are compared with those from traditional fixed control and the classic Q-learning-based traffic signal control schemes.

Figure 3 illustrates the total waiting time at a large single intersection, showing that congestion peaks around 1700 s as vehicles accumulate, followed by a gradual decline as congestion alleviates. Unlike the other two TSC agents using reinforcement learning methods, DQN and Q-learning, fixed control exhibits periodic peaks due to its preset phase sequence and cycle duration (see Figs. 3, 4 and 5). Figure 4 displays the average waiting time per stopped vehicle, revealing that fixed control does not show a decreasing trend over time, unlike the proposed DQN-TSC method, which gradually reduces average waiting time after the initial congestion peak. Figure 5 illustrates the trend in the total number of stopped vehicles, similar to Fig. 3, with an initial increase followed by a decrease post-peak.

To quantitatively assess traffic flow efficiency, mean values of total waiting time, average waiting time, and total stopped vehicles from Figs. 3, 4 and 5 were calculated and compared. Table 2 shows the percentage improvements of DQN over fixed control and Q-learning. Compared to fixed control, DQN significantly reduces total waiting time, average waiting time, and total stopped vehicles by 81.47%, 88.29%, and 53.82%, respectively, while achieving improvements of 29.97%, 45.07%, and 39.01% over Q-learning.

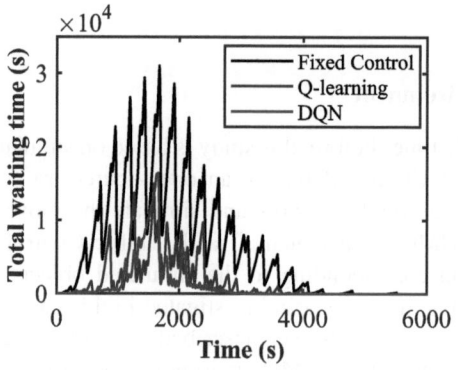

Fig. 3. Total waiting time of the vehicles.

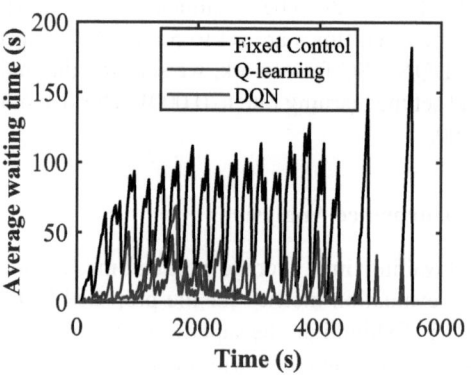

Fig. 4. Average waiting time of the vehicles

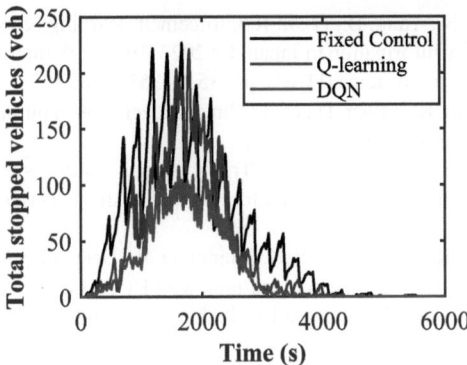

Fig. 5. Total number of the stopped vehicles.

Table 2. Enhancement (%) of DQN-TSC framework compared to fixed control and Q-learning

Evaluation Metrices	Enhancement (%)	
	DQN vs Fixed	DQN vs Q-learning
Total waiting time	81.47	29.97
Average waiting time	88.29	45.07
Total stopped vehicles	53.82	39.01

4 Conclusion

In this study, we developed a large single-intersection model within the SUMO environment and proposed an effective DQN-TSC framework. By carefully defining the state, action, and reward function, we evaluated the framework's impact on traffic flow efficiency through simulation experiments. Through comparative experiments with fixed control and Q-learning, results show that the DQN-TSC model can significantly improve total waiting time, average waiting time, and total number of stopped vehicles. Future work will extend beyond DQN to explore additional DRL methods, such as SARSA, A2C, and PPO, with comparative experiments. Research scenarios will also expand to more complex, multi-intersection models based on the real map. Additionally, while this study used cumulative waiting time as the reward function, future research will incorporate factors such as vehicle travel time and queue length to further enhance reward function design.

References

1. Ding, C., Ho, I.W.H.: Digital-twin-enabled city-model-aware deep learning for dynamic channel estimation in urban vehicular environments. IEEE Trans. Green Commun. Netw. **6**(3), 1604–1612 (2022)
2. Wei, H., Zheng, G., Gayah, V., et al.: A survey on traffic signal control methods, arXiv preprint arXiv:1904.08117 (2019)

3. Mei, X., Fukushima, N., Yang, B., et al.: Reinforcement learning based traffic signal control considering the railway information in Japan. In: 2023 IEEE 26th International Conference on Intelligent Transportation Systems (ITSC), pp. 3533–3538 (2022)
4. Mnih, V., Kavukcuoglu, K., Silver, D., et al.: Human-level control through deep reinforcement learning. Nature **518**(7540), 529–533 (2015)
5. Kodama, N., Harada, T., Miyazaki, K.: Traffic signal control system using deep reinforcement learning with emphasis on reinforcing successful experiences. IEEE Access **10**, 128943–128950 (2022)
6. Rao, P.S., Polisetty, V.R.M., Jayanth, K.K., Manoj, et al.: Deep adaptive algorithms for local urban traffic control: deep reinforcement learning with DQN. In: 2024 2nd International Conference on Intelligent Data Communication Technologies and Internet of Things (IDCIoT), pp. 592–598 (2024)
7. Haddad, T.A., Hedjazi, D., Aouag, S.: A deep reinforcement learning-based cooperative approach for multi-intersection traffic signal control. Eng. Appl. Artif. Intell. **114**, 105019 (2022)
8. Böhm, P., Pounds, P., Chapman, A.C.: Feature extraction for effective and efficient deep reinforcement learning on real robotic platforms. In: 2023 IEEE International Conference on Robotics and Automation (ICRA), pp. 7126–7132 (2023)
9. Mei, X., Fukushima, N., Yang, B., et al.: Reinforcement learning based intelligent traffic signal control considering sensing information of railway. IEEE Sens. J. **23**(24), 31125–31136 (2023)

DCA-YOLO: Non-Prominent Feature Object Detection Using the Dynamic Convolution Attention YOLO Model

Yang Li[1], Xiaolong Yang[2], Yuekun Hei[2], and Xuting Duan[2(✉)]

[1] School of Data Science, City University of Hong Kong, Kowloon, Hong Kong
yli669c@gmail.com
[2] School of Transportation Science and Engineering, Beihang University, Beijing, China
duanxuting@buaa.edu.cn

Abstract. Camouflaged object detection is one of the most challenging problems in computer vision. Object detection depends on feature extraction and processing, so detecting targets with less distinct features is difficult. To enrich the experiments regarding the performance of such objects on YOLO-related models, this paper conducts comparative experiments on a non-prominent feature objects dataset and explores the impact of dynamic convolution and attention mechanisms on the detection capability of YOLO models. This paper proposed a YOLO-based model called DCA-YOLO, which combines dynamic convolution and attention mechanisms. Dynamic convolution provides flexible and powerful feature extraction capabilities, while attentional scale sequence fusion further improves detection performance through effective feature fusion and weight assignment. Our YOLO based model with the proposed components, performs well in diverse scenarios. The proposed model and other 4 YOLO models were tested on certain real-world dataset about targets disguised in the background. Results showed that our proposed model can effectively detect non-distinctive targets.

Keywords: Camouflaged Objective Detection · Computer Vision · Attention Mechanism · Deep Learning · You Only Look Once (YOLO)

1 Introduction

Object Detection, one of the most basic and challenging tasks in computer vision, is used to detect all instances of predefined classes appearing in the image or video and assign them corresponding class tags. Object detection answers a fundamental question in computer vision: What objects are where? Object detection is widely used in vehicle counting and facial recognition fields. Furthermore, it provides powerful support for more advanced tasks such as trajectory tracking, behavior analysis, and semantic segmentation.

In the past two decades, with the continuous updating of deep learning technology, object detection has been rapidly developed, which has extensively promoted the progress of autonomous driving, medical image analysis, industrial automation, and other fields.

However, many object detection challenges are still waiting to be solved in complex, realistic scenes, including camouflaged objects, occlusion, and small objects. The main subject of the camouflaged object detection task is objects appearing in pictures or videos with similar color, texture, and brightness to the background, such as polar bears in the snow and lizards in the desert. In this paper, we call them non-prominent feature objects. Because similar areas in the background can be mistaken for targets, it is easy to confuse the visual feature when detecting the non-prominent feature objects, which leads to a high false detection rate.

Dynamic Convolution Attention YOLO (DCA-YOLO) is an improved model of the YOLO V8 framework, which in backbone part, adds dynamic convolution into C2f modules [2,3] and in the Neck part, uses attention mechanisms promoted by ASF-YOLO [4]. Dynamic convolution makes the parameters of the convolution kernel adaptive and allows the model to capture more context information. Attention mechanisms fuse features at different scales while dynamically assigning more weight to essential features. The combination of the two improves the accuracy of the detection task.

- the design of a model named Dynamic Convolution Attention YOLO (DCA-YOLO), which performs well on non-prominent feature objects in a real-world dataset MODD-λ [1]
- On this non-prominent feature objects dataset, we have conducted systematic experiments using multiple different versions of the YOLO series models. Based on these comparisons and analyses, we can more clearly grasp the advantages and limitations of each YOLO model in handling non-prominent feature objects, thereby providing an important reference for the selection and optimization of models in subsequent related tasks.

The remainder of the paper is organized as follows. The second briefly reviews classical algorithms and cutting-edge algorithms in the field of target detection. At the same time, we make a preliminary introduction about how to evaluate the object detection model. Section 3 introduces the model we will be using in this project and explains the principles and structure of our model. Section 4 is the introduction to the dataset, environment, and device. Section 5 is the experimental process and analysis of the results. Section 6 summarizes our contributions and provides directions for future research.

2 Related Work

The early object detection models were based on machine learning techniques. In 2001, the Viola-Jones object detector was introduced, a face detection detector [5, 6]. It searches for Haar-like features by sliding through the window, and after passing through the integral image, the trained Adaboost cascades each feature classifier. Dalal and Triggs proposed the Histogram of Oriented Gradients (HOG) four years later [7]. HOC creates histograms on images divided into grids and generates features. These features are fed into a linear SVM classifier for detection.

The rise of object detection can be attributed to three factors:

- The widespread use of GPUs. The increase in computer processing power speeds up the operation of complex algorithms and models, which makes more complex calculations possible.

- The disclosure of large data sets. The performance of the target detection model depends on the training of rich data resources to some extent. The establishment and opening of large-scale and diverse data sets (such as ImageNet, COCO, etc.) provide rich nutrients for the training of algorithms.
- Most importantly, deep learning techniques are applied.

Scholars have found that deep learning techniques, particularly convolutional neural networks (CNNS), have achieved great success in computer vision and image processing tasks [8]. With the rise of deep learning, object detection has also ushered in a period of rapid development. In 2014, The Region-based Convolutional Neural Network (R-CNN) was the cornerstone of the object detection model using deep learning [9, 10]. At that time, the algorithm made a remarkable breakthrough that had a significant influence on research in the field of object detection. RCNN uses CNN to extract features and Selective Search to generate a region proposal and then classifies the region proposal. This pioneering model not only improves the accuracy of target detection, but also avoids the intensive sliding-window search of the entire image, thus greatly improving the efficiency of the algorithm. However, the computational speed of RCNN is very slow and the algorithm is also very complex. These shortcomings have prompted researchers to propose improved algorithms based on RCNN, such as Fast R-CNN [11], Faster R-CNN [12] and Mask R-CNN [13].

You Only Look Once (YOLO)
Object detection consists of two subtasks: recognition and classification. An object detection algorithm in which two subtasks are carried out simultaneously is called One-Stage, while an object detection algorithm in which two subtasks are identified first and then classified is called two-stage. One-stage target detection is the mainstream at present, among which there are many famous algorithms such as YOLO (You Only Look Once) [14], SSD (Single Shot Multibox Detector) [15], and so on.

In 2016, Joseph Redmon, Santosh Divvala, Ross Girshick, and others pro- posed a one-stage object detection network called YOLO V1 (You Only Look Once). The core idea of YOLO is to transform target detection into a regression problem, using the whole graph as the network's input, just through a neural network, to get the location of the bounding box and its category. Since then, the authors have continued to improve on the YOLO V1, and as of 2024, the latest version of YOLO V10 has been announced. However, because each version has a different focus on improvement, the new version of the model may not perform as well as the old model in a particular dataset or application scenario. Tradeoffs in model training and optimization are also a reason for this.

Camouflaged Object Detection (COD)
Deng-Ping Fan et al. present the first systematic study on concealed object detection and design of a famous model, the Search identification network (SINet) [19]. Another clever idea is to adopt step-by-step thinking. SegMaR utilizes an attention-based sampler to magnify object regions progressively, achieving a step-by-step refinement in detection [20]. In 2023, the COD field again saw progress, and the FEDER model addressed the intrinsic similarity of targets and backgrounds by using learnable wavelets to decompose features into different frequency bands [21]. It then focuses on the bands with the most

information to mine for clues that distinguish targets and backgrounds. The FEDER model performed better than SINet and SegMaR on the real datasets.

Other Object Detection Problem
Small objects have less pixel information and are easily lost in the down- sampling process. A classical method is to use the image pyramid method for multi-scale variation enhancement [22–24]. One of the main problems of FPN is plodding training speed, and layers of different scales are easy to overfit [25]. Thus, some researchers try to use another way, which is to build a parallel multi-branch structure called Trident, allowing the efficient detection of objects of different sizes.

Occlusion can be divided into two cases: the mutual occlusion between the detected targets and the other is the occlusion of the detected targets by interfering items [26]. Making the model judge occlusion spontaneously is the key in this direction. If the surrounding ground truth of the target contains objects other than the object, the Repulsion Loss [26] requires that the proposal of the prediction be removed from all of them. Another way is scores the visibility of the subareas of the candidate areas and judges occlusion by comparing the scores [27].

Blurry images can be caused by bad weather (e.g., fog, night) because of the loss of spatial position information and the lack of features for small-scale targets. Some GAN-based models can up-sample small fuzzy images to enrich image details [28]. Another easy way to think about it is to dilute the effects of weather-specific information through image preprocessing [29].

3 Methodology

The DCA-YOLO model is modified on the basis of the framework of YOLO V8, shown as Fig. 1. There are 3 parts in DCA-YOLO framework, the Backbone part, the Neck part, and the Head part.

3.1 Backbone

Except for replacing C2f modules with C2f_DyConv modules, backbone part has the exact same structure in DCA-YOLO and YOLO V8.

The backbone section consists of five convolutional layers and four C2f modules. The C2f(Channel-to-Pixel) module is one of the critical components used for feature fusion in YOLO V8. It is essentially a residual block that directly transmits the input signal to the output signal through the residual connection to learn the direct mapping relationship between the input and output. To improve feature extraction capabilities, the C2f modules were replaced with C2f modules incorporating dynamic convolution.

C2f modules with dynamic convolution is dynamically aggregated ac- cording to the attention of multiple parallel convolution kernels [2, 3].

The static perceptron is defined as follow:

$$y = g(\tilde{W}^T(x)x + b(x)) \tag{1}$$

where W and b are weight matrix and bias vector, and g is an activation function.

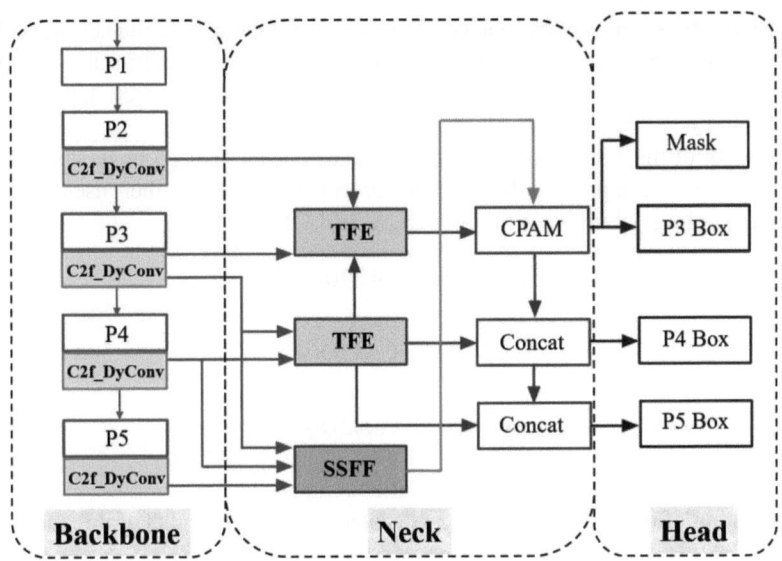

Fig. 1. Brief Overview Framework of DCA-YOLO

The dynamic perceptron by aggregating multiple (K) linear functions $\{\tilde{W}_k^T x + \tilde{b}_k\}$ is defined as follows:

$$\tilde{W}(x) = \sum_{k=1}^{K} \pi_k(x) \tilde{W}_k, \tag{2}$$

$$\tilde{b}(x) = \sum_{k=1}^{K} \pi_k(x) b_k \tag{3}$$

$$\text{s.t. } 0 \leq \pi_k(x) \leq 1, \ \sum_{k=1}^{K} \pi_k(x) = 1$$

where π_ks are same in Equation (2) and (3), which is the attention weight for the kth linear function $\tilde{W}_k^T x + b_k$. $\{\pi_k(x)\}$ is varied attention weight that correspond the optimal aggregation of linear models for a given input x. However, $\tilde{W}^T(x)x + b(x)$ is a non-linear function that make C2f modules with dynamic convolution has more representation power.

3.2 Neck

DCA-YOLO use the modules that proposed by M. Kang et al. [4]. M. Kang et al. build the Scale Sequence Feature Fusion module (SSFF) and a Triple Feature Encoder module (TFE) to combines spatial and scale features for accurate and detailed detection of small objects with blurred boundaries. Non-prominent feature objects and objects with blurred borders face similar problems because they are easily confused with backgrounds.

SSFF module mainly corresponds to improving the feature pyramid net- work (FPN) in the Neck section. The module enhances the fusion ability of multi-scale features by sequence fusion of features at different scales, thus improving the detection performance of small objects.

The input of the SSFF module is feature maps P3, P4, and P5 generated from the backbone part. It compresses the input feature map in half and then uses a multiple maximum pooling operation (3 times in DCA-YOLO).

$$y_1 = \text{MaxPool2D}(input') \tag{4}$$

$$y_2 = \text{MaxPool2D}(y_1) \tag{5}$$

$$y_3 = \text{MaxPool2D}(y_2) \tag{6}$$

where $input'$ is the input of SSFF module after compressing.

The output of the SSFF module is a concatenation of the results of three maximum pooling.

$$Output\_SSFF = \text{Conv}(\text{Concat}(input', y\_1, y\_2, y\_3)) \tag{7}$$

TFE module improves the accuracy and speed of the model. The inputs of the TFE module are three feature maps of different sizes(large l, medium m, and small s). Before feature encoding, the number of channels for large and small feature maps is adjusted to be the same as medium-scale feature maps's number of channels.

Then, large-size feature maps experience maximum pooling and average pooling for downsampling. For small-size feature maps, the nearest neighbor interpolation method is used for upsampling.

$$l' = \text{AdaptiveMaxPool}(l, m\_size) + \text{AdaptiveAvgPool}(l, m\_size) \tag{8}$$

$$s' = \text{Nearest}(s, \text{size} = m\_size) \tag{9}$$

TFE module output ($Output_{TFE}$) is a concatenation feature map with first dimension.

$$Output_{TFE} = \text{Concat}(l', m, s') \tag{10}$$

4 Experiments

4.1 Dataset

This paper uses the aerial view part of the MODD-λ dataset[3] [1]. MODD-λ can be classified as a COD dataset, which mainly consists of objects captured in[1] military scenes, i.e. with personnel wearing camouflage uniforms and vehicles painted with camouflage paint.

---

[1] Data address: https://github.com/RyanBlack5728/MODD-Lambda.

This dataset has three classes of objects: soldier, armored car, and tank. The total number of images in each category is 22,834 number of soldiers, 3437 for armored cars, and 2729 for tanks. This dataset is imbalanced, with number of soldiers more than six times that of armored cars and more than eight times that of class tanks.

MODD-λ includes 5916 images with 19020 x 1080 pixels. About 83 percent of the data sets were used as training set, about 8.5 percent were used as validation set, and the rest were used as test set.

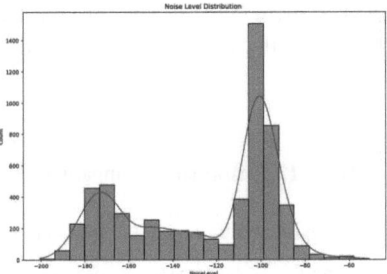

Fig. 2. Noise Level Distribution

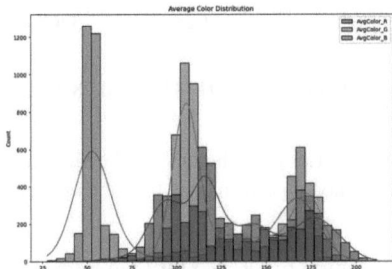

Fig. 3. RGB Distribution

Figure 2 shows the noise level as a bimodal distribution. The two major peaks are between about −180 and −100, indicating two different types of images in the dataset: one that is more noisy and one that is less noisy. Images with high noise levels can adversely affect object detection algorithms because noise interferes with image details.

According to Fig. 3, although the distribution of red, green, and blue channels is bimodal, the peaks are obviously different. This shows that the images in the dataset have a great variety of colors.

4.2 Implementation Details

All experiment of this paper is implemented on an NVIDIA GeForce 4060 GPU, using Pytorch 1.12.1 and CUDA 11.3 dependencies. The YOLO V8 model in this paper is the 8.1.9 version. The initial weights of all models in this paper are derived from training the YOLO V8 model on the large COCO and ImageNet datasets. The input image size is 640 x 640 pixels. The optimization function of the experiment is Stochastic Gradient Descent (SGD). The loss function is CIoU.

5 Ablation Study

5.1 Model Performance

There are two main detection error types:

- Missed Detection Error(Miss Error): the number of non-detected objects.
- Classification Error(Cls Error): the number of objects that are classified with the wrong class.

Table 1. Performance comparison

	mAP50 ↑	mAP50:95 ↑	Precision↑	Recall↑	Miss Error↓	Cls Error↓
YOLO V6	0.82197	0.62774	0.85719	0.78011	337	13
YOLO V8	0.81817	0.63216	0.87087	0.74193	350	24
YOLO V10	0.78373	0.56741	0.79251	0.69632	361	30
ASF-YOLO V8	0.83901	0.63509	0.86249	**0.78968**	324	31
DCA-YOLO V8 (Ours)	**0.85483**	**0.64149**	**0.91732**	0.78297	**274**	**11**

This table lists the performance metrics of each model at the highest epoch of the *mAP50*:95. The bolded values represent the best model performance for each indicator.

Table 1 shows the contribution of DCA-YOLO in improving the objective detection performance. Since its release, the YOLO V8 [17] has been welcomed for its combination of performance and precision. Compared to its predecessor, the YOLO V6 [16], and the latest version, the YOLO V10 [18], the YOLO V8 is not the best in every aspect but embodies its balanced and robust characteristics. As an improved model for the YOLO V8, the ASF-YOLO has the highest recall (around 79%), the second highest *mAP50*:95, and the highest classification error, which suggests that it is good at detecting the presence of objects but has weaknesses in feature fusion and final classification.

Our DCA-YOLO model has high precision (around 87%) and highest mAP, which means it detects and classifies any possible target area. Moreover, this well-rounded model has the lowest classification error (11 error objectives) and missed detection errors (274 error objectives), which suggests it has strong feature extraction and classification capabilities.

Figure 4 compares the detection results of different models across three sample images. Only test results with a confidence level greater than 0.2 are retained. Three example graphs represent each of the three error cases. The original image in the left column (Fig. (4a)) has only two targets, but YOLO V8 and ASF-YOLO incorrectly detect the background as the target. Only DSF-YOLO is correct.

The middle column also has two goals, which are smaller and less obvious than in the first sample. YOLO V8 gives many false detection results, as shown in Fig. (4e). ASF-YOLO and DCA-YOLO accurately detect these two objects, but there is a bounding box overlap when drawing the target in the lower part of the image. During detection, the model will produce a large number of candidate boxes for the same target, and these candidate boxes will overlap with each other. This is one of the common errors of object detection models. This error has been resolved by filtering detection results through Non-Maximum Suppression (NMS) to remove redundant overlapping boxes. No model fine-tuning was conducted for this problem to maintain consistent settings and facilitate more meaningful comparisons.

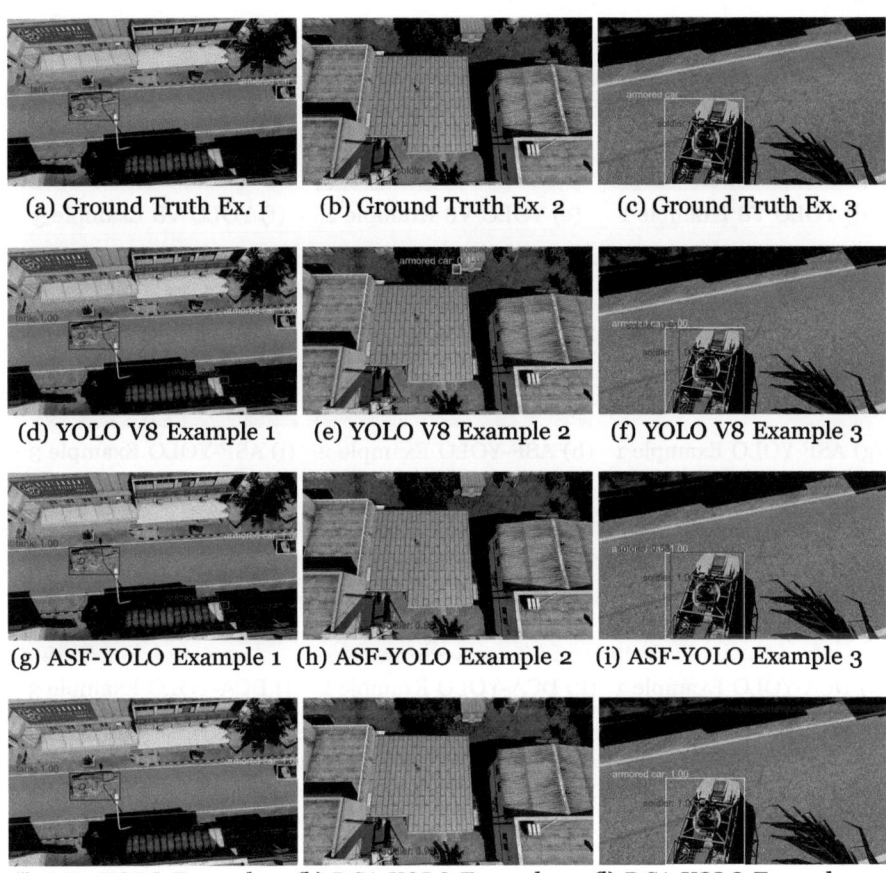

Fig. 4. Result Visualization. Figures in the same row are generated from same model. Figures in the same column come from same original image.

The image's targets are apparent but difficult to detect in the right column. Because when the soldier is driving the armored car, the soldier is only partially exposed, and its region exists in the region of the armored car. The YOLO V8 and ASF-YOLO models give a ludicrous result, drawing bounding boxes for soldiers about the same size as the armored cars, with the two frames mostly overlapping. Only DCA-YOLO did not have this error.

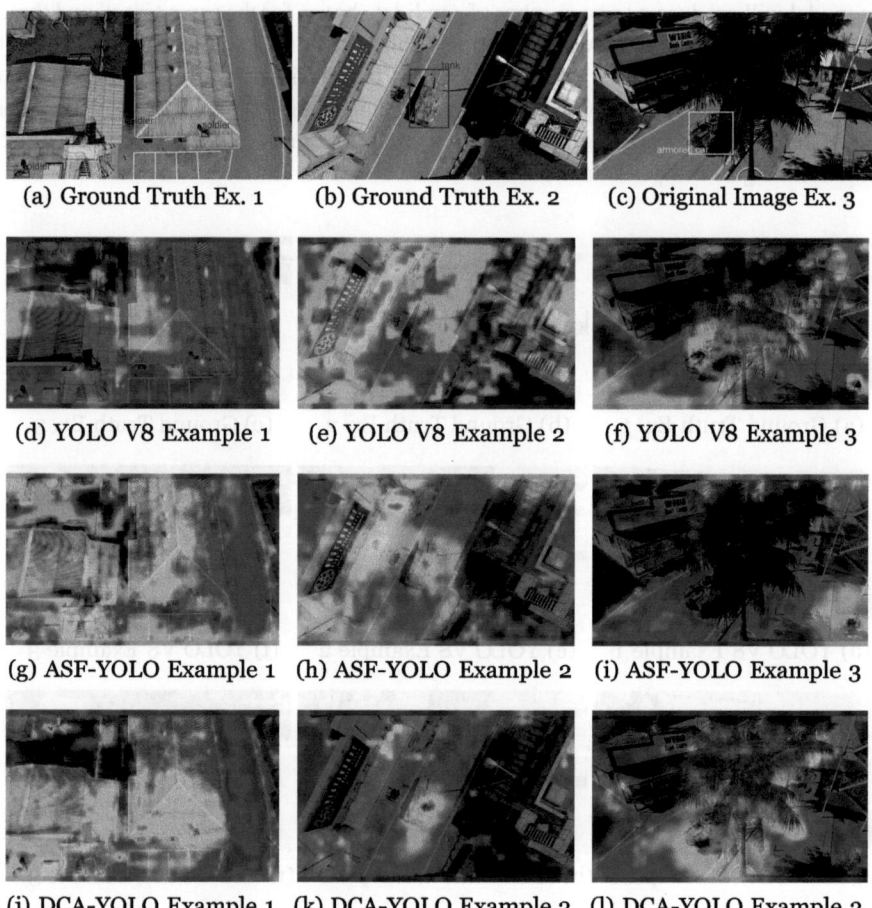

Fig. 5. Heatmaps of different models. Figures in the same row are generated from same model, the figures in first row are original images not heatmap, it's for comparison. Figures in the same column come from same original image. Example 1,2 and 3 are represented multi-object, single-object, and obscured respectively.

Figure 5 shows the focus areas of the different models on three sample images. Which area of the network is more focused on, the image's corresponding part is brighter. In other words, the information in the red areas of the image contributes the most to the prediction result, which are called high-response areas. The high-response region attracts the most attention of the model, so we can observe the model's training effect and prediction results by observing whether the high- response region falls on the target region.

As shown in Fig. (5d), the red part is concentrated in the upper right corner of the image. However, the four targets almost do not entirely attract the attention of the YOLO V8 model because we can see that the areas around the targets are not even yellow and green. About half of the area in Fig. (5g) height attracted the attention of the ASF-YOLO model, but this prevented the ASF- YOLO model from correctly finding the target. Figure (5j) is a visualization of the attention distribution results of the DCA-YOLO model. Although the high-response region did not accurately fall on the target, much attention was not allocated to the background, which significantly improved the accuracy of feature extraction of the model and laid a good foundation for the subsequent detection task.

In Fig. (5e), most of the attention of the YOLO V8 model is focused on the billboard on the left side of the image. The ASF-YOLO model takes its attention away from the wrong target and successfully notices the tank target, but the rest of the image still receives some attention. Figure (5k) shows the high precision of the DCA-YOLO model, as it focuses entirely on the single target of the image.

The right column is the most complicated case, including multiple different classes of targets, and the barrier half obscures the larger target. The YOLO V8 model (Fig. (5f)) notices two objects but also allocates some attention to the barrier. The occlusion fools the ASF-YOLO model (Fig. (5i)), so the ASF- YOLO model only notices the most obvious target in the lower right corner. The DCA-YOLO model is smart enough to recognize occluders, focusing the image's high-response area only on the not-occluded part, but it ignores two other small targets.

5.2 C2f Dynamic Convolution (C2f-DyConv) Module

Table 2 compares three distinct placement strategies of C2f modules and C2f- DyConv modules. When all C2f modules in the backbone part are replaced by the C2f-DyConv modules, the overall performance achieves the best. By com- paring **All** situation and **Backbone** situation, we discover that replacing the C2f module in the head part with the C2F-Dyconv module will decrease the model's performance. One possible reason is that the C2f-DyConv module adds computational overhead or introduces overfitting.

Table 2. Performance Comparison of different C2f-DyConv module locations

	mAP50 ↑	mAP50:95 ↑	Precision↑	Recall↑	Miss Error↓	Cls Error↓
None	0.83901	0.63509	0.86249	**0.78968**	324	31
Backbone	**0.85483**	**0.64149**	**0.91732**	0.78297	**274**	11
All	0.84115	0.63603	0.86503	0.78556	307	7

The best results are in bold. **None** represents there does not exit the C2f-DyConv module in model, that is ASF-YOLO. **Backbone** represents C2f-modules in backbone part are replaced, that is DCA-YOLO **All** represents all C2f-modules in model are replaced.

5.3 Model Efficiency

It can be seen from Table 3 that DCA-YOLO has a relatively large number of layers, and the number of parameters and gradients are the largest among these models. DCA-YOLO is a fast model in the training and inference phases (GFLOPs = 8.1 and GFLOPs during inference = 7.3).

Table 3. Efficiency comparison

	No. of layers	No. of parameters	Gradients	GFLOPs	GFLOPs (inference)
YOLO V6	195	4238441	4238425	11.9	11.8
YOLO V8	225	3011433	3011417	8.9	8.1
YOLO V10	385	2708210	2708194	8.4	6.5
ASF-YOLO V8	247	3051561	3051545	9.3	8.5
DCA-YOLO V8 (Ours)	278	4471057	4471041	8.1	7.3

This table lists the efficiency metrics of each model during training and GFLOPs during inference.

6 Conclusions

This paper proposes a camouflaged object detection model DCA-YOLO that combines dynamic convolution and attention mechanisms. Compared with the other four YOLO models, DCA-YOLO achieves the best overall performance on the MODD-λ non-prominent feature object dataset. It improves detection accuracy for non-prominent feature objects, achieving the highest mAP 50 and mAP 50:95. It also reduces missed detections and classification errors and decreases background interference by allocating attention more reasonably. YOLO V6 is characterised by a lightweight, modular structure. While it balances speed and accuracy well, its feature extraction capability is limited in complex scenarios, resulting in more missed detections. YOLO V8 demonstrates stable, comprehensive performance thanks to the balanced design of CSPDarknet53 and PANet; however, it struggles to distinguish non-prominent feature objects. YOLO V10 has been adapted for edge deployment through lightweight and robustness optimization; however, its accuracy in experiments is not as good as that of models designed for more specific purposes. Despite improving the recall rate of small target detection with the help of the SSFF and TFE modules, ASF-YOLO has the highest classification error rate due to structural defects in the feature fusion and classification stages.

However, due to the size and imbalance classes of the dataset MODD-λ in this paper, the model's generalization ability is a major concern in future research. The DCA-YOLO model can be further improved by experimenting with other camouflaged object detection datasets and further changing the overall structure.

Acknowledgments. We sincerely thank our supervisor's valuable guidance and insightful advice throughout the research project. We would also like to thank the members of our group for their continued support and positive discussions. Everyone played an essential role in the completion of this paper. At the same time, we are very grateful to the research team for permitting us to use the MODD-λ dataset and allowing us to train and test our model effectively.

References

1. Hei, Y., Duan, X., Yang, X., Zhou, J., Lin, C.: MODD-λ: military Object Detection Dataset for Land-Air Integration and Cross-Domain Collaborative Unmmanned Swarm Systems (2024)
2. Chen, Y., Dai, X., Liu, M., Chen, D., Yuan, L., Liu, Z.: Dynamic convolution: attention over convolution kernels. In: 2020 IEEE/CVF Conference on Computer Vision and Pattern Recognition (CVPR), pp. 11027–11036 (2019)
3. Han, K., Wang, Y., Guo, J., Wu, E.: ParameterNet: Parameters Are All You Need for Large-scale Visual Pretraining of Mobile Networks. ArXiv, abs/2306.14525 (2023)
4. Kang, M., Ting, C., Ting, F.F., Phan, R.C.: ASF-YOLO: A Novel YOLO Model with Attentional Scale Sequence Fusion for Cell Instance Segmentation. ArXiv, abs/2312.06458 (2023)
5. Viola, P.A., Jones, M.J.: Rapid object detection using a boosted cascade of simple features. In: Proceedings of the 2001 IEEE Computer Society Conference on Computer Vision and Pattern Recognition, CVPR 2001, vol. 1, p. I (2001)
6. Viola, P.A., Jones, M.J.: Robust real-time face detection. Int. J. Comput. Vision **57**, 137–154 (2001)
7. Dalal, N., Triggs, B.: Histograms of oriented gradients for human detection. In: 2005 IEEE Computer Society Conference on Computer Vision and Pattern Recognition (CVPR 2005), vol. 1, pp. 886–893 (2005)
8. Krizhevsky, A., Sutskever, I., Hinton, G.E.: ImageNet classification with deep convolutional neural networks. Commun. ACM **60**, 84–90 (2012)
9. Girshick, R.B., Donahue, J., Darrell, T., Malik, J.: Rich feature hierarchies for accurate object detection and semantic segmentation. In: 2014 IEEE Conference on Computer Vision and Pattern Recognition, pp. 580–587 (2013)
10. Girshick, R.B., Donahue, J., Darrell, T., Malik, J.: Region-based convolutional networks for accurate object detection and segmentation. IEEE Trans. Patt. Anal. Mach. Intell. **38**, 142–158 (2016)
11. Girshick, R.B.: Fast R-CNN (2015)
12. Ren, S., He, K., Girshick, R.B., Sun, J.: Faster R-CNN: towards real-time object detection with region proposal networks. IEEE Trans. Pattern Anal. Mach. Intell. **39**, 1137–1149 (2015)
13. He, K., Gkioxari, G., Dollár, P., Girshick, R.: Mask r-CNN. IEEE Trans. Patt. Anal. Mach. Intell. (2017)
14. Redmon, J., Divvala, S.K., Girshick, R.B., Farhadi, A.: You only look once: unified, real-time object detection. In: 2016 IEEE Conference on Computer Vision and Pattern Recognition (CVPR), pp. 779–788 (2015)
15. Liu, W., et al.: SSD: Single shot MultiBox detector. In: European Conference on Computer Vision (2015)
16. Li, C., et al.: YOLOv6: A Single-Stage Object Detection Framework for Industrial Applications. ArXiv, abs/2209.02976 (2022)
17. Varghese, R., Sambath, M.: YOLOv8: a novel object detection algorithm with enhanced performance and robustness. In: 2024 International Conference on Advances in Data Engineering and Intelligent Computing Systems (ADICS), pp. 1–6 (2024)
18. Wang, A., et al.: YOLOv10: Real-Time End-to-End Object Detection. ArXiv, abs/2405.14458 (2024)

19. Fan, D., Ji, G., Sun, G., Cheng, M., Shen, J., Shao, L.: Camouflaged object detection. In: 2020 IEEE/CVF Conference on Computer Vision and Pattern Recognition (CVPR), pp. 2774–2784 (2020)
20. Jia, Q., Yao, S., Liu, Y., Fan, X., Liu, R., Luo, Z.: Segment, magnify and reiterate: detecting camouflaged objects the hard way. In: 2022 IEEE/CVF Conference on Computer Vision and Pattern Recognition (CVPR), pp. 4703–4712 (2022)
21. He, C., et al.: Camouflaged object detection with feature decomposition and edge reconstruction. In: 2023 IEEE/CVF Conference on Computer Vision and Pattern Recognition (CVPR), pp. 22046–22055 (2023)
22. Lin, T., Dollár, P., Girshick, R.B., He, K., Hariharan, B., Belongie, S.J.: Feature pyramid networks for object detection. In: 2017 IEEE Conference on Computer Vision and Pattern Recognition (CVPR), pp. 936–944 (2016)
23. Liu, S., Qi, L., Qin, H., Shi, J., Jia, J.: Path aggregation network for instance segmentation. In: 2018 IEEE/CVF Conference on Computer Vision and Pattern Recognition, pp. 8759–8768 (2018)
24. Guo, C., Fan, B., Zhang, Q., Xiang, S., Pan, C.: AugFPN: improving multi-scale feature learning for object detection. In: 2020 IEEE/CVF Conference on Computer Vision and Pattern Recognition (CVPR), pp. 12592–12601 (2019)
25. Li, Y., Chen, Y., Wang, N., Zhang, Z.: Scale-aware trident networks for object detection. In: 2019 IEEE/CVF International Conference on Computer Vision (ICCV), pp. 6053–6062 (2019)
26. Wang, X., Xiao, T., Jiang, Y., Shao, S., Sun, J., Shen, C.: Repulsion loss: detecting pedestrians in a crowd. In: 2018 IEEE/CVF Conference on Computer Vision and Pattern Recognition, pp. 7774–7783 (2017)
27. Zhang, S., Wen, L., Bian, X., Lei, Z., Li, S.: Occlusion-aware R-CNN: detecting Pedestrians in a Crowd. In: European Conference on Computer Vision (2018)
28. Bai, Y., Zhang, Y., Ding, M., Ghanem, B.: SOD-MTGAN: small object detection via multi-task generative adversarial network. In: European Conference on Computer Vision (2018)
29. Liu, W., Ren, G., Yu, R., Guo, S., Zhu, J., Zhang, L.: Image-adaptive YOLO for object detection in adverse weather conditions. In: AAAI Conference on Artificial Intelligence (2021)

A Cross-Layer Congestion-Aware Routing Protocol for UAV-Aided VANETs with Enhanced Line-of-Sight Communication

Prangya Priyadarshini[1], Lopamudra Hota[1], Arun Kumar[1(✉)], and Peter Han Joo Chong[2]

[1] Department of Computer Science and Engineering, National Institute of Technology, Rourkela, Rourkela 769008, India
{522CS3005,hotal,kumararun}@nitrkl.ac.in
[2] School of Engineering, Computer and Mathematical Sciences, Auckland University of Technology, Auckland, New Zealand
peter.chong@aut.ac.nz

Abstract. Vehicular Ad-hoc Network (VANET) is a pivotal factor in an Intelligent Transportation System (ITS) that improves traffic management, road safety, and infotainment features. Routing in VANET is impeded by frequent link disconnection due to roadblocks, high mobility, and rapid topological changes. An Unmanned Aerial Vehicle (UAV) with three-dimensional movement capacity may significantly enhance a VANET's routing experience by boosting the likelihood of a line-of-sight, improving connection, and implementing an effective store-carry-forward mechanism. This also enables efficient data transmission by minimizing free-space path loss, a key contributor to signal degradation. The proposed approach addresses connectivity and congestion issues in vehicular networks by utilizing UAVs as relay nodes and implementing a congestion-aware routing protocol based on Q-learning. This method leverages vehicle density patterns, network state monitoring, and hierarchical packet routing to ensure continuous connectivity, reduce communication overhead, and enhance packet delivery reliability. The results show that the proposed approach significantly enhances packet survivability and packet delivery ratio (PDR).

Keywords: Unmanned Aerial Vehicle · Vehicular Ad-hoc Network · Routing · Congestion Control

1 Introduction

The Internet of Things (IoT) integrated into ITS, particularly within the Internet of Vehicles (IoV), to transform traditional transportation networks into smart, interconnected ecosystems, revolutionizing how we perceive and navigate the urban landscape [9]. Improving the Vehicle-to-Everything (V2X) communication connection and efficiency is the main objective of the Internet of Things in Automotive technology [12]. IoT enables more rapid and effective data distribution for non-safety and safety-related signals, such as infotainment and accident alarms. Cutting-edge sensor technologies can be deployed in a sophisticated vehicular control system to precisely regulate the vehicle's acceleration, direction, and speed. Using state-of-the-art Artificial Intelligence (AI) algorithms, this system incorporates an Adaptive Cruise Control (ACC) mechanism. It delivers a sophisticated driving experience with unmatched efficiency and responsiveness, optimizes vehicle performance, and increases safety by seamlessly integrating sensor data and AI-driven decision-making. When applied to ground transportation, ITS uses sensing, analysis, control, and communications technology to boost security, convenience, and productivity. To reduce wait times, enhance traffic management, lessen adverse effects on the environment, and provide more advantages to business users and the general public, ITS incorporates various applications that process and communicate information [5].

IoV has the potential to improve customer satisfaction and safety while driving by integrating informatics and wireless communication technologies with ITS. Vehicle-to-vehicle (V2V) connection and communication are the core tasks of ITS. IoV routing is hampered by rapid vehicle movement, which also results in unequal node distribution, frequent topology changes, and fluctuating environmental circumstances [4]. ITS is seriously endangered by these issues. Dynamic vehicles and base stations can be linked via wireless networks that utilize protocols like 802.11p, 5G-V2X, or LTE-V, which are particularly vulnerable to variables like physical distance, obstructions, and interference from other radio signals [6]. The networking infrastructure is not capable of solving these issues. Therefore, researchers have lately explored different options, including using aids like UAVs to avoid impediments and increase the coverage of infrastructures and vehicles.

UAVs or Drones in the sky are more accessible to move around than their road-bound counterparts. This capability allows UAVs to effectively utilize various mobility models that are both quicker and more directional-specific [18]. Equipped with onboard communication devices, UAVs can perform network activities and link characteristics similar to urban vehicles. Despite their versatility, UAVs are energy-constrained nodes requiring meticulous management. UAVs can be utilized for traffic control and reporting potential infractions in ITS.

UAV-assisted Vehicular Ad-Hoc Networks (UAV-assisted VANETs) involve UAVs collecting and distributing data from vehicles. Flying RSUs, like those carried by UAVs, may collect data from and about vehicles and relay it to far-flung locations like mobility service centers [14]. Thanks to their ability to operate at higher altitudes, these cost-effective multirotor UAVs are more likely to establish line-of-sight (LOS) communication links with ground vehicles. By integrating with preexisting IoVs, UAVs may avoid obstructions and dependably participate in data transmission. UAVs create an aerial coverage network that supports ground-based IoVs, serving as intermediary relays during network disconnections. Their flexibility also allows them to cover traffic incidents, particularly in emergencies efficiently [15].

The article is structured as follows: Sect. 2 delivers an in-depth literature review, followed by the introduction of the proposed cross-layer congestion-aware routing protocol in Sect. 3. Section 4 discusses the analysis of the results, and Sect. 5 provides the concluding remarks.

Fig. 1. System Model for UAV-Aided VANET

2 Literature Review

The three-dimensional mobility of UAVs greatly improves the routing performance of VANETs, leading to higher line-of-sight probabilities, improved connection, and an optimized store-and-carry-forward mechanism. To further optimize the routing experience in VANETs, various routing protocols leveraging GPS or position-based methodologies have been developed.

To find the best route that provides the maximum transmission rate, a delay-constrained UAV-assisted VANET routing protocol is suggested in the paper [2]. The protocol ensures that the transmission delay remains below a specified threshold. The study [11] enhances urban vehicular ad-hoc networks by proposing a cooperative communication system employing numerous UAVs. UAVs are strategically deployed depending on projected terrestrial traffic circumstances to solve obstructions, isolated vehicles, and uneven traffic loads. The Multimodal Nomad Algorithm (MNA) coordinates UAVs, which maximizes network efficiency and draws inspiration from nomadic behavior.

In [13], the author presented an algorithm that improves data connectivity in a VANET environment by using UAVs. Here, UAV plays a crucial role in facilitating data packet transmission between vehicles when there is a lack of adequate fixed infrastructure, especially during emergency situations. Based on movement directions and SINR from UAVs, the article clusters vehicles using an unsupervised machine learning approach called FGKMs. Clusters are formed with centroid points acting as cluster heads (CHs). By employing minimal overhead to receive queue status information from Ground Vehicle Nodes (GVNs) for the UAV Relay Node (URN), [17] suggests a unique method for assessing network demand. After overhearing and broadcasting messages, the URN gathers information from a wider area than the GVNs. Additionally, load balancing based on Q-learning (Q-LBR) is provided as a way to dynamically adjust network load within URN capacity without relying on ground network routing. Q-LBR incorporates a reward control function to adjust reward values rapidly depending on ground network congestion and URN load, facilitating adaptive learning in dynamic network environments.

Location-based geographical routing stands out as a superior solution to other routing protocols in UAV-assisted VANET as the solution of dynamic network topology. Ground vehicles and UAVs utilize GPS technology to obtain their positions and subsequently share their status information with nearby nodes. Thereby reducing the latency and routing overhead and eliminating the need for complex routing tables and frequent route updates. Additionally, geographical routing improves scalability and robustness in a UAV-assisted VANET environment. A proposed Q-learning-based geographical routing, supported by UAVs [7]is proposed, in which, with the help of an effective reward function and a fixsized Q-table, the aerial component leverages UAV-collected data to construct a global routing scheme based on fuzzy logic and the depth-first-search method. For UAV based VANETs, the Zone-Based AOMDV (ZAOMDV) routing protocol [1] is suggested as a way to improve routing efficiency. By evaluating physical distance, spatial distance, and energy consumption, the protocol addresses connection failures by introducing zone-based spatial coverage, which reduces computing cost and latency.

By incorporating UAV assistance and prioritizing vehicle speeds on unidirectional roadways, this study [10] provides an innovative approach for congestion control in VANETs. By splitting cars into several speed-based priority groups and using UAVs for uplink transmission calculations, the system efficiently controls congestion by assigning resources depending on vehicle priorities. To reduce congestion in vehicular networks, this method [8] uses dynamic route planning and real-time data accumulation. Taking into account real-time traffic data,

Dijkstra's algorithm determines the shortest path between the current and destination points. f congestion is detected along the selected route, the algorithm revises and replans the route, selecting an alternative path to avoid traffic congestion. Furthermore, when RSU capacity exceeds a certain threshold, the algorithm directs UAV deployment to crowded crossroads, therefore increasing RSU capacity and streamlining traffic.

3 Methodology

The system model presented in Fig. 1 depicts a two-way road scenario with OBUs. The UAVs operate as dynamic Roadside Units (RSUs) as they soar over the OBUs in a spring motion. Operating at elevations between 300 and 1500 m, these UAVs cover an area of 10 to 100 km [16]. Depending on the transmission range, communication occurs via UAV-to-UAV (U2U), Vehicle-to-Vehicle (V2V), and Vehicle-to-UAV (V2U) connections. Cooperative communication enhances data transmission efficiency. OBUs and RSUs can access GPS signals, and Messages are generated at the beginning of the control channel interval, followed by data dissemination. For V2U communication, as soon as an OBU generates a packet, a Request to Send (RTS) is sent to the RSU. Upon receiving the Clear to Send (CTS) signal, data is transmitted to the RSU after a Short Interframe Space (SIFS) period. If the transaction is successful, an Acknowledgment (ACK) will be sent after another SIFS period. Subsequent transmissions occur after a Distributed Interframe Space (DIFS) period. For V2V and U2U communications, data is transmitted directly without the RTS/CTS handshake, maintaining the SIFS and DIFS time intervals.

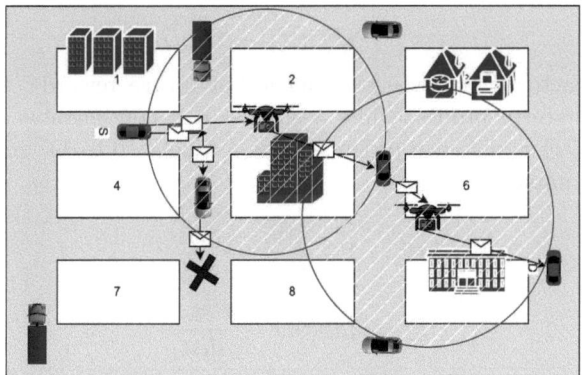

Fig. 2. Cross Layer Congestion-Aware Routing Protocol for UAV-Assisted VANET

The server utilizes historical traffic flow data from different segments to train the Q-learning model and then distributes the Q-table to the deployed UAVs.

These UAVs consult the table to determine the best road segment for packet forwarding by locating the highest Q-value, as illustrated in Fig. 2. This Q-learning algorithm's seamless integration aligns with the routing model's optimal control [12] strategy and routing path. Here, the server functions as the agent, leveraging historical traffic flow information to learn and make decisions. It improves routing efficiency by continually adjusting control strategies in response to environmental changes. As shown in Eq. 1, r_t represents the reward an agent receives after performing action a_t and switching between states s_t and s_{t+1}. Q-values for every potential state-action pair are kept in the Q-table, where $Q(s_t, a_t)$ represents the expected reward for completing action a_t while in state s_t. The agent's objective is to develop a strategy π that maximizes its total accumulated reward by exploring its environment. The function assesses the policy π's effectiveness using the function:

$$Q^{\pi}(s, a) = E[r_t(s_t, a_t) + \gamma Q^{\pi}(s_{t+1}, a_{t+1})] \quad (1)$$

To update the Q-table iteratively, the action-utility function is defined as follows:

$$Q(I_i^t, D_k, a_r^t) \leftarrow (1-\alpha) * Q(I_i^t, D_k, a_r^t) + \alpha * [R_t(I_i^t, D_k, a_r^t) + max_{a^{t+1}} Q(I_j^{t+1}, D_k, a^{t+1})) * \gamma_t] \quad (2)$$

The learning rate, represented by α and empirically set to 0.1, controls the extent to which new information updates existing knowledge. To be more precise, when $\alpha = 0$, the agent is unable to absorb fresh information; on the other hand, when $\alpha = 1$, the agent only uses the most recent information. To go to the destination D_k, the function, in this case, calculates the Q-value of carrying out action a_t for road segment r at the present intersection I_t.

$$\gamma_t = \beta * SP_t + (1-\beta) * DP_t \quad (3)$$

The discount factor γ sets the significance of future rewards; a larger value emphasizes long-term profits, while a smaller one concentrates on immediate results. Here, DP_t is distance progress, β is a weight (0 to 1), and SP_t reflects vehicle density impact.

$$SP_t = 1 - \frac{|S_{ij} - S_O|}{S_{max} - S_{min}} \quad (4)$$

$$DP_t = max(0, 1 - \frac{dist_{t+1}}{dist_t}) \quad (5)$$

$$dist = \sqrt{(x_1 - x_D)^2 + (y_1 - y_D)^2} \quad (6)$$

On road segments, the highest vehicle density is denoted by S_{max}, the minimum by S_{min}, and the ideal vehicle density is denoted by S_O. The distance between the destination D_k and the current road segment I_i^t is denoted by $dist_t$, while the distance between the destination D_k and the next road segment I_j^{t+1} is denoted by $dist_{t+1}$. Exploration-exploitation is accomplished by adopting a

ϵ-greedy approach. With a probability of ϵ, the agent picks an action at random from the available action space A_r, whereas, with a probability of $1-\epsilon$, it opts for the best possible action based on the given conditions.

The Reward can be calculated as follows:

$$r^j = K_1 \zeta_j + K_2(S\_score_j^t) + K_3 G(C_{j,R}^t - C_{j,R}^{min}) \tag{7}$$

The weighting elements that are utilized to balance the reward are K_1 through K_3. A step-wise function $G(x)$ is provided by

$$G(x) = \begin{cases} A, & \text{if } x \geq 0, \\ 0, & \text{if } x < 0, \end{cases} \tag{8}$$

where $A > 0$ is the constant to indicate the revenue. ζ_j is the message size that is to be transferred by time t. The data rate between node j and RSU is $C_{j,R}^t$, and the minimum data rate required for V2I communication is C_j^{min}. The S_score is calculated using 16.

The source UAV is calculated by using the Euclidean distance and given as

$$U_k = \min_{i=1}^{n} \sqrt{(X_s - X_i)^2 + (Y_s - Y_i)^2} \tag{9}$$

$U(X_i, Y_i)$ is the candidate source UAV, and $U(X_s, Y_s)$ is the source vehicle that has the data to be delivered.

Congestion at a node, caused by high data rates, interference, and frequent link disruptions, leads to increased queue sizes and delays, often resulting in packet loss due to Time-to-Live (TTL) expiration or buffer overflow [3].

Take into consideration a $G/M/1/\infty$ queuing system When the channel opens up, these packets are transferred one at a time while being stored in FIFO order.

Every packet has a fixed TTL value allocated to it. The packet is removed from the queue by a node when its Time-To-Expire (TTE) value drops to zero. This method makes sure that even in cases when the node has a limited but large enough buffer, packets are not discarded for no other reason than buffer overflow. This method's implementation effectively regulates packet management, enabling better handling and less loss from buffer restrictions. The value of Time-to-Expire is computed as

$$TTE = TTL - W, where W = \frac{\lambda}{\mu(\mu - \lambda)} \tag{10}$$

W denotes the average queuing delay for a packet, μ is the average packet service rate, and λ indicates the mean arrival rate of packets.

The total anticipated delay a packet will encounter while traveling from node i to the destination along route R is referred to as the Estimated Time to Destination (ETD) at node i. It is calculated as follows:

$$ETD_r(i) = \sum_{J \in R^i} \left[\frac{1}{|P_j|} \sum_{p \in P_j} (PST)_p \right]_j \tag{11}$$

In this case, P_j denotes the data packets that have been successfully transmitted by node j, while $R(i)$ represents the nodes along route R from node i to the destination.

Packet service time (PST) is the duration of a packet p in the node's MAC queue, or from the time it enters the queue until it is routed to the next hop node and an acknowledgment (ACK) packet is received.

For every node I in such a system, its average PST of packets is calculated as follows:

$$(PST)_p = \frac{1}{\mu_i - \lambda} \tag{12}$$

$$\mu_i = \frac{Q_i}{S * IL_i} \tag{13}$$

$$\lambda = \frac{C_{j,R}^t}{S} \tag{14}$$

The packet size is denoted by S in bits, while the channel rate at node i is indicated by Q_i in bits per second. The parameter μ_i declines as the number of active or interfering connections, represented as IL_i, rises in the vicinity of node i. The cumulative count of interfering links from node i to the destination along route R is known as the interfering link score at node i, denoted as $IL_R(i)$.

R^i denotes the nodes along route R that connect node i to the destination. Once data transmission on route R starts, IL_j^ϕ indicates the new intra-flow interfering connections at node j, while IL_j^θ represents the latest interfering link value for node j received via the control packet.

$$IL_R(i) = \sum_{J \in R^i} [IL_j^\theta + IL_j^\phi] \tag{15}$$

Rather than being organized in FIFO order, the packets in a node's queue are sorted in ascending order based on their survivability score (S_score).

$$S\_score = \frac{TTE}{ETD} \tag{16}$$

Low survival score packets are, therefore, given priority during transmission, increasing the likelihood that they will reach the target node before their TTL expires. Dropped packets are those whose survival score falls below a certain level. It is most likely not possible for these packets to reach the destination node before they expire due to the constraints imposed by the present network design and traffic.

A new, shorter route with a low ETD could eventually become accessible, though, as network architecture is vulnerable to frequent changes. Thus, beginning from the head of the line, the scheme only discards the first M packets. Every node uses the aforementioned policy to regularly assess its queue.

Algorithm 1. Pseudocode for the Packet Routing

Input: $A, S, \alpha, \beta, \epsilon$
Output: Q-table, A_r
1: Initialize Q-table and R-matrix as **0**
2: **for** each $r_k \in r$ **do**
3:     $R[r_k] \leftarrow \phi$
4:     **for** episode 1 to M **do**
5:         Set initial road segment
6:         **for** time step 1 to N **do**
7:             Generate $r_n \in (0, 1)$
8:             **if** $r_n \leq \epsilon$ **then**
9:                 Select random A_r
10:             **else**
11:                 Select $\arg \max Q(s, a)$
12:             **end if**
13:             Calculate γ_t
14:             Update Q value
15:             **if** $S_{t+1} = D_k$ **then**
16:                 **break**
17:             **end if**
18:         **end for**
19:         $R[r_k] \leftarrow 0$
20:     **end for**
21: **end for**

Figure 3 delineates the operational framework of the cross-layer routing protocol incorporating a congestion control mechanism. Initially, control packets encompassing historical traffic data, IL, and PST values are utilized to construct a network table. The routing method based on Q-learning uses this table as an input. The resultant Q-values of the Q table are subsequently passed to the MAC layer, where the survivability score is computed. Each node's queue rearranges packets according to their survivability score, giving priority to those with lower scores for transmission, while packets with scores falling below a certain threshold are discarded. The active source-destination pairs, along with their respective TTE values, are then employed in the calculation of the Q-table values.

Algorithm 2. Routing Path Selection and Congestion Control

Input: Q_table
Output: Relay node
1: Identify source UAV
2: **for** $UAV = 1$ to j **do**
3:     **for** $P_i \in P$ **do**
4:         **if** $V_i \in \{V\}$ **then**
5:             $V_i \to$ Relay
6:         **else if** $U_{j+1} \in \{U\}$ **then**
7:             $U_{j+1} \to$ Relay
8:         **else**
9:             Discard packet
10:         **end if**
11:     **end for**
12:     Determine current state (r_k, D_k)
13:     **for** $r \in \{N, S, E, W\}$ **do**
14:         $A_r = \arg\max Q(s, a)$
15:     **end for**
16:     **for** P_i from V_i, U_i **do**
17:         Compute S_score (Eq. 16)
18:     **end for**
19:     Sort buffer by S_score
20:     **if** $\overline{S\_score} > \theta$ **then**
21:         $A_r = \arg\max_2 Q(s, a)$
22:     **else**
23:         Discard packet
24:     **end if**
25: **end for**

4 Results and Discussions

In VANETs, packet drops occur due to several factors: transmission over broken links, channel fading leading to erroneous packet reception, packet collisions, and congestion-induced buffer overflow or packet expiry. High mobility in VANETs frequently causes link breaks, necessitating our scheme's preemptive switching to alternative routes to mitigate mobility-induced packet drops. Assuming an error-free channel with line-of-sight communication, channel fading, and packet collisions remain the primary causes of unsuccessful packet receptions. Transmitters retain data packets in their MAC queue until an acknowledgment from the receiver or until the maximum retransmission limit is reached, leading to head-of-line (HOL) blocking and increased queuing delay. The cumulative impact of packet collision, link breaks, and channel fading exacerbates congestion, further increasing queuing delays, especially under high traffic loads from elevated data generation rates or multiple traffic flows. FIFO ordering is used in a $G/M/1/\infty$ queuing system, where source nodes generate packets at a fixed mean arrival rate (λ), store them sequentially, and deliver them based on channel availability.

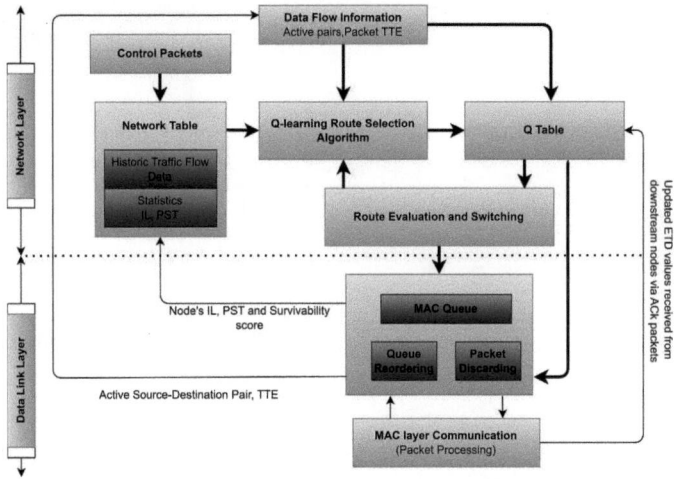

Fig. 3. Flow Chart

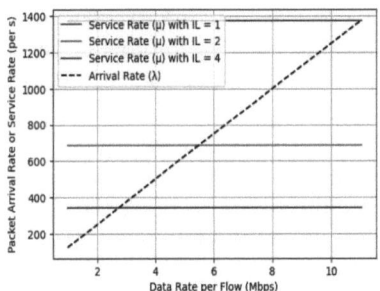

Fig. 4. Packet arrival rate (λ) versus packet service rate (μ) for different data rates and IL values

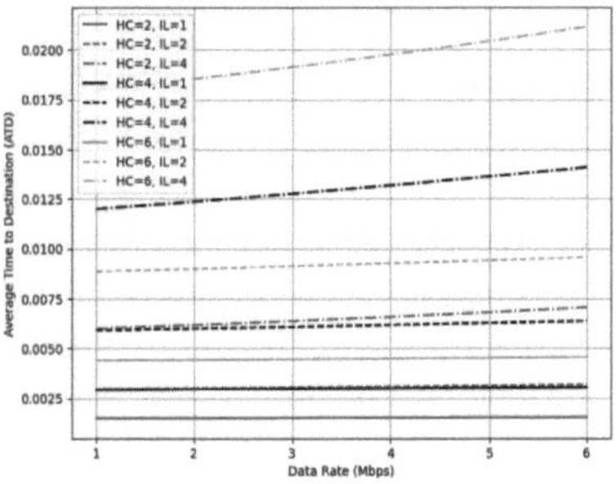

Fig. 5. Estimated Time to Destination vs Data Rate for Different HC and IL Values

Queueing delays are considered as independent random variables with identical distribution and a fixed time-to-live (TTL) value for every packet.

Figure 4 illustrates that an increase in the data generation rate and/or Interference Level (IL) in the neighborhood of a node results in the condition where $\lambda > \mu$, indicating that the arrival rate exceeds the service rate. This condition leads to congestion at the node, thereby increasing packet queuing delay and subsequently the Average Transmission Delay (ATD), as observed in Fig. 5.

The resultant increase in ATD reduces the packet survivability score, leading to packet losses owing to expiry. Moreover, a longer route (higher hop count, HC) results in a higher ATD and a lower packet survivability score. In order to improve packet survivability and, in turn, the Packet Delivery Ratio (PDR), a routing protocol must dynamically select or switch to shorter, less congested

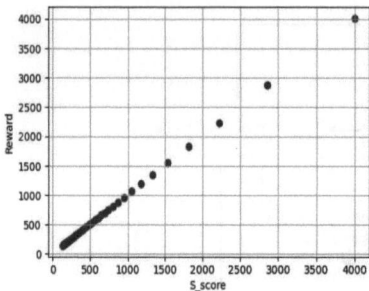 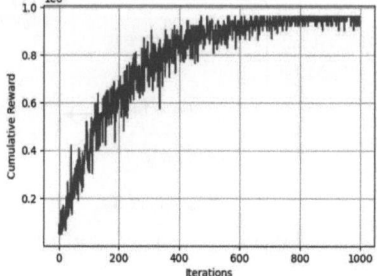

Fig. 6. Survivability score vs Reward

Fig. 7. Q-learning Cumulative Reward over Iterations

routes (with lower IL), given that IL and HC values might fluctuate frequently owing to changes in VANET architecture and traffic circumstances.

The likelihood of a packet reaching its destination is minimal for those with low survivability scores. To optimize resource utilization, nodes should discard these packets using the proposed buffer management scheme. This strategy reallocates resources to packets with higher survivability scores, improving their chances of successful delivery and enhancing the overall Packet Delivery Ratio (PDR).

Our scheme integrates these observations into route selection, switching, and queue management. It prioritizes routes with lower IL values to maximize μ and continually observes the ETD and packet survivability score to track the time-varying μ of the present route. In this way, it proactively changes to a different path prior to the occurrence of the $\lambda > \mu$ condition.

The Fig. 6 illustrates that as the survivability score increases, the corresponding reward also rises. In Q-learning, an elevated reward indicates that the agent is making more optimal decisions, effectively discerning the best actions to undertake in various states. This results in enhanced performance, with the agent progressively achieving higher cumulative rewards over time, as shown in Fig. 7, thereby optimizing its overall efficiency in navigating the environment. As the training progresses, the graph demonstrates convergence, signifying that the agent has stabilized in its learning process and is consistently making optimal decisions.

5 Conclusion

This paper presents a novel congestion-aware routing mechanism for UAV-aided VANET. The proposed algorithm designs a Q-learning mechanism to optimize the route and dynamically manage congestion. The UAVs are considered mobile relays that enhance the LoS that is common in smart city scenarios. The integration of Q-learning into the path selection and congestion control mechanism allows the system model to adapt to dynamic network conditions, learning optimal routes to balance traffic loads and minimize congestion. The proposed model enhances the network performance showing challenging results in terms of packet service time and PDR. Further, The cross-layer design ensures efficient use of resources by considering both the MAC and network layers.

As a part of future work, the model has a scope for incorporation of advanced learning mechanisms and also few other matrices of cross-layer design such as throughput, and energy efficiency are to be considered in the routing process of UAVs.

References

1. Al-Dolaimy, F., Alkhafaji, M.A., Abbas, F.H., Hassan, M.H., Alkhayyat, A.H., Mahmood, S.N.: A collaborative routing protocol for the internet of drone things in the VANET environment. In: Al-Sadiq International Conference on Communication and Information Technology (AICCIT), pp. 7–12. IEEE (2023)
2. Fan, X., Huang, C., Fu, B., Wen, S., Chen, X.: UAV-assisted data dissemination in delay-constrained VANETs. Mob. Inf. Syst. (1), 8548301 (2018)
3. Garg, S., Ihler, A., Bentley, E.S., Kumar, S.: A cross-layer, mobility, and congestion-aware routing protocol for UAV networks. IEEE Trans. Aerosp. Electron. Syst. **59**(4), 3778–3796 (2022)
4. Hota, L., Dash, P.K.: A pervasive study on the internet of vehicles (IoVs). In: Internet of Things, pp. 141–161. Apple Academic Press (2023)
5. Hota, L., Nayak, B.P., Jain, P.K., Kumar, A.: Recent trends in artificial intelligence applications for smart cities: a review. In: Emerging Electrical and Computer Technologies for Smart Cities, pp. 51–68 (2024)
6. Hota, L., Nayak, B.P., Kumar, A., Ali, G.M.N., Chong, P.H.J.: An analysis on contemporary MAC layer protocols in vehicular networks: state-of-the-art and future directions. Future Internet **13**(11), 287 (2021)
7. Jiang, S., Huang, Z., Ji, Y.: Adaptive UAV-assisted geographic routing with q-learning in VANET. IEEE Commun. Lett. **25**(4), 1358–1362 (2020)
8. Jobaer, S., Zhang, Y., Iqbal Hussain, M.A., Ahmed, F.: UAV-assisted hybrid scheme for urban road safety based on VANETs. Electronics **9**(9), 1499 (2020)
9. Khan, I.U., et al.: RSSI-controlled long-range communication in secured IoT-enabled unmanned aerial vehicles. Mob. Inf. Syst. (1), 5523553 (2021)
10. Li, J., Han, T., Guan, W., Lian, X.: A preemptive-resume priority mac protocol for efficient BSM transmission in UAV-assisted VANETs. Appl. Sci. **14**(5), 2151 (2024)
11. Lin, N., Fu, L., Zhao, L., Min, G., Al-Dubai, A., Gacanin, H.: A novel multimodal collaborative drone-assisted VANET networking model. IEEE Trans. Wirel. Commun. **19**(7), 4919–4933 (2020)
12. Luo, L., Sheng, L., Yu, H., Sun, G.: Intersection-based v2x routing via reinforcement learning in vehicular ad hoc networks. IEEE Trans. Intell. Transp. Syst. **23**(6), 5446–5459 (2021)
13. Mokhtari, S., Nouri, N., Abouei, J., Avokh, A., Plataniotis, K.N.: Relaying data with joint optimization of energy and delay in cluster-based UAV-assisted VANETs. IEEE Internet Things J. **9**(23), 24541–24559 (2022)
14. Nazib, R.A., Moh, S.: Routing protocols for unmanned aerial vehicle-aided vehicular ad hoc networks: a survey. IEEE Access **8**, 77535–77560 (2020)

15. Oubbati, O.S., Chaib, N., Lakas, A., Lorenz, P., Rachedi, A.: UAV-assisted supporting services connectivity in urban VANETs. IEEE Trans. Veh. Technol. **68**(4), 3944–3951 (2019)
16. Pasandideh, F., et al.: A review of flying ad hoc networks: key characteristics, applications, and wireless technologies. Remote Sens. **14**(18), 4459 (2022)
17. Roh, B.S., Han, M.H., Ham, J.H., Kim, K.I.: Q-LBR: Q-learning based load balancing routing for UAV-assisted VANET. Sensors **20**(19), 5685 (2020)
18. Sharma, P.K., Kim, D.I.: Random 3D mobile UAV networks: mobility modeling and coverage probability. IEEE Trans. Wirel. Commun. **18**(5), 2527–2538 (2019)

Communication Technologies I

Communication Technologies 1

Pointing Errors Analysis for Inter-satellite MRR PNC System

Hangfei Zhang[1,2], Audrey Christine Guo[3], Lu Lu[1,2], and Yanmei Jia[1,2(✉)]

[1] Technology and Engineering Center for Space Utilization, CAS, Beijing 100094, China
jiayanmei@csu.ac.cn
[2] University of Chinese Academy of Sciences, Beijing 100049, China
[3] Alabama School of Fine Arts, Birmingham, AL 35203, USA

Abstract. Large-scale networking of micro-satellites needs to meet the requirements of rapid interaction, information sharing and autonomous management, which requires low SWaP communication terminals for multi-point communication. We propose a physical layer network coding (PNC) architecture based on modulated retro-reflector (MRR) that can fulfill the new requirements in micro-satellites with symmetric channels. We evaluate performance of MRR PNC under Additive White Gaussian Noise (AWGN) channel with pointing errors. We obtain the impact of pointing error to the outage probability and bit error rate (BER) by theoretical calculation and numerical simulation. Parameters used are designed under joint constraints. Simulation results indicate the proposed scheme's BER performance and outage probability can achieve better than 10^{-10} level.

Keywords: Modulated retro reflector · Inter-satellite optical communication · Micro-satellite networking · Physical layer network coding

1 Introduction

The rapid development of large-scale Micro-satellite networking necessitates new communication paradigms to manage the increasing complexity and demand for efficient data exchange [1,2]. As the number of satellites in a constellation grows, the traditional one-to-one communication strategy [3,4] creates huge resource requirements and a lot of channel wastage [5–7].

Future constellations of autonomously operating satellites [2,8] will require larger volumes of communications data and lower tolerance for communications

---

Y. Jia—This work was supported in part by the Key Research Program of the Chinese Academy of Sciences (CAS), under Grant ZDRW-KT-2019-1-0103, and in part by the Youth Innovation Promotion Association Project of CAS.

outages. Moreover, the inherent challenges of long-distance space communication, such as unavoidable pointing errors [9], further exacerbate the need for increased redundancy.

Considering satellites in close proximity share similar information [10], adoption of cluster-based communication [11] can be more efficient and coordinate, which also forming a directed graph topology, aligns well with the application of planning and distribution algorithms traditionally used in graph theory [11,12]. Additionally, dual communication techniques offer significant potential for enhancing communication error correction capabilities – by enabling real-time bit error rate assessments and allowing for dynamic redundancy adjustments, further optimizing channel capacity [13].

Therefore, space free network for Micro-satellites is urgently needed to meet requirements of rapid interaction, information sharing and scheduling, space based real time information transferring support [14]. The communication terminals must be miniaturized, integrated, high speed and have low SWaP (Size, Weight and Power) value.

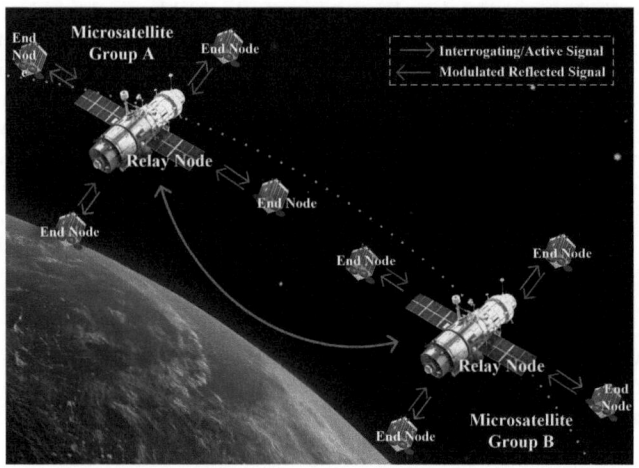

Fig. 1. Laser communication network topology based on MRR.

MRR does not rely on Micro-satellite platform for pointing which will not introduce complex optical mechanical design and real time correction of optical axis wobble deviation. Compared with many projects such as CLICK [16] VSOTA [17] FITSAT [18] and Cloud T5, MRR can not only meet the requirements of Micro-satellite communications [19], but also can realize "one point to multi points" communication. ISOC (Inter Spacecraft Omni Irectional Optical Communication) [20] with the fast MEMS reflector has achieved Space-wide Angle coverage by assembling multiple transmitting and receiving units into array sphere, but does not solve the problem of real-time and efficient information exchange.

We propose MRR-based free network topology as Fig. 1 shows, which takes one or more main satellites installed interrogator as network nodes.

MRR-based PNC enables the exchange of two packets between end nodes in two time slots, enhancing throughput in a two-way relay channel (TWRC), as well as simplify Pointing, Acquiring and Tracking (PAT) and electronic devices of end nodes. In our previous work, we have investigated MRR PNC for space to ground TWRC scenario without considering the impact of pointing error [21]. In this paper, we investigated the outage probability and BER performance of the given system. We evaluated the feasibility by considering greater attenuation than traditional FSOC, multiple noise terms (each bidirectional MRR FSOC link has two noise items) [22] and the main detrimental factor of pointing errors for Inter-satellite MRR FSOC link.

The general system model and related definition are introduced in Sect. 2. Section 3 makes the bit error rate estimation for Inter-satellite MRR PNC. In Sect. 4, we analyze the proposed system's outage probability. In Sect. 5, simulation results and discussion are given. In Sect. 6, we provide concluding remarks. In our results, outage probability and BER for MRR PNC could reach 10^{-10} level on the designed parameters in our simulation.

2 System Model and Definition

MRR related tests can be traced back to the 1990s, and MRR can be realized in two forms, cat's eye and angle reflector [23]. The modulator includes liquid crystal [24,25], small dust motes [26], MEMS [27–30], multi-quantum well [31], etc. Monostatic systems isolate transmission and reception using fiber circulators, beam splitters, or polarizers, with varying degrees of success [32–35].

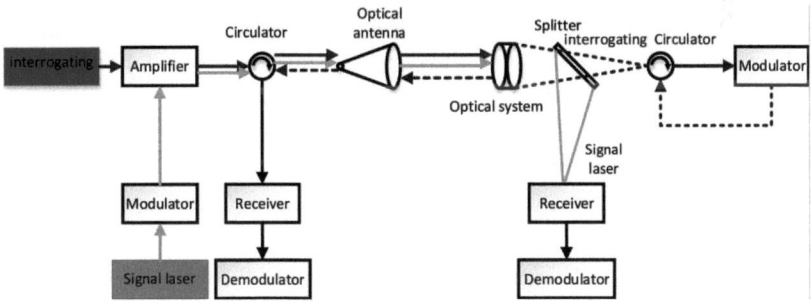

Fig. 2. Typical MRR communication system framework [36].

Considering the requirement of simultaneous transmission, high data rates, and practical implementation, an MRR scheme using an electro-optic modulator is proposed, as illustrated in Fig. 2. The full duplex MRR system is monostatic system made with beam splitters, using wavelength to isolate transmission and reception, and fiber circulators are used to reflect modulated signals. The communication system consists of the interrogator terminal and modulated reflection end.

Our focus is on MRR-based PNC in TWRC, as illustrated in Fig. 3. The system comprises source nodes and relay node. The relay node is interrogator terminal, and the two source nodes are modulated reflection terminals.

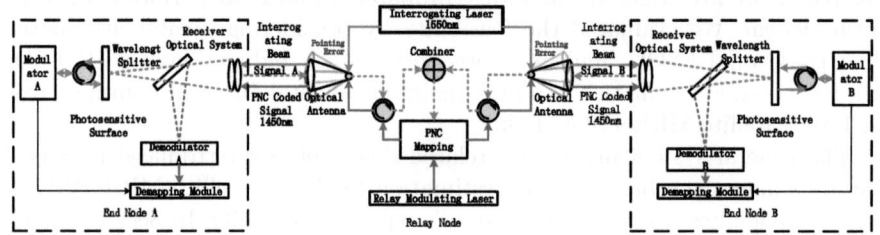

Fig. 3. MRR PNC communication system with pointing error

The relay node is set to be interrogator, so as to send interrogating beams to MRR end. Two MRR nodes modulate their data onto the interrogating beam and reflect it to the interrogator. The interrogator combines signal beams from nodes A and B, demodulates and maps. The mapped signal is sent to nodes A and B using another wavelength. Nodes A and B get data of each other by demodulating and demapping.

2.1 Signal Model

In intensity modulation/direct detection (IM/DD) channels, the receiver integrates the photocurrent over each bit period, removing constant background bias. The the resulting electrical signal y experiences intensity fluctuations caused by misalignment and noise and can be modeled as, x the transmitted intensity, h the channel state, η the receiver's effective photo-current conversion ratio, and n the signal-independent AWGN with variance σ_n^2.

$$y = \eta h x + n. \tag{1}$$

h represents the stochastic loss along the propagation path, results from path loss. h_{Tl} and h_{Rl} are the channel states for the interrogating and retro-reflected paths. While h_p refers to a statistical distribution function that models the geometric spread caused by pointing errors. We consider the channel is symmetric, therefore assume $h_{Tl} = h_{Rl} = h_l$, so the channel state is written as [38]:

$$h = h_l h_l h_p. \tag{2}$$

Here we consider $h_l = 1$ since there is no atmosphere for Inter-satellite laser link.

The MRR link is expressed as [39]:

$$P_{sig} = P_{Las}G_T L_T L_R T_{atm} G_{MRR} L_{MRR} M L_R T_{atm} G_{rec} L_{rec}.$$

P_{sig} : the power of retro-reflected signal,

P_{Las} : the power of laser,

G_T : the interrogator's transmit optics's optical antenna gain,

L_T : the transmit optics's loss,

L_R : the loss of free space range,

T_{atm} : the transmission in the atmospheric, assuming $T_{atm} = 1$,

L_{MRR} : the MRR's optical loss, excluding modulator loss,

G_{rec} : the interrogator's receiver's optical antenna gain,

L_{rec} : the receiver's optical losses,

M : the electric-optic modulator's insert loss,

G_{MRR} : the retro reflector's gain.

(3)

Considering that there are two AWGN noises per MRR FSOC link, the received electrical signal-to-noise ratio (SNR) for MPSK signal of MRR in a weak fading channel is characterized as:

$$SNR(h_p) = \frac{\eta^2 h_p^2 P_{sig}}{2\sigma_n^2}. \tag{4}$$

For MRR PNC system, MRR nodes receive the interrogating optical signal and then modulate the source data with the BPSK scheme. Modulated signals are reflected and go back through the optical system to the relay node.

We consider synchronous and symmetric PNC, signal received by the relay node R is the added signals with no phase offset and symbol offset. R processes Y_R to generate network-coded signal $X_R = f(Y_R)$ for transmission.

It is known that $x_i[n] \in \{-1,1\}$ in BPSK. Let $x_i = 1$ for bit 0 and $x_i = -1$ for bit 1. Assuming BPSK is used in the backward link, the PNC output x_R is mapped as $x_R = x_A \oplus x_B$.

As stated in [41],

$$U \triangleq \arg\min_{U \in \{\pm x_A \pm x_B\}} \left\{ |y_R - U|^2 \right\}, \tag{5}$$

the decision rule for mapping y_R to x_R is as shown in Table 1:

R encodes the mapped data a_R using a 1450 nm laser with BPSK, generating the transmitted signal S_R.

These data signals travel through the optical systems and are reflected back to the end nodes. After demodulating the transmitted signal S_R, the mapped data a_R is recovered. The source nodes then perform an XOR operation on the mapped data a_R along with their own data S_A or S_B, enabling them to retrieve the data sent by the other node.

Table 1. XOR mapping rules

U	$x_R = x_A \oplus x_B$
$x_A + x_B$	1
$x_A - x_B$	−1
$-x_A + x_B$	−1
$-x_A - x_B$	1

2.2 Pointing Errors Model

According to the generalized pointing error probability distribution model, the PDF for h_p is [42]:

$$f_{h_p}(h_p) = \frac{\partial^2}{A_0^{\partial^2}}(h_p)^{\partial^2 - 1}, 0 \leq h_p \leq A_0, \tag{6}$$

where $\partial = W_{z_{eq}}/2\sigma_s$ represents the ratio of the equivalent beam radius at the receiver. σ_s^2 is the jitter variance at the receiver. Decrease in the value of the ∂ parameter indicates a stronger effect of pointing errors. The equivalent beam width $W_{Z_{eq}}$ is given by:

$$W_{Z_{eq}}{}^2 = W_z^2 \frac{\sqrt{\pi}\, erfc(v)}{2v \exp(-v^2)},$$

$$v = \frac{a\sqrt{\pi}}{\sqrt{2}W_z}, \tag{7}$$

$$W_z = z \tan\left(\frac{\theta_{div}}{2}\right),$$

$$A_0 = [erfc(v)]^2.$$

a is the transverse plane of the incident wave's receiver radius. W_z denotes the beam waist at the distance of z. θ_{div} stands for the corresponding divergence angle. A_0 the fraction of the collected power when the radial distance is 0, $erfc(\cdot)$ the error function.

3 Average Bit Error Rate Estimation

As mentioned in Sect. 2, we consider coherent modulation in RF domain. We choose BPSK modulation method since BPSK offers better performances under the same condition [43].

A communication system's performance is often evaluated by a key metric BER, defined as [44]:

$$BER = \int_0^\infty P_e(h_p) f_{h_p}(h_p) dh_p, \tag{8}$$

where the conditional probability of error $P_e(h_p)$ is given by:

$$P_e(h_p) = Q\left(\sqrt{2SNR(h_p)}\right) = \frac{1}{2}erfc\left(\sqrt{SNR(h_p)}\right). \tag{9}$$

The modulated IM/DD signal bit error rate (BER) using BPSK can be computed by substituting (7) and (9) into (8).

$$BER_{FSOC} = \frac{\partial^2 A_0^{-\partial^2}}{2} \int_0^\infty erfc\left(\frac{\eta h_p \sqrt{P_{sig}}}{\sqrt{2}\sigma_n}\right) h_p^{\partial^2 - 1} dh_p. \tag{10}$$

This integral involves complex hypergeometric functions [45], but efficient numerical methods are used for its computation in this paper. According to [46], we derive the $P_e(h_p)$ of BPSK modulated MRR PNC:

$$\begin{aligned}
P_e(h_p) = & Q\left(\sqrt{2SNR(h_p)} + \frac{\ln\left(1+\sqrt{1-e^{-8SNR(h_p)}}\right)}{2\sqrt{2SNR(h_p)}}\right) \\
& -\frac{1}{2}Q\left(3\sqrt{2SNR(h_p)} + \frac{\ln\left(1+\sqrt{1-e^{-8SNR(h_p)}}\right)}{2\sqrt{2SNR(h_p)}}\right) \\
& +\frac{1}{2}Q\left(\sqrt{2SNR(h_p)} - \frac{\ln\left(1+\sqrt{1-e^{-8SNR(h_p)}}\right)}{2\sqrt{2SNR(h_p)}}\right).
\end{aligned} \tag{11}$$

We can get the BER of MRR PNC relay node by substituting (11) into (8). This integral can be represented using complex hypergeometric functions. We use efficient numerical techniques to compute this integral:

$$BER_{MRRPNC} = \partial^2 A_0^{-\partial^2} \times \int_0^\infty P_e(h_p) h_p^{\partial^2 - 1} dh_p. \tag{12}$$

4 Outage Probability

Outage probability is a useful metric to evaluate the MRR PNC system's performance. To be more specific, the outage probability and average capacity, we define instantaneous SNR. Based on (1) and (3), and as aforementioned that IM/DD method is used, the instantaneous SNR is [9]:

$$\gamma = \frac{\eta^2 h_p^2 P_{sig}}{2\sigma_n^2} = \frac{\eta^2 h_p^2 \tilde{P}_{sig}}{N_0}, \tag{13}$$

where P_{sig} is the average transmitted optical power, and $\tilde{P}_{sig}$ and N_0 denote the PSD of signal and noise optical. The cumulative density function (CDF) is given by integrating (5) as:

$$F_{h_p}(h_p) = A_0^{-\partial^2} h_p^{\partial^2}, 0 \le h_p \le A_0. \tag{14}$$

The instantaneous SNR follows the same distribution as h_p^2. The CDF of h_p^2 is derived from (14):

$$F_{h_p^2}(x) = F_{h_p}(\sqrt{x}) \triangleq \int_0^{\sqrt{x}} f_{h_p}(y)\,dy = \frac{1}{A_0^{\partial^2}}(x)^{\partial^2/2}, 0 \le x \le A_0^2. \quad (15)$$

Hence, its PDF is given by:

$$f_{h_p^2}(x) = dF_{h_p^2}(x)/dx = \frac{\partial^2}{2A_0^{\partial^2}}(x)^{\frac{\partial^2}{2}-1}. \quad (16)$$

The outage probability fall below a corresponding predetermined threshold, γ_{th}:

$$P_o(\gamma_{th}) = P_r(\gamma \le \gamma_{th}). \quad (17)$$

$P_o(\gamma_{th})$ can be obtained based on (13) and (15):

$$\begin{aligned}
P_o(\gamma_{th}) &= P_r\left(h_p^2 \le \frac{2\sigma_n^2 \gamma_{th}}{\eta^2 \tilde{P}_{sig}}\right) \\
&= F_{h_p^2}\left(\frac{2\sigma_n^2 \gamma_{th}}{\eta^2 \tilde{P}_{sig}}\right) \\
&= \left(\frac{\partial^2}{\partial^2+2}\right)^{\partial^2/2} \tilde{\gamma}^{-\partial^2/2} \gamma_{th}^{\frac{\partial^2}{2}}, \gamma_{th} \le \frac{\partial^2+2}{\partial^2}\tilde{\gamma},
\end{aligned} \quad (18)$$

where $\tilde{\gamma} = \frac{\partial^2 A_0^2 \eta^2 \tilde{P}_{sig}}{2(\partial^2+2)\sigma_n^2}$

The outage probability of the MRR PNC can be obtain by:

$$P_{oPNC}(\gamma_{th}) = 2P_o(\gamma_{th}) - [P_o(\gamma_{th})]^2. \quad (19)$$

5 Simulation Results and Discussion

We calculated link budget under perfect condition at first. Then we analysed the effects of SNR threshold, distance and jitter standard deviation on outage probability. Last but not least, we made numerical simulations of the BER of MRR PNC system with pointing errors.

5.1 Simulation Parameter and Link Budget

The most advanced reported MRR FSO system to date is 200 km, 1 Gbps Intersatellite link between cubesates using MEMS modulating retro reflector [47]. We made optical link budget for MRR PNC system. Table 2 lists parameters under consideration, some of them are from [48]. Our goal is to obtain a BER of 10^{-9}, and data rate of 1 Gbps at 200 km.

Table 2. Parameters used for Link Budget Calculations

Expression	Value
Transmitter Power	37 dBm
Tx loss	−1.0 dB
Tx antenna gain	105.5 dB
Interrogator range loss	−249.4 dB
MRR loss	−0.7 dB
MRR Antenna gain	213.8 dB
Range loss of retro	−249.4 dB
Receiver antenna gain	117.4 dB
Rx loss	−1 dB
Rx sensitivity	−38.0 dB
Predicted Rx power	−31.8 dB

Link budget calculated in the subsection does not consider power variations due to pointing errors in Inter-satellite communication, we assume perfect pointing here. However, the satellites are in motion, so the interrogating beam remains centered on the MRR surface for a limited time. However, discrepancies between theory and practice arise due to deviations from an ideal diffraction-limited return from the retroreflector. Pointing error effection will be discussed later.

5.2 Outage Probability Results

The parameters used for investigation are presented in Table 2 and Table 3 [48].

Table 3. Parameters used for simulations

Term	parameter	value
Transmission rate	Rate	1 Gbps
T/R optics efficiency	$\eta_T = \eta_R$	0.8
Responsivity	R	0.5
Receiver sensitivity	S_v	−38.0 dB
Noise standard deviation	σ_n	$10^{-7} A/\sqrt{Hz}$
Beam radius at 1km	W_z	15 cm
Pointing errors	θ_s	1 μrad
Jitter standard deviation	σ_s	≅10 cm

In Fig. 4(a), the outage probability performs as a function of the $\tilde{\gamma}/\gamma_{th}$ for different σ_s. The outage probability increases with more severe pointing errors for

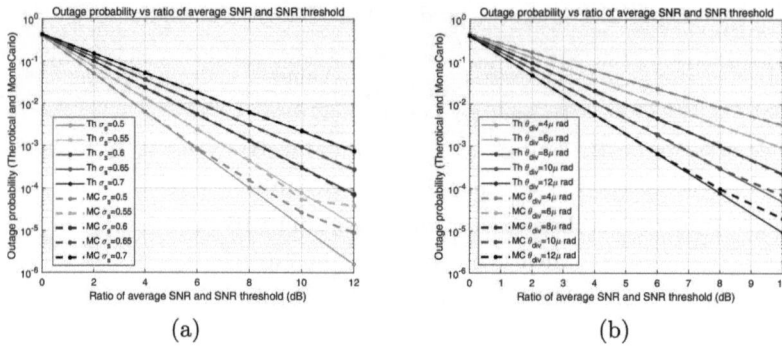

Fig. 4. (a) Outage probability vs ratio of average SNR and SNR threshold. (b) Variation of Outage Probability with Different Divergence Angle.

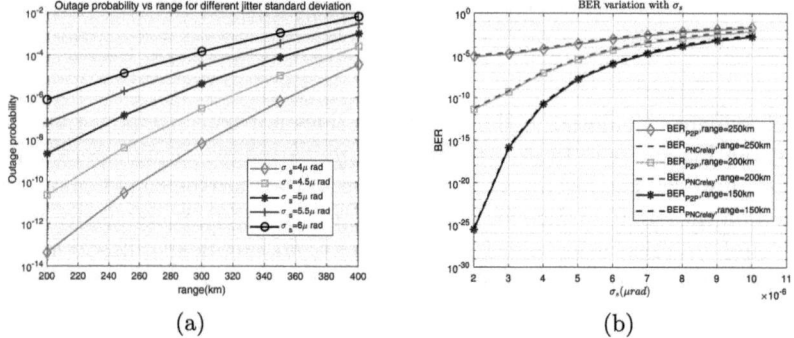

Fig. 5. (a) Outage probability vs range of Inter-satellite for different SNR threshold, for $\lambda = 850$ nm. (b) BER Variation with Jitter Standard Deviation, for $\lambda = 850$ nm, $P_{sig} = -38$ dBm.

a fixed $\tilde{\gamma}/\gamma_{th}$ when range is 200 km. We observed from Fig. 4(b) that the larger the beam divergence angle, the smaller the probability of outage probability. This may be that as the signal divergence angle becomes larger, the range over which the signal can be received becomes larger, and the effects of pointing error caused by electrical noise, mechanical vibration etc. are weakened, so the probability of interruption is reduced, but the received signal strength is reduced for the same transmitter power, and hence the BER is reduced. The result shows that the antenna gain will decrease and BER will deteriorate with the increase of divergence angle.

In Fig. 5(a), outage probability varies with the Inter-satellite range for different jitter standard deviation with fixed γ_{th}. The outage probability increases as the jitter standard deviation becomes larger. For the same jitter standard deviation, the outage probability increases when the range is longer. It can be seen that the pointing error effects the outage probability more severely than range does. For a fixed distance, the outage probability becomes larger as σ_s increases.

5.3 BER Performance Results

We analyze the BER of the BPSK-modulated MRR PNC system. Based on (10) and (15). We studied varying misalignment-induced fading strengths ∂^2 by setting σ_s and $range$ which will cause different beam waste values. Different pointing errors will occur by setting σ_s, $range$ and divergence angle θ_{div}. Various analytical results are presented below for assumed parameters.

Figure 5(b) illustrates that BER of both "point to point (P2P)" and PNC relay node increase as the jitter standard deviation becomes larger, and BER go higher due to distance enlarging on the fixed jitter standard deviation. BER of MRR PNC relay node and end node are close to each other.

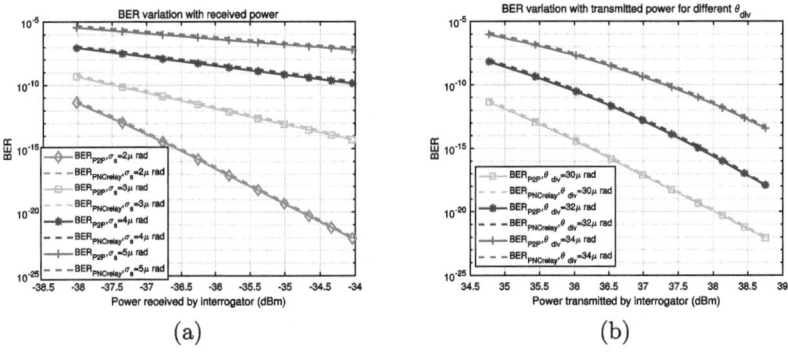

Fig. 6. (a) BER variation with received power, for $\lambda = 850$ nm. (b) BER variation with transmitted power for different θ_{div}, $\lambda = 850$ nm, $range = 200$ km, $\sigma_s = 2\,\mu$rad.

Figure 6(a) depicts that weaker pointing errors corresponding to higher received power by interrogator. For a fixed received power, the impact of pointing errors is getting stronger due to larger jitter standard deviation. It should be noted that BER is less than 10^{-10} for $1\,\mu$rad jitter standard deviation and -38 dBm received power. The result illustrates that parameters we designed in Sect. 5.1 are reasonable.

Figure 6(b) shows BER varies with power transmitted by interrogator and beam divergence angle θ_{div} for a fixed jitter standard deviation $\sigma_s = 2\,\mu$rad. BER decreases due to higher transmitted power and smaller divergence angle.

6 Conclusion

In this work, we proposed an MRR based network topology and introduced MRR PNC to meet the real time and efficient information exchange requirements of formation flying Micro-satellite groups.

MRR PNC has low SWaP value, simplifies the system design complexity by reducing PATs of the end nodes compared to traditional "point to point" FSOC. By virtue of the rapid reconstruction capability of MRR based network topology, this design can realize real-time and efficient information exchange.

Our results indicate that parameters designed for the system are appropriate to maintain the constraint conditions of Micro-satellites. We explored the impacts of Pointing Errors. Outage probability and BER for MRR PNC could reach 10^{-10} level on the designed parameters.

Note that this paper assumes end nodes channel symmetry, therefore, future work needs to consider the asynchrony and Doppler effects on the MRR PNC system. We also need to investigate channel coding suitable for the system to improve performance further.

References

1. Zhiquan, L., Huizhong, Z., Zhaoguang, B., Zhi, Y.: Review and prospect of small satellite structures. J. Astronaut. **42**(9), 1067–1077 (2021)
2. Jinping, X., Ying, W., Sunmei, L., Yi, X., Fuqiang, L.: Research on autonomous collaborative control technology of intelligent micro-nano satellite cluster. Artif. Intell. Robot. Res. **12**(3), 226–235 (2023)
3. Bibi, S., Baig, M.I., Qamar, F., Shahzadi, R.: A comprehensive survey of free-space optical communication-modulation schemes, advantages, challenges and mitigations. J. Opt. Commun. (2023)
4. Yunyi, Q., et al.: Performance analysis of modulating retro-reflector optical communication system based on an airy beam. J. Mod. Opt. **70**, 1–8 (2023)
5. Runnan, Q., Xiaodong, P., Wenming, X., Jianjiang, H., Weichun, F., Jiahong, J.: Design of publish/subscribe system for big-data security transmission of spacecraft. Syst. Eng. Electron. **46**(3), 963–971 (2024)
6. Shanzhi, C., Zhiwen, F., Jiade, J., Yun, C.: Analysis and suggestions on intersatellite laser communication of satellite internet. Telecommun. Sci. **40**(2), 1–10 (2024)
7. Xinyue, L., Ran, Z., Zhengxuan, H., Jiang, L., Qinqin, T., Tao, H.: Review on networking and control technologies of space satellite network. Space-Integrated-Ground Inf. Netw. **4**(3), 48–58 (2023)
8. Li, Y., Shuyi, W.: A review on development of intelligent health management technology for spacecraft control systems. Acta Aeronauticaet Astronautica Sinica **42**(4), 525044 (2021)
9. Trevlakis, S.E., et al.: Outage performance of transdermal optical wireless links in the presence of pointing errors. In: 2018 IEEE 19th International Workshop on Signal Processing Advances in Wireless Communications (SPAWC), pp. 1–5 (2018)
10. Dudu, Z., Xu, H., Xiaoxiao, J., Xuemin, J.: Direct trajectory optimization of underactuated spacecraft formation reconfiguration in elliptic orbits. Aerosp. Control **37**(6), 35–41+72 (2019)
11. Xue, B., Xiaoyu, Z., Tianji, C., Ming, X.: Space mission planning and control method of small satellite swarm system. Aerosp. Control **40**(4), 61–68 (2022)
12. Yongming, W., Xiaorong, S., Xuemei, H., Yue, Y.: An intelligent decision-making method for multi-coupling tasks of UAV cluster countermeasure. J. Astronaut. **42**(4), 504–512 (2021)

13. Jiangchun, G., Guoru, D., Haichao, W., Yitao, X.: Integrated communications and jamming: toward dual-functional wireless networks under antagonistic environment. IEEE Commun. Mag. **61**(5), 181–187 (2023)
14. Xibin, C., Zhaoweir, S.: Rapid Response Micro Satellite Design, 1st edn. Science Press (2016)
15. Chaudhry, A.U., Yanikomeroglu, H.: Laser inter-satellite links in a starlink constellation. IEEE Veh. Technol. Mag. **16**(2), 48–56 (2021)
16. Cahoy, K., Grenfell, P., et al.: The cubesat laser infrared crosslink mission (CLICK). In: International Conference on Space Optics - ICSO 2018. LNCS, pp. 111800Y-2–111800Y-11 (2018)
17. Kuwahara, T., et al.: Laser data downlink system of micro-satellite RISESAT. In: Proceedings of the 27th Annual AIAA/USU Conference on Small Satellites, pp. 1–10 (2013)
18. Tanaka, T., et al.: Development and operations of nano-satellite FITSAT-1 (NIWAKA). Acta Astronautica **1**(8), 1–10 (2015)
19. Rabinovich, W.S., et al.: Modulating retro-reflectors links in high turbulence: challenges and solutions. In: Applications of Lasers for Sensing and Free Space Communications, pp. 1–5 (2015)
20. Velazco, J.E., et al.: Inter-satellite omnidirectional optical communicator for remote sensing. In: CubeSats and NanoSats for Remote Sensing II, p. 107690L (2018)
21. Yanmei, J., Congmin, L., et al.: Modulated retro-reflector-based physical-layer network coding for space optical communications. J. IEEE Access **9**, 44868–44880 (2021)
22. Zhang, P., Wang, T., et al.: Performance evaluation of full-duplex free space laser communication system based on modulating retro-reflector. J. Infrared Laser Eng. **44**(8), 2506–2510 (2015)
23. Biermann, M.L., et al.: Design and analysis of a diffraction-limited cat's-eye retroreflector. J. Opt. Eng. **41**, 1655–16600 (2002)
24. Swenson, C.M., et al.: Low-power FLC-based retromodulator communications system. J. Photonics West **72090C**, 1–5 (1997)
25. Kullander, F., Sakari, P., et al.: System trials with modulated retroreflective optical communication. In: Unmanned/Unattended Sensors and Sensor Networks II, pp. 598–612 (2005)
26. Brien, O., Dominic, C., et al.: Design and implementation of optical wireless communications with optically powered smart dust motes. IEEE J. Sel. Areas Commun. **27**, 1646–1653 (2009)
27. Changping, L., Goosen, K.W.: Optical microelectromechanical system array for free-space retrocommunication. IEEE Photonics Technol. Lett. **16**, 2045–2047 (2004)
28. Chan, T.K., Ford, J.E.: Retroreflecting optical modulator using an MEMS deformable micromirror array. J. Lightwave Technol. **24**, 516–525 (2006)
29. Jenkins, C., Brown, J., et al.: MEMS retro-phase-modulator for free-space coherent optical communications. IEEE J. Sel. Top. Quantum Electron. **13**, 330–335 (2007)
30. Ziph-Schatzberg, L., Bifano, T., et al.: Secure optical communication system utilizing deformable MEMS mirrors. In: Proceedings of SPIE - The International Society for Optical Engineering, vol. 7318, pp. 1–6 (2009)
31. Rabinovich, W.S.: Free-space optical communication link across 16 kilometers over the Chesapeake Bay to a modulated retroreflector array. Opt. Eng. **47**, 40–45 (2008)

32. Pen, Z., Tianshu, W., et al.: Performance evaluation of full-duplex reverse modulation recovery space optical communication system. Infrared Laser Eng. **44**, 2506–2510 (2015)
33. Xianglian, F., Hexin, J., et al.: Single-source duplex high-speed FSO communications using electro-optic modulator-based MRR. In: Unmanned/Unattended Sensors and Sensor Networks II, pp. JTu2A–54 (2018)
34. Xianlian, F., Hexin, J., et al.: Demonstration of modulating retro-reflection FSO transmission using 80 Gb/s Pol-MUX QPSK signal in simulated atmosphere environment. Electron. Lett. **56**, 93–95 (2019)
35. Liu, R.D., et al.: Performance analysis of laser communication system based on circular polarization modulating retro-reflector. In: 2019 IEEE 4th Advanced Information Technology, Electronic and Automation Control Conference (IAEAC), pp. 218–221 (2019)
36. Yanmei, J., Congmin, L., Pengfei, S., Lu, L.: Modulated retro-reflector based physical-layer network coding for space optical communications. IEEE Access (2021)
37. William, W.: Advanced Optical Wireless Communication Systems: Optical Modulating Retro-Reflectors, 1st edn. Cambridge University Press (2012)
38. Gil, Y., Rotter, N., et al.: Feasibility of retroreflective transdermal optical wireless communication. Appl. Opt. **51**(18), 4232–4239 (2012)
39. Majumdar, A.K.: Modulating retroreflector-based free-space optical (FSO) communications. In: William, T., et al. (eds.) Advanced Free Space Optics (FSO). SSOS, vol. 186, pp. 243–293. Springer, New York (2015). https://doi.org/10.1007/978-1-4939-0918-6_8
40. Liew, S.C., Zhang, S., Lu, L.: Physical-layer network coding: tutorial, survey, and beyond. Phys. Commun. **6**, 4–42 (2013). Network Coding and its Applications to Wireless Communications. ISSN 1874-4907
41. Lu, L., Wang, T., et al.: Implementation of physical-layer network coding. Phys. Commun. **6**, 74–87 (2013)
42. Bag, B., et al.: Design, Implementation, and Analysis of Next Generation Optical Networks: Emerging Research and Opportunities, 1st edn. IGI Global (2020)
43. Kaur, P., et al.: Effect of atmospheric conditions and aperture averaging on capacity of free space optical links. Opt. Quantum Electron. **46**, 1139–1148 (2014)
44. Kumar, P., et al.: Performance improvement of OFDM-FSO multi-user communication system with combined transmit frequency diversity and receive space diversity. Opt. Commun. **366**, 410–418 (2016)
45. Adamchik, V.S., Marichev, O.I.: The algorithm for calculating integrals of hypergeometric type functions and its realization in REDUCE system. In: Proceedings of the International Symposium on Symbolic and Algebraic Computation, pp. 212–224 (1990)
46. Zhang, S.L., Liew, S.C., et al.: Hot topic: physical-layer network coding. In: Proceedings of the 12th Annual International Conference on Mobile Computing and Networking, pp. 358–365
47. Velazco, J.E., et al.: High data rate inter-satellite omnidirectional optical communicator. In: 2019 IEEE Aerospace Conference, pp. 1–5
48. Goetz, P.G., et al.: Multiple quantum well-based modulating retroreflectors for inter- and intra-spacecraft communications. In: Proceedings of SPIE - The International Society for Optical Engineering, vol. 6308, p. 12 (2006)

Hy-LiRF: Hybrid LiFi and WiFi Network Supporting Seamless Real-Time Transmissions

Menghan Li[1,2], Runxin Zhang[1,2], Yuheng Zhang[1,2], Yongsheng Gong[2(✉)], Jianhua He[2], and Lu Lu[1,2]

[1] University of Chinese Academy of Sciences, Beijing 100049, China
{limenghan21,zhangrunxin20,zhangyuheng221}@mails.ucas.ac.cn,
lulu@csu.ac.cn
[2] Technology and Engineering Center for Space Utilization, Chinese Academy of Sciences, Beijing 100094, China
{gys,hejianhua}@csu.ac.cn

Abstract. With rapid advances of visible light communications techniques, also known as light fidelity (LiFi), its integration with ubiquitous WiFi network interface cards (NICs) has been finalized in the latest IEEE 802.11bb standard in 2023. Although LiFi has abundant bandwidth resources that can support higher physical-layer (PHY-layer) data rates over WiFi, pure LiFi communication links are easily interrupted by blockage, which becomes a big barrier for its widely applications. To tackle this problem in LiFi, this paper proposes a hybrid LiFi and WiFi communication design (Hy-LiRF) in which PHY-layer packets are parallelly transmitted using two RF ports of the WiFi NIC, one for LiFi and the other for conventional WiFi. Since the LiFi link has a frequency up-conversion and down-conversion module to match the low-pass characteristics of LED and photo-diode, additional carrier frequency offset (CFO) which may greatly degrade the system BER performance is introduced because WiFi NICs do not know what happened to its PHY-layer. In this paper, we propose a well-designed precoding matrix that is updated in real time based on channel status information to mitigate effects of additional CFO. Simulation results show that this approach effectively lowers the system's bit error rate to the level where CFO is negligible. Besides, we build a prototype on top of the WiFi NICs' 2×2 MIMO RF ports, which achieves a real-time data rate of 140 Mbps within a 40 MHz bandwidth. To the best of our knowledge, Hy-LiRF is the first real-time bidirectional communication system. Experimental results show that Hy-LiRF can maintain communication regardless of obstacles blocking the optical path or radio frequency interference, and restore to the highest communication rate 3 s after the blockage or interference sources are removed, supporting seamless real-time transmissions.

This work was supported in part by the Key Research Program of the Chinese Academy of Sciences (CAS), under Grant ZDRW-KT-2019-1-0103, and in part by the Youth Innovation Promotion Association Project of CAS.

Keywords: Visible Light Communications · WiFi · LiFi · Hybrid Communication System

1 Introduction

Traditional radio frequency (RF) communication is encountering a significant challenge owing to the limited bandwidth, exacerbated by the continuous surge in wireless data traffic [1–3]. In this context, optical wireless communication (OWC) with ultra-high bandwidth stands out as a promising addition to RF communication [3–5]. Specifically, OWC harnessing the visible light spectrum is recognized as visible light communications (VLC), also known as light fidelity (LiFi).

VLC is a promising technology for future communication scenarios. In addition to the advantage of wide bandwidth, visible light also enjoys robustness to electromagnetic interference and higher security, which makes it convenient to construct cellular networks in 5G and higher generations. In recent years, several standardization activities are being carried out on VLC and LiFi, including IEEE 802.15.7 Standard [6], ITU-T G.9991 Standard [7] and IEEE 802.15.13 Standard [8]. These standards make provisions and modifications to the physical-layer (PHY-layer) and medium access control (MAC) layer of VLC. In June 2023, IEEE 802.11bb Standard was approved and defined modifications to existing physical layers and MAC layer to enable transparent operation of IEEE 802.11 over the wireless light medium [9], which makes the integration of VLC and existing wireless communication technologies more convenient.

However, the high dependence on line-of-sight (LoS) links has become a major obstacle to the widespread application of LiFi. Once the LoS link is blocked, VLC will be interrupted. Unlike VLC, RF communication exhibits completely different characteristics. Radio waves can propagate through multi-paths, resulting in more homogeneous coverage and robustness to shadows. However, RF communication is susceptible to electromagnetic interference, and the available bandwidth of RF band is limited, which restricts the achievable data rates [10].

The different characteristics of wireless fidelity (WiFi) and LiFi make them natural complementary technologies. In this case, using the two technologies simultaneously can achieve both high throughput and reliability of communication systems [11]. Researchers have already done some work on such aggregation. In 2011, [12] proposed the concept of hybrid LiFi and WiFi network (HLWNet). The authors of [13] designed a hybrid RF and VLC system with multiple VLC and RF access points. An exhaustive survey on HLWNets is given in [11] and validated the superiority of HLWNets over the stand-alone LiFi or WiFi systems. There is also some work devoted to system implementation. The authors of [14] designed a complete VLC transceiver system and experimentally demonstrated the performance of unidirectional VLC transmission. Later, a prototype using separate components and two IEEE 802.11ax network interface cards (NICs) in 5 GHz channel named LiRF is proposed for bidirectional data transmissions with real-time applications support capability [15,16]. However, pure LiFi systems are susceptible to obstacles. Communication will be interrupted once the optical path is blocked. Combining the LiFi system with the RF communication system can utilize the RF link to communicate when obstacles block the VLC link, thereby effectively counteracting obstruction. In addition, when the RF link is interfered, the system can also rely on the VLC link to maintain communication. [17] proposed the aggregation of LiFi and RF communication, which is called "Hy-Fi". Hy-Fi used multiple input multiple output (MIMO) capabilities of WiFi to aggregate LiFi and RF signals directly at the physical layer. In 2022, the authors further studied the solution of applying Hy-Fi as a wireless access technology to the next generation indoor enterprise network [18]. Nevertheless, the existing work on hybrid LiFi and WiFi systems, including Hy-Fi, only took unidirectional communication into consideration, where the problem of real-time bidirectional communication remains unsolved.

To address this research gap, this paper put forth a hybrid LiFi and WiFi communication design (Hy-LiRF) in which physical-layer packets are parallelly transmitted using two RF ports of the WiFi NIC, one for LiFi and the other for conventional WiFi. That is, Hy-LiRF can support parallel LiFi and WiFi transmissions by building on top of the WiFi NICs's 2×2 MIMO RF ports. A comparison of our work against existing studies is summarized in Table 1.

Table 1. Comparison with Existing Works

References	System Design	Implementation		VLC	VLC+RF
		Unidirectional	Bidirectional		
[12]	✓				
[13]	✓				
[14]	✓	✓		✓	
[15]	✓		✓	✓	
[16]	✓		✓	✓	
[17]	✓	✓			✓
[18]	✓	✓			✓
This work	✓		✓		✓

Our main contributions are listed as follows:

- We propose a straightforward and practical hybrid LiFi and WiFi communication system framework named Hy-LiRF. Building on a WiFi NIC, Hy-LiRF uses two RF ports of the NIC to transmit LiFi and WiFi signals parallelly. Compared to pure LiFi systems, Hy-LiRF provides an additional RF link to maintain communication when the optical path is blocked, improving the robustness of the communication system when obstruction exists.
- We reveal the key to doubling the throughput of Hy-LiRF compared to a single-antenna communication system. Replacing one of the two RF antennas with a VLC module introduces additional carrier frequency offset (CFO)

to Hy-LiRF. This CFO cannot be mitigated by standard commercial WiFi NICs. As a result, it can seriously diminish the throughput of the system. To eliminate the impact of additional CFO, we propose a well-designed precoding matrix. Simulation results indicate that this approach effectively lowers the system's bit error rate (BER) to the level where CFO is negligible.
- We establish a prototype using commercial WiFi NICs and discrete components to validate the feasibility of Hy-LiRF. To the best of our knowledge, this is the first real-time bidirectional hybrid LiFi and WiFi communication system. Experimental results show that Hy-LiRF can achieve a real-time data rate of 140 Mbps within a 40 MHz bandwidth. Besides, Hy-LiRF is able to maintain communication over the RF link when the VLC link is obstructed, or via the VLC link when the RF link is interfered. After the blockage or interference sources are removed, it can restore to the highest communication rate within 3 s. These experimental results prove the ability of Hy-LiRF to support seamless real-time transmissions.

The remainder of this paper is organized as follows: Sect. 2 introduces the system model, including hardware composition and mathematical representation of signal flow. Section 3 analyzes the impact of CFO through simulation and introduces a precoding matrix to mitigate its effects. Experimental results are given in Sect. 4 and Sect. 5 concludes the paper.

2 System Model

Building on a commercial WiFi NIC, Hy-LiRF uses two RF ports of it. One port is connected to an RF antenna and the other is connected to the VLC module. How to make the VLC module seamlessly connect with the NIC and how to solve the bidirectional communication of the VLC module are important issues. This section first overviews the architecture of Hy-LiRF, and then the mathematical representation of signal flow is established and analyzed.

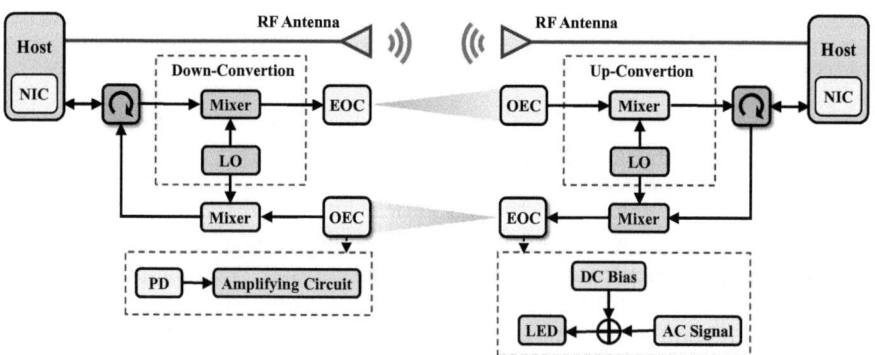

Fig. 1. Architecture of the proposed Hy-LiRF transceiver.

2.1 Overview

Figure 1 shows the main architecture of the proposed Hy-LiRF system, consisting of a pair of communication nodes. Each communication node mainly includes a host computer, an RF antenna, a circulator and a visible light transceiver module, simultaneously utilizing the RF link and the VLC link to transmit signals generated by the NIC. Each visible light transceiver module contains an up-and-down frequency conversion module, an electro-optical conversion (EOC) module and an optical-electro conversion (OEC) module. The specific functions of each module are as follows:

- **Host computer**: equipped with commercial IEEE 802.11 WiFi NICs. Generate and process signals.
- **Circulator**: isolate the transmitted and received signals of the VLC link. Since both LEDs and PDs can only support unidirectional signal transmission, it is essential to separate the bidirectional RF signals into two unidirectional signals.
- **Up-and-down frequency conversion module**: composed of two mixers and a local oscillator (LO). The RF signal from NIC needs to be downconverted to an intermediate frequency (IF) suitable for EOC, while the IF signal received by OEC needs the reverse operation.
- **EOC module**: consists of a drive circuit and an LED [19]. This module converts electrical signals into optical signals.
- **OEC module**: consists of a photodetector (PD) and amplifying circuits. This module converts photocurrent into voltage and amplifies it.

It is worth mentioning that attenuators are needed since the input power requirements of each component are different. Experiments have shown that both the value and position of attenuators will affect system performance, so adjustment according to actual situation is necessary. In addition, we have put a lens in front of the PD to enhance the intensity of the received light.

2.2 Mathematical Representation of Signal Flow

As shown in Fig. 1, we consider a 2×2 MIMO system transmitting orthogonal frequency division multiplexing (OFDM) signals. $X[k]$ represents a frequency domain baseband quadrature amplitude modulation (QAM) symbol, where $k = 0, 1, \ldots, N-1$ represents the subcarrier index. Then a baseband OFDM symbol can be obtained by performing inverse discrete Fourier transform (IDFT) on $X[k]$:

$$x[n] = \frac{1}{\sqrt{N}} \sum_{k=0}^{N-1} X[k] e^{\frac{j2\pi kn}{N}}, \quad n = 0, 1, \ldots, N-1. \tag{1}$$

Modulate the signal onto the carrier and we get:

$$s[n] = Re[x[n] e^{-j2\pi f_c T n}], \tag{2}$$

where f_{cT} is the carrier frequency at the transmitter.

After transmitting through the RF channel and the VLC channel respectively, we derive the two received signals at the receiver. Since the crystal oscillators of the transmitter and receiver are not synchronized, the CFO will inevitably be introduced. Represent the carrier frequency at the receiver as f_{cR} and specify $f_{cT} - f_{cR} = \varepsilon_0$. Both the two received signals have the CFO ε_0. Besides, compared with the RF link, the VLC link has undergone an additional up and down frequency conversion, which introduces additional CFO to the received signal. Denote the frequency of LO1 as f_{VT} and the frequency of LO2 as f_{VR} respectively, and specify $f_{VR} - f_{VT} = \varepsilon_1$, which is the extra CFO of the VLC link relative to the RF link.

Usually, a general 2×2 MIMO system is expressed as:

$$\begin{bmatrix} y_1 \\ y_2 \end{bmatrix} = \begin{bmatrix} h_{11} & h_{12} \\ h_{21} & h_{22} \end{bmatrix} \begin{bmatrix} s_1 \\ s_2 \end{bmatrix} + \begin{bmatrix} z_1 \\ z_2 \end{bmatrix}, \qquad (3)$$

where s_1 and s_2 represent the signals sent by the transmitter RF antenna and EOC module respectively; y_1 and y_2 represent the signals received by the receiver RF antenna and OEC module respectively; $h_{ij}, i, j = 1, 2$ represents channel impulse response; $z_i, i = 1, 2$ is the additive Gaussian white noise.

Taking aforementioned CFO into consideration, 2×2 Hy-LiRF system can be expressed as:

$$\begin{bmatrix} y_1 \\ y_2 \end{bmatrix} = \begin{bmatrix} h_{11} & h_{12} \\ h_{21} & h_{22}e^{-j2\pi\varepsilon_1 n} \end{bmatrix} \begin{bmatrix} s_1 \\ s_2 \end{bmatrix} + \begin{bmatrix} z_1 \\ z_2 \end{bmatrix}, \qquad (4)$$

where we write $e^{-j2\pi\varepsilon_1 n}$ separately outside h_{ij} to emphasize the additional CFO introduced by the VLC link.

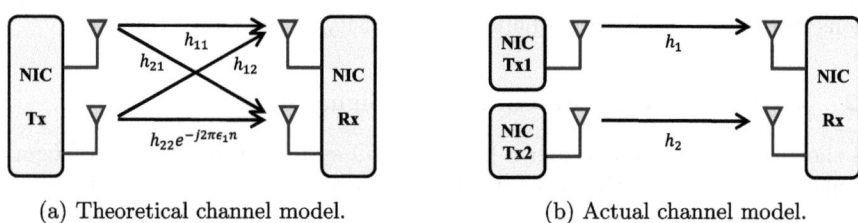

(a) Theoretical channel model.   (b) Actual channel model.

Fig. 2. Channel model.

Ideally, there are only two completely independent orthogonal channels h_{RF} and h_{VLC} between the transmitter and receiver. That is to say, $h_{12} = h_{21} = 0$, $h_{RF} = h_{11}$, and $h_{VLC} = h_{22}$. Then (4) can be written as:

$$\begin{bmatrix} y_1 \\ y_2 \end{bmatrix} = \begin{bmatrix} h_{RF} & 0 \\ 0 & h_{VLC}e^{-j2\pi\varepsilon_1 n} \end{bmatrix} \begin{bmatrix} s_1 \\ s_2 \end{bmatrix} + \begin{bmatrix} z_1 \\ z_2 \end{bmatrix}. \qquad (5)$$

However, the leakage of RF signals from the NIC antenna port is difficult to avoid, which means that h_{12} and h_{21} are not actually equal to 0. At this time, the system model is as described in (4), as shown in Fig. 2a.

Generally, commercial NICs can compensate for the frequency offset ε_0, but cannot handle the additional frequency offset ε_1. This makes it appear to the receiver that it is receiving signals from two different transmitters, as shown in Fig. 2b. Unfortunately, current NICs cannot work in such situation [14]. As a result, the signal multiplied with h_{12} and h_{21} is regarded as interference, which makes the NIC think that the channel condition is poor. Commercial NICs adaptively choose diversity technology under poor channel conditions. At this time, the Hy-LiRF system cannot obtain multiplexing gain, which means that the system throughput cannot reach twice that of a single-antenna system.

At the receiver, the NIC regards the signal multiplied with h_{12} and h_{21} as interference, so (4) can be rewritten as:

$$\begin{bmatrix} y_1 \\ y_2 \end{bmatrix} = \begin{bmatrix} h_{11} & 0 \\ 0 & h_{22}e^{-j2\pi\varepsilon_1 n} \end{bmatrix} \begin{bmatrix} s_1 \\ s_2 \end{bmatrix} + \begin{bmatrix} z'_1 \\ z'_2 \end{bmatrix}, \quad (6)$$

where $z'_1 = z_1 + h_{12}s_1$ and $z'_2 = z_2 + h_{21}s_2$. Replace h_{11} and h_{22} with h_{RF} and h_{VLC} respectively. It can be seen that (6) and (5) have the same channel matrix, and the only difference is the noise. Additionally, note that $s_1 = s_2$, rewritten (6) as:

$$\begin{bmatrix} y_1 \\ y_2 \end{bmatrix} = \begin{bmatrix} h_{RF} \\ h_{VLC}e^{-j2\pi\varepsilon_1 n} \end{bmatrix} s + \begin{bmatrix} z_{RF} \\ z_{VLC} \end{bmatrix}. \quad (7)$$

In (7), z_1 and z'_1 are uniformly written as z_{RF}, and z_2 and z'_2 are uniformly written as z_{VLC}. Combining the two signals using maximum ratio combining (MRC), we get:

$$\hat{s} = \boldsymbol{w}^H \boldsymbol{y} = [w^*_{RF}\ w^*_{VLC}] \left(\begin{bmatrix} h_{RF} \\ h_{VLC}e^{-j2\pi\varepsilon_1 n} \end{bmatrix} s + \begin{bmatrix} z_{RF} \\ z_{VLC} \end{bmatrix} \right), \quad (8)$$

where $\boldsymbol{w} = \left[\frac{h_{RF}}{|h|^2}\ \frac{h_{VLC}}{|h|^2} \right]^T$. And then remove the carrier of signal $\hat{s}[n]$ to get $\hat{x}[n]$. Here the common CFO ε_0 is introduced. Since NICs can compensate for ε_0 while cannot deal with ε_1, we only consider ε_1 in the following derivation.

Denote $\frac{|h_{RF}|^2}{|h_{RF}|^2+|h_{VLC}|^2}$ as α and $\frac{|h_{VLC}|^2}{|h_{RF}|^2+|h_{VLC}|^2}$ as β. Performing discrete Fourier transform (DFT) to recover QAM symbols, we get:

$$\hat{X}[k] = \sum_{n=0}^{N-1} \hat{x}[n]e^{-\frac{j2\pi nk}{N}} = \sum_{n=0}^{N-1} (\alpha x[n] + \beta x[n]e^{-j2\pi\varepsilon_1 n})e^{-\frac{j2\pi nk}{N}}$$

$$= \alpha \sum_{n=0}^{N-1} x[n]e^{-\frac{j2\pi nk}{N}} + \beta \sum_{n=0}^{N-1} x[n]e^{-j2\pi\varepsilon_1 n} \cdot e^{-\frac{j2\pi nk}{N}}. \quad (9)$$

It is clear that the frequency offset ε_1 introduced by the additional up and down conversion of the VLC link still remains in the signal. This will cause the second term of (9) looks like an interference of the first term, and vice versa. This is the reason that the communication data rate of Hy-LiRF system without any processing cannot be equal to the rate of a stand-alone 2 × 2 WiFi or 2 × 2 LiFi system.

3 Simulation Results

As pointed out in the previous section, the CFO of the VLC link has a crucial impact on the throughput of Hy-LiRF. In this section, we first simulate the influence of CFO ε_1, and then propose a solution to combat it by designing a precoding matrix. The simulation results verify the effectiveness of this method.

3.1 Impact of CFO

We simulate a 2 × 2 MIMO system using diversity technology in MATLAB. Considering that in actual systems, NICs can compensate for the common CFO ε_0, we only artificially introduce CFO ε_1 of the VLC link. The transmitter sends an OFDM signal modulated with 64-QAM, and the receiver utilizes MRC to combine signals.

Figure 3 shows the impact of CFO ε_1 on bit error rate (BER). For each fixed SNR, BER increases with increasing CFO ε_1. When CFO is lower than 200 Hz, BER improves significantly as SNR increases. However, when CFO increases further, BER no longer gets better with increasing SNR. It is easy to explain, because no matter how high the SNR is, the constellation points will deviate too much from the reference point when CFO exceeds a certain value, causing the failure of normal decoding.

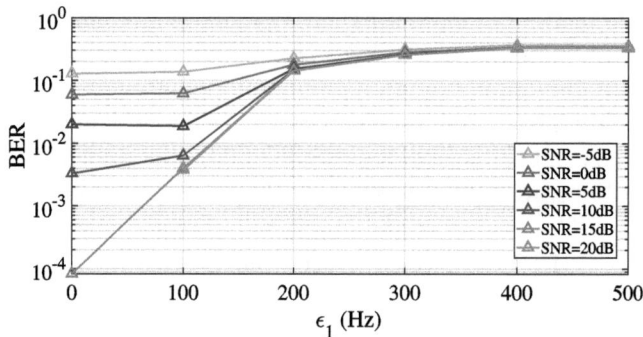

Fig. 3. The impact of CFO ε_1 on system BER under different SNRs.

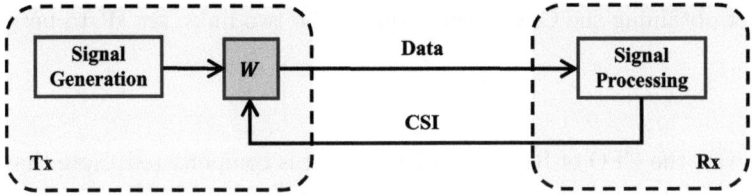

Fig. 4. Adding a precoding matrix to compensate for CFO.

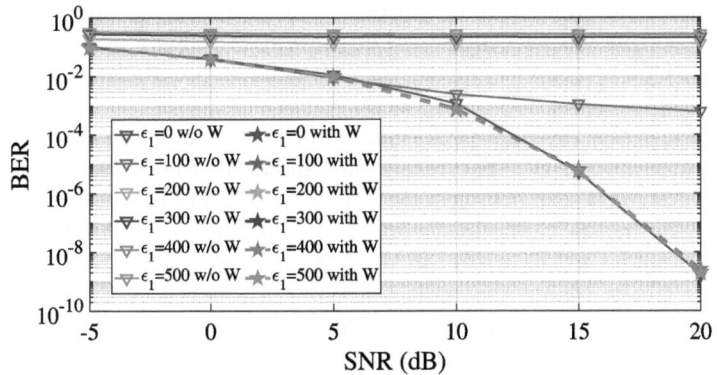

Fig. 5. Comparison of system BER with and without the precoding matrix W.

3.2 Compensation for CFO

In this paper, we propose a precoding method to counter the additional CFO. As shown in Fig. 4, a precoding matrix W is added to the transmitter. Before sending the data signal, first send the known signal using only the RF antenna and VLC frontend respectively, which can be achieved by configuring the matrix W. More specifically, first set W to be:

$$W = \begin{bmatrix} 1 & 0 \\ 0 & 0 \end{bmatrix}, \quad (10)$$

and then the transmitter only transmits the known RF signal using RF antenna. After receiving the known signal, the receiver performs channel estimation and feeds back the channel status information (CSI) to the transmitter, which includes the estimation of the RF link frequency offset $\hat{\varepsilon}_0$. Next W is set to be:

$$W = \begin{bmatrix} 0 & 0 \\ 0 & 1 \end{bmatrix}, \quad (11)$$

and then the transmitter only transmits the known VLC signal using VLC frontend. In the same way, the receiver feeds back CSI of the VLC channel to the transmitter, and the transmitter learns the estimation of the VLC link frequency offset $\hat{\varepsilon}$, where $\varepsilon = \varepsilon_0 + \varepsilon_1$.

After obtaining the CFO estimations of the two links, set $\boldsymbol{W}$ to be:

$$\boldsymbol{W} = \begin{bmatrix} e^{j2\pi\hat{\varepsilon}_0} & 0 \\ 0 & e^{j2\pi\hat{\varepsilon}} \end{bmatrix}. \tag{12}$$

In this way, the CFO of RF link and VLC link is compensated. Note that in the case of RF signal leakage, multiplying the precoding matrix $\boldsymbol{W}$ cannot eliminate the leaked RF signal. However, it can be considered that the power of the leaked RF signal is small, so the signal to interference plus noise ratio (SINR) is still at a high level. In addition, a timer can be added in actual implementation. Every time a certain backoff time passes, the transmitter sends a detection signal to re-estimate CSI to prevent changes of the channel conditions caused by user movement, interference and other circumstances.

We demonstrate the BER performance of the system before and after adding the precoding matrix $\boldsymbol{W}$. The results are shown in Fig. 5. Obviously, adding precoding matrix $\boldsymbol{W}$ can significantly reduce the BER of the system to the level where no CFO exists, and the system can maintain a good BER performance even when a high CFO exists in the VLC link, indicating that precoding matrix $\boldsymbol{W}$ can effectively combat the additional CFO introduced by the VLC link.

As can be seen from the above simulation results, when CFO exceeds a certain value, the receiver can no longer decode normally, and the simulation results are consistent with the phenomenon we find in experiments. That is, if the CFO ε_1 introduced by VLC link is not compensated, the data rate of the hybrid system will be lower than that of a single-antenna WiFi or LiFi system. Adding the proposed precoding matrix at the transmitter can effectively counter the impact.

4 Experiment

In this section, we build a prototype to verify the feasibility and robustness of the Hy-LiRF architecture, on which real-time bidirectional data rate tests are conducted.

4.1 Experimental Platform Setup

Based on the description in Sect. 2, we establish an experimental platform as shown in Fig. 6. At each communication node, we use a mini computer connected to a router that equipped with an IEEE 802.11 NIC as the host. We enable two antenna ports of the NIC in this work. One of the ports is connected to an RF antenna, and the other is connected to the visible light transceiver module through a circulator that is used to isolate the sending and receiving signals of the VLC link. *Iperf3* [20] is utilized to test the real-time communication data rate between the two communication nodes.

Since our current prototype uses commercial NICs and *iperf3* is also a packaged software, we cannot directly apply the proposed precoding matrix $\boldsymbol{W}$ to offset CFO in the actual system. As an alternative solution, we use the same

Fig. 6. Hy-LiRF Experiment Platform.

LO in one VLC link to conduct both the up and down conversion and set the oscillators on both sides to the same frequency to ensure the precision of the carrier frequency.

The selection of some components mentioned above are shown in Table 2. When testing, set the NIC to operate in 5 GHz frequency band and use 40 MHz bandwidth.

Table 2. Component Selection

Component	Type
NIC	IPQ4018
Circulator	UIYCC2528A
Mixer	Mini-Circuits ZX05-C60-S+
LO	ADF5355
EOC	Self-designed
PD	HAMAMATSU C5658

4.2 Real-Time Data Rate

Figure 7 illustrates the real-time data rate of Hy-LiRF system. We draw the rate curve of WiFi system with dual antennas and a single antenna simultaneously as the benchmark. It can be seen from the figure that in the absence of interference, the rate of Hy-LiRF system is stable at 140 Mbps. We can draw the conclusion that Hy-LiRF system realizes the cooperative work of VLC and RF communication at the PHY-layer. Under the conditions where no interference exists and the impact of CFO of the VLC link is eliminated, Hy-LiRF system can achieve a data rate comparable to the rate of WiFi system with dual antennas, which is twice that of a single-antenna WiFi system. Besides, we test the

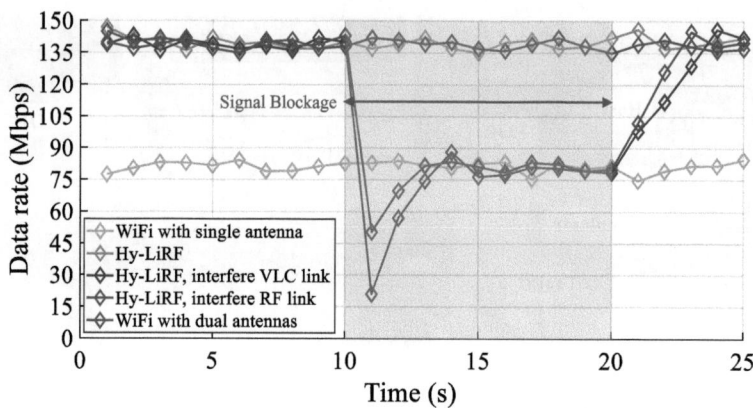

Fig. 7. Real-time data rate of Hy-LiRF system with and without interference.

system's response to interferences. Adding interferences to the RF link and VLC link at the 10th second of the test respectively, the date rate of Hy-LiRF system quickly drops to 50 Mbps and 20 Mbps, which is lower than that of a single-antenna WiFi system. The reason should be that the system has not yet had time to switch from multiplexing technology to diversity technology, resulting in data reception errors and thus requires data retransmission. This causes the data rate to drop temporarily and return to the rate of the single-antenna WiFi system after 2 to 3 s. In addition, changes of channel conditions will also cause the NIC to reconfigure modulation and coding scheme (MCS), which specifies the modulation format and code rate of the transmitted data. NICs need to wait until the data packets under the current MCS are sent before sending new data packets under the new MCS. After the interference is removed at the 20th second of the test, the data rate takes 3 s to return to 140 Mbps. We speculate the reasons why the system cannot restore to the maximum rate immediately when the channel conditions improve are still that it takes time to switch from diversity technology to multiplexing technology and change the MCS configuration. In general, although the system throughput decreases when a certain link is interfered, the communication is not interrupted, and the system can recover to the highest throughput in a short time after the interference is removed, which is a significant advantage over the pure WiFi or LiFi system.

5 Conclusion

This paper introduces Hy-LiRF, a bidirectional seamless hybrid LiFi and WiFi communication architecture that enables simultaneous PHY-layer packet transmission over both VLC and RF links, and demonstrates the first real-time prototype using the 2 × 2 MIMO RF ports of commercial WiFi NICs. To address the additional CFO introduced by the optical link, which standard commercial NICs cannot eliminate, we propose a carefully designed precoding matrix.

Simulations confirm the effectiveness of this matrix. Furthermore, experimental results from the prototype align with these simulations, achieving a real-time data rate of 140 Mbps within a 40 MHz bandwidth. The proposed Hy-LiRF system maintains communication over the RF link when the VLC link is obstructed and continues via the optical path when the RF link is interfered, demonstrating strong resilience to blockages and interference.

The Hy-LiRF prototype confirms the integration of RF and VLC links at the PHY layer, enabling seamless real-time transmissions with significant potential for indoor communication scenarios that demand more reliable connections and higher throughput. Hy-LiRF shows promise in delivering high-speed wireless communication in future networks, where it can capitalize on VLC's benefits while remaining compatible with ubiquitous RF networks. Rather than replacing RF technology, Hy-LiRF complements it by enabling parallel RF and LiFi transmissions. Moving forward, our focus will shift toward exploring Gbps data rates by leveraging broader bandwidth and shortening the time it takes to recover to the highest data rate after removing interferences.

References

1. Zhang, R., Shao, Y., Li, M., Lu, L.: Optical integrated sensing and communication. arXiv preprint arXiv:2305.04395 (2023)
2. Shao, Y., Gündüz, D., Liew, S.C.: Federated edge learning with misaligned over-the-air computation. IEEE Trans. Wirel. Commun. **21**(6), 3951–3964 (2022)
3. Chi, N., Zhou, Y., Wei, Y., Hu, F.: Visible light communication in 6G: advances, challenges, and prospects. IEEE Veh. Technol. Mag. **15**(4), 93–102 (2020)
4. You, X., et al.: Towards 6g wireless communication networks: vision, enabling technologies, and new paradigm shifts. Sci. China Inf. Sci. **64**, 1–74 (2021)
5. Rahman, M.T., Bakibillah, A.S.M., Parthiban, R., Bakaul, M.: Review of advanced techniques for multi-gigabit visible light communication. IET Optoelectron. **14**(6), 359–373 (2020)
6. IEEE Computer Society LAN/MAN Standards Committee. IEEE Standard for Local and Metropolitan Area Networks–Part 15.7: Short-Range Wireless Optical Communication Using Visible Light. IEEE Std 802.15.7-2011 (2011)
7. ITU-T. High-speed Indoor Visible Light Communication Transceiver - System Architecture, Physical Layer and Data Link Layer Specification. ITU-T Rec. G.9991 (2019)
8. IEEE Computer Society LAN/MAN Standards Committee. IEEE Standard for Multi-Gigabit per Second Optical Wireless Communications (OWC), with Ranges up to 200 m, for Both Stationary and Mobile Devices. IEEE Std 802.15.13-2023 (2023)
9. IEEE Computer Society LAN/MAN Standards Committee et al.: IEEE Standard for Information Technology-Telecommunications and Information Exchange Between Systems-Local and Metropolitan Area Networks-Specific Requirements Part 11: Wireless LAN Medium Access Control (MAC) and Physical Layer (PHY) Specifications. IEEE Std 802.11 (2007)
10. Shaik, P., Keçeci, C., Garg, K.K., Boyaci, A., Ismail, M., Serpedin, E.: Hybrid RF-VLC communication system: performance analysis and deep learning detection in the presence of blockages. IEEE Trans. Veh. Technol. (2024)

11. Wu, X., Soltani, M.D., Zhou, L., Safari, M., Haas, H.: Hybrid LiFi and WiFi networks: a survey. IEEE Commun. Surv. Tutor. **23**(2), 1398–1420 (2021)
12. Rahaim, M.B., Vegni, A.M., Little, T.D.C.: A hybrid radio frequency and broadcast visible light communication system. In: 2011 IEEE GLOBECOM Workshops (GC Wkshps), pp. 792–796. IEEE (2011)
13. Basnayaka, D.A., Haas, H.: Hybrid RF and VLC systems: improving user data rate performance of VLC systems. In: 2015 IEEE 81st Vehicular Technology Conference (VTC Spring), pp. 1–5. IEEE (2015)
14. Gawłowicz, P., Jarchlo, E.A., Zubow, A.: WiFi over VLC using COTS devices. In: IEEE INFOCOM 2020-IEEE Conference on Computer Communications Workshops (INFOCOM WKSHPS), pp. 340–345. IEEE (2020)
15. Zhang, R., Zhang, Y., Li, M., Liu, Q., Lu, L.: Realization of RF signal over bidirectional optical wireless communication links. In: 2024 IEEE International Conference on Communications Workshops (ICC Workshops), pp. 714–719. IEEE (2024)
16. Zhang, R., Li, M., Zhang, Y., Xiong, J., Lu, L.: LiRF: light-based wireless communications supporting ubiquitous radio frequency signals. IEEE Photonics J. (2024)
17. Zubow, A., Gawłowicz, P., Bober, K.L., Jungnickel, V., Habel, K., Dressler, F.: Hy-Fi: aggregation of LiFi and WiFi using MIMO in IEEE 802.11. In: 2021 IEEE 22nd International Symposium on a World of Wireless, Mobile and Multimedia Networks (WoWMoM), pp. 100–108. IEEE (2021)
18. Zubow, A., et al.: Hybrid-fidelity: utilizing IEEE 802.11 MIMO for practical aggregation of LiFi and WiFi. IEEE Trans. Mob. Comput. **22**(8), 4682–4697 (2022)
19. Zhang, R., Xiong, J., Li, M., Lu, L.: Design and implementation of low-complexity pre-equalizer for 1.5 GHz VLC system. IEEE Photonics J. (2024)
20. Iperf3. iPerf - The ultimate speed test tool for TCP, UDP and SCTP. https://iperf.fr/

UAVs-Enabled Maritime Communications: Control Barrier Functions for Physical Secure Systems

Zhitao Yu[1], Wake Shu[1], Xuanzhi Guo[1], Liang Mao[2], Guanchong Niu[1(✉)], Man-On Pun[3], and Zhiming Cheng[4]

[1] Guangzhou Institute of Technology, Xidian University, Guangzhou 510700, China
22011210877@stu.xidian.edu.cn, niuguanchong@xidian.edu.cn
[2] Shenzhen Polytechnic University, Shenzhen 518055, China
maoliangscau@szpu.edu.cn
[3] The Chinese University of Hong Kong, Shenzhen 518172, China
SimonPun@cuhk.edu.cn
[4] China Academy of Telecommunications Technology, Beijing 100191, China
chengzhimi@cictmobile.com

Abstract. In modern maritime communication, although UAVs provide better line-of-sight and data transmission capabilities, ensuring secure and reliable transmission has become increasingly difficult due to unstable channel conditions and the ever-present threat of eavesdropping. This work considers a scenario in which a formation of UAVs communicates with USVs on the sea surface in the presence of eavesdroppers (EDs). To prevent eavesdropping and ensure the safety of the UAV formation, a distributed control strategy based on Control Barrier Functions (CBFs) is introduced. Unlike previous methods, the proposed CBFs are suitable for dynamic maritime environments and can easily adapt to various control constraints, such as collision avoidance and eavesdropping prevention, as discussed in this paper. The simulation results demonstrate the stability of the control strategy, providing new insights for the use of UAV-based systems in critical applications such as military operations, rescue missions, and marine transport.

Keywords: UAVs · Physical Secure Communications · Control Barrier Functions

1 Introduction

With the rapid advancement of UAVs technology, the application of UAVs as mobile communication repeaters has provided a flexible and efficient solution for modern maritime communications [1,2]. However, due to the instability of

---

This work was supported by National Key Research and Development Program of China under Grant No. 2020YFB1807700.

maritime channels, the harshness of the environment such as weather changes, and the potential threat of eavesdropping, ensuring the reliability and security of communications faces huge challenges. These challenges not only affect the quality of communication, but also pose a threat to the privacy of information transmission, especially in application scenarios such as military, rescue, and marine transportation that have extremely high requirements for information security [3].

Traditional maritime communication methods usually rely on satellite systems or shore-based signal towers, but these methods face a series of challenges in practical applications. The main problem is that although satellite communication has a wide coverage area, its cost is relatively high, and due to the orbital altitude of the satellite, signal transmission often has a certain delay, which affects the real-time nature of communication. Although shore-based signal towers can provide relatively stable signal coverage in offshore areas, as the ship moves away from the shore, the signal strength will decay rapidly, resulting in communication interruption or quality degradation. This limitation is particularly evident in ocean voyages or offshore operations, and a more flexible and efficient communication solution is urgently needed. By deploying communication equipment on UAVs, they can significantly expand the coverage of maritime communications and quickly respond to communication needs [2]. However, as an open wireless communication network, UAV systems are also susceptible to attacks by EDs, which poses a serious challenge to the security of data transmission.

This paper studies the integration of CBFS in UAV systems, with particular emphasis on their role in improving system safety and reliability. CBFs are increasingly popular in the fields of control and robotics as a favorable approach to solving safety control problems [4,5]. This paper uses CBFs to define safe areas and restrict the movement of UAVs to ensure that they do not violate preset safety standards during operation. Reference [6] takes the expansion of maritime communication coverage as its starting point, while references [7] and [8] focus on improving maritime communication network performance and effective maritime communication scheduling, respectively. They demonstrate the advantages of UAV maritime communications but do not focus on how to avoid ED attacks. Reference [9] uses Q-learning and deep deterministic policy gradient (DDPG) algorithms to solve discrete and continuous UAV trajectory design problems, respectively, to ensure secure communications, but has problems such as unstable training and impracticality in dynamic environments.

In addition to helping UAV systems avoid collisions with obstacles, CBFs also play an important role in avoiding the threat of EDs. By optimizing movement and communication strategies, CBFs enhance the adaptability of UAVs in harsh environments and reduce the chance of being exposed to potential attacks. Specifically, CBFs can adjust the communication parameters of drones in real time to cope with changes in environmental conditions and ensure the stability and security of data transmission. This ability to dynamically monitor and reasonably allocate system resources enables drones to effectively avoid being attacked by EDs, thereby improving the security and efficiency of communications.

This paper proposes a CBFs-based solution to the problem of physical security system (PLS) for drone maritime communications. The core idea of CBFs is to limit the flight range of drones by planning the flight path of drones, avoid collisions with obstacles or other drones, and improve the ability to prevent potential eavesdropping threats.

The contributions of this work can be elabo-rated as follows:

1. The UAV security control scheme based on CBFs is proposed, which can effectively avoid UAV collisions in the maritime environment and reduce the risk of EDs obtaining sensitive information by dynamically adjusting communication paths and parameters.
2. By introducing a distributed control strategy, each UAV can autonomously make decisions based on local information, thereby freeing the system from centralized control in dynamic maritime environments.
3. The effectiveness of the proposed method was verified through simulation, showing that CBFs can significantly improve the operational efficiency and safety level of UAVs in maritime communications.

Notations: Uppercase boldface and lowercase boldface letters are used to denote matrices and vectors, respectively. $\|\mathbf{A}\|$ stands for the $\mathcal{L}_2$ norm of $\mathbf{A}$ while $|A|$ denotes the absolute value of real number A. $\mathbf{A}^T$ denote the transpose of $\mathbf{A}$. Finally, $\nabla f(\mathbf{A})$ represents the gradient of function $f(\mathbf{A})$.

2 Preliminaries

2.1 System Overview

The system framework is shown in Fig. 1, where a formation of multiple UAVs, each equipped with a mmWave base station, moves between USVs. To enable communication for each UAVS in the formation, it is equipped with a antenna, continuously transmitting data to Z USVs, each equipped with a receiving antenna, and M EDs. It is assumed that the UAV formation communicates with and locates Z UEs simultaneously. The horizontal position of the z-th USV and the i-th UAVs can be denoted as $\mathbf{p}_z^G = [x_z^G, y_z^G, z_z^G]$ and $\mathbf{p}_i^U = [x_i^U, y_i^U, z_i^U]$, respectively, with M EDs located at $\mathbf{p}_m^{ED} = [x_m^{ED}, y_m^{ED}, z_m^{ED}]$.

2.2 CBFs for Multi-UAV System

Consider a multi-UAV system (MAS) with N UAVs, indexed by $\mathcal{I} = \{1, 2, \ldots, N\}$. The dynamics of agent $i \in \mathcal{I}$ is given by $\dot{\mathbf{x}}_i = \mathbf{f}_i(\mathbf{x}_i) + \mathbf{g}_i(\mathbf{x}_i)\mathbf{u}_i$, where the state $\mathbf{x}_i \in \mathbb{R}^{n_i}$, and the control input $\mathbf{u}_i \in \mathbb{R}^{m_i}$, $\mathbf{f}_i(\mathbf{x}_i)$, $\mathbf{g}_i(\mathbf{x}_i)$ are locally Lipschitz functions in $\dot{\mathbf{x}}_i$. $\mathrm{blk}(\mathbf{g}_1, \mathbf{g}_2, \ldots, \mathbf{g}_N)$ denotes a block diagonal matrix with diagonal blocks $\mathbf{g}_1, \mathbf{g}_2, \ldots, \mathbf{g}_N$, which can be either a vector or a matrix. This paper denotes the stacked state $\mathbf{x} := \left(\mathbf{x}_1^\top, \mathbf{x}_2^\top, \ldots, \mathbf{x}_N^\top\right)^\top \in \mathbb{R}^n$,

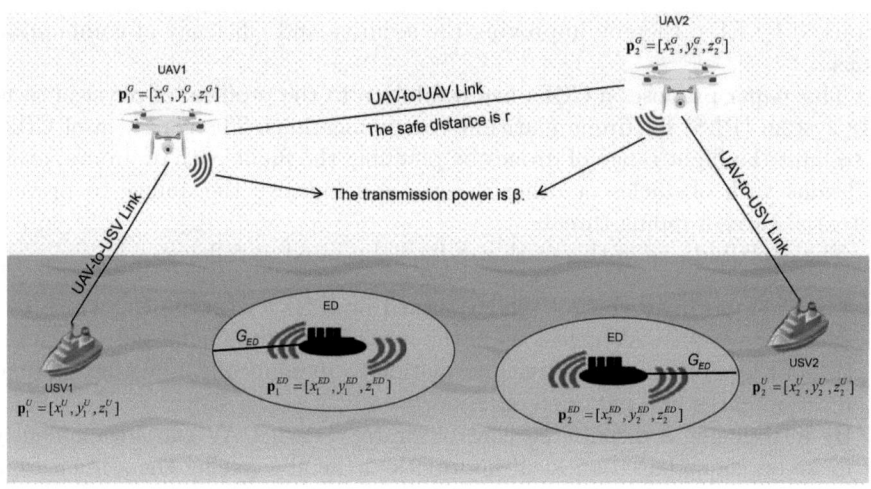

Fig. 1. Multiple UAVs communicate with multiple USVs at different time slots. The EDs are randomly distributed on the sea surface.

$n := \sum_{i \in \mathcal{I}} n_i$, the stacked control input $\mathbf{u} := \left(\mathbf{u}_1^\top, \mathbf{u}_2^\top, \ldots, \mathbf{u}_N^\top\right)^\top \in \mathbb{R}^m$, $m = \sum_{i \in \mathcal{I}} m_i$, the stacked vector $\mathbf{f} = \left(\mathbf{f}_1^\top, \mathbf{f}_2^\top, \ldots, \mathbf{f}_N^\top\right)^\top$ and $\mathbf{g} = \text{blk}(\mathbf{g}_1, \mathbf{g}_2, \ldots, \mathbf{g}_N)$. Thus, the stacked dynamics is obtained as

$$\dot{\mathbf{x}} = \mathbf{f}(\mathbf{x}) + \mathbf{g}(\mathbf{x})\mathbf{u}. \tag{1}$$

The communication topology of the MAS is represented by the graph $\mathcal{G} = (\mathcal{I}, E)$, where $\mathcal{I}$ stands for the set of nodes or agents, and E represents the edges connecting these nodes, facilitating the exchange of information between them. The Laplacian matrix corresponding to the connections is denoted by L. This work assumeS a 1-hop communication framework, meaning that each agent can access its own state and the states of its immediate neighbors, denoted by $N_i := \{j \in \mathcal{I} : (i,j) \in E\}$. The locally available state for agent i is given by $\mathbf{x}_{\text{loc},i} := (\mathbf{x}_i^\top, \mathbf{x}_{j_1}^\top, \ldots, \mathbf{x}_{j_{|N_i|}}^\top)^\top$, where $j_k \in N_i$ for $k \in \{1, 2, \ldots, |N_i|\}$. In essence, $\mathbf{x}_{\text{loc},i}$ stores the state information of agent i along with that of all its neighboring agents $j \in N_i$.

The safety set $\mathcal{C}$ represents a region in the state space where a certain safety constraint is satisfied. This set is defined as:

$$\mathcal{C} = \{\mathbf{x} \in \mathbb{R}^n : h(\mathbf{x}) \geq 0\}, \tag{2}$$

where $h(\mathbf{x})$ is a continuously differentiable function. The safety set $\mathcal{C}$ consists of the interior and boundary, where the condition $h(\mathbf{x}) > 0$ defines the interior of the safe region, and $h(\mathbf{x}) = 0$ defines the boundary between the safe and unsafe regions. In contrast, the condition $h(\mathbf{x}) < 0$ characterizes the unsafe region, indicating states that violate the safety constraints.

To further clarify, the boundary of the safety set is represented by the equation $h(\mathbf{x}) = 0$, which forms the dividing line between safe and unsafe regions. The interior of the set, where $h(\mathbf{x}) > 0$, defines the states that strictly satisfy the safety constraints. The unsafe region, defined by $h(\mathbf{x}) < 0$, includes states that fall outside the safety constraints.

The set $\mathcal{D}$ is considered as a superset of the safety set $\mathcal{C}$, which may include both the safe region and the unsafe region. This geometric representation is useful in control design and verification processes, where maintaining the system state within the safe region $\mathcal{C}$ is critical for ensuring the system's safety.

Definition 1 (CBF). Let set $\mathcal{C}$ be defined by (2). $h(\mathbf{x})$ is a CBF for the stacked system (1) if there exists a locally Lipschitz extended class $\mathcal{K}$ function α such that:
$$\sup_{\mathbf{u} \in \mathbb{R}^m} [L_f h(\mathbf{x}) + L_g h(\mathbf{x})\mathbf{u} + \alpha(h(\mathbf{x}))] \geq 0, \quad \forall \mathbf{x} \in \mathbb{R}^n. \tag{3}$$

It has been shown [10] that any locally Lipschitz control input $\mathbf{u}$ that satisfies the CBF constraint (3) renders the set $\mathcal{C}$ forward invariant and, if $\mathcal{C}$ is compact, asymptotically stable.

Assumption 1. Based on [11], the expression in (4) is assumed to be linear in $\mathbf{u}$, as shown in (5):
$$\sum_{i \in \mathcal{I}} \mathbf{a}_i^\top (\mathbf{x}_{\text{loc},i})\mathbf{u}_i + \sum_{i \in \mathcal{I}} b_i(\mathbf{x}_{\text{loc},i}) \leq 0, \tag{4}$$

where $\mathbf{a}_i \in \mathbb{R}^{m_i}$ and $b_i \in \mathbb{R}$ correspond to the agent-specific components of the terms $-L_g h(\mathbf{x})$ and $-L_f h(\mathbf{x}) - \alpha(h(\mathbf{x}))$ derived from (4), respectively.

The detailed computation of these terms will be elaborated in the following section.

2.3 Large-Scale Fading

Modeling wireless channels over sea wave propagation is an emerging and relatively novel research area. Traditional channel models, such as the air-to-ground path loss model outlined in [12], typically rely on the urban environment model. These models incorporate an additional loss to the free space path loss, which is dependent on the presence of a line of sight (LOS) between the UAV and the users. However, due to the distinct characteristics of the sea surface environment, these models may not fully capture the complexities involved in wireless propagation over water. The roughness of the sea surface, combined with specific atmospheric phenomena over the sea, such as humidity and evaporation ducting, introduces unique challenges to accurate channel modeling.

The inadequacy of traditional air-to-ground models when applied to sea environments has prompted researchers to explore alternative wireless channel models for air-to-sea communications. However, the development of a robust and standardized air-to-sea wave propagation model is still in its infancy. Existing approaches in the literature vary considerably depending on factors such as the frequency of operation, the communication technology being used, and the specific implementation scenario. These models range from simplified two-ray models to more complex models that take into account environmental and atmospheric factors.

In [13], similar to most channel models proposed in the literature, the assumption is made that the sea surface is smooth, and any ducting effects are neglected. As a result, a two-ray model is employed, which considers the reflection component from the sea surface. The path loss for this model is expressed as follows:

$$L(d) = -20 \log_{10} \left(\frac{\lambda}{4\pi d} \left[2 \sin \left(\frac{2\pi h_t h_r}{\lambda d} \right) \right] \right), \quad (5)$$

where d represents the distance between the UAV and the user, λ denotes the signal wavelength, and h_t and h_r are the heights of the transmitting and receiving antennas, respectively. This model captures the key elements of path loss by considering both the direct line of sight component and the reflection from the sea surface.

While the two-ray model provides a basic approximation for path loss over the sea, it is important to note that it does not account for more complex factors such as sea surface roughness or the aforementioned atmospheric ducting effects. Therefore, further research is required to refine these models and better capture the nuances of air-to-sea wireless communications.

2.4 Location-Aware Physical Layer Security

Since EDs are present in the system, the UAVS needs to avoid transmitting data to the regions where EDs might intercept the signal. Recalling (5), the received signal power must meet the following constraint:

$$\beta_{ED} - L(d)_{ED} \leq T_{ED}, \quad (6)$$

where T_{ED} denotes the minimum power that an ED can receive to successfully decode the signal, and β_{ED} represents the transmission power of the UAVS.

Now that the positions of each fixed ED are known, and the receiving antennas are fixed on each USV and ED with a height of h_r, while the transmitting antennas are fixed on each UAV, the height h_t of the transmitting antenna can be determined based on the path loss in (5).

3 CBF-Based Path-Planning for PLS

Referring to (5), it is obtained that the UAVs move in a plane with a fixed altitude denoted by h_t. Therefore, the critical radius beyond which the UAVs must avoid the ED can be determined. Consequently, the undesirable radius G_{ED} can be calculated.

3.1 Distributed Implementation

The deployment of a multi-UAV formation in a maritime environment will encounter multiple security constraints. A general controller that would always satisfy the constraints is given by the following Quadratic Problem

$$\min_{\mathbf{u}} \quad \|\mathbf{u} - \mathbf{u}_{\text{nom}}\|^2$$
$$\text{s.t.} \quad \sum_{i \in \mathcal{I}} (\mathbf{a}_i^q)^\top (\mathbf{x}_{\text{loc},i}) \mathbf{u}_i + \sum_{i \in \mathcal{I}} b_i^q(\mathbf{x}_{\text{loc},i}) \leq 0, \quad (7)$$
$$\text{for } q = 1, 2, \ldots, Q.$$

where Q is the total number of all the safety constraints.

It has been proposed in [13] that instead of solving a single centralized local QP, each individual UAV $i \in \mathcal{I}$ should solve an equivalent QP.

$$\min_{\mathbf{u}_i \in \mathbb{R}^{m_i}} \quad \|\mathbf{u}_i - \mathbf{u}_{\text{nom},i}\|^2$$
$$\text{s.t.} \quad \mathbf{a}_i^\top (\mathbf{x}_{\text{loc},i}) \mathbf{u}_i + \sum_{j \in N_i} (y_i - y_j) + b_i(\mathbf{x}_{\text{loc},i}) \leq 0, \quad (8)$$

where $\mathbf{y} = (y_1, y_2, \ldots, y_N) \in \mathbb{R}^N$ is an auxiliary variable.

Two classes of functions are recognized, where the CBF condition can be expressed as (7). This work considers two types of constraints. The first type is individual constraints, denoted by $h_k(\mathbf{x}_i)$, while the second type is dual constraints, denoted by $h_e(\mathbf{x}_i, \mathbf{x}_j)$.

Below, the work will integrate these two types of constraints based on the maritime environment and the need to avoid eavesdropping by EDs.

3.2 Main Result

To achieve the system's security constraints, it is required that $\min_{e \in E} h_e(\mathbf{x}_i, \mathbf{x}_j) \geq 0$. However, to ensure the distributed implementation of the CBF for the MAS, the results observed in [11] will be adopted by

$$\min_{e \in E} h_e(\mathbf{x}_i, \mathbf{x}_j) \geq -\frac{1}{p} \log \left(\sum_{e \in E} e^{-p h_e(\mathbf{x}_i, \mathbf{x}_j)} \right). \quad (9)$$

Through calculation, the following can be obtained:

$$h(x) = \sum_{e \in E} \left(\frac{1}{|E|} - e^{-p h_e} \right) =: \sum_{e \in E} \tilde{h}_e(\mathbf{x}_i, \mathbf{x}_j) \geq 0, \quad (10)$$

where $|E|$ denotes the cardinality of the set E. Based on this, a formulation for dual constraints of the same type was proposed in [14], as shown below

$$\mathbf{a}_{i,\text{dual}} = -\sum_{e \in E} I_e(i) \nabla_{\mathbf{x}_i} \tilde{h}_e(\mathbf{x}_i, \mathbf{x}_j) \mathbf{g}_i^\top, \quad (11)$$

$$b_{i,\text{dual}} = -\sum_{e \in E} I_e(i) \left(\nabla_{\mathbf{x}_i} \tilde{h}_e(\mathbf{x}_i, \mathbf{x}_j)\right)^\top \mathbf{f}_i$$
$$+ \frac{a}{2}\left(\frac{1}{\beta} - e^{-ph_e(\mathbf{x}_i, \mathbf{x}_j)}\right), \tag{12}$$

In this context, $\beta = |E|$ when all the functions $\tilde{h}_e$ belong to the same category, such as collision avoidance between neighboring agents in the network. The indicator function $I_e(i)$ is defined as

$$I_e(i) = \begin{cases} 1, & \text{if edge } e \text{ contains } i, \\ 0, & \text{if edge } e \text{ does not contain } i. \end{cases} \tag{13}$$

Similar to the dual constraint case, the individual constraint can be found in [14]

$$\mathbf{a}_{i,\text{ind}} = -\sum \nabla \tilde{h}_k(\mathbf{x}_i) \mathbf{g}_i^\top, \tag{14}$$

$$b_{i,\text{ind}} = -\sum_{k \in K} \left(\nabla \tilde{h}_k(\mathbf{x}_i)^\top \mathbf{f}_i\right) + a\left(\frac{1}{\beta} - e^{-ph_k(\mathbf{x}_i)}\right), \tag{15}$$

where $\beta = |\mathcal{I}||K|$, and K represents the number of individual constraints of the same type imposed on each UAV $i \in \mathcal{I}$. Finally, it can be formulated based on multiple constraints, as shown below.

$$\mathbf{S}_i = \sum_{l_e \in L_E} \mathbf{S}_{i,\text{dual}}^{l_e} + \sum_{l_k \in L_K} \mathbf{S}_{i,\text{ind}}^{l_k}, \tag{16}$$

where L_E and L_K are the different type of dual and individual constraints and $\mathbf{S}_i$ is a vector composed of $\mathbf{a}_i$ and $\mathbf{b}_i$.

Based on the results from [14], the problem is formulated according to the maritime environment. The main objective is to avoid eavesdropping by EDs, and since the range G_{ED} that prevents eavesdropping has already been obtained, the following can be derived.

$$h_i(\mathbf{x}_i) = \|\mathbf{x}_i - \mathbf{p}_m^{ED}\|^2 - G_{ED}^2, \tag{17}$$

where $\mathbf{x}_i = \mathbf{p}_i^G$, and this is clearly a individual constraint. It can be obtained that

$$\nabla h_i = \begin{bmatrix} 2\left(x_i^U - x_m^{ED}\right) \\ 2\left(y_i^U - y_m^{ED}\right) \\ 2\left(z_i^U - z_m^{ED}\right) \end{bmatrix}. \tag{18}$$

Computing the $\mathbf{a}_{i,\text{ind}}$ and $b_{i,\text{ind}}$ terms using (14) and (15).

For the dual constraints, the primary focus is on the issue of collision avoidance at sea, from which the following can be derived:

$$h_e(\mathbf{x}_i, \mathbf{x}_j) = \|\mathbf{x}_i - \mathbf{x}_j\|^2 - r^2 \geq 0, \tag{19}$$

where r is the minimum distance between UAVs to ensure collision avoidance. And $\mathbf{x}_i = \mathbf{p}_i^G$, $\mathbf{x}_j = \mathbf{p}_j^G$. The following gradient can be obtained:

$$\nabla h_e(\mathbf{x}_i, \mathbf{x}_j) = \begin{bmatrix} 2(x_i^U - x_j^U) \\ 2(y_i^U - y_j^U) \\ 2(z_i^U - z_j^U) \\ -2(x_i^U - x_j^U) \\ -2(y_i^U - y_j^U) \\ -2(z_i^U - z_j^U) \end{bmatrix}. \quad (20)$$

Using (11) and (12), the $\mathbf{a}_{i,\text{dual}}$ and $b_{i,\text{dual}}$ terms for the QP can be computed.

Based on the above solution, $\mathbf{a}_i$ and $\mathbf{b}_i$ can be solved using (16), thereby completing the solution to this quadratic programming problem.

4 Experimental Results

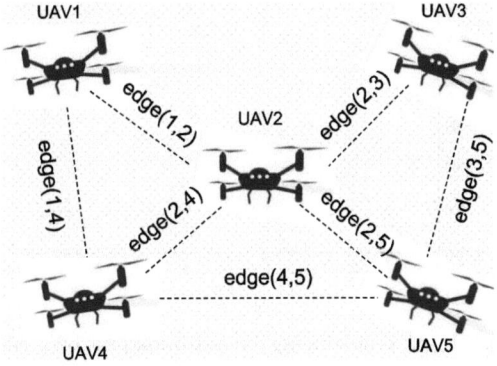

Fig. 2. Communication topology of the MAS.

In this section, we present our findings for a MAS consisting of $N = 5$ agents. The communication graph, denoted as $(\mathcal{I}, E)$, is illustrated in Fig. 2. We now implement our findings on the same multi-agent system for a consensus control scenario, introducing a stacked state boundedness constraint as described below. For $i \in \mathcal{I}$, where $\mathbf{x}_i \in \mathbb{R}^2$ represents the state vector of the agent, the system dynamics are $\dot{\mathbf{x}}_i = \mathbf{u}_i$, with the initial condition given as $\mathbf{x}_1 = (0, 0, 10)$, $\mathbf{x}_2 = (3, 1, 10)$, $\mathbf{x}_3 = (6, 2, 10)$, $\mathbf{x}_4 = (1, 4, 10)$, and $\mathbf{x}_5 = (5, 5, 10)$. Additionally, the initial position of the receiving antenna of a certain ED is given by $\mathbf{x}_{ED} = (50, 50, 1)$.

In Fig. 3, the effect of CBFs in preventing collisions within the MAS is presented. The figure shows the changes in the constraint function $h(x)$ over time as it applies to the CBF constraints. Initially, some UAV states are outside the

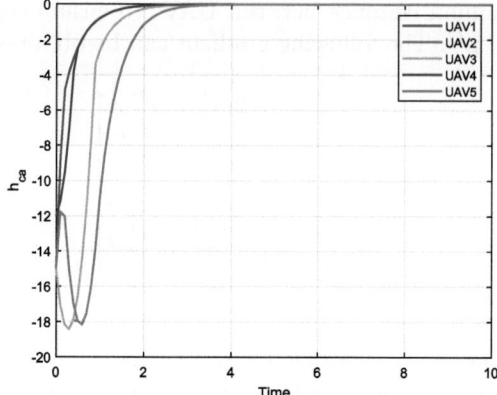

Fig. 3. Collision avoidance between UAVs.

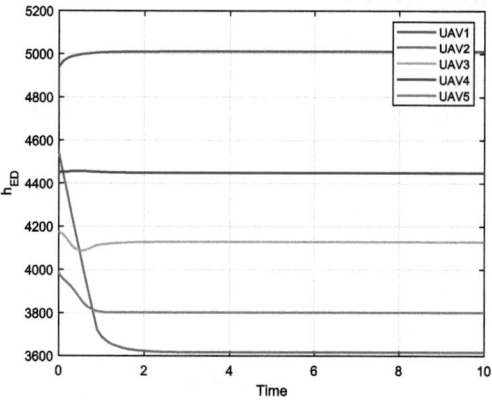

Fig. 4. Each UAV avoids being eavesdropped on by a certain ED.

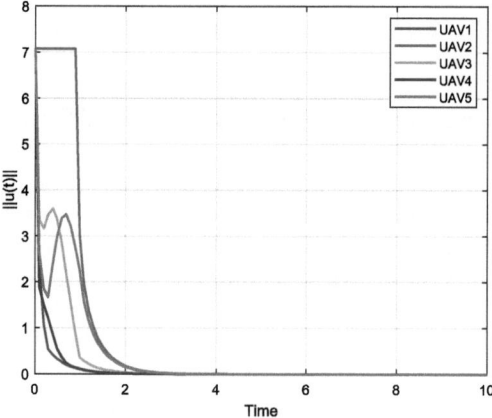

Fig. 5. Time evolution of $\|\mathbf{u}(t)\|$.

safety boundary, indicating potential collision risks. However, as the CBF strategy is applied, the values of $h(x)$ adjust gradually, ensuring that all UAV states enter and remain within the safe region. This figure illustrates that CBFs effectively constrain the movement of UAVs, ensuring they comply with the collision avoidance rules throughout their operation.

Figure 4 demonstrates how the UAV system maintains PLS in the presence of EDs by using CBF constraints. The figure reflects the dynamic changes in the constraint function $h(x)$, describing how the UAVs adjust their states to avoid the threat of eavesdropping. Initially, some UAVs are within the threat region, meaning their communications are vulnerable to interception. However, after applying the CBF control strategy, the values of $h(x)$ change, ensuring that the UAVs move into the safe zone, far from the EDs' detection range. This figure shows that the CBFs successfully prevent eavesdropping, enhancing the physical security of the system.

Figure 5 illustrates the time evolution of the norm of the control input vector $\|u(t)\|$ for each UAV during the simulation. At the beginning of the simulation, the control inputs are relatively large, as the UAVs make significant adjustments to their states to avoid collisions and stay clear of EDs. These adjustments require higher control efforts due to the rapid changes in direction and speed. As the simulation progresses, and the UAVs reach trajectories that satisfy all safety and security constraints, the required control inputs gradually decrease and eventually stabilize. This stabilization of control inputs indicates that the UAVs have settled into efficient and safe paths, requiring minimal adjustments to maintain the desired operational behavior, showcasing the effectiveness of the CBF-based control strategy.

The experimental results confirm that the introduced CBF method effectively ensures both collision avoidance and secure communication in the MAS. Figure 3 demonstrates successful collision prevention, while Fig. 4 shows how UAVs avoid EDs. Figure 5 highlights the stability of the control inputs, demonstrating the efficiency of the CBF strategy. Overall, the CBF-based approach provides a robust solution for safe and secure UAV operations in dynamic environments.

5 Conclusion

This paper proposes a UAV-enabled maritime communication system that integrates CBF to enhance physical security and operational safety. The use of CBFs allows for effective collision avoidance and minimizes the risk of eavesdropping by dynamically adjusting UAV communication paths and parameters. The simulation results demonstrate that the approach significantly improves the reliability and efficiency of UAV operations under dynamic maritime conditions. By ensuring that UAVs remain within a well-defined safety region, the system achieves secure communication even in challenging environments, making it suitable for a wide range of maritime applications where security and resilience are critical.

References

1. Wang, Y., Feng, W., Wang, J., Quek, T.Q.S.: Hybrid satellite-UAV-terrestrial networks for 6G ubiquitous coverage: a maritime communications perspective. IEEE J. Sel. Areas Commun. **39**(11), 3475–3490 (2021)
2. Nomikos, N., Gkonis, P.K., Bithas, P.S., Trakadas, P.: A survey on UAV-aided maritime communications: deployment considerations, applications, and future challenges. IEEE Open J. Commun. Soc. **4**, 56–78 (2022)
3. Arbanas, B., Ivanovic, A., Car, M., Orsag, M., Petrovic, T., Bogdan, S.: Decentralized planning and control for UAV-UGV cooperative teams. Auton. Robot. **42**(8), 1601–1618 (2018)
4. Choi, J.J., Lee, D., Sreenath, K., Tomlin, C.J., Herbert, S.L.: Robust control barrier-value functions for safety-critical control. In: 2021 60th IEEE Conference on Decision and Control (CDC), pp. 6814–6821. IEEE (2021)
5. Ames, A.D., Xu, X., Grizzle, J.W., Tabuada, P.: Control barrier function based quadratic programs for safety critical systems. IEEE Trans. Autom. Control **62**(8), 3861–3876 (2016)
6. Tang, R., Feng, W., Chen, Y., Ge, N.: Noma-based UAV communications for maritime coverage enhancement. China Commun. **18**(4), 230–243 (2021)
7. Cao, X., Yan, S., Peng, M.: MMWave-based beamforming for capacity maximization in UAV-aided maritime communication networks. In: 2021 IEEE/CIC International Conference on Communications in China (ICCC), pp. 451–456. IEEE (2021)
8. Xin, Y., Wang, J., Zhao, W., Zhang, J., Shi, P.: Multi-UAV assisted maritime communication scheduling strategy. In: 2024 IEEE International Conference on Communications Workshops (ICC Workshops), pp. 499–504. IEEE (2024)
9. Liu, J., Zeng, F., Wang, W., Sheng, Z., Wei, X., Cumanan, K.: Trajectory design for UAV-enabled maritime secure communications: a reinforcement learning approach. China Commun. **19**(9), 26–36 (2022)
10. Xu, X., Tabuada, P., Grizzle, J.W., Ames, A.D.: Robustness of control barrier functions for safety critical control. IFAC-PapersOnLine **48**(27), 54–61 (2015)
11. Tan, X., Dimarogonas, D.V.: Distributed implementation of control barrier functions for multi-agent systems. IEEE Control Syst. Lett. **6**, 1879–1884 (2021)
12. Al-Hourani, A., Kandeepan, S., Jamalipour, A.: Modeling air-to-ground path loss for low altitude platforms in urban environments. In: 2014 IEEE Global Communications Conference, pp. 2898–2904. IEEE (2014)
13. Wang, J., et al.: Wireless channel models for maritime communications. IEEE Access **6**, 68070–68088 (2018)
14. Fernandez-Ayala, V.N., Tan, X., Dimarogonas, D.V.: Distributed barrier function-enabled human-in-the-loop control for multi-robot systems. In: 2023 IEEE International Conference on Robotics and Automation (ICRA), pp. 7706–7712. IEEE (2023)

A Low-Complexity and High-Performance K-Best GFSK MSDD with LLRs Outputs

Jiajun Zhu and Francis C. M. Lau

Department of Electrical and Electronic Engineering, The Hong Kong Polytechnic University, Kowloon, Hong Kong SAR, China
jiajun.zhu@connect.polyu.hk, francis-cm.lau@polyu.edu.hk

Abstract. In the field of wireless communications, particularly within the Internet of Things (IoT) domain, efficient and reliable modulation techniques are paramount. Gaussian Frequency Shift Keying (GFSK) is a favored modulation scheme due to its good spectral efficiency and its resilience to impairment of radio frequency (RF) circuits. However, the challenge of achieving high performance in terms of Bit Error Rate (BER) and Packet Error Rate (PER) while maintaining low complexity in the detector design remains a significant issue. Addressing this challenge, this paper introduces a novel K-best based GFSK detector that not only approaches the optimal performance in BER and PER, but also manages to do so with reduced computational complexity. Further, another key feature of our technique is the generation of Log-Likelihood Ratios (LLRs), which are crucial for subsequent soft channel decoding stages. By providing LLR outputs, our detector facilitates a more refined decoding process, enhancing the overall error correction capabilities of the system.

Keywords: GFSK · GMSK · Bluetooth · K-best detector · LLR

1 Introduction

Gaussian Frequency Shift Keying (GFSK), a digital modulation technique, is extensively utilized in Internet of Things (IoT) communications, including Bluetooth protocols. In the realm of IoT, there is a high demand for low energy consumption, cost-effectiveness, and long-range transmission capabilities. Hence, this work is dedicated to deriving a GFSK detector designed for low complexity and enhanced performance at the receiver end.

The traditional GFSK detectors, including the limiter-discriminator with integrator (LDI) detector [1], the non-coherent phase differential detector [1,2], the phase averaging detector [3], and the zero-crossing detector [4], are appreciated for their simplicity. These detectors are known for their low complexity, albeit at the expense of diminished error performance. High-performance GFSK detectors often employ a sophisticated filter system to align with expected waveforms by a maximum likelihood (ML) criterion for detecting multiple symbols

[5], akin to the approach of multiple symbols differential detection (MSDD) as introduced in [6]. However, the complexity of such high-precision detectors can be excessively demanding. To address these concerns, [7] introduced a recursive, low-cost solution aimed at reducing computational requirements while still achieving high error performance. On another front, [8] explored an algorithm that leverages known or estimated symbols through a decision-feedback strategy, aiming to cut down on complexity without significantly sacrificing performance. Despite these advancements, the recursive method proposed in [7] still necessitates a considerable amount of computational effort. Furthermore, the decision-feedback technique detailed in [8] has been found to introduce instability due to its feedback control mechanism, as observed in our experiments. This instability complicates the generation of viable Log-Likelihood Ratios (LLRs), which are crucial for boosting performance when combined with channel decoders.

In this paper, a K-best Gaussian Frequency Shift Keying Multi-Symbol Differential Detection (GFSK MSDD) with LLRs output is proposed. This technique, in contrast to [5] and [7], adopts the K-best method to narrow down potential candidates through recursive implementation during GFSK MSDD, aiming for near-optimal performance. Compared with [8], although complexity remains a drawback, our proposed method is more stable and provides LLR output which significantly enhances performance when combined with channel coding.

This paper is organized as follows. Section 2 describes traditional GFSK MSDD and its disadvantage in terms of complexity. Subsequently, the proposed K-best based on the GFSK detector and the generation of LLRs are introduced in Sects. 3 and 4, respectively. Finally, the simulation results and conclusion are presented in Sects. 5 and 6, respectively.

2 Traditional GFSK MSDD

Figure 1 shows the block diagram of a GFSK modulator. We assume an observation interval of T (in terms of number of bit periods) and we denote the input bit stream as $[p_1, p_2, \ldots, p_T]$ which consists of ± 1. We also assume that the input bits are sampled at a rate of M samples per bit. Then the sampled signal $\mathbf{p}$ is convolved with a digital Gaussian filter $\mathbf{g}$. The output of the Gaussian filter, which represents the instantaneous phase, is given by

$$w_{n,t} = 2\pi\beta \left(\mathbf{p}_{n,t} * \mathbf{g}\right) \tag{1}$$

where β is the modulation index, $t = 1, 2, \ldots, T$ denotes the index of symbol or bit, $n = 1, 2, \ldots, M$ denotes the index of sample per symbol, and $*$ represents the convolution operator. Since the accumulation of the instantaneous phase becomes the phase of the GFSK signal, the baseband complex signal is given by

$$s_{n,t} = \exp\left(j \sum_{i=-\infty}^{n} \sum_{j=-\infty}^{t} w_{i,j}\right), \tag{2}$$

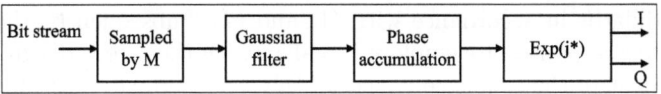

Fig. 1. GFSK modulator at transmitter

where j denotes $\sqrt{-1}$ and $\exp(\cdot)$ represents the exponential function.

At the receiver, we denote the received baseband signal by

$$r_{n,t} = h s_{n,t} + z_{n,t}, \tag{3}$$

where h is the complex channel gain assumed to be $e^{j\theta}$ with $\theta \in [0, 2\pi)$, and $z_{n,t}$ is a complex Gaussian noise with variance σ^2 in each dimension. The GFSK MSDD employs a maximum likelihood detection over a group of multiple symbols. The output of MSDD is given by

$$\hat{\mathbf{p}} = \arg\max_{\check{s} \in \Theta} \left| \sum_{t=1}^{T} \sum_{n=1}^{M} r_{n,t} \check{s}_{n,t}^{*} \right|^2. \tag{4}$$

where Θ is the set of 2^T matched filter responses; $\check{s}_{n,t}$ is one of the 2^T matched filter responses; $\hat{\mathbf{p}}$ is a $T \times 1$ vector of the detected bit sequence $[\hat{p}_1, \hat{p}_2, \ldots, \hat{p}_T]^H$ in which H denotes the transpose operator; and $(\cdot)^*$ is the conjugate operator.

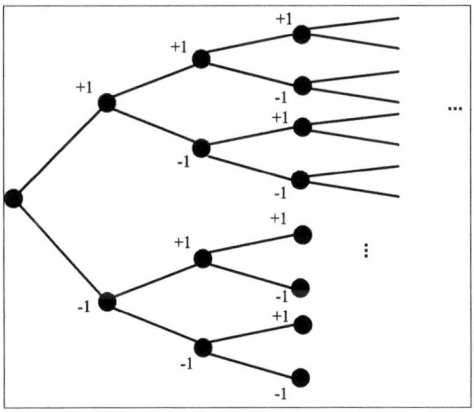

Fig. 2. A tree diagram to display MSDD

The process of MSDD can be depicted through the tree diagram shown in Fig. 2. In this diagram, the levels of the tree and the branches at each level signify the index of symbol and the respective potential candidates. Each node within the tree symbolizes a viable bit candidate for its corresponding level. The potential matched filter responses are generated by sequences of nodes, using a

GFSK modulator in accordance with (1) and (2). Subsequently, these derived matched filter responses are employed to align with the received signal $r_{n,t}$. The aim is to identify the sequence of most likely bit candidates within the observation interval T. Theoretically as T increases, the error performance of MSDD improves. Moreover, the number of possible candidates and the computational resource increase exponentially.

3 K-Best Based GFSK Detector

In this work, we introduce a K-best algorithm tailored to the ML tree diagram for GFSK MSDD. The K-best algorithm operates as follows. When the number of nodes at a certain level is less than K, all nodes are retained. On the other hand, if the node count exceeds K, a pruning process is applied where only the K nodes with the highest likelihoods, as determined by the maximum likelihood criterion, are kept. We consider, for example, setting $K = 4$. As depicted in Fig. 3, at level 3, where there are 8 nodes, only the 4 nodes deemed most likely are retained. These retained nodes then further extend their branches to the next level, ensuring that the search space is effectively managed by focusing on the most probable candidates while progressing through the levels.

According to the tree-fashion processing, we have the matrix $\hat{\mathbf{P}}$ which records the potential bit candidates within the observation interval T. Thus, the size of $\hat{\mathbf{P}}$ increases as the tree level increases. For example, the size of $\hat{\mathbf{P}}$ increases from 2×1 at level 1 to 4×2 at level 2, expressed by

$$\begin{bmatrix} p_1^+ \\ p_1^- \end{bmatrix} \rightarrow \begin{bmatrix} p_1^+ & p_2^+ \\ p_1^+ & p_2^- \\ p_1^- & p_2^+ \\ p_1^- & p_2^- \end{bmatrix}, \quad (5)$$

where p_t^+ and p_t^- denote the candidates of $+1$ and -1 at the t-th level respectively. If $K = 4$, at level 3 the size of matrix $\hat{\mathbf{P}}$ increases from 4×2 to 8×3 firstly, and then shrinks to 4×3 by discarding 4 rows due to the K-best method, expressed by

$$\begin{bmatrix} p_1^+ & p_2^+ \\ p_1^+ & p_2^- \\ p_1^- & p_2^+ \\ p_1^- & p_2^- \end{bmatrix} \rightarrow \begin{bmatrix} p_1^+ & p_2^+ & p_3^+ \\ p_1^+ & p_2^+ & p_3^- \\ p_1^+ & p_2^- & p_3^+ \\ p_1^+ & p_2^- & p_3^- \\ p_1^- & p_2^+ & p_3^+ \\ p_1^- & p_2^+ & p_3^- \\ p_1^- & p_2^- & p_3^+ \\ p_1^- & p_2^- & p_3^- \end{bmatrix} \rightarrow \begin{bmatrix} p_1^+ & p_2^+ & p_3^+ \\ p_1^+ & p_2^+ & p_3^+ \\ p_1^- & p_2^+ & p_3^+ \\ p_1^- & p_2^- & p_3^- \end{bmatrix}. \quad (6)$$

At each subsequent level, the matrix $\hat{\mathbf{P}}$ will be expanded to 8 rows before being reduced back to 4 rows using the K-best algorithm. Ultimately, the matrix $\hat{\mathbf{P}}$ will have a size of $4 \times T$. We use $\tilde{\mathbf{P}}$ to represent the expanded matrix with the

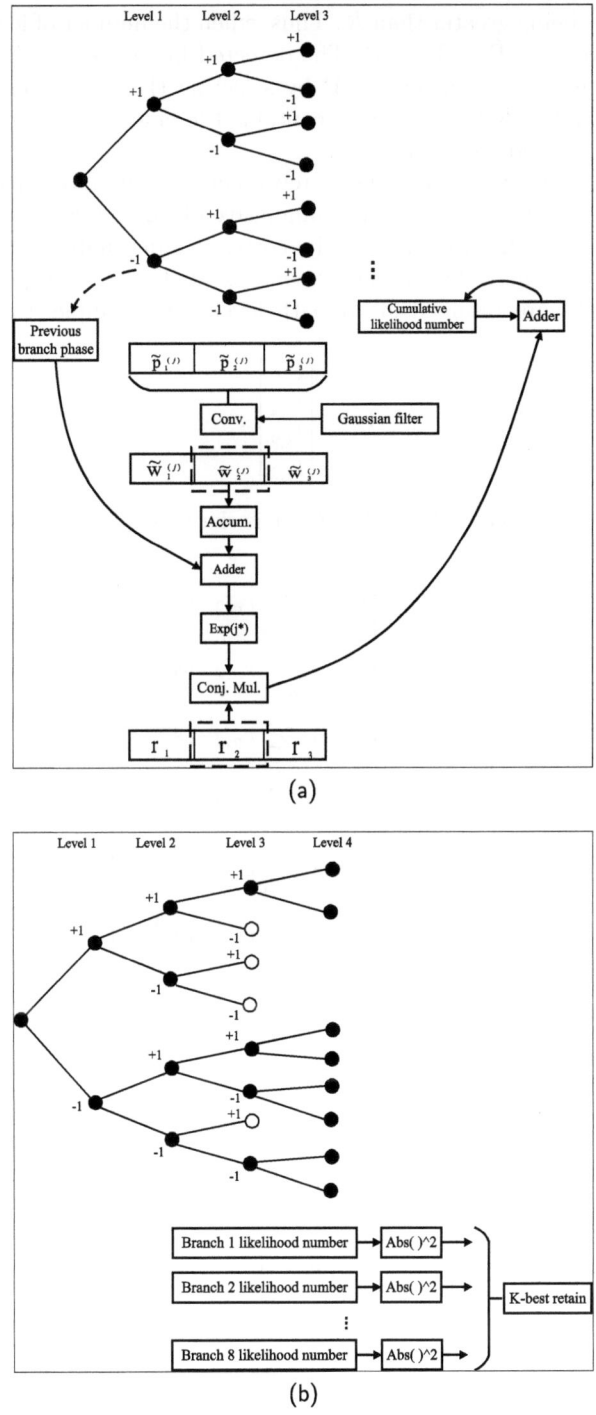

Fig. 3. An interpretation of K-best based GFSK detector.

number of rows being greater than K. Thus, when the number of levels is greater than $\log_2 K$, we have $\hat{\mathbf{P}} \to \tilde{\mathbf{P}} \to \hat{\mathbf{P}}$. The detected bit sequence will be obtained from the K candidate sequences of $\hat{\mathbf{P}}$ by selecting the index corresponding to $\max |\mathbf{l}_T|^2$, where the $K \times 1$ vector $\mathbf{l}_T$ contains the cumulative likelihood values related to the K candidate sequences.

We define a vector $\mathbf{l}_t$ whose elements represent the cumulative likelihood value of all nodes at level t. The higher the cumulative likelihood value, the higher the correlation between the candidate of the corresponding matched filter response and the received signal. Then, the elements of vector $\mathbf{l}_t$ corresponding to the highest K values are retained at the t-th level. For example, the vector $\mathbf{l}_2$ is given by

$$\mathbf{l}_2 = \begin{bmatrix} l_{1,2} \\ l_{2,2} \\ l_{3,2} \\ l_{4,2} \end{bmatrix}. \tag{7}$$

Then, if $K = 4$, the vector $\tilde{\mathbf{l}}_3$ of size 8×1 is derived from the vector $\mathbf{l}_2$ and is given by

$$\tilde{\mathbf{l}}_3 = \begin{bmatrix} \tilde{l}_1 \\ \tilde{l}_2 \\ \tilde{l}_3 \\ \tilde{l}_4 \\ \tilde{l}_5 \\ \tilde{l}_6 \\ \tilde{l}_7 \\ \tilde{l}_8 \end{bmatrix} = \begin{bmatrix} l_{1,2} + \sum_{n=1}^{M} r_{n,2} \cdot (\breve{s}_{n,2}^{(1)})^* \\ l_{1,2} + \sum_{n=1}^{M} r_{n,2} \cdot (\breve{s}_{n,2}^{(2)})^* \\ l_{2,2} + \sum_{n=1}^{M} r_{n,2} \cdot (\breve{s}_{n,2}^{(3)})^* \\ l_{2,2} + \sum_{n=1}^{M} r_{n,2} \cdot (\breve{s}_{n,2}^{(4)})^* \\ l_{3,2} + \sum_{n=1}^{M} r_{n,2} \cdot (\breve{s}_{n,2}^{(5)})^* \\ l_{3,2} + \sum_{n=1}^{M} r_{n,2} \cdot (\breve{s}_{n,2}^{(6)})^* \\ l_{4,2} + \sum_{n=1}^{M} r_{n,2} \cdot (\breve{s}_{n,2}^{(7)})^* \\ l_{4,2} + \sum_{n=1}^{M} r_{n,2} \cdot (\breve{s}_{n,2}^{(8)})^* \end{bmatrix}, \tag{8}$$

where $\breve{s}_{n,2}^{(j)}$ denotes the j-th potential matched filter response corresponding to the 2nd symbol. Since the number of nodes at level 3 is greater than $K = 4$, we retain $K = 4$ elements in the vector $\mathbf{l}_3$ with

$$\mathbf{l}_3 = \text{Top-K} \left| \tilde{\mathbf{l}}_3 \right|^2, \tag{9}$$

where Top-K($\cdot$) denotes selecting the largest K values. The sequence $\mathbf{l}_t$ is also obtained by Top-K $\left|\tilde{\mathbf{l}}_t\right|^2$ where $\tilde{\mathbf{l}}_t$ is updated by adding the corresponding $\sum_{n=1}^{M} r_{n,t} \cdot (\check{s}_{n,t}^{(j)})^*$. Finally from the vector $\mathbf{l}_T$, the detected bit sequence is obtained by selecting the row from $\hat{\mathbf{P}}$ corresponding to largest cumulative likelihood value.

Note that the t-th matched filter response candidates are composed of the three symbols at positions $t-1$, t, and $t+1$ because the Gaussian filter is associated with these three symbols. We refer to Level 3 in Fig. 3a. In order to generate the candidates of $\check{s}_{n,2}^{(j)}$, we pick up the elements of $\tilde{p}_{j,1}$, $\tilde{p}_{j,2}$, and $\tilde{p}_{j,3}$ from the matrix $\tilde{\mathbf{P}}$, and obtain the candidate symbol sequence $\tilde{\mathbf{p}}^{(j)}$ which is expressed by

$$\tilde{\mathbf{p}}^{(j)} = \left[\tilde{\mathbf{p}}_1^{(j)}, \tilde{\mathbf{p}}_2^{(j)}, \tilde{\mathbf{p}}_3^{(j)}\right], \tag{10}$$

where $\tilde{\mathbf{p}}_i^{(j)}$ contains M elements $\tilde{p}_{j,i}$. Then, the Gaussian filtered sequence $\tilde{\mathbf{w}}^{(j)}$ is obtained by convoluting the candidate symbol sequence $\tilde{\mathbf{p}}^{(j)}$ with the Gaussian filter. The Gaussian filtered sequence $\tilde{\mathbf{w}}^{(j)}$ is depicted by

$$\tilde{\mathbf{w}}^{(j)} = \left[\tilde{\mathbf{w}}_1^{(j)}, \tilde{\mathbf{w}}_2^{(j)}, \tilde{\mathbf{w}}_3^{(j)}\right], \tag{11}$$

where $\tilde{\mathbf{w}}_i^{(j)} = \left[\tilde{w}_{i,1}^{(j)}, \tilde{w}_{i,2}^{(j)}, \cdots, \tilde{w}_{i,M}^{(j)}\right]$. Finally, $\check{s}_{n,2}^{(j)}$ is given by

$$\check{s}_{n,2}^{(j)} = \exp\left[j \cdot \left(\tilde{\Theta}_2^{(j)} + \sum_{n=1}^{M} \tilde{w}_{2,n}^{(j)}\right)\right]. \tag{12}$$

In (12), the matrix $\tilde{\Theta}_2^{(j)}$ is expanded from $\Theta_1^{(j)}$ and is given by

$$\Theta_1^{(j)} = \begin{bmatrix} \theta_1^{(1)} \\ \theta_1^{(2)} \\ \theta_1^{(3)} \\ \theta_1^{(4)} \end{bmatrix} \rightarrow \tilde{\Theta}_2^{(j)} = \begin{bmatrix} \tilde{\theta}_2^{(1)} \\ \tilde{\theta}_2^{(1)} \\ \tilde{\theta}_2^{(2)} \\ \tilde{\theta}_2^{(2)} \\ \tilde{\theta}_2^{(3)} \\ \tilde{\theta}_2^{(3)} \\ \tilde{\theta}_2^{(4)} \\ \tilde{\theta}_2^{(4)} \end{bmatrix} \tag{13}$$

where $\theta_1^{(j)}$ denotes the accumulated phase at Level 1. Then, the updated accumulated phase vector $\hat{\mathbf{\Theta}}_2^{(j)}$ at Level 3 is given by

$$\hat{\mathbf{\Theta}}_2^{(j)} = \begin{bmatrix} \hat{\theta}_2^{(1)} \\ \hat{\theta}_2^{(2)} \\ \hat{\theta}_2^{(3)} \\ \hat{\theta}_2^{(4)} \\ \hat{\theta}_2^{(5)} \\ \hat{\theta}_2^{(6)} \\ \hat{\theta}_2^{(7)} \\ \hat{\theta}_2^{(8)} \end{bmatrix} = \begin{bmatrix} \tilde{\theta}_2^{(1)} + \sum_{n=1}^{M} \tilde{\mathbf{w}}_{2,n}^{(1)} \\ \tilde{\theta}_2^{(1)} + \sum_{n=1}^{M} \tilde{\mathbf{w}}_{2,n}^{(2)} \\ \tilde{\theta}_2^{(2)} + \sum_{n=1}^{M} \tilde{\mathbf{w}}_{2,n}^{(3)} \\ \tilde{\theta}_2^{(2)} + \sum_{n=1}^{M} \tilde{\mathbf{w}}_{2,n}^{(4)} \\ \tilde{\theta}_2^{(3)} + \sum_{n=1}^{M} \tilde{\mathbf{w}}_{2,n}^{(5)} \\ \tilde{\theta}_2^{(3)} + \sum_{n=1}^{M} \tilde{\mathbf{w}}_{2,n}^{(6)} \\ \tilde{\theta}_2^{(4)} + \sum_{n=1}^{M} \tilde{\mathbf{w}}_{2,n}^{(7)} \\ \tilde{\theta}_2^{(4)} + \sum_{n=1}^{M} \tilde{\mathbf{w}}_{2,n}^{(8)} \end{bmatrix}. \quad (14)$$

After that, the $K \times 1$ vector $\mathbf{\Theta}_3^{(j)}$ is obtained by retaining K rows of $\hat{\mathbf{\Theta}}_2^{(j)}$ according to the K-best indices.

4 K-Best Based GFSK Detector with LLR Outputs

In an IoT communication system, the long-distance transmission requirement is crucial. In this case, channel coding is an efficient way to improve the communication distance. Instead of a hard-decision channel decoder, a soft-decision channel decoder can bring significant improvement in terms of improved error performance as well as communication distance. However, the soft-decision channel decoder generally requires LLR from the detector. Thus, this paper proposed a K-best GFSK MSDD with LLR outputs. According to [9], $LLR_k = \ln \frac{p(p_k=+1|\mathbf{r})}{p(p_k=-1|\mathbf{r})}$. The LLR output of a GFSK MSDD can be expressed as

$$\ln \frac{p(p_k=+1|\mathbf{r})}{p(p_k=-1|\mathbf{r})} = \min_{p_k \in \Delta_k^-} \frac{1}{2\sigma^2} \sum_{n=1}^{TM} |r_n - \check{s}_n(p_k)|^2 - \min_{p_k \in \Delta_k^+} \frac{1}{2\sigma^2} \sum_{n=1}^{TM} |r_n - \check{s}_n(p_k)|^2 \quad (15)$$

where $\mathbf{r}$ is a vector representing the received signal and containing $r_1, r_2, \cdots, r_{TM}$; $\check{s}_n(p_k)$ denotes the reconstructed transmit symbols upon the assumed p_k. Δ_k^+ and Δ_k^- represents the set of reconstructed transmit samples with $p_k = +1$ and $p_k = -1$ respectively.

In (15), $\sum_{n=1}^{TM} |r_n - \check{s}_n(p_k)|^2$ can be rewritten as:

$$\sum_{n=1}^{TM}|r_n - \breve{s}_n(p_k)|^2 = \sum_{n=1}^{TM}(|r_n|^2 - |\breve{s}_n(p_k)|^2) - 2\Re(\sum_{n=1}^{TM} r_n \breve{s}_n^*(p_k))\cos(\psi)$$
$$-2\Im(\sum_{n=1}^{TM} r_n \breve{s}_n^*(p_k))\cos(\psi) \quad (16)$$
$$= \sum_{n=1}^{TM}(|r_n|^2 - |\breve{s}_n(p_k)|^2) - 2\left|\sum_{n=1}^{TM} r_n \breve{s}_n^*(p_k)\right|\cos(\psi - \alpha)$$

where $\Re()$ and $\Im()$ refer to the real and imaginary parts, respectively; ψ is a random phase error between transmitter and receiver; and α is given by

$$\alpha = \tan^{-1}\frac{\Im\left(\sum_{n=1}^{TM} r_n \breve{s}_n^*(p_k)\right)}{\Re\left(\sum_{n=1}^{TM} r_n \breve{s}_n^*(p_k)\right)}. \quad (17)$$

Since GFSK is a constant amplitude signal, $|\breve{s}_n^*(p_k)|^2$ can be assumed as '1'. Hence, the GFSK MSDD LLR output can be rewritten as

$$LLR_k = \min_{p_k \in \Delta_k^-} \frac{1}{2\sigma^2}\left(-\left|\sum_{n=1}^{TM} r_n \breve{s}_n^*(p_k)\right|\cos(\psi - \alpha)\right)$$
$$- \min_{p_k \in \Delta_k^+} \frac{1}{2\sigma^2}\left(-\left|\sum_{n=1}^{TM} r_n \breve{s}_n^*(p_k)\right|\cos(\psi - \alpha)\right). \quad (18)$$

However, the phase error ψ is unknown in the non-coherent detection. Thereby, we assume that $\psi = \angle\left(\arg_{l_{i,T}} \max |\mathbf{l}_T|^2\right)$.

As for the K-best-based GFSK detector, the LLR generator also employs (18). The critical difference is that the K-best method removes some branches, and then Δ_k^- or Δ_k^+ may be empty. In this case, in terms of the empty set, the LLR is set to be the maximum or minimum value. In other words, if Δ_k^- is empty, $LLR_k = +\rho$; if Δ_k^+ is empty, $LLR_k = -\rho$, where ρ is the maximum absolute value of LLR. For LLR output, we can modify it to

$$LLR_k = \min_{p_k \in \Delta_k^-} \frac{1}{2\sigma^2}\left(-|\mathbf{l}_T|\cdot\cos(\psi - \alpha)\right)$$
$$- \min_{p_k \in \Delta_k^+} \frac{1}{2\sigma^2}\left(-|\mathbf{l}_T|\cdot\cos(\psi - \alpha)\right). \quad (19)$$

5 Simulation Results

In our simulation, we examine the performance of the novel GFSK MSDD under various values of K. The aim is to compare its performance against the theoretical limits of GFSK, focusing on both BER and PER metrics. The packet length is fixed at 37 bytes, aligning with one of the standard lengths specified in Bluetooth protocol test suites. An Additive White Gaussian Noise (AWGN) channel model is assumed in the simulation environment. Moreover, as illustrated in the subsequent figures, we adopt the convolutional coding scheme from Bluetooth standard [10] with a coding rate of 1/2. At the receiving end, two types of decoders are considered: one employing a hard-decision Viterbi algorithm and the other a soft-decision Viterbi algorithm. The soft-decision decoder is designed to receive Log-Likelihood Ratios (LLRs) from the K-best GFSK MSDD detector. The comparative analysis delves into the performance differences between soft- and hard-decision decoding in terms of BER and PER.

Figures 4 and 5 reveal that with an increase in the value of K, both PER and BER performances are enhanced. Notably, when K equals 16, the disparity between the K-best GFSK MSDD's performance and the theoretical performance limit is a mere 0.6 dB at BER = 10^{-3} and 0.2 dB at PER = 10^{-1}. This indicates that the K-best GFSK MSDD can closely approximate the performance limit even with a relatively modest value of K.

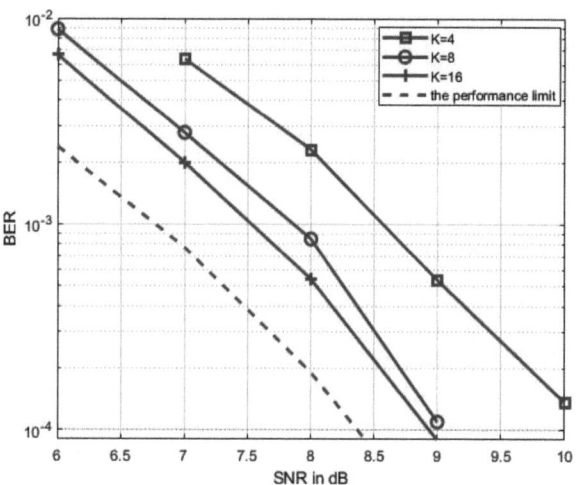

Fig. 4. BER performance of K-best GFSK MSDD $K = 4, 8, 16$.

The efficacy of the K-best GFSK MSDD is further evaluated in Figs. 6 and 7. The BER performance is notably enhanced when employing a soft-decision Viterbi decoder, achieving an approximate gain of 1.2 dB at BER = 10^{-3} and a substantial 2 dB improvement at BER = 10^{-4} over the hard-decision Viterbi decoder. Similarly, the PER performance benefits from the soft-decision Viterbi decoder, with an improvement of about 1.2 dB at PER = 10^{-1} and 2 dB at PER = 10^{-2} compared to the hard-decision counterpart. Furthermore, it is evident that the K-best GFSK MSDD with channel coding consistently surpasses the performance of the system without channel coding in both BER and

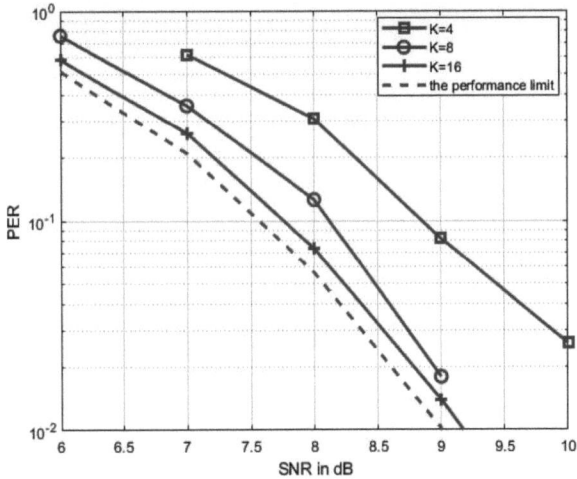

Fig. 5. PER performance of K-best GFSK MSDD $K = 4, 8, 16$.

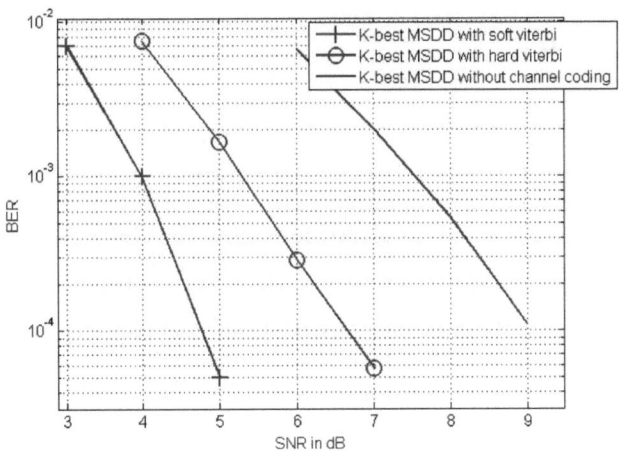

Fig. 6. BER performances of K-best GFSK MSDDs without channel coding; and with channel coding using soft-decision Viterbi and hard-decision Viterbi decoders $K = 16$.

PER assessments, regardless of the decoding strategy—hard-decision or soft-decision—employed by the Viterbi decoder. These findings highlight the significant advantages of integrating soft-decision decoding with K-best detection in GFSK MSDD systems for more reliable wireless communication.

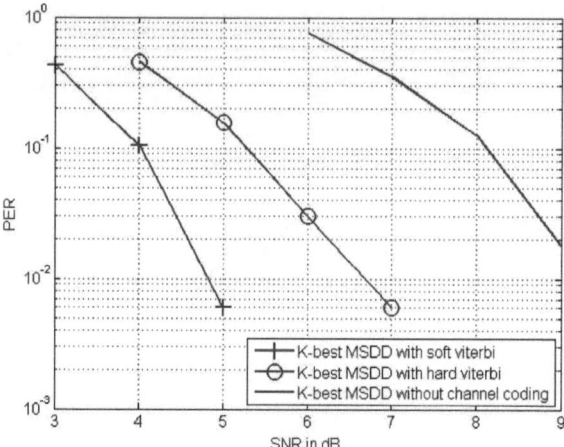

Fig. 7. PER performances of K-best GFSK MSDDs without CC as well as with soft-decision viterbi and hard-decision viterbi decoders for CC, where $K = 16$.

6 Conclusion

In this paper, we have presented a novel approach to GFSK detection by introducing the K-best MSDD technique. This method not only demonstrates the potential to approach the theoretical performance limit of GFSK but also does so with relatively low decoder complexity. The essence of our contribution lies in the strategic integration of a K-best algorithm within the GFSK MSDD framework, which streamlines the detection process without sacrificing accuracy. Moreover, we have designed a Log-Likelihood Ratio (LLR) generation technique tailored specifically for the K-best GFSK MSDD. This technique is a cornerstone in harnessing the full potential of soft channel decoders. By providing LLRs as inputs to these decoders, we facilitate a more effective decoding process, thereby enhancing error correction capabilities. Through rigorous simulation and analysis, our results indicate that the proposed detector can achieve near-optimal performance levels, coming within a fraction of a decibel of the GFSK limit.

References

1. Simon, M., Wang, C.: Differential versus limiter - discriminator detection of narrow-band FM. IEEE Trans. Commun. **31**(11), 1227–1234 (1983)
2. Soltanian, A., Van Dyck, R.: Performance of the Bluetooth system in fading dispersive channels and interference. In: GLOBECOM 2001 - IEEE Global Telecommunications Conference (Cat. No. 01CH37270), vol. 6, pp. 3499–3503 (2001)
3. Yu, B., Yang, L., Chong, C.-C.: Optimized differential GFSK demodulator. IEEE Trans. Commun. **59**(6), 1497–1501 (2011)
4. Scholand, T., Jung, P.: Novel receiver structure for Bluetooth based on modified zero-crossing demodulation. In: GLOBECOM 2003 - IEEE Global Telecommunications Conference (IEEE Cat. No. 03CH37489), vol. 2, pp. 729–733 (2003)

5. Osborne, W., Luntz, M.: Coherent and noncoherent detection CPFSK. IEEE Trans. Commun. **22**(8), 1023–1036 (1974)
6. Divsalar, D., Simon, M.: Multiple-symbol differential detection of MPSK. IEEE Trans. Commun. **38**(3), 300–308 (1990)
7. Tibenderana, C., Weiss, S.: Low-complexity high-performance GFSK receiver with carrier frequency offset correction. In: 2004 IEEE International Conference on Acoustics, Speech, and Signal Processing, vol. 4, pp. iv–933 (2004)
8. He, J., Cui, J., Yang, L., Wang, Z.: A low-complexity high-performance noncoherent receiver for GFSK signals. In: 2008 IEEE International Symposium on Circuits and Systems (ISCAS), pp. 1256–1259 (2008)
9. Kim, S.W., Kim, K.P.: Log-likelihood-ratio-based detection ordering in V-BLAST. IEEE Trans. Commun. **54**(2), 302–307 (2006)
10. Core Specification Working Group. Bluetooth Core Specification v2.1. Bluetooth Specification (2007)

Introduction of Direction of Arrival (DOA) Indoor and Outdoor Navigation Based on Machine Learning

Tong Liu and Wei Lin(✉)

Department of Electrical and Electronic Engineering, The Hong Kong Polytechnic University, Hong Kong SAR, China
tong1997.liu@connect.polyu.hk, w.lin@polyu.edu.hk

Abstract. Direction of arrival (DOA) estimation is a significant technology in navigation and positioning systems. With the development of machine learning, DOA estimation methods based on machine learning have shown great potential in indoor and outdoor navigation. This paper reviews the theoretical background and models of DOA and gives an overview of machine learning methods applied to DOA estimation. It also discusses DOA estimation methods based on machine learning and their applications in navigation. Machine learning can be divided into traditional machine learning methods, deep learning methods, and reinforcement learning methods. Traditional machine learning methods are support vector machines, k-nearest neighbor classification, etc. Deep learning methods consist of deep neural networks, convolutional neural networks, etc. By analyzing the challenges faced by current applications and future development directions, potential strategies for enhancing the performance of DOA estimation are proposed. This study aims to provide a comprehensive technical framework and a reference for future research for researchers in related fields.

Keywords: Direction of arrival · machine learning · navigation systems

1 Introduction

With the development of IoT technology, demand for navigation systems is increasing [1, 2]. DOA (Direction of Arrival) is used to identify the direction of the signal source [3, 4]. In indoor and outdoor navigation systems, DOA can be used to locate and track mobile targets. Although traditional DOA estimation methods, such as MUSIC [5, 6] and ESPRIT [7, 8] perform well under certain conditions, they often have limitations in environments with high noise and strong signal coherence. The emergence of machine learning, especially deep learning technology [9–11], has introduced novel strategies for DOA estimation. Machine learning technology can better capture the propagation characteristics of signals in complex environments and improve positioning accuracy and robustness.

This paper aims to introduce the theoretical background of DOA, analyze the DOA estimation methods using machine learning, explore the current challenges, and propose future research directions.

2 DOA Principles and Models

2.1 DOA Definition

DOA estimation is a positioning technology that determines the direction of a signal source by analyzing the phase or time difference. By measuring the arrival time difference or phase difference of the signal, the azimuth can be estimated [12]. Specifically, when a signal source is near the antenna array, the signal will be received at each antenna on the array with different phases and time differences. This difference in phase and time reflects the azimuth of the signal source relative to the antenna array. By analyzing and processing these phase differences or time differences, the azimuth of the signal source can be determined [3, 4].

2.2 DOA Estimation Model

DOA estimation usually uses an array model to receive signals. Assume there is a uniform linear array (ULA), as shown in Fig. 1. The signal model can be expressed as:

$$X(t) = A \cdot s(t) + n(t) \tag{1}$$

where $X(t)$ is the received signal, A is the array response matrix, $s(t)$ is the signal source, and $n(t)$ is the noise.

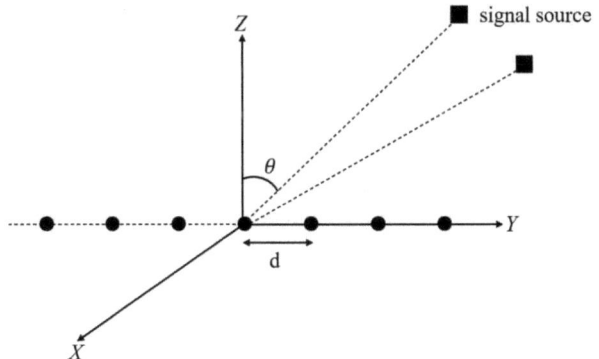

Fig. 1. Uniform linear array (ULA) model.

The response matrix describes the phase difference and amplitude of different signal sources reaching each antenna. Using the received signal and the array response model, various algorithms (such as MUSIC, ESPRIT, machine learning methods, etc.) are applied to estimate DOA.

2.3 Traditional DOA Estimation Methods

Traditional DOA estimation methods include:

Multiple Signal Classification (MUSIC): This technique utilizes eigenvalue decomposition of the signal to process the received signal covariance matrix [5, 6]. It separates between the signal and the noise, utilizing the orthogonality of the noise subspace to identify the maximum spectrum peak for estimating the DOA.

Estimation of Signal Parameters via Rotational Invariance Techniques (ESPRIT): This technique utilizes rotational invariance to model the phase difference of the signal [7, 8]. It directly estimates the DOA by solving a set of linear equations.

Although these methods are effective under specific conditions, they often perform poorly in complex environments.

3 DOA Estimation Based on Traditional Machine Learning Methods

Although traditional methods can achieve good performance when there is a good command of the system, they suffer from a low generation ability and a high correlation between target and noise. Machine learning (ML) and deep learning (DL) have recently made great progress with their strong information extraction ability. Many DOA methods based on ML and DL have been proposed in recent years. In this section, DOA methods based on ML are introduced and discussed.

3.1 Support Vector Machines

The support vector machine (SVM) aims to give a hyperplane to achieve classification or regression and the support vector is the point that is close to the hyperplane, contributing to the search for the optimal hyperplane [2].

In recent years, researchers have applied SVM to DOA estimation. SVM is introduced in [13]. A 4×4 planar sensor array is used, the amount of training data is 400, and the maximum number of incident signals is 4. It generates a rough probability map of DOA from training sets, then classifies the test data using SVM, and performs synthetic scaling on the angle region of interest with high probability. Compared with traditional methods, it performs better in different scenarios and shows better generalization ability, especially in complex electromagnetic environments. The SVM-based method can estimate DOA of both single and multiple signals than the traditional eigenvalue decomposition method allows.

A theoretical relationship is established between the minimum variance distortionless response (MVDR) [14] and MUSIC in [15], which leads to the MVDR-MUSIC and SVM-MUSIC algorithms. This combines the advantages of subspace methods and SVM. The SVM-MUSIC algorithm is obtained by replacing the autocorrelation matrix. Experiments show that the algorithm outperforms MVDR and MUSIC algorithms when dealing with both incoherent and coherent signals.

Gridless DOA estimation is achieved in [16] through 1-b measurement, and DOA estimation is combined with the classification problem. The algorithm is applicable to

ULA and sparse linear array (SLA), and SVM is used for classification to calculate DOA. Then optimization based on Taylor expansion is performed to achieve off-grid DOA estimation. In comparison to Binary Iterative Hard Thresholding (BIHT) [17] and ESPRIT methods, the proposed method performs better in the mean absolute error of DOA estimation to some extent.

SVM is applied in [18] to improve DOA estimation of an electronically steerable parasitic array radiator (ESPAR) antenna [19] by applying SVM to received signal strength (RSS) values recorded at an antenna's output port. The method is based on the radiation patterns and these patterns are used for SVM training. Experiment results show that the SVM algorithm outperforms others in DOA estimation.

SVM is introduced to perform DOA estimation by using its ability to handle nonlinear problems in [20]. First, signal samples are collected through a ULA with a signal-to-noise ratio (SNR) range of 26dB to 6dB and a DOA angle range of 0° to 90°. Then, spatial features and amplitude information are extracted from the received signal. Experimental results show that this method outperforms traditional methods under different SNR conditions, especially providing higher accuracy under low SNR conditions.

3.2 K-Nearest Neighbors Classification

The K-Nearest Neighbors (KNN) can be used to achieve classification or regression. Specifically, the core of KNN is to recognize the unseen sample according to the label of its nearest labeled samples.

A novel locating method named D-KNN is performed by the intersection of directions obtained by adaptive antennas in [21]. D-KNN selects K nearest neighbors based on the minimum Euclidean distance of RSS between the user and the reference point (RP), then selects the best RP in the positioning area. The performance of D-KNN is better than that of traditional KNN, with a smaller mean estimation error (MEE).

A high-frequency positioning method based on 60 GHz millimeter wave is proposed in [22]. This method combines the access point (AP) DOA information with the received signal strength indicator (RSSI) of AP to build a new offline database for online matching. By selecting reference points (RP) with similar characteristics, the weighted K nearest neighbor (WKNN) algorithm is applied to calculate the final position.

A novel WKNN algorithm is proposed in [23]. The algorithm balances RSS difference and signal propagation distance difference to calculate weighted Euclidean distance (WED). Then, the approximate position distance (APD) is obtained. Finally, the nearest RP is selected more accurately based on the APD (APD-WKNN) algorithm to estimate user location. The algorithm performs better in positioning accuracy and has lower complexity.

3.3 Decision Trees and Random Forest

Decision Tree (DT) continuously chooses the optimal feature to divide the training data and build the tree. During testing phase, DT will traverse the tree according to the feature value of the test sample and figure out which tree leaf (representing a class or regression value) the sample belongs to. The random forest consists of multiple DTs. It gives the final classification or regression considering all the results of each DT. Thus, the random forest can achieve a higher accuracy and robustness than DT.

A DT model is trained to estimate the azimuth and elevation in [24]. The DT-based method has robustness and good generalization ability in DOA estimation under various conditions. Comparative analysis demonstrates that performance using DT outperforms the MUSIC algorithm, with an average decrease of over 90% in prediction error and an average reduction of 50% in prediction time.

A radio frequency-based indoor positioning system is implemented in [25]. The KNN, rule-based classifier (JRip), and random forest algorithms are studied. The data is collected to make radio maps of features for indoor positioning purposes. It shows that random forest is the best classifier with more than 91% accuracy compared to KNN and JRip.

A random forest algorithm is proposed to optimize the time difference of arrival (TDOA) positioning system in [26] by utilizing multipath information. The method is applied to outdoor scenarios with "non-cooperative" transmitters, where the sensor is unaware of the signal. Orthogonal frequency division multiplexing (OFDM) signals at 2.45 GHz are located using a vertical whip antenna. Experimental results show that the algorithm achieves accurate predictions.

A machine learning-enabled metasurface is proposed for DOA estimation in [27]. The tunable metasurface is sequentially controlled to produce a range of field intensities at a single receiving probe. The sensed data is processed by a pre-trained random forest model to obtain the incident angle. The metasurface achieves good performance with an accuracy of more than 95% and an error of less than $0.5°$.

3.4 Logistic Regression

Logistic regression (LR) aims to find the optimal parameters to transform input data to a class or value(regression). During the LR training phase, the gradient descent method is employed to update the parameters and minimize the difference in predicted values and labels.

LR model is used to estimate the azimuth using modified total least squares techniques in [28]. A method based on a non-uniform linear sensor array combined with an LR model is proposed in [29]. It is used for multiple incoherent source signals. Unlike previous DOA estimation methods that rely on spatial features, this approach integrates known waveforms and independent sensor noise to construct a maximum likelihood estimation problem associated with multiple LR models. The coefficients are estimated by regression analysis, and the estimated values of angle and gain are obtained from them using the generalized least squares method.

Overall, the traditional machine learning method can help to learn the data pattern and achieve a relatively good performance on DOA tasks. However, the traditional machine learning method highly depends on feature selection. The identification of features needs expert knowledge and cannot be transferred. Besides, a decrease may be observed when there are some redundant features in the data. In addition, due to the development of IoT technology, the scale of the sensor data is too large for traditional machine learning methods to process.

4 DOA Estimation Based on Deep Learning Methods

Deep learning method can automatically extract latent features from the origin input. Thus, feature identification or feature selection is not compulsory for deep learning methods. Besides, the deep learning method contains large quantities of parameters and can perform good learning capacity and robustness. In this section, DOA methods based on DL are reviewed.

4.1 Deep Neural Network

Deep neural network (DNN) achieves strong capacity by introducing multiple layers and activation functions. A simple example of DNN is shown in Fig. 2. DNN mainly contains three parts: the input layer, the hidden layer, and the output layer.

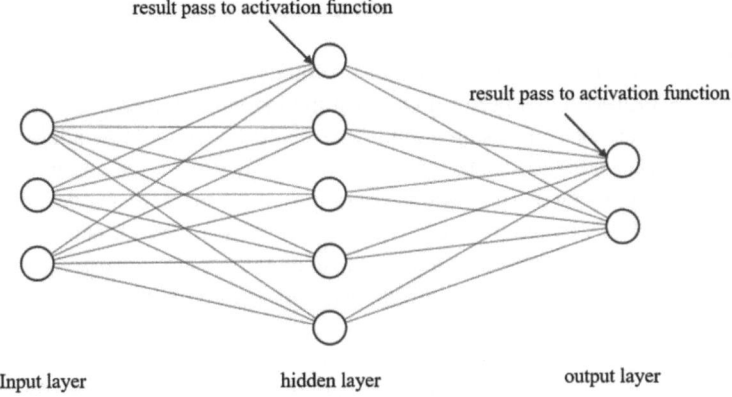

Fig. 2. An example of DNN models.

Specifically, a standard training process is shown below.

1. The origin data is transformed into the numerical value
2. The data is fed into the input layer, which calculates the output based on its weights and biases. This output is then sent to the activation function. At last, the output from the activation function serves as the input for the next layer. We denote the X, y, σ, W, and b as the input of the layer, the output of the layer, the activation function, weight, and bias of the certain layer, then the calculation of a DNN layer is as:

$$y = \sigma(X \times W + b) \qquad (2)$$

3. Each layer in the model follows the step 2 to calculate the output
4. The loss function measures the discrepancy between label and model output. Subsequently, an optimization method is employed to update the model parameters based on the calculated loss.

Specifically, we denote lf, Y_{pred}, Y_{label}, as the loss function, the model output, and the label. Then, the loss of the model can be calculated as follows:

$$loss = lf(Y_{pred}, Y_{label}) \tag{3}$$

We denote W, $W\prime$ and lr as the model parameters, the update model parameters, and the learning rate. Then the updated model parameters can be calculated as follows:

$$W\prime = W - lr * \partial \frac{loss}{W} \tag{4}$$

5. Repeat steps 2–5 until the loss decreases to an ideal level.

By training with large amounts of collected sensor data, DNN shows good performance in DOA research.

A new framework integrating massive multiple-input multiple-output (MIMO) [30] into deep learning is introduced in [31]. First, the DNN is trained offline under different channel conditions with simulation data, and then the estimated DOA spatial spectrum is generated according to the current input data in online learning. Two deep learning-based algorithms are proposed that perform DOA estimation without increasing complexity.

A DNN framework comprising a multi-task autoencoder and a parallel multi-layer classifier is introduced in [32]. The autoencoder is similar to a filter, and multiple components in different spatial sub-regions decomposed by the autoencoder are used as the input of the DNN to reduce the generalization burden. The classifier uses a one-versus-all classification criterion to determine whether there are signal components near a preset direction grid. Compared with the MUSIC algorithm, this method has better performance.

A DNN-based phase enhancement strategy is proposed in [33]. The analysis indicates that the phase feature is crucial for DOA estimation. The DNN only trains for the phase feature. Compared with other methods, this technique performs better in estimation error and goodness of fit (GoF).

A nonlinear mapping is established between the receiving antenna output and its related DOA through DNN in [34]. The detection network significantly reduces the training set size. After training is completed, the testing phase identifies the corresponding DOA based on the current input. The performance of this technology is close to MUSIC and SVR with a relatively low computational complexity.

A novel DNN model is introduced in [35]. Residual technology is introduced to improve the resolution and generalization ability of DNN. The model is applicable to a random number of signals without knowing the number of signals in advance, and can effectively avoid the edge aggravation problem of sub-regions and adapt to larger spatial areas. The model can maintain high resolution with a minimum number of antenna elements and is almost applicable under large SNR differences.

A scheme named DAE-DNN consists of a denoising autoencoder (DAE) and a DNN is proposed in [36]. The DAE improves the robustness under low SNR and the DNN enhances the detection accuracy. The proposed DAE-DNN model outperforms the traditional methods in terms of accuracy and robustness.

4.2 Convolutional Neural Network

Convolutional neural network (CNN) can extract information directly from the origin image data. A simple example of CNN is shown in Fig. 3. The typical CNN mainly contains two parts: the convolution layer and the pooling layer. The convolution layer uses a convolution kernel to extract information. Usually, the kernel size is much smaller than the input feature. Thus, to extract latent features, multiple layers are needed which would lead to a high computation cost and model complexity. To fix this problem, generally, the pooling layer is deployed between convolution layers. The pooling layer can help to decrease the computation cost and improve model robustness.

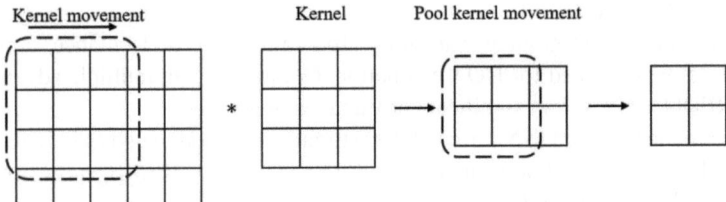

Fig. 3. An example of CNN models.

With the convolution operation, CNN can extract local information or learn the correlation between the different features. Besides, the CNN model contains fewer parameters because of the pooling layer and parameter sharing of the convolution layer. Thus, much DOA research based on CNN is proposed.

A DL network based on CNN is introduced in [37]. Data received by a uniform circular array (UCA) is converted into a directional image, which is formed by the phase component. A CNN is constructed to map from the antenna excitation space to the signal source. Each DOA label consists of the sine and cosine values. The model performs well in mean absolute error (MAE), root mean square error (RMSE), and success rate.

A positioning model based on Wi-Fi RSSI fingerprint data combining CNN and GPR is proposed in [38]. The model is adapted to complex scenarios with multipath effects and multiple APs. The preprocessing algorithm enables CNN to process RSSI vectors from different access points. In addition, the GPR algorithm is utilized to adjust the target point coordinates, further mitigating the overfitting issue of the CNN.

Three neural network models, namely DNN, one-dimensional convolutional neural network (1-D CNN), and two-dimensional convolutional neural network (2-D CNN) are proposed in [39] to minimize the phase distortion and enhance the phase characteristics. A phase enhancement framework is constructed for DOA estimation. RMSE is used to estimate the accuracy and compare each model.

A deep ensemble learning method to achieve fast and accurate two-dimensional DOA estimation is introduced in [40]. The proposed method uses a CNN to map between the spatial covariance matrix and DOA. The output layer contains three neurons: sine and cosine values of the azimuth, and the normalized value of the elevation. To improve prediction performance, an ensemble learning method is proposed to independently train five distinct CNN networks. The final estimation is derived by averaging the prediction results from each CNN. The model performance is compared by MAE, RMSE, and success rate.

A framework that consists of an autoencoder, a feedforward network, a network parameter database, and a series of parallel directed acyclic graph networks (DAGNs) is proposed to improve the DOA estimation performance in non-ideal environments in [41]. Each parallel DAGN subnetwork contains a CNN and two bidirectional long short-term memory (BiLSTM) [42] networks to obtain DOA estimates through regression.

CNN network is used to estimate DOA in extreme noise in [43]. The problem is converted to a multi-label classification by adopting an on-gird approach. The CNN is then trained using the multi-channel data from the true array manifold matrix.

A multi-module CNN, named RFDOA-Net, is proposed in [44]. The network utilizes convolutional layers with different filter sizes. Residual connections are deployed inside each module to prevent gradient vanishing. To evaluate the performance, a synthetic signal dataset is generated for DOA estimation. Compared with multiple advanced DL models, RFDOA-Net shows significant advantages in accuracy.

There are many other CNN-based DOA estimation methods, such as [45, 46], which have also shown advanced performance in terms of accuracy, RSME, success rate, etc. compared with other methods.

4.3 Recurrent Neural Network

Recurrent neural network (RNN) is proposed to learn the relationship between different steps in series data. A simple example of RNN is shown in Fig. 4.

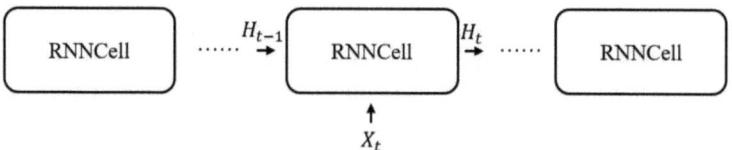

Fig. 4. An example of RNN models.

To explain the mechanism, the schedule of time t is taken as an example. We denote the X_t, H_{t-1}, H_t and W as input of time t, hidden state of t-1, hidden state of t, and model parameters. Then, the calculation of time t is as follows:

$$H_t = W[H_{t-1}, X_t] \tag{5}$$

Through the flow of the hidden state, RNN catches the dependency of different time steps. For DOA research, the input of the model can also be a signal series, thus, there are some DOA models based on the RNN model in recent years.

RNN is used to predict the UAV DOA under the 5G IoT network in [47, 48]. A new framework to combine parallel DOA estimators with Toeplitz matrix reconstruction is proposed in [49]. Each estimator forms an alternative CNN and RNN structure. With the assistance of the Toeplitz source number determination method, the spatial spectrum is recovered more accurately.

A DOA estimation method using a long short-term memory (LSTM) neural network is proposed in [50]. Considering the sequence characteristics of moving targets and the relationship of multi-frame data, LSTM is employed to minimize phase distortion and enhance the accuracy and generalization capability. RNN can mine the statistical characteristics of data and extract more detailed features than traditional DNN methods, so it is used to learn the phase sequence characteristics of moving targets.

A novel DOA estimation method treats DOA estimation as a time series problem through a signal processing algorithm and an RNN to improve the performance is introduced in [51]. It utilizes the spatial power spectrum (SPS) as the input feature of the gated recurrent unit (GRU) to learn the spatial power spectrum features.

5 DOA Estimation Based on Reinforcement Learning

DOA-based AI model needs to face the complexity and the dynamicity of the environment. Although online training can help alleviate the problem of data shift between offline training and real-time environment, the model structure is usually fixed and shows poor generalization ability when facing a dynamic environment. In this circumstance, re-modeling is required to achieve the ideal performance in a real-time application, which is time-consuming. To alleviate this problem, reinforcement learning has been utilized in DOA in recent research. A simple example of reinforcement learning is shown in Fig. 5.

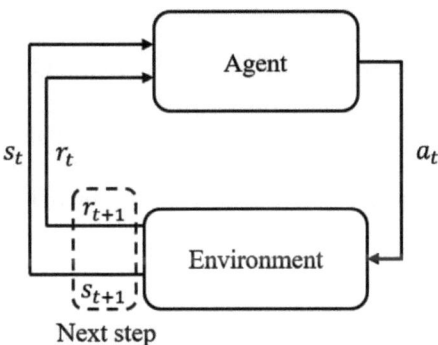

Fig. 5. An example of reinforcement learning models.

We denote $s_t, r_t, a_t, r_{t+1}, S_{t+1}$ as the state of time t, reward of time t, action of time t, state of time t + 1, reward of time t + 1. Then, the schedule of reinforcement learning at time t is as follows:

1. The agent observes the s_t and r_t. The agent optimizes its strategy according to the r_t. Then, the agent gives the a_t to the environment.
2. Taking the a_t, the environment gives the r_{t+1} and S_{t+1}

When the reinforcement learning model faces a different environment, the model can adjust the strategy to adapt to the new environment. It is pointed out in [52] that deep reinforcement learning can be used for DOA estimation, which can improve the generalization ability and reduce the time cost.

Combining massive MIMO technology with deep reinforcement learning, a UAV navigation method is proposed in [53]. A deep Q network (DQN) is designed to extract features of MIMO. After training, DQN can make decisions based on RSS and obtain the best location selection strategy, realizing UAV navigation based on Q-learning.

A reinforcement learning-based multi-target detection algorithm for a massive MIMO cognitive radar (MMIMO CR) system is proposed in [54]. The algorithm is fully data-driven and does not require offline knowledge about the interference distribution or its covariance matrix, thus avoiding the model mismatch problem.

Several multi-agent deep reinforcement learning (MDRL) [55] models are proposed to achieve target localization for UAV in [56]. Reinforcement learning is used to enable intelligent agents to learn in complex environments. The actor-critic structure is combined with CNN. The centralized learning and decentralized exection method is used to ensure the scalability of the number of agents, making the solution adaptable to complex and dynamic environments.

A fingerprint-based positioning method combines deep reinforcement learning (DRL) and intelligent reflective surface (IRS) is proposed in [57]. Firstly, a fingerprint positioning system supporting the IRS is constructed, and a list of regularly configured RSSIs is collected into a database. When the receiver sends a positioning request, the database is compared with the RSSI data measured online, and the best position estimate is determined using KNN. In addition, a DRL-based IRS configuration selector is developed to optimize the IRS configuration and minimize positioning errors.

6 Application Challenges and Future Prospects

In indoor navigation, DOA estimation based on machine learning can be combined with Wi-Fi signals for positioning. In outdoor navigation, DOA estimation of GPS signals can improve positioning accuracy, especially in urban environments.

6.1 Application Challenges

Although machine learning-based DOA estimation methods have made some progress, they still face the following challenges:

Low accuracy with insufficient data: Machine learning models usually require a large amount of data for training, and the cost of data collection and annotation is high.

High accuracy with high cost: In practical applications, DOA estimation requires real-time processing capabilities, and the computational complexity of machine learning methods may affect real-time performance.

Environmental changes: Different environmental conditions will affect the signal propagation characteristics, resulting in insufficient model generalization capabilities.

6.2 Future Prospects

Future research can focus on the following directions:

Data enhancement: Generate more samples through data enhancement technology to improve the robustness.

Model compression: Design the model considering both accuracy and efficiency. Model optimization techniques, such as Bayesian optimization methods [58], can be used to reduce model parameters while maintaining high accuracy. Besides, knowledge distillation [59] can be used to generate lightweight and high-performance models from large models, which are trained with large numbers of data and have high accuracy.

Domain adaptation: Domain adaptation (DA) [60] aims to achieve the knowledge transfer between different but related domains. In the DOA estimation task, DA techniques can be utilized to help the AI model obtain more generalization ability when facing different environments such as the level of noise and the arrived angle range.

7 Conclusion

DOA estimation based on machine learning has broad application prospects in indoor and outdoor navigation, and can effectively improve positioning accuracy and robustness. Although there are still some challenges, with the development of technology, more efficient and accurate DOA estimation is expected to be achieved in the future. This paper provides researchers with a comprehensive technical framework and hopes to inspire more research and application exploration.

Acknowledgement. This work was supported in part by the Research Grants Council of the Hong Kong, SAR, China, under Project PolyU 25213623 and Project AoE/E-101/23-N, and in part by Hong Kong Innovation and Technology Fund, under Project PRP/047/24FX.

References

1. Chen, L., et al.: Robustness, security and privacy in location-based services for future IoT: a survey. IEEE Access **5**, 8956–8977 (2017)
2. Hung, J.C., et al.: Innovative computing. In: Proceedings of the 4th International Conference on Innovative Computing (IC 2021), vol. 791 (2022)
3. Krim, H., Viberg, M.: Two decades of array signal processing research: the parametric approach. IEEE Sig. Process. Mag. **13**(4), 67–94 (1996)
4. Bekkerman, I., Tabrikian, J.: Target detection and localization using MIMO radars and sonars. IEEE Trans. Signal Process. **54**(10), 3873–3883 (2006)
5. Schmidt, R.: Multiple emitter location and signal parameter estimation. IEEE Trans. Antennas Propag. **34**(3), 276–280 (1986)
6. Swindlehurst, A.L., Kailath, T.: A performance analysis of subspace-based methods in the presence of model errors. I. The MUSIC algorithm. IEEE Trans. Sig. Process. **40**(7), 1758–1774 (1992)
7. Roy, R., Kailath, T.: ESPRIT-estimation of signal parameters via rotational invariance techniques. IEEE Trans. Acoust. Speech Signal Process. **37**(7), 984–995 (1989)
8. Zoltowski, M.D., Haardt, M., Mathews, C.P.: Closed-form 2-D angle estimation with rectangular arrays in element space or beamspace via unitary ESPRIT. IEEE Trans. Signal Process. **44**(2), 316–328 (1996)

9. Du, K.-L., et al.: Neural methods for antenna array signal processing: a review. Sig. Process. **82**(4), 547–561 (2002)
10. Rawat, A., Yadav, R.N., Shrivastava, S.C.: Neural network applications in smart antenna arrays: a review. AEU-Int. J. Elec. Commun. **66**(11), 903–912 (2012)
11. LeCun, Y., Bengio, Y., Hinton, G.: Deep learning. Nature **521**, 7553, 436–444 (2015)
12. Simon, B.C., Supriya, M.H., Jayanthi, V.S.: Deep neural based beamforming techniques for Direction of Arrival (DOA) estimation. In: 2021 International Symposium on Ocean Technology (SYMPOL). IEEE (2021)
13. Donelli, M., et al.: An innovative multiresolution approach for DOA estimation based on a support vector classification. IEEE Trans. Antennas Propag. **57**(8), 2279–2292 (2009)
14. Wolfel, M., McDonough, J.: Minimum variance distortionless response spectral estimation. IEEE Signal Process. Mag. **22**(5), 117–126 (2005)
15. El Gonnouni, A., et al.: A support vector machine MUSIC algorithm. IEEE Trans. Antennas and Propagation **60**(10), 4901–4910 (2012)
16. Gao, Y., et al.: Gridless 1-b DOA estimation exploiting SVM approach. IEEE Commun. Lett. **21**(10), 2210–2213 (2017)
17. Koep, N., Mathar, R.: Binary iterative hard thresholding for frequency-sparse signal recovery. In: WSA 2017, 21th International ITG Workshop on Smart Antennas. VDE (2017)
18. Tarkowski, M., Kulas, L.: RSS-based DoA estimation for ESPAR antennas using support vector machine. IEEE Antennas Wirel. Propag. Lett. **18**(4), 561–565 (2019)
19. Ohira, T., Iigusa, K.: Electronically steerable parasitic array radiator antenna. Electron. Commun. Japan (Part II: Electronics) **87**(10), 25–45 (2004)
20. Yadav, S., Wajid, M., Usman, M.: Support vector machine-based direction of arrival estimation with uniform linear array. Adv. Comput. Intell. Tech. **1**, 253–264 (2020)
21. Roshanaei, M., Maleki, M.: Dynamic-KNN: a novel locating method in WLAN based on angle of arrival. In: 2009 IEEE Symposium on Industrial Electronics and Applications, vol. 2, no. 1, pp. 722–726 (2009)
22. Wei, Z., et al.: DoA-LF: a location fingerprint positioning algorithm with millimeter-wave. IEEE Access **5**, 22678–22688 (2017)
23. Wang, B., et al.: A novel weighted KNN algorithm based on RSS similarity and position distance for Wi-Fi fingerprint positioning. IEEE Access **8**, 30591–30602 (2020)
24. Carballeira, A.R., de Figueiredo, F.A.P., Brito, J.M.C.: Simultaneous estimation of azimuth and elevation angles using a decision tree-based method. Sensors **23**(16), 7114 (2023)
25. Jedari, E., et al.: Wi-Fi based indoor location positioning employing random forest classifier. In: 2015 International Conference on Indoor Positioning and Indoor Navigation (IPIN), vol. 1, pp. 1–5. IEEE (2015)
26. de Sousa, M.N., Thomä, R.S.: Applying random forest and multipath fingerprints to enhance TDOA localization systems. IEEE Antennas Wirel. Propag. Lett. **18**(11), 2316–2320 (2019)
27. Huang, M., et al.: Machine–learning-enabled metasurface for direction of arrival estimation. Nanophotonics **11**(9), 2001–2010 (2022)
28. Gu, J.-F., Zhu, W.-P., Swamy, M.N.S.: Joint 2-D DOA estimation via sparse L-shaped array. IEEE Trans. Sig. Process. **63**(5), 1171–1182 (2015)
29. Gu, J.-F., Zhu, W.-P., Swamy, M.N.S.: Fast and efficient DOA estimation method for signals with known waveforms using nonuniform linear arrays. Sig. Process. **114**, 265–276 (2015)
30. Catbas, F.N., Brown, D.L., Emin Aktan, A.: Parameter estimation for multiple-input multiple-output modal analysis of large structures. J. Eng. Mech. **130**(8), 921–930 (2004)
31. Huang, H., et al.: Deep learning for super-resolution channel estimation and DOA estimation based massive MIMO system. IEEE Trans. Veh. Technol. **67**(9), 8549–8560 (2018)
32. Liu, Z.-M., Zhang, C., Yu Philip, S.: Direction-of-arrival estimation based on deep neural networks with robustness to array imperfections. IEEE Trans. Antennas Propag. **66**(12), 7315–7327 (2018)

33. Xiang, H., et al.: A novel phase enhancement method for low-angle estimation based on supervised DNN learning. IEEE Access **7**, 82329–82336 (2019)
34. Chen, M., Gong, Y., Mao, X.: Deep neural network for estimation of direction of arrival with antenna array. IEEE Access **8**, 140688–140698 (2020)
35. Liu, W.: Super resolution DOA estimation based on deep neural network. Sci. Rep. **10**(1), 19859 (2020)
36. Chen, D., et al.: Robust DoA estimation using denoising autoencoder and deep neural networks. IEEE Access **10**, 52551–52564 (2022)
37. Zhu, W., Zhang, M.: A deep learning architecture for broadband DOA estimation. In: 2019 IEEE 19th International Conference on Communication Technology (ICCT), vol. 1, pp. 244–247. IEEE (2019)
38. Zhang, G., et al.: Wireless indoor localization using convolutional neural network and Gaussian process regression. Sensors **19**(11), 2508 (2019)
39. Xiang, H., et al.: Improved de-multipath neural network models with self-paced feature-to-feature learning for DOA estimation in multipath environment. IEEE Trans. Veh. Technol. **69**(5), 5068–5078 (2020)
40. Zhu, W., et al.: Two-dimensional DOA estimation via deep ensemble learning. IEEE Access **8**, 124544–124552 (2020)
41. Cong, J., et al.: Robust DOA estimation method for MIMO radar via deep neural networks. IEEE Sens. J. **21**(6), 7498–7507 (2020)
42. Graves, A., Graves, A.: Long short-term memory. In: Supervised Sequence Labelling with Recurrent Neural Networks, pp. 37–45 (2012)
43. Papageorgiou, G.K., Sellathurai, M., Eldar, Y.C.: Deep networks for direction-of-arrival estimation in low SNR. IEEE Trans. Sig. Process. **69**, 3714–3729 (2021)
44. Akter, R., et al.: RFDOA-Net: an efficient ConvNet for RF-based DOA estimation in UAV surveillance systems. IEEE Trans. Veh. Technol. **70**(11), 12209–12214 (2021)
45. Zhao, F., et al.: DOA estimation method based on improved deep convolutional neural network. Sensors **22**(4), 1305 (2022)
46. Wu, X., et al. A gridless DOA estimation method based on convolutional neural network with Toeplitz prior. IEEE Sig. Process. Lett. **29**, 1247–1251 (2022)
47. Xiao, K., et al.: Trajectory prediction of UAV in smart city using recurrent neural networks. In: ICC 2019–2019 IEEE International Conference on Communications (ICC), vol. 1, pp. 1–6. IEEE (2019)
48. Xiao, K., et al.: Abnormal behavior detection scheme of UAV using recurrent neural networks. IEEE Access **7**, 110293–110305 (2019)
49. Yao, Y., Lei, H., He, W.: A-CRNN-based method for coherent DOA estimation with unknown source number. Sensors **20**(8), 2296 (2020)
50. Xiang, H., et al.: Improved direction-of-arrival estimation method based on LSTM neural networks with robustness to array imperfections. Appl. Intell. **51**, 4420–4433 (2021)
51. Babakhani, P., et al.: Bluetooth direction finding using recurrent neural network. In: 2021 International Conference on Indoor Positioning and Indoor Navigation (IPIN), vol. 1, pp. 1–7. IEEE (2021)
52. Luong, N.C., et al.: Applications of deep reinforcement learning in communications and networking: a survey. IEEE Commun. Surv. Tutor. **21**(4), 3133–3174 (2019)
53. Huang, H., et al.: Deep reinforcement learning for UAV navigation through massive MIMO technique. IEEE Trans. Veh. Technol. **69**(1), 1117–1121 (2019)
54. Ahmed, A.M., et al.: A reinforcement learning based approach for multitarget detection in massive MIMO radar. IEEE Trans. Aerosp. Elec. Syst. **57**(5), 2622–2636 (2021)
55. Gronauer, S., Diepold, K.: Multi-agent deep reinforcement learning: a survey. Artif. Intell. Rev. **55**(2), 895–943 (2022)

56. Alagha, A., et al.: Target localization using multi-agent deep reinforcement learning with proximal policy optimization. Fut. Gener. Comput. Syst. **136**, 342–357 (2022)
57. Wang, Y., et al.: Intelligent reflecting surface enabled fingerprinting-based localization with deep reinforcement learning. IEEE Trans. Veh. Technol. **72**(10), 13162–13172 (2023)
58. Snoek, J., Larochelle, H., Adams, R.P.: Practical bayesian optimization of machine learning algorithms. Adv. Neural. Inf. Process. Syst. **25**, 1–9 (2012)
59. Gou, J., et al.: Knowledge distillation: a survey. Int. J. Comput. Vis. **129**(6), 1789–1819 (2021)
60. Farahani, A., et al.: A brief review of domain adaptation. In: Advances in Data Science and Information Engineering: Proceedings from ICDATA 2020 and IKE 2020, pp. 877–894 (2021)

Automatic Preamble Extraction System for LPWAN Signals

Chun Ho Kong and Haibo Hu(✉)

The Hong Kong Polytechnic University, Kowloon, Hong Kong
hopkins.kong@connect.polyu.hk, haibo.hu@polyu.edu.hk

Abstract. With the global adoption of Internet-of-Things (IoT) technologies, inexpensive IoT devices with various IoT wireless protocols are deployed in license-free ISM bands. These Low-Power Wide-Area Network (LPWAN) signals can be in open or proprietary standards with different security implications. Preambles that are prefixed in the packets are often found in these protocols and are normally used for tasks like signal detection and Automatic Gain Control (AGC). In terms of unintended uses, they can be used for device identification, reverse engineering of protocol features, intrusion detection of wireless attacks, performing jamming attacks, and more. Therefore, it is important to localize and extract the preamble portion of LPWAN signals for physical layer reverse engineering, especially for proprietary protocols and further enhancing the security of the spectrum. In this regard, we provide an automatic preamble extraction system that seeks the common prefix of arbitrary frequency-varying LPWAN signals from the IQ data received by Software-Defined Radios (SDRs). Existing methods usually employ supervised machine learning algorithms with labeled data for training. Our algorithm eliminates the need to use labeled data and only relies on the constant nature of the preamble in the spectrogram to perform extractions. Experimental results demonstrate an average precision (IoU@0.75) of up to 96.3% for LoRa signals with varying bandwidth, spreading factors, data, and preamble lengths.

Keywords: Internet of Things · Preamble Extraction · Radio Frequency

1 Introduction

With the emergence and the global deployment of Internet of Things (IoT) technologies, plenty of inexpensive IoT devices with different Low-Power Wide-Area Network (LPWAN) IoT Wireless Protocols are installed on a large scale. This involves various areas including security, smart grid, smart cities, smart homes, healthcare, etc., [15,26] with a huge global market share of over 8 trillion U.S. dollars by the year 2030. [3] However, due to limited computation power on these IoT devices, concerns regarding information security [8,16,27] and privacy issues [5,14,28] including counterfeit and rogue [2] IoT Devices have been raised.

Regardless of open or proprietary standards, these LPWAN IoT wireless protocols are often transmitted with preambles that are prefixed on the packets before the actual payload. This could be useful to wake up a transceiver in low power mode, identify the start of a new packet frame, or even perform Automatic Gain/Frequency Control (AGC/AFC) on the receiver front end. [12] The existence of preamble fields in the physical (PHY) layers can be seen in various protocols, including BLE [4], LoRa [1], UNB [7] and more. Due to the essential nature of preambles in wireless protocols for a wireless receiver to function properly, with the fact that they are usually unencrypted and constant, disallowing the preamble to be received by a legitimate receiver with methods like reactive jamming [18] would cause degradation of wireless networks, or even denial of services [19]. Moreover, other uses that exploit the unique nature of the preambles can also be found, such as RF fingerprinting for device classification and identifications [21–23], or performing PHY level wireless intrusion detection system [20].

Enabled by Software-Defined Radios (SDRs), [10] Commercial, Off The Shelf (COTS) radio frontend are widely available on the market, which can be purchased and connected to a regular PC for performing most of the signal processing tasks. The usage of SDRs is closely related to Cognitive Radio (CR) [9], which provides reconfigurability for radios to adapt to variations of new wireless standards and incorporate new services and applications when they arise. By utilizing SDRs and continuously acquiring Inphase, Quadrature (IQ) data to a computer, it is possible to effortlessly reconfigure the radio receiver on the fly and receive different LPWAN signals across the ISM bands of various bandwidth, protocol parameters, or modulation schemes, with minimal costs.

To this end, with COTS SDRs as the means to access the Radio Frequency (RF) spectrum and the underlying LPWAN signals in the ISM bands, we provide a system that performs automatic LPWAN signals preamble extraction, by exploiting the nature of the preambles that are fixed and located at the start of the packet in PHY layer. This system processes the spectrogram of arbitrary frequency-varying LPWAN signals and works on multiple LPWAN signals containing different protocol parameters, preamble lengths, and RF bandwidths. In recent research, techniques, like supervised Machine Learning (ML), are often used that require running an algorithm on expensive GPUs with labeled data for training, or only apply to specific protocols and protocol parameters. Hence, we aim to provide an alternate system that eliminates the need to perform ML and is generic enough to work on multiple LPWAN IoT wireless protocols.

The remainder of the paper is organized as follows. In Sect. 2, related work in the field of preamble extraction and their applications are outlined. Section 3 presents the design of our system. Section 4 shows empirical evaluation results against different protocol parameters.

2 Related Work

To perform preamble extractions, researchers were often presented as a standalone algorithm, or as a part of an attack procedure that requires usage of preamble. These works can be broadly categorized by the involvement of using ML techniques.

For ML approaches, existing work such as [21] performed cross-correlation on slides of IQ data in the time domain, generating a feature map for ML uses. Similar to this work, it aims to exploit the nature of the preamble but in the application of identifying UAV drones. However, these UAVs wireless protocols inherently bear with large bandwidth ($\geq$ 10 MHz) ranges, which unlike those in LPWAN IoT signals, are narrow band in nature and inherently contain less information available for extractions. For works like [11,17,24], they utilize a custom deep neural network to detect the preamble without localizing and extracting the relevant preambles, and some require prior knowledge of the signals.

Same with the issues above, non-ML approaches like [13,23,29] often rely on the prior knowledge of the signal, including the underlying protocol format and modulation schemes to perform preamble extractions or detections. In [25], demonstrated a method that employed Discrete Fourier Transform (DFT), which is similar to our method, but they worked on the overall samples to obtain the Power Spectral Density (PSD) of them and find cross-correlation of different PSD sequences. It assumes high bandwidth Wi-Fi signals and only performs feature extraction of the preamble for classification without localization.

To close the research gap, we present a method that does not involve labeling datasets for training ML models, while allowing preamble localization on narrowband LPWAN signals, especially Sub-GHz ones. This is achieved by using the spectrogram traces which will be outlined in the next section.

3 System Design

The overview of the system is outlined in Fig. 1. LPWAN signals from the SDR are extracted and processed on the computer and fed into our proposed signal comparison and extraction engine, before outputting the localization information of the preamble for extraction.

3.1 LPWAN Packets IQ Extraction

After the LPWAN signals are received by the SDR, these complex IQ data are processed on the computer for individual LPWAN packet extraction. IQ data can be represented as:

$$x[k] = \text{Re}(x[k]) + j\,\text{Im}(x[k]) = I[k] + jQ[k], \tag{1}$$

where k is the IQ sample index and $I[k]$ and $Q[k]$ represent the real (in-phase) and imaginary (quadrature) parts of the signal, respectively.

In our experiment, we generated an annotated IQ dataset for individual LPWAN packets across the spectrum with random frequency and bandwidth, whereas in reality, algorithms like Variance Trajectory or simply performing RF Squelch [6] can be used to split the LPWAN Packets IQ data for further processing. Formally, individual LPWAN packets IQ data can be represented as:

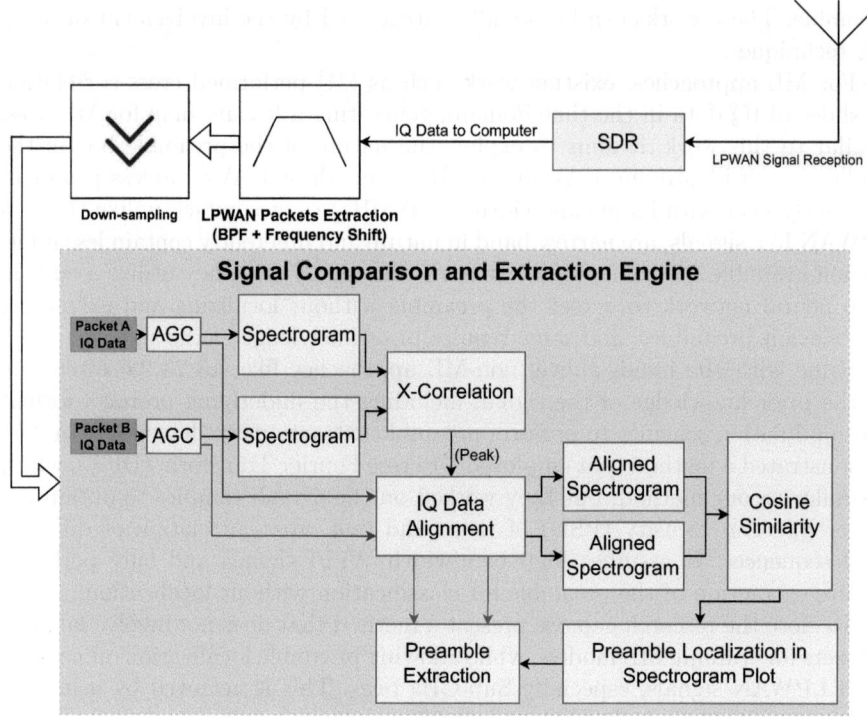

Fig. 1. System Overview

$$x[n,k] = \text{Re}(x[n,k]) + j\,\text{Im}(x[n,k]) = I[n,k] + jQ[n,k], \quad (2)$$

where n is the LPWAN packet index, k is the IQ sample index in n and $I[n,k]$ and $Q[n,k]$ represent the in-phase and quadrature parts of n LPWAN packet, respectively.

To decrease the data required for signal processing, while allowing higher frequency resolution in the subsequent steps, the overall sample rate of the IQ data will be reduced.

An FIR band-pass filter on the LPWAN packet n will first be designed:

$$h_n[m] = \sum_{k=-\infty}^{\infty} H(e^{j\omega}) e^{j\omega m} d\omega, \quad (3)$$

where $h_n[m]$ is the impulse response of the FIR filter for specific LPWAN signal, and $H(e^{j\omega})$ is the desired frequency response that encompasses the bandwidth of the actual LPWAN signal. Then this filter is applied to the wide-band SDR baseband signal:

$$y[n,k] = \sum_{m=0}^{M-1} h[m] x[n, k-m], \quad (4)$$

where $y[n, k]$ is the filtered output for packet n, $x[n, k]$ is the input signal, and M is the filter order.

The filtered LPWAN signal is then shifted to 0 Hz by multiplying the frequency offset:

$$z[n, k] = y[n, k] \cdot e^{-j2\pi f_c k / f_s}, \tag{5}$$

where $z[n, k]$ is the new baseband signal, f_c is the center frequency of the LPWAN packet, and f_s is the original sampling rate.

To reduce the sampling rate, which is subject to the Nyquist rate:

$$w[n, l] = z[n, kD], \tag{6}$$

where $w[n, l]$ is the downsampled signal, D is the downsampling factor, and $l = \lfloor k/D \rfloor$.

The new sampling rate is subjected to the Nyquist rate: $f_{s,new} = f_s/D \geq 2B$, where B is the actual bandwidth of the LPWAN signal, to satisfy the Nyquist criterion.

3.2 Signal Comparison and Extraction Engine

This engine performs actual LPWAN packets IQ data comparison and preamble extraction. To ascertain the consistency of the signal power of IQ data, Automatic Gain Control (AGC) is used by iteratively applying the following algorithm to all input IQ samples:

1. Apply current gain (initial gain is 1):

$$y[n] = G[n] \cdot x[n] \tag{7}$$

2. Calculate sample power:

$$|y[n]|^2 = \Re(y[n])^2 + \Im(y[n])^2 \tag{8}$$

3. Calculate error:

$$e[n] = |y[n]|^2 - R^2, \tag{9}$$

where $R = 1$ is the reference magnitude.
4. Calculate scaled error:

$$e_{scaled}[n] = \frac{\alpha^2 \cdot e[n]}{\alpha^2 \cdot |y[n]|^2 + \epsilon}, \tag{10}$$

where α is the adaptation rate and $\epsilon = 1 \times 10^{-10}$ is a small constant to provide stability and to prevent division by zero.
5. Update gain:

$$G[n+1] = G[n] \cdot (1 - e_{scaled}[n]) \tag{11}$$

6. Limit gain:

$$G[n+1] = \text{clip}(G[n+1], G_{min}, G_{max}), \tag{12}$$

where $G_{min} = 1 \times 10^{-6}$ and $G_{max} = 65536$ are the minimum and maximum allowable gains, respectively.

After AGC, Short-Time Fourier Transforms (STFTs) are taken to generate spectrograms of individual LPWAN packets. STFT operation on $x[n]$ (which is the downsampled $w[n,l]$) to produce $X[k]$ can be expressed as:

$$X[k,m] = \sum_{n=kR}^{kR+N-1} x[n]W[n-kR]e^{-j\frac{2\pi mn}{N}}, \tag{13}$$

where:

- k is the index of the time bin.
- m is the index of the frequency bin.
- $W[n-kR]$ is the window function
- N is the FFT size, and in our case $N = 2048$ to balance computation efficiency and frequency resolution.
- R is the hop size, and in our case $R = N = 2048$.

Here, Blackman window in $W[n-KR]$ is utilized, which is given by the following equation:

$$W[n] = 0.42 - 0.5\cos\left(\frac{2\pi n}{N-1}\right) + 0.08\cos\left(\frac{4\pi n}{N-1}\right), \tag{14}$$

where n is the sample index, and N is the total number of samples in the window.

After obtaining the STFT vectors in (13), to obtain a spectrogram, the magnitudes of the STFT bins are squared:

$$P[k,m] = |X[k,m]|^2 \tag{15}$$

Aiming further aligning the LPWAN signals, cross-correlation is performed for two LPWAN packet spectrograms:

$$R_{x_1 x_2}[l] = \sum_{n=-\infty}^{\infty} x_1[n] \cdot x_2^*[n-l], \tag{16}$$

where x_2^* denotes the complex conjugate of x_2.

The peak magnitude of the output is used to align both IQ data:

$$l_{peak} = \arg\max_{l} |R_{x_1 x_2}[l]| \tag{17}$$

The second LPWAN signals are aligned to the first by shifting it by l_{peak} samples:

$$x_2^{aligned}[n] = x_2[n + l_{peak}] \tag{18}$$

For each pair of LPWAN packets, cosine similarity is calculated along the aligned spectrogram to acquire the overall similarity metric along the frequency-time spectrogram plot:

Let $P_1[k,m]$ and $P_2[k,m]$ be the aligned spectrograms of two LPWAN packets, where k represents the frequency bin and m represents the time frame. For a window of size $WinSz$, the cosine similarity at time index i is given by:

$$CS(i) = \frac{\sum_{k=0}^{K-1} \sum_{j=0}^{WinSz-1} P_1[k, i+j] \cdot P_2[k, i+j]}{\sqrt{\sum_{k=0}^{K-1} \sum_{j=0}^{WinSz-1} P_1[k, i+j]^2} \sqrt{\sum_{k=0}^{K-1} \sum_{j=0}^{WinSz-1} P_2[k, i+j]^2}}, \tag{19}$$

where K is the number of frequency bins, $WinSz$ is the window size, and i ranges from 0 to $M - WinSz$, with M being the total number of time frames.

Finally, the localization and extraction of the preambles are executed according to a certain similarity threshold $T_{SimStart}, T_{SimEnd}$ which denotes the threshold that considers the two LPWAN signals started to be similar and dissimilar, respectively, from the aligned spectrogram plot.

4 Result and Discussions

To evaluate the performance of the proposed system, we have generated 10 batches of fully annotated LoRa signal datasets, with each batch containing 300 LoRa packets varied in transmission power, frequency, signal bandwidth, spreading factor, random data payload, and most importantly, preamble lengths. The following table describes the datasets for evaluation (Table 1):

Table 1. Dataset description for each batch

Bandwidth	Spreading Factor	Preamble Length (Symbols)	Number of Packets
125 KHz	7	6	25
		12	25
	11	6	25
		12	25
250 KHz	7	6	25
		12	25
	11	6	25
		12	25
500 KHz	7	6	25
		12	25
	11	6	25
		12	25

Here are the parameters supplied to the algorithm:

- AGC $\alpha = 1 \times 10^{-8}$
- Cosine similarity matching window size $WinSz = 32$
- Cosine similarity similar thresholds $T_{SimStart} = 0.35$, $T_{SimEnd} = 0.2$

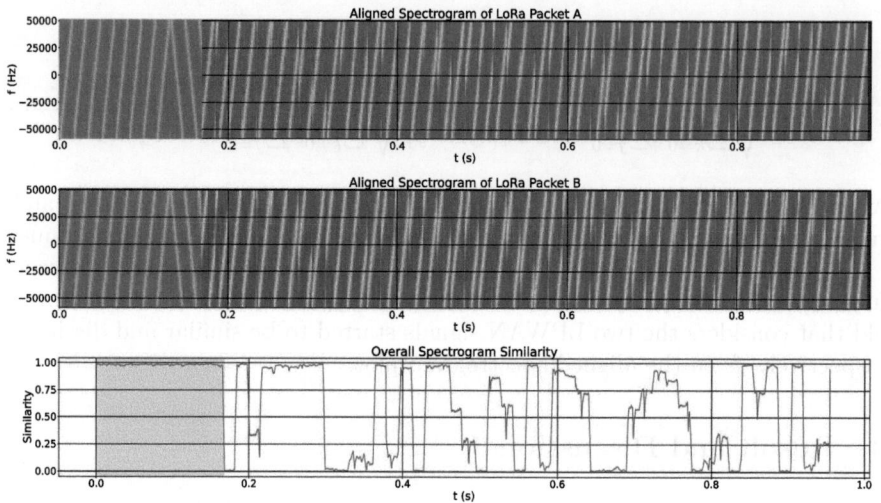

Fig. 2. Comparison and Extraction Example (BW = 125 KHz, SF = 11, Preamble Length = 6), areas in red indicates detected preamble locations

All of the LPWAN packets of the same class are supplied to the system for comparison, resulting in 300 comparisons for each class. To evaluate the performance of the system, we calculated the Intersection over Union (IoU) against the preamble range of the ground truth of the actual common prefix of the LPWAN signals, which is given by:

$$\text{IoU} = \frac{|P \cap G|}{|P \cup G|}, \quad (20)$$

where P denotes the prediction interval, G the ground truth interval, $|\cdot|$ denotes the length of the interval. Two IoU thresholds are selected $t \in \{0.5, 0.75\}$, and their Average Precision (AP) is calculated by:

$$\text{AP} = \sum_{k=1}^{N} P(k) \cdot \Delta R(k) \quad (21)$$

where:

- N is the total number of predictions.
- $P(k) = \frac{\sum_{i=1}^{k} \mathbb{K}[\text{IoU}_i \geq t]}{k}$ is the precision at position k.
- $R(k) = \frac{\sum_{i=1}^{k} \mathbb{K}[\text{IoU}_i \geq t]}{N}$ is the recall at position k.
- $\Delta R(k) = R(k) - R(k-1)$ is the change in recall between position k and $k-1$.
- $\mathbb{K}[\text{IoU}_i \geq t] = 1$ if $\text{IoU}_i \geq t$, 0 otherwise.

For each signal class, the AP is given in Table 2. An example comparison and extraction result can be found in Fig. 2.

Table 2. AP of each class

Bandwidth	Spreading Factor	Preamble Length (Symbols)	AP@0.5	AP@0.75
125 KHz	7	6	95.67%	75.33%
		12	98.33%	84.00%
	11	6	100.00%	96.33%
		12	100.00%	96.33%
250 KHz	7	6	97.67%	79.67%
		12	99.33%	85.67%
	11	6	99.67%	94.67%
		12	100.00%	94.67%
500 KHz	7	6	74.00%	56.00%
		12	78.33%	64.33%
	11	6	89.00%	71.67%
		12	83.67%	73.67%

For narrow-band signals, AP of above 95.6% can be observed, especially for longer preamble lengths and spreading factors because of more time-axis features. If the signal is higher in bandwidth (i.e. 500 KHz), there is a drop in AP which indicates the frequency-axis features do not benefit from the increasing amount of data. This is anticipated as larger bandwidth signals result in higher noise power (AWGN in this case), which reduces correlation. Moreover, these signals could also dilute the usable features as a fixed number of STFT bins is used in correlation. In general, this algorithm shows promising results in localizing and extracting LPWAN preambles that bear different protocol parameters, bandwidth, and preamble lengths.

5 Conclusion

In this paper, we proposed a system that allows preamble localization and extraction on arbitrary frequency-varying LPWAN signals, without the need to label training datasets for Machine Learning. We experimented on multiple frequencies, bandwidth, and protocol parameters of LoRa packets and discovered that over 95.6% AP can be achieved with narrow-band signals. In the future, we plan to extend the algorithm to more real-world LPWAN technologies, especially those that are not frequency-varying in nature, like Phase-Shift Keying (PSK). We believe that the existing phase information inside the spectrogram can be obtained and used against preamble extraction, given that the original phase and frequency offset are correctly compensated. We will also explore a hybrid lightweight ML approach that combines the current algorithm to further enhance this system, especially for signals that are larger in bandwidth.

References

1. Lora alliance (2024). https://lora-alliance.org/. Accessed 24 July 2024
2. Afzal, S., Faisal, A., Siddique, I., Afzal, M.: Internet of things (IoT) security: issues, challenges and solutions. Int. J. Sci. Eng. Res. **12**(6), 52 (2021)
3. Al-Sarawi, S., Anbar, M., Abdullah, R., Al Hawari, A.B.: Internet of things market analysis forecasts, 2020-2030. In: 2020 Fourth World Conference on Smart Trends in Systems, Security and Sustainability (WorldS4), pp. 449–453 (2020). https://doi.org/10.1109/WorldS450073.2020.9210375
4. BluetoothSIG: Specification of the Bluetooth System, Core Version 4.0. Bluetooth SIG (2010). https://www.bluetooth.org/docman/handlers/downloaddoc.ashx?doc_id=229737
5. Chen, Z., Hu, H., Yu, J.: Privacy-preserving large-scale location monitoring using bluetooth low energy. In: 2015 11th International Conference on Mobile Ad-Hoc and Sensor Networks (MSN), pp. 69–78. IEEE (2015)
6. Damak, N., Krall, C., Storn, R.: Optimization of squelch parameters for efficient resource allocation in software defined radios. In: Proceedings of SDR-WInnComm-Europe 2013, pp. 57–63 (2013)
7. Ferré, G., Simon, E.P.: An introduction to Sigfox and LoRa PHY and MAC layers (2018). https://hal.archives-ouvertes.fr/hal-01774080. Working paper or preprint
8. Hassija, V., Chamola, V., Saxena, V., Jain, D., Goyal, P., Sikdar, B.: A survey on IoT security: application areas, security threats, and solution architectures. IEEE Access **7**, 82721–82743 (2019). https://doi.org/10.1109/ACCESS.2019.2924045
9. Haykin, S.: Cognitive radio: brain-empowered wireless communications. IEEE J. Sel. Areas Commun. **23**(2), 201–220 (2005)
10. Jondral, F.K.: Software-defined radio–basics and evolution to cognitive radio. EURASIP J. Wirel. Commun. Netw. **2005**, 1–9 (2005)
11. Khan, M.U., Testi, E., Paolini, E., Chiani, M.: Preamble detection in asynchronous random access using deep learning. IEEE Wirel. Commun. Lett. **13**(2), 279–283 (2024). https://doi.org/10.1109/LWC.2023.3325918
12. Lee, Y.S., Park, Y.O.: BER performance of AGC in high-speed portable internet system. In: IEEE 60th Vehicular Technology Conference, 2004. VTC2004-Fall, vol. 7, pp. 4794–4797 (2004). https://doi.org/10.1109/VETECF.2004.1405004
13. Leonardi, M., Di Fausto, D.: ADS-B signal signature extraction for intrusion detection in the air traffic surveillance system. In: 2018 26th European Signal Processing Conference (EUSIPCO), pp. 2564–2568. IEEE (2018)
14. Li, R., Hu, H., Ye, Q.: Rftrack: stealthy location inference and tracking attack on wi-fi devices. IEEE Trans. Inf. Forensics Secur. (2024)
15. Mahmood, S.: Review of internet of things in different sectors: recent advances, technologies, and challenges. J. Internet Things **3**(1), 19 (2021)
16. Neshenko, N., Bou-Harb, E., Crichigno, J., Kaddoum, G., Ghani, N.: Demystifying IoT security: an exhaustive survey on IoT vulnerabilities and a first empirical look on internet-scale IoT exploitations. IEEE Commun. Surv. Tutor. **21**(3), 2702–2733 (2019). https://doi.org/10.1109/COMST.2019.2910750
17. Ninkovic, V., Vukobratovic, D., Valka, A., Dumic, D.: Preamble-based packet detection in wi-fi: a deep learning approach. In: 2020 IEEE 92nd Vehicular Technology Conference (VTC2020-Fall), pp. 1–5 (2020). https://doi.org/10.1109/VTC2020-Fall49728.2020.9348765
18. Pirayesh, H., Zeng, H.: Jamming attacks and anti-jamming strategies in wireless networks: a comprehensive survey. IEEE Commun. Surv. Tutor. **24**(2), 767–809 (2022)

19. Rahbari, H., Krunz, M., Lazos, L.: Swift jamming attack on frequency offset estimation: the achilles' heel of OFDM systems. IEEE Trans. Mob. Comput. **15**(5), 1264–1278 (2015)
20. Ramsey, B.W., Mullins, B.E., Temple, M.A., Grimaila, M.R.: Wireless intrusion detection and device fingerprinting through preamble manipulation. IEEE Trans. Dependable Secure Comput. **12**(5), 585–596 (2014)
21. Reus-Muns, G., Chowdhury, K.R.: Classifying UAVs with proprietary waveforms via preamble feature extraction and federated learning. IEEE Trans. Veh. Technol. **70**(7), 6279–6290 (2021). https://doi.org/10.1109/TVT.2021.3081049
22. Scanlon, P., Kennedy, I.O., Liu, Y.: Feature extraction approaches to RF fingerprinting for device identification in femtocells. Bell Labs Tech. J. **15**(3), 141–151 (2010)
23. Schnur, S.R.: Identification and classification of OFDM based signals using preamble correlation and cyclostationary feature extraction. Ph.D. thesis, Citeseer (2009)
24. Sun, H., Kaya, A.O., Macdonald, M., Viswanathan, H., Hong, M.: Deep learning based preamble detection and TOA estimation. In: 2019 IEEE Global Communications Conference (GLOBECOM), pp. 1–6. IEEE (2019)
25. Suski II, W.C., Temple, M.A., Mendenhall, M.J., Mills, R.F.: Using spectral fingerprints to improve wireless network security. In: IEEE GLOBECOM 2008 - 2008 IEEE Global Telecommunications Conference, pp. 1–5 (2008). https://doi.org/10.1109/GLOCOM.2008.ECP.421
26. Fernández-Caramés, T.M., Fraga-Lamas, P.: A review on the use of blockchain for the internet of things. IEEE Access **6**, 32979–33001 (2018)
27. Tang, L., Hu, H.: Ohea: secure data aggregation in wireless sensor networks against untrusted sensors. In: Proceedings of the 29th ACM International Conference on Information & Knowledge Management, pp. 1425–1434 (2020)
28. Zheng, H., Hu, H.: Missile: a system of mobile inertial sensor-based sensitive indoor location eavesdropping. IEEE Trans. Inf. Forensics Secur. **15**, 3137–3151 (2019)
29. Zou, H., Ban, T., Zhuang, Z.: An S mode ADS-B preamble detection algorithm. In: 2019 IEEE 5th International Conference on Computer and Communications (ICCC), pp. 178–182. IEEE (2019)

AI and Information Security

An Automated Smart Contract Framework for NFT-Based Warranty Management System with Account Abstraction

Sai Sambhab Chaini[1], Lopamudra Hota[1], Arun Kumar[1(✉)], and Peter Han Joo Chong[2]

[1] Department of Computer Science and Engineering, National Institute of Technology, Rourkela, Rourkela 769008, India
kumararun@nitrkl.ac.in
[2] School of Engineering, Computer and Mathematical Sciences, Auckland University of Technology, Auckland, New Zealand

Abstract. Current warranty systems for businesses with diverse products or extensive customer bases are bogged down by complexity. Traditional warranty management often faces challenges such as complexity, fraud, cost, customer dissatisfaction, and inefficiency. Businesses need to address these issues to effectively manage warranties, reduce costs, and improve customer satisfaction. For example, by implementing blockchain-based solutions, businesses can streamline warranty processes, reduce fraud, and enhance transparency. This research work presents an innovative, blockchain-powered solution to mitigate the above-stated issues. Each product is assigned an unique and secure warranty in the form of a Non-Fungible Token (NFT). This NFT tracks ownership and expiry directly on the blockchain, guaranteeing its validity and eliminating potential fraud. To ensure a user-friendly experience, account abstraction simplifies interaction with the system and reduces transaction fees. Finally, Gelato Ops automates the secure burning of expired NFTs upon reaching their designated date. This system streamlines warranty management for businesses, enhances trust through automation, and leverages the security and immutability of blockchain technology.

Keywords: NFT Warranty · Smart Contract Automation · Blockchain · Account Abstraction · Verification of warranties

1 Introduction

According to a forecast by eMarketer [1], global retail e-commerce sales in the year 2022 exceeded an impressive amount of 4.9 trillion USD, which is an increase from the previous year's figure of 4.2 trillion USD. This signifies a compound annual growth rate (CAGR) of 10.2% as compared to a 2.1% CAGR for global offline retail sales. According to Statista, electronics accounted for 30.6% of total global online retail sales in 2023 [2]. This is the largest share of any product category, followed by apparel and fashion (22.2%) and home and garden (17.9%) [2]. Nevertheless, a difficulty emerges in the dissemination of warranties for these commodities, as it is imperative to authenticate the possessor and the expiration of the warranty. Presently, there exist two classifications of guarantees: first, physical warranties that necessitate documentation, are vulnerable to manipulation, and are not transferable. Second, digital warranties are preserved in a centralized system and do not ensure comprehensive transfers of ownership. NFTs began gaining massive attraction with CryptoPunks in October 2017 due to the most significant art sale in history by Mike Winkelmann, a digital artist who sold his work for nearly $70 million [3]. The art industry has commercialized and popularized NFTs, and the volume and value of NFT transactions are rapidly growing [3]. NFT-based warranties have the ability to offer a resolution to all of these aforementioned challenges. The issuance of NFT-based warranties can be executed with swiftness and ease.

Once an NFT warranty has been minted, it can be transferred to the customer without any difficulty. Moreover, NFT-based warranties can streamline the procedure of warranty servicing. Furthermore, NFT-based warranties possess the added benefit of being resistant to tampering and easily verifiable. NFT-based warranties can revolutionize the warranty industry by making it more secure, transparent, and efficient. They offer benefits like reduced fraud, improved customer satisfaction, and increased sales. Additionally, they can enhance sustainability by reducing paper waste and conserving resources. Previous scholarly works pertaining to NFT-based systems offer illustrations of various methodologies for utilizing NFTs, such as the car rental paradigm [4], the house rent resolver [6], and the renting of playing cards [4]. Furthermore, these NFTs prove beneficial in addressing challenges necessitating the verification of assets and their proprietors.

1.1 Motivation

The act of issuing warranties presents a dilemma that is anticipated to expand exponentially in the forthcoming years due to the forecasts on retail sales, an expanding customer base, and the assortment of items dispatched. NFTs will prove to be a valuable approach in addressing the challenge of issuing, verifying, and disposing of warranties whenever the need arises.

1.2 Objectives

- To create a NFT-based Warranty Issue System for implementation by various manufacturers and retail sellers in order to distribute NFTs upon sale of warranted items.
- To provide an algorithm to verify and authenticate valid owners of the warranties.
- To automate the burning process of NFT for expired warranties.
- To implement account abstraction to decrease gas cost on user.

2 Literature Review

The authors in [7] define the characteristics of the OpenSea NFT marketplace, which is one of the largest platforms for trading NFTs. The researchers collected and analyzed sales data from January 2019 to December 2021, focusing on user behaviour, economic trends, and network properties. Their research concludes that a small subset of buyers and sellers, known as heavy-hitters, dominated the marketplace. They have also observed a shift in sales from gaming-related NFTs to art and collectibles. The findings contribute to a better understanding of the NFT market and its development. The authors suggest that further research is needed to explore market trends within specific NFT categories and across different platforms. On the other hand, the authors in [3] offer a comprehensive examination of the potential influence of NFTs within the realm of electronic commerce. The researchers systematically collected and organized research papers, in addition to conducting a survey aimed at gauging public perspectives on NFTs. The outcomes suggest that the majority of respondents hold a positive view on the potential benefits of NFTs for e-commerce, citing various factors such as authentication, trust, customer value, commodity, security, and proof of ownership. The article emphasizes the necessity for industry-wide security standards and further research to address concerns pertaining to environmental impact, security, fraud, and intellectual property rights. Figure 1 and Fig. 2 present the familiarity with digital assets and familiarity ratings with digital assets among users respectively.

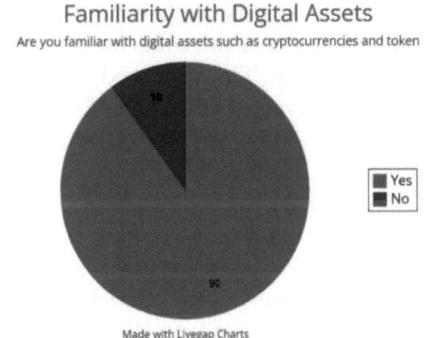

Fig. 1. Demographic representation of Familiarity with Digital Assets [3].

The authors in [4] focus on Ethereum Improvement Proposal (EIP) ERC-4519, which aims to standardize the definition of NFTs on the Ethereum blockchain. NFTs are unique assets that can generate their own Ethereum addresses [4] and have different owners. The article illuminates the benefits of ERC-4519 in diverse scenarios, encompassing tangible resources such as IoT devices. The Ethereum blockchain is explained as a public blockchain that allows

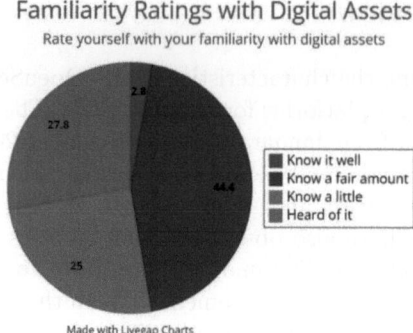

Fig. 2. Representation of Familiarity ratings with digital assets [3].

for the execution of smart contracts [5]. The benefits of ERC-4519 in diverse utilization scenarios are illustrated. Instances encompass the application of ERC-4519 non-fungible tokens in the realm of the digital art market, where individuals may grant or lease their creative masterpieces. In music platforms, the melodies can be vented and their permits can be shared temporarily.

The authors in [6] present a proof of concept for renting and selling smart homes using blockchain technology, specifically the Ethereum network. The study explores the features of ERC-4519 NFTs and discusses their application in the rental process. By deploying a smart contract on the Goerli Testnet and utilizing a Pycom Wipy 3.0 device as the smart home gateway [6], the researchers successfully demonstrated the feasibility of their proposed rental solution. Overall, the research work presents a promising solution for renting and selling smart homes using blockchain technology. The proposed system has the potential to improve the security, transparency, and efficiency of smart home rental transactions.

The research work in [8] put forward a proposal for a warranty system that is based on blockchain technology and utilizes NFTs as a means to tackle the challenges associated with traditional physical and digital warranties. The proposed system generates product warranties that possess unique token IDs, with the product and warranty details being stored in the metadata. Additionally, the image and metadata are uploaded to the InterPlanetary File System (IPFS) for permanent storage on the blockchain. This ensures that the warranties are resistant to tampering, can be verified, and transferred, and their ownership can be tracked. The system offers various advantages, such as protection against physical damage, evidence of ownership, authenticity, the ability to trace the history of the product, and simplified transfer of ownership in the event of resale.

The authors in [9] discuss the significance of safeguarding NFTs and digital artworks in the long run. It delves into the existing body of literature on blockchain technology in the management of art and heritage, with a specific focus on NFT-based digital art.

The research work presented in [10,11] explores the integration of EIP-4337 as a foundational standard for account abstraction (AA) in Ethereum's Splurge phase, aiming to enhance user accessibility and expand DApp functionalities. The study delves into the operating mechanisms of account abstraction, advancements in accounts, wallets, and standards related to its development, and conducts a preliminary security evaluation. The paper recognizes the potential security enhancements achieved through AA updates and provides an in-depth analysis of security vulnerabilities and their mitigation with the adoption of account abstraction. The analysis covers various Ethereum account-related vulnerabilities and demonstrates that account abstraction can mitigate these issues by introducing a set of security enhancements. The research work provides a comprehensive overview and evaluation of the concept of account abstraction and its potential impact on Ethereum's ecosystem [10].

2.1 Research Gap

Previous research conducted on NFT-based systems works with standards which are not widespread, thereby rendering the adoption challenging with exceedingly limited documentation and support. Certain systems also employ centralized databases, which undermine the fundamental nature of Decentralized Applications. Additionally, the utilization of automation is exceedingly sparse necessitating further research. The scalability and security concerns are also matters that promote the use of account abstraction to reduce cost to end users.

3 Methodology

3.1 System Environments

To ensure the secure storage and management of accounts, both the seller and buyer are required to have a Metamask wallet [12]. These wallets serve as a platform for issuing and receiving warranties. The buyer's wallet address is crucial for authentication purposes.

To address warranties that have expired, a resolver contract must be uploaded to Gelato Ops. Gelato Network is a web3 automation network that allows developers to automate and relay smart contract executions across EVM-based blockchains like Ethereum [13].

To optimize the user experience, a Paymaster is set as an entry point into the Warranty Manager contract. This ensures that the Paymaster contract covers the total gas costs, eliminating the need for users to pay gas fees directly. The Paymaster and Account Abstraction are configured using Alchemy's Account Abstraction Infrastructure.

The prerequisites for minting the NFT encompass the following elements: the wallet address of the seller and buyer, a unique product ID, the URI of the product image, the time of creation, and the expiration time. Technologies used are: React, Gelato Network, Gelato Ops, Alchemy, Polygon Testnet, Solidity, and IPFS.

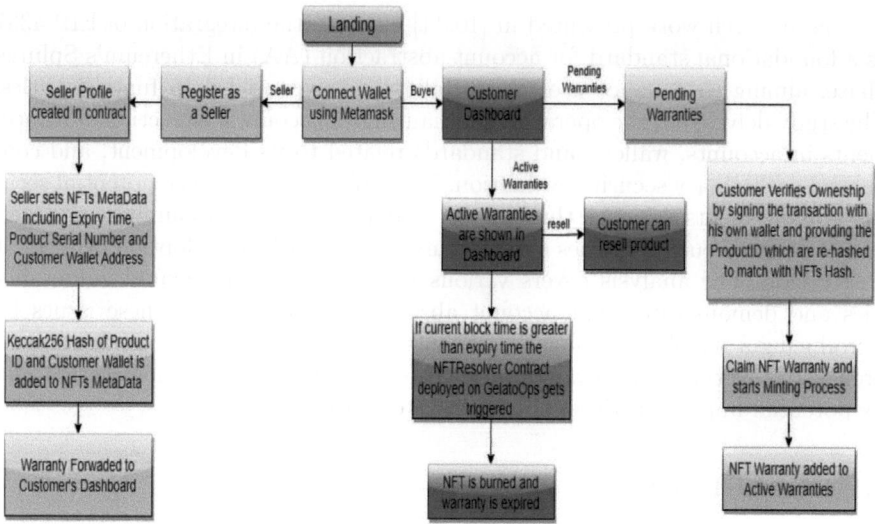

Fig. 3. Schematic Representation of the proposed NFT Warranty system

3.2 Proposed Approach

The proposed methodology involves the seller generating a new NFT Warranty on their dashboard by providing essential information. A bundler then validates the transaction and forwards it to the Entry Point Contract. A unique identifier is created using the seller's address and product ID. A verifyHash is generated to authenticate the seller, and the warranty metadata is updated to include the verifyHash and ID. This process ensures the security and integrity of the NFT Warranties.

Creating a New NFT Warranty. To begin, the seller generates a new NFT Warranty on their Dashboard by providing the seller's address, Expiry Date, and Product ID. Then, the bundler contacts the Paymaster to validate the transaction and after validation forwards the user operation to the Entry Point Contract. The Seller's Address and Product ID are combined to form a unique identifier for the specific warranty, which is then used to associate it with the various products sold by the seller and the corresponding warranties issued for each. Next, a verifyHash is generated, which is a hash produced through the utilization of the keccak 256 hashing mechanism. This hashing mechanism encodes both the buyer address and the productId simultaneously. This hash is subsequently employed to authenticate the specific seller who possesses the corresponding warranty. The metadata of the NFT Warranty is then amended to encompass all the essential information, including the verifyHash and ID.

Verifying and Claiming Warranty. The NFTs are displayed in the buyer's Dashboard as a Pending Warranty that requires verification and must be claimed

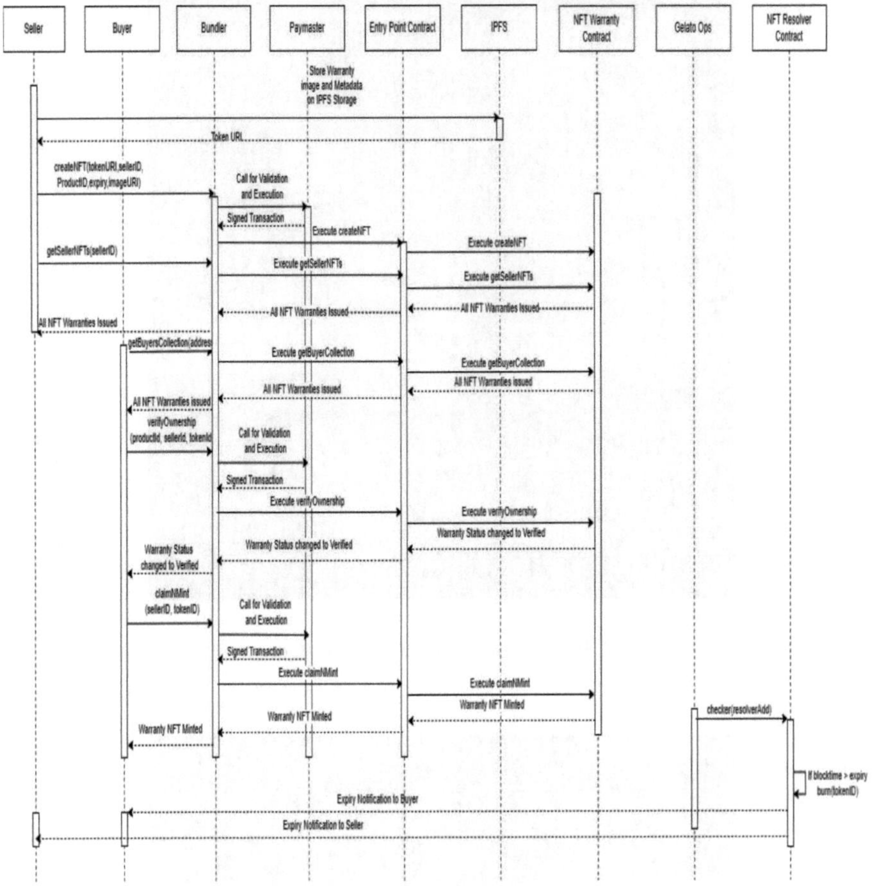

An Automated Smart Contract Framework   235

Fig. 4. Sequence Diagram of proposed NFT Warranty System

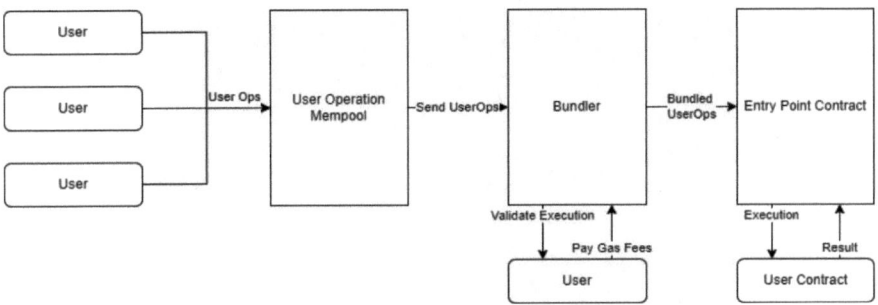

Fig. 5. User Operations using Account Abstraction

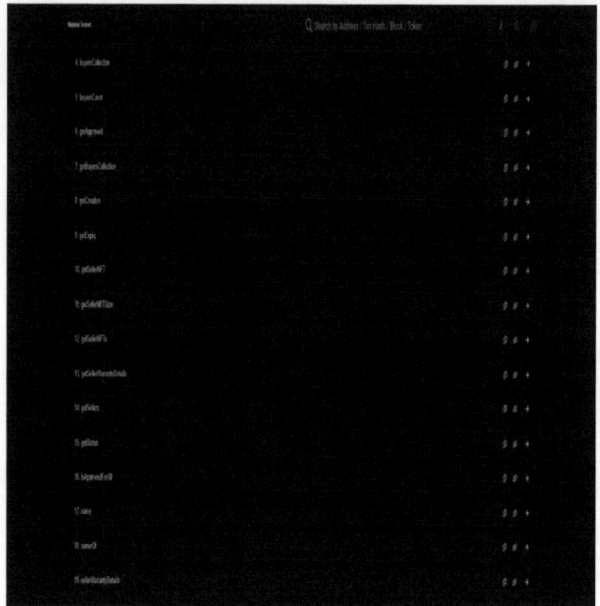

Fig. 6. Read Operations in Smart Contract

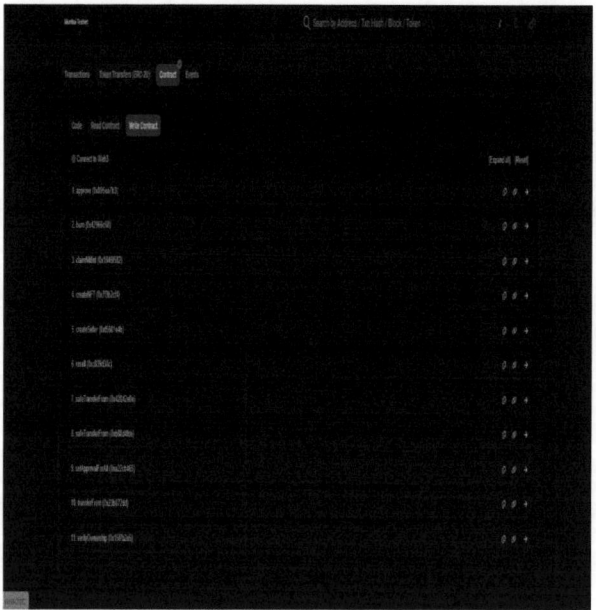

Fig. 7. Write Operations in Smart Contract

by the Buyer. To authenticate ownership of a specific warranty, a hash is once again generated using the keccak 256 hashing functions. The input for this process includes the user address and the product ID of the purchased item. This resulting hash is compared with the verifyHash variable found in the NFTs metadata. If these hashes are a match, the owner's identity is confirmed, granting them the ability to claim and create the NFT. Consequently, the NFT Warranty is activated, enabling the buyer to utilize any services offered under the warranty.

Expiry of Warranty. The burn function is an uncomplicated function that dispatches the non-fungible token (NFT) to a wallet that cannot be spent and is inaccessible to any individual. In addition, the NFT Warranty is designated as Expired. When the current block time surpasses the expiry time linked to the warranty, a Gelato Ops-uploaded NFT Resolver contract triggers the burn function for a specific warranty ID. However, the seller retains the ability to peruse the preceding data.

Sponsoring Gas Fees Using Paymaster. All user operations that require a gas fee to be paid are first validated by the bundler with the paymaster. So the user just signs the transaction then the paymaster signs the transaction with the gas fees and it is then forwarded to the entry point contract that executes the user operation using the NFT Warranty Contract.

Figure 3 represents the flow diagram of the proposed system and Fig. 4 shows the sequence diagram of the proposed NFT Warranty System and represents the seller and buyer interaction with the proposed system. User Operations in Account Abstraction is represented in Fig. 5.

4 Results and Analysis

4.1 Requirements

Table 1 lists all software and frameworks required for the proposed system.

4.2 Results

Figure 6 and Fig. 7 show the read and write functions of the deployed and verified smart contracts on Polygon Mumbai [12] Testnet. By implementing Account Abstraction we have successfully sponsored the gas fees of all write operations. This has decreased the gas cost on the user from 0.0007555 ETH per warranty created to zero wei per warranty thus decreasing the burden on users and acting as an incentive for users to use the proposed system over other traditional systems.

Table 2 represents the difference in gas paid by the users while using different gas options. However, as there is a single Entry Point Contract and one Paymaster, it increases the time taken for a transaction to be included in a block.

Table 1. Requirements of the proposed system

S. no	Software	Version
1.	Solidity	0.8.0
2.	React	18.1.0
3.	React Router	6.3.0
4.	Web3.js	1.7.3
5.	Tailwind CSS	3.3.1
6.	IPFS	56.0.1
7.	Gelato Ops	2.0.0
8.	Ethereum	1.12.2
9.	Polygon	4.4.5

Table 2. Gas fees paid by users

Gas Options	Traditional Systems	Proposed System
Low	0.0005545 ETH	0 ETH
Market	0.0007555 ETH	0 ETH
Aggressive	0.0009564 ETH	0 ETH

Even though the time taken is not significantly large for a small number of users the effect is significantly large for a large number of users.

To overcome this bottleneck the proposed approach has a Bundler to bundle user ops to decrease the time required to complete a transaction by bundling some user operations in the mempool and sending them for validation and execution by the handleOps function in the Entry Point Contract.

5 Conclusion

The proposed warranty system employs an innovative methodology that utilizes NFTs, web3 automation, and account abstraction to enhance the security, transparency, effectiveness, and convenience of warranties for both purchasers and vendors. The system operates by generating an NFT Warranty for each item, subsequently associating it with the purchaser's wallet address. The NFT Warranty encompasses all pertinent warranty details, such as the expiration date and the terms and conditions. Upon the expiration of the warranty, a Gelato Ops-uploaded NFT Resolver contract automatically eliminates the NFT Warranty, guaranteeing that it cannot be reused or redeemed. The proposed framework is substantiated by preceding investigations on the utilization of NFTs for warranties and the potential advantages of NFTs for e-commerce. Nonetheless, it is imperative to acknowledge that there are certain difficulties linked to NFTs, such as the danger of misplacement. It is crucial to implement suitable precautions to safeguard NFTs and ensure their enduring conservation.

The future work considers planned improvements to the proposed mechanism, focusing on scalability, security, real-world deployment challenges, and user experience enhancements. By addressing these areas, the mechanism can be further refined to provide a more secure, scalable, and user-friendly warranty experience.

References

1. eMarketer. Worldwide ecommerce will approach $ 5 trillion this year. Insider Intelligence. Association for Computing Machinery (2021). https://www.emarketer.com/content/worldwide-ecommerce-will-approach-5-trillion-this-year
2. Statista. Global online retail sales by product category 2023. https://www.statista.com/topics/871/online-shopping/#topicOverview
3. Blancaflor, E., Aladin, K.: Analysis of the NFT's potential impact in an e-commerce platform: a systematic review. In: Proceedings of the 10th International Conference on Computer and Communications Management, New York, NY, USA, pp. 239–245 (2022)
4. Arcenegui, J., Arjona, R., Baturone, I.: Use case examples of ethereum non-fungible tokens tied to assets using ERC-4519. In: IEEE International Conference on Omnilayer Intelligent Systems (COINS) (2023)
5. Tiwari, S.D., Hota, L., Nayak, B.P., Kumar, A.: Beyond trust: leveraging blockchain for privacy-centric VANET authentication. In: 2024 IEEE 9th International Conference for Convergence in Technology (I2CT), pp. 1–7. IEEE (2024)
6. Arcenegui, J., Arjona, R., Baturone, I.: Non-fungible tokens based on ERC-4519 for the rental of smart homes. Sensors **23**(16), 7101 (2023)
7. White, B., Mahanti, A., Passi, K.: Characterizing the OpenSea NFT marketplace. In: Companion Proceedings of the Web Conference, New York, NY, USA, pp. 488–496 (2022)
8. Ali, A., Agrawal, S., Pisalkar, T., Dongre, S.: Modernising e-commerce warranties using non-fungible tokens on the blockchain. In: OPJU International Technology Conference on Emerging Technologies for Sustainable Development (OTCON) (2022)
9. Nogueira, A., Marques, C.G., Manso, A., Almeida, P.: NFTs and the danger of loss. Heritage **6**(7), 5410–5423 (2023)
10. Wang, Q., Chen, S.: Account abstraction, analysed. In: IEEE International Conference on Blockchain (Blockchain), pp. 323–331 (2023)
11. Singh, A.K., Hassan, I.U., Kaur, G., Kumar, S., Anmol. Account abstraction via singleton entrypoint contract and verifying paymaster. In: 2nd International Conference on Edge Computing and Applications (ICECAA), pp. 1598–1605 (2023)
12. Lee, W.M.: Using the MetaMask crypto-wallet. In: Beginning Ethereum Smart Contracts Programming. Apress, Berkeley, CA (2023)
13. Gelato Network. Introducing gelato ops: Web3's multi-chain smart contract automation hub. https://medium.com/gelato-network/introducing-gelato-ops-web3s-multi-chain-smart-contract-automation-hub-713dbcf2dad1

LTTS-GAN: A Long-Term Time Series Generative Adversarial Network

Xiangyu Cui[1], Xianping Ma[1], Man-On Pun[1(✉)], and Zhimin Cheng[2]

[1] School of Science and Engineering, The Chinese University of Hong Kong,
Shenzhen 518172, Guangdong, China
SimonPun@cuhk.edu.cn
[2] China Academy of Telecommunications Technology, Beijing 100191, China

Abstract. This study focuses on generating long-term time series data. Existing deep learning-based methods for generating long-term sequences face two main challenges: limited ability in capturing long-term temporal relationships and gradient problems during training. To address these issues, we propose a long-term time series generative adversarial network (LTTS-GAN) by exploiting a multi-channel progressive decomposition generator. Both the generator and discriminator in LTTS-GAN are built upon the transformer encoder structure. In addition, we enhance the generator's architecture by incorporating multiple channels of trend information from real data, aiming to improve the quality of the generated data. Furthermore, we employ the Auto-Correlation mechanism to identify period-wise relationships while introducing a global-local attention mechanism to balance local and long-range information. As a result, LTTS-GAN demonstrates superior capability in capturing long-term sequence features compared to other models. We validate the effectiveness of LTTS-GAN through a real-world classification application, confirming its performance across various scenarios.

Keywords: Generative Adversarial Network · Transformer · Auto-Correlation · Time series Generation

1 Introduction

Time series data are commonly used in various fields such as finance, economics, meteorology, and medicine. However, obtaining real-life time series data directly from the field can be challenging. The data are often collected over a long period and may not be easily accessible for analysis. To overcome this challenge, deep learning-based methods have been explored to generate realistic data that captures the temporal dynamics of real-life measurements. However, existing approaches mainly focus on generating shorter sequences and struggle to reliably capture long-term features. These models face distribution shifts [1] when generating lengthy sequences. However, some time series exhibit cyclical trends that require longer periods to represent accurately. Therefore, it is of great practical interest to investigate the generation of long sequences.

Recently, several generative adversarial network (GAN)-based models have been proposed in the literature [2–8] for time series generation. For instance, [2–6] were designed with Recurrent Neural Networks (RNNs) [9] while [7] adopted a transformer-based framework [10]. However, it is well-known that conventional RNNs suffer from inherent problems such as gradient vanishing and explosion. To cope with the gradient problem, Long Short-Term Memory (LSTM) [11] and Gated Recurrent Unit (GRU) [12] have been developed, though the gradient decay over layers remains to be a problem for them [13]. As a result, it is challenging to train GAN-based models equipped with RNNs for long-term time series generation. Recently, the transformer architecture has attracted much attention due to its remarkable performance in many applications including natural language processing (NLP) [10,14,15], computer vision (CV) [16–18], audio processing [19–21]. However, it is non-trivial to introduce the transformer architecture to generate long-term sequences due to the quadratic complexity of self-attention required [14]. Some pioneering works on sparse and truncated self-attention schemes have been devised for long-term time series generation at the cost of information loss [7].

One of the primary challenges in generating time series is the limited capability of models in capturing long-term temporal patterns. However, time series data of the same type typically share common temporal characteristics, particularly in their trend-cyclical components. Such inspired, this work proposes a novel approach that leverages the long-term trend information from real time series data during the generation process. Besides, the outputs of internal modules of the generator are decomposed into the trend-cyclical and seasonal components. Furthermore, to detect the periodic dependence between time series, the Auto-Correlation mechanism [22–24] is adopted to replace the conventional self-attention mechanism. However, the improvement on capturing the long-term features may incur a loss of local details. To achieve a better balance between global information and local details, this work proposes to employ the global-local attention. This mechanism involves constructing the global branch using the Auto-Correlation mechanism while incorporating two one-dimensional convolutional layers for the local branch.

In summary, we propose a novel GAN-based model with a multi-channel progressive decomposition generator for long-term time series generation by overcoming the issue pertaining to the limited capacity of existing models in capturing robust long-term features. The contributions of this work can be summarized as follows:

- A multi-channel progressive decomposition architecture is proposed for the generator to separate trend-cyclical components and seasonal components of synthetic data in the long-term time series generating progress;
- The global-local mechanism is applied to compensate missing local information and balance the relationship between global information and local details;

- The performance of the proposed LTTS-GAN is validated using four real-life datasets. Our experimental results confirm the good performance of the proposed LTTS-GAN.

2 Related Work

2.1 Time Series Generation Based on GANs

GANs have received a lot of attention since the first GAN model was proposed in 2014 [25]. The inaugural study to employ GANs for the generation of continuous sequential data is C-RNN-GAN [26], where both the generator and discriminator are constructed utilizing LSTMs. The model's capacity to generate continuous data is exemplified through music generation, although there remains a need for further improvement in the quality of synthetic data. Furthermore, Recurrent Conditional GAN (RCGAN) [3] similarly employs RNNs to construct its generator and discriminator components, albeit with a slightly distinct architectural approach when compared to C-RNN-GAN. The outputs of RCGAN's generator are not fed back as inputs for the next time step, and additional information is input to build a Conditional GAN (CGAN) [27]. The application of RCGAN in the generation of medical data has demonstrated its ability to generate real-valued multi-dimensional time series. However, both C-RNN-GAN and RCGAN fail to consider the distinctive temporal correlations inherent in time series data. To effectively preserve temporal dynamics, TimeGAN [4] proposes a novel architecture for time series generation that integrates the GAN model with an autoregressive model. Embedding and recovery are applied to convert data between the time domain and the embedding space. Subsequently, the generation process occurs within this embedding space.

2.2 Transformers for Long Sequences

This work primarily concentrates on addressing the challenge of long-term time series generation. With the objective of addressing this challenge, several variants of transformers have been developed. Informer [28] is a transformer-based model designed to tackle long-term forecasting problems. It incorporates a ProbSparse self-attention mechanism and self-attention distilling as key components in its architecture. For the same long-term series forecasting problem, Autoformer [24] is designed as a novel decomposition architecture with the Auto-Correlation mechanism. Nevertheless, these models are specifically engineered for forecasting problems utilizing encoder-decoder architectures, which may not be well-suited for time series generation tasks.

2.3 Transformer-Based GAN for Time Series Generation

Recently, the remarkable achievements of transformers across diverse tasks have sparked interest in exploring their potential in the domain of data generation.

For instance, [29] uses two pure transformers to construct a GAN and verifies its performance on image generation tasks. In light of this, Transformer-based Time-Series GAN (TTS-GAN) [7] is proposed for continuous time series generation tasks, where both the generator and discriminator are constructed using a pure transformer encoder architecture. Because of the robust performance of transformers across distinct domains, transformers are employed as the fundamental building blocks. To leverage the valuable insights gained from prior research endeavors, we embark on an investigation and exploration of integrating GANs with various transformer architectures to handle long sequences. Subsequently, we conduct a comprehensive comparative analysis to discern the distinctions in performance. Furthermore, given the distinctive characteristics of long-term time series data, we enhance the GAN architecture to maximize the efficient utilization of input data information.

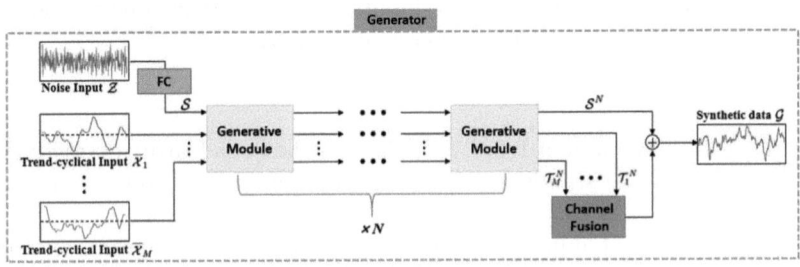

(a) Generator Architecture

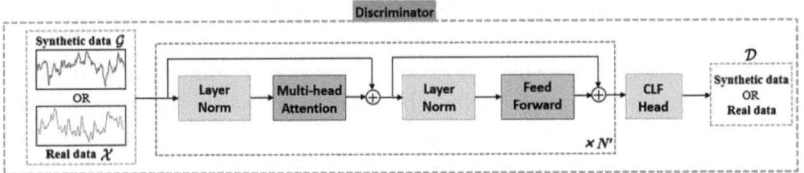

(b) Discriminator Architecture

Fig. 1. (a) The architecture diagram of the generator. (b) The architecture diagram of the discriminator.

3 Proposed Model

LTTS-GAN, a generative adversarial network model, comprises two distinct components: a generator and a discriminator. Figure 1 provides a high-level block diagram of the proposed LTTS-GAN.

3.1 The Generator Architecture

Since the primary focus of this work is centered around the generation of long-term time series data, the major challenges pertaining to capturing temporal features and the associated trade-offs become increasingly complex. In addition, the substantial computational and memory requirements also pose significant challenges during the training process of GANs.

To cope with the aforementioned challenges, we first introduce a multi-channel progressive decomposition architecture to design our generator. Different from vanilla GANs that solely utilize noise as input, we leverage the complete long-term trend information extracted from the real data to serve as auxiliary input. As shown in Fig. 1(a), the proposed generator consists of multiple input channels, including a regular noise input channel and several additional trend channels that provide trend characteristics of the real data. By utilizing the multi-channel auxiliary inputs, the generator is capable of effectively comprehending the temporal characteristics of the real data and accurately simulating the distribution of authentic data.

More specifically, we denote by $\mathcal{X} \in \mathbb{R}^{I \times d}$ the real time series data of d channels and length I. The auxiliary inputs to the trend channels denoted by $\overline{\mathcal{X}}_m$ are the features extracted from the real data given by:

$$\overline{\mathcal{X}}_m = f(\mathcal{X}, \ell_m), \tag{1}$$

where $\overline{\mathcal{X}}_m \in \mathbb{R}^{I \times d}$ with $m = 1, 2, \ldots, M$ denotes the m-th feature extracted from real data whereas $f(\cdot)$ stands for the feature extraction function parameterized by ℓ_m.

Clearly, there exist numerous alternative choices for the feature extraction function $f(\cdot)$, which can be selected based on the specific requirements of the tasks. In this work, the proposed $f(\cdot)$ takes the form of moving average with distinct window sizes, which yields trend-cyclical inputs exhibiting varying degrees of smoothness.

Such a design facilitates the utilization of trend components of real data with different frequencies while enhancing the realism of synthetic data by fusing it with more accurate long-term temporal characteristics. Thus, $\overline{\mathcal{X}}_m$ denotes the mean of the padding-added moving average of $\mathcal{X}$ by channel. The only difference among $\overline{\mathcal{X}}_m$ is the moving average window size ℓ_m from which they are derived. It is noteworthy that the operation of padding ensures that all $\overline{\mathcal{X}}_m$ possess equal length as the real data $\mathcal{X}$.

In addition, the input noise initially undergoes a transformation through a fully connected layer, yielding a sequence of the same length but higher channel dimensions as compared to $\overline{\mathcal{X}}_m$. Subsequently, it proceeds to traverse through iterative generation blocks in order to generate the synthetic time series. The overall generation process can be formalized as follows:

$$\mathcal{S} = \text{FC}(\mathcal{Z}), \tag{2}$$

where $\mathcal{S} \in \mathbb{R}^{I \times c}$ represents the transformation output with c being the intermediate channel dimension. Furthermore, $\text{FC}(\cdot)$ denotes the fully connected layer whereas the input $\mathcal{Z}$ stands for Gaussian noise vectors.

Subsequently, the combination of $\mathcal{S}$ and $\{\overline{\mathcal{X}}_m\}$ undergoes a sequence of N generative modules whose details are reported in Sect. 3.3. Finally, the seasonal output from the final generative module $\mathcal{S}^N$ is combined with the fused trend-cyclical outputs from multiple channels $\{\mathcal{T}_m^N\}$ to yield the synthetic data:

$$\mathcal{G} = \mathcal{S}^N + \text{Fusion}(\mathcal{T}_1^N, \mathcal{T}_2^N, \ldots, \mathcal{T}_M^N), \tag{3}$$

where $\mathcal{G} \in \mathbb{R}^{I \times d}$ represents the generated time series data while $\text{Fusion}(\cdot)$ denotes the channel fusion block. Details pertaining to the design of $\text{Fusion}(\cdot)$ are provided in Sect. 3.4.

3.2 The Discriminator Architecture

As shown in Fig. 1(b), the discriminator functions as a binary classifier, tasked with discerning the authenticity of the input by determining whether it originates from real or synthetic sources. The inputs to the discriminator consist of either real time series or synthetic time series. They traverse through N' layers of transformer encoder blocks before being subjected to classification by the classification head, distinguishing them as either real or synthetic. Details are shown as follows:

$$\mathcal{D} = \text{CLF}(\text{Encoder}(\mathcal{X} \text{ or } \mathcal{G})_{\times N'}), \tag{4}$$

where $\text{Encoder}(\cdot)_{\times N'}$ represents N' identical transformer encoder blocks that are sequentially linked. The function $\text{CLF}(\cdot)$ denotes the classification head. Additionally, $\mathcal{D} \in \mathbb{R}^1$ refers to the final output of the proposed discriminator, which signifies the authenticity of the input time series data.

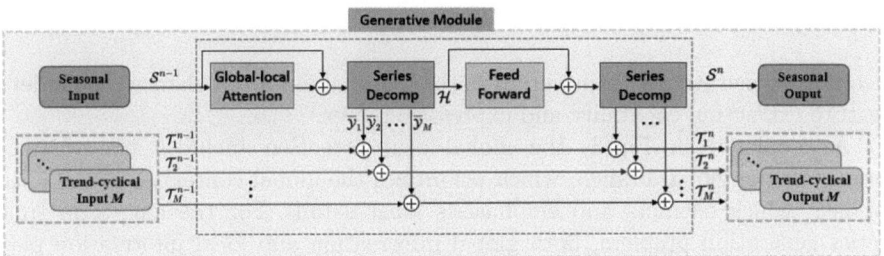

Fig. 2. The architecture of the generative module.

3.3 The Generative Module

The generative module serves as the pivotal component within the generator, responsible for extracting temporal features from the input data and decomposing the input information into distinct components, namely the seasonal and the trend-cyclical components. The architecture of the proposed generative module is depicted in Fig. 2. First, a global-local attention block is utilized to extract the

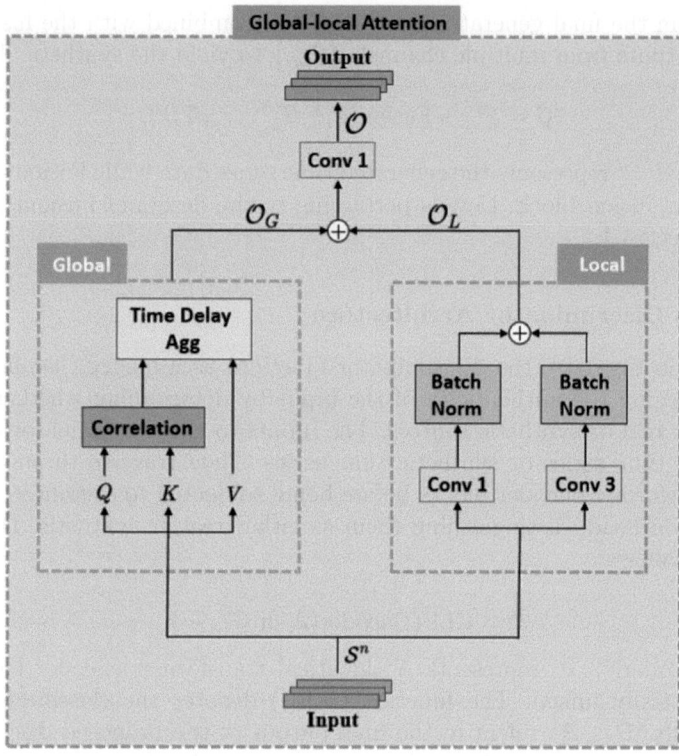

Fig. 3. Global-local Attention. The global branch is constructed by Auto-Correlation Mechanism and the local branch consists of two one-dimensional local convolutions.

necessary generative information from the seasonal input to enhance the model's feature extraction capability and expressive power.

As depicted in Fig. 3, the global-local attention includes two distinct branches: the global branch, which prioritizes the global context, and the local branch, which extracts and emphasizes local details. For the long-term time series generation problem, both global information and local information play essential roles. The global information provides insights into potential periods and the cyclical trend, whereas the local details retain the temporal dynamics among neighboring time points.

The architecture of the global-local attention block is shown in Fig. 3. In an effort to mitigate the complexity associated with module generation and enhance the model's capacity to extract comprehensive global information from extended sequences, the Auto-Correlation mechanism [22,23] is employed to construct the global branch. Additionally, the local branch is constructed using two 1D convolutional layers of distinct kernel sizes, connected before batch normalization layers. Mathematically, the global-local attention can be expressed as follows:

$$\mathcal{O}_G = \text{Auto} - \text{Correlation}(Q, K, V), \quad (5)$$

and
$$\mathcal{O}_L = \text{BatchNorm}(\text{Conv}_1(\mathcal{S}^n)) + \text{BatchNorm}(\text{Conv}_3(\mathcal{S}^n)), \tag{6}$$

where Q, K and V are the Query, Key, and Value matrices, respectively. In addition, $\mathcal{S}^n$ for $n = 1, 2, \ldots, N$ represents the seasonal output of the n-th generative module. $\mathcal{O}_G$ and $\mathcal{O}_L$ are the outputs of the global branch and local branch, respectively. Furthermore, BatchNorm($\cdot$) denotes the batch normalization layer whereas Conv_k is a 1D convolutional layer of kernel size k. The output of the global-local attention block, denoted as $\mathcal{O} \in \mathbb{R}^{I \times c}$, is obtained by combining the local output $\mathcal{O}_L$ and the global output $\mathcal{O}_G$ through a convolution operation.

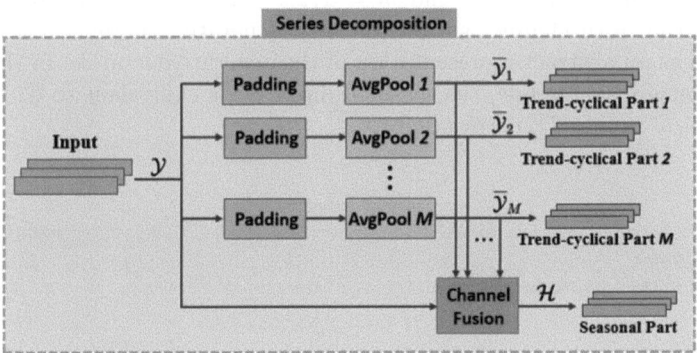

Fig. 4. The architecture of series decomposition block. This block decomposes internal results into a trend-cyclical part and several seasonal parts.

Next, we introduce a series decomposition block as shown in Fig. 4. The series decomposition module decomposes inputs into a seasonal component and M trend-cyclical components. These trend-cyclical components are obtained by the moving average operation of different window sizes after padding. Because they are extracted by windows of distinct lengths, they represent different levels of smoothness of realistic trend information with frequency information derived from real data. The results obtained from subtracting the trend-cyclical components from the inputs in distinct channels are fused by the channel fusion module to obtain the seasonal component of this decomposition module. This series decomposition module can be mathematically modeled as follows:

$$\overline{\mathcal{Y}}_m = \text{AvgPool}(\text{Padding}(\mathcal{Y})), \tag{7}$$

and
$$\mathcal{H} = \text{Fusion}(\mathcal{Y} - \overline{\mathcal{Y}}_1, \mathcal{Y} - \overline{\mathcal{Y}}_2, \ldots, \mathcal{Y} - \overline{\mathcal{Y}}_M), \tag{8}$$

where $\mathcal{Y}$ is the input of the series decomposition module. Furthermore, $\overline{\mathcal{Y}}_m$ with $m = 1, 2, \ldots, M$ denotes the moving average of $\mathcal{Y}$ after padding by channel, corresponding to the trend-cyclical outputs of the individual channels. Additionally,

$\mathcal{H}$ denotes the seasonal component resulting from the fusion of channels, serving as the seasonal output of this module.

The subsequent operations entail the utilization of a feed-forward network for projection and information propagation, as well as the inclusion of another series decomposition block that functions similarly to the initial decomposition block. The seasonal information, after undergoing the second series decomposition block, along with several trend-cyclical components, serves as the input for the subsequent generative module. The generative module can be formalized as follows:

$$\mathcal{S}^n, \mathcal{T}_1^n, \ldots, \mathcal{T}_M^n = g(\mathcal{S}^{n-1}, \mathcal{T}_1^{n-1}, \ldots, \mathcal{T}_M^{n-1}), \qquad (9)$$

where $\mathcal{T}_m^n$ for $n = 1, 2, \ldots, N$ and $m = 1, 2, \ldots, M$ denotes the trend-cyclical output of the m-th channel within the n-th generative module. The function $g(\cdot)$ serves as an abstract representation of the generative module. In the case of the first generative module, the seasonal input $\mathcal{S}^0$ is equivalent to $\mathcal{S}$, while the trend-cyclical inputs $\mathcal{T}_m^0$ correspond to $\overline{\mathcal{X}}_m$.

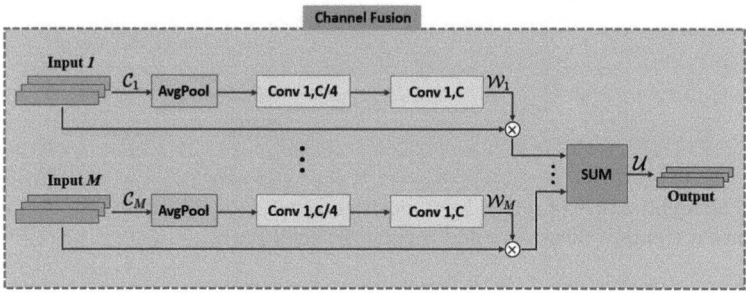

Fig. 5. The architecture of channel fusion block. The primary function of this module is to enable the fusion of multi-channel data.

3.4 Channel Fusion

The act of simply adding the trend-cyclical information from different channels lacks practical significance. Therefore, we introduce a channel fusion module [30] designed to merge and integrate these channels effectively. As shown in Fig. 5, the inputs of this module are first reweighted by channel and then summed element-wisely. The reweighting operation is performed through an average pool layer and two convolutional layers, which evaluates the importance and weighting methods of distinct inputs by channel. The process can be mathematically expressed as:

$$\mathcal{U} = \sum_{m=1}^{M} \mathcal{W}_m \times \mathcal{C}_m, \qquad (10)$$

where $\mathcal{C}_m \in \mathbb{R}^{I \times d}$ and $\mathcal{U} \in \mathbb{R}^{I \times d}$ denote the input and output of the channel fusion module, respectively. Furthermore, $\mathcal{W}_m \in \mathbb{R}^{1 \times d}$ with $m = 1, 2, \ldots, M$ are learnable weights of M distinct channels and takes the following form:

$$\mathcal{W}_m = \text{Conv}_1(\text{Conv}_1(\text{AvgPool}(\mathcal{C}_m))), \qquad (11)$$

with the function $\text{Conv}_1(\cdot)$ represents the one-dimensional convolution. The channel fusion module is employed both at the end of the generator and within the series decomposition module. Within the generator, inputs $\mathcal{C}_m$ correspond to T_m^N. And in the series decomposition module, inputs $\mathcal{C}_m$ correspond to $\overline{\mathcal{Y}}_m$, while the output $\mathcal{U}$ corresponds to $\mathcal{H}$.

4 Experiments

Datasets. We evaluate the proposed LTTS-GAN on four distinct datasets: UniMiB human activity recognition (UMB) dataset [31], CinC ECG torso (CECG) dataset [32], Star Light Curves (SLC) dataset [33], and the Pressure Sensor (PS) dataset collected by ourselves. All data in the four datasets are normalized to be zero-mean and unit-variance by channel in the data preprocessing stage.

Baselines and Evaluation. We conduct a comparative analysis between the proposed LTTS-GAN and three existing generative models, namely RCGAN [3], TimeGAN [4], and TTS-GAN [7]. RCGAN and TimeGAN are both RNN-based generative models, while TTS-GAN is a transformer-based model. Due to the limited availability of methods specifically designed for generating time series in long-term scenarios, we employ the ProbSparse self-attention mechanism, as introduced in Informer [28], to enhance TTS-GAN. In the sequel, the improved TTS-GAN is referred to as IFGAN and considered as a baseline for comparison alongside LTTS-GAN.

Qualitative Visualization. The nonlinear dimensionality reduction algorithm t-SNE [34] is a prevalent technique employed in deep learning for non-linear dimensionality reduction. It facilitates the exploration of two-dimensional representations of high-dimensional data. When the inherent characteristics of the original high-dimensional data are closely related, the points obtained after dimensionality reduction should exhibit a significant degree of overlap. Based on this, we can apply the t-SNE algorithm to effectively demonstrate the similarity between real data and synthetic data, utilizing an intuitive visualization approach.

Quantitative Scores. To quantitatively assess the proximity between synthetic data and real data, we utilize two established metrics: Jensen-Shannon Distance (JSD) [35] and Maximum Mean Discrepancy (MMD) [36].

(1) JSD can be employed as a metric to quantify the dissimilarity between two probability distributions, and it can be computed as follows:

$$\text{JSD} = \sqrt{\frac{\text{KL}(f_{real} \| f_{avg}) + \text{KL}(f_{syn} \| f_{avg})}{2}}, \qquad (12)$$

where f_{real} and f_{syn} denote feature vectors of real and synthetic data, respectively. $KL(A||B)$ represents the Kullback-Leibler divergence between A and B whereas $f_{avg} = (f_{real} + f_{syn})/2$.

(2) MMD is employed as a metric for quantifying the distance between the distributions of two distinct yet interconnected random variables. In practical applications, the squared value of MMD holds greater significance, and it can be computed as follows:

$$\text{MMD}^2 = \left\| \frac{1}{n^2} \sum_{i=1}^{n} \sum_{i'=1}^{n} K(r_i, r_{i'}) - \frac{2}{nm} \sum_{i=1}^{n} \sum_{j=1}^{m} K(r_i, s_j) + \frac{1}{m^2} \sum_{j=1}^{m} \sum_{j'=1}^{m} K(s_j, s_{j'}) \right\|, \quad (13)$$

where $\{r_i\}_{i=1}^{n}$ and $\{s_j\}_{j=1}^{m}$ stand for the real and synthetic time series, respectively. Furthermore, $K(\cdot)$ is a kernel function and we use the radial basis function (RBF) kernel in experiments.

Table 1. Results on different datasets (Bold is the best result).

Models		RCGAN		TimeGAN		TTSGAN		IFGAN		LTTS-GAN	
Metric		JSD	MMD²	JSD	MMD²	JSD	MMD²	JSD	MMD²	JSD	MMD²
UMB	150	0.116	0.265	0.107	0.441	0.070	0.041	0.071	0.039	**0.065**	**0.033**
CECG	600	0.399	2.497	0.220	2.945	0.234	1.015	0.188	0.442	**0.154**	**0.110**
	900	0.344	4.088	0.374	2.984	\	\	0.295	0.283	**0.138**	**0.116**
	1200	0.441	6.185	0.431	3.001	\	\	0.334	0.509	**0.141**	**0.135**
	1500	0.443	6.189	0.436	3.140	\	\	0.369	1.807	**0.151**	**0.167**
PS	600	0.203	1.168	0.131	1.221	0.289	0.871	0.179	0.983	**0.127**	**0.431**
	900	0.238	1.470	0.454	2.611	\	\	0.234	1.035	**0.135**	**0.488**
	1200	0.301	2.360	0.504	4.098	\	\	0.242	1.609	**0.156**	**0.521**
	1500	0.304	3.513	0.541	5.865	\	\	0.250	2.140	**0.143**	**0.559**
SLC	400	0.273	1.748	**0.149**	**0.386**	0.248	1.861	0.291	0.932	0.159	**0.307**
	600	0.192	1.627	0.144	**0.470**	0.174	1.844	0.254	0.591	**0.107**	**0.279**
	800	0.154	1.506	0.191	0.447	0.151	1.809	0.258	0.493	**0.098**	**0.267**
	1000	0.141	1.386	0.214	0.444	\	\	0.225	0.457	**0.072**	**0.270**

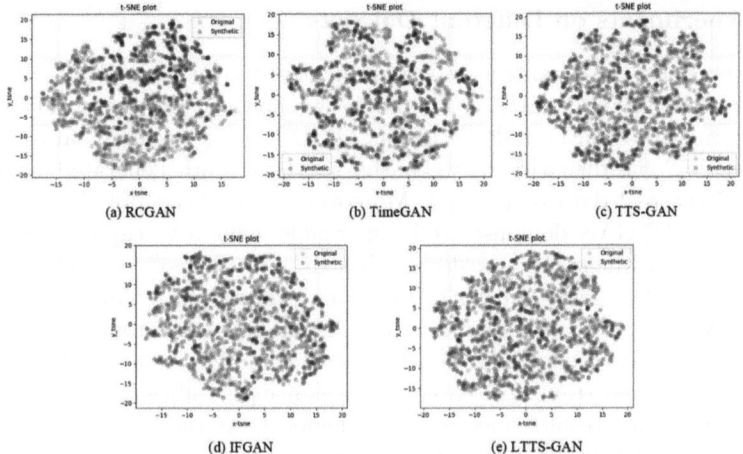

Fig. 6. Visualization results on UniMiB Running dataset with length 150.

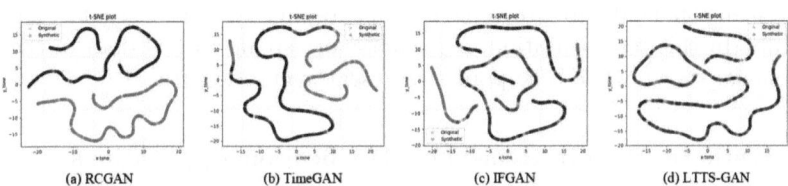

Fig. 7. Visualization results on different CECG dataset with length 900.

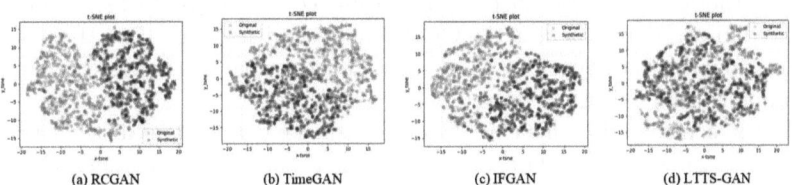

Fig. 8. Visualization results on different PS dataset with length 1500.

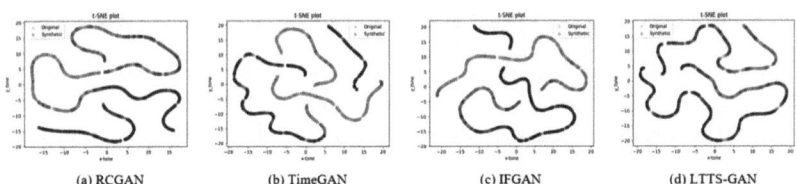

Fig. 9. Visualization results on different SLC dataset with length 1000.

4.1 Experiments on Different Datasets

Table 1 presents the quantitative scores achieved by the models across four datasets with varying lengths of real data. As shown in this table, LTTS-GAN achieved the lowest JSD and the lowest MMD^2 across the four datasets. This indicates that the disparity between the synthetic data generated by LTTS-GAN and the real data is minimal. Moreover, as the length of the input data increases, LTTS-GAN demonstrated remarkable generative capabilities. Under the long-term settings, the transformer-based model TTS-GAN appeared more susceptible to divergence during the training process and exhibited an inability to effectively capture the characteristics of long-term time series inputs. Furthermore, it is evident that the RNN-based models, namely RCGAN and TimeGAN, suffered from noticeable performance degradation as compared to ours. The obtained results unequivocally demonstrate the limited capability of the previous models in handling long-term sequences, thereby affirming the effectiveness and significance of our proposed LTTS-GAN.

Figure 6, 7, 8 and 9 show the t-SNE visualization of real and synthetic data. High-dimensional data are projected onto a two-dimensional space and visualized as points. In this representation, red points correspond to real data in the two-dimensional space, while blue points represent synthetic data.

4.2 Synthetic Data in Real-Life Classification Applications

In this section, we focus on investigating the role of synthetic data within a real-life classification task. Our objective is to explore the potential of leveraging synthetic data to enhance the performance of realistic tasks. The dataset employed in this experiment is the CECG dataset with length 1500. This dataset contains four distinct types of ECG data and the goal of the experiment is to determine the type of ECG data.

More specifically, for this classification task, we employ two distinct training sets, one comprising real data and the other consisting of synthetic data. We employed the proposed LTTS-GAN as the generative model to model the real data. A classifier based on the transformer architecture has been constructed to discern the categories of the data. This classifier shares the same architectural framework as the discriminator component of our LTTS-GAN, as both are employed for classification purposes.

Experiment Details. In this classification task, a combined total of 1400 real data samples have been employed, with each of the four categories contributing 350 samples. A fixed set of 200 data instances per category has been designated as the training set, while the remaining 150 data instances per category have been allocated for testing purposes. To generate four distinct categories of data, four separate LTTS-GAN models are trained, each trained on one of the four categories of data. In this process, all 350 samples from each category are utilized for training the corresponding LTTS-GAN. Following the completion of the training process, a combined total of 1000 synthetic data samples, along with 200 real data samples for each category, are employed as the comprehensive training set.

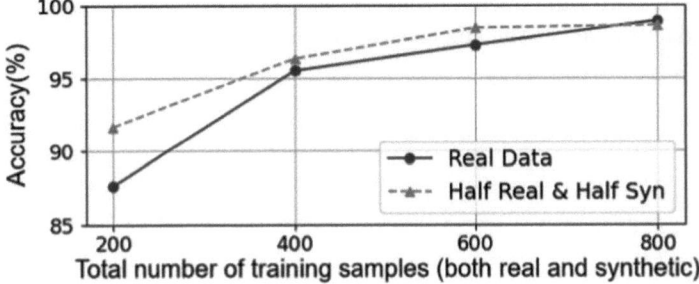

Fig. 10. Accuracy as a function of total number of training samples: The solid line with circular markers denotes the training set only includes real data, whereas the dashed line with triangular markers denotes the same amount of training samples composed of half real data and half synthetic data.

Main Results. Figure 10 shows the performance of synthetic data in the classification task. The solid line with circular markers denotes a training set composed solely of real data, while the dashed line with triangular markers signifies a training set comprising an equal distribution of both real and synthetic data. Figure 10 substantiates the observation in [37] that the substitution of a portion of real data with synthetic data can yield comparable or even superior outcomes, thereby illustrating the potential for synthetic data to replace real data in this particular classification task.

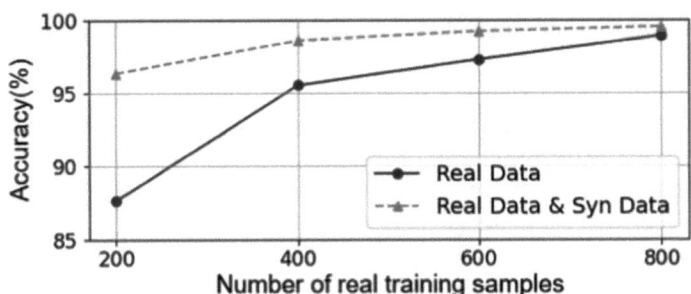

Fig. 11. Accuracy as a function of the number of *real* training samples: The solid line marked with circles represents a training set consisting solely of real data, while the dashed line marked with triangles indicates a training set that includes an equal amount of synthetic data alongside the real data.

Furthermore, Fig. 11 provides evidence of the utility of synthetic data in realworld tasks. The dashed line with triangular markers represents a training set that comprises an equal quantity of real data and synthetic data. Importantly, the solid line with circular markers corresponds to a training set comprising exclusively real data. Based on the consistent vertical offset between the dashed and solid lines, we can conclude that the inclusion of an appropriate amount of synthetic data enhances the efficacy of real data utilization and proves beneficial for practical applications.

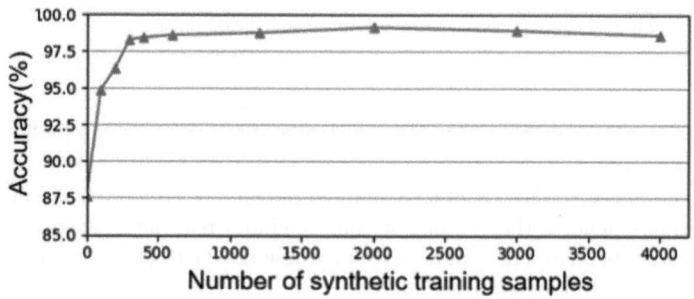

Fig. 12. Accuracy as a function of the number of *synthetic* training samples: The amount of real data is fixed at 200 while varying the amount of synthetic data.

Finally, to ascertain the optimal quantity of synthetic data deemed as the "appropriate" amount, we maintained a constant quantity of real data (i.e., 200 samples) while systematically varying the amount of synthetic data as illustrated in Fig. 12. As we increased the amount of synthetic data, there was an initial trend of improved accuracy, followed by saturation, and ultimately a slight decline. Within this experiment, the determination of the "appropriate" amount can be established as any value within the range of 400 to 2000. However, it is important to note that this definition may vary across diverse applications and datasets.

In conclusion, the inclusion of appropriate synthetic data, either through direct substitution of real data or as an addition to real data, offers potential benefits for real-world tasks. However, in practical mission scenarios, the recommendation is to opt for the latter approach of incorporating synthetic data alongside real data. Besides, it is essential to note that the definition of the "appropriate" amount may vary across different applications and datasets, necessitating a determination based on specific circumstances and requirements.

5 Conclusion

In this paper, a generative model based on GANs called LTTS-GAN has been proposed by exploiting a multi-channel progressive decomposition generator. Through the utilization of the decomposition method, the model prioritizes the generation of seasonal components, while relying on the trend information from real data to predominantly contribute towards the generation of the trend-cyclical information. The Auto-Correlation mechanism is introduced as a replacement for self-attention, facilitating the detection of period-dependencies among sub-series. Additionally, the global-local mechanism has been developed to effectively balance the integration of global information and local details. Extensive experiments on four datasets have confirmed that the proposed model exhibited substantial performance enhancement, surpassing previous benchmarks. Finally, to assess the performance of synthetic data in practical applications, we have designed a realistic classification task. The results obtained have effectively showcased the advantageous influence of the synthetic data generated by our model on real-world applications. This finding significantly bolsters the case for employing generated data in lieu of real data, particularly in scenarios where acquiring real data poses challenges or limitations.

References

1. Wang, L., Zeng, L., Li, J.: AEC-GAN: adversarial error correction GANs for autoregressive long time-series generation. In: Proceedings of the AAAI Conference on Artificial Intelligence, vol. 37 (2023)
2. Yu, L., Zhang, W., Wang, J., Yu, Y.: SeqGAN: sequence generative adversarial nets with policy gradient. In: Proceedings of the AAAI Conference on Artificial Intelligence, vol. 31 (2017)
3. Hyland, S.L., Esteban, C., Rätsch, G.: Real-valued (medical) time series generation with recurrent conditional GANs. Stat **1050**(8) (2017)
4. Yoon, J., Jarrett, D., Van der Schaar, M.: Time-series generative adversarial networks. In: Advances in Neural Information Processing Systems, vol. 32 (2019)
5. Liao, S., Ni, H., Sabate-Vidales, M., Szpruch, L., Wiese, M., Xiao, B.: Sig-Wasserstein GANs for conditional time series generation. Math. Financ. **34**(2), 622–670 (2023)
6. Hazra, D., Byun, Y.-C.: SynSigGAN: generative adversarial networks for synthetic biomedical signal generation. Biology **9**(12), 441 (2020)
7. Li, X., Metsis, V., Wang, H., Ngu, A.H.H.: TTS-GAN: a transformer-based time-series generative adversarial network. In: Michalowski, M., Abidi, S.S.R., Abidi, S. (eds.) AIME 2022. LNCS, vol. 13263, pp. 133–143. Springer, Cham (2022). https://doi.org/10.1007/978-3-031-09342-5_13
8. Sun, H., Deng, Z., Chen, H., Parkes, D.: Decision-aware conditional GANs for time series data. In: Proceedings of the ACM International Conference on AI in Finance, pp. 36–45 (2023)
9. Jordan, M.I.: Serial order: a parallel distributed processing approach. Adv. Psychol. **121**, 471–495 (1997)
10. Vaswani, A., et al.: Attention is all you need. In: Advances in Neural Information Processing Systems, vol. 30 (2017)
11. Jozefowicz, R., Zaremba, W., Sutskever, I.: An empirical exploration of recurrent network architectures. In: Proceedings of the International Conference on Machine Learning, pp. 2342–2350 (2015)
12. Cho, K., et al.: Learning phrase representations using RNN encoder-decoder for statistical machine translation. In: Proceedings of the Conference on Empirical Methods in Natural Language Processing (2014)

13. Li, S., Li, W., Cook, C., Zhu, C., Gao, Y.: Independently recurrent neural network (INDRNN): building a longer and deeper RNN. In: Proceedings of the IEEE Conference on Computer Vision and Pattern Recognition, pp. 5457–5466 (2018)
14. Beltagy, I., Peters, M.E., Cohan, A.: Longformer: the long-document transformer. arXiv preprint arXiv:2004.05150 (2020)
15. Lu, S., Zhou, C., Xie, K., Lin, J., Wang, Z.: Fast and accurate FSA system using ELBERT: an efficient and lightweight BERT. IEEE Trans. Signal Process. **71**, 3821–3834 (2023)
16. Parmar, N., et al.: Image transformer. In: Proceedings of the International Conference on Machine Learning, pp. 4055–4064 (2018)
17. Carion, N., Massa, F., Synnaeve, G., Usunier, N., Kirillov, A., Zagoruyko, S.: End-to-end object detection with transformers. In: Vedaldi, A., Bischof, H., Brox, T., Frahm, J.-M. (eds.) ECCV 2020. LNCS, vol. 12346, pp. 213–229. Springer, Cham (2020). https://doi.org/10.1007/978-3-030-58452-8_13
18. Dosovitskiy, A., et al.: An image is worth 16x16 words: transformers for image recognition at scale. arXiv preprint arXiv:2010.11929 (2020)
19. Dong, L., Xu, S., Xu, B.: Speech-transformer: a no-recurrence sequence-to-sequence model for speech recognition. In: Proceedings of the IEEE International Conference on Acoustics, Speech and Signal Processing, pp. 5884–5888 (2018)
20. Gulati, A., et al.: Conformer: convolution-augmented transformer for speech recognition. In: Interspeech (2020)
21. Chen, X., Wu, Y., Wang, Z., Liu, S., Li, J.: Developing real-time streaming transformer transducer for speech recognition on large-scale dataset. In: Proceedings of the IEEE International Conference on Acoustics, Speech and Signal Processing, pp. 5904–5908 (2021)
22. Papoulis, A., Unnikrishna Pillai, S.: Probability, random variables and stochastic processes (2002)
23. Kirchgässner, G., Wolters, J., Hassler, U.: Introduction to Modern Time Series Analysis. Springer (2012)
24. Wu, H., Xu, J., Wang, J., Long, M.: Autoformer: decomposition transformers with auto-correlation for long-term series forecasting. Adv. Neural. Inf. Process. Syst. **34**, 22419–22430 (2021)
25. Goodfellow, I., et al.: Generative adversarial networks. Commun. ACM **63**(11), 139–144 (2020)
26. Mogren, O.: C-RNN-GAN: continuous recurrent neural networks with adversarial training. arXiv preprint arXiv:1611.09904 (2016)
27. Mirza, M., Osindero, S.: Conditional generative adversarial nets. arXiv preprint arXiv:1411.1784 (2014)
28. Zhou, H., et al.: Informer: beyond efficient transformer for long sequence time-series forecasting. In: Proceedings of the AAAI Conference on Artificial Intelligence, vol. 35, pp. 11106–11115 (2021)
29. Jiang, Y., Chang, S., Wang, Z.: TransGAN: two pure transformers can make one strong GAN, and that can scale up. In: Advances in Neural Information Processing Systems, vol. 34 (2021)
30. Seichter, D., Köhler, M., Lewandowski, B., Wengefeld, T., Gross, H.-M.: Efficient RGB-D semantic segmentation for indoor scene analysis. In: Proceedings of the IEEE International Conference on Robotics and Automation, pp. 13525–13531 (2021)
31. Micucci, D., Mobilio, M., Napoletano, P.: UniMiB SHAR: a dataset for human activity recognition using acceleration data from smartphones. Appl. Sci. **7**(10), 1101 (2017)

32. The UCR Time Series Classification Archive. www.cs.ucr.edu/~eamonn/time_series_data/. Accessed 30 May 2024
33. Rebbapragada, U., Protopapas, P., Brodley, C.E., Alcock, C.: Finding anomalous periodic time series: an application to catalogs of periodic variable stars. Mach. Learn. **74**, 281–313 (2009)
34. Van der Maaten, L., Hinton, G.: Visualizing data using t-SNE. J. Mach. Learn. Res. **9**(11) (2008)
35. Fuglede, B., Topsoe, F.: Jensen-Shannon divergence and Hilbert space embedding. In: Proceedings of the International Symposium on Information Theory, p. 31 (2004)
36. Gretton, A., Borgwardt, K., Rasch, M., Schölkopf, B., Smola, A.: A kernel method for the two-sample-problem. In: Advances in Neural Information Processing Systems, vol. 19 (2006)
37. Jahanian, A., Puig, X., Tian, Y., Isola, P.: Generative models as a data source for multiview representation learning. In: Proceedings of the International Conference on Learning Representations (2021)

A Lightweight Encrypted JPEG Image Retrieval Model Based on Self-attention Networks

Yanfeng Chen, Jing Liang, and Peiya Li(✉)

Jinan University, Guangzhou, China
frankz@stu2022.jnu.edu.cn, liangjing99@stu.jnu.edu.cn, lpy0303@jnu.edu.cn

Abstract. The widespread adoption of the Internet of Things (IoT) has led to a surge in image generation, with many being outsourced to the cloud to reduce storage pressures. To prevent from privacy leakage, it is wise to upload the encrypted form of images to the cloud server, however, encryption often leads to difficulty to image retrieval. Thus, the field of encrypted image retrieval has garnered significant interest for researchers. In this paper, a new encrypted JPEG image retrieval scheme using new adaptive images encryption algorithm and neural network is proposed. Specifically, the histograms of DCT coefficients are extracted from the cipher images as features vectors. These features vectors are then sent into a highly lightweight self-attention based neural network in retrieval process. Experiments results reveal that our scheme can attain enhanced retrieval precision with less computational cost compared to previous neural network based schemes. The lightweight self-attention networks (LSAN) we proposed can directly run with CPU, the GPU accelerated computing is not necessarily required. We upload our code at https://github.com/FrankZanyar/LSAN.

Keywords: Internet of Things (IoT) · Cipher-image retrieval · privacy preservation · neural network

1 Introduction

Nowadays, Internet of Things (IoT) devices such as smart cameras and visible doorbells are widely used, these devices generate vast amount of multimedia data, including images, every day. [1]. However, these smart devices have a disadvantages of constrained storage space and inferior computing power [2]. To save storage space and preserve this large amount of image data, users typically outsource their image data to third party storage services provider like cloud servers, for IoT applications. However, the cloud servers cannot be fully

---

Supported by the National Key R&D Program of China under Grant 2022YFB3103500, in part by the National Natural Science Foundation of China under Grants 62302195, and in part by the GuangDong Basic and Applied Basic Research Foundation under Grant 2022A1515011960.

trusted because they may sell users' privacy for profit or leak privacy through hacker attacks. Additionally, images generated by IoT devices usually contain users' privacy, as these devices are often used in people's homes. Thus, for privacy security, it is wise to encrypt images prior to transferring them to cloud servers [3].

Content-based image retrieval (CBIR) is a technique that can retrieve similar images from a database using an input image [4]. However, CBIR is not suitable for encrypted images since the visual features in ciphertext images are destroyed. Thus, encrypted image retrieval (EIR) has been developed, which aims at extracting high level features from ciphertext images to perform retrieval. Currently, EIR schemes can be mainly classified into two types. The first type of the EIR schemes extracts features before image encryption [5–10]. Specifically, the features are extracted from plain images by the image owners, then they encrypts the extracted features and images respectively. After that, the encrypted images and the encrypted features are uploaded to the cloud server. However, these schemes often use homomorphic encryption algorithms, which have high computational complexity [11]. Additionally, the separate encryption and feature extraction operations further increase the image owner's computational workload. Therefore, to reduce the computational burden for image owners, a second type of EIR has been developed. This type of schemes extracts features after image encryption [12–17]. The advantage of this type of scheme is that it significantly reduces the computation burden for image owner, since he/she only needs to encrypt the images, other operations can be performed on cloud servers. Our paper follows the approach that extracts features after encryption. The main challenge is how to use ciphertext features to represent plaintext images. Liang et al. [12] used Huffman-code histogram extracted from encrypted JPEG images as features for retrieval. Xia et al. [13,17] utilized the Bag of Words (BOW) model and K-means algorithm to construct a vocabulary of visual words for encrypted images through calculating the color histograms. Then, the histogram of visual words can be used as feature vectors for retrieval. Though these schemes achieve efficient images retrieval while preserving users' privacy, they suffer from low retrieval accuracy and they are not suitable for large database. As the swift advancement of deep learning, neural network models are being utilized in the EIR domain to enhance retrieval accuracy. Feng et al. [15] used Vision Transformer (ViT) to directly learn the high-dimensional features from partial encrypted images. Ma et al. [16] designed a DenseNet model to mine the CNN features in encrypted images for retrieval.

The usage of neural network models greatly improves the retrieval accuracy, but these models usually have deep and complex network structure in order to obtain good performance, and requiring GPUs for accelerated computation. GPU is far more expensive than CPU in cloud environment, it consumes more energy and produces more greenhouse gas as well. It is not economical and environmental friendly if all retrieval process needs GPU for computation. To solve this problem, we design a novel model named lightweight self-attention network (LSAN) for encrypted JPEG image retrieval. The model structure of

LSAN is very simple and has fewer parameters than traditional deep learning models while experiment results show that our scheme maintains satisfactory retrieval performance. Once trained, the model can use CPU to provide retrieval service, which can reduce the finance cost for users. We design a new adaptive JPEG encryption algorithm to protect the images. Specifically, we extract DCT coefficients from plain images, then use it to generate the encryption keys. The DC and AC coefficients are encrypted respectively, for each coefficient, it has a different encryption key. In addition, we add a 8 × 8 block permutation for confusion. After encryption, we compute histograms for transformed coefficients situated at various frequency positions, which are sent into LSAN to train the retrieval model. The primary contributions of this work are outlined below:

(1) In retrieval model, we apply concepts from natural language processing to process images' features, which improves the retrieval performance.
(2) The proposed LSAN significantly diminishes the quantity of model parameters and the computational expense. After training, the model can be deployed on servers without GPU, which can reduce the financial expense for users.
(3) We design an adaptive image encryption algorithm, where each image has a corresponding encryption key, which ensures image security while improving retrieval accuracy.

2 Proposed Scheme

In our proposed scheme, we consider a scenario with the following three different types of entities: image owner, cloud server and authorized user. The image owner are the users of the IoT devices, they encrypts images for privacy protection and then uploads the cipher images to the cloud server. The cloud server provides storage and retrieval services, it firstly extracts features from the uploaded cipher images, then uses these features to train a retrieval model. An authorized user can upload an encrypted query image to the server to require retrieval service. Upon receiving the query image, the cloud server computes the similarities with the database images based on the trained model. Then, the top-K similar results are returned to the authorized user. Ultimately, the authorized user decrypts the returned results from the cloud server to access the corresponding decrypted similar images. The encryption key is shared between image owner and the authorized users, and the cloud server doesn't know any knowledge about encryption key. We will discuss the encryption process and retrieval process in detail at below.

2.1 Key Generation

In order to improve the safety, we use the plaintext images to generate encryption keys. Every JPEG image comprises three color components: Y, U, and V, and each component has a corresponding DCT coefficient matrix. We extract DCT coefficients for each component and input these coefficients respectively to the SHA-256 hash function to generate three different 256-bit hash values. We use these three hash value as secret key to encrypt the corresponding color component in plaintext images, and we denote these secret keys as IEK_*, where $* \in \{Y, U, V\}$. We further extent the 256-bit hash value to a longer key stream using RC4 algorithm, and the long key stream is directly used in encryption process. Thus, one image is encrypted with three 256-bit keys, and it is enough to resist ciphertext-only attacks. However, the original plain-images are needed for decryption which the authorized user may not have. What's more, different images have different keys and it is not suitable for authorized user to storage the corresponding keys for all images. The reversible data hiding technology (RDH) [18] can assist us to handle this problem. The image owner and all authorized users share three predefined 256-bit keys PDK_*, and these predefined keys are used to encrypt the three hash values, which is shown as follows,

$$IEK'_* = IEK_* \oplus PDK_* \qquad (1)$$

where $* \in \{Y, U, V\}$ and $\oplus$ is the XOR operation. Then we embed IEK'_* into the corresponding cipher image's component as [18] put forward. When an authorized user receives an image, he/she can use the predefined key to perform another XOR operation on the key IEK'_* which can be extracted from the retrieval image to get the original secret keys IEK_* for decryption (Fig. 1).

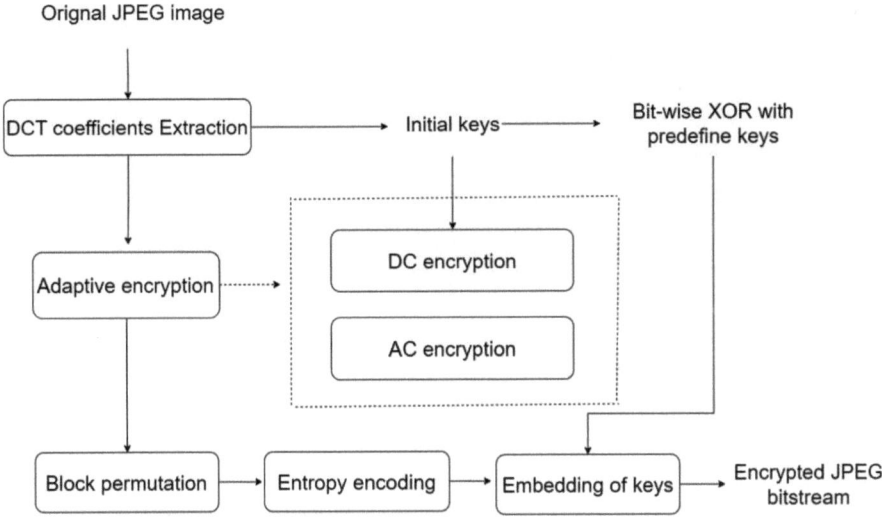

Fig. 1. The proposed adaptive image encryption method.

2.2 Adaptive Image Encryption

The JPEG format images are widely used in nowadays internet environment, that is why our proposed scheme uses JPEG images to conduct retrieval. To ensure effective retrieval, it is imperative to extract ruled weak features from cipher-images. However, the encryption of spatial content, including pixel-level information, poses challenges for feature extraction. Inspired by encryption techniques employed in JPEG compression [15,19,20], which simultaneously safeguards visual spatial content while preserving weak features. We design an adaptive image encryption algorithm which involves three steps: DCT coefficients extraction, adaptive encryption, and block permutation.

Step 1: DCT Coefficients Extraction. Given a plain-image I, the width and height of the image I are W and H, respectively. For each plain color image, We extract the DCT coefficient matrix of each component $I_i(i \in \{R,G,B\})$ from the bitstream of the JPEG image. We denote the blocks of component I_i as $B^* = \{B_j^*\}$, where $j \in [1, 2, ..., blknum]$, and $blknum = \frac{W \times H}{8 \times 8}$. A block B_j^* consists of 64 coefficients, which include one DC coefficient and 63 AC coefficients.

Step 2: Adaptive Encryption. We use different methods to encrypt DC and AC coefficients. We encrypt the DC coefficients using a random short sequence k_1 of initial keys obtained from the plaintext image, which is described as

$$DC' = \begin{cases} -(-DC) \oplus k_1 & DC < 0 \\ DC \oplus k_1 & DC \geq 0 \end{cases} \quad (2)$$

where $\oplus$ is exclusive-or operator.

For AC coefficients in each block B^*, we first adopt zigzag scan to arrange them. Then, we denote len as the length of AC coefficient when it is binary and $k_2(x)$ as a random short sequence with length of x obtained from IEK_*. The AC after encryption can be defined as

$$AC' = \begin{cases} AC \oplus k_2(len) & len \geq T \\ AC \oplus k_2(T) & len < T \end{cases} \quad (3)$$

where T is a set number that can be modified and $\oplus$ is exclusive-or operator. If len is greater than the given T, the length of the encryption key k_2 will be adaptively adjusted to be consistent with len. Otherwise, the encryption key length will not change.

Step 3: Block Permutation. We use $Yates\_shuffle$ [21] algorithm to shuffle the position of all blocks, and it is controlled by the key stream IEK_*. After entropy encoding, we embed the key IEK'_* into the bitstream and get the encrypted JPEG bitstream.

2.3 Image Retrieval

Though the visual features of the encrypted images are destroyed by encryption algorithm, the DCT coefficients histograms of JPEG images still carry many high-dimensional features [20], therefore, it is practicable to use DCT coefficients histograms to represent features of encrypted images. Specifically, during the feature extraction process, the cloud server initially decodes the Huffman codes, subsequently reorganizes all coefficients into 8 × 8 blocks, and finally applies JPEG's quantization table for dequantization. Every 8 × 8 dequantized block contains 64 coefficients positioned at various frequency locations, with each frequency position being categorized into a distinct group. The coefficients at the same group in all 8 × 8 blocks are counted by a histogram. Note that coefficients from different color components are calculated separately. As a result, each color component can generate 64 different histograms, and one image is represented by $64 \times 3 = 192$ histograms.

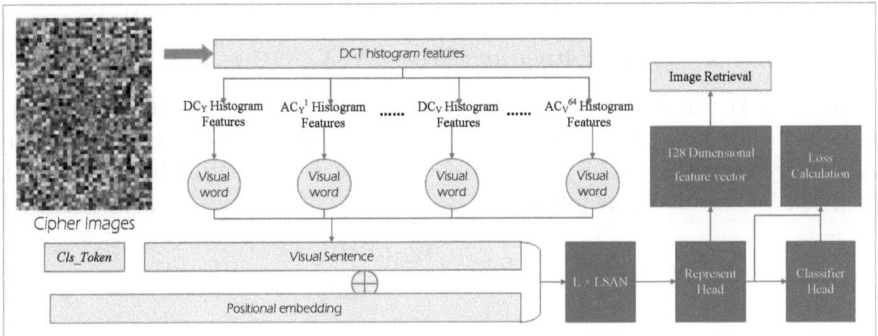

Fig. 2. The proposed retrieval model.

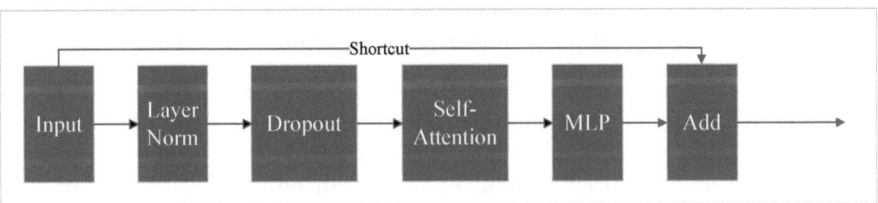

Fig. 3. Diagram of LSAN architecture.

In our scheme, each histogram has 64 bins. Inspired by word embedding technology in natural language processing (NLP) area [22], we treat each histogram as a "word" with 64 embedding dimensions, and each image can seen as a "sentence" with 192 "words", then we can use techniques in NLP to processing images' features. Self-attention is widely used in NLP tasks especially when Transformer is proposed in [23], its special structure can catch the high dimensional feature from input data and it has good ability to learn global dependencies relations, that is why we choose self-attention as backbone in our model. Our retrieval model is shown at Fig. 2. An image is represented by 192 histograms, and each histogram is a 64 dimension vector. Furthermore, we append a learnable embedding vector Cls_Token, as introduced in [24], to the feature vector. The Cls_Token can be seen as a summary of all the features. What's more, another learnable positional embedding vector is added to the feature vector, and the positional embedding vector shares the same shape with the feature vector. Positional embedding is first proposed in [23], which is used to learn the positional relationship between words in a sentence. The coefficients used in our scheme also have positional relationship, as DC coefficients usually carry more information, and AC coefficients located at back often are zeros, which means less information is carried. As shown in Fig. 3, the calculation of our proposed LSAN module is outlined below:

$$X_i = MLP(Attention(Drop(LN(X_{i-1})))) + X_{i-1} \qquad (4)$$

where X_{i-1} is the $i^{th}(i = 1, 2, ..., L)$ input, LN is Layer Normalization [25], $Drop$ is the Dropout layer, $Attention$ is the self-attention block, MLP is the Multilayer Perception (MLP) block. To be specific, self-attention block and MLP block can be calculated as follows:

$$Attention(X) = Softmax(\frac{W_Q(X)W_K(X)^T}{\sqrt{d_k}})W_V(X) \qquad (5)$$

$$MLP(X) = W_2(Drop(\sigma(W_1(X)))) \qquad (6)$$

where W_Q, W_K, W_V, W_1, W_2 are fully-connected layers, d_k is the embedding dimension, which is 64 in our model, and σ is the activation function Switch [26]. After L rounds calculation with LSAN, which we set $L = 8$, we extract the Cls_Token_L from X_L for classification purposes, and the process can be detailed as follows:

$$ft = BN(W_3(Cls\_Token)) , prediction = W_4(ft) \qquad (7)$$

where W_3, W_4 are fully-connected layers, BN is batch normalization [27]. The $prediction$ is used for computing cross entropy loss L_{CE} in supervised learning. And ft represents the ultimate representation vector, encapsulating the deep features of the associated cipher-image, and it can be used for classification in retrieval through computing consine distance between different ft. What's more, we use it to compute Proxy Anchor loss [28] L_{PA} in training stage. Therefore, the loss function we use is defined as

$$L = L_{PA} + \alpha L_{CE} \qquad (8)$$

In addition, we replace the original activation function ReLU with the Swish activation function [26] which can make training more stable and improve retrieval accuracy.

Once the model is trained, the cloud server can employ the trained model to construct a feature vector database from the uploaded encrypted images. Thus, two types of data is preserved in the cloud server, which is the encrypted images and their corresponding feature vectors. Upon the authorized user uploading a query image, the cloud server initially extracts the DCT histograms from the image and subsequently obtains its feature vector using the trained model. Through computing the cosine similarity between the query feature and the database features, the Top K most similar images are then returned to the authorized user.

3 Experiments and Analyses

We conduct experiment on Corel 1K and Corel 10K dataset [29], which contains 1000 and 10000 images of 10 and 100 different categories, respectively. We commence by encrypting the images using our encryption technique, followed by feature extraction from the encrypted images. For the training of the retrieval neural network, we allocate 70% of the images to the training set and reserve 30% for the testing set. Our model is optimized by Adam optimizer [30] with a learning rate of 0.0004 during training, and we employ the Cosine annealing strategy. The batch size is 100 and the number of epoch is 500. In addition, we set $\alpha = 0.8$ in Eq. 8.

3.1 Security Analyses

Because our proposed scheme aims at designing a privacy-preserving retrieval model, it is imperative to assess the security of our encrypted model.

Differential Attack. Differential attack method makes subtle changes to the original plaintext image, and encrypts the original plaintext image and the modified image separately. Through the comparison of two encrypted ciphertext images, an attacker discerns the correlation between the original plaintext image and the encrypted ciphertext image, leveraging this association and pattern to deduce the information of encryption key. To resist differential attacks, even a minor alteration in the plain-image should yield a significant discrepancy in the corresponding encrypted images. Number of pixels change rate (NPCR) and unified average changing intensity (UACI) are two indicators to evaluate resistance ability against differential attack. The ideal result of NPCR and UACI is 99.6094% and 33.4635%. The result of our scheme is shown at Table 1, we choose the first five classes from Corel1K dataset to conduct experiment. The results are close to ideal results, demonstrating that our scheme has a strong capability to withstand differential attacks.

Visual Security. The Peak Signal-to-Noise Ratio (PSNR) and Structural Similarity (SSIM) are used to assess the visual safety of our scheme. We encrypt 10000 images from Corel10K dataset and calculate the mean PSNR and SSIM values using different encryption schemes. Lower PSNR and SSIM means better

Table 1. NPCR and UACI values of Corel1K dataset.

Classes	NPCR	UACI
African	99.22	31.881
Beach	99.288	32.275
Architecture	99.341	32.064
Buses	99.233	32.332
Dinosaur	99.212	32.401

visual security. The experiment result is shown in Table 2, from which is obviously that our scheme exhibits the minimum values for both PSNR and SSIM, signifying the greatest level of visual security. What's more, example from Fig. 2 shows that the encrypted image is sufficiently chaotic that no information can be gleaned from it.

Table 2. Comparison of visual security for different schemes.

Schemes	Li [14]	Feng [15]	Lu [19]	Proposed
PSNR	13.189	9.754	8.866	**8.844**
SSIM	0.0327	0.04538	0.1309	**0.0271**

3.2 Retrieval Accuracy

We use images from testing set to search the Top-100 similar images from training set. The Mean Average Precision (mAP) metric is employed to assess the retrieval accuracy of the proposed model, with a higher mAP denoting greater accuracy in retrieval. The Top-30 accuracy is also calculated, which is more intuitive for evaluating models in practical scenario. We utilize K-reciprocal reranking algorithm [31] to further increase the retrieval accuracy especially for large dataset. According to Table 3, our model can achieve 0.847 mAP on Corel1K, and 0.5932 mAP on Corel10K. Compared with previous non deep learning based models [13,14,17], our model has significant improvement on both Corel1K and Corel10K dataset. Compared with state-of-the-art deep learning based models [15,16,32], our model also has advance in mAP. What's more, the Top-30 accuracy of our model is also higher in both Corel 1K and Corel 10K datasets.

3.3 Efficiency Comparison

Deep learning based neural network improves the accuracy of retrieval, however, it brings additional computational cost. Usually, neural network needs to be run on GPU for accelerating computation. In cloud server business, computing power

Table 3. Retrieval performance of different schemes.

Schemes	Corel 1K		Corel 10K	
	mAP	Top-30	mAP	Top-30
Xia [13]	0.4984	0.4491	0.2351	0.1798
Li [14]	0.4526	0.4412	0.2698	0.1910
Xia [17]	0.4018	0.4211	0.2062	0.1669
Ma [16]	0.5517	0.5296	0.2996	0.2413
Lu [32]	0.8034	0.7852	0.4301	0.3942
Feng [15]	0.6196	0.6076	0.5519	0.4716
Proposed	**0.8479**	**0.8344**	**0.5932**	**0.5731**

Table 4. Efficiency comparison for different models.

Models	Ma [16]	Feng [15]	Lu [19]	Proposed
Parameters	176.54M	35.775M	3.997M	**0.407M**
FLOPs	158.21M	20.524G	307.39M	**70.05M**

from GPU is much more expensive than CPU. What's more, the frequency of image owner and authorized user to apply for retrieval service may not be high, so it's a waste for image owner to rent a cloud server equipped with GPU. The LSAN model we designed highly reduces the computational cost, compared with traditional deep learning models, since it can be run on CPU with an acceptable time. The cloud server can concentrate all training tasks on machine equipped with GPU, then the trained model can be deployed to servers only with CPU to provide retrieval service. Table 4 shows the parameters and floating point operations (FLOPs) of different models, which are indicators to measure a model's computational cost. It can be seen that the parameters of our model is only 10% and even 0.2% of the compared model, and the FLOPs are smaller than compared model, but the retrieval accuracy of our model is higher than others. Lower numbers of parameters and FLOPs mean that our model has lower time and space complexity, as a result, our model is more efficient that others.

To be more intuitive, we calculate the time consumption of processing 10000 features from Corel10K dataset, the CPU we use is Intel Core(TM) i5-12600KF 3.70 GHz. The result is shown at Table 5. Note that the "*" sign in the table means this data is calculated using GPU, which is collected in paper [16]. It's obvious that our model uses the least time to process 10000 images' features.

Table 5. Time usage comparison for different models to process Corel10K with CPU.

Model	Ma [16]	Feng [15]	Lu [19]	Proposed
Time usage	67.2 s*	2220 s	51.03 s	**18.81 s**

4 Conclusion

In this paper, we propose a new encrypted JPEG image retrieval scheme in the Internet of Things environment using adaptive image encryption and lightweight self-attention network called LSAN. The encryption method we used can protect encrypted images ciphertext-only attack. Furthermore, because the encryption key is generated with the plain-image, our encryption method can resist differential attack as well. Assisted by the reversible data hiding technology, the encryption key can be transmitted undetectable. Experiment results demonstrate that the our proposed LSAN model has significant improvement on retrieval accuracy with minimum computational cost compared with other deep learning based model. How to mine more deep features for encrypted JPEG images and how to enhance the precision of retrieval will be our future work's priority.

References

1. Yan, H., Chen, Z., Jia, C.: SSIR: secure similarity image retrieval in IoT. Inf. Sci. **479**, 153–163 (2019)
2. Song, L., Miao, Y., Weng, J., Choo, K.-K.R., Liu, X., Deng, R.H.: Privacy-preserving threshold-based image retrieval in cloud-assisted internet of things. IEEE Internet Things J. **9**(15), 13598–13611 (2022)
3. Yuan, J., Yu, S., Guo, L.: SEISA: secure and efficient encrypted image search with access control. In: 2015 IEEE Conference on Computer Communications (INFOCOM), pp. 2083–2091. IEEE (2015)
4. Li, X., Yang, J., Ma, J.: Recent developments of content-based image retrieval (CBIR). Neurocomputing **452**, 675–689 (2021)
5. Lu, W., Varna, A.L., Swaminathan, A., Wu, M.: Secure image retrieval through feature protection. In: 2009 IEEE International Conference on Acoustics, Speech and Signal Processing, pp. 1533–1536 (2009). https://doi.org/10.1109/ICASSP.2009.4959888
6. Xia, Z., Zhu, Y., Sun, X., Qin, Z., Ren, K.: Towards privacy-preserving content-based image retrieval in cloud computing. IEEE Trans. Cloud Comput. **6**(1), 276–286 (2015)
7. Xia, Z., Wang, X., Zhang, L., Qin, Z., Sun, X., Ren, K.: A privacy-preserving and copy-deterrence content-based image retrieval scheme in cloud computing. IEEE Trans. Inf. Forensics Secur. **11**(11), 2594–2608 (2016)
8. Zhang, L., et al.: PIC: enable large-scale privacy preserving content-based image search on cloud. IEEE Trans. Parallel Distrib. Syst. **28**(11), 3258–3271 (2017)
9. Liang, H., Zhang, X., Cheng, H., Wei, Q.: Secure and efficient image retrieval over encrypted cloud data. Secur. Commun. Netw. **2018** (2018)
10. Shen, M., Cheng, G., Zhu, L., Xiaojiang, D., Jiankun, H.: Content-based multi-source encrypted image retrieval in clouds with privacy preservation. Futur. Gener. Comput. Syst. **109**, 621–632 (2020)
11. Gentry, C., Halevi, S., Smart, N.P.: Homomorphic evaluation of the AES circuit. In: Safavi-Naini, R., Canetti, R. (eds.) CRYPTO 2012. LNCS, vol. 7417, pp. 850–867. Springer, Heidelberg (2012). https://doi.org/10.1007/978-3-642-32009-5_49
12. Liang, H., Zhang, X., Cheng, H.: Huffman-code based retrieval for encrypted JPEG images. J. Vis. Commun. Image Represent. **61**, 149–156 (2019)

13. Xia, Z., Jiang, L., Liu, D., Lihua, L., Jeon, B.: BOEW: a content-based image retrieval scheme using bag-of-encrypted-words in cloud computing. IEEE Trans. Serv. Comput. **15**(1), 202–214 (2019)
14. Li, P., Situ, Z.: Encrypted JPEG image retrieval using histograms of transformed coefficients. In: 2019 Asia-Pacific Signal and Information Processing Association Annual Summit and Conference (APSIPA ASC), pp. 1140–1144. IEEE (2019)
15. Feng, Q., Li, P., Lu, Z., Liu, G., Huang, F.: End-to-end learning for encrypted image retrieval. In: 2021 Asia-Pacific Signal and Information Processing Association Annual Summit and Conference (APSIPA ASC), pp. 1839–1845. IEEE (2021)
16. Ma, W., Zhou, T., Qin, J., Xiang, X., Tan, Y., Cai, Z.: A privacy-preserving content-based image retrieval method based on deep learning in cloud computing. Expert Syst. Appl. **203**, 117508 (2022)
17. Xia, Z., Wang, L., Tang, J., Xiong, N.N., Weng, J.: A privacy-preserving image retrieval scheme using secure local binary pattern in cloud computing. IEEE Trans. Netw. Sci. Eng. **8**(1), 318–330 (2020)
18. Yang, D., Yin, Z.: New framework for code-mapping-based reversible data hiding in JPEG images. Inf. Sci. **609**, 319–338 (2022)
19. Lu, Z., Feng, Q., Li, P., Lo, K.-T., Huang, F.: A privacy-preserving image retrieval scheme based on 16×16 DCT and deep learning. IEEE Trans. Cloud Comput. **11**(3), 3314–3325 (2023)
20. Feng, Q., et al.: DHAN: encrypted JPEG image retrieval via DCT histograms-based attention networks. Appl. Soft Comput. **133**, 109935 (2023)
21. Fisher, R.A., Yates, F.: Statistical tables for biological, agricultural and medical research. Edinburgh and London, p. 44 (1957)
22. Goldberg, Y., Levy, O.: Word2vec explained: deriving Mikolov et al.'s negative-sampling word-embedding method. arXiv preprint arXiv:1402.3722 (2014)
23. Vaswani, A., et al.: Attention is all you need. In: Advances in Neural Information Processing Systems, vol. 30 (2017)
24. Devlin, J., Chang, M.W., Lee, K., Toutanova, K.: Bert: pre-training of deep bidirectional transformers for language understanding. arXiv preprint arXiv:1810.04805 (2018)
25. Ba, J.L., Kiros, J.R., Hinton, G.E.: Layer normalization (2016). arXiv:1607.06450
26. Ramachandran, P., Zoph, B., Le, Q.V.: Searching for activation functions. arXiv preprint arXiv:1710.05941 (2017)
27. Ioffe, S., Szegedy, C.: Batch normalization: accelerating deep network training by reducing internal covariate shift. In: International Conference on Machine Learning, pp. 448–456. PMLR (2015)
28. Kim, S., Kim, D., Cho, M., Kwak, S.: Proxy anchor loss for deep metric learning. In: Proceedings of the IEEE/CVF Conference on Computer Vision and Pattern Recognition, pp. 3238–3247 (2020)
29. Wang, J.Z., Li, J., Wiederhold, G.: Simplicity: semantics-sensitive integrated matching for picture libraries. IEEE Trans. Pattern Anal. Mach. Intell. **23**(9), 947–963 (2001)
30. Kingma, D.P., Ba, J.: Adam: a method for stochastic optimization. arXiv preprint arXiv:1412.6980 (2014)

31. Zhong, Z., Zheng, L., Cao, D., Li, S.: Re-ranking person re-identification with k-reciprocal encoding. In: 2017 IEEE Conference on Computer Vision and Pattern Recognition (CVPR), pp. 3652–3661 (2017). https://doi.org/10.1109/CVPR.2017.389
32. Lu, Z., Feng, Q., Li, P.: Encrypted JPEG image retrieval via Huffman-code based self-attention networks. In: 2022 Asia-Pacific Signal and Information Processing Association Annual Summit and Conference (APSIPA ASC), pp. 1–6. IEEE (2022)

Local-Channel Large Separable Kernel Attention

Zengjie Deng, Tao Lei[✉], and Haixia Cui[✉]

School of Electronic Science and Engineering, South China Normal University,
Foshan 528225, China
{2022024826,leitao,cuihaixia}@m.scnu.edu.cn

Abstract. Large Kernel Attention (LKA) has demonstrated superior performance in image classification/segmentation and surpassing transformer-based visual tasks. However, using 1×1 Conv for full-channel interaction in Large Kernel Separable Attention (LSKA) results in quadratic growth in computational complexity and memory usage as the number of channels increases. To alleviate this issue, this study proposes a Local-channel Large Separable Kernel Attention (LLSKA) module where the group convolution is employed to focus module solely on local-channel information to reduce the model complexity while maintaining system performance. The number of groups is determined by an adaptive strategy to determine the local-channel receptive ranges.

Keywords: CNN · local-channel information · Large Kernel Attention (LKA)

1 Introduction

Adding visual attention mechanisms to Convolutional Neural Networks (CNNs) [11] can significantly enhance the system performance. However, the recent research indicates that the self-attention-based models, such as Vision Transformer (ViT) [4] and its variants, demonstrate superior scalability and ability to model the long-range dependencies within input images by introducing multi-fead self-attention mechanisms. In response to the characteristics, the researchers have proposed a series of large attention mechanisms, such as Large Kernel Attention (LKA) [5] and Large Separable Kernel Attention (LSKA) [10]. These large kernel attention mechanisms not only leverage the advantages of convolution in capturing local structural information but also incorporate the strengths of self-attention in modeling long-range dependencies while avoiding their drawbacks in neglecting adaptivity in the channel dimension. Yet, when handling the high-resolution images, the computational complexity and memory consumption

---

This work was supported in part by the GuangDong Basic and Applied Basic Research Foundation under Grant 2024A1515012052, in part by the National Natural Science Foundation of China under Grant 61871433, 61828103, and in part by the Research Platform of South China Normal University.

of ViTs increase quadratically with the image resolution, making them significantly more costly compared to the CNNs.

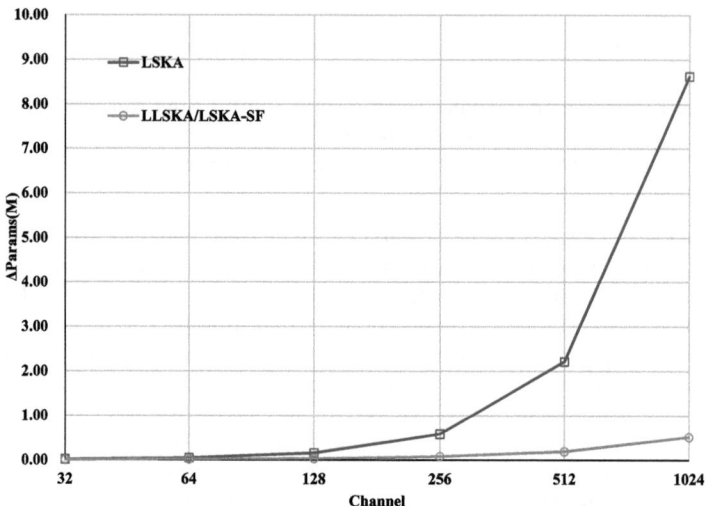

Fig. 1. Parameter increments of LSKA, LLSKA, and LSKA-SF with increasing channels. Parameter increments are generated by adding eight modules at the same number of channels of the convolutional network.

To reduce the parameters and computational burden, many lightweight CNN models have been proposed. MobileNets [7] employed depthwise separable convolutions, breaking down the regular convolutional operations into depth-wise convolution and point-wise convolution. However, the point-wise convolutions still result in a significant increase in parameters. ShuffleNet [14] introduced the group convolutions combined with the Shuffle operation, as shown in Fig. 3b. Recently, FalconNet [2] introduced sparsity to channel connections to maintain a sufficient receptive range with minimal parameters and FLOPs. However, such large kernel attention mechanisms all use 1×1 Conv to focus on the channel information of feature maps, leading to quadratic growth in module parameter count with increasing channel numbers. As the number of channels increases, this results in larger memory and computational overhead, impacting the computational efficiency of the model.

In this paper, we first study the effect of the number of feature map channels C on the number of parameters in LSKA, introduce the sparsity of group convolution [9] into LSKA, and propose the Sparse Full-channel LSKA (LSKA-SF) module. Secondly, comparing the full-channel interaction and local-channel interaction, the proposed Local-channel Large Separable Kernel Attention (LLSKA) implements the local-channel interaction, which significantly reduces the quadratic growth of the number of parameters with the size of the number of channels by the LLSKA module of the VAN, while keeping other factors constant. The proposed LLSKA enables VAN to obtain similar performance to LSKA in CIFAR-10 [8], CIFAR-100 [8], and Tiny-Imagenet-200. In short, the main contributions of this paper are summarised as follows.

- This study proposes to replace the given 1 × 1 Conv with two cascaded group convolutions to achieve local-channel interaction, effectively addressing the inefficiency of depth convolutional kernels in large kernel attention due to the increasing number of channels.
- The proposed channel-adaptive strategy automatically adjusts the channel receptive ranges, allowing the module to have larger receptive ranges for feature maps with a large number of channels and smaller receptive ranges for feature maps with a small number of channels.
- Experimental validation confirms the effectiveness of LLSKA in image classification and segmentation tasks. Compared to LSKA, LLSKA exhibits a reduced inference time. In VAN-LLSKA-Tiny, the proposed module achieves accuracies of 97.47% and 84.09% on the CIFAR-10 and CIFAR-100 datasets, respectively. On the Tiny-ImageNet-200 dataset, it achieves an accuracy of 73.64%, with a 5.2% reduction in parameters, a 6.0% decrease in computation, and a 2.7% increase in inference speed compared to LSKA.

2 Method

In this section, we first reduce parameter and computational overhead by employing sparse full-channel interaction. Subsequently, contrasting sparse full-channel interaction with local-channel interaction prompts the introduction of Local-channel Large Separable Kernel Attention (LLSKA). Moreover, a channel adaptive strategy is adopted to determine the receptive ranges of group convolutions. Finally, a comparative analysis of the complexities of LSKA and LLSKA is conducted.

2.1 Sparse Full-Channel Interaction

In Fig. 2a, the use of 1 × 1 Conv in LSKA enables attention to full-channel information. The connectivity pattern between the output neurons and input neurons in the 1 × 1 Conv is illustrated in Fig. 3a, where the connections between output neurons and input neurons are highly dense, resulting in channel receptive ranges of C. On the other hand, in Fig. 2b, two GConvs (i.e., group convolutions, referring to GConv1 and GConv2 in this paper) and Shuffle are employed to attend to full-channel information. The connectivity pattern between the output neurons and input neurons is depicted in Fig. 3b, where output neurons are indirectly connected to all input neurons, resulting in channel receptive ranges of C. We refer to this improved module of LSKA as Sparse Full-channel LSKA(LSKA-SF).

To ensure that the receptive ranges of two cascaded GConv layers match that of a Conv layer while maintaining minimal parameters, we employ the sparse

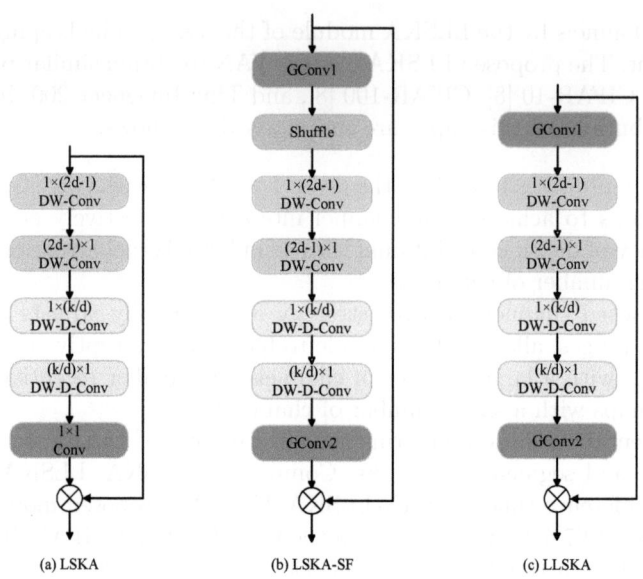

Fig. 2. Comparison of different designs of large kernel attention modules.

decomposition technique from FalconNet. In Fig. 4, suppose the input feature map $Input \in R^{H \times W \times C}$, the middle output feature map $Feature \in R^{H \times W \times \frac{C}{R}}$, the output feature map $Output \in R^{H \times W \times C}$, where the size of the input and output space are both H, W, the input and output channels are both C, and the channel reduction ratio R (hyperparameter, default is 2). As in Fig. 4, The sensory range k of GConnv1 is the number of groups $G_1 = \frac{C}{k}$, the number of input channels C, and the number of output channels $\frac{C}{R}$. At this point, the number of GConv1 parameters $\frac{Ck}{R}$.

To ensure that the channel receptive range is consistent with the 1×1 Conv, GConnv2 is the number of groups $G_2 = \frac{C}{RG_1}$, the number of input channels $\frac{C}{R}$, and the number of output channels C. At this point, the number of GConv2 parameters $\frac{C^2}{k}$. The total number of parameters in the two GConvs is $\frac{Ck}{R} + \frac{C^2}{k}$. To minimize the number of parameters one should make $k = \sqrt{CR}$, which is dynamically adjusted according to C,R. The total number of parameters in the GConvs is $2C\sqrt{\frac{C}{R}}$. LSKA-SF introduces channel sparsity while maintaining the sensory range of the channel and reducing the number of parameters.

2.2 Local-Channel Interaction

As illustrated in Fig. 2c, we utilize only two group convolutions to achieve local-channel interaction. As previously mentioned, while group convolutions and channel shuffling can reduce parameters and maintain full-channel interaction, the sparse connections among neurons may limit the information available to

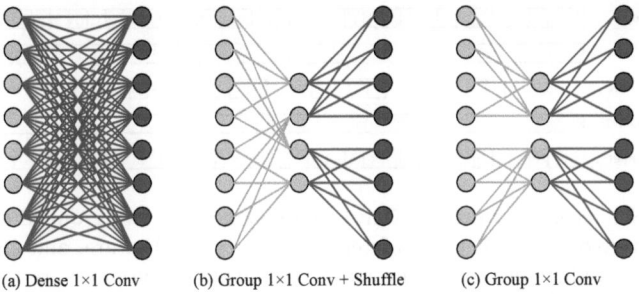

Fig. 3. Connections and corresponding receptive ranges of different 1×1 Convs.

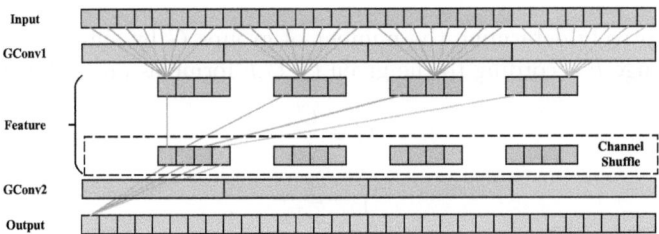

Fig. 4. LSKA-SF receptive range. GConv1 and GConv2 are two grouped convolutions, with different colors representing different groups. Input, Feature, and Output represent the input, middle output feature map, and output feature map, respectively. The number of blocks indicates the number of channels in the feature map, and blocks of different colors represent the operations performed by different convolution groups.

each neuron from its inputs, thereby reducing representational capacity. Therefore, we only employ group convolutions without channel shuffling to ensure denser connections between output and input neurons. As shown in Fig. 3b, a single output neuron from group convolution plus shuffling connects with only four input neurons. In Fig. 3c, a single output neuron from plain group convolution connects with eight input neurons. This denser connection pattern enhances the model's representative capacity.

In LLSKA, we maintain consistency with LSKA-SF by setting the number of group convolutions groups to be identical, ensuring parity in the number of parameters between the two modules. However, the channel receptive ranges of LLSKA, depicted in Fig. 5, reveal that the receptive ranges of each output are limited to k.

2.3 Channel Adaptive Strategy

As our module uses local-channel interactions, there is a need to determine the range of receptivity of the channel interactions. The number of channels may be different for different feature maps at different locations in the network, and thus the number of channel interactions needs to be dynamically adjusted. Thus

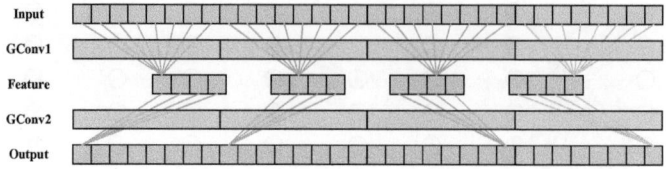

Fig. 5. LLSKA receptive range. GConv1 and GConv2 are two grouped convolutions, with different colors representing different groups. Input, Feature, and Output represent the input, middle output feature map, and output feature map, respectively. The number of blocks indicates the number of channels in the feature map, and blocks of different colors represent the operations performed by different convolution groups.

we can adaptively determine the number of groups G by simply adjusting the receptive range k according to the given C. G,k formulas are as follows:

$$G = \frac{C}{k} \tag{1}$$

$$k = \begin{cases} \frac{C}{\lfloor \frac{\sqrt{C}}{\gamma} \rfloor \times \gamma}, \\ \sqrt{CR}. \end{cases} \tag{2}$$

where $\lfloor t \rfloor$ denotes the nearest integer to t taken downwards. Since the number of channels in the feature map in the network is usually an integer multiple of 4 and G needs to be divisible by C, we set the value of γ to 4. R is the channel reduction factor (hyperparameter, $R = 2$ by default). Our priority is to ensure that the parameters of LSKA-SF and LLSKA modules are consistent and minimized, thus we first use $\sqrt{CR}$ to calculate the value of k. When $\sqrt{CR}$ is not an integer, we use $\frac{C}{\lfloor \frac{\sqrt{C}}{\gamma} \rfloor \times \gamma}$ to calculate the k value. By employing the aforementioned strategy, feature maps with a larger number of channels possess broader receptive ranges, whereas those with fewer channels exhibit narrower receptive ranges. This approach also helps to maintain relatively lower parameters.

2.4 Complexity Analysis of LLSKA

The LSKA structure, as depicted in Fig. 2a, assumes that the input and output sizes of LSKA feature maps are the same (i.e., $H \times W \times C$). We compute the floating-point operations (FLOPs) and parameters (Params) for LSKA as follows:

$$Params = (2d - 1) \times C \times 2 + \lceil \frac{k}{d} \rceil \times C \times 2 + C \times C \tag{3}$$

$$FLOPs = ((2d - 1) \times C \times 2 + \lceil \frac{k}{d} \rceil \times C \times 2 + C \times C) \times H \times W \tag{4}$$

where k is the convolution kernel size and d is the expansion rate.

The number of parameters and FLOPs for LLSKA are calculated as follows:

$$Params = (2d - 1) \times \frac{C}{R} \times 2 + \lceil \frac{k}{d} \rceil \times \frac{C}{R} \times 2 + \frac{C^2}{RG_1} \times CG_1 \tag{5}$$

$$FLOPs = ((2d-1) \times \frac{C}{R} \times 2 + [\frac{k}{d}] \times \frac{C}{R} \times 2 + \frac{C^2}{RG_1} \times CG_1) \times H \times W \quad (6)$$

From Sect. 2.1, to minimize Eq. 5 and 6 with C, R, d, and k constant, $G_1 = \sqrt{\frac{C}{R}}$ is required. In this case, Eq. 7 and 8 are obtained as follows:

$$Params = (2d-1) \times \frac{C}{R} \times 2 + [\frac{k}{d}] \times \frac{C}{R} \times 2 + 2C\sqrt{\frac{C}{R}} \quad (7)$$

$$FLOPs = ((2d-1) \times \frac{C}{R} \times 2 + [\frac{k}{d}] \times \frac{C}{R} \times 2 + 2C\sqrt{\frac{C}{R}}) \times H \times W \quad (8)$$

By the first two terms of Eq. 7 and 3, the number of parameters of the spatial convolutional layer of LLSKA is the number of parameters of LSKA. Again, when comparing the third term, it changes from C^2 to $C^{\frac{3}{2}}$. The variation of LSKA parameters to channel numbers is illustrated in Fig. 1, showing a quadratic growth trend. Simultaneously, it can be observed that LLSKA addresses the issue of quadratic growth in parameters, exhibiting fewer parameters and FLOPs compared to LSKA.

3 Experiment

To validate the effectiveness of the proposed LLSKA, a comparative analysis of its performance in image classification tasks was conducted against LSKA. Additionally, experiments were conducted on ResNet, FasterNet, and D-LKA Net to validate the effectiveness of the proposed module in other models.

3.1 Settings

Image Classification. We conducted experiments on CIFAR-10/100 and Tiny-ImageNet-200 datasets, following the training setup described in [10]. During the testing phase, we reported the Top-1 accuracy and parameter count on the validation sets of CIFAR-10/100 and Tiny-ImageNet-200. Additionally, we reported the inference speed (examples per second) on the Tiny-ImageNet-200 validation set.

Skin Lesion Segmentation. Experiments were conducted on the skin lesion segmentation datasets ISIC2017 and ISIC2018. The data preprocessing and training process parameter settings were consistent with those described in the reference [1].

3.2 Ablation Study

Local-Channel Interaction. The study conducted ablation experiments to demonstrate the effectiveness of each module within LLSKA. Utilizing the Tiny model as the baseline, we initially compared LSKA-SF and LLSKA to ascertain the necessity of full-channel interaction versus local-channel interaction. Following the dataset settings described previously, experiments were conducted on CIFAR-10/100. The experimental results, as shown in Table 1, indicate that LLSKA achieved the optimal Top-1 accuracy, confirming the superiority of local channel interaction over sparse global channel interaction and no channel interaction.

Table 1. Ablation of the local-channel and full-channel interaction on CIFAR-10/100.

Index	GConv1,GConv2	Shuffle	Input Resolution	CIFAR-10	CIFAR-100
A	✓	✓	32^2	88.91	67.47
B	✓	✗	32^2	**89.18**	**67.54**
C	✗	✗	32^2	88.98	67.52

Channel Adaptive Strategy. As shown in Eq. 1 and 2, the size of k in our LLSKA module affects the size of the channel receptive ranges. Here, we evaluate the effectiveness of the Channel Adaptive Strategy on LLSKA. We set k to 4, 8, 16, and adaptive strategy on VAN-LLSKA-Tiny and then train it. The results are shown in Fig. 6. The size of k has an impact on the accuracy of the model. The model setting a fixed value of k cannot adapt to the change in the number of channels of the feature map while using an adaptive strategy to set different feeling ranges for feature maps with different numbers of channels can make the model more accurate.

3.3 Comparison with Existing Methods

Table 2 and Table 3 indicate that LLSKA maintains similar performance to LSKA within VAN while reducing both parameters and computational load. The results of LLSKA on CIFAR-10 and CIFAR-100 are comparable, with an analysis based on CIFAR-10 experimental results presented in Table 2. Compared to VAN-LSKA-Tiny, VAN-LLSKA-Tiny exhibits comparable performance while reducing parameters by 7.8% and computational load by 5.8%. Relative to VAN-LSKA-Small, VAN-LLSKA-Small shows a slight performance improvement with parameters reduced by 6.8% and computational load decreased by 6.1%. In comparison to VAN-LSKA-Base, VAN-LLSKA-Base experiences a slight performance decline with parameters reduced by 7.7% and computational load decreased by 6.9%.

Furthermore, LLSKA was experimented with and subjected to inference speed tests on Tiny-Imagenet-200, with the results presented in Table 3. Table 3 records the parameters, FLOPs, inference speed, and Top-1 accuracy of LLSKA. Compared to VAN-LSKA-Tiny, VAN-LLSKA-Tiny shows a slight performance

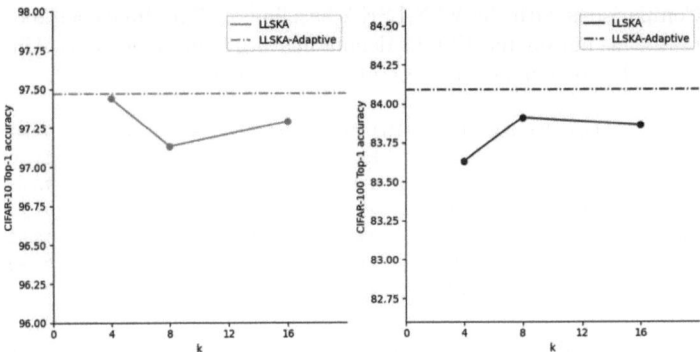

Fig. 6. LLSKA Receptive Range.

improvement with parameters reduced by 5.2%, computational load decreased by 6.0%, and an increase in inference speed by 2.7%. Relative to VAN-LSKA-Small, VAN-LLSKA-Small experiences a slight performance decline with parameters reduced by 6.7%, computational load decreased by 6.1%, and an increase in inference speed by 4.7%. In comparison to VAN-LSKA-Base, VAN-LLSKA-Base demonstrates comparable performance with parameters reduced by 7.7%, computational load decreased by 6.9%, and an increase in inference speed by 4.8%. Notably, the inference speed of LLSKA is slightly higher than that of LSKA.

The above results indicate that as the model scale increases, the reduction in parameters and FLOPs becomes more pronounced when employing LLSKA, leading to a more significant change in inference speed. This suggests that LLSKA exhibits higher operational efficiency while utilizing fewer parameters and computational resources while maintaining performance similar to LSKA.

Table 2. Comparisons with the VAN-LSKA baseline on CIFAR-10/100, Tiny-Imagenet-200 classification. Params means parameter. FLOPs denote floating point operations.

Model	Input Resolution	Params(M)	FLOPs(M)	Model Type	CIFAR-10	CIFAR-100	Tiny-Imagenet-200
CRTATE-S [13]	224^2	13.12	-	Transformer	96	81.0	-
CRTATE-B [13]	224^2	22.80	-	Transformer	96.8	82.7	-
CRTATE-L [13]	224^2	77.64	-	Transformer	97.2	83.6	-
ResNet XnIDR [12]	224^2	23.86	-	Convolution	96.87	-	-
MobileNetV1 [7]	224^2	4.23	588.91	Convolution	93.18	72.47	64.36
FasterNet-T0 [3]	224^2	2.63	339.37	Convolution	95.77	79.43	58.32
FalconNet [2]	224^2	2.39	333.14	Convolution	94.85	78.04	69.46
VAN-LSKA-Tiny	224^2	3.8	838.92	Convolution	97.44	84.3	73.24
VAN-LLSKA-Tiny(Ours)	224^2	**3.5**	**788.18**	Convolution	**97.47**	84.09	**73.64**
VAN-LSKA-Small	224^2	13.2	2459.93	Convolution	97.58	83.82	73.25
VAN-LLSKA-Small(Ours)	224^2	**12.3**	**2308.4**	Convolution	**97.68**	**84.19**	**73.92**
VAN-LSKA-Base	224^2	25.8	4922.67	Convolution	**97.88**	84.29	**74.82**
VAN-LLSKA-Base(Ours)	224^2	**23.8**	**4580.97**	Convolution	97.68	**84.38**	74.62

Table 3. Comparisons with the VAN-LSKA baseline on Tiny-Imagenet-200 classification. Params means parameter. FLOPs denote floating point operations. The inference speed is the number of samples per second (higher is better).

Model	Input Resolution	Params(M)	FLOPs(M)	Inference Speed(example/secs)	Tiny-Imagenet-200
VAN-LSKA-Tiny	224^2	3.8	839.0	2052	73.24
VAN-LLSKA-Tiny(Ours)	224^2	**3.6**	**788.2**	**2109**	**73.64**
VAN-LSKA-Small	224^2	13.3	2460.0	1350	73.25
VAN-LLSKA-Small(Ours)	224^2	**12.4**	**2308.5**	**1414**	**73.92**
VAN-LSKA-Base	224^2	25.9	4922.8	736	**74.82**
VAN-LLSKA-Base(Ours)	224^2	**23.9**	**4581.1**	**772**	74.62

Table 4. Experimental results of the proposed module on other image classification models.

Model	Input Resolution	Params(M)	FLOPs(M)	CIFAR-10	CIFAR-100
ResNet-18 [6]	224^2	11.18	1823.5	96.80	80.73
ResNet-18-LSKA	224^2	11.93	1944.32	96.85	81.12
ResNet-18-LLSKA	224^2	11.26	1844.57	96.82	81.09
FasterNet-T0 [3]	224^2	2.63	339.37	95.77	79.43
FasterNet-T0-LSKA	224^2	3.12	339.37	95.87	79.87
FasterNet-T0-LLSKA	224^2	2.71	339.37	95.91	79.85

3.4 The Proposed Modules Performance On Other Methods

LSKA and LLSKA modules were integrated into ResNet-18 and FasterNet-T0 for performance evaluation in detection tasks. As shown in Table 4, both LLSKA and LSKA demonstrate accuracy improvements within ResNet-18. While LLSKA and LSKA exhibit similar accuracy enhancements in ResNet-18 and FasterNet-T0, LLSKA achieves fewer parameters and FLOPs compared to LSKA. In the segmentation task model, D-LKA was replaced with LLSKA and compared with the original D-LKA Net on skin lesion segmentation. Experimental results, as shown in Table 5, indicate improved ACC and SP on ISIC2017/ISIC2018 compared to the original model. These results underscore the efficacy of our module in both classification and segmentation tasks.

Table 5. Experimental results of the proposed module on other image segmentation models.

Methods	ISIC 2017				ISIC 2018			
	DSC	SE	SP	**ACC**	DSC	SE	SP	**ACC**
LKA [1]	0.9229	0.9192	0.9824	0.9704	0.9118	0.8984	0.9802	0.9632
D-LKA Net [1]	0.9254	0.9327	0.9793	0.9705	0.9177	0.9164	0.9773	0.9647
LLSKA	0.9152	0.8907	0.9882	**0.9709**	0.9159	0.8957	0.9851	**0.9673**

4 Conclusion

This paper maintains the spatial perception range of LSKA and introduces the local-channel interaction to address the quadratic growth issue in 1×1 Conv parameters with the number of channels in the LSKA module increasing. An effective LLSKA module is proposed where the group convolution generates the channel attention and the channel adaptive strategy determines the channel receptive range. Experimental results demonstrate that incorporating the LLSKA module into ResNet and FasterNet can improve the model's accuracy while reducing the parameter count compared to LSKA. Through this research, we aim to enhance the model performance on mobile devices using the LLSKA module.

References

1. Azad, R., et al.: Beyond self-attention: deformable large kernel attention for medical image segmentation. In: Proceedings of the IEEE/CVF Winter Conference on Applications of Computer Vision, pp. 1287–1297 (2024)
2. Cai, Z., Shen, Q.: Falconnet: factorization for the light-weight convnets. In: International Conference on Neural Information Processing, pp. 368–380. Springer (2023)
3. Chen, J., et al.: Run, don't walk: chasing higher flops for faster neural networks. In: Proceedings of the IEEE/CVF Conference on Computer Vision and Pattern Recognition, pp. 12021–12031 (2023)
4. Dosovitskiy, A., et al.: An image is worth 16x16 words: transformers for image recognition at scale. arXiv preprint arXiv:2010.11929 (2020)
5. Guo, M.H., Lu, C.Z., Liu, Z.N., Cheng, M.M., Hu, S.M.: Visual attention network. Comput. Vis. Media **9**(4), 733–752 (2023)
6. He, K., Zhang, X., Ren, S., Sun, J.: Deep residual learning for image recognition. In: Proceedings of the IEEE Conference on Computer Vision and Pattern Recognition, pp. 770–778 (2016)
7. Howard, A.G., et al.: Mobilenets: efficient convolutional neural networks for mobile vision applications. arXiv preprint arXiv:1704.04861 (2017)
8. Krizhevsky, A., Hinton, G., et al.: Learning multiple layers of features from tiny images (2009)
9. Krizhevsky, A., Sutskever, I., Hinton, G.E.: Imagenet classification with deep convolutional neural networks. In: Advances in Neural Information Processing Systems, vol. 25 (2012)
10. Lau, K.W., Po, L.M., Rehman, Y.A.U.: Large separable kernel attention: rethinking the large kernel attention design in CNN. Expert Syst. Appl. **236**, 121352 (2024)
11. LeCun, Y., Bottou, L., Bengio, Y., Haffner, P.: Gradient-based learning applied to document recognition. Proc. IEEE **86**(11), 2278–2324 (1998)
12. Sun, J., Fard, A.P., Mahoor, M.H.: XnODR and XnIDR: two accurate and fast fully connected layers for convolutional neural networks. J. Intell. Robot. Syst. **109**(1), 17 (2023)
13. Yu, Y., et al.: White-box transformers via sparse rate reduction. In: Advances in Neural Information Processing Systems, vol. 36 (2024)
14. Zhang, X., Zhou, X., Lin, M., Sun, J.: Shufflenet: an extremely efficient convolutional neural network for mobile devices. In: Proceedings of the IEEE Conference on Computer Vision and Pattern Recognition, pp. 6848–6856 (2018)

FLTP: A Fast and Low-Bandwidth Transaction Propagation Protocol in Ethereum

Deen Ma, Chonghe Zhao, Shengli Zhang[✉], Taotao Wang, and Qing Yang

College of Electronic and Information Engineering, Shenzhen University, Shenzhen, China
zsl@szu.edu.cn

Abstract. Blockchain technology, exemplified by Ethereum, relies on P2P networks for transaction and block propagation. Ethereum uses a hybrid transaction propagation protocol to conserve bandwidth, where nodes forward either full transactions or transaction hashes to their neighbors. While this approach saves bandwidth, it can introduce delays in transaction propagation, especially when nodes must request full transactions using *GetData* messages. In this paper, we introduce FLTP, a fast and low-bandwidth transaction propagation protocol designed to improve bandwidth efficiency and reduce propagation delays. Our analysis of Ethereum's transaction propagation process reveals that nodes with higher connectivity tend to receive transactions faster due to fewer *GetData* requests. Based on these insights, in FLTP, each node maintains a table to track the frequency of *GetData* requests from each neighbor. This allows nodes to prioritize propagation transactions to those with a history of needing more data. Experiments conducted in a simulated Ethereum environment demonstrate that, compared to transaction propagation protocol in Ethereum, FLTP reduces data by 14.36% and decreases transaction propagation time by 38.61%, demonstrating its effectiveness in optimizing transaction propagation.

Keywords: Ethereum Blockchain · Peer-to-Peer Network · Transaction Propagation Protocol · Bandwidth · Transaction Propagation Time

1 Introduction

Blockchain technology, first introduced by Satoshi Nakamoto in Bitcoin, is a secure, verifiable, and tamper-resistant distributed ledger that supports digital asset transactions [18]. Blockchain can achieve consensus in permissionless decentralized networks [7,19], and has become a disruptive technology in the

---

This work was supported in part by the Guangdong Basic and Applied Basic Research Foundation (2024A1515012407), in part by Research Center for FinTech and Digital-Intelligent Management, Shenzhen University, and in part by Shenzhen Key Research Project (JSGG20220831095603007, JCYJ20220818100810023).

fields of fintech [6], the Internet of Things (IoT) [5,11], Metaverse [12,13,24], and supply chain management [1]. In 2014, Ethereum introduced smart contracts and the Ethereum Virtual Machine (EVM) [10], enabling decentralized execution of Turing-complete computational tasks [3]. By leveraging smart contracts, Ethereum greatly expanded the application scope of blockchain, allowing users to develop various decentralized applications (DApps). The next generation of blockchains will further enhance performance by adopting novel consensus protocols, cross-chain methods, and sharding technologies.

As a fully distributed system, Ethereum exploits a Peer-to-Peer (P2P) network to build its communication infrastructure [14]. A new node participates in the system by discovering and connecting with other nodes in the P2P network. All nodes exchange transactions and blocks over the P2P network to maintain a consistent ledger. The basic performance and stability of Ethereum are thereby influenced by message propagation protocols. For instance, the propagation time for blocks and transactions in the network is a key factor that affects the security and transaction processing capacity of Ethereum [28]. Speeding up the propagation of blocks and transactions would enhance both the robustness and transaction processing capacity of Ethereum.

Generally, flooding [15] is employed in Peer-to-Peer (P2P) networks to quickly forward messages. Unfortunately, this method is inefficient in terms of bandwidth, as each node forwards messages to all its neighboring nodes, resulting in the same message being received multiple times from different neighbors. To improve bandwidth efficiency, the Ethereum community has proposed a hybrid transaction propagation protocol [22]. In this protocol, a node randomly selects a subset of its neighbors to forward full transactions, while sending only the transaction hashes to the remaining neighbors. When a node receives a transaction hash but does not have the corresponding transaction, it can send a *GetData* packet to request the complete transaction from the node that sent the hash. This mechanism effectively saves bandwidth; however, it can increase transaction propagation delays, as some nodes may require up to 1.5 Time To Live (TTL) intervals to obtain the complete transactions [23].

Although numerous studies have focused on analyzing and optimizing these processes [17,25,26], most have primarily concentrated on block propagation [20], leaving transaction propagation with insufficient attention. In this paper, we introduce a novel transaction propagation protocol called FLTP, designed to save bandwidth and accelerate the propagation process. The primary contributions of this work are as follows:

- We simulate and analyze the transaction propagation process within an environment that closely mimics the Ethereum network. Our findings reveal that certain nodes consistently receive transactions earlier than others. These early-receiving nodes share a common characteristic: they tend to have a higher degree of connectivity, which enables them to reduce the number of *GetData* messages needed during transaction propagation.
- We propose FLTP, a fast and low-bandwidth transaction propagation protocol that optimizes the use of *GetData* messages. Based on our analysis, to

minimize the number of nodes retrieving transactions via *GetData*, each node can forward transaction hashes to high-degree neighbors while propagating full transactions to low-degree neighbors. However, obtaining a real-time list of a neighbor's neighbors in Ethereum is not feasible. To address this, FLTP maintains a table that records the historical number of *GetData* requests from each neighbor. Using this table, each node prioritizes propagating full transactions to neighbors with a high number of *GetData* requests while propagating transaction hashes to those with fewer requests.
- We implement FLTP and evaluate its performance in a simulated environment that closely resembles the Ethereum network. The experimental results indicate that FLTP achieves a 14.36% reduction in data and reduces transaction propagation time across the network by 38.61%. This demonstrates that FLTP not only conserves bandwidth but also significantly decreases propagation latency.

2 Background

This section first introduces the two types of P2P network structures: structured P2P networks and unstructured P2P networks. Ethereum utilizes a structured P2P network. Following this, we describe the transaction propagation protocol of Ethereum and analyze its shortcomings.

2.1 P2P Network

P2P (Peer-to-Peer) networks allow each device to freely join or leave the network, becoming a node. When node A connects to node B, they become each other's neighbors. In contrast to the client-server architecture, each node in a P2P network can act as both a client and a server, requesting and providing services. This eliminates single points of failure and decentralizes data storage, enhancing privacy [4]. Based on whether nodes and network storage content are organized or added in a deterministic manner, P2P networks can be classified into structured P2P networks and unstructured P2P networks.

Structured P2P Networks. When a P2P network does not impose much structure on the connections between nodes, and the storage of network content is independent of the network topology, it is classified as an unstructured P2P network. In this type of network, content needs to be located using specific methods. These include broadcasting request messages throughout the network until the desired content is found, like Flooding [9], or using more refined methods such as the Random Walk mechanism [2].

In Flooding, to prevent messages from propagating endlessly, recipients perform several checks. First, each node records the identifiers of previously received messages in a list. If they encounter the same message again, they discard the duplicate. Second, to avoid indefinite storage of seen messages, which would increase storage capacity, each message is assigned a Time To Live (TTL). The message originator sets the TTL, and it is decremented by one at each node that receives the message. When the TTL reaches zero, the message is no longer propagated.

In Random Walk, a single request message is sent to a randomly chosen neighbor, and this message has a TTL value that decreases with each hop. If the message is received by a node that has the requested content, the message propagation process terminates, and the found content is returned. Otherwise, the request fails, and the requester can choose to initiate the request again on another path. To shorten response time, multiple random walks can be initiated in parallel on different paths. The key to this method is the random selection of the next hop, which helps avoid propagating the query back to nodes that have already received it.

Unstructured P2P Networks. Early P2P networks were unstructured, making them easy to implement but inefficient in routing and unable to locate rare objects. These disadvantages led to the development of structured P2P networks with deterministic routing mechanisms [16] that ensure any object stored in the network can be located. Most of these designs use specific routing geometries and are called structured P2P networks.

Structured P2P networks support key-based routing, mapping object identifiers to peer identifier address spaces, and routing object requests to the closest node in the address space. These systems are known as Distributed Object Location and Routing (DOLR) systems, with one specific type being the Distributed Hash Table (DHT) [29]. In DHTs, identifiers are computed using consistent hashing, and each node holds a specific range of the hash table.

Various implementations of structured P2P networks have been proposed, such as Chord [21], which organizes peers in a logical ring and maintains neighbor pointers at logarithmic intervals around the ring. Each peer also links to its predecessor and successor. Chord's routing table is known as the Finger Table. Other classic implementations include Pastry and Tapestry.

2.2 Ethereum Transaction Relay Protocol

The Ethereum Wire Protocol (ETH) [8] is used for exchanging blockchain messages between Ethereum nodes. It requires establishing connections between nodes and primarily accomplishes three tasks: chain synchronization, block propagation, and transaction propagation. This section introduces the transaction propagation process.

Transaction propagation takes place when nodes synchronize their transaction pools or when new transactions are generated and need to be sent out.

In the Ethereum transaction propagation protocol, suppose there is a node A that wants to forward a transaction to its neighbor nodes. Among its neighbors, there are N nodes that have not received the transaction or transaction hash from node A. In this scenario, node A randomly selects $\sqrt{N}$ neighbor nodes from these N neighbors to directly forward the transaction, while the remaining $N - \sqrt{N}$ neighbor nodes receive the transaction hash. Neighbor nodes that receive the transaction will choose to accept it if needed. Neighbor nodes that receive the transaction hash will check if they have already received the transaction. If not, they will request the transaction from node A by send *Getdata* messages. Upon receiving the *Getdata*, node A will then send the transaction to the requesting neighbor node. This process is illustrated in Fig. 1.

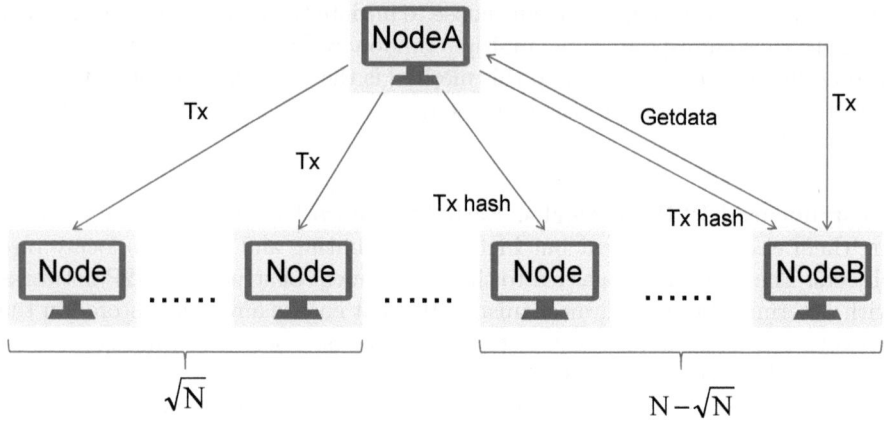

Fig. 1. Ethereum transaction propagation.

For the existing propagation protocol data consumption, assume the total number of nodes in the network is M, and each node has N neighbors (where N depends on the number of nodes that the node is connected to in the network topology). The transaction byte size is S_t, the transaction hash byte size is S_{hash}, the *Getdata* message byte size is S_{get}. In an ideal scenario, each node in the entire network only needs to receive a transaction once. In this case, the data consumption for propagating the transaction across the entire network would be:

$$D_{ini} = M \cdot S_t \tag{1}$$

In reality, according to the transaction propagation protocol, the data consumption starts with a transaction being generated by a node is

$$D_{create} = S_t \tag{2}$$

Afterward, the transaction starts propagating throughout the entire network. Except for the node that generated the transaction, all other nodes need to obtain the transaction. Assuming a node has N neighbors, the probability of it receiving the transaction hash from one of its neighbor nodes is: $P = \frac{N-\sqrt{N}}{N}$. The average number of transaction hashes received from N neighbor nodes is $N - \sqrt{N}$. The number of bytes consumed by all nodes receiving the transaction hash from their neighbor nodes is:

$$D_{hash} = \sum_{i=1}^{M-1} \left(N_i - \sqrt{N_i}\right) \cdot S_{hash} \tag{3}$$

After receiving the transaction hash, if the node does not have the transaction, it will only send a *GetData* request for the transaction only to one of the neighbor nodes that sent the transaction hash. It will not request the transaction from any other neighbors. The neighbor node that receives this request will then send the transaction back to the requesting node. The number of bytes consumed in this process is:

$$D_{reply} = (M-1) \cdot (S_t + S_{get}) \tag{4}$$

The probability that each node directly receives the transaction from one neighbor node is $\frac{1}{\sqrt{N}}$, on average, each node receives $\sqrt{N}$ transactions from N neighbor nodes. Due to the randomness of transaction propagation, nodes will still receive duplicate transactions even if they already have the transaction. The number of bytes consumed by all nodes when directly receiving transactions from neighbor nodes is:

$$D_{tx} = \sum_{i=1}^{M-1} \sqrt{N_i} \cdot S_t \tag{5}$$

Therefore, for the propagation of a single transaction across the entire network, the additional data generated by the transaction propagation protocol is:

$$D_{more} = D_{total} - D_{ini} = (M-1) \cdot S_{get} + D_{tx} + D_{hash} \tag{6}$$

where D_{total} can be expressed as $D_{total} = D_{create} + D_{tx} + D_{hash} + DD_{reply}$. It can be seen that the additional data D_{more} is much greater than D_{ini}, and the additional data increases linearly with the number of nodes in the entire network and increases with the number of neighbor nodes. This results in unnecessary bandwidth resource wastage.

3 Ethereum Transaction Propagation Protocol Test

Through the analysis in Sect. 2.2, we can identify the issues with the current Ethereum transaction propagation protocol. Because transactions are propagated randomly, it is possible to forward transactions to neighboring nodes that already have the transaction (and do not require it), while propagating transaction hashes to neighboring nodes that do not have the transaction (and do require it). The key to solving this problem lies in predicting the likelihood that a neighboring node needs the transaction. If the likelihood that a neighboring node needs the transaction is low, there is no need to forward the transaction to that node; instead, just propagating the smaller transaction hash is sufficient. If a neighboring node already has the transaction, it will discard the received transaction hash without needing to reply, thus saving more data compared to directly propagating the transaction. In case the prediction is incorrect and the neighboring node does not possess the transaction, since the node has received the transaction hash, it will subsequently request the transaction through a *GetData* request, ensuring that the node will eventually obtain the transaction. If the likelihood that a neighboring node needs the transaction is high, then the transaction can be propagated directly to that node, as the node is likely to accept the transaction and will probably not discard it.

3.1 Experimental Design and Parameter Settings

To analyze the method for predicting the likelihood that a node needs a transaction, we first conduct a simulation experiment using MATLAB to measure the transaction propagation process in Ethereum. To ensure that the simulation is as consistent as possible with the real Ethereum network, we have designed the experiment meticulously:

First, in the selection of the number of nodes, to simulate a sizable Ethereum network, we referenced a tested Ethereum network topology [27] and extracted a subset of 100 nodes. We generated a network topology of 100 nodes by reading the topology file through MATLAB. To simulate the real environment as closely as possible when creating nodes, we set a bandwidth limit of 25 MBit/sec for the nodes and allocated IP to the nodes according to the actual Ethereum node distribution ratio. We then generated 100 transactions, each 100 bytes in size, and randomly selected nodes to broadcast these transactions. When a node broadcasts a transaction, a delay is first caused due to the bandwidth limit, and then a propagation delay is added based on the IP of the sending and receiving nodes. These two factors are crucial in affecting the transaction propagation

Table 1. Experimental Parameters and Settings.

Experimental Parameter	Parameter Value
Total Number of Nodes	100
Node Bandwidth	25 MBit/sec
Packet Loss Rate	0-0.01 Random
Transaction Message Size	100 Bytes
Transaction Hash Message Size	32 Bytes
Getdata Message Size	145 Bytes
Number of Broadcast Transactions	100
Propagation Delay	Assigned refer to Node IP

speed. Regarding the settings for message sizes, we refer to the actual message sizes in Ethereum. The transaction message size is 100 bytes, the transaction hash message size is 32 bytes, and the *GetData* message size is 145 bytes. The packet loss rate is set to a random value between 0 and 0.01. The parameter settings are shown in Table 1.

3.2 Experimental Results and Analysis

In the experiment, we recorded the time and content of messages sent and received by each node. By analyzing the logs and experimental data, we identified the correlation between the number of neighbors of a node and the time taken to receive a transaction. This relationship is illustrated in Fig. 2.

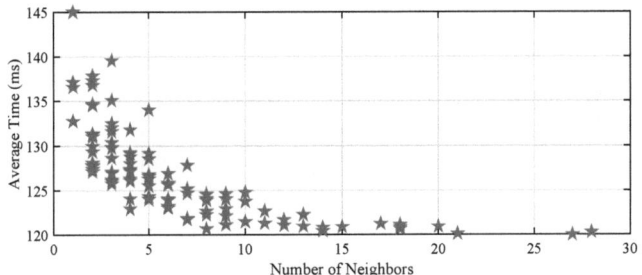

Fig. 2. Relationship Between Number of Neighbors and Average Time to Receive Transaction.

By calculating the correlation between the number of neighboring nodes and the time taken to receive a transaction, we obtained a Spearman correlation coefficient $R = -0.886058$. This indicates a very strong negative correlation between the number of neighbor nodes and the time taken to receive a message. In other words, the more neighbors a node has, the shorter the time it takes to receive a transaction.

According to the above analysis, the more neighbors a node has, the shorter the time it takes to receive a transaction. Conversely, nodes with fewer neighbors take longer to receive a transaction. These nodes often receive the transaction hash first and then request the transaction from their neighbors via *GetData*. The neighbors then send the transaction to the node. Compared to directly sending the transaction to the node, this process involves additional data for the transaction hash and *GetData*, which increases data consumption and prolongs the time for the transaction to be broadcast across the entire network.

To reduce data consumption during transaction broadcasting and speed up the transaction broadcast across the entire network, we consider broadcasting the transaction first to nodes with fewer neighbors. The specific design of the protocol is as follows:

Before a node decides to forward a received transaction, it first obtains the number of neighbors for each of its neighboring nodes and sorts them in ascending order. The node then sends the transaction to the $\sqrt{N}$ neighbors with the fewest neighbors and sends the transaction hash to the remaining $N - \sqrt{N}$ neighbors. The rest of the process remains the same as the original Ethereum protocol.

The new experiment only modifies the transaction propagation protocol, while other experimental settings remain the same as in Sect. 3.1. By testing and organizing data based on the neighbor count-optimized transaction propagation protocol, we obtained the following metrics under this protocol: the average time for each transaction to propagate across the entire network, the average amount of transaction data sent, the average amount of transaction hash data sent, the average amount of *GetData* sent, and the average total data sent. The comparison with the original Ethereum protocol is illustrated in Figs. 3 and 4.

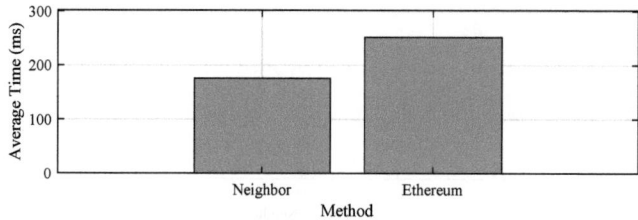

Fig. 3. Comparison of Average Time for Two Methods.

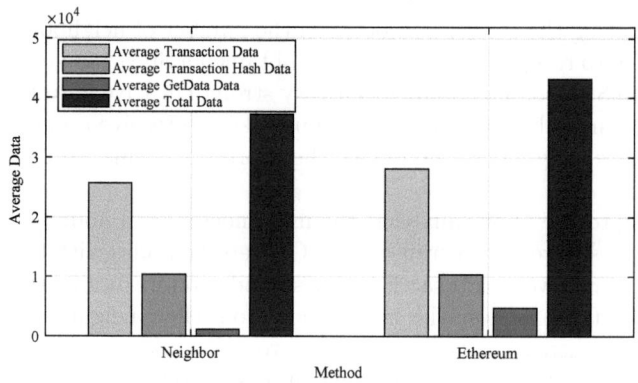

Fig. 4. Comparison of Average Data for Two Methods.

Compared to the original Ethereum transaction propagation protocol, there are improvements in both transaction propagation time and data reduction. The time to broadcast a transaction across the entire network improved by 30.24%, the propagation data of transactions improved by 8.61%, the transaction hash data remained approximately the same, the *GetData* data improved by 75.82%, and the total data was reduced by 13.92%.

4 System Design and Experimental Testing

In the Ethereum network, obtaining the neighbor counts of neighboring nodes presents a significant challenge. While theoretically, optimization methods based on these counts have demonstrated considerable effectiveness, their practical application in Ethereum is difficult. The network's decentralization and anonymity make acquiring this information highly challenging. As a result, although these strategies may enhance performance in simulated environments, their real-world application remains limited.

4.1 System Design

In equation Eq. (6), we observe that *GetData* significantly affects the data propagation process, influencing transaction propagation speed. Typically, *GetData* messages accompany transaction requests, meaning that each additional *GetData* message increases transaction propagation occurrences. By reducing the number of *GetData* messages, we can concurrently decrease the number of transaction messages. Moreover, the history of *GetData* in Ethereum is traceable and does not raise privacy concerns.

By plotting the relationship between the number of *GetData* messages and the average transaction reception time of nodes, we can observe a strong correlation in Fig. 5.

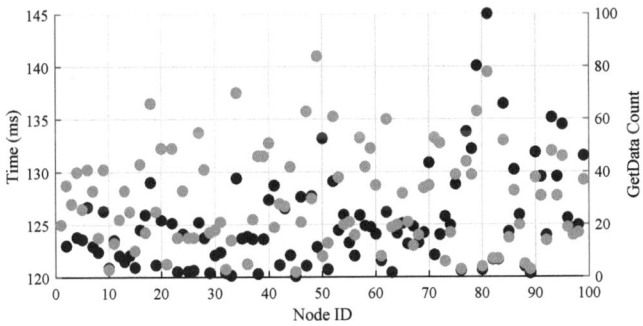

Fig. 5. GetData Count and Time per Node.

In our proposed optimization protocol, FLTP (Fast and Low-bandwidth Transaction Propagation Protocol), we enhance the prioritization of transaction propagation by considering the historical forwarding records of neighboring nodes. Specifically, we assign priority to nodes based on the frequency of *GetData* messages they have sent in previous transactions. This method ensures that nodes with a higher frequency of *GetData* requests receive complete transaction data more expeditiously, thereby enhancing the efficiency of transaction propagation and ensuring faster and more reliable data distribution across the network. Moreover, all experimental parameters were meticulously configured as outlined in Subsect. 3.1, ensuring a thorough evaluation of the protocol's performance.

To determine the optimal number of historical *GetData* messages to consider, we evaluated the optimization effects using transaction histories of 10, 30, 50, 70, 100, and 200 transactions. We collected statistical data and illustrated the results in Figs. 6 and 7. From these figures, it is evident that the optimization effect nearly reaches its peak when considering 100 transactions. Increasing the number of queries beyond this point offers negligible improvement.

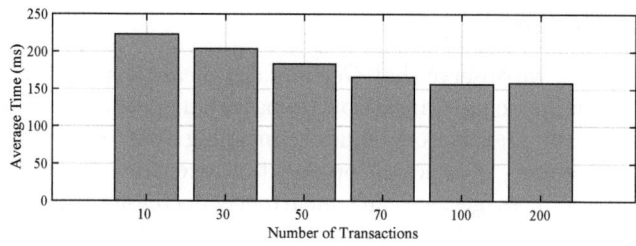

Fig. 6. FLTP's Effect for Different Number of Transactions - Average Time.

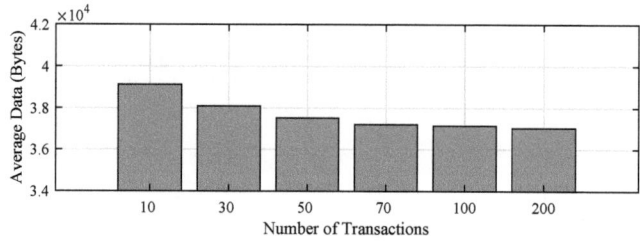

Fig. 7. FLTP's Effect for Different Number of Transactions - Average Data.

4.2 FLTP Protocol Testing

Based on the tests conducted in Sect. 4.1, querying the *GetData* history for 100 transactions provides a satisfactory level of optimization for the FLTP protocol. Consequently, we have set the number of queries to 100 for our experiments. To assess the effectiveness of our approach, we compared the statistical data obtained using the original Ethereum protocol with our optimized protocol, which takes into account the number of neighboring nodes. The results of this comparison are illustrated in Figs. 8 and 9.

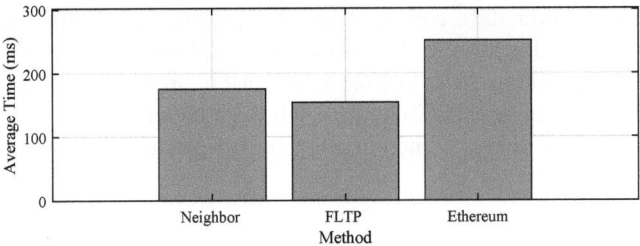

Fig. 8. Comparison of Average Time for Three Methods.

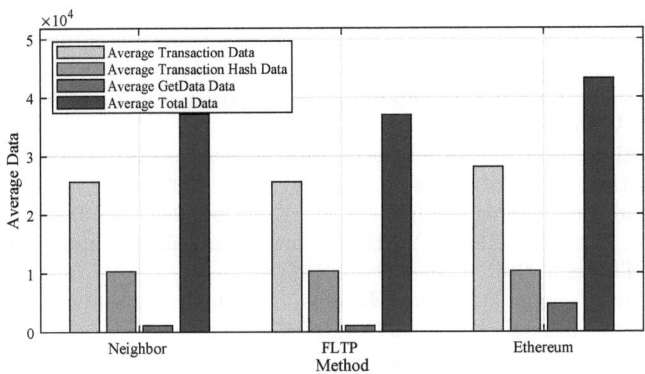

Fig. 9. Comparison of Average Data for Three Methods.

The FLTP Protocol shows significant improvements compared to the original Ethereum protocol. The time taken for transaction propagation across the entire network is accelerated by 38.61%, and the data consumption for propagation each transaction is reduced by 8.84%. The data consumption for transaction hashes remains almost unchanged, while the data consumption for *Getdata* messages is reduced by 78.42%. Overall, the total data consumption is reduced by 14.36%. While protecting node privacy and ensuring applicability, the performance shows a slight improvement compared to the optimization protocol based on the number of neighboring nodes and a great improvement over the original Ethereum protocol, offering faster broadcast speeds and lower data consumption.

5 Conclusion

In this paper, we propose FLTP, a fast and low-bandwidth transaction propagation protocol that employs a novel method where nodes prioritize transaction propagation based on the frequency of *GetData* requests from their neighbors. By testing the transaction propagation in Ethereum, we analyzed the impact of node connectivity on Ethereum's performance, revealing that nodes with higher connectivity benefit from fewer *GetData* requests, resulting in faster transaction propagation and lower data consumption. Leveraging this characteristic, FLTP enables nodes to maintain a table to query the *GetData* request history of each neighbor, allowing them to prioritize transaction propagation to those neighbors with higher data needs. This approach improves bandwidth efficiency and reduces propagation delays while ensuring better privacy and practical applicability.

References

1. Abeyratne, S.A., Monfared, R.P.: Blockchain ready manufacturing supply chain using distributed ledger. Int. J. Res. Eng. Technol. **5**(9), 1–10 (2016)
2. Bisnik, N., Abouzeid, A.A.: Optimizing random walk search algorithms in P2P networks. Comput. Netw. **51**(6), 1499–1514 (2007)
3. Buterin, V., et al.: A next-generation smart contract and decentralized application platform. White Paper **3**(37), 2–1 (2014)
4. Conoscenti, M., Vetro, A., De Martin, J.C.: Peer to peer for privacy and decentralization in the internet of things. In: 2017 IEEE/ACM 39th International Conference on Software Engineering Companion (ICSE-C), pp. 288–290. IEEE (2017)
5. Dai, H.N., Zheng, Z., Zhang, Y.: Blockchain for internet of things: a survey. IEEE Internet Things J. **6**(5), 8076–8094 (2019)
6. Fanning, K., Centers, D.P.: Blockchain and its coming impact on financial services. J. Corporate Account. Financ. **27**(5), 53–57 (2016)
7. Garay, J., Kiayias, A., Leonardos, N.: The bitcoin backbone protocol: analysis and applications. J. ACM **71**(4), 1–49 (2024)
8. Gencer, A.E., Basu, S., Eyal, I., van Renesse, R., Sirer, E.G.: Decentralization in bitcoin and Ethereum networks. In: Meiklejohn, S., Sako, K. (eds.) FC 2018. LNCS, vol. 10957, pp. 439–457. Springer, Heidelberg (2018). https://doi.org/10.1007/978-3-662-58387-6_24
9. Grubmüller, H.: Predicting slow structural transitions in macromolecular systems: conformational flooding. Phys. Rev. E **52**(3), 2893 (1995)
10. Hildenbrandt, E., et al.: KEVM: a complete formal semantics of the Ethereum virtual machine. In: 2018 IEEE 31st Computer Security Foundations Symposium (CSF), pp. 204–217. IEEE (2018)
11. Hu, K., Liao, H., Li, M., Wang, F.: MMcount: stationary crowd counting system based on commodity millimeter-wave radar. In: ICASSP 2024-2024 IEEE International Conference on Acoustics, Speech and Signal Processing (ICASSP), pp. 56–60. IEEE (2024)
12. Jin, Y., Hu, K., Liu, J., Wang, F., Liu, X.: From capture to display: a survey on volumetric video (2023). https://arxiv.org/abs/2309.05658
13. Jin, Y., Liu, J., Hu, K., Wang, F.: A networking perspective of volumetric video service: architecture, opportunities and case study. IEEE Network, p. 1 (2024). https://doi.org/10.1109/MNET.2024.3442210
14. Kim, S.K., Ma, Z., Murali, S., Mason, J., Miller, A., Bailey, M.: Measuring Ethereum network peers. In: Proceedings of the Internet Measurement Conference 2018, pp. 91–104 (2018)
15. Liu-Zhang, C.D., Matt, C., Maurer, U., Rito, G., Thomsen, S.E.: Practical provably secure flooding for blockchains. In: International Conference on the Theory and Application of Cryptology and Information Security, pp. 774–805. Springer, Cham (2022). https://doi.org/10.1007/978-3-031-22963-3_26

16. Manku, G.S., Naor, M., Wieder, U.: Know thy neighbor's neighbor: the power of lookahead in randomized p2p networks. In: Proceedings of the Thirty-Sixth Annual ACM Symposium on Theory of Computing, pp. 54–63 (2004)
17. Mighan, S.N., Mišić, J., Mišić, V.B.: On block delivery time in Ethereum network. In: GLOBECOM 2022 - 2022 IEEE Global Communications Conference, pp. 2867–2872 (2022https://doi.org/10.1109/GLOBECOM48099.2022.10001081
18. Nakamoto, S.: Bitcoin: A peer-to-peer electronic cash system. Satoshi Nakamoto (2008)
19. Pass, R., Seeman, L., Shelat, A.: Analysis of the blockchain protocol in asynchronous networks. In: Coron, J.-S., Nielsen, J.B. (eds.) EUROCRYPT 2017. LNCS, vol. 10211, pp. 643–673. Springer, Cham (2017). https://doi.org/10.1007/978-3-319-56614-6_22
20. Silva, P., Vavricka, D., Barreto, J., Matos, M.: Impact of geo-distribution and mining pools on blockchains: a study of ethereum. In: 2020 50th Annual IEEE/IFIP International Conference on Dependable Systems and Networks (DSN), pp. 245–252. IEEE (2020)
21. Stoica, I., et al.: A scalable peer-to-peer lookup protocol for internet applications. IEEE/ACM Trans. Netw. **11**(1), 17–32 (2003)
22. Vyzovitis, D., Napora, Y., McCormick, D., Dias, D., Psaras, Y.: GossipSUB: attack-resilient message propagation in the filecoin and eth2. 0 networks. arXiv preprint arXiv:2007.02754 (2020)
23. Wang, T., Zhao, C., Yang, Q., Zhang, S., Liew, S.C.: Ethna: analyzing the underlying peer-to-peer network of Ethereum blockchain. IEEE Trans. Netw. Sci. Eng. **8**(3), 2131–2146 (2021). https://doi.org/10.1109/TNSE.2021.3078181
24. Wu, Y., Hu, K., Shao, Q., Chen, J., Chen, D.Z., Wu, J.: TeleOR: real-time telemedicine system for full-scene operating room . In: proceedings of Medical Image Computing and Computer Assisted Intervention – MICCAI 2024, vol. LNCS 15006. Springer Nature Switzerland (2024)
25. Zhao, C., Wang, T., Zhang, S., Liew, S.C.: HCB: enabling compact block in Ethereum network with secondary pool and transaction prediction. IEEE Trans. Netw. Sci. Eng. **11**(1), 1077–1092 (2024). https://doi.org/10.1109/TNSE.2023.3321063
26. Zhao, C., Zhang, S., Wang, T., Liew, S.C.: Bodyless block propagation: TPS fully scalable blockchain with pre-validation. Futur. Gener. Comput. Syst. **163**, 107516 (2025). https://doi.org/10.1016/j.future.2024.107516, https://www.sciencedirect.com/science/article/pii/S0167739X24004801
27. Zhao, C., Zhou, Y., Zhang, S., Wang, T., Sheng, Q.Z., Guo, S.: DEthna: Accurate Ethereum network topology discovery with marked transactions. In: IEEE INFOCOM 2024 - IEEE Conference on Computer Communications, pp. 1711–1720 (2024). https://doi.org/10.1109/INFOCOM52122.2024.10621281
28. Zhao, L., Sen Gupta, S., Khan, A., Luo, R.: Temporal analysis of the entire ethereum blockchain network. In: Proceedings of the Web Conference 2021, pp. 2258–2269 (2021)
29. Zhu, Y., Hu, Y.: Efficient, proximity-aware load balancing for DHT-based p2p systems. IEEE Trans. Parallel Distrib. Syst. **16**(4), 349–361 (2005)

Communication Technologies II

Communication Technologies II

Automated Topology Exploration and Design of Passive Microstrip Filters Based on Grid-Like Topology

Jingyun Bi(✉) and Xinyu Zhou

Department of Electrical and Electronic Engineering, The Hong Kong Polytechnic University,
Hong Kong SAR, China
2537503782@qq.com

Abstract. This paper proposes an automated design method for microstrip filters which comprises topology exploration and parameter optimization stages. In the topology exploration stage, a novel grid-like topology is utilized in conjunction with an efficient generation and deduplication algorithm based on VF2++ isomorphism detection, significantly expanding the available design freedom of RF filter. The parameter optimization depends on a hybrid mode combining simulated annealing and gradient optimization, reducing computation time and simplifying the design process. To validate the method's effectiveness and practicality, a dual-band bandpass filter for 6G communication (1.8–2.7GHz and 3.4–3.7GHz) was successfully designed and implemented within 5 h (4 h of computation and 1 h of manual layout design). The electromagnetic (EM) simulation results show that the filter, within a compact size of $0.275\lambda_g \times 0.285\lambda_g$, achieves frequency selectivity with an insertion loss below 0.6 dB in the passband, roll-off rates of 71/100 dB/GHz and 180/87 dB/GHz for the first and second frequency passbands respectively, and effective out-of-band suppression.

Keywords: Microstrip band pass filter · Passive circuits · RF filter · Simulated annealing (SA)

1 Introduction

Passive microstrip filters play a crucial role in RF and microwave communication systems, directly affecting the signal quality and spectral efficiency of the entire system. With the rapid development of modern communication technologies, the requirements for filters have become increasingly stringent, especially in complex multi-band application scenarios, such as the design of dual-band bandpass filters [1]. Traditional filter design methods primarily rely on the experience and calculations of designers, which is not only time-consuming and labor-intensive but also challenging to guarantee the optimality of the design results. In the current design paradigm, the performance of a filter is mainly determined by its topology, which affects both the frequency response and the complexity of physical implementation.

In recent years, computational intelligence and optimization algorithms have been increasingly applied in RF filter design [2]. Jamshidi et al. proposed an intelligent design method using dynamic neural networks and Bayesian regularized backpropagation, successfully optimizing a low-pass filter's performance using artificial neural networks [3]. Gao et al. developed an automated design method for distributed filter circuits using reinforcement learning algorithms, which significantly improved design efficiency and quality by reducing subjectivity and constraints [4]. Kabir et al. introduced a neural network inverse model with electrical parameters as input and geometric parameters as output, addressing non-uniqueness issues through data grouping and sub-model creation [5]. Their method was successfully tested on waveguide filters. However, these related studies are all based on optimization design for a specific topology. Limited research has addressed the systematic application of these optimization techniques to microstrip filter topology synthesis.

This paper proposes an automatic microstrip filter design method based on a novel grid-like topology, combined with topology traversal, simulated annealing optimization, and gradient optimization techniques. The proposed approach focuses on forward modeling and optimization methods to determine structural parameters, eliminating the need for an inverse model. This method aims to address the challenges of complex filter design by systematically exploring the design space and optimizing both the topology and parameters of microstrip filters. By leveraging advanced optimization techniques, the proposed approach seeks to enhance the efficiency and effectiveness of microstrip filter design, potentially leading to improved performance in various communication applications.

2 Generation Strategy for Traversing Topologies

2.1 Grid-Like Topology

To achieve automated topology exploration, a universal topological template capable of transforming into specific filter topologies was required. As a result, a novel grid-like microstrips topology composed of interconnected nodes and edges was designed and introduced, where each edge represents an ideal microstrip line segment, while each node is formed by the intersection of four microstrip lines. This grid-like topology allows for flexible representation of various series and parallel relationships between microstrip lines, with independently adjustable length and width parameters for each segment. The specific dimensions of the topology are determined by the impedance and electrical angle parameters of each microstrip line segment, with each line controlled by a dedicated variable (Var) for its parameters (as shown in Fig. 1). The overall size of the topology is flexibly adjustable according to different design requirements.

This grid-like topology exhibits high flexibility and effectively combines into various Π-type and T-type microstrip line networks, achieving capacitive and inductive effects through multiple series and parallel combinations. It effectively reproduces the topology of traditional branch-line networks. In subsequent topology exploration, the target topology is obtained through simple activation and deactivation of microstrip lines. As illustrated in Fig. 1, microstrip lines without red frames are activated, while those enclosed in red frames are deactivated. This design method significantly increases

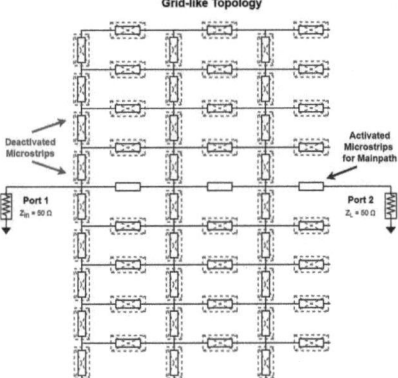

Fig. 1. Grid-like topology template for traversal exploration, where a 9 × 6 grid example is shown with 9 horizontal and 6 vertical microstrip line segments defining the grid dimensions

the degrees of freedom in filter design, enabling better fulfillment of complex filtering requirements.

In this grid-like topology, each segment of microstrip line is treated as an equivalent unit, possessing identical default parameter settings and optimization ranges. To strike a balance between microstrip line dimensions and design flexibility, this study sets the electrical angle range for each microstrip line segment from 0.1 to 60°, and the impedance range from 5 to 100 Ω, serving as the foundation for parameter exploration.

2.2 Generation and De-duplication of Topologies

Based on the proposed grid-like topology template, this study developed an topology traversal and deduplication algorithm to efficiently explore the design space of microstrip filters. The method starts with three main path microstrip lines and systematically generating more complex sub-topologies by increasing the number of microstrip lines. This process encompassed configurations with 4, 5, and more microstrip lines, enabling a comprehensive exploration of the design space.

To precisely describe these topologies, a directed graph representation was adopted [6]. Main paths were depicted by unidirectional arrows, reflecting the primary signal propagation direction, while other connections were represented by bidirectional arrows. This graphical representation provided intuitive visualization and established a clear basis for subsequent analysis and optimization. Through the introduction of a special visualization method, Figs. 2(a) and (b) showed a pair of topologies that appeared different but were isomorphic.

To avoid redundancy and ensure efficient exploration, a topology deduplication mechanism based on the VF2++ isomorphism detection algorithm was introduced [7]. This process effectively compared generated graphs, identifying and eliminating duplicate topologies. By retaining only one representative instance for each unique topology, the algorithm significantly reduced the number of topologies to be analyzed and substantially improved the efficiency of subsequent design and optimization stages.

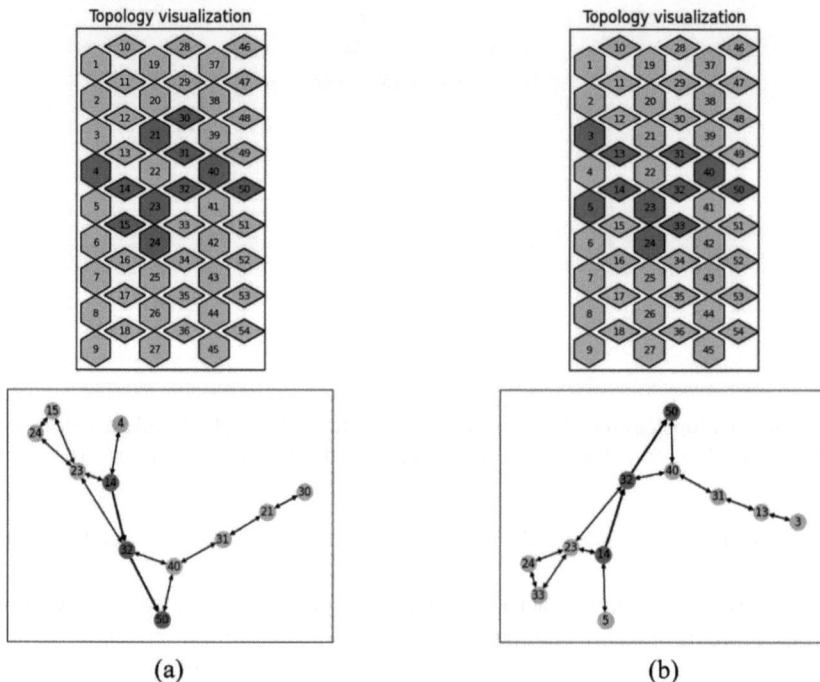

Fig. 2. Directed graphs for topology deduplication, where (a) and (b) are isomorphic

3 Parameter Optimization for Specific Topologies

3.1 Goal for Optimization

In the filter design process, performance goals focused on S-parameter behavior across different frequency ranges. The method involved dividing the frequency range into subbands (passbands, stopbands, and transition bands) and setting specific goals for S_{21} and S_{11} in each sub-band, aiming to precisely define the desired filter performance while balancing different objectives through weight allocation.

To address issues with weight assignment, particularly at transition points, a more nuanced approach was adopted. Weights gradually varied in transition regions between passbands and stopbands, or some frequency ranges were left without defined goals. By creating a smoother optimization landscape and preventing the optimizer from overfocusing on or neglecting certain points, this strategy enabled balanced optimization across the entire frequency range, resulting in filter responses that closely matched the desired characteristics.

3.2 Establishing the Error Function

This study employed the L2 Least Squares Error (LSE) as the Error Function (EF). The L2 LSE is a canonical error metric in optimization problems and data fitting. This function quantifies model performance by computing the sum of squared deviations between predicted and target values. In the context of filter design optimization, the L2 LSE function was utilized to assess the quality of optimization solutions by evaluating the discrepancy between the optimized frequency response and the prescribed goals. For proposed optimization problem, the L2 least squares EF can be expressed as:

$$EF = \sum_j \frac{(\sum_f [\sum_i W_{ij} * e_{ij}(f)])}{N_j} \quad (1)$$

where i denotes the response index, j denotes the frequency range index, f denotes the frequency point, F_j is the set of frequencies in the j th frequency range, W_{ij} is the weight factor associated with response $R_{ij}(f)$ and goal g_{ij}, $e_{ij}(f)$ is the error between $R_{ij}(f)$ and g_{ij} at frequency f, and N_j is the number of frequency points in frequency range F_j. The calculation of the error contribution $e_{ij}(f)$ depends on the optimization goal specification, involving specified relational operators (equal to, less than, or greater than). For standard least squares, define:

$$e_{ij}(f) = \left(\frac{|R_{ij}(f) - g_{ij}|}{d_i}\right)^2 \quad (2)$$

where d_i is the goal normalization factor, used to ensure fair comparison of goals with different scales. Equations (1) and (2) together form the core error measurement framework for this optimization problem. This framework considers multiple frequency ranges, various response types, and error contributions from each frequency point, providing a comprehensive performance evaluation standard. The introduction of weight factors W_{ij} allows us to finely adjust the importance of different responses and frequency ranges, which is particularly important in practical engineering optimization.

3.3 Two-Phase Exploration-Design Optimization Approach

This study used a two-stage optimization strategy for filter design. The first stage employed simulated annealing to explore diverse filter topologies, prioritizing structural variety. Top-performing topologies then underwent parameter fine-tuning using a Gradient Optimizer in the second stage. This approach combined simulated annealing's global search with the gradient optimizer's local optimization, aiming for high-quality filter designs within reasonable computational times. The method allowed for broad exploration of the design space followed by refined optimization of promising solutions.

Topology Exploration Phase - Simulated Annealing Corana. Simulated annealing, inspired by the metallurgical annealing process, was chosen for its effectiveness in handling complex problems with numerous variables or multiple local minima. This method uses an abstract "temperature" concept to guide its search process. The core of simulated annealing is based on the Boltzmann distribution, allowing the algorithm to occasionally accept sub-optimal solutions to explore a broader solution space and avoid local minima. This study specifically employed the Corana simulated annealing optimizer, which retains the fundamental principles of simulated annealing while introducing features suited for complex optimization problems [8]. By reducing the EF through variable alterations, this approach aimed to find optimal filter designs within a diverse solution landscape.

The probability of accepting a new solution was based on the Metropolis criterion, given by the following formula:

$$P(\Delta E) = exp(\frac{-\Delta E}{T}) \tag{3}$$

where ΔE represented the change in the error function, and T denoted the current temperature. The temperature decreased gradually throughout the optimization process, following a cooling schedule:

$$T(i+1) = \alpha * T(i) \tag{4}$$

where α was the cooling ratio.

A key feature of the Corana optimizer was its use of dynamically adjusted step sizes for each optimization variable. This adaptive mechanism enabled more effective exploration of the search space, particularly when dealing with variables of different scales and sensitivities. The approach retained the ability to avoid local minima while improving convergence efficiency. Through careful selection of initial parameters such as temperature, cooling rate, and iteration count, the study aimed to find near-globally optimal solutions within reasonable computational timeframes. This method was particularly suited for complex filter design problems, allowing for more effective balancing of different performance metrics in multi-objective optimization environments.

Parameter Design Phase - Gradient Optimizer. In this subsequent phase, a gradient optimizer was introduced for parameter optimization, leveraging its ability to effectively locate local minima and produce stable solutions. This optimizer uses gradient information from the EF to minimize a least-squares error function, achieving desired performance goals. The gradient optimizer proved particularly effective for simple circuit designs with straightforward requirements, excelling in convergence and following complex contours.

4 Experimental Design and Results Analysis

4.1 Introduction to the Design Case Process

To validate the effectiveness and practicality of this method, a specific design case is described in detail: a dual-band bandpass filter for 6G communication (1.8–2.7GHz and 3.4–3.7GHz) was successfully designed and implemented in just 5 h (4 h of computation time and 1 h of manual layout design). The engineering design process, simulation results, and actual performance of this filter are presented, focusing on analyzing its frequency selectivity and out-of-band suppression characteristics.

Figure 3 illustrates the design process integrating Python scripts with the Keysight Advanced Design System (ADS) AEL environment. Python-generated topologies are passed to ADS, which creates a proposed grid-like topology and realizes filter designs by activating or deactivating microstrip lines. ADS then simulates and calculates the EF,

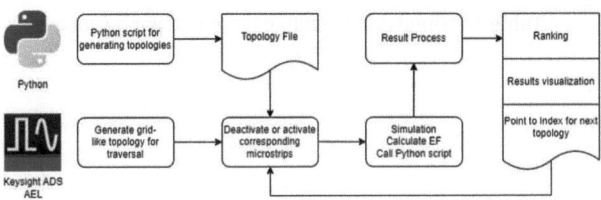

Fig. 3. Flowchart of the automated design process

while calling Python scripts for optimization. Result processing includes performance ranking and visualization, guiding subsequent topology optimization. Post-ranking, gradient parameter optimization will be executed. The results will be then manually converted into microstrip lines and layout design (Fig. 4).

4.2 Generation of Topology Traversal Strategies

```
(5, 6, 14, 29, 30, 32, 38, 39, 40, 49, 50)
(5, 6, 14, 29, 31, 32, 37, 38, 39, 40, 50)
(3, 5, 13, 14, 29, 31, 32, 38, 39, 40, 50)
(5, 14, 15, 20, 29, 32, 38, 39, 40, 48, 50)
(5, 6, 7, 14, 17, 29, 32, 38, 39, 40, 50)
(5, 14, 22, 29, 31, 32, 38, 39, 40, 49, 50)
(5, 14, 15, 21, 29, 31, 32, 38, 39, 40, 50)
(5, 14, 20, 29, 31, 32, 38, 39, 40, 48, 50)
(5, 14, 29, 32, 33, 38, 39, 40, 41, 50)
(5, 14, 28, 29, 32, 37, 38, 39, 40, 47, 50)
(5, 14, 22, 29, 32, 38, 39, 40, 50)
(5, 11, 14, 15, 29, 32, 38, 39, 40, 50)
(5, 14, 20, 22, 29, 32, 38, 39, 40, 48, 50)
(5, 14, 29, 30, 31, 32, 38, 39, 40, 47, 50)
(5, 6, 7, 14, 22, 29, 32, 38, 39, 40, 50)
(5, 14, 29, 31, 32, 38, 39, 40, 47, 49, 50)
```

Fig. 4. Representation of 7,712 non-isomorphic topologies as ordered tuples, where each topology is uniquely encoded as a sequence of microstrip line numbers. Each row represents one topology in the form of (n_1, n_2,..., n_k), where n_i indicates the number assigned to each microstrip line as a node in the topology.

4.3 Setting Optimization Objectives and Optimizer Parameters

Based on the design objectives, optimization goals and weights for S_{21} and S_{11} were established, and the EF was calculated by combining these two optimization goals. Within each optimization target, the relative importance of different limits was determined by their weight ratios, while the weight ratio between the two optimization goals were set to 1:5 to balance the number of limits in each target and prevent underestimation of the S response error. The detailed optimization constraints for the filter will be presented in Fig. 8.

To strike an optimal balance between exploration space and computational efficiency, the simulated annealing optimizer parameters were configured as presented in Table 1. The table exhibited a large initial temperature, which indicated a higher probability for the algorithm to accept cost-increasing moves (i.e., unfavorable moves). This characteristic facilitated the algorithm's ability to escape local minima [9]. Utilizing an Intel i5-13490F processor platform, the optimization of a single topology was achieved within a one-minute timeframe.

Table 1. Simulated annealing optimizer parameters

Parameter	Value
Initial Temperature	50
Temperature Cooling Ratio	0.7
Number of Trials per Iteration	20
Number of Shoots per Trial	20
MaxIters	10

4.4 Schematic Optimization Results

After automatically executing the loop illustrated in Fig. 3 for 500 iterations, the top 10 topologies ranked according to EF values (where lower values indicate superior performance) were identified as potentially significant reference points, as shown in Fig. 5. Subsequent analysis and refinement efforts were concentrated on these ten high-performing topological configurations.

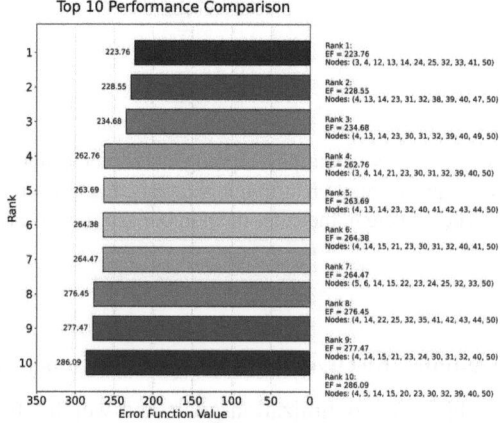

Fig. 5. Ranking of lowest EF values (Top 10)

These top 10 topologies were all subjected to gradient optimization to obtain their respective optimal solutions. Through a comprehensive evaluation of the post-secondary optimization Values and routing complexity, a specific topology was selected (see Fig. 6). This selection process integrated both performance metrics and practical implementation factors, particularly the physical clearance requirements between microstrip lines and layout routing complexity, to identify the most promising configuration for further development.

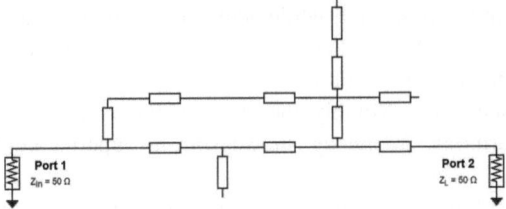

Fig. 6. Ideal microstrip topology considering error and layout

4.5 Layout Design Results

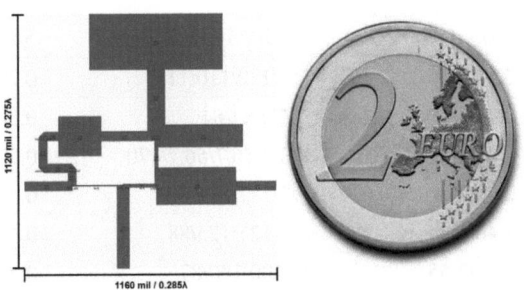

Fig. 7. 1:1 scale layout size comparison

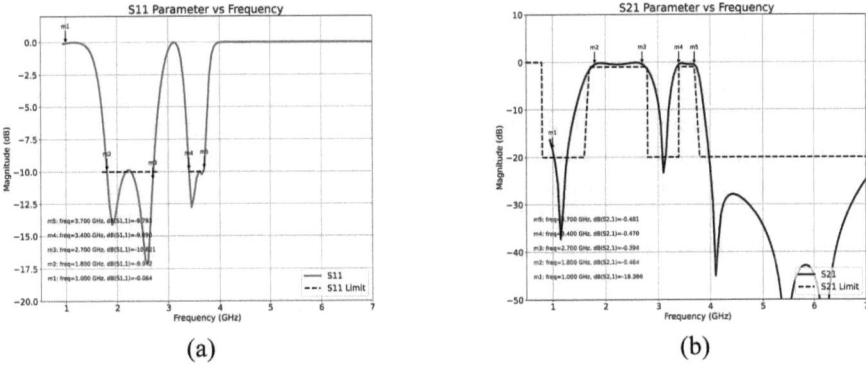

Fig. 8. S-parameters obtained from EM simulation of the proposed microstrip topology (a) S_{11} (b) S_{21}

Through multiple iterations of gradient optimization, a filter design solution meeting the performance specifications was ultimately obtained. Based on the schematic diagram, the layout design was manually performed with deliberately bent microstrip lines (see Fig. 7) and finally controlled the layout to dimensions of $0.275\lambda_g \times 0.285\lambda_g$, which is comparable to the size of a two-euro coin.

Using ADS Momentum electromagnetic (EM) simulation software for analysis, results demonstrate that the filter exhibits excellent frequency selectivity and out-of-band suppression characteristics (as shown in Fig. 8). It maintains a low insertion loss of less than 0.6 dB in the passband, while achieving high attenuation in the stopband. The frequency response exhibits sharp roll-off characteristics, with the first and second frequency passbands demonstrating measured roll-off rates of 71/100 dB/GHz and 180/87 dB/GHz, respectively. Notably, the filter maintained a selectivity below –20 dB up to the second harmonic frequency, showcasing its superior nonlinear suppression capability.

The topology explored using the proposed design method demonstrates practical value compared to some existing topologies, as shown in Table 2.

Table 2. Related works performance table

Ref	f_1/f_2 (GHz)	ξ_R (dB/GHz)	Size ($\lambda_g \times \lambda_g$)
[10]	2.33/4.36	119/130/110/115	0.28 × 0.23
[11]	3.4/5.4	70/70/64/64	0.24 × 0.25
[12]	3/4.35	113.3/56.7/56.7/170	0.22 × 0.19
[13]	2.4/3.8	177/177/191/191	0.46 × 0.68
[14]	3.46/5.34	100/125/125/88	0.15 × 0.16
This work*	2.25/3.55	71/100/180/87	0.27 × 0.28

* This work was in EM simulation level.

5 Conclusion

An automated design method for microstrip filters was proposed, combining topology exploration and parameter optimization. The effectiveness of this approach was demonstrated through a dual-band bandpass filter designed for 6G communication (1.8–2.7GHz and 3.4–3.7GHz). The novel grid-like topology, integrated with VF2++ isomorphism detection, successfully identified 7,712 unique topologies from over 1.3 million potential configurations. The hybrid optimization strategy incorporating simulated annealing and gradient optimization achieved significant performance improvements while maintaining computational efficiency. The designed filter exhibited exceptional characteristics within a compact size of $0.275\lambda_g \times 0.285\lambda_g$, achieving insertion loss below 0.6 dB and roll-off rates of 71/100 dB/GHz and 180/87 dB/GHz for the respective passbands. The filter's selectivity remained below –20dB up to the second harmonic frequency, demonstrating superior out-of-band suppression. The automated design methodology presented in this work established a systematic framework that significantly enhanced design efficiency while maintaining high performance standards. This approach showed promising potential for broader applications in RF and microwave circuit design, particularly in scenarios requiring rapid prototyping and optimization of complex filter specifications.

References

1. Pereira, L.A.M., et al.: Implementation of a multiband 5G NR fiber-wireless system using analog radio over fiber technology. Optics Commun. **474**, 126112 (2020)

2. Feng, F., Na, W., Jin, J., et al.: Artificial neural networks for microwave computer-aided design: the state of the art. IEEE Trans. Microw. Theory Tech. **70**(11), 4597–4619 (2022)
3. Jamshidi, M.B., Lalbakhsh, A., Mohamadzade, B., Siahkamari, H., Mousavi, S.M.H.: A novel neural-based approach for design of microstrip filters. AEU-Int. J. Electron. C. **110**, 152847 (2019)
4. Gao, P., Yu, T., Wang, F., Yuan, R.Y.: Automated design and optimization of distributed filter circuits using reinforcement learning. J. Comput. Des. Eng. qwae066 (2024)
5. Kabir, H., Wang, Y., Yu, M., Zhang, Q.J.: Neural network inverse modeling and applications to microwave filter design. IEEE Trans. Microw. Theory Tech. **56**(4), 867–879 (2008)
6. Somani, A., Chakrabarti, P.P., Patra, A.: An evolutionary algorithm-based approach to automated design of analog and RF circuits using adaptive normalized cost functions. IEEE Trans. Evol. Comput. **11**(3), 336–353 (2007)
7. Jüttner, A., Madarasi, P.: VF2++—an improved subgraph isomorphism algorithm. Discret. Appl. Math. **242**, 69–81 (2018)
8. Corana, A., Marchesi, M., Martini, C., Ridella, S.: Minimizing multimodal functions of continuous variables with the "simulated annealing" algorithm. ACM Tran. Math. Softw. **13**(3), 262–280 (1987)
9. Ben-Ameur, W.: Computing the initial temperature of simulated annealing. Comput. Optim. Appl. **29**, 369–385 (2004)
10. Li, D., Wang, J.A., Liu, Y., Chen, Z., Yang, L.: Selectivity-enhancement technique for parallel-coupled SIR based dual-band bandpass filter. Microw. Opt. Technol. Lett. **63**, 787–792 (2021)
11. Moattari, A.M., Bijari, A., Razavi, S.M.: A new compact microstrip dual bandpass filter using stepped impedance and $\lambda/2$ bended resonators. Int J RF Microw Comput Aided Eng **31**, e22568 (2021)
12. Zhang, Z., Xia, M., Li, G.: Compact dual-band bandpass filter with high selectivity using stub-loaded stepped-impedance resonators. Prog. Electromagn. Res. Lett. **2022**(102), 101–107 (2022)
13. Kim, C., Hyeon Lee, T., Shrestha, B., Chul Son, K.: Miniaturized dual-band bandpass filter based on stepped impedance resonators. Microw. Opt. Technol. Lett. **59**(5), 1116–1119 (2017)
14. Yue, J., Zhang, G., Che, Z., Lun, Y., Li, Z., Suo, J.: Compact dual-band bandpass filter based on SSL-SIR with sharp roll-off. Appl. Comput. Electromagn. Soc. J.Electromagn. Soc. J. **36**(12), 1623–1629 (2021)

Physical Layer Security for Omni-DRIS Enhanced Visible Light Communications

Mengda Liu[1,2], Xinyan Xie[1,2], Defan Shen[1,2], Jianhua He[2(✉)], Yanmei Jia[2], and Lu Lu[1,2]

[1] University of Chinese Academy of Sciences, Beijing 100049, China
{liumengda22,xiexinyan20,shendefan23}@mails.ucas.ac.cn
[2] Technology and Engineering Center for Space Utilization, Chinese Academy of Sciences, Beijing 100094, China
{hejianhua,jiayanmei,lulu}@csu.ac.cn

Abstract. Omni-digital reconfigurable intelligent surfaces (Omni-DRIS) has been proposed to enhance the coverage of visible light communication (VLC) systems in recent years. Compared with traditional optical RIS using only reflections, Omni-DRIS is capable of extending the communication range of VLC even further, using both refection and refraction. Although RIS VLC system's security performance inside one room has been studied in the literature, the security communication data rate is not directly applicable to Omni-DRIS systems, which cover two rooms simultaneously, using bi-directions transmissions. In this paper, we focus on the system where two rooms are interconnected using one Omni-DRIS in the middle. Alice node's information is transmitted using both signal light emitting diodes (LEDs) and noise LEDs on the ceilings. The Eve node can appear in any room to eavesdropping Bob users. However, we argue that the minimum-secrecy-rate maximization problem in the Omni-DRIS setting is non-deterministic polynomial-time (NP) hard. To solve the optimization problem, we first make use of an alternating optimization (AO) algorithm to transform the original problem into two sub-problems, and then we adopt the successive convex approximation (SCA) method to solve the sub-problems. Simulation results show that, when the number of user is 2 and the LED transmitting power is 25 dBm, the minimum secrecy rate of the Omni-DRIS system is approximately 105% and 1425% larger compared with state-of-the-art RIS-VLC and non-precoding benchmark systems, respectively. In addition, we find that increasing the number of Omni-DRIS elements can significantly enhance the security performance. Our findings have important implications for the large-scale deployment of secured Omni-DRIS enhanced VLC systems in the future.

This work was supported in part by the Key Research Program of the Chinese Academy of Sciences (CAS), under Grant ZDRW-KT-2019-1-0103, and in part by the Youth Innovation Promotion Association Project of CAS.

Keywords: Visible light communications · Omni-DRIS · physical-layer security · secrecy rate

1 Introduction

As a key component of future wireless communication networks, visible light communication (VLC) has garnered increasing attention due to its abundant spectrum resources and enhanced security [1]. Compared with radio frequency (RF) communication, VLC also exhibits superior security attributes, such as line-of-sight propagation [2]. However, due to the broadcast nature of the VLC [3], preventing eavesdropping and unauthorized access becomes critical. Therefore, enhancing the security performance of VLC systems has become a significant research topic.

Reconfigurable intelligent surface (RIS) enhances physical layer security by actively configuring channels through electromagnetic wave manipulation . Recent research on RIS enhanced VLC systems focuses on optimizing secrecy capacity and rates in non-orthogonal multiple access (NOMA) based and multi-user scenarios through channel adjustments [4,5]. Additionally, deep reinforcement learning [6] and jamming techniques [7] have been employed to further protect VLC systems from eavesdropping. Specific studies also address maximizing secrecy rates in RIS assisted VLC systems with multiple users and eavesdroppers [5]. Although traditional RIS can enhance the security of VLC systems in some scenarios, it also has a limited coverage area, which can only cover one room.

Given the limitation of traditional RIS, where the transmitter and receiver are located on the same side, omni-digital reconfigurable intelligent surfaces (Omni-DRIS) were proposed as a variant of RIS, capable of simultaneously connecting users on both sides and enabling dual-sided beam management [9,10]. Traditional RIS can only reflect signals, restricting communication to a single room. In contrast, Omni-DRIS allows simultaneous coverage of two rooms, significantly extending communication coverage by simultaneously reflecting and refracting signals, effectively treating them as a unified system [8]. While the security performance of RIS in a single room has been explored, these findings do not directly translate to Omni-DRIS systems that facilitate bi-directional transmissions across two rooms simultaneously. A comparison between this work and existing studies is summarized in Table 1.

The main contributions of this paper are listed as follows: This paper is the first study to investigate the problem of maximizing the minimum secure rate in Omni-DRIS enhanced VLC systems. We propose a model for improving the secure rate of VLC systems using Omni-DRIS, which transmits noise signals towards the eavesdropper while employing precoding to reduce multiuser interference. Instead of using conventional RIS to enhance the security performance of VLC systems, we employ Omni-DRIS, which not only extends the coverage area but also enhances system security. Additionally, our approach does not restrict the service targets of the LEDs, as described in [6,11], where the transmission model is unicast. To solve the non-deterministic polynomial-time

Table 1. Comparison between our works and the literature.

References	RIS type		Transmission type		Precoding	Security
	RIS	Omni-DRIS	unicast	broadcast		
[5,9]	✓		✓		✗	✗
[10,11]	✓			✓	✓	✗
[4,6,7]	✓			✓	✗	✓
[12,13]		✓		✓	✗	✗
This work		✓		✓	✓	✓

(NP-hard) problem of secure rate maximization, we developed an alternating optimization (AO) algorithm to decompose the original problem into two sub-problems. Each sub-problem is transformed into a convex problem using successive convex approximation (SCA) and solved by CVX. Simulation results show that, compared to the RIS system and non-precoding system, the Omni-DRIS system can significantly improve the secrecy performance of VLC systems.

Notations: In this paper, normal letters a (A), boldface letters $\boldsymbol{a}$, boldface uppercase letters $\boldsymbol{A}$ and calligraphic letters $\mathcal{A}$ represent scalar values, vectors, matrices and the defined index sets, respectively. Moreover, $(\cdot)^T$ represents matrix transpose.

2 System Model and Problem Formulation

As shown in Fig. 1, Omni-DRIS enhanced VLC system with an eavesdropper. In the room, there are one eavesdropper named Eve and K legitimate users named Bob, two LED arrays consisting of L LEDs named Alice. N Omni-DRIS elements are deployed on the adjacent wall of the two rooms, which can act as either reflective elements or refractive elements [13]. In the system, only the noise LED can emit unintended signal, while other LEDs can only emit normal signals. The following part of this section provides a detailed explanation of this system.

2.1 Channel Model

In this system, Eve attempts to eavesdrop on a certain user while Omni-DRIS elements use noise LED to transmit the intended signals precisely towards Eve, which ensures that there is no interference with other users. Then, we introduce an association matrices $\boldsymbol{G} \triangleq [\boldsymbol{g}_1, \ldots, \boldsymbol{g}_K]^{N \times K}$ where $\boldsymbol{g}_k \triangleq [g_{1,k}, \ldots, g_{N,k}]^T \in \{0,1\}$ to represent the association behavior between Omni-DRIS and users, which transforms the Omni-DRIS configuration problem into an allocation problem [10]. Specifically, one Omni-DRIS element can be assigned to at most one user, which $g_{n,k} = 1$ means the n-th element transmits the incident signal to the k-th user. This system includes both LoS and NLoS channel.

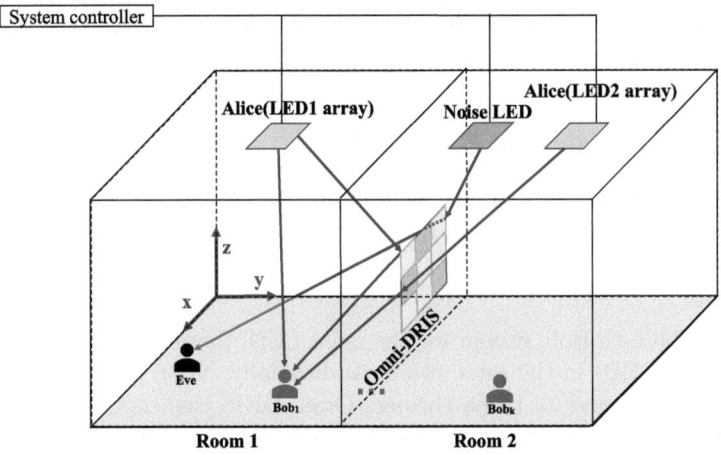

Fig. 1. Omni-DRIS Enhanced VLC System with an Eavesdropper.

LoS Channel. Generally, the LoS channel in VLC can be modeled by Lambertian radiant formulation [1]. Therefore, the LoS channel gain for the k-th PD is defined as follows :

$$h^{(1)}_{k,l} = \frac{(m+1)A_{PD}}{2\pi d^2_{k,l}} \cos^m(\phi) \cos(\psi) T(\psi) g(\psi), \tag{1}$$

where A_{PD} represents the detection area of the PD, $d_{k,l}$ is the Euclidean distance between the l-th LED and the k-th PD, ϕ is the irradiance angle. Then the parameters m, ψ, $T(\psi)$ and $g(\psi)$ denote the Lambertian index, incidence angle, gain of an optical filter and optical concentrator gain, respectively. Moreover, a matrix $\boldsymbol{h}^{(1)}_k \triangleq \left[h^{(1)}_{k,1}, \ldots, h^{(1)}_{k,L}\right]^T$ is defined as the LoS channel gain between LEDs and the k-th PD where $h^{(1)}_{k,l}$ can be calculated as (1).

NLoS Channel. In VLC, because of the huge number of reflections, the channel gain of diffuse reflection link is in a multiplicative form, resulting in insignificant energy and can be ignored [3]. Otherwise, the NLoS link through the Omni-DRIS is only one reflection or refraction so that it follows an additive model. The NLoS channel gain between the l-th LED, n-th Omni-DRIS element and the k-th PD can be expressed as [14]:

$$h^{(2)}_{k,n,l} = \frac{(m+1)A_{PD}}{2\pi(d_{n,l} + d_{k,n})^2} \cos^m(\phi) \cos(\psi) T(\psi) g(\psi), \tag{2}$$

where $d_{n,l}$ is the distances between the LED and the Omni-DRIS element, $d_{k,n}$ is the distances between the Omni-DRIS element and the PD. Additionally, a matrix $\boldsymbol{h}^{(2)}_k \triangleq \left[h^{(2)}_{k,1}, \ldots, h^{(2)}_{k,L}\right]^T$ is defined as the NLoS channel gain between

LEDs and the k-th PD where $\boldsymbol{h}_{k,l}^{(2)} \triangleq \left[h_{k,1,l}^{(2)}, \ldots, h_{k,N,l}^{(2)}\right]$, moreover $h_{k,n,l}^{(2)}$ can be calculated as (2).

2.2 Received Signals of Bob and Eve

To reduce multi-user interference, we suppose the transmission signal vector and the precoding matrix are $\boldsymbol{s} \triangleq [s_1, \cdots, s_k]^T$ and $\boldsymbol{P} \triangleq [\boldsymbol{p}_1, \ldots, \boldsymbol{p}_K]^{L \times K}$, respectively.

Bob. For the k-th Bob, except for the noise LED, there are LoS paths between them and all LEDs in the same room. Additionally, NLoS paths can be formed between the Bob and all LEDs through Omni-DRIS elements.

In summary, the received signals of the k-th Bob after removing the DC value can be represented as follows:

$$y_k = \underbrace{\rho_k \left(\mathbf{h}_k^{(1)} + \mathbf{h}_k^{(2)} \mathbf{g}_k\right)^T \mathbf{p}_k s_k}_{\text{Desired signals}}$$
$$+ \underbrace{\rho_k \sum_{\substack{i=1 \\ i \neq k}}^{K} \left(\mathbf{h}_k^{(1)} + \mathbf{h}_k^{(2)} \mathbf{g}_k\right)^T \mathbf{p}_i s_i}_{\text{Interference signals}} + n_k, \qquad (3)$$

where n_k represents additive white Gaussian noise (AWGN) with zero mean and a variance σ_k^2 of the k-th Bob; ρ_k is the responsivity of the k-th Bob's PD. The achievable rate of k-th Bob R_k can be represented as follows [12]:

$$R_k = \frac{1}{2} W \log_2 \left(1 + \frac{e}{2\pi} \frac{|\boldsymbol{h}_k^T \boldsymbol{p}_k|^2}{\sum_{i=1, i \neq k}^{K} |\boldsymbol{h}_k^T \boldsymbol{p}_i|^2 + \sigma^2}\right), \qquad (4)$$

where W and e are the signal bandwidth and the base of natural logarithms, respectively. For the convenience of expression, the channel gain of the k-th user is represented by the matrix $\boldsymbol{h}_k = \boldsymbol{h}_k^{(1)} + \boldsymbol{h}_k^{(2)} \boldsymbol{g}_k$.

Eve. Compared to Bob, Eve is considered as a special element. We denote the relationship between the noise LED and the Omni-DRIS with the vector $\boldsymbol{g_0} \in \{0,1\}^{N \times 1}$. The received signals after removing the DC value and the achievable rate of Eve can be expressed as follows:

$$y_{e,k} = \rho_e \underbrace{\sum_{\substack{i=1 \\ i \neq k}}^{K} \left(h_e^{(1)}\right)^T p_i s_i + \left(h_e^{(2)} g_0\right)^T p_{an} s_{an} + n_e}_{\text{Interference signals}}$$

$$+ \underbrace{\rho_e \left(h_e^{(1)}\right)^T p_k s_k}_{\text{Desired signals}}, \qquad (5)$$

where p_{an} and s_{an} represent the power and signals of artificial noise to interfere Eve eavesdropping on the k-th user.

$$R_{e,k} = \frac{1}{2} W \log_2 \left(1 + \frac{e}{2\pi} \frac{\left|\left(h_e^{(1)}\right)^T p_k\right|^2}{I_{k,e}^2 + \left|\left(h_e^{(2)} g_0\right)^T p_{an}\right|^2 + \sigma^2}\right), \qquad (6)$$

where the multi-user interference power is denoted as

$$I_{k,e} = \sum_{\substack{i=1 \\ i \neq k}}^{K} \left(h_e^{(1)}\right)^T p_i. \qquad (7)$$

2.3 Security Performance Formulation

To guarantee that each legitimate user in this system can transmit information securely and equitably, our goal is to maximize the secrecy rate of the worst legitimate user. Hence, this paper is concentrated on maximize the minimum secure rate for the k-th user in this system. Secrecy capacity refers to the difference in data rates between the Bob and Eve. Additionally, considering the power limitation of each LED is P_{max}. Similar to the security performance formulation in [5], the optimization problem can be formulated as follows:

$$\mathbf{P1}: \underset{P,G}{\text{maximize}} \underset{k \in \mathcal{K}}{\text{minimize}} \ (R_k - R_{e,k}) \qquad (8a)$$

$$\text{s.t.} \& \|p_l\|^2 \leq P_{max}, \quad \forall l \in \mathcal{L}, \qquad (8b)$$

$$g_{n,k} \in \{0,1\}, \quad \forall n \in \mathcal{N}, k \in \mathcal{K}, \qquad (8c)$$

$$\sum_{k=1}^{K} g_{n,k} = 1, \quad \forall n \in \mathcal{N}. \qquad (8d)$$

The constraints in Eqs. (8c) and (8d) means one Omni-DRIS element can be assigned to at most one user; the constraints in Eq. (8b) means the limitation of the LED transmission power need to satisfy. We note that constraint Eq. (8c) indicates that the Omni-DRIS element can cover any user in either of the two rooms, which is different from the constraint in conventional RIS [5].

Due to the coupling of variables G and P, $P1$ is a NP hard and non-convex problem [11]. Simultaneously finding the precoding matrix and the alignment matrix is an extremely difficult optimization problem.

3 AO Based Secrecy Rate Max-Min Algorithm

In this section, we propose an AO algorithm that decouples the original problem into two independent sub-problems. In the optimization algorithm, assuming the value of one matrix is fixed, we optimize the other matrix, and in the next step, we reverse the roles. We repeat this process until the algorithm converges. For these two sub-problems, we solve them using SCA respectively. The secrecy rate of the k-th Bob can be equivalently rewritten as

$$R_k - R_{E,k} = \log_2\left(T_k^1\right) + \log_2\left(T_k^2\right) - \log_2\left(T_k^3\right) - \log_2\left(T_k^4\right), \tag{9}$$

where

$$T_k^1 = \sum_{i=1}^{K} |\boldsymbol{p}_i^T \boldsymbol{h}_k^{(1)} + \boldsymbol{p}_i^T \boldsymbol{h}_k^{(2)} \boldsymbol{g}_k|^2 + \sigma^2, \tag{10a}$$

$$T_k^2 = \sum_{\substack{i=1 \\ i \neq k}}^{K} |\left(\boldsymbol{h}_e^{(1)}\right)^T \boldsymbol{p}_i|^2 + |p_{an}\left(\boldsymbol{h}_e^{(2)}\right)^T \boldsymbol{g}_0|^2 + \sigma^2, \tag{10b}$$

$$T_k^3 = \sum_{\substack{i=1 \\ i \neq k}}^{K} |\boldsymbol{p}_i^T \boldsymbol{h}_k^{(1)} + \boldsymbol{p}_i^T \boldsymbol{h}_k^{(2)} \boldsymbol{g}_k|^2 + \sigma^2, \tag{10c}$$

$$T_k^4 = \sum_{i=1}^{K} |\left(\boldsymbol{h}_e^{(1)}\right)^T \boldsymbol{p}_i|^2 + |p_{an}\left(\boldsymbol{h}_e^{(2)}\right)^T \boldsymbol{g}_0|^2 + \sigma^2, \tag{10d}$$

to efficiently address the max-min problem, we introduce an auxiliary variable u into the formulation [15]. Consequently, $P1$ can be rewritten as

$$P2: \underset{P,G}{\text{maximize}}\ u \tag{11a}$$

$$\text{s.t.} \& u \leq \log_2\left(T_k^1\right) + \log_2\left(T_k^2\right) - \log_2\left(T_k^3\right) - \log_2\left(T_k^4\right), \tag{11b}$$

$$\|\boldsymbol{p}_l\|^2 \leq P_{max}, \quad \forall l \in \mathcal{L}, \tag{11c}$$

$$g_{n,k} \in \{0,1\}, \quad \forall n \in \mathcal{N}, k \in \mathcal{K}, \tag{11d}$$

$$\sum_{k=1}^{K} g_{n,k} = 1, \quad \forall n \in \mathcal{N}. \tag{11e}$$

The constraints (11b) is non-convex, we introduce auxiliary variables $s_{k,1}$, $s_{k,2}$, $s_{k,3}$, $s_{k,4}$ and $r_{k,1}$, $r_{k,2}$, $r_{k,3}$, $r_{k,4}$, the constraints (11b) is transformed to

$$\log_2(r_{k,1}) \geq s_{k,1}, \tag{12a}$$
$$\log_2(r_{k,2}) \geq s_{k,2}, \tag{12b}$$
$$T_k^3 \leq r_{k,3}, \tag{12c}$$
$$T_k^4 \leq r_{k,4}, \tag{12d}$$
$$T_k^1 \geq r_{k,1}, \tag{12e}$$
$$T_k^2 \geq r_{k,2}, \tag{12f}$$
$$\log_2(r_{k,3}) \leq s_{k,3}, \tag{12g}$$
$$\log_2(r_{k,4}) \leq s_{k,4}, \tag{12h}$$

it can be observed that constraints (12e)-(12h) are convex while other constraints are still non-convex.

3.1 Optimization of Precoding Matrix

Given the allocation matrix $\boldsymbol{G}$, the optimization of the precoding matrix $\boldsymbol{P}$ is performed. The sub-optimization problem is transformed to:

$$\boldsymbol{P3}: \underset{\boldsymbol{P}}{\text{maximize}} \ u \tag{13a}$$
$$\text{s.t.} \& u \leq s_{k,1} + s_{k,2} - s_{k,3} - s_{k,4}, \tag{13b}$$
$$(12a) - (12h), \tag{13c}$$
$$\|\boldsymbol{p}_l\|^2 \leq P_{max}, \quad \forall l \in \mathcal{L}. \tag{13d}$$

However, the constraints (12e)-(12h) are non-convex. To tackle these non-convex problems, the first-order Taylor expansion method is applied to obtain a convex upper bound. As a result, these non-convex constraints can be upper-bounded as

$$\sum_{i=1}^{K} 2\boldsymbol{p}_i \boldsymbol{h}_k \boldsymbol{h}_k^T \boldsymbol{p}_i^t - |\boldsymbol{h}_k^T \boldsymbol{p}_i^t|^2 + \sigma^2 \geq r_{k,1}, \tag{14a}$$

$$\sum_{\substack{i=1 \\ i \neq k}}^{K} 2\boldsymbol{p}_i^T \boldsymbol{h}_e^{(1)} \left(\boldsymbol{h}_e^{(1)}\right)^T \boldsymbol{p}_i^t - |\left(\boldsymbol{h}_e^{(1)}\right)^T \boldsymbol{p}_i^t|^2 + \sigma^2 \geq r_{k,2}, \tag{14b}$$

$$\log_2\left(r_{k,3}^t\right) + \left(\frac{r_{k,3} - r_{k,3}^t}{\ln 2 r_{k,3}^t}\right) \leq s_{k,3}, \tag{14c}$$

$$\log_2\left(r_{k,4}^t\right) + \left(\frac{r_{k,4} - r_{k,4}^t}{\ln 2 r_{k,4}^t}\right) \leq s_{k,4}, \tag{14d}$$

where t is the iteration index. Therefore, the $\boldsymbol{P3}$ problem can be rewritten as

$$\boldsymbol{P4}: \underset{\boldsymbol{P}}{\text{maximize}} \quad u \tag{15a}$$

$$\text{s.t.} \& u \leq s_{k,1} + s_{k,2} - s_{k,3} - s_{k,4}, \tag{15b}$$

$$(12a) - (12d) \quad (14a) - (14d), \tag{15c}$$

$$\|\boldsymbol{p}_l\|^2 \leq P_{max}, \quad \forall l \in \mathcal{L}. \tag{15d}$$

It can be observed that the sub-problem $\boldsymbol{P4}$ is a convex problem with its convex constraints and can be solved by CVX.

3.2 Optimization of Alignment Matrix

Given the precoding matrix $\boldsymbol{P}$, the optimization of the allocation matrix $\boldsymbol{G}$ for Omni-DRIS is performed. Then the constraint (11d) (11e) are relaxed to $0 \leq g_{n,k} \leq 1$, and the sub-optimization problem is transformed to:

$$\boldsymbol{P5}: \underset{\boldsymbol{G}}{\text{maximize}} \quad u \tag{16a}$$

$$\text{s.t.} \& u \leq s_{k,1} + s_{k,2} - s_{k,3} - s_{k,4}, \tag{16b}$$

$$(12a) - (12d), \tag{16c}$$

$$g_{n,k} \in [0,1], \quad \forall n \in \mathcal{N}, k \in \mathcal{K}, \tag{16d}$$

$$\sum_{k=1}^{K} g_{n,k} = 1, \quad \forall n \in \mathcal{N}. \tag{16e}$$

Similarly, we also use SCA to transform the constraints ((12e))-((12h)) into a convex problem. The first-order Taylor expansion of constraints ((12g)) and ((12h)) are the same as that of constraints ((14c)) and ((14d)). Therefore, the constraints ((12e)) and ((12f)) can be rewritten as the constraints ((17a)) and ((17b)).

$$\sum_{i=1}^{K} |\boldsymbol{p}_i^T \boldsymbol{h}_k^{(1)}|^2 + 2\left(\left(\boldsymbol{h}_k^{(1)}\right)^T \boldsymbol{p}_i \boldsymbol{p}_i^T \boldsymbol{h}_k^{(2)} + (\boldsymbol{g}_k^t)^T \left(\boldsymbol{h}_k^{(2)}\right)^T \boldsymbol{p}_i \boldsymbol{p}_i^T \boldsymbol{h}_k^{(2)} \right) \boldsymbol{g}_k - (\boldsymbol{g}_k^t)^T \left(\boldsymbol{h}_k^{(2)}\right)^T \boldsymbol{p}_i \boldsymbol{p}_i^T \boldsymbol{h}_k^{(2)} \boldsymbol{g}_k^t + \sigma^2 \geq r_{k,1},$$

$$\tag{17a}$$

$$\sum_{\substack{i=1 \\ i \neq k}}^{K} |\left(\boldsymbol{h}_e^{(1)}\right)^T \boldsymbol{p}_i|^2 + 2p_{an}^2 \boldsymbol{g}_0^T \boldsymbol{h}_e^{(2)} \left(\boldsymbol{h}_e^{(2)}\right)^T \boldsymbol{g}_0^t - p_{an}^2 (\boldsymbol{g}_0^t)^T \boldsymbol{h}_e^{(2)} \left(\boldsymbol{h}_e^{(2)}\right)^T \boldsymbol{g}_0^t + \sigma^2 \geq r_{k,2},$$

$$\tag{17b}$$

Then the sub-problem **P6** can be rewritten as

$$\mathbf{P6}: \underset{G}{\text{maximize}} \ u \tag{18a}$$

$$\text{s.t.} \ \& u \leq s_{k,1} + s_{k,2} - s_{k,3} - s_{k,4}, \tag{18b}$$

$$(12a) - (12d) \ (14c) - (14d) \ (17a) - (17b) \tag{18c}$$

$$g_{n,k} \in [0,1], \quad \forall n \in \mathcal{N}, k \in \mathcal{K}, \tag{18d}$$

$$\sum_{k=1}^{K} g_{n,k} = 1, \quad \forall n \in \mathcal{N}. \tag{18e}$$

Similarly, sub-problem **P6**, with its convex constraints, can be solved by CVX.

Given initial random matrix G and P, the general algorithm for the joint design of precoding and alignment matrices is outlined in Algorithm 1.

Algorithm 1. AO based secrecy rate max-min algorithm.

Input: $h_{k,l}^{(1)}$, $h_{k,n,l}^{(2)}$, $t \leftarrow 0$
Initialize: $G \epsilon R^{N \times K}$, $P \epsilon R^{L \times K}$
repeat
    calculate P with P_{t+1} by solving **P4** with fixed $G = G_t$ using CVX method
    calculate G with G_{t+1} by solving **P6** with fixed $P = P_t$ using CVX method
    set $t = t + 1$
until convergence
Output: P, G

---

4 Simulation Results

In this section, we present the simulation results for the security performance of the Omni-DRIS Enhanced VLC System with an Eavesdropper. Specifically, two 8 m× 8 m ×3 m rooms are considered. The users and eavesdroppers are randomly distributed in both rooms. We primarily refer to the parameter configurations described in [5,11], which are listed in Table 2.

To demonstrate the superiority of our proposed system named Omni-DRIS system, we use the following two systems as benchmarks in our simulations: (1) RIS-VLC system: This system deploys a conventional optical RIS in Room 1, which can only reflect signals and cannot cover Room 2. (2) non-precoding system: This system does not use precoding, only optimizes the allocation matrix G.

Figure 2 illustrates the variation in the minimum secrecy rate of the system with the number of iterations for different K and N. It can be observed that the minimum secrecy rate of the system increases with the number of iterations and eventually stabilizes. When $N = 4$ and $K = 4$, the system converges the

Table 2. Simulation setup

Parameters	Symbols	Values(SI)
Transmitter semi-angle	ϕ	80°
Detector area	Apd	1 cm²
Field of view of PD	FOV	80°
Received noise power	σ_k^2	10^{-10} W
System bandwidth	W	20 MHz
Omni-DRIS element size		0.2×0.2
Center of Omni-DRIS		(4,8,1.5)
LED location of Room 1		(3,2,3);(3,7,3);(6,2,3);(6,6,3)
LED location of Room 2		(1,9,3);(1,14,3);(7,10,3);(7,14,3)
Noise LED location		(4,12,3)

fastest. In comparison, for $N = 25$ with $K = 4$ and $K = 6$, the convergence occurs almost simultaneously. It can be shown that N may play a dominant role in influencing the convergence speed of the system. The proposed algorithm ultimately converges for different system parameters, which demonstrate its effectiveness.

Figure 3 shows the relationship between the transmit power P_t and the minimum secrecy rate of the system for $N = 36$, $K = 2$, and $K = 6$. As shown, for the same system, a smaller K results in better system security performance. Under the same K, the Omni-DRIS system significantly improves the minimum secrecy rate compared to the RIS-VLC and non-precoding systems. For example, when $K = 2$ and $P_t = 25$ dBm, the minimum secrecy rate of the Omni-DRIS system is approximately 2.05 times and 15.25 times higher than RIS-VLC and non-precoding systems, respectively. We observe that the minimum secrecy rate increases the transmit power in all three cases, but the rate of increase is much slower for the non-precoding system, which means precoding is important to enhance the security performance of multi-user VLC system.

To further investigate the impact of the number of Omni-DRIS elements on the minimum secrecy rate, we compare the Omni-DRIS system with the RIS-VLC system under different N. As shown in Fig. 4, for the Omni-DRIS system, increasing N and P_t can significantly enhance the minimum secrecy rate. When $K = 2$ and $P_t = 25$ dBm, the minimum secrecy rate with $N = 225$ is approximately 1.39, 2.31, and 3.24 times higher than that $N = 100$, $N = 25$, and the RIS-VLC system, respectively. Moreover, it can be observed that when N increases by 25 from 0, the system's security rate increases by 1.40 times. When N increases by 75 from 25, the security rate increases by 1.66 times, and N increases by 125 from 100, the rate increases by only 1.38 times. This indicates that as N grows, the rate of improvement in system security slows down, underscoring the importance of deploying Omni-DRIS to enhance system performance. It also suggests that in practical scenarios, factors such as the

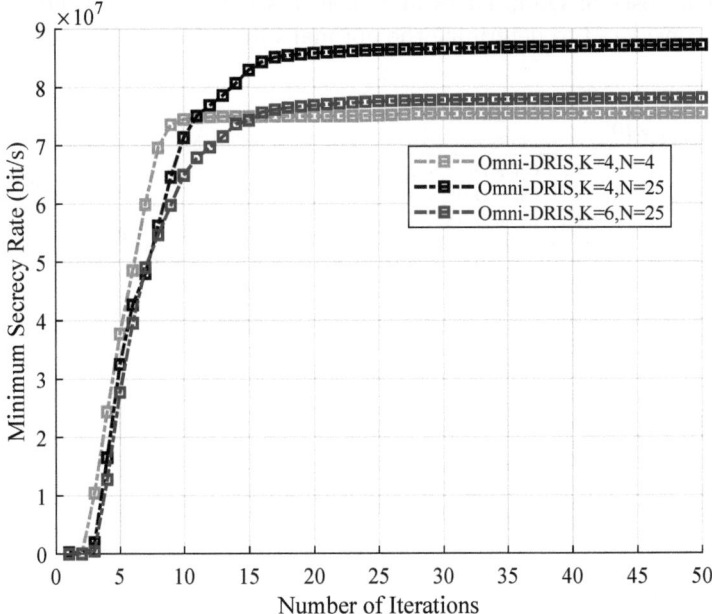

Fig. 2. Convergence rate of proposed AO algorithm.

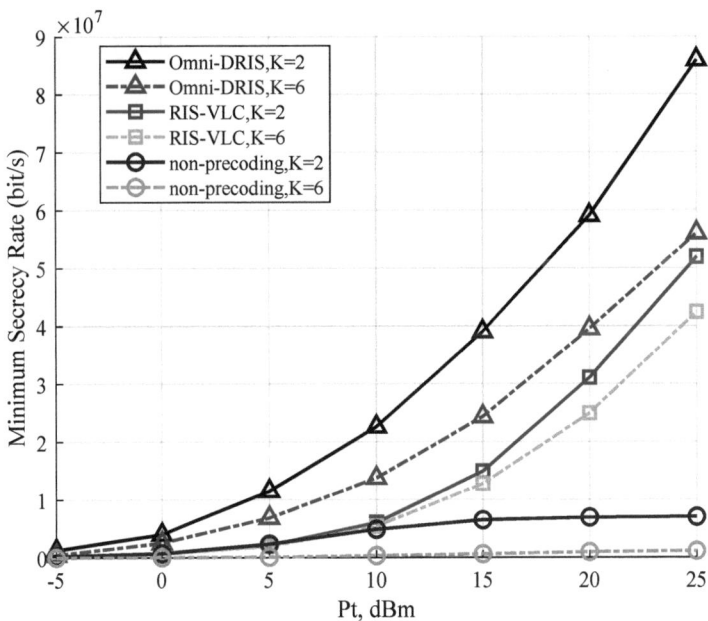

Fig. 3. Minimum secrecy rate versus the transmit power with N = 36 and K = 2,6 for Omni-DRIS, RIS-VLC and non-precoding systems.

deployment costs of Omni-DRIS and specific security requirements should be carefully considered to determine the optimal value of N.

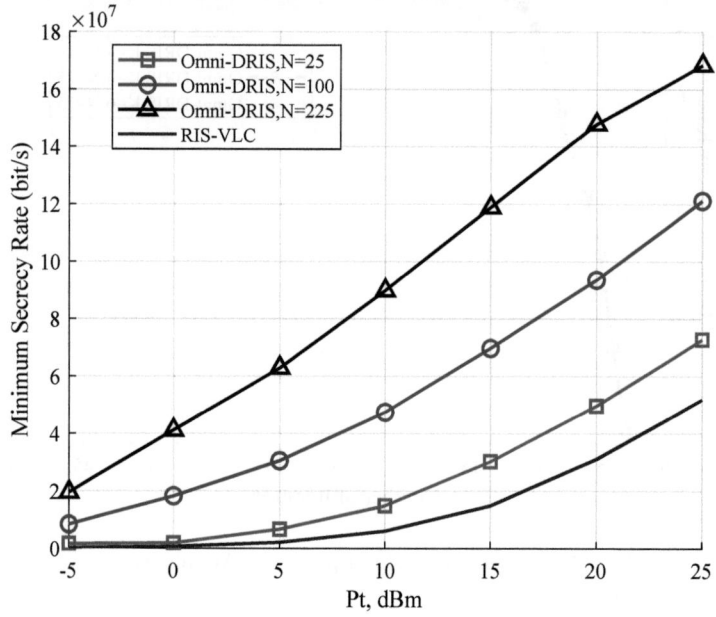

Fig. 4. Minimum secrecy rate versus the transmit power with $K = 2$ and $N = 25, 100, 225$ for Omni-DRIS and RIS-VLC systems.

5 Conclusion

In this paper, we propose an Omni-DRIS enhanced VLC system with an eavesdropper. For the security performance of this system, we use an AO algorithm, transforming the original optimization problem into a series of sub-problems, which can be solved by SCA method. The numerical results demonstrate that the Omni-DRIS system achieves a minimum secrecy rate that is approximately 105% higher than the state-of-the-art RIS-VLC system and 1425% higher than the non-precoding system. Additionally, as the number of Omni-DRIS element increases, the minimum secure rate of the Omni-DRIS system grows more slowly. In future research, the utilization of Omni-DRIS to enhance the physical layer security could demonstrate great potential for large-scale deployment in next-generation VLC systems.

References

1. Aboagye, S., Ndjiongue, A.R., Ngatched, T.M., Dobre, O.A., Poor, H.V.: RIS-assisted visible light communication systems: a tutorial. IEEE Commun. Surv. Tutorials **25**, 251–288 (2023)
2. Su, N., Panayirci, E., Koca, M., Yesilkaya, A., Poor, H.V., Haas, H.: Physical layer security for multi-user MIMO visible light communication systems with generalized space shift keying. IEEE Trans. Commun. **69**, 2585–2598 (2021)
3. Obeed, M., Salhab, A.M., Alouini, M.S., Zummo, S.A.: On optimizing VLC networks for downlink multi-user transmission: a survey. IEEE Commun. Surv. Tutorials **21**, 2947–2976 (2019)
4. Abumarshoud, H., Chen, C., Tavakkolnia, I., Haas, H., Imran, M.A.: Intelligent reflecting surfaces for enhanced physical layer security in NOMA VLC systems. In: ICC 2023 - IEEE International Conference on Communications (2023)
5. Sun, S., Yang, F., Song, J., Han, Z.: Optimization on multiuser physical layer security of intelligent reflecting surface-aided VLC. IEEE Wireless Commun. Lett. **11**, 1344–1348 (2022)
6. Saifaldeen, D.A., Ciftler, B.S., Abdallah, M.M., Qaraqe, K.A.: DRL-based IRS-assisted secure visible light communications. IEEE Photon. J. **14**, 1–9 (2022)
7. Soderi, S., Brighente, A., Turrin, F., Conti, M.: VLC physical layer security through RIS-aided jamming receiver for 6G wireless networks. In: 2022 19th Annual IEEE International Conference on Sensing, Communication, and Networking (SECON) (2022)
8. Zhang, H., Di, B.: Intelligent omni-surfaces: simultaneous refraction and reflection for full-dimensional wireless communications. IEEE Commun. Surv. Tutorials **24**, 1997–2028 (2022)
9. Sun, S., Yang, F., Song, J.: Sum rate maximization for intelligent reflecting surface-aided visible light communications. IEEE Commun. Lett. **25**, 3619–3623 (2021)
10. Sun, S., Yang, F., Song, J., Zhang, R.: Intelligent reflecting surface for MIMO VLC: Joint design of surface configuration and transceiver signal processing. IEEE Trans. Wireless Commun. **22**, 5785–5799 (2023)
11. Atashbar, M., Ghazijahani, H.A., Guan, Y.L., Yang, Z.: A precoding for ORIS-assisted MIMO multi-user VLC system. arXiv preprint arXiv:2312.08214 (2023)
12. Ndjiongue, A.R., Dobre, O.A., Shin, H.: Maximal transmission rate in Omni-DRIS-assisted indoor visible light communication systems. IEEE Trans. Veh. Technol. **73**, 13956–13961 (2024)
13. Ndjiongue, A.R., Ngatched, T.M.N., Dobre, O.A., Haas, H., Shin, H.: Double-sided beamforming in VLC systems using omni-digital reconfigurable intelligent surfaces. IEEE Commun. Mag. **62**, 150–155 (2024)
14. Abdelhady, A.M., Sultan Salem, A.K., Amin, O., Shihada, B., Alouini, M.-S.: Visible light communications via intelligent reflecting surfaces: Metasurfaces vs mirror arrays. IEEE Open J. Commun. Soc. **2**, 1–20 (2021)
15. Wei, M., Xu, X., Jin, L., Li, Y., Han, S., Liu, B.: Secure transmission fairness in IRS-assisted cell-free network. In: 2023 IEEE Wireless Communications and Networking Conference (WCNC) (2023)

A Hybrid Topological Heterostructure for Communication

Xinyu Zhang[1(✉)], Yueyao Li[1,2], Sijie Li[1], and Menglin L. N. Chen[1]

[1] Department of Electrical and Electronic Engineering, The Hong Kong Polytechnic University, Hong Kong, China
{menglin.chen,menglin.chen}@polyu.edu.hk
xinyu-eee.zhang@connect.polyu.hk
[2] School of Automation, Northwestern Polytechnical University, Xi'an, China

Abstract. Topological photonic crystals have emerged as an important branch of physics for their excellent ability to manipulate light. Furthermore, a large-area photonic crystal can provide an additional degree of freedom by inserting a photonic crystal structure without a band gap between topologically distinct photonic crystals. In this article, we propose a hybrid topological heterostructure with the potential to be applied in modern communication. The time-reversal symmetry is broken by applying an external magnetic field while the spatial-inversion symmetry is broken by rotating the dielectric components. Our system exhibits the characteristics of large-area one-way transmission that evenly distributes over the middle domain. The unidirectional excitation properties and inherent robustness are verified in a Z-shaped channel. The proposed heterostructure provides broad application prospects in photonic integrated networks and on-chip integrated communication systems.

Keywords: Photonic crystals · Large-area state · Topological edge state

1 Introduction

In recent years, photonic crystals have been of great importance in the research fields of fundamental materials and photonic devices, and researchers now have drawn their attention to topological photonic crystals with great robust properties [1–4]. The most significant features of the topological photonic crystals are their non-trivial topological phases and the associated robust topological edge states. The edge states protected by topological invariants are immune to the interference that is caused by defects and random disorder, resulting in low-loss transmission of photonic information. The topological edge states provide a great platform for designing modern communication devices.

Due to the extension of quantum Hall physics from the field of electron gas to photons, photonic quantum Hall [5–7], quantum spin Hall [8–10], and quantum valley Hall [11–13] states are proposed and demonstrated by researchers. Furthermore, the presence of an external magnetic field imposed in magneto-optical photonic crystal leads to quantum anomalous Hall, as a result of the broken of the time-reversal symmetry. Also, when both time-reversal symmetry and space-inversion symmetry are broken, an unpaired Dirac point at K and K' points will appear [14]. However, to our best knowledge, no further application is proposed based on this combination.

Recent works introduce a new width degree of freedom to the topological photonic crystal by inserting an additional photonic crystal domain featuring ungapped Dirac degeneracies into the conventional double-layer topological photonic crystal [4]. Compared with the conventional way to build topological photonic crystals, that is, interfacing two photonic crystals with different topological invariants, whose topological edge states are mostly confined at the interface, the three-layer model features a wide and tunable transmission width.

Here, we propose a 2D heterostructure consisting of three domains, which supports backscattering-immune large-area transmission. Band gaps of the upper and lower PCs occur due to broken parity symmetry and time-reversal symmetry, respectively, and the middle domain features unpaired Dirac points. Both the inherent brilliant topological properties and the flexibility of transmission width are demonstrated. Many practical communication devices can be further designed based on our model.

2 Unit Cell Design

Three distinct kinds of hexagonal unit cells are shown in Fig. 1(a). Each unit cell has the same lattice constant and comprises three same round dielectric pillars as well as a larger gyromagnetic/dielectric rod in the center. An orientation angle is applied to the three small dielectric pillars, which causes the in-plane parity symmetry breaking. The central rods in unit cells of domains A and B are made of yttrium iron garnet (YIG), which is magnetized by the presence of an external magnetic field H_0 along the z-axis. The time-reversal symmetry is broken due to the gyromagnetic anisotropy property of the YIG rods. The relative magnetic permeability of the YIG has form

$$\tilde{\mu} = \begin{bmatrix} \mu_r & i\kappa & 0 \\ -i\kappa & \mu_r & 0 \\ 0 & 0 & 1 \end{bmatrix} \quad (1)$$

where $\mu_r = \frac{(\omega_0+i\alpha\omega)\omega_m}{(\omega_0+i\alpha\omega)^2-\omega^2}$, $\kappa = \frac{\omega\omega_m}{(\omega_0+i\alpha\omega)^2-\omega^2}$, $\omega_m = \gamma M_s$ is the characteristic circular frequency with the saturation magnetization M_s, $\omega_0 = \gamma H_0$ is the resonance frequency, H_0 is the external magnetic field, γ is the gyromagnetic ratio, α is the damping coefficient, and ω is the operating frequency. The central rods in domain C are dielectric cylinders without gyromagnetic properties, where the time-reversal symmetry is preserved. The band structures of three different unit cells are shown in Fig. 1(b), where only the TM polarization is considered, that is, the E-field parallel to the central rods. As a result of breaking time-reversal and parity symmetry in domains A and C, gaps appear in their band structure, while both time-reversal and parity symmetry are broken in the inserted part, namely domain B, resulting in an unpaired photonic Dirac point.

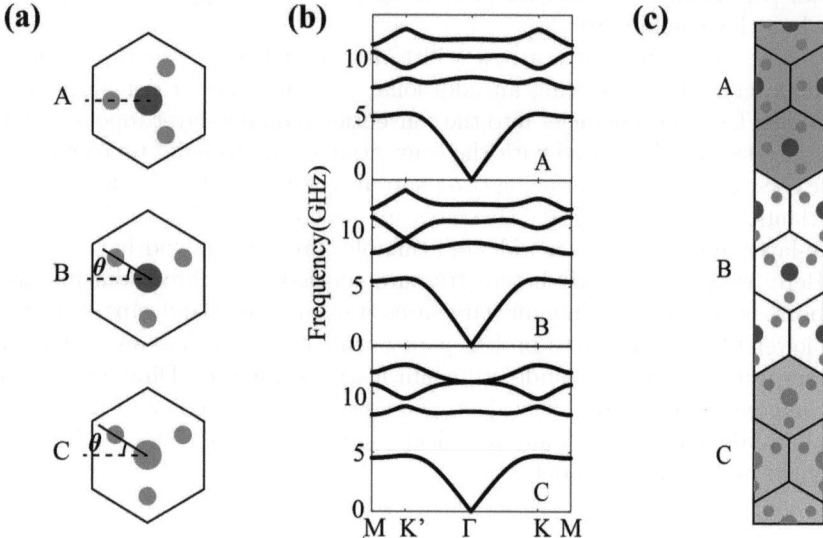

Fig. 1. Schematic of proposed unit cells and band structures. (a) Illustration of unit cells in domains A, B, and C, where the red rods are gyromagnetic and the blue rods are dielectric. (b) Corresponding band structure of unit cell in domains A, B, and C when unit cells A and B are biased by $+H$. (c) Combination of three PCs, where different colors indicate different unit cells. (Color figure online)

3 Large-Area Topological Waveguide States

A three-layer heterostructure system is proposed with three kinds of PCs mentioned above, which support edge states distributed over the middle domain. The unit cells with unpaired Dirac points are inserted between two topological nontrivial domains (A and C) as depicted in Fig. 1(c). The schemes of all these domains are well designed to make sure that the bandgaps of domain A and domain C are at the same frequency and that the Dirac point of domain B precisely aligns in the frequency range. The corresponding dispersion curve of the supercell is depicted in Fig. 2(a), where the red dots indicate the edge state and the black dots show the bulk state. The edge state only exits at the K' Valley point with a negative slope, showing the unidirectional waveguide state located in the band gap.

As for the mode width, a degree of freedom (DOF) that has been newly introduced, three supercells with different widths of the middle domain are constructed as shown in Fig. 2(b). The three models are designed with mid-domain

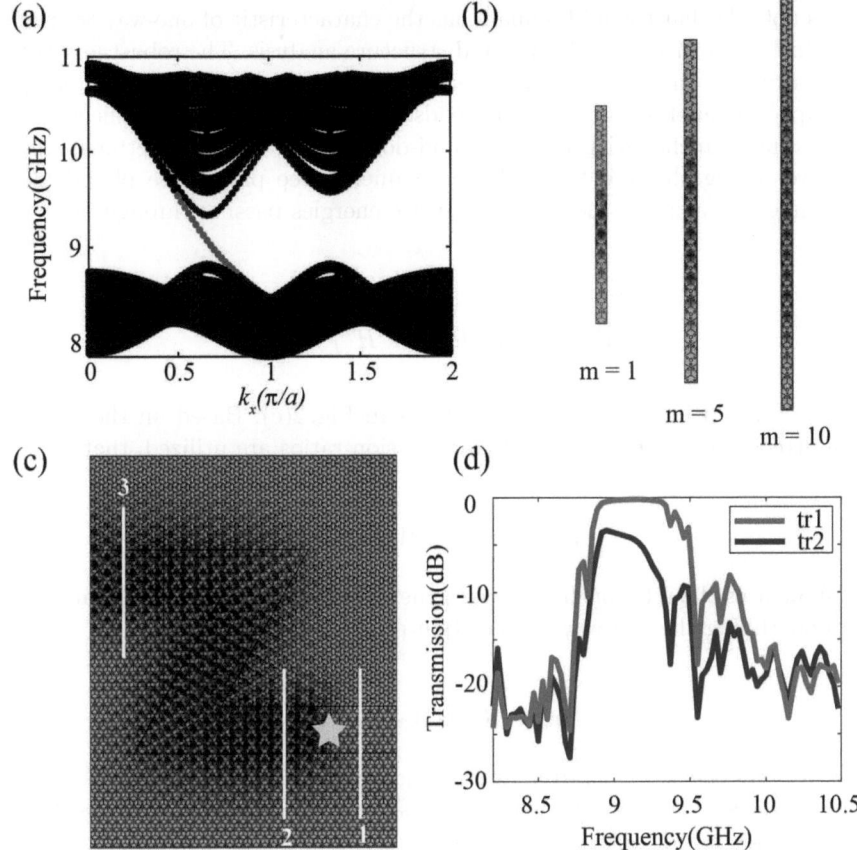

Fig. 2. (a) Projected band structures of the supercell, where the red dots indicate the topological edge state. (b) Electric field distribution of the supercells with different widths of the middle domain (m = 1, 5, 10). (c) A Z-shape waveguiding channel with sharp bends. The yellow star indicates the energy source, and the white lines indicate the planes for energy extraction. (d) Simulated transmission profiles for the Z-shape channel. (Color figure online)

width m = 1, m = 5, and m = 10, respectively, where m indicates the number of layers in domain B. From the normalized electric field distributions, it can be found that the energy is mainly distributed in the middle domain B, indicating that the large-area transmission function has been achieved. Moreover, it is evident that the energy transported has a linear relationship with the mid-domain width m, which means when increasing the number of layers in domain B, the power transmitted grows simultaneously. In particular, compared with the conventional edge states that waves can pass through at the interface of two PCs, our model enables electromagnetic waves to transmit in the entire middle domain and thus much more information along with energy could be carried.

It is notable that the mid-domain has the characteristic of one-way transmission, which is consistent with the band structure analysis. The robustness of the model is further investigated by a Z-shaped channel. As depicted in Fig. 2(c), a Z-shaped channel with two sharp bends is constructed, which connects three waveguiding branches with the same mid-domain width m. To better quantify the power going through the Z-shape channel, three planes are placed along the channel to calculate the electromagnetic energies passing through, with the formula

$$W_i = \frac{1}{2} * \int_{S_i} Re(E \times H^*) \cdot dS, \quad (2)$$

where $i = 1, 2, 3$ indicates the three planes in Fig. 2(c). Based on the energies transmitted, two different types of transmission ratios are utilized, that is,

$$tr1 = 10log(W_3/W_3 + W_1), \quad (3)$$

that showcases the relationship between the excited forward and backward energies, underlining the one-way propagation property, and

$$tr2 = 10log(W_3/W_2), \quad (4)$$

which reflects the reflection-free interfacing and backscattering-immune propagation features by showing the energy transport efficiency. The simulated transmission ratios are depicted in Fig. 2(d), and it is clear that in the topological bandgap, they both perform much better than out of it. The transmission ratios of the topological states are both near-zero dB, which indicates that most of the excited energies are transported to the left end of the Z-shape channel. Its excellent properties of unidirectional and robust propagation against sharp bends and reflection-free interfacing provide a potential platform for communication devices.

4 Conclusion

In conclusion, we have investigated a novel three-layer heterostructure system that supports topological unidirectional transmission, exhibiting both topological quantum valley Hall and topological quantum anomalous Hall properties. Also, a new degree of freedom, transmission width, is introduced resulting in much more energy and information can be transmitted. In addition, a Z-shaped channel is constructed, demonstrating the robust backscattering-immune transmission, inherent reflection-free interfacing, and unidirectional propagation characteristics of our proposed heterostructure.

References

1. Ozawa, T., et al.: Topological photonics. Rev. Mod. Phys. **91**(1) (2019). https://doi.org/10.1103/RevModPhys.91.015006
2. Yan, B., et al.: Multifrequency and multimode topological waveguides in a Stampfli-Triangle photonic crystal with large valley chern numbers. Laser Photonics Rev. **18**(6), 2300686 (2024). https://doi.org/10.1002/lpor.202300686
3. Shi, A., et al.: Observation of topological corner state arrays in photonic quasicrystals. Laser Photonics Rev. **18**(7), 2300956 (2024). https://doi.org/10.1002/lpor.202300956
4. Zhang, X., Li, S., Lan, Z., Gao, W., Chen, M.L.N.: Reconfigurable photonic valley filter in hybrid topological heterostructures. Laser & Photonics Rev., 2400797. https://doi.org/10.1002/lpor.202400797
5. Raghu, S., Haldane, F.D.M.: Analogs of quantum-hall-effect edge states in photonic crystals. Phys. Rev. A **78**(3), 033834 (2008). https://doi.org/10.1103/PhysRevA.78.033834
6. Haldane, F.D.M., Raghu, S.: Possible realization of directional optical waveguides in photonic crystals with broken time-reversal symmetry. Phys. Rev. Lett. **100**(1), 013904 (2008). https://doi.org/10.1103/PhysRevLett.100.013904
7. Wang, Z., Chong, Y.D., Joannopoulos, J.D., Soljačić, M.: Reflection-free one-way edge modes in a gyromagnetic photonic crystal. Phys. Rev. Lett. **100**, 013905 (2008). https://doi.org/10.1103/PhysRevLett.100.013905
8. Khanikaev, A.B., Hossein Mousavi, S., Tse, W.K., Kargarian, M., MacDonald, A.H., Shvets, G.: Photonic topological insulators. Nat. Mater. **12**(3), 233–239 (2013). https://doi.org/10.1038/nmat3520
9. Chen, W.J., et al.: Experimental realization of photonic topological insulator in a uniaxial metacrystal waveguide. Nat. Commun. **5**(1), 5782 (2014). https://doi.org/10.1038/ncomms6782
10. Ma, T., Khanikaev, A.B., Mousavi, S.H., Shvets, G.: Guiding electromagnetic waves around sharp corners: topologically protected photonic transport in metawaveguides. Phys. Rev. Lett. **114**(12), 127401 (2015). https://doi.org/10.1103/PhysRevLett.114.127401
11. Ma, T., Shvets, G.: All-Si valley-Hall photonic topological insulator. New J. Phys. **18**(2), 025012 (2016). https://doi.org/10.1088/1367-2630/18/2/025012
12. Wu, X., et al.: Direct observation of valley-polarized topological edge states in designer surface plasmon crystals. Nat. Commun. **8**(1), 1304 (2017). https://doi.org/10.1038/s41467-017-01515-2
13. Gao, F., et al.: Topologically protected refraction of robust kink states in valley photonic crystals. Nat. Phys. **14**(2), 140–144 (2018). https://doi.org/10.1038/nphys4304
14. Liu, G.G., et al.: Observation of an unpaired photonic DIRAC point. Nat. Commun. **11**(1), 1873 (2020). https://doi.org/10.1038/s41467-020-15801-z

Zero-Shot Learning-Based Maritime Semantic Communication System

Lanxiang Hou[1], Jiayi Sun[1], Haoqi Liang[1], Liang Mao[2], Guanchong Niu[1(✉)], Man-On Pun[3], and Zhiming Cheng[4]

[1] Guangzhou Institute of Technology, Xidian University, Guangzhou 510700, China
{24181214360,24181214361,24181214196}@stu.xidian.edu.cn,
niuguanchong@xidian.edu.cn
[2] Shenzhen Polytechnic University, Shenzhen 518055, China
maoliangscau@szpu.edu.cn
[3] The Chinese Univeristy of Hong Kong, Shenzhen 518172, China
simonpun@cuhk.edu.cn
[4] China Academy of Telecommunications Technology, Beijing 100191, China
chengzhimi@cictmobile.com

Abstract. Semantic communication (SC) is critical for the efficient and accurate transmission of data in complex environments, especially for unmanned surface vehicles (USVs) operating in marine settings characterized by strong interference and limited bandwidth. Traditional methods of transmitting large volumes of raw data are inefficient and susceptible to errors. Additionally, semantic communication systems, which depend on labeled datasets, have limited capacity to handle unfamiliar objects in dynamic marine environments. The long-tailed data distribution further complicates the recognition and processing of novel data types. To address these issues, this paper presents a novel approach that integrates zero-shot learning (ZSL) with SC, effectively enhancing image transmission and recognition tasks accuracy in various conditions. The proposed method employs semantic encoding and decoding to prioritize meaningful data, thereby enhancing transmission efficiency and accuracy. Additionally, we introduce semantic metrics for training and evaluating system performance, improving the ability to handle unfamiliar data types. Experimental results demonstrate that our algorithm significantly outperforms traditional methods in image transmission.

Keywords: UAVs · Semantic Communication · Zero-Shot Learning

1 Introduction

The growing use of Unmanned Surface Vehicles (USVs) in maritime operations necessitates robust communication systems capable of handling complex environments. In maritime communications, tough conditions such as poor signal quality, strong interference, and limited bandwidth further compound the challenges

---

This work was supported by National Key Research and Development Program of China under Grant No. 2020YFB1807700.

faced by conventional image transmission technologies in achieving efficient data transfer. The instability of the sea surface in open ocean environments induces multipath propagation, which intensifies Rayleigh fading and frequency-selective fading, further complicating frequency dispersion. These conditions increase the likelihood of issues such as signal loss, image distortion, and the theft or tampering of image data [1]. Traditional communication systems typically require the transmission of complete raw data or continuous streams, resulting in high bandwidth consumption. This not only amplifies transmission errors in maritime communications but also leads to inefficient data transfer. In this case, the quantification and compression of information become essential [2].

Considering that the marine environment typically features a relatively simple background and a limited range of target types, semantic communication (SC) [3] surpasses traditional raw data transmission by prioritizing the comprehension of the intrinsic meaning of the information rather than focusing solely on individual pixels. Unlike traditional communication, which focuses on the exchange of data bits, SC ensures that the transmitted information is contextually relevant and readily interpretable by the receiver. This capability enhances data security and improves communication efficiency, while significantly reducing the demand for communication resources. Consequently, SC is widely recognized as a new paradigm for the future of communication technology.

In recent years, the rapid advancement of deep learning (DL) technologies and their applications in natural language processing, computer vision, and other fields have provided significant insights for the development of SC in image transmission [4,5]. Current SC systems [6] rely on deep learning techniques, improving efficiency by training and utilizing a shared understanding or background knowledge database between the sender and receiver. These foundational knowledge databases, which include experiential data and corresponding semantic information, are critical for accurately interpreting and processing transmitted data. However, due to the dynamic nature of the data and the frequent appearance of unfamiliar object types, training DL-based SC models heavily relies on large amounts of labeled data. Additionally, the long-tail distribution effect of the data exacerbates this dependency, resulting in the trained knowledge database being insufficient for the recognition of unfamiliar objects. Therefore, SC systems must be both flexible and context-aware, with the capability to identify unknown categories.

This paper proposes a hybrid model combining zero-shot learning (ZSL) and SC, referred to as ZSL-SC, to improve image transmission and recognition for maritime USVs. The model leverages information from various modalities, such as text, images, and audio, to improve the system's adaptability to new tasks. DL-based SC models typically rely heavily on large amounts of labeled data for training. In contrast, multimodal ZSL enables the model to leverage existing knowledge to perform efficient reasoning and decision-making, even in the absence of training samples. Additionally, the integration of ZSL within the system enables USVs to recognize and comprehend objects or concepts that were not encountered in the knowledge database during the training phase.

The core concept of ZSL involves using shared intermediate representations, such as attributes and semantic embeddings, to connect known and unknown classes [7]. Attributes are high-level semantic features describing interpretable class characteristics, while semantic embeddings use continuous vector representations to capture semantic similarities between classes, thereby constructing mappings between them in high-dimensional space.

By utilizing ZSL, the SC framework reduces its reliance on large annotated datasets in maritime communication. This reduction is particularly important in situations where obtaining labeled data is challenging or time-consuming. The ZSL-SC system can leverage existing knowledge and apply it to the maritime communication domain, minimizing semantic errors in data transmission and achieving effective communication with minimal data requirements. This approach enhances the semantic transmission efficiency of maritime communications and adapts to the evolving maritime SC environment.

The main contributions of this paper are summarized below:

1. **SC framework based on ZSL and generative models:** We propose a SC framework combining ZSL with generative models, where the transmitter describes the objects, and the receiver retrieves the object using ZSL.If the object is absent in the knowledge database, the receiver synthesizes it using a ZSL-based generative model to complete the communication.
2. **Dynamically updated knowledge database:** The knowledge database updates automatically with each new object or sample, enhancing future ZSL processes and improving the efficiency and accuracy of SC systems, even in constrained maritime environments.
3. **Efficient multimodal ZSL method:** We significantly enhance SC performance, by integrating CLIP (Contrastive Language-Image Pretraining) and CLAP (Contrastive Language-Audio Pretraining) from different modalities, with multimodal approaches outperforming single-modality ZSL in maritime communication tasks.

2 System Model

In a communication system that employs ZSL and multimodal data, a comprehensive architecture has been developed. As illustrated in Fig. 1, this architecture encompasses several key stages, including preprocessing, input, encoding at the transmitter, as well as decoding, output, retrieval, and generation at the receiver.

2.1 Overview of the System Model

SC System is typically task-oriented. In image transmission, semantic information refers to the meaning of the image content. By extracting task-relevant semantic information and removing irrelevant details, the volume of data transmitted can be reduced. This relevant information includes maritime targets collected by USVs, such as ships and buoys, while background information like the

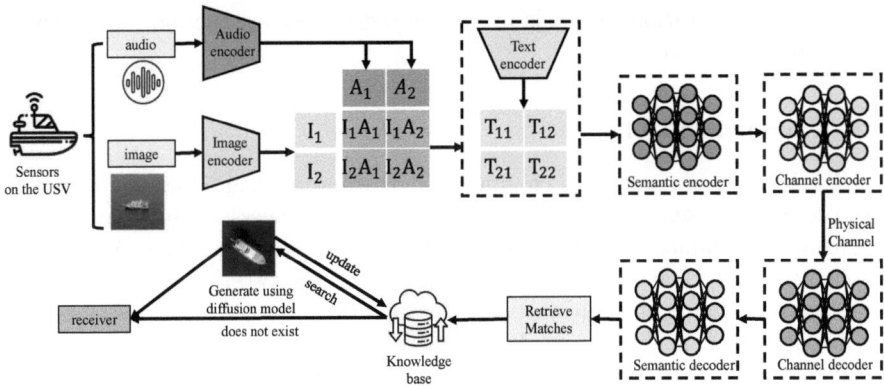

Fig. 1. The USVs Communication System Based on ZSL and Multimodality.

ocean and sky is considered irrelevant. Compared to general SC frameworks, the ZSL-SC system requires multimodal data preprocessing at the input stage. Additionally, output data must be retrieved or generated from a cloud-based semantic library to fully reconstruct multimodal data.

The system diagram is shown in Fig. 1. The system employs the CLIP-CLAP (CLAIP) model to map images and audio into a shared textual encoding vector space [8,9]. A nearest-neighbor search threshold τ is applied to evaluate output validity. Valid outputs are used for decision-making, while invalid outputs are sent via API to the USV's real-time model database for accurate descriptions. A fixed input format is used for auxiliary environmental sensing to reduce computational overhead.

The communication process begins at the input stage, where raw image data from USV sensors enters the system. In the context of ZSL, these new images are not part of the training dataset, requiring the transmitter to generate descriptions of observed marine objects, represented as $T = f(I)$. During the encoding stage, the system verifies whether predefined processing conditions are met and performs tasks such as normalization and feature extraction. The encoder transforms raw image data into a format suitable for the channel, expressed as $Z = E(T)$. In the channel phase, the encoded semantic information is transmitted while preserving key features and minimizing noise. This stage is crucial for maintaining the integrity of the semantic content. The decoding stage follows, where the system interprets the transmitted semantic data through hierarchical analysis, particularly focusing on zero-shot scenarios. The decoder applies generalized knowledge to interpret new marine images, represented as $\hat{T} = D(Z)$. After decoding, the system produces output reflecting the semantic interpretation of the marine images, including object classifications and environmental descriptions.

Finally, the system retrieves multimodal output data from the cloud-based library for scene reconstruction. If matching data is found, it is presented to the user; if not, generation methods are employed for reconstruction, emphasizing zero-shot generation.

2.2 Channel Model

The inadequacy of traditional channel models when applied to sea environments has prompted researchers to explore alternative wireless channel models for maritime communications. In maritime channel simulation of [10], Assuming a smooth sea surface and neglecting ducting effects, the two-ray model provides a basic approximation of maritime path loss and fits up to 86% of the measurement results. However, it neglects weaker scattered paths, sea surface roughness, and atmospheric ducting effects. Given the high transmitter altitude, signal scattering frequently occurs near the receiver. Therefore, the maritime channel model can be represented as:

$$h_{3Ray}(t,\tau) = h_{2Ray}(t,\tau) + z_3(t)a_3(t)\exp\left(j\varphi_3(t)\right)\delta\left(\tau - \tau_3(t)\right), \qquad (1)$$

where a_3, τ_3, and φ_3 are the time-varying amplitude, propagation delay, and phase shift of the third multipath component, respectively. Here, z_3 is generated from a random process that controls the occurrence possibility of the third multipath component, and $h_{2Ray}(t,\tau)$ is the CE2R model with

$$h_{2Ray}(t,\tau) = \delta\left(\tau - \tau_0(t)\right) + \alpha_s(t)\exp\left(j\varphi_s(t)\right)\delta\left(\tau - \tau_s(t)\right), \qquad (2)$$

where $\alpha_s(t)$ is the amplitude of the surface reflection wave, and $\varphi_s(t)$ is the relative phase shift to the direct path. $\alpha_s(t)$ might be affected by parameters including the reflection coefficient, shadowing factor, divergence factor, and the surface roughness factor, and $\varphi_s(t)$ can be geometrically calculated according to the Sea level curved approximation.

In most semantic transmissions, the transmitter maps the source signal s to a symbol stream x, which is subsequently transmitted through a physical channel that experiences transmission impairments. The received symbol stream y is decoded at the receiver to produce an estimate of the source signal $\hat{s}$. Both the transmitter and receiver are represented by deep neural networks (DNNs) that are jointly designed. Specifically, the DNN at the transmitter comprises a semantic encoder and a channel encoder, while the DNN at the receiver consists of a channel decoder and a semantic decoder. The semantic encoder learns to extract semantic information from the transmitted data and transforms it int4o an encoded feature vector, whereas the semantic decoder learns to recover the transmitted data from the received signals. Additionally, the channel encoder and decoder are designed to mitigate signal distortions caused by the wireless channel.

Assuming that the input consists of data preprocessed by CLAIP, we consider a system with N_t transmit antennas and N_r receive antennas. The encoded symbol stream can be represented as

$$\mathbf{x} = f_2(f_1(s;\theta_1);\theta_2), \qquad (3)$$

where $\mathbf{x} \in \mathbb{C}^{N_t \times 1}$, and θ_1 and θ_2 denote the trainable parameters of the semantic encoder $f_1(\cdot)$ and the channel encoder $f_2(\cdot)$, respectively. Subsequently, the received signal y is expressed as

$$y = \mathbf{H}\mathbf{x} + n, \tag{4}$$

where $\mathbf{H} \in \mathbb{C}^{N_r \times N_t}$ signifies the channel matrix, and $n \in \mathbb{C}^{N_r \times 1} \sim \mathcal{N}(0, \sigma^2 I)$ represents the additive white Gaussian noise (AWGN). Accordingly, the decoded signal is expressed as

$$\hat{s} = g_1(g_2(y; \Theta_2); \Theta_1), \tag{5}$$

where Θ_1 and Θ_2 denote the trainable parameters of the semantic decoder $g_1(\cdot)$ and the channel decoder $g_2(\cdot)$, respectively.

It is worth noting that the channel model incorporating AWGN simulates the information distortion in a real physical channel by accounting for channel gain h and independent Gaussian noise n. This enhances the robustness of the USV visual image transmission system against noise and improves its reliability. For clarity, we denote θ as the set of trainable parameters in the DNNs of the considered SC system. Therefore, we have $\hat{s} = f_\theta(s)$. The goal of this system is to minimize semantic errors while simultaneously reducing the number of symbols that need to be transmitted.

2.3 Problem Fomulation

In the context of USVs operating in complex marine environments, efficient and accurate image transmission is essential. Traditional communication methods frequently encounter bandwidth limitations and environmental interference, leading to suboptimal performance. This underscores the necessity for a transmission method that is less dependent on bandwidth and less susceptible to environmental factors. SC presents a promising solution by concentrating on the transmission of relevant semantic information instead of raw data, thus improving transmission efficiency. However, within the framework of ZSL, since the new image does not belong to the training dataset, it is challenging to generate an accurate description of marine objects, and a single image data cannot achieve a comprehensive perception of the marine environment. Therefore, our objectives are to investigate the following:

CLIP and CLAP are employed to convert image and audio data into transmittable semantic information. Let I represent the image data captured by the USV and A represent the corresponding audio data. A semantic extraction function E is applied to the image and audio inputs, transforming them into semantic embeddings $Z_I = E_I(I)$ and $Z_A = E_A(A)$, where E_I and E_A are the semantic encoders for image and audio data, respectively. These embeddings capture the essential information needed for communication, significantly reducing the bandwidth required for transmission.

For efficient data transfer, the CLIP and CLAP models help us convert image and audio data into a shared vector space. The embeddings Z_I and Z_A are projected into a common semantic space T using a shared mapping function

g_{shared}, resulting in $T = g_{\text{shared}}(Z_I, Z_A)$. This allows both image and audio data to be integrated and transmitted as semantic information in a multimodal form, ensuring that only the most relevant content is communicated.

ZSL is leveraged to handle the transmission of unseen objects or new data that are not part of the training set. Using a generative model G, meaningful descriptions D of unseen objects are generated based on the semantic embeddings, as $D = G(Z_I, Z_A)$. This allows the system to adapt to new inputs without the need for extensive retraining, a critical feature for dynamic marine environments where new objects or conditions may frequently arise.

We aim to evaluate the effectiveness of our approach using metrics such as Peak Signal-to-Noise Ratio (PSNR), Structural Similarity Index (SSIM), and Video Multi-Method Assessment Fusion (VMAF).

3 Methodology of ZSL-Based SC System

This section provides a detailed description of the SC system equipped with ZSL, including the transmitter responsible for generating descriptions of observed objects and the receiver integrated with ZSL capabilities and a generative model.

3.1 CLAIP Based Preprocessing

At the sender end, after preliminary denoising and normalization, the input text data is rendered suitable for direct processing by the semantic encoder. For image and audio data, the system implements an advanced information preprocessing technique based on the CLAIP model, thereby significantly enhancing its processing efficiency for these data modalities. In this model, the input images I and audio A are processed concurrently, enabling them to be mapped to distinct vector spaces I_1 and A_1. This mapping is accomplished through encoding functions $I_1 = E_I(I)$ for images and $A_1 = E_A(A)$ for audio. Here, E_I and E_A denote the encoding functions that convert the raw inputs into their corresponding vector representations.

This dual mapping process not only enriches the semantic understanding of both modalities but also ensures their effective integration and utilization within the communication framework.

In this architecture, a local multimodal database L is established, which can map local text information T into the vector space V_T. This setup supports efficient nearest neighbor searches, enabling the system to identify the most suitable textual descriptions corresponding to the audio or image input data. This process can be expressed as $V_T = E_T(T)$, where E_T is the semantic encoding function for the text that maps it into the vector space.

The system then calculates the similarity between the text and audio or image input through nearest neighbor search using cosine similarity (CS):

$$\text{CS}_{T,M} = \frac{V_T \cdot V_M}{\|V_T\|\|V_M\|}, \quad M \in \{\text{image}, \text{audio}\}, \tag{6}$$

where, V_T represents the textual features in the vector space, V_M denotes the modal features corresponding to the modality M (image or audio), $CS_{T,M}$ indicates the cosine similarity between the text and the modality M.

To address potential issues related to the absence of audio or image data descriptions, a distance threshold is established in the vector space. If the minimum similarity between text-image and text-audio does not meet the predefined threshold, the system will invoke the API of the multimodal model to retrieve or generate descriptions. Conversely, if the predefined threshold is met, the system considers that a matching text description has been found, as detailed below:

$$\min\left(CS_{T,I}, CS_{T,A}\right) \geq \text{threshold}, \tag{7}$$

where $CS_{T,I}$ represents the CS between the textual information T and the image modality I, and $CS_{T,A}$ represents the CS between the textual information T and the audio modality A. This method guarantees that the minimum similarity between text and audio or image meets or exceeds the predetermined threshold, thereby enhancing matching efficiency and optimizing the processing of audio or image data.

3.2 Transmitter and Receiver Architecture in System Model

Transmitter: The transmitter in the ZSL-SC system model includes a semantic encoder and an integrated dynamic knowledge database D, responsible for processing and transmitting semantic information. The semantic encoder E extracts semantic features from the source input data X_{in}, refining the high-level semantic information S, ensuring that the transmitted data is semantically rich and highly adaptable. Subsequently, the knowledge database D is continuously updated and integrated into the transmitter's processing as ZSL identifies new categories, enabling the USV to adapt to new data types and scenarios in maritime environments.

Receiver: The receiver consists of a ZSL module and a semantic decoder, tasked with interpreting and reconstructing the transmitted semantic information. The ZSL module Z processes the received semantic representation S along with the dynamic dataset D, generating semantic embeddings T. The semantic decoder D then reconstructs the semantic content into the output Y_{out}. The receiver function R integrates these processes to ensure accurate interpretation and reconstruction of the transmitted semantic content, including previously unseen data types.

Knowledge Database: In our maritime ZSL-SC system, the database design is essential for efficient semantic transfer. The system includes two databases: the sender database D_s and the receiver database D_r. Both databases contain semantic-image pairs, which form the core data structure for supporting comprehension and reasoning at the receiver.

The sender database D_s contains semantic descriptions s_i and their corresponding images I_{s_i}, with N_s representing the total number of semantic-image pairs. These pairs represent the semantic information at the sender and are used for semantic encoding and compression within the system.

The receiver database D_r contains semantic descriptions r_i and corresponding images I_{r_i}, with N_r representing the total number of semantic-image pairs. Typically, the receiver database is larger than the sender database ($N_s < N_r$), indicating that the receiver has more extensive background information and reference data to support decoding and reasoning. This database design allows the system to interpret and transmit previously unseen semantic information without the need for explicit syntax.

The ZSL-SC system leverages this database structure to implement ZSL, enabling the receiver to accurately interpret semantic information absent from the sender's database through reasoning and mapping mechanisms. This process continuously enriches the receiver's database, enhancing the system's robustness and adaptability when handling unknown semantic content.

3.3 Generation Architecture in the System Model

At the output end, our ZSL-SC system integrates both cloud retrieval and generation methods. Cloud retrieval: if the corresponding feature data previously generated by ZSL exists in the knowledge database, it is retrieved directly. Otherwise, the system employs the ZSL generation method to produce relevant data for new categories directly.

In the ZSL-SC system, the semantic encoder E at the transmitter transforms the raw input data X_{in} into the semantic representation S. Additionally, AWGN is incorporated into the channel model during training, represented by

$$\hat{y} = h\hat{w} + n, \tag{8}$$

where $\hat{y}$ represents the output of the channel coding, h denotes the channel gain, and n signifies the independent Gaussian noise, *i.e.*,

$$y = g(\hat{y}), \tag{9}$$

The reconstructed data y is generated using the zero-shot generator G. This process leverages the generative capability of ZSL to reconstruct audio or image data based on the received semantic information.

Within the ZSL framework, raw audio or image data x undergoes feature extraction via a semantic encoder and is then decoded by a semantic decoder endowed with ZSL capabilities. During this process, data features are aligned with semantic features of unseen categories within a shared semantic space to generate reconstructed data y. The generation process can be optimized using the following objective function:

$$E(x) = \alpha V(x, g(x)) + \beta S(x, g(x)), \tag{10}$$

where $V(x, g(x))$ and $S(x, g(x))$ represent image quality metrics, namely, VMAF and SSIM, respectively, while α and β are the weight parameters.

The distribution probability of the original image is recorded as P_x. while the distribution of the ZSL-generated data is P_y. A discriminator D is employed in adversarial learning to handle both the original data x and the generated feature data y. After sufficient training, the discriminator becomes proficient in extracting features aligned with the original data's distribution P_x, thereby effectively distinguishing original data from newly generated features. This capability allows the system to accurately generate and recognize images from unseen categories. Ultimately, these features are archived in a knowledge database to facilitate retrieval for subsequent semantic communications, thereby enhancing the system's efficiency.

In practical communication scenarios, the system may encounter an unfamiliar entity u. If the sender's database D_s contains the entity u, only the relevant textual information T is transmitted, thereby minimizing the data volume.

In this study, a pre-trained classification model Φ has been adapted to fit the application of ZSL within SC systems. The specific adjustment is represented as:

$$\Phi = (F, W_s), \tag{11}$$

where F is the feature extractor, and W_s is the weight matrix of the classifier. Through this adjustment, the system is capable of classifying unseen categories of images without training images, ensuring accurate semantic understanding in dynamic environments.

Through the integration of ZSL and multimodal data processing capabilities, the system accurately transmits semantic information for maritime scenarios requiring a combination of auditory and visual data, even amid unfamiliar entities at sea. This integration establishes a robust foundation for precise communication in narrow band maritime environments.

3.4 Practical Implementation

As shown in Fig. 2, The practical implementation of the proposed SC system follows a structured approach aligned with the described architecture. The transmitter monitors messages and employs a CLAIP-based multimodal model to generate a semantic description of the observed object while providing audio input. This multimodal data is encoded and transmitted to a ZSL-equipped receiver. The ZSL module searches for the relevant object in the knowledge database; if a match is found, communication is efficiently completed. If no match is found, the receiver uses the generative model to synthesize a new image based on the description, thereby updating the knowledge database to improve adaptation to the new entity.

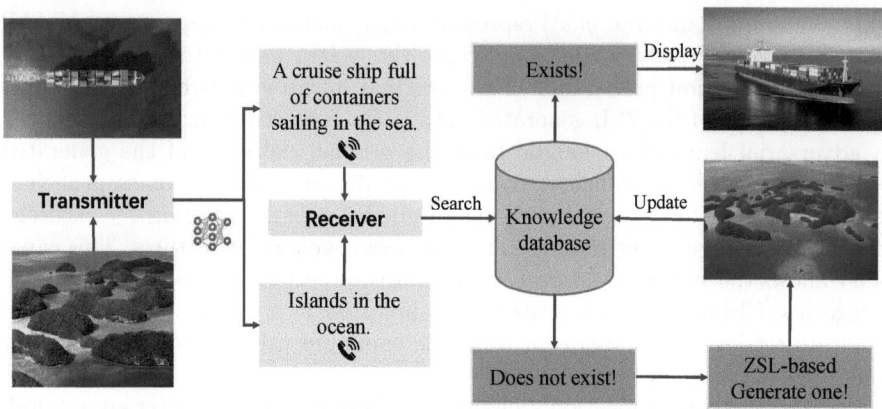

Fig. 2. A Practical application of ZSL-SC system in maritime communications.

4 Experimental And Results

4.1 Metrics

PSNR, SSIM, and VMAF are key metrics for evaluating the quality of transmitted images and videos. Similar to many experiments that assess reconstructed images against their originals, this paper utilizes PSNR, SSIM, and VMAF to validate the effectiveness of the proposed methods.

PSNR is a metric based on pixel differences, indicating the maximum possible difference between the reconstructed and original images. Its relatively straightforward calculation method makes it widely used in numerous experiments. PSNR can be calculated using the Mean Squared Error (MSE) with the following formula:

$$PSNR = 10 \times \log_{10}\left(\frac{MAX^2}{MSE}\right), \tag{12}$$

where MAX is the maximum possible pixel value in the image.

SSIM is a quality assessment metric that aligns closely with human visual perception. It evaluates similarity by comparing the brightness, contrast, and structural information of two images within local regions, offering a more accurate reflection of perceived image quality.

VMAF is a video quality assessment tool developed by Netflix, trained with machine learning models to generate a score from 0 to 100, where higher scores indicate better perceived quality.

4.2 Evaluation

To demonstrate the superiority of our proposed method in maritime communication, we compared it against CADA-VAE [11], DeML [12], ZSL-GAN [13], ResNet-ZSL [14] and LATEM [15]. The results are depicted as follows.

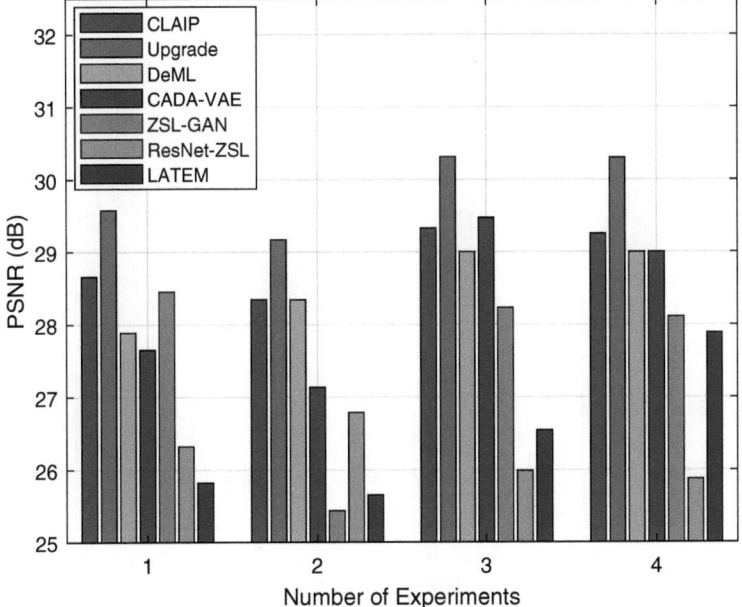

Fig. 3. PSNR.

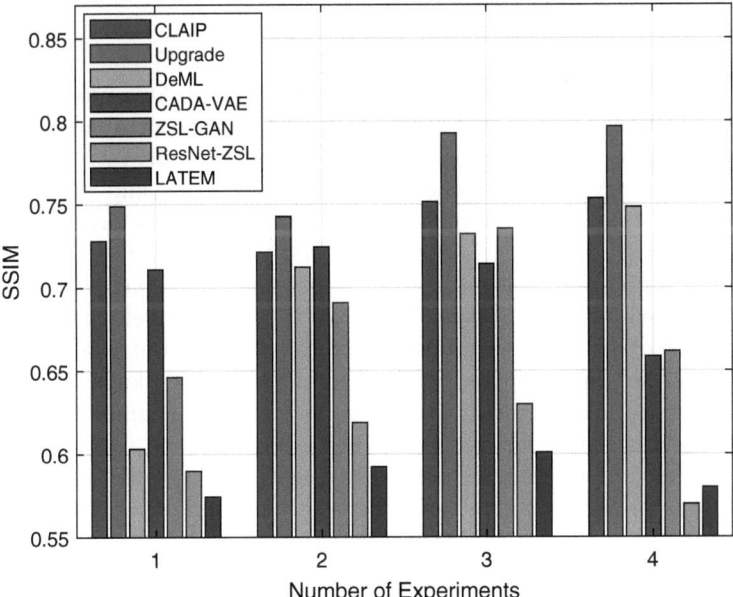

Fig. 4. SSIM.

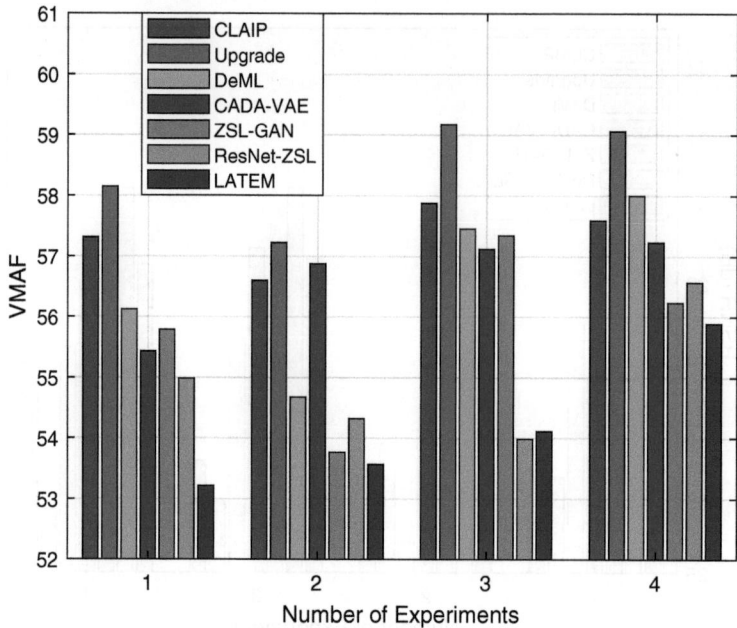

Fig. 5. Aggregated VMAF Data.

In the Figs. 3, 4 and 5, the vertical axis denotes the datasets utilized in the experiments. In the context of USVs, we employed 4 types of datasets: boats, ships, islands, and vast ocean expanses for training. Different from the above five algorithms that rely on static knowledge database. Our proposed method leverages the multimodal capabilities of CLIP-CLAP to continuously enhance semantic recognition. Newly identified data is systematically integrated into the dynamic knowledge database, enabling adaptive learning and further improving semantic recognition performance. This dynamic update process allows the system to manage novel and previously unobserved objects in the marine environment with greater precision, thereby enhancing the accuracy and efficiency of data transmission. Additionally, it enables the system to effectively address a broader range of maritime scenarios. As demonstrated by the experimental comparative analyses, our proposed method employs dynamic knowledge database enhancements to minimize semantic errors and improve communication performance. It achieves superior results across all four datasets, with SSIM, PSNR, and VMAF metrics ranking highest. Consequently, in complex and variable offshore USV scenarios, this approach consistently outperforms existing methods.

5 Conclusion

This paper presents a novel SC framework that utilizes ZSL and generative models to enhance the efficiency and adaptability of communication in dynamic marine environments. By leveraging the strengths of the CLIP and CLAP models, our proposed ZSL method effectively maps images and audio to a shared textual encoding vector space, facilitating robust semantic understanding. This framework is particularly well-suited for applications in complex marine environments characterized by poor communication conditions, as it can process and analyze data from various sensors on USVs in real time. The integration of a dynamically updated knowledge database ensures continuous learning and performance enhancement, reducing reliance on large labeled datasets and addressing the limitations of traditional SC systems. This framework can interpret novel, unseen data, thereby enhancing the reliability and efficiency of marine communications. Finally, the superiority of the proposed algorithm is validated through comparative analysis against several existing methods, evaluated using PSNR, SSIM, and VMAF.

References

1. Giger, A., Barnett, W.: Effects of multipath propagation on digital radio. IEEE Trans. Commun. **29**(9), 1345–1352 (1981)
2. Biing Hwang Juang: Quantification and transmission of information and intelligence–History and outlook [DSP history]. IEEE Signal Process. Mag. **28**(4), 90–101 (2011)
3. Luo, X., Chen, H.-H., Guo, Q.: Semantic communications: overview, open issues, and future research directions. IEEE Wirel. Commun. **29**(1), 210–219 (2022)
4. Qin, Z., Ye, H., Li, G.Y., Juang, B.H.F.: Deep learning in physical layer communications. IEEE Wireless Commun. **26**(2), 93–99 (2019)
5. Chen, Y., Hong, X., Chen, W., Wang, H., Fan, T.: Experimental research on overwater and underwater visual image stitching and fusion technology of offshore operation and maintenance of unmanned ship. J. Marine Sci. Eng. **10**(6), 747 (2022)
6. Weng, Z., Qin, Z., Li, G.Y.: Semantic communications for speech signals. In: ICC 2021-IEEE International Conference on Communications, pp. 1–6. IEEE (2021)
7. Geng, Y., et al.: Ontology-enhanced zero-shot learning. In: Proceedings of the Web Conference, vol. 2021, pp. 3325–3336 (2021)
8. Radford, A., et al. Learning transferable visual models from natural language supervision. In: International Conference on Machine Learning, pp. 8748–8763. PMLR (2021)
9. Elizalde, B., Deshmukh, S., Al Ismail, M., Wang, H.: CLAP: Learning audio concepts from natural language supervision. In: ICASSP 2023-2023 IEEE International Conference on Acoustics, Speech and Signal Processing (ICASSP), pp. 1–5. IEEE (2023)
10. Wang, J., et al.: Wireless channel models for maritime communications. IEEE Access **6**, 68070–68088 (2018)
11. Schonfeld, E., Ebrahimi, S., Sinha, S., Darrell, T., Akata, Z.: Generalized zero- and few-shot learning via aligned variational autoencoders. In: Proceedings of the IEEE/CVF Conference on Computer Vision and Pattern Recognition, pp. 8247–8255 (2019)
12. Chen., B., Deng, W.: Hybrid-attention based decoupled metric learning for zero-shot image retrieval. In: Proceedings of the IEEE/CVF Conference on Computer Vision and Pattern Recognition, pp. 2750–2759 (2019)

13. Talkani, A., Bhojan, A.: Approaching zero-shot learning from a text-to-image GAN perspective. In: 2022 IEEE 24th International Workshop on Multimedia Signal Processing (MMSP), pp. 1–6. IEEE (2022)
14. Luo, Y., Wang, X., Cao, W.: A novel dataset-specific feature extractor for zero-shot learning. Neurocomputing **391**, 74–82 (2020)
15. Xian, Y., et al.: Latent embeddings for zero-shot classification. In: Proceedings of the IEEE Conference on Computer Vision and Pattern Recognition, pp. 69–77 (2016)

Rate Optimization for Visible Light Communications Using Asymmetric Bridged-T Pre-Equalizer

Hewei Tian[1,2]([✉]), Runxin Zhang[1,2], Jian Xiong[1,3], Jianhua He[2], and Lu Lu[1,2]

[1] University of Chinese Academy of Sciences, Beijing, China
{tianhewei22,zhangrunxin20}@mails.ucas.ac.cn, xiongjian@ucas.ac.cn,
lulu@csu.ac.cn
[2] Technology and Engineering Center for Space Utilization, Beijing, China
hejianhua@csu.ac.cn
[3] Hangzhou Institute for Advanced Study, Hangzhou, China

Abstract. In ultra-high speed visible light communications (VLC) with light emitting diodes (LEDs) as the transmitter, analog pre-equalizers are often adopted to extend the modulation bandwidth. However, pre-equalizer may severely degrade the signal-to-noise-ratio (SNR) in the low frequency if we only focus on its bandwidth extending feature. And therefore, an important issue is that there exists a tradeoff between extending the system bandwidth and improving the SNR. In this paper, we first study the small signal characteristics of LEDs using the ABC parameters by taking into account of its internal quantum efficiency. And then, we propose an asymmetric bridged-T pre-equalizer considering an impedance matching network, based on which we study the bandwidth-SNR tradeoff problem via analytical derivations. We formulate a data rate maximization problem by considering the above tradeoff issue. Interestingly, different from common intuition, simulations results indicate that when the LED driving current and modulation bandwidth both reach maximal values, the achievable rate cannot reach the highest point. Specifically, using an OSRAM green LED, a maximum data rate of 1.15 Gbps can be achieved with a bias current of 378.63 mA and transmitter bandwidth of 163.31 MHz. The simulated data rate is 1.47 times higher than that of the literature using similar LED with 1/2 of the signal power attenuation. In the future, we will based on the optimized LED driving and equalization circuit to design PCB and test its impacts in real deployments.

Keywords: Visible light communications · Optimization · Equalizer circuit · Rate optimization

---

This work was supported in part by the Key Research Program of the Chinese Academy of Sciences, under Grant ZDRW-KT-2019-1-0103, and in part by the Youth Innovation Promotion Association Project of CAS.

1 Introduction

With the aim of achieving further enhancements in mobile broadband, ultra-massive machine type communications, and enhanced ultra-reliable and low latency communications, the key performance indicators of 6G technologies have become increasingly stringent and diverse [1–3]. In this context, visible light communications (VLC) stands out as a promising technology, thanks to its ultra-high bandwidth, absence of electromagnetic interference, and high security features [3–5]. Consequently, VLC is viewed as a vital complement to radio frequency technology in the future wireless networks.

Especially with the rapid advancement of semiconductor technology, LEDs have become ubiquitous in almost every indoor spaces and many outdoor settings for lighting. However, their typical bandwidth, which falls within the tens of megahertz (MHz) range constrained by factors including resistance-capacitance time delay and the quantum-confined Stark effect of quantum wells (QWs) [5], poses limitations on the capabilities of optical systems that employ them. While equalization is a commonly employed technique to broaden the bandwidth of optical links, extending the system's bandwidth inevitably results in a decrease in signal power or the modulation depth of the LED [6]. Since channel capacity is typically the optimization goal for wireless communications [7], where both signal power and bandwidth play crucial roles, this tradeoff makes it challenging to achieve a delicate balance. In addition, the direct current (DC) component of the signals used to drive LEDs has a significant impact on the electro-optical (EO) conversion efficiency of the light source [8] and its bandwidth, as it influences the lifespan of carriers [5,9].

In recent years, numerous studies have focused on optimizing the design of VLC transmitters. However, there still exist the following gaps in optimizing the VLC transmitter: 1) Establishing a mathematical model that links the characteristics of LEDs with their operating points, also known as Q points. 2) Jointly optimizing LED efficiency and the equalizer for the VLC transmitter. Ref. [10] unveiled the phenomenon of LED frequency response altering with injected DC and measured the average spectral efficiency affected by the bias current through experimental analysis, but the relationship between efficiency and DC current is not analyzed, which means repeated experiments should be conducted to find the optimal DC with different light source. In the meantime, signal power attenuation resulting from the introduction of the equalizer has been observed through simulations and measurements in [6,11,12], but extent of attenuation was not quantitatively described. The authors of [13] introduced the concept of OMA-bandwidth product (OBP) to illustrate the tradeoff in LED performance. They showed that LEDs with a larger OBP demonstrate better bit error rate performance, but did not specifically address the effect of bias current on LED performance. Previous studies on equalization have not considered the mathematical relationship between the operational efficiency of LEDs and DC [14,15]. Additionally, they have not addressed the mathematical relationship between bandwidth expansion and the signal power attenuation introduced by equalization.

In this light, we aim to present an efficient VLC transmitter design to maximize the achievable data rates while considering the tradeoff between bandwidth and signal power arising from both the small signal characteristics of LEDs and the parameters of the equalizer circuit. The main contributions of this paper can be summarized as follows.

- We establish a mathematical relationship for the tradeoff between bandwidth and signal power considering both of the LEDs' small signal characteristics and the parameters of the equalizer circuit. With the aim of maximizing rate, we then design an asymmetric bridged-T equalizer to tackle concerns regarding impedance matching.
- Through simulation, we achieved a maximum rate of 1.15 Gbps with a driving current of 378.628 mA and an extended system bandwidth of 163.31 MHz. The simulated data rate is 1.47 times higher than that of the literature using similar LED with 1/2 of the signal power attenuation

The remainder of this paper is organized as follows: Sect. 2 is an overview on the transmitter of VLC and formulates the LED and equalizer model. Section 3 discusses the achievable rate optimization and propose the optimal solution. Section 4 demonstrates the simulation and Sect. 5 concludes this paper.

2 System Model

2.1 Overview

A typical VLC transmitter comprises essential components, as illustrated in Fig. 1, including a power amplifier (PA), an equalizer circuit, a Bias-Tee circuit, and a light source. While the architecture effectively facilitates a functional optical link, there are still challenges regarding the optimization of the maximum achievable rate, specifically concerning the trade-off between bandwidth and signal power. In Fig. 2, we outline the primary factors including the LED's Q point, and the bandwidth and attenuation of equalizer. This paper summaries all these factors into the following two trade-offs to further enhance the capacity of the optical channel:

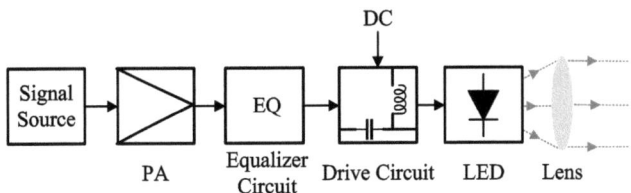

Fig. 1. The structure of the VLC transmitter.

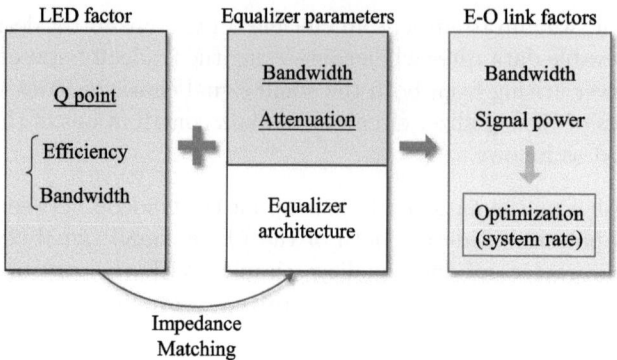

Fig. 2. Tradeoff between bandwidth and signal power for VLC with the constraint of an equalizer.

- Q point is the steady-state DC of LED with no signal input, and plays a crucial role in both the efficiency of EO conversion and the 3 dB bandwidth of a raw LED. EO conversion efficiency typically shows an initial rise with the Q point, followed by a decline, whereas bandwidth consistently extends as the Q point increases. Hence, it is necessary to establish the tradeoff and identify the optimal Q point.
- Another tradeoff arises in the design of the equalizer, which involves balancing system bandwidth and attenuation. Also we consider the impedance matching for reduce reflection when transmitting high frequency signal, and ultimately ensure that the LED absorbs the maximum signal power available.

2.2 LED Model

The luminous efficiency and bandwidth of the raw LED both depend on the static working current [10], known as the Q point of the LED. In this section, we establish the connection between luminous efficiency and bandwidth via carrier concentration, which directly correlates with the Q point.

The luminous efficiency of an LED is correlated with the input current or Q point. As the current increases, the recombination time of carriers decreases, leading to an expansion of the LED's 3 dB bandwidth [16]. The DC can be expressed according to the LED model using recombination coefficients A, B and C [17]:

$$I_{\text{IN}}(N_{\text{QW}}) = A_{\text{LED}}\zeta q(A N_{\text{QW}} + B N_{\text{QW}}^2 + C N_{\text{QW}}^3), \tag{1}$$

where A_{LED} is the active region of LED; ζ is a scaling factor; and q is the elementary charge. N_{QW} represents the number of carriers in QWs under constant current. A, B and C are the coefficients characterizing Shockley–Read–Hall (SRH) trap-assisted recombination, bimolecular radiative recombination, and Auger recombination, respectively [18]. In order to facilitate the visual representation of the VLC system under the influence of DC, the inverse function of 1 is expressed as [19]:

$$N_{\text{QW}}(I_{\text{IN}}) = \frac{-B + \sqrt{B^2 - 3AC}(g(I_{\text{IN}}) + \frac{1}{g(I_{\text{IN}})})}{3C} \qquad (2)$$

where

$$g(I_{\text{IN}}) = \sqrt[3]{\chi(I_{\text{IN}}) + \sqrt{\chi(I_{\text{IN}})^2 - 1}} \qquad (3)$$

$$\chi(I_{\text{IN}}) = \frac{9ABC - 2B^3 - 27C^2 \frac{I_{\text{IN}}}{A_{\text{LED}}\zeta q}}{2(\sqrt{B^2 - 3AC})^3} \qquad (4)$$

In the small signal model [17], the internal quantum efficiency (IQE) can be expressed as a function of DC:

$$\eta_{\text{IQE}}(I_{\text{IN}}) = \frac{2BN_{\text{QW}}(I_{\text{IN}})}{A + 2BN_{\text{QW}}(I_{\text{IN}}) + 3CN_{\text{QW}}^2(I_{\text{IN}})}. \qquad (5)$$

According to 1 and 5, the curve of IQE η_{IQE} with respect to DC current I_{IN} can be obtained, from which it can be told that IQE increases first and then decreases with the current. This is because Bimolecular recombination is the main part of carrier recombination at small current, which is the only one that results in light emission. When the current rises, Auger recombination becomes significant and causes LED efficiency droop.

Then, we obtain the EO conversion efficiency η_{EO}:

$$\begin{aligned}\eta_{\text{EO}}(I_{\text{IN}}) &= \eta_i \cdot \eta_{\text{IQE}}(I_{\text{IN}}) \cdot \frac{h\nu}{q} \\ &= \eta_i \cdot \frac{2BN_{\text{QW}}(I_{\text{IN}})}{A + 2BN_{\text{QW}}(I_{\text{IN}}) + 3CN_{\text{QW}}^2(I_{\text{IN}})} \cdot \frac{h\nu}{q},\end{aligned} \qquad (6)$$

where η_i is light extraction efficiency (LEE), h is the Planck's constant, and ν is the light frequency. When considering 1 and 6 together, we observe that η_{EO} sharply decreases with I_{IN} after a brief initial increase.

The 3 dB bandwidth of an LED can also be described using the ABC parameters [20,21]. Assuming the LED material is undoped and carriers are uniformly distributed, the 3 dB bandwidth of the LED can also be expressed as a function of DC:

$$f_{\text{3dB}}(I_{\text{IN}}) = \frac{\sqrt{3}}{2\pi}(A + 2B\frac{N_{\text{QW}}(I_{\text{IN}})}{V} + 3C\frac{N_{\text{QW}}^2(I_{\text{IN}})}{V^2}), \qquad (7)$$

where V is the volume given the number of carriers. 7 demonstrates that $f_{3\text{ dB}}$ increases monotonically with the DC.

Since the opposing variations of the luminous efficiency and the 3 dB bandwidth with the increase of I_{IN}, we will further discuss the maximum achievable rate considering 6 and 7.

2.3 An Asymmetric Bridged-T Equalizer

Since the LED's raw bandwidth of several MHz is insufficient for achieving high-speed communication rates, the equalizer is important in extending the bandwidth of the optical link. As a passive analog equalizer, while it can extend the bandwidth, it also entails some attenuation as a trade-off [7]. Therefore, the corner frequency of the equalizer needs to be carefully designed to prevent excessive attenuation. Additionally, the impedance matching determined by the structure of the equalizer also affects the power transfer efficiency.

The specific relationship between bandwidth and attenuation is dictated by the structure of the equalizer. This paper explores the tradeoff issue introduced by the equalizer, focusing on an asymmetric bridged-T equalizer. The symmetric bridged-T equalizer demonstrates a characteristic where the input and output impedance become equal and constant under certain conditions [12]. However, due to the small impedance of the LED, which differs significantly from that of the source, the traditional symmetric equalizer circuit can cause severe reflection when transmitting high-frequency signals. Therefore, we propose the asymmetric architecture allowing for simultaneously matching the output impedance of the signal source and the input impedance of the LED.

Figure 3(a) illustrates the general structure of bridged-T equalizer composed of four components: Z_x, Z_y, Z_1, and Z_2. To reach the maximum transmission power, the input impedance of the equalizer requires to match the conjugate of the source impedance Z_s, and the output impedance requires to align with the conjugate of the load impedance Z_L. In order to facilitate the construction of equalizer circuit, we present a simplified cascade circuit to approximate an asymmetric bridged-T equalizer, as depicted in Fig. 3(b). The orange part represents the symmetric bridged-T equalizer, while the blue section is the impedance matching network. The symmetric bridged-T equalizer satisfies the following impedance limitations:

$$Z'_1 Z'_2 = R_0^2 \tag{8}$$

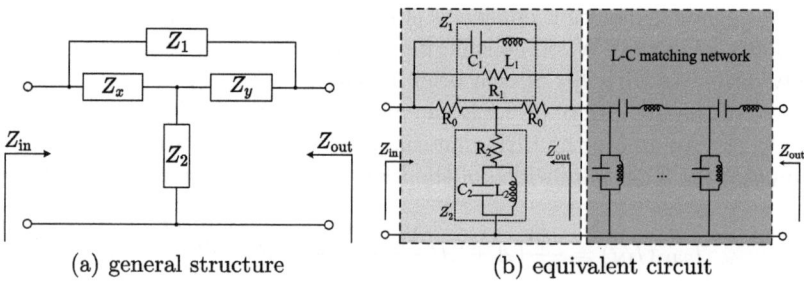

(a) general structure   (b) equivalent circuit

Fig. 3. The structure of bridged-T equalizer

With the equalizer structure shown in Fig. 3(b), we can establish the relationship between the attenuation caused by the equalizer and the increased 3 dB bandwidth. The impedance matching network is composed of inductors and capacitors. Unlike radio frequency system, the impedance matching is designed for wide-band applications because the impedance of LEDs varies with frequency [22], and the input signal in VLC systems is typically a broadband signal. The design of components satisfies the following equations:

$$\begin{aligned} Z_{\text{out}}(\omega) &= Z_{\text{LED}}^*(\omega), \\ Z_{\text{out}}'(\omega) &= Z_{\text{in}} = R_0, (\omega_1 \leq \omega \leq \omega_2) \end{aligned} \quad (9)$$

where ω is the angular frequency; Z_{LED}^* is the conjugation of LED impedance; ω values from ω_1 to ω_2 satisfying the wide-band requirement. Since no resistance elements is introduced into the impedance matching network, signal attenuation is not introduced.

Then, we analyze the influence of equalization structure on the signal in VLC systems. The transfer function of the asymmetric bridged-T equalizer is defined as the ratio of the output signal's amplitude to that of the input signal, which can be expressed as

$$H_{\text{eq}}(s) = \frac{R_0}{R_0 + R_1} \frac{1 + R_1 C_1 s + L_1 C_1 s^2}{1 + \frac{R_0 R_1 C_1}{R_0 + R_1} s + L_1 C_1 s^2} \cdot H_{\text{LC}}(s), \quad (10)$$

where $s = j\omega$ is the complex frequency domain parameter with angular frequency ω and imaginary unit j. The gain of the response function is written as:

$$\alpha = \frac{R_0}{R_0 + R_1}. \quad (11)$$

The zero-pole matching method is applied to the equalization structure to achieve bandwidth expansion [11]. In order to achieve a more intuitive zero-pole matching, the transfer function $H_{\text{eq}}(s)$ is decomposed into the product of α, $H_1(s)$ and $H_2(s)$, which is expressed as:

$$H_{\text{eq}}(s) = \alpha \cdot H_1(s) \cdot H_2(s), \quad (12)$$

where $H_1(s) = \frac{1}{1+s \cdot \frac{R_0 R_1 C_1}{R_0+R_1}+s^2 \cdot C_1 L_1}$ is a second order oscillation element, the natural frequency $\omega_{\text{n1}} = \frac{1}{\sqrt{C_1 L_1}}$, the damping ratio $\zeta_1 = \frac{R_1}{2}\sqrt{\frac{C_1}{L_1}} \cdot \alpha$; $H_2(s) = 1 + s \cdot C_1 R_1 + s^2 \cdot C_1 L_1$ is a second order differentiation element, the natural frequency $\omega_{\text{n2}} = \frac{1}{\sqrt{C_1 L_1}}$, the damping ratio $\zeta_2 = \frac{R_1}{2}\sqrt{\frac{C_1}{L_1}}$. Because α is less than 10^{-2} and R_1 is more than 10^2, $0 < \zeta_1 \ll 0.7$ and $\zeta_2 \gg 1$. Thus, $H_2(s)$ can be expressed as the product of two first order differentiation elements. According to the modulus of the transfer function $|H_{\text{eq}}(s)| = \alpha |H_1(s)||H_2(s)|$, the following equations are satisfied:

$$\begin{cases} \frac{R_1}{2L_1} - \sqrt{\frac{R_1^2}{4L_1^2} - \frac{1}{C_1 L_1}} = \omega_{\text{3dB}} \\ \frac{1}{\sqrt{C_1 L_1}} = \omega_{\text{B}}, \end{cases} \quad (13)$$

where $\omega_{3\text{dB}} = 2\pi f_{3\text{dB}}$, $\omega_\text{B} = 2\pi f_\text{B}$ and f_B is system bandwidth after equalization. The components in the equalizer circuit satisfy the following relation:

$$\begin{cases} R_1(I_\text{IN}, f_\text{B}) = 2L_1 \frac{(2\pi f_{3\text{dB}}(I_\text{IN}))^2 + (2\pi f_\text{B})^2}{2(2\pi f_{3\text{dB}}(I_\text{IN}))} \\ C_1(I_\text{IN}, f_\text{B}) = \frac{1}{L_1(2\pi f_\text{B}(I_\text{IN}))^2}. \end{cases} \quad (14)$$

According to 11, the attenuation introduced from the equalizer is:

$$\alpha(I_\text{IN}, f_\text{B}) = \frac{R_0}{R_0 + 2L_1 \frac{(2\pi f_{3\text{dB}}(I_\text{IN}))^2 + (2\pi f_\text{B})^2}{2(2\pi f_{3\text{dB}}(I_\text{IN}))}}. \quad (15)$$

Since the zero of the equalizer remains consistent for a given LED Q point following the zero-pole matching approach, broadening the bandwidth requires choosing a small value for C_1 alongside a substantial L_1 and R_1, consequently resulting in a reduction in α. We will delve into this tradeoff in the subsequent section.

3 Maximum Rate Optimization

In the previous section, we discussed the balance issue between LED efficiency and bandwidth, as well as the the balance issue between equalizer bandwidth and attenuation. This section will propose an optimization problem combing both trade-off into consideration to enhance channel capacity. The optimal solution is given using the particle swarm optimization (PSO) algorithm.

3.1 Optimization Problem

In the previous section, we obtained the trade-offs discussed for the raw LED and the gain of the response function α and bandwidth f_B. Our aim is to determine the optimal Q point and optical system bandwidth to maximize the channel rate.

The power driving LED is divided into DC power P_0 and signal power p_s. With a constant input signal power, the signal power of the VLC system is expressed as the square of voltage:

$$P_\text{S}(I_\text{IN}, f_\text{B}) = \left[\frac{\sqrt{p_s R_0} \cdot \alpha(I_\text{IN}, f_\text{B})}{r_\text{LED}} \eta_\text{EO}(I_\text{IN}) \cdot R_\text{F} R_\text{PD} \right]^2, \quad (16)$$

where R_0 is the source impedance, which is usually 50 Ω; r_LED is the internal resistance of LED; α is given in 15; η_EO is given in 6; R_F is the transimpedance; R_PD is the responsivity of the photo detector (PD). Given that the transceivers remain stationary and only the line of sight (LoS) channel is considered, the SNR and the achievable data rate R are [23]:

$$\text{SNR}(I_\text{IN}, f_\text{B}) = \frac{P_\text{S}(I_\text{IN}, f_\text{B})}{\sigma_n^2}, \quad (17)$$

$$R(I_\text{IN}, f_\text{B}) = f_\text{B} \log_2 \left[1 + \frac{\text{SNR}(I_\text{IN}, f_\text{B})}{\Gamma} \right], \quad (18)$$

where Γ is the SNR gap. PIN is used as a photodetector in our VLC system. Due to its small detection area, the interference of ambient light to the VLC system is negligible, so it is assumed that the noise is mainly from the thermal noise inside the system. The noise primarily consists of thermal noise with variance $\sigma_n^2 = N_0 f_B = 4\kappa T R_F F_n f_B$, where κ is the Boltzmann constant, T is the temperature, and F_n is the noise figure of amplifiers.

$$\{\hat{I}_{IN}, \hat{f}_B\} = \arg \max_{\{I_{IN}, f_B\}} f_B \log_2 \left(1 + \frac{P_S(I_{IN}, f_B)}{4\kappa T F_n R_F \alpha \cdot f_B}\right) \tag{19}$$

$$\text{s.t.} \quad P_0(I_{IN}) \leq P_{\max} \tag{20}$$

$$f_B \gg \frac{\sqrt{3}}{2\pi}(A + 2B\frac{N_{QW}(I_{IN})}{V} + 3C\frac{N_{QW}^2(I_{IN})}{V^2}) \tag{21}$$

To maximize the channel rate, we formulate an optimization problem as shown in 19 considering both tradeoffs discussed in 2.2 and 2.3. DC power P_0 is a function of I_{IN} according to the LED datasheet. Considering the power consumption, P_0 is confined to a range less than $P_{\max}$, which affects the range of DC I_{IN}. System bandwidth after equalization is considered far more than LED bandwidth.

3.2 Optimization Problem Solving

The challenges for solving 19 lie in the nonlinearity of the optimization problem and the non-convex constraint 19g. To solve the optimization problem expressed in 19, the particle swarm optimization (PSO) algorithm is used to find the optimal solution, which has an outstanding performance in solving non-convex and nonlinear optimization problems. PSO algorithm finds the global optimal solution by searching individual optimal solutions for each particle and sharing values with other particles. Each particle has two properties of the position and the velocity. In order to find the optimal value of I_{IN} and f_B to achieve the max achievable rate, the position of each particle is a bivector $\mathbf{x}_i = (I_{IN,i}, f_{B,i})^T (\forall i = 1, 2, ..., N)$, where N is the number of particles. The velocity vector $\mathbf{v}_i$ is also a bivector. At the beginning of each iteration, particles first update the velocity and position vectors according to the historical and global optimal. The update rule of velocity and position vectors satisfies the following formula:

$$\mathbf{v}_i^n = w \cdot \mathbf{v}_i^{n-1} + c_1 r_1 \cdot (\mathbf{P}_i^{n-1} - \mathbf{x}_i^{n-1})$$
$$+ c_2 r_2 \cdot (\mathbf{P}_{\text{global}}^{n-1} - \mathbf{x}_i^{n-1}); \tag{20}$$
$$\mathbf{x}_i^n = \mathbf{x}_i^{n-1} + \mathbf{v}_i^{n-1}, \tag{21}$$

where $\mathbf{v}_i^n$ and $\mathbf{x}_i^n$ are the velocity and position vector of the ith particle for the $n^{\text{th}}(\forall n = 1, 2, ..., N_{\text{iter}})$ iteration; N_{iter} is the total iteration number; $\mathbf{P}_i^{n-1}$

Algorithm 1. The optimal value solution via PSO.

Input: Constants in objective function 19, the max DC power $P_{\max}$, the particle number N and the iteration number N_{iter}.
Output: $\mathbf{P}_{\text{global}}$ and corresponding maximum achievable rate.
  Initialize $\mathbf{x}_i$ and $\mathbf{v}_i$ for N particles randomly;
  Initialize $\mathbf{P}_i$ and $\mathbf{P}_{\text{global}}$ by evaluating each particles;
  repeat
    for $i = 1$ to N **do**
      Update velocity and position vectors of the ith particle by using 20 and 21;
      Check if particles are out of bounds;
      Update $\mathbf{P}_i$ of each particles;
      Update $\mathbf{P}_{\text{global}}$ of the swarm;
    end for
  until $n \geq N_{\text{iter}}$
---

is the ith particle best solution after $(n-1)$ iterations; $\mathbf{P}_{\text{global}}^{n-1}$ is the global best solution in the swarm after $(n-1)$ iterations; w is the inertia weight, and the global search ability is stronger when the value is larger; c_1 and c_2 are learning factors; r_1 and r_2 are random numbers between (0,1). After the update is complete, the values beyond the boundary are adjusted. The values of the objective function R_i corresponding to $\mathbf{x}_i$ is calculated according to 17, so that the velocity vectors are assigned to $\mathbf{P}_i$ and $\mathbf{P}_{\text{global}}$ in terms of fitness function. The PSO approach finding the optimal value is summarized in Algorithm 1.

4 Results and Discussion

This section presents simulation results for the VLC transmitter setup employing the proposed asymmetric bridged-T equalizer, and all used parameters are detailed in Table 1.

4.1 LED Characteristics

In order to make the simulation results useful for the design of the actual system, we first measured the characteristics of the commercial LED. As shown in Fig. 4(a), the relationship between relative luminous flux and power consumption with current can be obtained from the LED datasheet. The luminous flux is normalized with that at 350 mA. Considering the VLC system as a power limited system, the maximum DC power $P_{\max}$ in 19g is 1 W and the corresponding DC is $I_{\max}$. Figure 4(b) plots the EO conversion efficiency η_{EO} and 3 dB bandwidth $f_{3\text{ dB}}$ of LED as a function of injected DC I_{IN}. We normalized the efficiency to intuitively reflect the characteristics of LED. As I_{IN} increases, η_{EO} initially rises and then decline, while $f_{3\text{ dB}}$ consistently increases. The scattered data points in the figure sampled by experimental testbed and aligns well with the simulation

Table 1. Simulation Parameters

Parameter	Description	Value
N_{QW}	Number of carriers in QWs	$\sim 10^{14}$
A	Recombination parameters of LED model	5.7×10^7
B		1.528×10^{-8}
C		2.04×10^{-23}
V	Volume given the number of carriers	$2.1\,\text{cm}^3$
A_{LED}	Active region of LED	$1.2\,\text{mm}^2$
λ	LED peak wavelength	$521\,\text{nm}$
P_0	Input electrical power	$1\,\text{mW}$
R_{PD}	The responsivity of PD	$0.6\,\text{A/W}$
F_n	Noise figure of amplifiers	30
Γ	SNR gap	2.6

results, particularly for current exceeding 50 mA. It can be told from the result that the LED model with ABC parameters can well describe the characteristics of the LED. As a result, Fig. 4(b) shows that the maximum efficiency is attained at 75.6 mA, which correspond to a raw bandwidth of 2.6 MHz.

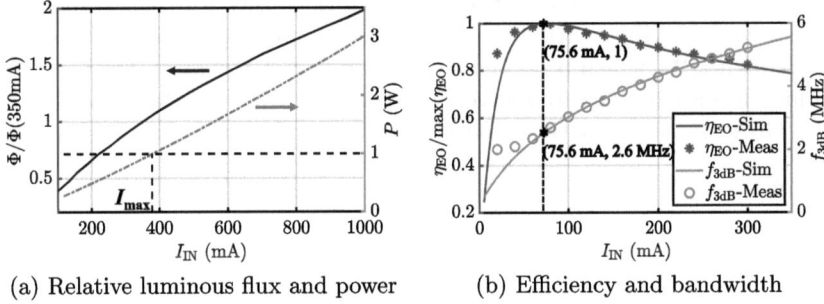

(a) Relative luminous flux and power (b) Efficiency and bandwidth

Fig. 4. The characteristics of the used LED: variation of luminous flux and power as well as the efficiency and bandwidth with current

4.2 Maximum Rate

We first determine the maximum channel rate using numerical results as shown in Fig. 5. Figure 5 illustrates the SNR and achievable rate R varying with different LED DC I_{IN} and system bandwidth f_B. As shown in Fig. 5(a), SNR is a function of I_{IN} and f_B, which forms a three-dimensional plane. The red line on the plane represents the limitation of power of 1 W, which means the DC should be under

I_{max}. Meanwhile, as shown in Fig. 5(b), the achievable rate is also a function of I_{IN} and f_B. It can be told from the figure that the function is convex, meaning that the extreme value can be solved through optimization algorithms. The red line on the plane is also the limitation of power.

On one hand, with a fixed I_{IN}, the SNR decreases as the bandwidth extends. However, the rate R initially increases and then decreases as f_B keeps increasing. On the other hand, with a fixed f_B, both SNR and R increases with injected DC I_{IN}, which is limited by the max DC power consumption. Consequently, the VLC link achieves its maximum rate as the solution to the optimization problem defined in 19 with the simulation parameters listed in Table 1. The maximum achievable rate is 1.15 Gbps with I_{IN} = 378.63 mA and f_B = 163.31 MHz, at which point the DC power of LED is 1 W. This illustrates that when employing high-order modulation in VLC systems, while the utilization of an equalizer allows for wider bandwidth expansion, the consequent sharp decrease in SNR adversely affects system performance.

Finally, we compare our transmitter optimal parameter setting with the state-of-the-art analogue equalizer proposed in [24], which is an active-passive single-order equalizer extending the bandwidth of RGBY LED from 9 MHz to 181 MHz. The equalizer circuit is composed of a passive RC equalizer and an active triode circuit, and the pass-band signal attenuation of the equalizer is approximately 38 dB. By applying the technique of wavelength division multiplexing (WDM), the achievable data rate reaches 3.12 Gbps. By contrast, as shown in Fig. 5, the optimal VLC transmitter for a green LED front-end with 378.63 mA DC and extended system bandwidth of 163.31 MHz can achieve a data rate of 1.15 Gbps with 1/2 of the signal power attenuation. Meanwhile, compared with [25] which proposed a single bridged-T equalizer, the bandwidth of a blue LED is extended from several MHz to 350 MHz and the achievable rate is 1.87 Gb/s. In terms of the same level of achievable rate, our work presents

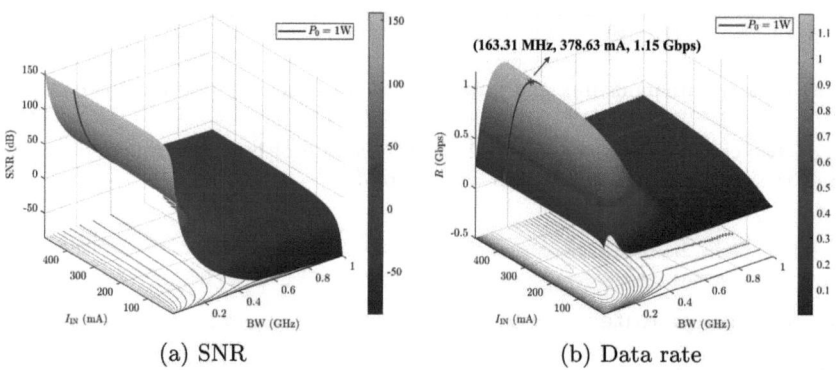

(a) SNR   (b) Data rate

Fig. 5. Simulation results about how the SNR and achievable data rate change with various LED input current (I_{IN}) and system bandwidths (f_B).

smaller bandwidth requirement of 163.31 MHz, meaning simpler design of the equalizer.

5 Conclusion

In this paper, we establish mathematical expressions for the EO conversion efficiency and the 3 dB bandwidth of a raw LED, and formulate the tradeoff problem between bandwidth and signal power considering both the LEDs' small signal characteristics and the parameters of the equalizer circuit. With the aim of maximizing the rate, we then design an asymmetric bridged-T equalizer to tackle concerns regarding impedance matching. Through simulation, we achieved a maximum rate of 1.15 Gbps with a 378.63 mA DC and an extended system bandwidth of 163.31 MHz. We validated the simulation results employing a COTS LED. The self-produced asymmetric bridged-T equalizer can achieve a reduction in reflection by 15 dB compared to a symmetric one.

Overall, we thoroughly discuss the tradeoff problem faced by VLC transmitters, and our proposed asymmetric bridged-T equalizer emerges as a promising solution for enhancing the optical channel rate, thereby paving the way for the practical deployment of VLC in future wireless networks.

References

1. Wang, C.-X., et al.: On the road to 6G: visions, requirements, key technologies, and testbeds. IEEE Commun. Surv. Tutorials **25**(2), 905–974 (2023)
2. Shao, Y., Gündüz, D., Liew, S.C.: Federated edge learning with misaligned over-the-air computation. IEEE Trans. Wireless Commun. **21**(6), 3951–3964 (2022)
3. Zhang, R., Shao, Y., Li, M., Lu, L.: Optical integrated sensing and communication. arXiv preprint arXiv:2305.04395 (2023)
4. Chi, N., Zhou, Y., Wei, Y., Fangchen, H.: Visible light communication in 6G: advances, challenges, and prospects. IEEE Veh. Technol. Mag. **15**(4), 93–102 (2020)
5. Wan, R., Wang, L., Huang, J., Yi, X., Kuo, H.-C., Li, J.: Improving the modulation bandwidth of GaN-based light-emitting diodes for high-speed visible light communication: countermeasures and challenges. Adv. Photonics Res. **2**(12), 2100093 (2021)
6. Wang, Y., Chen, X., Xu, Y.: Transmitter for 1.9 Gbps phosphor white light visible light communication without a blue filter based on OOK-NRZ modulation. Opt. Express **31**(5), 7933–7946 (2023)
7. Li, X., Ghassemlooy, Z., Zvanovec, S., Perez-Jimenez, R., Haigh, P.A.: Should analogue pre-equalisers be avoided in VLC systems? IEEE Photonics J. **12**(2), 1–14 (2020)
8. Piprek, J.: Efficiency models for GaN-based light-emitting diodes: status and challenges. Materials **13**(22), 5174 (2020)
9. Zhu, Z., et al.: Embedded electrode micro-LEDs with high modulation bandwidth for visible light communication. IEEE Trans. Electron Dev. **70**(2), 588–593 (2023)
10. Gao, X., et al.: Multi-Gb/s visible light communication based on AlGaInP amber micro-LED. Opt. Express **32**(6), 10732–10740 (2024)

11. Zhang, R., Xiong, J., Li, M., Lu, L.: Design and implementation of low-complexity pre-equalizer for 1.5 GHz VLC system. IEEE Photonics J. **16**(1), 1–10 (2024)
12. Min, C.: A novel method for constructing VLC equalizer with active-passive hybrid network. IEEE Photonics J. **12**(2), 1–10 (2020)
13. Chen, X., Wang, Y., Liu, X., Zhang, X., Deng, X., Zhou, F.: OMA bandwidth product: a preeminent performance metric for visible light communication. In: 2023 IEEE Globecom Workshops (GC Wkshps), pp. 967–972 (2023)
14. Xiong, J., Li, M., Zhang, R., Lu, L., Sun, Q.T., Long, K.: Precise frequency response of COTS LED for VLC using internal quantum efficiency metric. IEEE Open J. Commun. Soc. **5**, 1376–1386 (2024)
15. Shi, D., et al.: Energy efficiency optimization method of WDM visible light communication system for indoor broadcasting networks. IEEE Trans. Broadcast. **70**, 1207–1220 (024)
16. Wang, L., et al.: 1.3 GHz EO bandwidth GaN-based micro-LED for multi-gigabit visible light communication. Photonics Res. **9**(5), 792–802 (2021)
17. Romero, D.V., Cunha, T.E., Linnartz, J.P.: Optimizing LED performance for LiFi: bandwidth versus efficiency. In: 26th Annual Symposium of the IEEE Photonics Benelux Chapter (2022)
18. Alexeev, A., Linnartz, J.P.M., Arulandu, K., Deng, X.: Characterization of dynamic distortion in LED light output for optical wireless communications. Photonics Res. **9**(6), 916–928 (2021)
19. Deng, X., Wu, Y., Khalid, A.M., Long, X., Linnartz, J.P.M.: LED power consumption in joint illumination and communication system. Optics Express **25**(16), 18990–19003 (2017)
20. Yuan, Z., et al.: Investigation of modulation bandwidth of InGaN green micro-LEDs by varying quantum barrier thickness. IEEE Trans. Electron Dev. **69**(8), 4298–4305 (2022)
21. Zhu, Z., et al.: Embedded electrode micro-LEDs with high modulation bandwidth for visible light communication. IEEE Trans. Electron Dev. **70**(2), 588–593 (2023)
22. Li, X., Ghassemlooy, Z., Zvanovec, S., Alves, L.N.: An equivalent circuit model of a commercial LED with an ESD protection component for VLC. IEEE Photonics Technol. Lett. **33**(15), 777–779 (2021)
23. Sarbazi, E., Kazemi, H., Safari, M., Haas, H.: Imaging angle diversity receiver design for 6G optical wireless communications: performance tradeoffs and optimisation. In: GLOBECOM 2023 - 2023 IEEE Global Communications Conference, pp. 5555–5560 (2023)
24. Chen, X., et al.: A hybrid active-passive single-order equalizer for visible light communication systems. IEEE Photonics Technol. Lett. **35**(24), 1395–1398 (2023)
25. Cai, Y., et al.: Experimental demonstration of 16QAM/QPSK OFDM-NOMA VLC with LDPC codes and analog pre-equalization. Appl. Opt. **61**(19), 5585–5591 (2022)

Autonomous and Electric Vehicles

Mixed-Autonomy Traffic and Wireless Charging Problem for Autonomous Electric Vehicles Using Reinforcement Learning

Kai-Fung Chu[1(✉)], Yue Xie[1], Albert Y. S. Lam[2,3], and Fumiya Iida[1]

[1] University of Cambridge, Cambridge CB2 1PZ, UK
{kfc35,yx388,fi224}@cam.ac.uk
[2] The University of Hong Kong, Pok Fu Lam, Hong Kong
ayslam@eee.hku.hk
[3] Fano Labs, Sha Tin, Hong Kong

Abstract. As the adoption of electric vehicles (EVs) continues to increase, integrating vehicle-to-grid (V2G) technology while maintaining mobility and optimizing traffic flow becomes crucial. In this paper, we formulate a mixed-autonomy traffic and wireless charging problem where both autonomous and human-driven EVs coexist on the road. We aim to mitigate traffic congestion and improve V2G functionality, and therefore we propose a framework that adopts reinforcement learning, specifically the Soft Actor-Critic algorithm, to jointly enhance traffic throughput, balance the state-of-charge (SOC) among EVs, and maximize wireless charging energy in the mixed-autonomy ring-shaped road with wireless charging facilities. Experimental results demonstrate the effectiveness of our approach in stabilizing traffic, achieving SOC balance, and increasing the energy charged to EVs. This study showcases the potential for solving mixed-autonomy traffic and wireless charging problems in future wireless charging transportation systems.

Keywords: Mixed-autonomy traffic and wireless charging problem · Autonomous electric vehicles · Reinforcement learning · Reward

1 Introduction

The maturity of electric vehicle (EV) technology is one of the driving forces behind its commercialization. According to the International Energy Agency's Global EV Outlook 2024 [13], EV sales are projected to reach approximately 17 million in 2024, representing more than one in five cars sold globally. Given this vast amount of EV on the roads, the question of how to effectively and efficiently deliver energy to and from the grid using vehicle-to-grid (V2G) technologies [15] without sacrificing their mobility remains an active area of research [3,4]. Specifically, one may consider optimizing the placement of the charging stations

[17] and determining the optimal charging locations for each after-service EV [8]. However, EVs inevitably have to stop at the charging station to have the connector being plugged in, which limits the mobility of vehicles.

Alternatively, wireless charging technology for electric vehicles can support automated charging through three modes: 1) static charging; 2) quasi-dynamic charging; and 3) dynamic charging [1]. These modes offer several benefits, respectively, including the elimination of shock hazards associated with wires, the extension of vehicle range during short stops (e.g., at traffic lights), and the potential to increase driving range and reduce the battery size of the EV while en route. To facilitate this progress, the first wireless electric road in the US was installed in Detroit [19] and the UK conducted the first wireless electric charging trial in Nottingham [25] both in 2023. We can expect that EVs will connect to the grid through wireless charging roads seamlessly while en route in the near future, supporting various V2G and other applications such as carrying renewable energy from remote generating sites to urban demand regions through EVs [16]. Hence, we must consider traffic and wireless charging problems jointly to further boost the system's efficiency.

A common traffic problem affecting transportation efficiency is congestion, which emerges on the road when the traffic flow is high. In particular, it has been proven that congestion (also known as a shock wave) still emerges on the road even without bottlenecks [24]. One possible way to eliminate the shock wave is by controlling the speed of a vehicle in the platoon, thereby stabilizing the traffic and thus improving traffic throughput and energy consumption per unit of distance traveled [23]. This is an example of mixed-autonomy traffic which studies how autonomous vehicles should behave when human-driven vehicles coexist on the roads. Therefore, researchers have transformed it into a control problem and applied control methods such as reinforcement learning (RL) to handle it [27]. However, such an RL method highly relies on a predefined reference vehicle speed as the sole reward function, which may not automatically apply to other scenarios. Moverover, the charging problem in this microscopic speed-controlling scenario remains unexplored. Hence, we need to jointly investigate the mixed-autonomy traffic and wireless charging problem.

In this paper, we first formulate the mixed-autonomy traffic and wireless charging problem in which autonomous (AEVs) and human-driven EVs (HDEVs) coexist on a ring-shaped road, with a portion of the road segment embedded with wireless charging facilities. Our aim is to jointly enhance traffic throughput, balance the state-of-charge (SOC) among the EVs, and maximize the energy charged to EVs. Next, we propose using the Soft Actor-Critic algorithm with a composite reward function that can jointly enhance traffic throughput and balance the SOC among the EVs, thereby relaxing the requirement of prior knowledge of the reference vehicle speed and enhancing the V2G flexibility. We conduct experiments to evaluate the proposed method along with other reward functions, revealing the two-fold effectiveness of addressing traffic and wireless charging problems with a single method. This study serves as a preliminary exploration into the potential benefits of solving the mixed-autonomy traffic and wireless charging problem in future wireless charging transportation systems.

The main contributions of this paper are summarized as follows:

1. We formulate the mixed-autonomy traffic and wireless charging problem in which AEVs and HDEVs coexist within the system to optimize both traffic and V2G utilities.
2. We propose a solution framework that includes the design of problem settings, state space, action space, and reward function.
3. We conduct experiments to evaluate the effectiveness of the proposed method in solving the mixed-autonomy traffic and wireless charging problem.

This paper is organized as follows. The mixed-autonomy traffic and wireless charging problem is defined in Sect. 2, followed by the proposed method in Sect. 3. We present the experimental results in Sect. 4. The conclusion and discussion of future work are provided in Sect. 5.

2 Mixed-Autonomy Traffic and Wireless Charging Problem

In this section, we present the dynamics of the mixed-autonomy system and then define the corresponding traffic and wireless charging problem.

2.1 System Dynamics

Consider a vehicle fleet set $\mathcal{K}$ with $|\mathcal{K}|$ EVs, where each EV follows its preceding EV to form a vehicle platoon. Each EV $k \in \mathcal{K}$ is represented by a 6-tuple $\langle v_k, \eta_k, a_k, b_k, s_k, e_k \rangle$, denoting the vehicle speed, speed perturbation, acceleration, deceleration, bumper-to-bumper space headway, and SOC, respectively. In the vehicle set $\mathcal{K}$, N EV(s) are autonomous and the rest of the $|\mathcal{K}| - N$ EV(s) are driven by humans. The difference is that the accelerations of the AEVs are controllable by an agent trained by our proposed method while those of the HDEVs are controlled by a microscopic car-following model called the Intelligent Driver Model [26], which models the behavior of an intelligent driver such as decelerating to prevent a crash and accelerate to shorten the headway gap. This model describes the appropriate acceleration with the following equations:

$$a_k = \frac{dv_k}{dt} = a \left[1 - \left(\frac{v_k}{v_0} \right)^\delta - \left(\frac{s^*(v_k, \Delta v_k)}{s_k} \right)^2 \right] \quad (1)$$

$$s^*(v_k, \Delta v_k) = s_0 + v_k \tau_0 + \frac{v_k \Delta v_k}{2 a_k b_k} \quad (2)$$

where v_0, s_0, τ_0, δ and Δv_k are given parameters representing the free-flow speed, desired space headway, desired time headway, constant exponent, and speed difference, respectively.

To study the traffic problem, we reconstruct the traffic road similar to [24], which is a single-lane circular road like a ring. We follow the road length and number of vehicles used in [24]. In addition, we add a wireless charging facility with a length l_w to enable wireless charge. l_w must be larger than $Ml_k+(M-1)s_0$ so that M EVs can be charged on the wireless charging segment simultaneously. The mixed-autonomy traffic and wireless charging system is shown in Fig. 1.

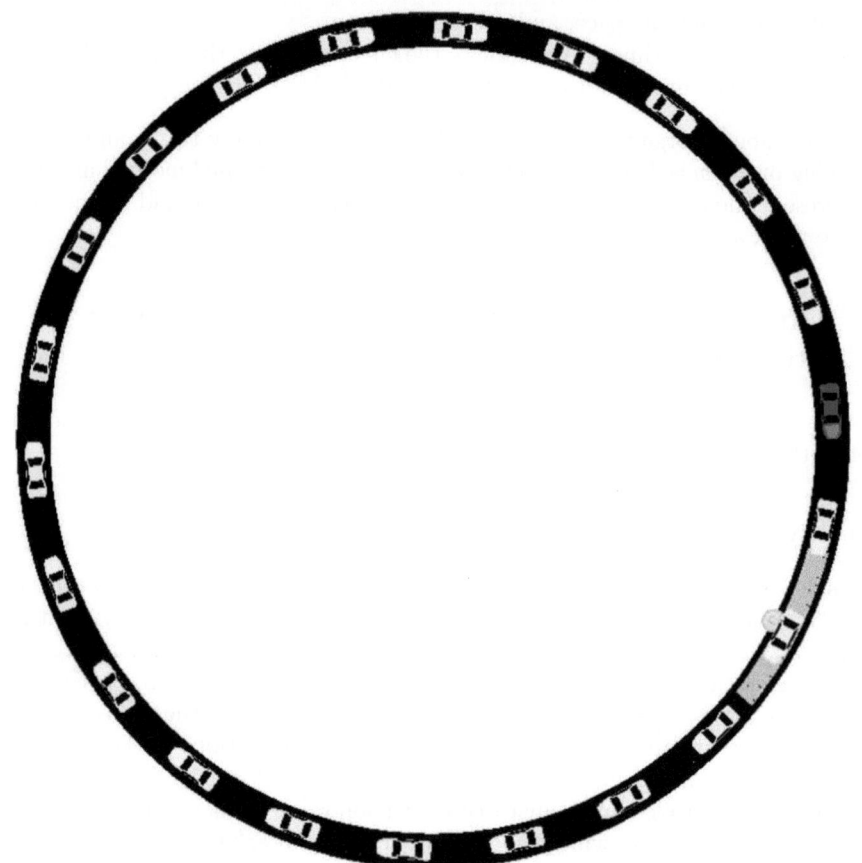

Fig. 1. An example of the mixed-autonomy traffic and wireless charging system. AEV and HDEV are indicated as red and yellow color, respectively. The blue segment is the wireless charging facility. (Color figure online)

2.2 Problem Setting

We study the mixed-autonomy traffic and wireless charging problem, i.e., how to control a set of AEVs on the roads together with other HDEVs such that objectives conforming to both traffic and V2G systems are optimized. We define the objectives as to maximize the traffic throughput, minimize the SOC difference among the EVs, and maximize the energy charged, thereby demonstrating the capability to eliminate traffic shock waves, increase the charging time, and balance the SOC for potential V2G applications, respectively.

As a preliminary study, we simplify the problem by considering only vehicle charging instead of both charging and discharging. Consequently, the action space of the agent is reduced to one dimension (vehicle acceleration). The charging factor is reflected by the time the vehicle staying over the wireless charging facilities, which is in turn revealed by the vehicular speed. In other words, the faster the vehicle, the less the charging time it has on the wireless charging segment for per move. Since action space is one dimensional, we can further simplify the problem to a centralized control and single-agent problem, and a distributed or multi-agent system is outside of the scope of this paper.

3 Methodology

In this section, we discuss the motivation for using RL to solve the mixed-autonomy traffic and wireless charging problem, and the Markov decision process (MDP) used to model it as a control problem.

3.1 Motivation

RL is capable of solving many complex problems, such as mastering the game of Go [22]. Despite its shortcomings [10], there are many successful applications to various engineering problems, such as the field of intelligent transportation system [12] and V2G [20]. For example, RL can be used to control traffic signals based solely on images of the intersection [9], recommend preferred transport modes in a mobility-as-a-service [5,6], and attack multi-modal transportation systems [7].

3.2 Markov Decision Process

We transform the mixed-autonomy traffic and wireless charging problem into a discrete-time MDP framework represented by $(\mathcal{S}, \mathcal{A}, \mathcal{P}, \mathcal{R})$, where $\mathcal{S} \subset \mathbb{R}^m$ is the m-dimensional state space, $\mathcal{A} \subset \mathbb{R}^n$ is the n-dimensional action space, $\mathcal{P} : \mathcal{S} \times \mathcal{A} \times \mathcal{S} \to \mathbb{R}+$ is the transition probability function, and $\mathcal{R} : \mathcal{S} \times \mathcal{A} \to \mathbb{R}$ is the reward function. The relationship between the attributes is that the agent determines an appropriate action $a_t \subset \mathcal{A}$ at time step t based on the given state $s_t \subset \mathcal{S}$. The transition to the next state s_{t+1} is governed by the transition probability $\mathcal{P}(s_{t+1}|s_t, a_t)$. The overall goal of the agent is to maximize the cumulative reward $\sum_{t=0}^{T} \gamma^t \mathcal{R}(s_t, a_t)$ over the time period T where $\gamma = [0, 1]$ is a given discount factor close to 1, accounting for the fact that immediate reward should be more favorable than delayed reward.

3.3 State Space

We assume the environment is fully observable to the agent, and thus the state can capture complete information about the EVs. However, we limit the state representation to vehicle speed v_k, position on the road $x_k = [0, l_r)$, SOC of EVs e_k, and charged energy c^i of the wireless charging facility i for implementation purposes. Since the road is ring-shaped, we assign a point as the starting point with a value of 0 or l_r. Those elements are concatenated together to form the overall state representation $s = [v_1, x_1, e_1, \ldots, v_{|\mathcal{K}|}, x_{|\mathcal{K}|}, e_{|\mathcal{K}|}, c^i]$.

3.4 Action Space

As discussed in Sect. 2, we are interested in controlling the set of AEVs. In the single-lane road setting, vehicle acceleration is the only degree of freedom for control. Hence, the action space is defined as the space between maximum deceleration and maximum acceleration, i.e., $a_k \in [-b_{max}, a_{max}]$. Although the agent can determine the acceleration value, the speed is bounded by an extra constraint layer for safety reasons. For example, the autonomous vehicle cannot accelerate if the preceding EV is too close. The speed can be changed only when within the safety bound $v_k \in [\underline{v}_{safe}, \overline{v}_{safe}]$, which is restricted by IDM. In other words, the actual vehicle speed $v_k := \max(\min(v_k + a_k, \overline{v}_{safe}), \underline{v}_{safe})$ is partially influenced by the environment, which is not controlled by the agent.

3.5 Reward Function

The objective of the problem is to maximize traffic and V2G utilities. Intuitively, we should define the reward function as a sum of two terms related to traffic and V2G, respectively. For the traffic reward term, we follow the definition in [27], which is:

$$R_{traffic} = \max\{0, ||v_{des} \cdot \mathbf{1}^{|\mathcal{K}|}||_2 - ||v - v_{des} \cdot \mathbf{1}^{|\mathcal{K}|}||_2\}, \tag{3}$$

where v_{des} is the desired speed. For V2G, one of the features is to balance the power demand through EV mobility [28], which provides flexible demand response management. However, the reference study examines a macroscopic scenario where EVs are routed on a V2G mobile energy network with multiple battery pools in different districts, which is not applicable to our microscopic case that examines vehicle acceleration and speed. Nevertheless, we can consider each EV on the road as an individual battery pool microscopically. Hence, the V2G utility can be transformed into balancing the SOC among the EVs and maximizing the energy charged to EVs, which is defined as:

$$R_{balance} = -\sigma(e) \tag{4}$$

and

$$R_{charge} = \sum_{t=0}^{T} \sum_{i} c_t^i \tag{5}$$

where $\sigma(e)$ is the standard deviation of the SOC of all EVs and c_t^i is the charged energy from wireless charging facility i at time t.

As a whole, the overall reward function is the weighted sum of the three terms, which are:

$$\mathcal{R} = \lambda_{traffic} R_{traffic} + \lambda_{balance} R_{balance} + \lambda_{charge} R_{charge} \qquad (6)$$

where the λs are the corresponding weighting factors to scale each term for fair summation.

4 Experiments

4.1 Experiment Settings

We conduct experiments to evaluate the effectiveness and efficiency of solving the mixed-autonomy traffic and wireless charging problem using the proposed method. To simulate the traffic and wireless charging scenario, we utilize the Simulation of Urban MObility (SUMO) [18] to model the system and set the parameters, interfaced by GYM [2], an open-source Python library that supports communication between the learning algorithm and the environments. SUMO is an open-source microscopic traffic simulator designed to replicate real-world traffic scenarios and simulate large-scale road networks with accurate dynamic models of individual vehicles on the road.

We place $|\mathcal{K}| = 22$ vehicles on a $l_r = 230$ m single-lane ring road, similar to the experiments in [24]. As a preliminary study, only one vehicle is autonomous, i.e. $N = 1$. The length of each vehicle l_k and desired space headway s_0 are 5 m and 2.5 m, respectively. The maximum acceleration and deceleration are both 1 ms^{-2}. We add a 0.1 deviation to the IDM to represent the imperfection of human drivers. For the electric specification, we follow the parameters of the Kia Soul EV 2020 [14] such as a 64 kWh maximum battery capacity and a 150 kW electric motor. The initial SOC is half of the maximum battery capacity. The length of the wireless charging segment is $l_w = 15$ m, which can support the wireless charging of $M = 2$ EVs simultaneously if the space headway between them is small.

For the RL algorithm, we use the Soft Actor-Critic (SAC) [11] implemented in Stable-Baselines3 [21]. The hyper-parameters are set by the default values in the Stable-Baselines3. Each training episode contains 2000 time steps, representing 200 s with the 0.1 step length setting in SUMO (i.e., one step represents 0.1 s in time). 100 training episodes were conducted for each experiment.

All models and parameters use the default settings in the above tools unless specified otherwise.

4.2 Experimental Results

We conduct the experiments to investigate three aspects: traffic flow, SOC balance, and wireless charging. Let A, B, and C be the methods trained with $R_{traffic}$, $R_{balance}$, and R_{charge}, respectively. Six ablated methods (A, B, C, A&B, A&C, B&C) are compared with the proposed one (A&B&C).

Traffic Flow. Figure 2 shows the traffic flow of the vehicle fleet. In general, the total traffic flow of methods with A (A, $A\&B$, $A\&C$, $A\&B\&C$) has a higher traffic flow than those with C (C, $A\&C$, $B\&C$, $A\&B\&C$). This is because the reward term $R_{traffic}$ facilitates the vehicle speed to a desired and stable value, eliminating congestion and enhancing the traffic flow. However, R_{charge} only encourages the charging of EVs, not the speed. Based on the low traffic flow of method C, we can interpret that EVs are stopped on the road, hindering the flow of vehicles. Among all the compared methods, $A\&B\&C$ trains the AEV agent that produces the highest traffic flow by adjusting its speed. This means that other terms related to V2G can facilitate the policy search related to traffic specifications, without solely relying on predefined speed references.

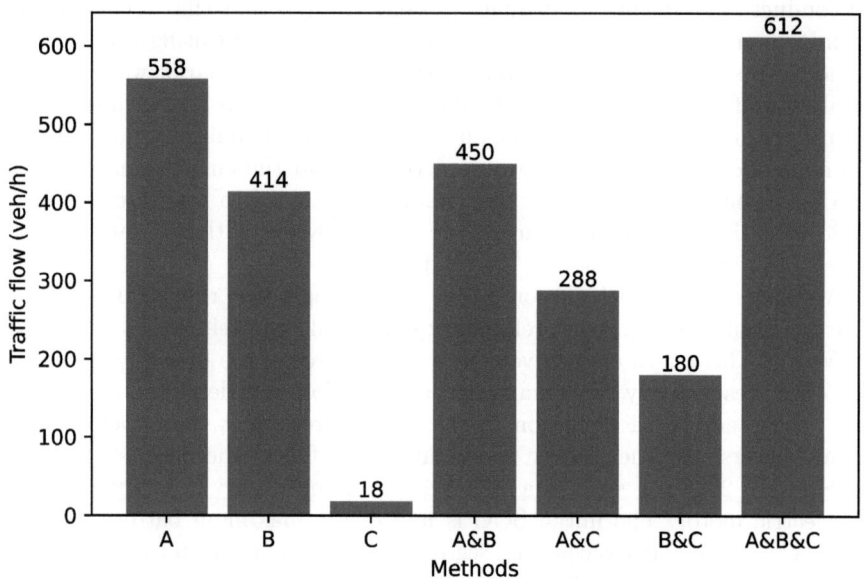

Fig. 2. Traffic flow against different methods upon testing.

SOC Balance. Figure 3 shows the standard deviation of EVs' SOC. Note that the SOC is affected by the energy consumption due to movement and wireless charging energy. Controlling the acceleration of a vehicle to balance the changing SOC of all EVs is not an trivial task. Since we aim to balance the SOC for V2G, a lower standard deviation means a better method. The methods converge to three groups: Method C is the lowest group; Methods $A\&B\&C$, A, $A\&B$, and B are the second group; Methods $B\&C$ and $A\&C$ are the group with the highest standard deviation. It is surprising that method C is the lowest since method C attempted to maximize the charging energy but not the SOC standard deviation. The reason is that the agent trained by C failed to move when combining the traffic flow results. Hence, if we ignore it, due to the extremely low traffic flow, the proposed $A\&B\&C$ method will be the best one. This shows that our proposed method can effectively balance the SOC by controlling the acceleration of an AEV.

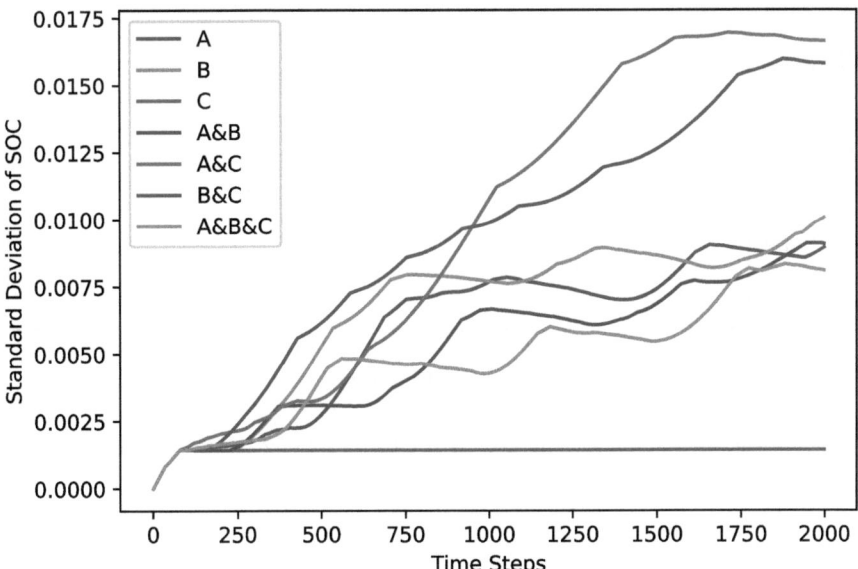

Fig. 3. Standard Deviation of SOC along vehicle traveling time steps upon testing.

Charged Energy. Figure 4 shows the cumulative charged energy to all EVs over the time steps. We can observe three groups from the figure. The best method for energy charging is $A\&C$ and $B\&C$. The second group is the methods A, B, $A\&B\&C$, and $A\&B$. The method with the lowest charged energy is C since the EVs do not stop on the wireless charging segment. Although it is obvious that stopping at the wireless charging segment can charge one or two EVs constantly, the agent still fails to discover this policy with only R_{charge}, implying R_{charge} should be combined with other terms such as $R_{traffic}$ and $R_{balance}$ that we proposed. Once it is combined with other terms, such as methods $A\&C$ and $B\&C$, the charged energy increases dramatically.

Combining the results from Figs. 2, 3 and 4, we can conclude that our proposed method $A\&B\&C$ can successfully stabilize traffic, balance the SOC, and increase the energy charged to EVs.

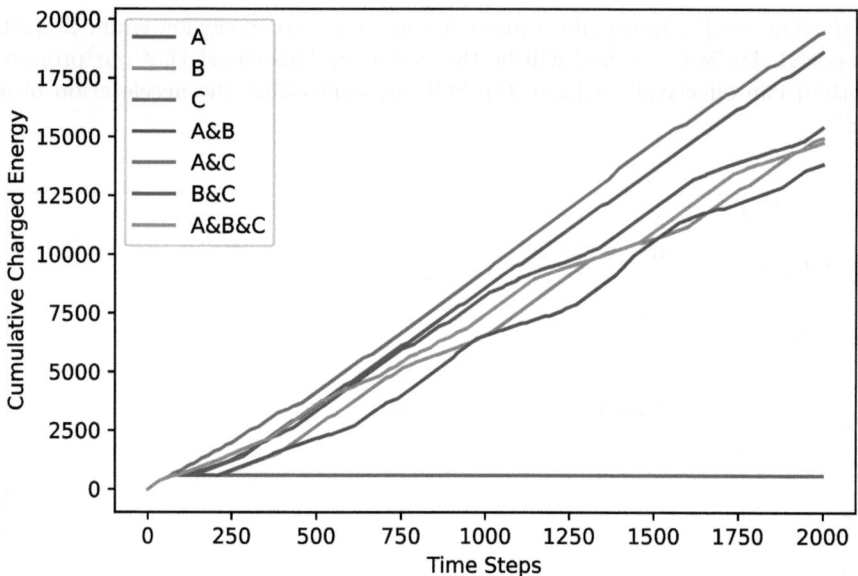

Fig. 4. Cumulative charged energy to EVs along the time steps.

5 Conclusion

This paper presents a new formulation of the mixed-autonomy traffic and wireless charging problem where AEVs and HDEVs coexist. By integrating wireless charging technology with traffic control mechanisms, the proposed method demonstrates its potential to enhance traffic throughput, balance the SOC among EVs, and increase the energy transfer from charging infrastructure, without relying heavily on predefined speed references. Our experiments, conducted on a simulated environment, show that the SAC method with a composite reward function effectively stabilizes traffic flow, maintains a balanced SOC across EVs, and optimizes energy charging during transit. The proposed method outperforms other approaches that focus on individual objectives, demonstrating the importance of this approach in solving mixed-autonomy traffic and wireless charging challenges.

This study serves as a preliminary exploration into the integration of traffic and wireless charging optimization, paving the way for more advanced and practical implementations in future wireless charging transportation systems. Future work may focus on extending the problem to multi-agent systems, incorporating more complex road networks, and exploring the impacts of different traffic conditions and wireless charging technologies on the system's overall performance.

Acknowledgements. This project has received funding from the European Union's Horizon 2020 research and innovation programme under the Marie Skłodowska-Curie grant agreement No 101034337.

References

1. Ahmad, A., Alam, M.S., Chabaan, R.: A comprehensive review of wireless charging technologies for electric vehicles. IEEE Trans. Transp. Electrif. **4**(1), 38–63 (2017)
2. Brockman, G., et al.: OpenAI gym (2016)
3. Chen, T., Chu, K.F., Lam, A.Y.S., Hill, D.J., Li, V.O.: Electric autonomous vehicle charging and parking coordination for vehicle-to-grid voltage regulation with renewable energy. In: 2020 IEEE Power & Energy Society General Meeting (PESGM). pp. 1–5. IEEE (2020)
4. Chu, K.F., Chen, T., Lam, A.Y.S., Song, Y.: Collaborative routing and charging/discharging scheduling of electric autonomous vehicles in coupled power-traffic networks. In: 2023 IEEE 97th Vehicular Technology Conference (VTC2023-Spring), pp. 1–6. IEEE (2023)
5. Chu, K.F., Guo, W.: Deep reinforcement learning of passenger behavior in multimodal journey planning with proportional fairness. Neural Comput. Appl. **35**(27), 20221–20240 (2023)
6. Chu, K.F., Guo, W.: Privacy-preserving federated deep reinforcement learning for mobility-as-a-service. IEEE Trans. Intell. Transp. Syst. (2023)
7. Chu, K.F., Guo, W.: Multi-agent reinforcement learning-based passenger spoofing attack on mobility-as-a-service. IEEE Trans. Dependable Secure Comput. (2024)
8. Chu, K.F., Lam, A.Y.S., Li, V.O.K.: Joint rebalancing and vehicle-to-grid coordination for autonomous vehicle public transportation system. IEEE Trans. Intell. Transp. Syst. **23**(7), 7156–7169 (2021)
9. Chu, K.F., Lam, A.Y.S., Li, V.O.K.: Traffic signal control using end-to-end off-policy deep reinforcement learning. IEEE Trans. Intell. Transp. Syst. **23**(7), 7184–7195 (2021)
10. Dulac-Arnold, G., et al.: Challenges of real-world reinforcement learning: definitions, benchmarks and analysis. Mach. Learn. **110**(9), 2419–2468 (2021). https://doi.org/10.1007/s10994-021-05961-4
11. Haarnoja, T., Zhou, A., Abbeel, P., Levine, S.: Soft actor-critic: off-policy maximum entropy deep reinforcement learning with a stochastic actor. In: International Conference on Machine Learning, pp. 1861–1870. PMLR (2018)
12. Haydari, A., Yılmaz, Y.: Deep reinforcement learning for intelligent transportation systems: a survey. IEEE Trans. Intell. Transp. Syst. **23**(1), 11–32 (2020)
13. IEA: Global EV outlook 2024 (2024). https://www.iea.org/reports/global-ev-outlook-2024
14. Kia: 2020 kia soul EV 64kwh - specifications and price (2020). https://www.evspecifications.com/en/model/e94fa0
15. Lam, A.Y.S.: Advanced vehicle-to-grid: architecture, applications, and smart city integration. In: Lee, C.H.T. (eds.) Emerging Technologies for Electric and Hybrid Vehicles. Green Energy and Technology, pp. 321–342. Springer, Singapore (2024). https://doi.org/10.1007/978-981-99-3060-9_11
16. Lam, A.Y.S., Leung, K.C., Li, V.O.K.: Vehicular energy network. IEEE Trans. Transp. Electrif. **3**(2), 392–404 (2017)
17. Lam, A.Y.S., Leung, Y.W., Chu, X.: Electric vehicle charging station placement: formulation, complexity, and solutions. IEEE Trans. Smart Grid **5**(6), 2846–2856 (2014)
18. Lopez, P.A., et al.: Microscopic traffic simulation using sumo. In: IEEE Intelligent Transportation Systems Conference (2018). https://doi.org/10.1109/ITSC.2018.8569938

19. Nissen, J.: First wireless charging road in U.S. unveiled in detroit (2023). https://www.fox2detroit.com/news/first-wireless-charging-road-in-u-s-set-to-be-unveiled-in-detroit
20. Qiu, D., Wang, Y., Hua, W., Strbac, G.: Reinforcement learning for electric vehicle applications in power systems: a critical review. Renew. Sustain. Energy Rev. **173**, 113052 (2023)
21. Raffin, A., Hill, A., Gleave, A., Kanervisto, A., Ernestus, M., Dormann, N.: Stable-baselines3: reliable reinforcement learning implementations. J. Mach. Learn. Res. **22**(268), 1–8 (2021). http://jmlr.org/papers/v22/20-1364.html
22. Silver, D., et al.: Mastering the game of go without human knowledge. Nature **550**(7676), 354–359 (2017)
23. Stern, R.E., et al.: Dissipation of stop-and-go waves via control of autonomous vehicles: field experiments. Transp. Res. Part C: Emerg. Technol. **89**, 205–221 (2018)
24. Sugiyama, Y., et al.: Traffic jams without bottlenecks—experimental evidence for the physical mechanism of the formation of a jam. New J. Phys. **10**(3), 033001 (2008)
25. Transport Nottingham: Nottingham wraps up UK-first wireless electric charging trial (2023). https://www.transportnottingham.com/nottingham-wraps-up-uk-first-wireless-electric-charging-trial/
26. Treiber, M., Hennecke, A., Helbing, D.: Congested traffic states in empirical observations and microscopic simulations. Phys. Rev. E **62**(2), 1805 (2000)
27. Wu, C., Kreidieh, A., Vinitsky, E., Bayen, A.M.: Emergent behaviors in mixed-autonomy traffic. In: Conference on Robot Learning, pp. 398–407. PMLR (2017)
28. Yu, R., Zhong, W., Xie, S., Yuen, C., Gjessing, S., Zhang, Y.: Balancing power demand through EV mobility in vehicle-to-grid mobile energy networks. IEEE Trans. Industr. Inf. **12**(1), 79–90 (2015)

A Review of Digital Twins for Electric Vehicles

Yangyang Zhou and Chao Huang(✉)

Department of Industrial and Systems Engineering, The Hong Kong Polytechnic University, Hung Hom, Hong Kong
22040432r@connect.polyu.hk, hchao.huang@polyu.edu.hk

Abstract. Traditional fuel vehicles emit large amounts of harmful gases, especially carbon dioxide. These gases will pose a huge threat to the ecological environment. With the emergence of electric vehicles (EVs), this problem has been alleviated and EVs have received more and more attention. Digital twin (DT) in EVs serve a pivotal role by creating a virtual model of a vehicle that mirrors the real-world vehicle. This technology enables real-time DT monitoring and diagnostics in all phases of EV production and operation. It permits the collection of data and analysis on how specific vehicles perform in different circumstances without physical testing. Therefore, the introduction of DT will bring significant potential for the development of EV. This paper explores the critical role of DT technology in EVs, specifically focusing on battery management systems, vehicle health monitoring, and propulsion drive systems. This will give readers a basic understanding of the DT technology and its potential future application in EVs.

Keywords: DT · EVs · Vehicle health monitoring · Battery management

1 Introduction

EV refers to a vehicle that uses one or more electric motors or traction motors as a power source. These vehicles are typically powered by a built-in battery pack that can be charged from an external power source and converts electrical energy into mechanical energy to drive the vehicle forward [1]. Vehicles using traditional internal combustion engines consume a large amount of fuel and emit exhaust containing harmful gases [2]. These gases cause serious pollution to the environment. In contrast, EVs not only contribute to reducing carbon emissions but also bring economic benefits by saving fuel costs [3]. As a result, they are receiving increasing attention.

This work was funded by the RIAIoT project, PolyU (Project ID: P0050293, Project Title: A Human-Guided Digital Twin Paradigm for the Training of Connected Autonomous Vehicles).

The origin of EVs can be traced back to 1834 when Thomas Davenport built the first EV driven by a DC motor [4]. This ushered in a new era of EV invention and application. The emergence of battery technology in 1859 made EVs widely used [5]. However, with the continuous advancement of internal combustion engine technology and the extensive development of petroleum resources, gasoline vehicles have gradually replaced EVs [6]. This has prompted EVs to face issues such as stagnant battery technology and high manufacturing costs. After the 21st century, breakthroughs in lithium-ion battery technology have provided essential technical support for the resurgence of EVs, and the endurance and performance of EVs have been remarkablely improved [4]. Compared with fuel cell vehicles and internal combustion engine vehicles, share of sales of EVs show substantial growth potential. Especially in 2020, the global EV market increased by approximately 43% compared with 2019 [7]. Information Handling Services Markit predicts that the market share of EVs will increase significantly, and by 2030, EVs will account for approximately 25% of the new passenger car market. By 2050, four out of five new passenger cars will be EVs [8]. These forecasts reflect the trend of the automotive industry towards electrification.

EV technology is developing rapidly, and the automobile system becomes more complex with a larger proportion of intelligence subsystems. Complexity due to the introduction of battery management, electric motor and hybrid drivetrain technologies into advanced driving systems. In addition, the integration of numerous sensors and interconnected electronic components that need to interact seamlessly with vehicle systems also increases complexity. The complexity of vehicle systems puts higher requirements on design, testing, operation and maintenance [9]. In addition, as the market demand for EVs continues to increase, the compression of development and production cycles has become a major challenge [10]. DT is deeply integrating the physical world with the virtual world through high-precision modeling and real-time data interaction by digital technology. Integrating DT technology into EVs will bring tremendous potential for the development of EVs. It enables the simulation and monitoring of EVs throughout their entire life-cycle [3]. By creating a complete virtual copy, engineers can test new designs and configurations without affecting the actual physical model [11]. This approach can shorten EVs development and production cycles and ensure the optimal designs.

The structure of the paper is as follows: Sect. 2 introduces the evolution of the DT concept and its common applications. Section 3 elaborates on the important applications of DT in EVs. The challenges and opportunities of DT deployment in EVs are discussed in Sect. 4. Finally, Sect. 5 summarizes this paper.

2 Development and Application Scenarios of DT

The concept of DTs can be traced back to National Aeronautics and Space Administration's Apollo mission in 1960 [12]. Subsequently, concepts related to DT such as mirror world and shadow system were proposed in 1993 and 1994 respectively [13]. The concept of DTs was first introduced by Dr. Grieves in a presentation on Product Life-cycle Management in 2003 [3]. Over the next decade, technologies such as Internet of Things, computer science and communication have significantly propelled DT. The first white paper on DT was released in 2014 [1]. Tao et al. divided DT into three stages in 2019: formation stage, incubation stage, and growth stage [14]. Additionally, in 2022, they expanded on the virtual models of DTs [15]. In 2024, the concept of DTs is currently being introduced into the metaverse [16].

DT technology has been employed in many sectors. This concept was first applied to manufacturing and products [17]. Due to its benefits such as improving efficiency and reducing operating costs, DT has further expanded its influence in other fields [18]. The common application areas of DT are depicted in Fig. 1. For example, DT allows engineers to monitor real-time data and predict potential failures of aircraft engines and components through advanced simulations. It can effectively reduce maintenance costs and increase the lifespan and reliability of aircraft [19]. In the field of construction, applying DT to construction for complex scenario simulation can provide engineers with a detailed digital description of the physical building [20]. In healthcare, DT can deliver even more positive aspects of medical services by enhancing quality and efficiency, as well as personalizing service. In the manufacturing industry, DT has been used to replicate and simulate the manufacturing process to optimize the production line [21]. Moreover, DTs can optimize urban planning and management in smart cities through highly detailed virtual models, achieving refined and sustainable urban operations [22].

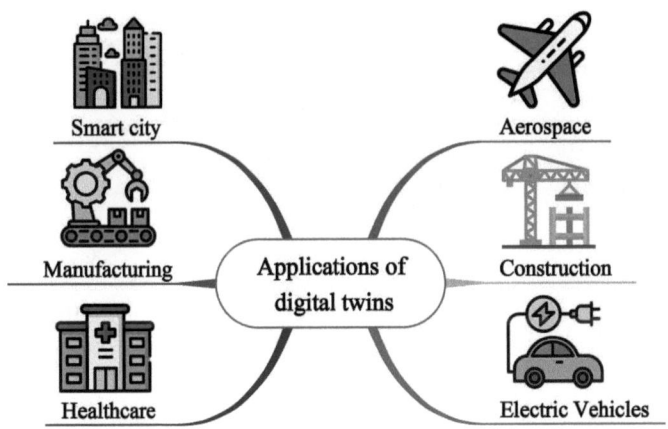

Fig. 1. Application of DTs in Different Fields

3 DTs Technology in Electric Vehicles

DT technology is an important branch connecting the physical and virtual worlds, with broad application in EVs. DT technology develops the intelligence of EV by constructing accurate digital replicas about those physical vehicles and production environments which realize real-time monitoring data analysis on physical vehicle. The subsequent sections will explore the critical functions and application examples of DT technology on different EV components, as well as other systems.

3.1 Battery Management Systems

Initially, DT technology was primarily utilized to monitor battery usage performance and overall condition. As DT technology evolves and innovates, the modeling process of its monitoring system becomes increasingly sophisticated. The whole system gradually integrates predictive performance, optimization techniques, control mechanisms, and the ecosystem of EV batteries [23]. The application of DT models has continued to evolve [24]. These DT models enable the implementation of advanced physics-based modeling. The rapid development of machine learning has provided new avenues for the advancement of DT technology. By combining DT technology with ML algorithms, EV battery management has been significantly improved [5]. DT technology is not only suitable for each single battery and vehicle, it even further extends to a larger-scale system. DT can integrate data from multiple vehicles and batteries into a unified model, a concept already being applied in EV fleets [25]. Figure 2 shows the practical application of DT technology on a Wireless battery management system (BMS).

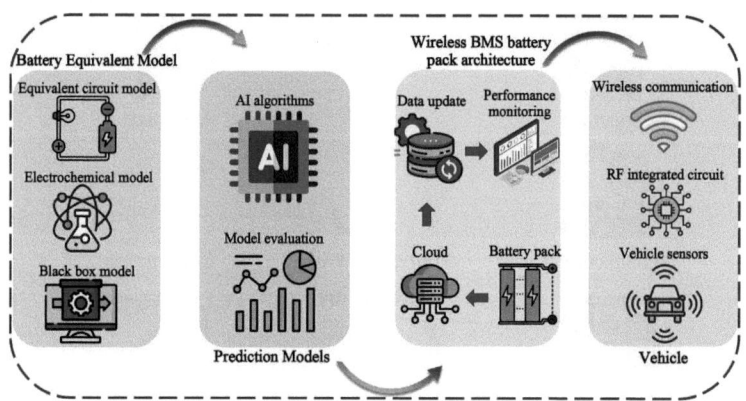

Fig. 2. Framework for a wireless battery management system

Battery Status Management: In BMS, the states of the battery include the state of charge, state of health, and state of power [1]. Accurate detection of these states is crucial for the healthy usage of batteries, as this information is used by algorithms responsible for monitoring, controlling, and protecting the battery pack. Due to CPU and memory limitations in BMS, implementing state-of-the-art battery state estimation algorithms can be challenging, leading to potential inaccuracies in battery state measurements and consequently, suboptimal battery performance and safety. DT technology, with its significantly higher computational resources compared to BMS, enables higher accuracy in these estimations.

Fault Diagnosis and Predictive Maintenance: EV's BMS requires regular service and maintenance. Traditional on-board BMS utilize classic fault detection and protection methods which typically apply sensors to monitor temperature, voltage, abnormal current and other data. After the data collection, sensors identify potential faults or anomalies through a preset threshold. However, the real-time processing of sensor data is insufficient and the recognition accuracy is limited, which will lead traditional production methods to be inefficient [12]. DT technology can utilize rich historical and real-time data combined with advanced multivariate condition monitoring to enhance the accuracy of fault detection and localization [25]. Physics-based battery models in DT technology can monitor specific behaviors or processes that may trigger faults. DT technology can also be utilized to support predictive fault maintenance and optimization of battery systems [5]. By continuously tracking battery performance, DT models can identify early signs of battery degradation and operational deviations. With the aid of predictive maintenance systems, maintenance tasks can be initiated once potential issues are anticipated.

Exploration of Battery Lifecycle: In EV battery management, DT technology facilitates continuous monitoring, analysis, and optimization of battery functions and states throughout their entire lifecycle [3]. It covers the detection and analysis of critical design structures, physical properties, and specific operational parameters within the system. The accumulation of long-term data and the construction of extensive databases facilitate the organization of rich historical data [1]. Using sophisticated deep learning algorithms, DT offers predictive analytics and data supported optimization of battery systems. These advancements help with the optimal utilisation of EVs, improved battery lifespan and capacity along with more insights regarding different stages of battery life cycle [12]. Moreover, with DT technology, the continuous estimation of battery health status and the storage of related data in databases offer new possibilities. This data can be optionally shared with battery manufacturers to inform future operational planning.

Thermal Management: Utilizing DT technology can identify the root causes of defects in the manufacturing process, ensuring quality and expediting completion times [26]. Another key optimization strategy is that of Thermal Management Systems (TMS) charged with energy management. This DT technology allows for smarter temperature management strategies using very accurate predictive approach to improve the working of TMS which subsequently increases battery life. For instance, a TMS integrated with DT technology can autonomously adjust battery temperatures several minutes before an EV arrives at a charging station. Design optimizations of TMS incorporating DT technology, as explored in literature [27], highlight the benefits of this integration.

3.2 Vehicle Health Monitoring and Management

Vehicle health monitoring and management (VHMM) is a framework that utilizes critical data from sensors to predict and diagnose vehicle faults. DT technology can be leveraged to evaluate and predict the health status key components [28]. Consequently, VHMM has transitioned from time-based or fault-driven maintenance to condition-based maintenance. In this mode, DT technology provides automakers with formidable capabilities in diagnosing abnormal states and predicting the rest life of vehicles. Figure 3 illustrates the framework of VHMM combined with DT technology. The contributions of DT in VHMM are summarized in Table 1.

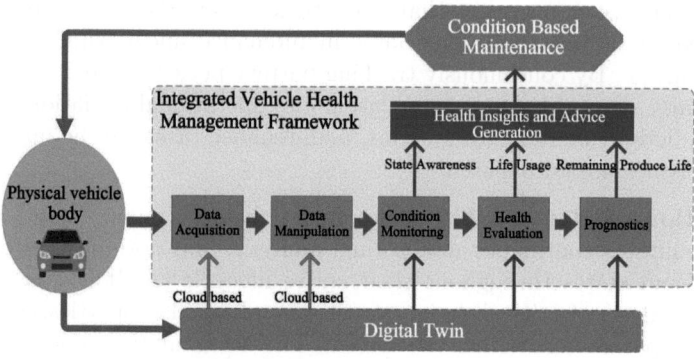

Fig. 3. Framework for DT-based integrated vehicle health management system

Entire Vehicle Health Monitoring: Vehicle health management aims to implies the monitoring, diagnosis and prognosis of systems in a vehicle to maintain their overall health status. To effectively diagnose and predict vehicle states, a comprehensive system rich in information and data is required for VHMM [29]. When utilizing DT technology for vehicle-level health monitoring, data-driven condition-based maintenance and repairs can be facilitated. It is this capability that has gradually propelled the adoption of DT technology in the realm of VHMM. DT technology can be viewed as a high-fidelity virtual simulation, providing a virtual representation of physical attributes in real-time or at a specific moment, and simulating system states under various conditions based on comprehensive data [30].

Health Management of Automotive Braking Systems: Currently, vehicle braking systems heavily rely on data [31] including simplified relationships and material data from the dynamic power system, which have limited practical value in engineering and physics. As a result, the pursuit of higher data value and more precise fault prediction and maintenance in the future. Specifically, DT technology provides automotive manufacturers with anomaly diagnosis and predictive services, enhancing the lifespan of materials in braking systems and improving driver safety and satisfaction. Modeling processes in the EV braking systems can incorporate physics-based modeling techniques to create a DT physical virtual model that predicts brake pad wear in traditional vehicle braking systems. Compared to purely physics-based modeling, the DT-based modeling approach generates a high-fidelity virtual model capable of predicting brake pad wear under different operating conditions.

Vehicle Motor Health Monitoring: To perform real-time health monitoring of automotive EV motors, DT technology constructs virtual models that mimic the physical systems to predict and anticipate their behavior. Permanent Magnet Synchronous Motors have become widely adopted in EVs due to their high efficiency, high power density, and consistent power range across various operating conditions [32]. The control of motor operating states and monitoring of its characteristics are intricately linked to intelligent transportation systems [31]. In addition, the advanced DT technology can be used to predict the lifespan of electric motors, which is a favorable measure to ensure the optimal reliability and maximum safety of the motor during operation, so as to ensure timely maintenance and preventive rescue for motor failures. Some studies have also provided research on DT technology used in motor health monitoring. Timimy et al. studied the impact of leakage flow caused by rotor penetration end covers on the performance of permanent magnet generators [33]. Zeng et al. proposed a new interturn fault diagnosis method for permanent magnet synchronous machines based on DT technology [34].

3.3 EV Propulsion Drive System

The powertrain system of an EV is the primary system that provides kinetic energy to the vehicle. It is a combination of electrical and mechanical components.

Energy Conversion Unit: In the Energy Conversion Unit (ECU) of EVs, DT technology also plays a pivotal role [1]. As the key equipment integrating energy storage systems, boost systems, DC-DC converters, and AC inverters, the ECU's performance directly impacts the energy utilization efficiency and power output of EVs [8]. When DT technology is applied to the power electronic converters within the ECU, it optimizes the energy conversion process by precisely controlling the switching of semiconductor devices [42]. Efficient modulation strategies with DT technology also improve the ECU energy conversion efficiency and reliability. Such advances further enhance the driving range of EVs and maturing a sustainable energy mode in the electric vehicle industry.

Traction Inverter: The traction inverter, a core component in EVs, is responsible for converting the direct current output from the traction battery into three-phase alternating current to drive the electric motor [3]. The application of DT

Table 1. Investigation of DT application in VHMM

Sl. No.	Methods	Functions	Year [Ref.No.]
1	A "5-D DT model for health prediction and management" system based on data fusion	Accurately assesses the vehicle's health and future maintenance demands	2018 [35]
2	DT system focused on collecting critical physical variables within EVs.	Monitoring health status of power system and predicting remaining life of permanent magnet.	2019 [36]
3	Establish an intelligent interface for monitoring vehicle age.	Monitoring the deterioration of vehicle health and optimize the EV servicing process	2019 [37]
4	Autonomous control subsystem of EV is constructed modularly according to the priority of the vehicle system	The construction efficiency of DTs on EVs has been greatly improved	2020 [38]
5	Constructed a multi-dimensional DT model to represent the complex relationship between objects and attributes	The DT modeling process is optimized and interaction mode of TRIZ has been improved	2021 [39]
6	Combination of DT technology and smart material technology with EV industry is comprehensively reviewed	Simplify the complexity of EV repair and maintenance; Reduced service and time costs	2022 [40]
7	Battery management for EVs through SoH cloud prediction and SoC vehicle estimation.	Improve the accuracy of SoH prediction and SoC estimation	2023 [41]

technology in the traction inverter has significantly enhanced the motor's control precision and dynamic performance [14]. DT technology enables the traction inverter to more accurately follow a driver's operating commands and achieve smooth acceleration and deceleration processes by directly controlling electromagnetic torque and flux linkage of motor. Additionally, when combined with advanced sensor technology and intelligent control algorithms, DT technology effectively suppresses torque ripples and harmonic interference, improving the ride comfort and safety of EVs [42]. In the practical application of traction inverter, DT technology has become one of the key technologies to improve EV dynamic performance and control accuracy in practical applications.

On-Board Charger: The On-Board Charger (OBC), an essential auxiliary device in EVs, directly influences the charging efficiency and user experience of these vehicles. The application of DT technology in OBC is primarily manifested in the optimized control of power electronic converters during the charging process [8]. By utilizing DT technology to control the power factor correction and DC/DC converters within the OBC, precise regulation of charging current and voltage is achieved, leading to improved charging efficiency and power factor [1]. Furthermore, when combined with advanced SiC semiconductor materials and intelligent control algorithms, DT technology further reduces the loss, volume, and weight of the OBC, enhancing the overall system performance.

4 Future Challenges and Opportunities

DT technology applied in the field of EV industry has reformed ways to design, produce and operate products. Despite the benefits that DT offers to EVs including enhanced design accuracy, optimized operational efficiency and lower maintenance costs, there are also multiple challenges it faces. The challenges of applying DT in EV are presented as follows.

Modeling complexity: Accuracy of the model is one of the main challenges faced while implementing DT technology in manufacturing EV models. It is easy to build accurate models of simple objects. However, for equipment that deals with complex structures, processes, and operating environments, the modeling difficulty increases significantly [42]. A further challenge arises from the fact that environmental and vehicle conditions for the model are continuously changing. How to quickly adjust the virtual model to reflect these changes is a major problem in technical implementation. This involves not only the model to be fit with substantial input data, but also that the algorithm can execute rapid decisions and predictions.

Cost-Effectiveness: DTs have high initial investment and maintenance costs in the deployment of EVs [17]. First of all, the implementation of DTs requires not only the purchase of high-performance hardware equipment but also investment in software development and system integration. In addition, the update and maintenance of these technologies is also a factor that demands a significant amount of financial investment. However, companies need to consider the long-term benefits of DT technology for EVs. Therefore, it is necessary to comprehensively evaluate its long-term returns and initial costs to make the application of DT technology in the EV industry more extensive and economical.

Privacy and Security: In EVs the convergence of DTs with Internet of Things requires assimilation, analytics and storage which are required in large volume for handling vehicle-related data along segment user related data. This results in the data being vulnerable during transmission, while hackers could take over or steal any information through cyberattacks. Therefore, strict data protection policies and technical solutions should be established. These technologies include encryption, access controls and real-time security monitoring systems.

5 Conclusions

Currently, DT is recognized as one of the most promising technology. From research and development to operation, integrating DT into EVs can pave the way for efficient and sustainable development of EVs. This paper starts by presenting the evolution of DT concept, and then it reviews its applications in different areas with a focus on the application of DT in EV battery management systems, vehicle health detection and management, and propulsion drive systems. Moreover, it elaborates the issues such as model complexity, cost-effectiveness faced by DT in EV applications. This paper hopes to offer a fundamental technical guideline for the innovation and development of DT technology in EVs in the future.

References

1. Bhatti, G., Mohan, H., Singh, R.R.: Towards the future of smart electric vehicles: digital twin technology. Renew. Sustain. Energy Rev. **141**, 110801 (2021)
2. Lü, X., Yinbo, W., Lian, J.: Energy management of hybrid electric vehicles: a review of energy optimization of fuel cell hybrid power system based on genetic algorithm. Energy Convers. Manage. **205**, 112474 (2020)
3. Deng, S., Ling, L.: A systematic review on the current research of digital twin in automotive application. Internet Things Cyber-Phys. Syst. **3**, 180–191 (2023)
4. AlZohbi, G.: An overview on electric vehicles. In: Smart Electric and Hybrid Vehicles: Fundamentals, Strategies and Applications, p. 1 (2024)
5. Rajesh, P.K., Soundarya, T., Jithin, K.V.: Driving sustainability - the role of digital twin in enhancing battery performance for electric vehicles. J. Power Sour. **604**, 234464 (2024)
6. Electric vehicles standards: charging infrastructure, and impact on grid integration: a technological review. Renew. Sustain. Energy Rev. **120**, 109618 (2020)
7. Sanguesa, J.A., Torres-Sanz, V., Garrido, P.: A review on electric vehicles: technologies and challenges. Smart Cities **4**(1), 372–404 (2021)
8. Ibrahim, M., Rassõlkin, A.: Overview on digital twin for autonomous electrical vehicles propulsion drive system. Sustainability **14**(2) (2022)
9. Lee, J., Bagheri, B., Kao, H.A.: A cyber-physical systems architecture for industry 4.0-based manufacturing systems. Manuf. Lett. **3**, 18–23 (2015)
10. Shikata, H., Yamashita, T.: Digital twin environment to integrate vehicle simulation and physical verification. SEI Tech. Rev. **88**, 18–21 (2019)
11. Glaessgen, E., Stargel, D.: The digital twin paradigm for future NASA and US air force vehicles. In: 53rd AIAA/ASME/ASCE/AHS/ASC Structures, Structural Dynamics and Materials Conference 20th AIAA/ASME/AHS Adaptive Structures Conference 14th AIAA, p. 1818 (2012)
12. Naseri, F., Gil, S., Barbu, C.: Digital twin of electric vehicle battery systems: comprehensive review of the use cases, requirements, and platforms. Renew. Sustain. Energy Rev. **179**, 113280 (2023)
13. Zhongxu, H., Lou, S., Xing, Y.: Review and perspectives on driver digital twin and its enabling technologies for intelligent vehicles. IEEE Trans. Intell. Veh. **7**(3), 417–440 (2022)
14. Tao, F., Zhang, H., Liu, A., Nee, A.Y.C.: Digital twin in industry: state-of-the-art. IEEE Trans. Industr. Inform. **15**(4), 2405–2415 (2019)

15. Tao, F., Xiao, B., Qi, Q., Cheng, J.: Digital twin modeling. J. Manuf. Syst. **64**, 372–389 (2022)
16. Sarwatt, D.S., Lin, Y., Ding, J., Sun, Y., Ning, H.: Metaverse for intelligent transportation systems (ITS): a comprehensive review of technologies, applications, implications, challenges and future directions. IEEE Trans. Intell. Transp. Syst. **25**(7), 6290–6308 (2024)
17. Liu, M., Fang, S.: Review of digital twin about concepts, technologies, and industrial applications. J. Manuf. Syst. **58**, 346–361 (2021). Digital Twin towards Smart Manufacturing and Industry 4.0
18. Thelen, A., Zhang, X., Fink, O., Yan, L., Ghosh, S.: A comprehensive review of digital twin–part 1: modeling and twinning enabling technologies. Struct. Multidiscip. Optim. **65**(12), 354 (2022)
19. Yang, W., Zheng, Y., Li, S.: Application status and prospect of digital twin for on-orbit spacecraft. IEEE Access **9**, 106489–106500 (2021)
20. Opoku, J., Perera, S.: Digital twin application in the construction industry: a literature review. J. Build. Eng. **40**, 102726 (2021)
21. Fuller, A., Fan, Z., Day, C., Barlow, C.: Digital twin: enabling technologies, challenges and open research. IEEE Access **8**, 108952–108971 (2020)
22. Mylonas, G., Kalogeras, A.: Digital twins from smart manufacturing to smart cities: a survey. IEEE Access **9**, 143222–143249 (2021)
23. Jafari, S., Byun, Y.-C.: Prediction of the battery state using the digital twin framework based on the battery management system. IEEE Access **10**, 124685–124696 (2022)
24. Parra, R.V., Pothureddy, G., Sanitas, T., Krishnamoorthy, V., Oluwafemi, O.: Digital twin-driven framework for EV batteries in automobile manufacturing. In: Transdisciplinary Engineering for Resilience: Responding to System Disruptions, pp. 181–190. IOS Press (2021)
25. Venturini, S., Rosso, C., Velardocchia, M.: An automotive steel wheel digital twin for failure identification under accelerated fatigue tests. Eng. Fail. Anal. **158**, 107979 (2024)
26. Söderberg, R.: Toward a digital twin for real-time geometry assurance in individualized production. CIRP Ann. **66**(1), 137–140 (2017)
27. Xu, Z., Jun, X., Guo, Z., Wang, H., Sun, Z., Mei, X.: Design and optimization of a novel microchannel battery thermal management system based on digital twin. Energies **15**(4), 1421 (2022)
28. Ezhilarasu, C.M.: The application of reasoning to aerospace integrated vehicle health management (IVHM): challenges and opportunities. Prog. Aerosp. Sci. **105**, 60–73 (2019)
29. Redding, L.: An introduction to integrated vehicle health management. In: Integrated Vehicle Health Management: Perspectives on an Emerging Field, p. 17 (2011)
30. Madni, A.M., Madni, C.C., Lucero, S.D.: Leveraging digital twin technology in model-based systems engineering. Systems **7**(1), 7 (2019)
31. Loureiro, R., Benmoussa, S.: Integration of fault diagnosis and fault-tolerant control for health monitoring of a class of MIMO intelligent autonomous vehicles. IEEE Trans. Veh. Technol. **63**(1), 30–39 (2014)
32. Gritli, Y., Rossi, C., Casadei, D., Zarri, L.: Demagnetizations diagnosis for permanent magnet synchronous motors based on advanced wavelet analysis. In: 2012 XXth International Conference on Electrical Machines, pp. 2397–2403 (2012)

33. Al-Timimy, A., Al-Ani, M., Degano, M., Giangrande, P., Gerada, C.: Influence of rotor endcaps on the electromagnetic performance of high-speed pm machine. IET Electr. Power Appl. **12**(8), 1142–1149 (2018)
34. Zeng, C., Huang, S., Yang, Y., Dun, W.: Inter-turn fault diagnosis of permanent magnet synchronous machine based on tooth magnetic flux analysis. IET Electr. Power Appl. **12**(6), 837–844 (2018)
35. Tao, F., Zhang, M., Liu, Y.: Digital twin driven prognostics and health management for complex equipment. CIRP Ann. **67**(1), 169–172 (2018)
36. Venkatesan, S., Manickavasagam, K.: Health monitoring and prognosis of electric vehicle motor using intelligent-digital twin. IET Electr. Power Appl. **13**(9), 1328–1335 (2019)
37. Ezhilarasu, C.M.:. Understanding the role of a digital twin in integrated vehicle health management (IVHM). In: 2019 IEEE International Conference on Systems, Man and Cybernetics (SMC), pp. 1484–1491 (2019)
38. Dygalo, V., Keller, A.: Principles of application of virtual and physical simulation technology in production of digital twin of active vehicle safety systems. Transp. Res. Procedia **50**, 121–129 (2020). XIV International Conference on Organization and Traffic Safety Management in Large Cities
39. Wu, C., Zhou, Y., Pessôa, M.V.P.: Conceptual digital twin modeling based on an integrated five-dimensional framework and TRIZ function model. J. Manuf. Syst. **58**, 79–93 (2021). Digital Twin towards Smart Manufacturing and Industry 4.0
40. Kamran, S.S., Haleem, A.: Role of smart materials and digital twin (DT) for the adoption of electric vehicles in India. Mater. Today: Proc. **52**, 2295–2304 (2022). International Conference on Advances in Mechanical Engineering: Transcending Boundaries-2021
41. Eaty, N.D.K.M., Bagade, P.: Digital twin for electric vehicle battery management with incremental learning. Expert Syst. Appl. **229**, 120444 (2023)
42. Li, X., Niu, W., Tian, H.: Application of digital twin in electric vehicle powertrain: a review. World Electr. Veh. J. **15**(5), 208 (2024)

Optimization of Orderly Charging Strategy of Electric Vehicles Based on GWO Algorithm

Shaokui Yan[1(✉)], Haili Ding[1], Fei Peng[2], Yuanfeng Zhou[1], and Ting Hu[1]

[1] State Grid Ningxia Marketing Services Center (State Grid Ningxia Metrology Center), Yinchuan 750002, China
sk.y@qq.com
[2] CET Shandong Electronic Co., Ltd., Jinan 250109, China

Abstract. Recently, the rapid increase in electric vehicles (EVs) has significantly raised their integration into the power grid. This overlap between EV charging times and daily routines has created 'peaks upon peaks,' exerting substantial pressure on distribution networks. Therefore, shifting EV charging loads to off-peak periods is essential. The existing time-of-use (TOU) static pricing is no longer suitable for current demands, leading to the introduction of a dynamic pricing mechanism. EV charging demand is highly adjustable yet unpredictable, necessitating the proposal of a compliance incentive coefficient. Based on this, a dual-objective function is established, aiming to minimize charging costs and the grid load peak-valley difference, thereby enhancing the predictability and controllability of the charging load. The existing Particle Swarm Optimization (PSO) algorithm faces issues with global search capability and convergence speed. To address these shortcomings, the Grey Wolf Optimization (GWO) algorithm is proposed. This algorithm can achieve an orderly charging strategy for EVs under dual constraints, effectively reducing user charging costs and minimizing the grid's peak-valley difference, successfully achieving the goal of peak shaving and valley filling.

Keywords: Electric Vehicles · Dynamic Pricing Mechanism · GWO Algorithm · Optimization Strategy · Orderly Charging

1 Introduction

The significant environmental and energy impacts of fuel-powered vehicles have driven increased research and development of green, clean, and efficient new energy vehicles [1–3]. Electric vehicles (EVs) are powered by onboard batteries [4] and integrate various technologies [5]. They offer high energy efficiency, environmental benefits, and low noise, making them essential devices for achieving cleaner energy [6]. Additionally, EVs have the advantages of low maintenance costs and simple operation. The electricity supply is diverse and controllable, with the ability to harness wind, solar, hydro, and nuclear power as clean energy sources [7], thereby reducing fossil fuel consumption and alleviating the pressure on fossil fuel supplies. Although EVs do not produce exhaust emissions during operation, their development has brought about some potential challenges. For example, large-scale EV charging can place a significant load on the power grid. Since charging times often overlap with people's work and daily routines, this can easily lead to the stacking of peak loads, putting tremendous pressure on the distribution network and causing a series of problems [8, 9]. To meet peak demand, the grid requires higher capacity, which is not conducive to the economic and sustainable development of the power grid. Therefore, optimizing EV charging scheduling has become a critical issue. Researchers have tackled this issue from two perspectives: the power supply side and the consumer side.

First, the power supply side focuses on power capacity and stability. In [10], an optimal EV charging scheduling strategy based on power supply capacity constraints is proposed. The strategy uses integer linear programming and genetic algorithms to maximize the satisfaction of charging demand while efficiently utilizing power supply capacity. However, using integer linear programming to solve large-scale problems is often time-consuming and complex. In [11], an optimization method based on a genetic algorithm is proposed for EV charging facility layout, which contributes to exploring economically efficient charging services and balancing grid loads. Although the effectiveness of the algorithm is validated, the impact of centralized charging on load was not fully analyzed. In [12], an optimization method combining a priority algorithm and a particle swarm optimization algorithm is proposed to address EV charging scheduling in microgrid environments that involve different charging scenarios across multiple time periods. The study considers multiple objectives, including grid operating costs, charging time, and battery life, and simulation results demonstrate the effectiveness of this method in reducing charging costs and extending battery life. This research provides valuable references for EV charging scheduling strategies in microgrid environments. However, relying solely on grid construction to solve EV charging issues is costly, challenging, and requires a long time. In [13], a linear programming method is used to model charging demand as an optimization problem that maximizes total charging volume, constrained by power supply capacity, to achieve sustainability and stability in power supply. However, linear programming may not effectively handle nonlinear and dynamic power supply constraints, limiting the accuracy and applicability of the model. In [14], a model is developed to analyze and optimize the flexibility of EV charging and discharging, aiming to minimize the operating costs of the power network. Similarly, in [15], an optimization scheduling model for charging stations is established, with the objective of maximizing total charging volume while adhering to power supply capacity constraints. These studies analyze and optimize from the perspective of grid operational efficiency, but they insufficiently consider the impact of user electricity consumption characteristics on scheduling.

Second, from the perspective of electricity consumers, [16] studies the impact of driving distance, time, and charging costs on consumers' choice of target charging stations. Additionally, due to differences in congestion levels at various charging stations, there is an imbalance between unit time profit and equipment utilization. In [17], an orderly charging and discharging strategy based on demand-side management is proposed to address the load fluctuations caused by large-scale EV integration into the grid.

The study also analyzes the spatiotemporal characteristics of EV charging loads and constructs a charging demand model considering electricity user preferences. However, the research primarily focuses on optimizing users' charging routes, with limited consideration of the impact of these routes on charging station loads. In [18], an EV group charging optimization method based on an improved particle swarm optimization (PSO) algorithm is proposed. The improvements to the traditional PSO algorithm enhance convergence speed and global search capability. Simulation experiments verify the effectiveness of the improved PSO algorithm in optimizing EV group charging, showing that the method can effectively reduce charging costs and mitigate the impact on the power grid. However, the study's scope is relatively limited, focusing mainly on specific charging scenarios and parameter settings, lacking verification for broader application scenarios. Moreover, the modeling of EV charging behavior in the study involves certain simplifying assumptions, failing to fully account for various uncertainties in the actual charging process, and lacks comparative analysis with other advanced optimization algorithms. In [19], the impact of EV integration on the distribution network is explored using probabilistic load flow calculation methods. The study analyzes the impact of EV charging behavior on the grid's acceptance capacity and the power system. Using the Monte Carlo method and a typical IEEE33 node distribution system as an example, the impact of EV charging loads on the distribution network under different penetration rates and integration methods is simulated. Furthermore, [20] proposes an EV charging load forecasting method that considers spatiotemporal distribution, conducting scheduling across time and space dimensions. By analyzing EV charging behavior in these two dimensions, a load forecasting model is established. This method helps accurately predict EV charging loads, optimizing the operation of the distribution network.

Most of the studies mentioned above focus primarily on either the supplier or the consumer side, which is not comprehensive for constructing orderly charging strategies. Therefore, some scholars have begun to explore the combined consideration of both suppliers and consumers for orderly charging. In [21], an orderly charging strategy for EVs based on time-of-use pricing is proposed. By designing a reasonable pricing mechanism, users are encouraged to charge during off-peak hours, thereby achieving peak load reduction. This strategy can effectively reduce grid load pressure and lower user charging costs. [22] proposes an EV charging load forecasting method based on user profiling, analyzing user behavior characteristics and charging habits to construct user profiles and improve load forecasting accuracy. The study's findings are of significant importance for intelligent charging management and grid planning. In [23], an orderly EV charging and discharging strategy based on particle swarm optimization (PSO) is proposed, using a two-stage optimization process to improve the orderliness of EV charging and the stability of the grid. This study provides a new solution for EV charging management, but the algorithm is prone to local optimization, leading to suboptimal results.

Therefore, based on the above research, this paper simultaneously considers two objective functions: minimizing charging costs and minimizing the peak-to-valley difference in grid load. This approach ensures that the charging strategy is not only cost-effective but also reduces grid load fluctuations. A dynamic pricing mechanism is also proposed, which, unlike traditional fixed time-of-use pricing (e.g., peak-valley pricing), adjusts prices in real-time based on the grid's real-time load, market electricity prices, and other influencing factors (such as weather conditions). This allows prices to flexibly change throughout the day. Through this dynamic pricing mechanism, EV users can be effectively guided to charge during off-peak periods, achieving the dual goals of reducing charging costs and minimizing the peak-to-valley difference in grid load. Additionally, by setting an economic incentive coefficient, users are encouraged to charge during periods of lower prices, increasing their responsiveness to scheduling. The effectiveness of this strategy is compared with uncontrolled charging to analyze its effectiveness.

2 EV Charging Load Modeling

2.1 Analysis of EV User Charging Behavior

EV users' charging behavior depends entirely on their habits. However, work and daily routines cause this behavior to follow certain patterns. Three main factors influence this behavior: charging start time, charging duration, and charging amount. Referring to the 2017 National Household Travel Survey (NHTS) in the United States, fuel-powered vehicles and EVs are typically used for commuting and leisure travel. Therefore, the general usage habits of these vehicles are similar, making the reference data highly relevant.

Charging Start Time. According to the NHTS survey of family cars, the probability distribution of electric vehicle users to start charging after they finish their daily work on weekdays is obtained, that is, the peak time is from 15:00 to 22:00. It can be assumed that the user charges immediately after returning home, and the probability distribution diagram of the charging time of the electric vehicle can be fitted (Fig. 1):

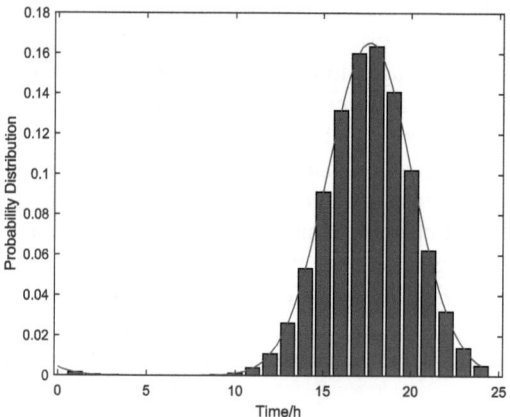

Fig. 1. Fitting diagram of the moment when an EV user starts charging

Based on the above analysis, the distribution of the start time for charging services can be represented by a normal distribution:

$$f(T_r) = \begin{cases} \frac{1}{\sqrt{2\pi}\sigma_r} \exp[-\frac{(T_r-\mu_r)^2}{2\sigma_r^2}], \mu_r - 12 < T_r \leq 24 \\ \frac{1}{\sqrt{2\pi}\sigma_r} \exp[-\frac{(T_r+24-\mu_r)^2}{2\sigma_r^2}], 0 < T \leq \mu_r - 12 \end{cases} \quad (1)$$

In the equation, μ_r and δ_r represent the expected value and standard deviation of the function, respectively, while t denotes the start time of charging. The start time for charging a home electric vehicle follows a normal distribution, $N(17.6, 3.4^2)$.

Charging Duration. The charging time of an EV is closely related to its daily driving distance. By analyzing the daily driving distance, the following probability distribution is obtained (Fig. 2):

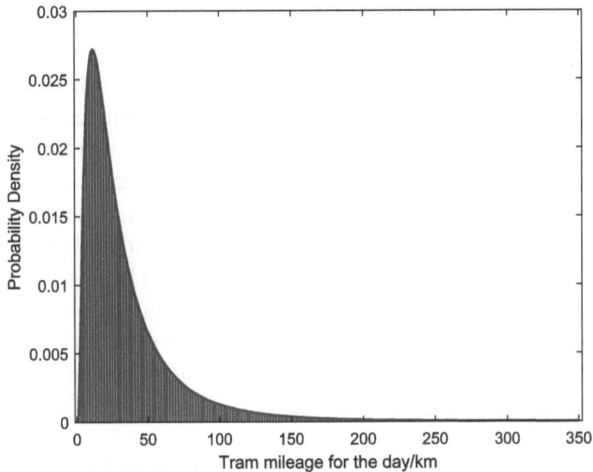

Fig. 2. Probability distribution of the daily distance traveled by a car

Since the driving habits of EVs are similar to those of fuel-powered vehicles, Fig. 3 can be used to simulate the driving distance of EVs. Based on this analysis, the daily driving distance f_L of an EV can be represented by a normal distribution, with the following distribution pattern:

$$f_L(x) = \frac{1}{x\sigma_D\sqrt{2\pi}} \exp[-\frac{(\ln x - \mu_D)^2}{2\sigma_D^2}] \quad (2)$$

The charging duration is:

$$T_c = \frac{WL}{100P_c} \quad (3)$$

where: $\mu_D = 3.20$, $\delta_D = 0.88$.

The following assumptions are made for the charging duration model:
The power consumption per 100 km is W.
The daily driving distance is L kilometers.
The charging power is P_c.
Through a series of calculations, W is found to be 17 kWh.

Charging Amount. The current EV charging environment is still underdeveloped, with a limited number of charging facilities and remote locations, which affects user charging behavior. Users typically do not wait until the battery is completely depleted ($SOC = 0$) to charge, nor do they overcharge, which could damage the battery. In real-world scenarios, due to time constraints or other reasons, users may leave the charging station before the battery is fully charged to 100%. For simplicity in this model, it is assumed that users charge the battery to an ideal state.

2.2 Dynamic Pricing Mechanism

In China, a common economic management strategy for electricity demand is the Time-of-Use (TOU) pricing system. This system, based on the grid load curve, divides the day into peak, mid-peak, and off-peak periods to regulate electricity consumption behavior. For these three periods, power companies set different pricing standards, aiming to guide electricity users to plan their consumption more rationally and adjust their usage patterns. This approach effectively mobilizes user participation, enhancing the stability of the entire power system with minimal modifications to the grid infrastructure. Although static TOU pricing has segmented periods, it does not adjust further, while basic electricity demand frequently fluctuates due to various external factors. Consequently, electricity demand often deviates from the initially set pricing intervals, leading to potential conflicts. Some studies propose a multi-period TOU pricing adjustment strategy based on day-ahead load forecasting to address these issues. Specifically, adjustment coefficients are added during peak and off-peak periods.

However, these adjustment coefficients are predetermined based on the composite conditions of the power system and primarily aim to guide user charging behavior by adjusting prices within fixed periods, thereby smoothing the grid load curve. While the multi-period TOU pricing introduces adjustment coefficients and improves upon traditional TOU pricing, its flexibility remains limited compared to dynamic pricing. It still relies on preset time intervals and prices, unable to adjust prices in real-time to respond to sudden load fluctuations or market price changes. Therefore, this paper proposes a more refined and real-time pricing control strategy: the Dynamic Pricing Mechanism (DPM).

The Dynamic Pricing Mechanism effectively optimizes electricity resource utilization and alleviates grid stress in managing EV charging loads.

Dynamic Pricing Model. The Dynamic Pricing Mechanism's core is a well-designed pricing model that reflects real-time electricity supply and demand conditions. This study adopts a dynamic pricing model based on load levels and market prices, expressed as follows:

$$C_t = C_{\text{base}} + \alpha L(t) + \beta M(t) \tag{4}$$

Where:

C_t is the electricity price at time t;
C_{base} is the base price, usually the minimum guaranteed price;
$L(t)$ represents the grid load at time t;
$M(t)$ represents the market electricity price at time t;
α and β are the weighting coefficients for load level and market price, reflecting the grid's sensitivity to these factors.

Impact of Grid Load. The grid load level $L(t)$ is a critical factor influencing dynamic pricing. when the grid load is high, the price will increase accordingly to suppress excessive charging demand and reduce grid load; when the grid load is low, the price will decrease to encourage users to charge during these periods, balancing the grid load. By adjusting the coefficient A, the responsiveness of the price to load levels can be controlled flexibly.

$$C_t = C_{base} + \alpha(\frac{L(t) - L_{min}}{L_{max} - L_{min}}) \tag{5}$$

Where L_{max} and L_{min} represent the maximum and minimum load in a day, respectively.

Impact of Market Prices. Market electricity price $M(t)$ reflects the supply and demand situation in the electricity market. When there is a shortage of electricity, market prices are usually high; when the supply is sufficient, prices are lower. Through the coefficient B in the dynamic pricing model, prices can fluctuate with market prices, encouraging users to charge during lower-priced periods, thereby reducing charging costs.

$$C_t = C_{base} + \beta(\frac{M(t) - M_{min}}{M_{max} - M_{min}}) \tag{6}$$

where M_{max} and M_{min} represent the highest and lowest market prices in a day, respectively

Comprehensive Dynamic Pricing Model. The final dynamic price can be derived by integrating both load levels and market prices into a more flexible pricing model:

$$C(t) = C_{base} + \alpha(\frac{L(t) - L_{min}}{L_{max} - L_{min}}) + \beta(\frac{M(t) - M_{min}}{M_{max} - M_{min}}) \tag{7}$$

Using the above formula, EV charging behavior can be optimally scheduled, guiding users to choose appropriate charging times to reduce costs and minimize grid load fluctuations. Additionally, this model can flexibly adapt to different power system environments, demonstrating strong practicality.

2.3 A Subsection Sample

As the number of electric vehicles grows, their charging behavior becomes more regular and can be predicted through stochastic simulation. Monte Carlo Simulation (MCS) is a tool that combines probability theory to analyze variables and construct probability distribution functions.

Assuming users start charging as soon as they return home from work. First, the factors influencing charging behavior are identified based on statistical data; then, random sampling is conducted through Monte Carlo simulation to initialize parameters. Next, these parameters are substituted into calculations to determine the charging duration for each vehicle; finally, the total charging load demand is obtained by summing the number of EVs charging in each period and multiplying by the charging power.

For instance, in a simulation using the Xiaomi SU7 standard version, which can travel 7.5 km per kWh, users start charging before the battery is fully depleted ($SOC = 0$), and overcharging is avoided to ensure battery lifecycle and safety.

Thus,

$$S_{soc=0\%} \leq S \leq S_{soc=100\%} \tag{8}$$

In real scenarios, users may leave the charging station before their vehicle is fully charged. Therefore, this model assumes that in practice, $SOC_{min} = 0.2$ and $SOC_{max} = 0.9$.

In Monte Carlo simulation, it is necessary to identify factors influencing charging behavior, such as daily travel needs, charging station distribution, and the number of charging piles. These factors determine charging demand and timing. Through statistical analysis, average daily mileage, average charging volume, and average charging time can be obtained as input variables for random sampling in the Monte Carlo simulation. The simulation results show that EV charging loads have distinct peak periods, typically concentrated after users return from work. As the number of EVs rapidly increases, charging loads rise, but due to the diversity of user charging behavior, peak loads become somewhat dispersed. The power system must adjust and optimize according to changing charging load trends to ensure stable grid operation.

3 Orderly Charging Strategy for Electric Vehicles Based on Dynamic Pricing Mechanism

3.1 Minimum Cost Model for Electric Vehicle Charging

The primary goal for EV users is to minimize charging costs.

Assume that during time period t, the charging station charges X_t electric vehicles. The latest start time for charging is given by:

$$T_i = \frac{T_{end,i}}{\Delta t} \tag{9}$$

where:

$T_{end,i}$ refers to the time when electric vehicle i finishes charging.

$\Delta t = 1$ indicates the duration of a time unit, where a day is divided into 24 segments.

The objective function to minimize the charging cost for user i is:

$$\min f_i = \sum_{i+1}^{T_i} P_r \Delta t C_t X_{i,t} \tag{10}$$

The overall objective function for minimizing the charging cost of all users is:

$$\min F = \sum_{i+1}^{T_i} f_i \qquad (11)$$

where:
f_i represents the charging cost for user i;
P_r represents the rated output power of the charging pile;
C_t is the electricity price at time t;
$X_{i,t}$ is a binary variable indicating whether user i is charging at time t (1 for charging, 0 for not charging).

EV users must adhere to the following constraints:

(1) Load Constraint:

$$\sum_{i=0}^{N} P_r X_{i,t} \le P_{max}, t = 1, 2, 3, \ldots, 48 \qquad (12)$$

(2) Charging Duration:

$$(T_{end,i} - T_{st,i}) \ge \frac{(SOC_{end,i} - SOC_{st,i})B}{P_r}, i = 1, 2, 3, \ldots, N \qquad (13)$$

(3) Charging Demand Constraint:

$$B \cdot SOC_{end,i} \le B \cdot SOC_{st,i} + \sum_{t=1}^{T_i} P_r X_{i,t} \Delta t \qquad (14)$$

where:
P_{max} is the maximum load the charging pile can provide;
$T_{end,i}$ is the time when user i finishes charging;
$T_{st,i}$ is the time when user i starts charging;
$SOC_{end,i}$ is the target state of charge after charging for user I;
$SOC_{st,i}$ is the initial state of charge before charging for user I;
B is the battery capacity.

Thus, within the framework of the smart grid, we can construct an orderly charging management model for electric vehicles. This model effectively collects various charging data from electric vehicles and performs detailed calculations with the objective of minimizing the charging cost, as represented by Eq. (11). Eventually, we will derive a strategy that can guide electric vehicle users to charge in an orderly manner.

3.2 Minimum Peak-To-Valley Difference Model for the Grid

Since there is no regular pattern in user charging behavior, and the number of charging users is vast, this can lead to an increase in the peak-to-valley difference in the grid, which in turn increases operational losses and affects the stability of the power system.

Therefore, while minimizing charging costs for users, we also need to ensure the smoothness of the load curve. This means that, besides pursuing the lowest charging cost, we should also minimize the peak-to-valley difference in the load curve as an important optimization goal.

The objective function is:

$$\min P = \max P_{(t)} - \min P_{(t)} \quad (15)$$

Subject to:

$$P_t = P_{0,t} + P_{EV,t} \quad (16)$$

$$P_{EV,t} = \sum_{i=1}^{N} P_r X_{i,t} \quad (17)$$

where:

$P_{0,t}$ is the original load on the grid during time period t;
$P_{EV,t}$ represents the load caused by user charging behavior during time period t;
P_r refers to the rated output power of the charging pile.

These three formulas are crucial for effectively guiding electric vehicle users' charging behavior and reducing the peak-to-valley difference in the grid load.

3.3 Orderly Charging Strategy Based on the Compliance Incentive Coefficient in the Dynamic Pricing Mechanism

Since users incur time costs and effort when shifting their charging time and location, the above model lacks flexibility. To maximize user compliance with scheduling, this paper adds a compliance incentive coefficient to the existing model.

Unlike general residential electricity use, the charging demand of electric vehicle users is highly adjustable and predictable. Users can determine when and how much to charge based on the battery status of their EV. Therefore, a reservation system is introduced, where users can reserve charging times based on their battery status and available time. This behavior will be rewarded with additional incentives, called compliance rewards.

The introduction of the compliance incentive coefficient not only helps smooth the grid load curve and improve the planning of power system operations but also provides users with a more complete and user-friendly service.

Compliance Incentive Coefficient. The compliance incentive coefficient encourages users to participate in grid stability strategies. If users charge within their reserved time slots, they will receive a compliance reward, calculated as follows:

$$C_t = (1 + \delta) C_c \quad (18)$$

where:

C_t is the compliance incentive price;
C_c is the peak-valley price for the time period;
δ is the compliance incentive coefficient.

Since this behavior is intended to encourage users to actively participate, no penalty coefficient for non-compliance is set. Therefore, the compliance incentive coefficient should be attractive enough to motivate users to comply.

Usually, users are discouraged from charging during peak periods, so the compliance incentive coefficient δ_p during peak periods is set to 0. Users charging during this time not only receive no reward, but also face the highest electricity prices, encouraging them to avoid peak period charging. Charging during normal periods can earn users a small reward, $\delta_n = 0$, but the incentive coefficient is small. To attract users to charge during off-peak periods, $\delta_v > \delta_n$, offering a higher incentive coefficient to better fulfill the charging agreement.

This strategy also addresses the issue of forming a "new peak" during off-peak periods. Its existence can reduce user queuing time, maximize the utilization of charging piles, reduce idle time, and improve charging efficiency.

Charging Reservation. Charging reservations are determined by the user's own needs, allowing the electricity provider to make reasonable arrangements. As mentioned in Sect. 1.1, charging user behavior includes three main factors: the start time of charging, the duration of charging, and the amount of charging. Therefore, when making a charging reservation, the user should provide the charging time window and the expected minimum and maximum charging amounts. The charging duration can be expressed as:

$$t_{n\min} = \frac{W_{n\min}}{P_r} \tag{19}$$

$$t_{n\max} = \frac{W_{n\max}}{P_r} \tag{20}$$

where:

P_r is the rated output power of the charging pile,

$W_{n\min}$ and $W_{n\max}$ are the user's expected minimum and maximum charging amounts.

In this model, users are discouraged from charging during peak periods. Therefore, the electricity provider can offer optimal solutions, suggesting users charge at other times and providing some rewards. If the user is unwilling to change due to personal reasons, despite the impact on the grid load, the advance knowledge allows for responsive measures, which is beneficial for overall grid management.

For users who charge during non-peak periods within their reserved time slots, higher rewards are provided to encourage off-peak charging. In this scenario:

$$\delta_p \ll \delta_n \leq \delta_v \tag{21}$$

In the context of a smart grid, it is possible to predict the charging load in future periods and calculate it synchronously with the charging reservation, preventing significant fluctuations in the load curve.

3.4 Grey Wolf Optimization Algorithm

The Grey Wolf Optimization (GWO) algorithm [24] plays a crucial role in orderly power usage strategies, especially in EV charging management. It can optimize two main objectives: minimizing charging costs and minimizing the peak-to-valley difference in the grid load. Both of these objectives are crucial for the stable operation of the power system and for economic benefits.

Firstly, minimizing charging costs is the primary consideration for users when selecting charging times and locations. EV users generally prefer charging during low-cost periods to minimize expenses. However, if this behavior is not properly guided, it could lead to a concentration of charging demand during specific periods, thereby undermining grid stability. The GWO algorithm simulates the hunting behavior of grey wolves, where each position in the search space represents a potential charging strategy, and the strategy with the lowest charging cost is considered the "prey." The algorithm continuously updates the wolves' positions (i.e., charging costs) to gradually approach this optimal solution.

Secondly, minimizing the peak-to-valley difference in the grid load is key to the stable operation of the power system. The GWO algorithm can optimize charging strategies by dynamically adjusting EV charging schedules based on the real-time load of the grid. This reduces charging loads during peak periods and encourages EV charging during low-load periods. Such optimization not only helps balance the grid load but also extends the lifespan of power equipment, reducing maintenance and replacement costs.

To meet these two objectives, they are combined into a multi-objective optimization problem, solved using the GWO algorithm. The algorithm introduces a weighting factor to balance the relative importance of these two objectives, ensuring grid stability while meeting user needs. In this way, the GWO algorithm not only enhances the efficiency of charging management but also improves the economic benefits and operational reliability of the grid.

In conclusion, the Grey Wolf Optimization algorithm has significant application value in orderly power usage strategies. By optimizing charging strategies, it can achieve the goals of minimizing charging costs and the peak-to-valley difference in the grid load, thereby improving the stability and economic efficiency of the power system.

4 Case Analysis

4.1 Data and Parameter Settings

Assume there are 330 electric vehicles in this community. The Xiaomi SU7 model is used as a simulation object, with a battery capacity of approximately 75 kWh. The rate at which the electric vehicle discharges power is 12 kW, and the charging power, which is the rate at which external energy is stored in the battery, is also 12 kW. The desired state of charge (SOC) for the electric vehicle is 0.9, meaning the battery is expected to be charged to 90% of its capacity. In real-world scenarios, charging users often leave the charging station before reaching their ideal charge level, so this model assumes that $SOC_{min} = 0.2$ and $SOC_{max} = 0.9$. The day is divided into 24 periods for the study.

In the Grey Wolf Optimization algorithm, the parameters are set as follows: a pack size of 650 and 500 iterations. The MatPower software package in Matlab, specifically Case33bw, is used, with 33 nodes loaded as input data. This package provides information such as node data, branch data, generator data, and load data for the power system. These data are loaded into the code for load flow and optimal power flow calculations to find the power distribution that minimizes a particular objective function within the system.

The charging power of disorderly charging of electric vehicles in a day is obtained through simulation that most charging behaviors occur from 15:00 to 24:00. Fig. 3 shows the base load and overall load demand under uncoordinated charging, where the significant difference between base and overall load demand during peak periods is evident.

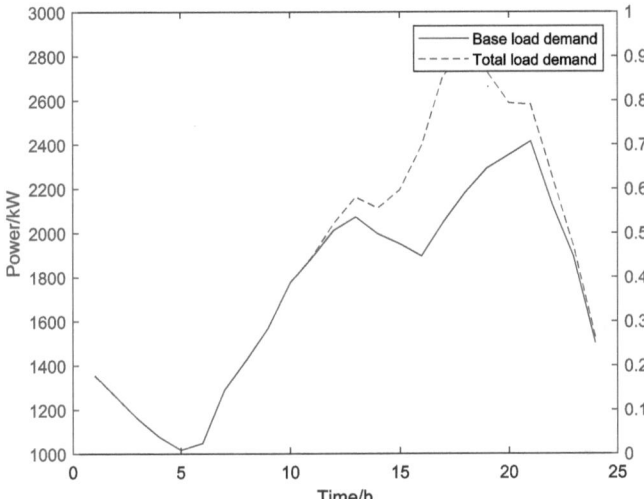

Fig. 3. Disorderly charging base load vs. total load

4.2 Analysis of Simulation Results for Coordinated Charging

Figure 4 presents a comparison between the peak-valley multi-time dynamic pricing based on the coordinated charging strategy and the original residential electricity pricing, as well as the comparison between base load demand and total load demand. From Fig. 4, it is evident that the peak-valley multi-time dynamic pricing, after applying the coordinated charging strategy, significantly improves the phenomenon of dual-peak overlap between actual load demand and base load demand. Compared to uncoordinated charging, the peak charging power decreases by approximately 14%. Additionally, the orderly charging strategy distributes the charging demand of electric vehicles reasonably to each node, and calculates the charging demand of electric vehicles at each node according to the optimal charging power distribution scheme, so that the charging power distribution is more uniform, rather than concentrating on 15:00 to 24:00. The comparison of peak and valley values, as well as electricity prices under different strategies, is shown in Table 1. This strategy significantly enhances the stability and efficiency of the power system.

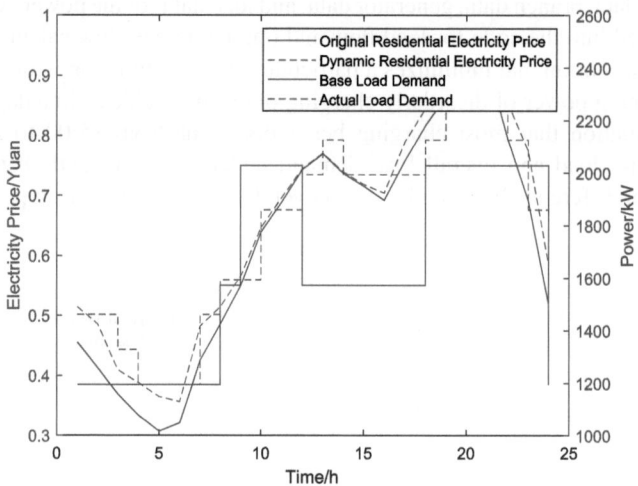

Fig. 4. Analysis of sequential charging strategies

Table 1. Comparison of peak-to-valley and electricity prices under different strategies.

Item category	Base load	Disorderly charging	Orderly charging
Peak load/Kw	2414.75	2810.8167	2452.4847
Load valley value	1016.6	1016.6	1204.3393
Load fluctuation standard deviation/Kw	432.7574	577.4169	377.3917

As shown in Table 1, simulation results show a 14% decrease in peak load and a 31% reduction in peak-valley difference. The user cost under uncoordinated charging is 1,293.74 yuan, while under the coordinated charging strategy, the user cost is reduced to 850.26 yuan, representing a 35% reduction in user costs. The results in Fig. 5 indicate that the gray wolf optimization algorithm used in this paper converges faster under the same conditions, which is more advantageous for determining the charging state. The horizontal axis represents the number of evolutions, while the vertical axis represents the objective function value.

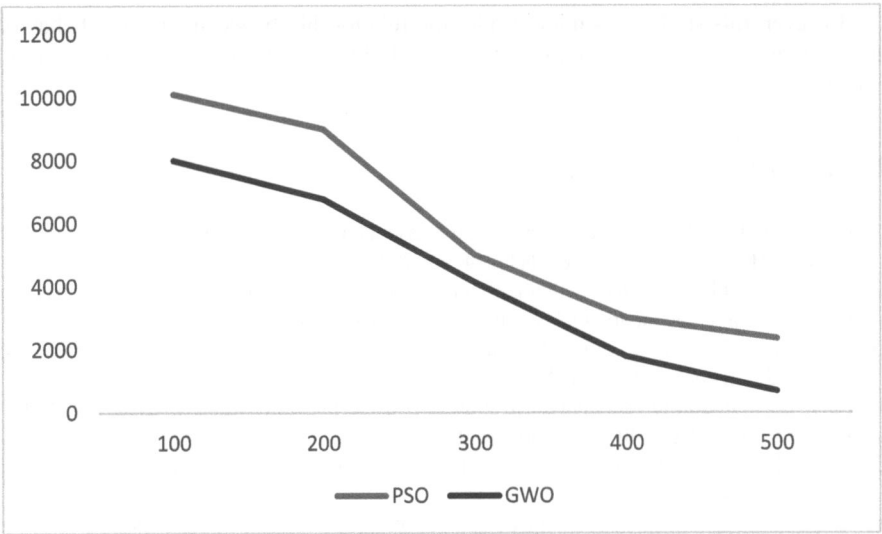

Fig. 5. PSO vs. GWO

5 Conclusion

Considering EV charging characteristics and user behavior, this study employs the Monte Carlo method to analyze user charging and daily behavior patterns. Furthermore, a peak-valley multi-time dynamic pricing strategy is proposed, guided by a time-of-use pricing strategy, and optimized using the Grey Wolf Optimization (GWO) algorithm. The load curves before and after optimization are obtained. A comprehensive analysis leads to the following conclusions:

- When electric vehicles engage in uncoordinated charging, i.e., unrestrained charging behavior, the dual-peak overlap between base load demand and total load demand is significant, which can cause a large peak-valley difference in the grid, affecting the stability of grid operation.
- By implementing a coordinated charging strategy with dual objectives of minimizing charging costs and reducing grid load peak-valley difference, dual-peak overlap is mitigated, the load curve is smoothed, grid stability is enhanced, and user charging costs are reduced by 35%.
- Compared to the Particle Swarm Optimization (PSO) algorithm, the GWO algorithm demonstrates better iteration results, improving global search capability and iteration speed.
- The peak-valley multi-time dynamic pricing mechanism is an improvement over traditional peak-valley pricing but lacks flexibility. Therefore, this study proposes a dynamic pricing mechanism, which provides more refined and real-time price regulation capabilities, suitable for addressing complex and changing power supply and demand scenarios.
- To ensure that charging users actively participate in this strategy, a compliance incentive coefficient is introduced to reduce user expenses.

However, this study does not consider the relationship between charging behavior and weather changes. In future in-depth research, introducing weather variables could make the model more universally applicable.

References

1. Connor, W.D.F.: Impact of connectivity on energy consumption and battery life for electric vehicles. IEEE Trans. Intell. Veh. **6**(1), 14–23 (2021)
2. Zhu, L.F.: Study on indirect network effects on the construction of electric vehicle charging piles based on game theory analysis. Energy Proc. **158**, 3853–3858 (2019)
3. Gao, C.F.: 2021 Electric vehicle 100 meeting: focus on new energy development pattern and industrial transformation. Auto Access. (3), 48–51 (2021)
4. Zhan, X.F.: Station-to-grid interactive strategy considering parking characteristics of electric vehicles. Smart Power **48**(9), 43–50 (2020)
5. Gan, L.F.: Optimal decentralized protocol for electric vehicle charging. IEEE Trans. Power Syst. **28**(2), 940–951 (2013)
6. Latifi, M.F.: Agent-based decentralized optimal charging strategy for plug-in electric vehicles. IEEE Trans. Ind. Elec. **66**(5), 3668–3680 (2019)
7. Zhou, J.F.: Optimal planning of wind-photovoltaic-hydrogen integrated energy system considering random charging of electric vehicles. Auto. Elec. Power Syst. **45**(24), 30–40 (2021)
8. Xin, B.F.: Research on the methodology of constructing new power systems. China Elec. Power News **001**(001), 1–18 (2023)
9. Hu, Z.F.: Impact and utilization of electric vehicles integration into power systems. Proc. CSEE **32**(4), 10 (2012)
10. Zhen, Q., Ren, B., Chi, H., Wang, W., Gao, S.: Robust optimal charging scheduling for electric vehicles considering the uncertainty of renewable energy output. In: 2023 7th International Conference on Smart Grid and Smart Cities (ICSGSC), Lanzhou, China, pp. 449–455 (2023)
11. Ling Li, F.: Layout planning of electric vehicle charging stations based on genetic algorithm. East China Elec. Power 116–119 (2011)
12. George Fernandez Savari, F.: Optimal charging scheduling of electric vehicles in micro grids using priority algorithms and particle swarm optimization. Mobile Netw. Appl. **24**(6), 1835–1847 (2019)
13. Liu, K.F.: Optimal charging strategy for large-scale electric buses considering resource constraints. Transp. Res. Part D: Transp. Environ. **99**, 103009.1–103009.18 (2021)
14. Yan, Z.F.: Research on large-scale electric vehicle charging and discharging system and its control based on MMC. North China Elec. Power Univ. (Beijing) (2018)
15. Qiwei, W.F.: Multi-objective optimal scheduling method for photovoltaic charging station of electric vehicle. 外文科技期刊数据库(文摘版)工程技术 (1), 981–984 (2021)
16. Lin, H.F.: Characteristics of electric vehicle charging demand at multiple types of location - application of an agent-based trip chain model. Energy **188**, 116122 (2019)
17. Sun, J.F.: Coordinated charging and discharging strategy for electric vehicles based on demand side management. Trans. China Electrotech. Soc. **29**(8), 64–69 (2014)
18. Wang, W.F.: Optimization method of electric vehicle group charging based on improved particle swarm optimization algorithm. Elec. Power Soc. **32**(6), 439–446 (2017)
19. Luo, Q.F.: Probabilistic load flow calculation and accommodated capacity analysis for distribution grid containing electric vehicle. Mech. Eng. **32**(11), 1498–1503 (2015)
20. Zhang, H.F.: A prediction method for electric vehicle charging load considering spatial and temporal distribution. Autom. Elec. Power Syst. **38**(1), 13–20 (2014)

21. Sun, X.F.: Coordinated charging strategy for electric vehicles based on time-of-use price. Autom. Elec. Power Syst. **37**(1), 191–195 (2013)
22. Huang, X.F.: Electric vehicle charging load forecasting method based on user portrait. J. Jilin Univ. (Engineering Science) (8), 2193–2200 (2023)
23. Zhang, L.F.: Two-stage optimization strategy for coordinated charging and discharging of EVs based on PSO algorithm. China Elec. Chin. J. Eng. **42**(5), 1837–1851 (2022)
24. Hatta, N.M., et al.: Recent studies on optimisation method of Grey Wolf Optimiser (GWO): a review (2014–2017). Artif. Intell. Rev. **52**, 2651–2683 (2019)

Optimized Global Path Planning Based on Terrain Traversability Analysis by Plane Fitting Approach

Ruiqi Ren[✉] and Zheng Zhang

College of Artificial Intelligence, Nankai University, Tianjin 300350, China
sory2008@163.com, 2120220569@mail.nankai.edu.cn

Abstract. The application of ground mobile robots in complex outdoor environments, particularly in rugged terrains, has been widely investigated to improve the capability. The terrain features significant variations in elevation, with dramatic surface undulations and diverse slope changes. In such terrain, path planning for mobile robots must balance both the distance of the path and safety considerations, and there are many safety issues that still need to be addressed. In unstructured environments, the determination of terrain traversability is crucial for generating global paths. This paper proposes a terrain traversability analysis based on Plane Fitting Rapidly-Exploring Random Trees* (PF-RRT*) to enhance the safety of ground mobile robots in outdoor terrains. The traversability metrics include sparsity and flatness of the planes containing the points along the PF-RRT* path, as well as the predicted pitch and roll angles of the mobile robot at those points. These metrics are incorporated into a cost function to assess the traversability of points along the path. The simulation results demonstrate that the proposed method could obtain safer paths with smoother velocities and has better performance compared with traditional strategies.

Keywords: intelligent system · traversability analysis · mobile robots · path planning

1 Introduction

With the rapid development of Simultaneous Localization and Mapping (SLAM) algorithms, the technology of autonomous navigation for ground mobile robots has also made significant progress. In complex outdoor 3D unstructured environments, particular in mountainous and rugged terrains, significant challenges arise for current technology. Rugged terrain is often characterized by steep slopes, irregular surfaces, obstacles, and changes in elevation, all of which make the path planning process more complex. Robots need to avoid or adapt to these obstacles during path planning to ensure safe passage. Due to the uneven ground, robots are prone to slipping, tilting, or even toppling over when navigating rugged terrain. Therefore, path planning must consider not only the shortest route but also the stability of navigation, avoiding overly steep or unstable paths. Rugged terrain places higher demands on path planning for mobile robots, affecting their safety, efficiency, and stability during navigation. In complex environments, the analysis of traversability is the fundamental prerequisite for autonomous navigation, where both safety and optimal trajectories require precise analysis of the surrounding environment information.

The goal of traversability analysis is to determine whether the robot can successfully navigate in a specific terrain and predict its performance and stability in that terrain. Traversability analysis methods can be categorized into ontology-based and external perception-based analysis methods, depending on the type of measurement data [3,7,14]. P. Abbeel [1] and X. Yao [12] used a proprioceptive perception method, where vehicles learn the difficulty of traversing different types of terrains by analyzing various sensor inputs such as vibration, wheel slippage, bumper collisions, etc. However, this approach requires a highly robust vehicle platform to handle potential failures such as tipping over or collisions. Therefore, proprioceptive perception is generally less preferred compared with external perception used for obstacle avoidance, and the traversability evaluation that can be adjusted in real complex traversal situations.

To this end, Philipp Krusi [6] represents traversability based on weighted and normalized roughness, roll angle, and pitch angle obtaining from point cloud maps. However, it does not consider the influence of sparsity on traversability, which can lead to increased risk of encountering difficult terrains or entering densely obstructed areas. Y. Tang [8] derives traversability based on the kinematic interaction between the ground and the robot using point cloud maps. Nevertheless, only the pose relationship between the robot and the ground was considered, and it does not take into account terrain flatness, sparsity, and other factors in the robot's path. H. Inotsume [4] evaluates terrain traversability based on inertial vision and predicts traversability using a multivariate Gaussian process that leverages past traversal experiences on multiple surface types. However, its feasibility has only been validated on gentle slopes. Z. Jian [5] calculates traversability based on weighted and normalized terrain flatness, sparsity, and the slope of fitted planes using point cloud maps. It lacks an analysis of the robot's posture in the path, which may lead to safety issues such as tipping. Xu [11] proposed a terrain traversability assessment method for autonomous navigation of mobile robots in unstructured outdoor environments. Xie [10] introduced a new method for local elevation mapping and traversability analysis using sparse data from a single LiDAR sensor.

However, neither of them predicted the posture of the vehicle along the trajectory, which cannot guarantee the safety of the vehicle during motion. To address these issues, this paper proposes a traversability analysis method based on Plane Fitting Rapidly-Exploring Random Trees* (PF-RRT*). This approach incorporates terrain flatness, sparsity, and predicts the pitch angle and roll angle of the ground mobile robot at fitting planes in the calculation of traversability. By weighting and normalizing these factors, the traversability of points in the path is determined. This method effectively addresses the limitations of the previous approaches and has been validated for its effectiveness through simulations. The contributions of this work can be summarized as follows: First, we present an accessible traversal analysis algorithm that considers both global factors, such as road flatness and sparsity. Moreover, some local factors, such as pitch angle and roll angle, are incorporated to improve the safety. Then, we test our algorithm in different simulation environments, and its feasibility and reliability in complex terrains are demonstrated.

2 Overview of The Framework

2.1 Problem Statement

Define S_w as the workspace, where $S_w \subset R^3$. S_{surf} represents the areas close to the ground and S_{obs} represents the occupied areas within the space. S_{free} is the remaining portion after removing of S_{obs} in S_w. S_{trav} represents the traversable subspace suitable for ground robots, which is the intersection of S_{free} and S_{surf}.

The problem is formally defined as follows: Given the initial state $s_{start} \in S_{trav}$ and the target state $s_{goal} \in S_{trav}$, the objective is to search for a safe trajectory S^*. The trajectory S^* takes s_{star} as input and guides the robot to move from s_{star} to s_{goal}. The trajectory S^* should satisfy the following conditions: 1) It must satisfy all kinematic and dynamic constraints; 2) It should avoid collision with obstacles along the path, and minimize the risk of unstable posture.

2.2 System Framework

The structure of the traversability analysis based PF-RRT* algorithm as shown in Fig. 1. The SLAM module is implemented using A-LOAM [15]. The SLAM module is responsible for mapping the robot's environment while simultaneously localizing the robot within that environment. The mapping module creates a point cloud map using a laser detection and ranging lidar and then generates a 3D grid map by applying point cloud filtering techniques. It then applies point cloud filtering techniques to enhance the map quality and creates a 3D grid map representation of the environment. The PF-RRT* module generates paths based on the 3D grid map and the traversability analysis module selects the path with the minimum cost function.

3 Approach Implementation

3.1 PF-RRT*

PF-RRT* is a random search tree algorithm that can be used for uneven terrain. Its framework is based on informed-RRT*. Unlike other algorithms that use 2D grid maps or 2.5D elevation maps [2,9–11,13], PF-RRT* directly uses a 3D map to represent the environment, enabling it to work in more complex 3D environments. The main process is shown in Fig. 1, and the variables closely related to it are defined as follows:

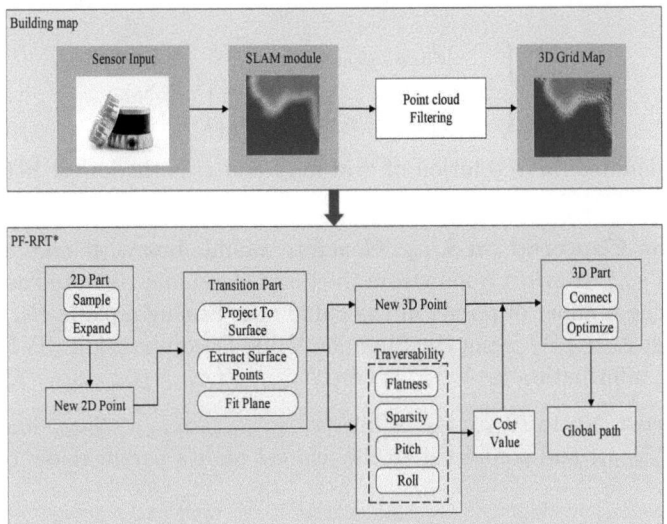

Fig. 1. Overview of system framework of traversability analysis based PF- RRT*. From top to bottom: lidar detects surrounding terrain and returns 3D grid map. Then, PF-RRT* generates paths on a 3D grid map. Finally, Compute the traversability of each point in the path and select the path with the minimum cost function.

- $s \subset R^3$ denotes a 3D point.
- $\bar{s} \subset R^2$ denotes a 2D point.
- $\tilde{s} \subset R^3$ denotes a 3D point.
- $\hat{s} \subset R^3$ denotes the position of the robot's center.
- S denotes a path that is a sequence of states.
- N denotes a node of the tree.

The principle of PF-RRT* is shown as follows:

Random Sampling. Get the coordinate $\bar{s}_{rand}$. Define $\bar{s}_{rand} = (x_{rand}, y_{rand})$.

Find the Nearest Node. Find the nearest node $N_{nearest}$ and get the coordinate $s_{nearest}$. Define the coordinate of $s_{nearest}$ as $s_{nearest} = (x_{nearest}, y_{nearest}, z_{nearest})$.

Project $s_{nearest}$ Onto the Plane. Project $s_{nearest}$ onto the plane and get it coordinate $\bar{s}_{nearest}$, where $\bar{s}_{nearest} = (x_{nearest}, y_{nearest})$.

Connect $\bar{s}_{rand}$ and $\bar{s}_{nearest}$. $\bar{s}_{new}$ is selected at a certain distance along the connection of $\bar{s}_{rand}$ and $\bar{s}_{nearest}$ where $\bar{s}_{new} = (x_{new}, y_{new})$.

Project $\bar{s}_{new}$ Onto the Surface. Project $\bar{s}_{new}$ onto the surface and get $\tilde{s}_{new}$. z_{new} satisfies

$$\min_{z_{new}} z_{new}$$

$$\text{s.t.} \begin{cases} [x_{\text{new}}, y_{\text{new}}, z_{\text{new}}]^T \in S_{\text{obs}} \\ [x_{\text{new}}, y_{\text{new}}, z_{\text{new}} + \text{res}]^T \in S_{\text{free}} \\ z_{\text{new}} - z_l = k \cdot \text{res}, k \in \mathbb{N} \end{cases} \quad (1)$$

where res denotes the resolution of grid map and z_l is the lowest height of grid map.

Fit a Plane Centered on $\tilde{s}_{new}$. Generate a cubic box with sides of length l_s centered on $\tilde{s}_{new}$ to select points from the point cloud map, denoted as $\Omega = \{\tilde{s}^j\}$, where j is the number of points in the cubic box. Fitting a plane P_{new} based on the point set $\Omega = \{\tilde{s}^j\}$ using the Singular Value Decomposition (SVD) method. Storing the information in N_{new}, Where $N_{new} = (x_{new}, y_{new}, z_{new}, P_{new})$.

Find Nearest Node $N_{nearest}$. While $(x_{new}, y_{new}, z_{new}) \in S_{trav}$, find the nearest node $N_{nearest}$ and connect it to the nearest node's parent node, recording it in the tree.

Iterate. Iterate continuously until reaching the target point and return the optimal solution $S*$.

The PF-RRT* algorithm has the advantages of real-time capability to complex environments and efficiency, making it suitable for fast and accurate path planning. It is particularly well-suited for complex 3D environments and scenarios that require real-time performance.

3.2 Traversability Analysis

The traditional traversability analysis mainly focuses on evaluation of individual points, which lacks assessment of the traversability of surfaces in the traversed area during ground robot locomotion. To address this problem, we extend the scope of traversability analysis to include an assessment of the terrain surfaces within the robot's vicinity. By evaluating the traversability of surfaces rather than just individual points, our approach provides a more comprehensive understanding of the robot's environment, leading to safer and more efficient navigation decisions.

Based on the point set $\Omega = \{\tilde{s}^j\}$, we use SVD method to fit a plane P_i, and get the normal vector n_i. The coordinate system of the plane can be defined based n_i. Define coordinate system by e_i^x, e_i^y, e_i^z.

$$e_i^z = n_i \quad (2)$$

$$e_i^x = \frac{p_i - k_i e_i^z}{\| p_i - k_i e_i^z \|} \quad (3)$$

$$e_i^y = e_i^z \times e_i^x \quad (4)$$

where $p_i = \tilde{s}_{i+1} - \tilde{s}_i$, $k_i = p_i^T \cdot e_i^z$ denotes the direction to the next node. The vector formed by the projection of p_i onto e_i^z. Then $R_i = [e_i^x, e_i^y, e_i^z]$, $t_i = \tilde{s}_i$ respectively represent the rotations and translations of the world coordinate system on the plane. Define e_i^x, e_i^y, e_i^z as: $(a_{11}, a_{21}, a_{31})^T$, $(a_{12}, a_{22}, a_{32})^T$, $(a_{13}, a_{23}, a_{33})^T$. Using this approach, each node N_i corresponds to a plane P_i. During the driving process, road conditions in small areas are often not taken into consideration. Instead, the focus is on the terrain undulation and flatness, as well as the vehicle's pitch and roll angles while on the ground, to ensure smooth and safe trajectory during vehicle operation. Therefore, we define traversability based on four criteria: flatness f, sparsity λ, pitch angle β on the plane, and roll angle γ:

$$\tau = \alpha_1 \frac{f}{f_{max}} + \alpha_2 \frac{\lambda}{\lambda_{max}} + \alpha_3 \frac{\beta}{\beta_{max}} + \alpha_4 \frac{\gamma}{\gamma_{max}} \tag{5}$$

where $\alpha_1, \alpha_2, \alpha_3, \alpha_4$ are weights which sum to 1. $f_{max}, \lambda_{max}, \beta_{max}, \gamma_{max}$ represent the maximum allowable flatness, maximum sparsity, maximum pitch angle, and maximum roll angle, respectively. These criteria are crucial for ground mobile robots during movement. Neglecting these criteria can potentially result in the vehicle being unable to move or even pose risks such as tipping over. A smaller value of τ represents higher traversability. While $\tau = 0$, it indicates that the terrain is suitable for vehicle traversal. On the contrary, when $\tau = 1$, it indicates that there is a high risk for the vehicle to traverse this area.

$$f = \beta_f \frac{\sum_{j=1}^{N} (e^z \cdot x^j)^4}{N} \tag{6}$$

$$\lambda = \begin{cases} 1, r > r_{max} \\ \frac{r - r_{min}}{r_{max} - r_{min}}, r \in [r_{min}, r_{max}] \\ 0, otherwise \end{cases} \tag{7}$$

$$\beta = \arctan 2(a_{32}, a_{33}) \tag{8}$$

$$\gamma = \arctan 2(-a_{31}, \sqrt{a_{11}^2 + a_{21}^2}) \tag{9}$$

where β_f is a constant coefficient. In the formula, r represents the proportion of empty space on the plane, while r_{min} and r_{max} represent the acceptable minimum and maximum ratios of empty space respectively. A higher empty space ratio indicates the possible presence of potholes on the plane.

$$f(N_i, N_{i+1}) = (1 + \omega(\frac{1}{1 - \tau_i} + \frac{1}{1 - \tau_{i+1}} - 2)) \cdot d_{i,i+1} \tag{10}$$

With traversability τ in place, we define the loss function as (10), where ω is a constant coefficient that represents the penalty scale factor, $d_{i,i+1}$ denotes the Euclidean distance between nodes N_i, N_{i+1}. By using this cost function, we are able to avoid planning paths that are difficult to traverse and, at the same time, shorten the path while ensuring sufficient safety.

4 Simulation Experiment

To validate the effectiveness and safety of the traversability analysis, we conducted simulation experiments by designing two types of field map with uneven terrains, as shown in Fig. 2 and Fig. 7.

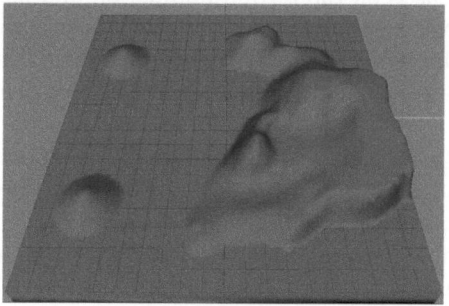

Fig. 2. The mountainous simulated map used in the simulations.

We set the starting point of the vehicle at the same elevated slope, and the endpoint at the bottom of the slope, where there is a steep slope between them. We compare our proposed traversability method with the traversability method in PUTN [7], using the PF-RRT* path generation method. The results are shown in Fig. 3.

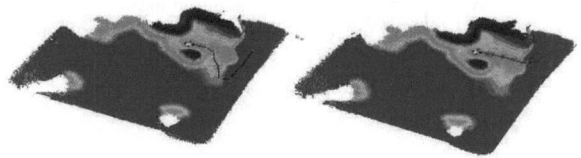

Fig. 3. Left figure is the path generated using the traversability analysis presented in this paper, and right figure is the path generated using the traversability analysis in PUTN.

It can be observed that the approach presented in this paper takes into account the pitch and roll angles of the vehicle on the plane. Therefore, by utilizing the traversability analysis method proposed in this paper, the vehicle is able to navigate around areas that pose a risk of rollover and other dangers. The obtaining trajectory of the vehicle after generating the path is shown in Fig. 4. The red lines depict the trajectory obtained using the method proposed in this paper, while the blue lines mean the trajectory generated by the PUTN method. We can see the vehicle overturned by PUTN method and it cannot reach the finish spots in Fig. 4.

In order to verify the effectiveness of the proposed method, we recorded the pitch angle of the vehicle during motion, as shown in Fig. 5. The red lines represent the variation of pitch angles during the vehicle's motion after applying the traversability analysis method proposed in this paper, while the blue lines represent the variation of pitch angles during the vehicle's motion after applying the PUTN method.

It can be observed that after applying the proposed traversability analysis method in this paper, the pitch angle of the vehicle during the motion remains within ±30°, indicating no safety issues. However, when using the traversability analysis method in PUTN, the vehicle's pitch angle exceeds −80° during the motion, resulting in a rollover. From this, it can be concluded that the proposed traversability analysis in this paper enhances the safety of the vehicle during the motion.

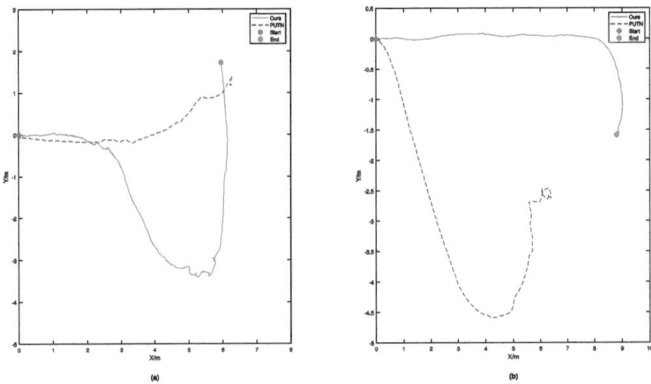

Fig. 4. The red lines represent the vehicle driving tracks by the traversability method in this paper, and the blue lines are the vehicle driving track by the PUTN traversability method. (Color figure online)

The speeds of the vehicle during motion are shown in Fig. 6, where the left figure represents the speed-time plot of the vehicle in simulation 1, and the right figure represents the speed-time plot of the vehicle in simulation 2. The red and blue lines represent the results obtained by applying the traversability analysis method proposed in this paper and the PUTN traversability analysis method, respectively. From the speed curves, it can be observed that the vehicle using the PUTN method experiences a sudden change in speed around 15 s, followed by a rollover that results in a constant speed of 0. On the other hand, the vehicle using the method proposed in this paper maintains a speed within the range of (0, 1) throughout the motion, whereas the vehicle using the PUTN method experiences drastic velocity changes when traversing pits and eventually falls into them. From the above experiments, we can see that our proposed traversability method exhibits high levels of safety and generates reasonable paths. It not only

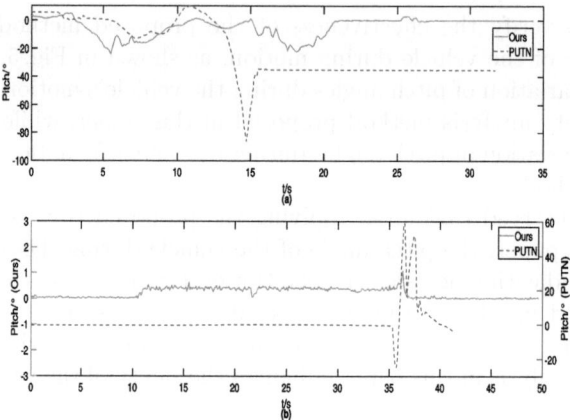

Fig. 5. The left figure represents the variation of the pitch angles during the vehicle's motion in simulation 1, while the right figure represents the variation of the pitch angles in simulation 2.

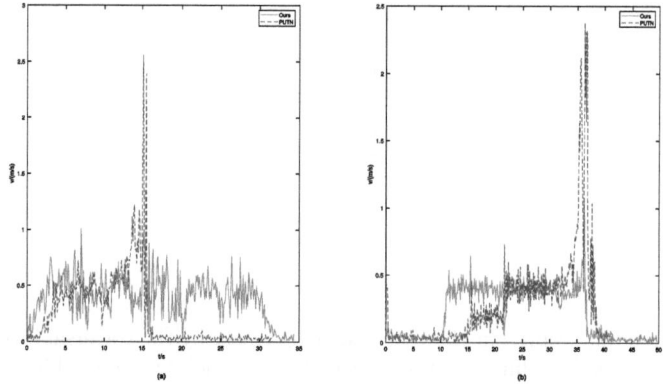

Fig. 6. The left represents the speeds of the vehicle during motion in simulation 1 and the right graph represents the speeds of the vehicle in simulation 2.

adapts well to mountainous terrain as shown in Fig. 3, but also accommodates terrain with pits as depicted in Fig. 8.

To demonstrate the effectiveness of our method in different scenarios, we also compared our algorithm with the traversability analysis of PUTN in the scenario depicted in Fig. 8. Unlike the mountainous terrain depicted in Fig. 3, Fig. 8 contains numerous potholes, posing significant challenges to traversability analysis methods. Our path proves to be more safer and feasible.

From the trajectory in Fig. 8, it can be seen that the vehicle on the left, utilizing our traversability assessment method, manages to reach the endpoint via a shorter path. In contrast, the vehicle using the PUTN traversability assessment method falls into a pit during the process and fails to reach the endpoint. Since

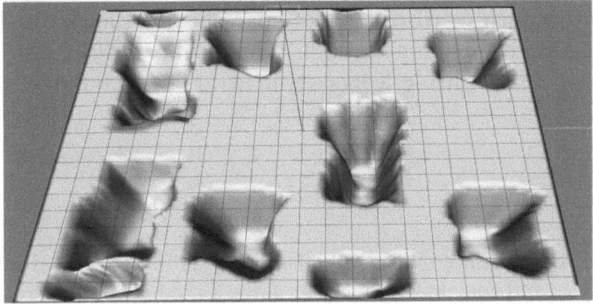

Fig. 7. The terrain with potholes used in the simulation experiments.

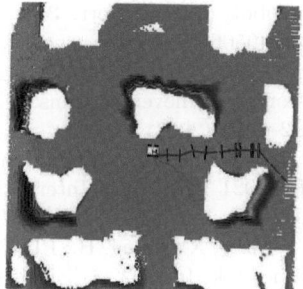 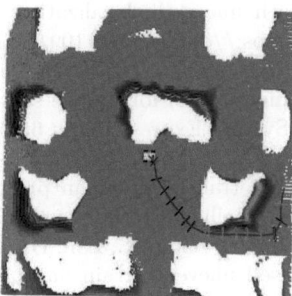

Fig. 8. The left figure displays the vehicle's driving track employing the traversability method outlined in this paper, while the right figure depicts the vehicle's driving track using the PUTN traversability method

the terrain in this multi-pit scenario is relatively flat, there are no significant changes in the pitch angle during the motion with our method. However, as shown in figures, the vehicle using the PUTN method falls into a pit, resulting in a drastic change in pitch angle during the descent.

5 Conclusion

The traversability analysis method proposed in this paper comprehensively considers several crucial factors that affect the vehicle's motion, including road flatness, sparsity, vehicle pitch angle, and roll angle. By incorporating these factors into the analysis, this method significantly improves the safety and smoothness of the vehicle's path during its motion. The proposed method ensures that the planned path avoids areas with excessive irregularities or inclinations, reducing the likelihood of accidents or rollovers by considering road flatness variations. Besides, the method aims to steer the vehicle away from such areas, prioritizing safer and more accessible paths with the aid of sparsity difference. Overall, the proposed traversability analysis method offers a comprehensive approach to enhance the safety and smoothness of the vehicle's path during motion. By considering factors such as road flatness, sparsity, pitch angle, and roll angle, it enables the vehicle to navigate through terrains more effectively, reducing the risks of accidents and ensuring a more comfortable and reliable motion experience.

References

1. Bermudez, F.L.G., Julian, R.C., Haldane, D.W., Abbeel, P., Fearing, R.S.: Performance analysis and terrain classification for a legged robot over rough terrain. In: 2012 IEEE/RSJ International Conference on Intelligent Robots and Systems, pp. 513–519. IEEE (2012)
2. Fankhauser, P., Bloesch, M., Hutter, M.: Probabilistic terrain mapping for mobile robots with uncertain localization. IEEE Robot. Autom. Lett. **3**(4), 3019–3026 (2018). https://doi.org/10.1109/LRA.2018.2849506
3. Ganganath, N., Yuan, W., Fernando, T., Iu, H.H.C., Cheng, C.T.: Energy-efficient anti-flocking control for mobile sensor networks on uneven terrains. IEEE Trans. Circuits Syst. II Express Briefs **65**(12), 2022–2026 (2018)
4. Inotsume, H., Kubota, T.: Adaptive terrain traversability prediction based on multi-source transfer gaussian processes. In: 2021 IEEE/RSJ International Conference on Intelligent Robots and Systems (IROS), pp. 2297–2304. IEEE (2021)
5. Jian, Z., Lu, Z., Zhou, X., Lan, B., Xiao, A., Wang, X., Liang, B.: PUTN: a plane-fitting based uneven terrain navigation framework. In: 2022 IEEE/RSJ International Conference on Intelligent Robots and Systems (IROS), pp. 7160–7166. IEEE (2022)
6. Krüsi, P., Furgale, P., Bosse, M., Siegwart, R.: Driving on point clouds: motion planning, trajectory optimization, and terrain assessment in generic nonplanar environments. J. Field Robot. **34**(5), 940–984 (2017)
7. Lv, W., Kang, Y., Zheng, W.X., Wu, Y., Li, Z.: Feature-temporal semi-supervised extreme learning machine for robotic terrain classification. IEEE Trans. Circuits Syst. II Express Briefs **67**(12), 3567–3571 (2020)
8. Tang, Y., Cai, J., Chen, M., Yan, X., Xie, Y.: An autonomous exploration algorithm using environment-robot interacted traversability analysis. In: 2019 IEEE/RSJ International Conference on Intelligent Robots and Systems (IROS), pp. 4885–4890. IEEE (2019)
9. Xiao, A., et al.: Robotic autonomous trolley collection with progressive perception and nonlinear model predictive control. In: 2022 International Conference on Robotics and Automation (ICRA), pp. 4480–4486 (2022). https://doi.org/10.1109/ICRA46639.2022.9812455
10. Xie, H., Zhong, X., Chen, B., Peng, P., Hu, H., Liu, Q.: Real-time elevation mapping with Bayesian ground filling and traversability analysis for UGV navigation. In: 2023 IEEE/RSJ International Conference on Intelligent Robots and Systems (IROS), pp. 7218–7225 (2023)
11. Xu, C., Zhang, B., Qiu, J., He, Z.: An unstructured terrain traversability mapping method fusing semantic and geometric features. In: 2023 IEEE International Conference on Unmanned Systems (ICUS), pp. 1142–1147 (2023)
12. Yao, X., Zhang, J., Oh, J.: RCA: ride comfort-aware visual navigation via self-supervised learning. In: 2022 IEEE/RSJ International Conference on Intelligent Robots and Systems (IROS), pp. 7847–7852. IEEE (2022)

13. Yuan, W., Li, Z., Su, C.Y.: Multisensor-based navigation and control of a mobile service robot. IEEE Trans. Syst. Cybern.: Syst. **51**(4), 2624–2634 (2021). https://doi.org/10.1109/TSMC.2019.2916932
14. Zhang, D., Zhang, P., Zhang, W., He, B., Zhu, G.: A weight adaptive Kalman information fusion method for attitude measurement. IEEE Sens. J. **23**, 30683–30690 (2023)
15. Zhang, J., Singh, S.: LOAM: Lidar odometry and mapping in real-time. In: Robotics: Science and Systems, Berkeley, CA, vol. 2, pp. 1–9 (2014)

GMLO: Ground and Memory Optimized LiDAR Odometry

Kaiduo Fang(✉) and Rui Song

Department of Electric and Electronic Engineering, The Hong Kong Polytechnic University, Hung Hom, Kowloon, Hong Kong, China
`kaiduo8.fang@connect.polyu.hk, rui23.song@polyu.edu.hk`

Abstract. As a sensor providing long-range perception and precise measurements, Light Detection and Ranging (LiDAR) can assist the development of smart cities in various aspects, which raises the rising interest in the topic of LiDAR Odometry (LO) research. Despite the popular application of LiDAR Odometry for the localization purpose, existing LiDAR Odometry methods are still limited by the estimation error in the elevation direction due to the low vertical resolution of LiDAR and the increasing storage cost with time. To address these issues, we propose Ground and Memory Optimized LiDAR Odometry (GMLO) for autonomous vehicles by integrating a joint scan-matching optimization between consecutive LiDAR frames. In addition, an efficient and robust ground extraction method, Polar Region Ground Plane Fitting (PR-GPF), is integrated into GMLO. Finally, we propose a novel scan-to-mapping scheme to eliminate accumulated errors with low storage cost and good efficiency in updating historical mapping data. To evaluate the performance of GMLO in various aspects, we have conducted extensive experiments based on the KITTI Odometry and Semantic-KITTI datasets, and the test results show that GMLO is effective with 1.03% average drifting error and over 25 Hz tracking frequency.

Keywords: Autonomous Driving · LiDAR Odometry · SLAM · 3D Point Cloud

1 Introduction

Intelligent vehicles, also referred to as self-driving vehicles are becoming an important technology for the development of intelligent transportation systems (ITS), e.g., smart cities [1,3]. As a powerful sensor with long-range perception and precise measurements [6], Light Detection and Ranging (LiDAR) could be widely applied in developing and managing smart cities for different aspects, including 3D Mapping and Modeling, Environmental Monitoring, Internet of

---

This work was supported in part by the Otto Poon Charitable Foundation Smart Cities Research Institute (Projects Q-CDA8 and Q-CDAS) and the Department of Electrical and Electronic Engineering (Project 4-ZZRM) at The Hong Kong Polytechnic University.

Things (IoT) integration, etc. The topic of LiDAR Odometry (LO) significantly contributes to the development of smart cities by providing precise localization and orientation estimations, which allows the creation of high-precision 3D maps of urban environments for safe and efficient navigation of different types of robotics platforms [4,5].

In the past decade, the research topic of LiDAR Odometry has been extensively investigated, and the algorithms can be divided into registration-based methods and feature-based methods based on point cloud data pre-processing [23]. Registration-based methods mostly use the Iterative Closest Point (ICP) algorithm [7] and its variants to retrieve the pose from the registration results of the consecutive point cloud pairs, while feature-based methods often get limited points with the hand-crafted extractor from the raw data, then the pose is computed from the extracted points. However, registration-based methods are often considered too time-consuming to support real-time localization performance. And feature-based methods are less robust in conditions where the feature extractor cannot get enough data to compute the pose.

In addition to the balance between accuracy and efficiency, one of the major existing problems in LiDAR Odometry is the poor performance in estimating the vertical direction, which often results in an accumulation of estimation errors on the z-axis of the LiDAR's local coordinate frame. This problem exists because the mechanical LiDAR has a low resolution in the vertical direction. For example, the azimuth resolution of VLP-64 is 0.08° and the elevation resolution is 0.4° [34]. This type of property results in point clouds from mechanical LiDAR being sparse in the vertical direction, which causes point cloud registration to lose accuracy in the associated degree of freedom (DoF). For autonomous driving scenarios, using points from the ground part in LiDAR odometry can improve the z-axis related estimation [18–20], but ground segmentation in point clouds is still an open problem.

To address the aforementioned issues, we propose the Ground and Memory Optimized LiDAR Odometry (GMLO) method in this paper. Unlike most of the existing feature-based LiDAR Odometry methods, GMLO utilizes a novel registration-based method to avoid estimation degeneration problems and is able to support real-time performance, which is better than most registration-based LiDAR Odometry methods. The ground points are segmented by a novel extraction algorithm, and GMLO is enhanced with the ground information by integrating ground optimization into the pose estimation process. In addition, the growing memory cost problem in the existing LiDAR Odometry methods is optimized in GMLO by a novel Scan-to-Mapping method. The main contributions of this paper are summarized as follows:

- A lightweight, robust point cloud registration method based on Generalized ICP (GICP) [9], called Voxel-to-Voxel GICP, is proposed to balance the accuracy and efficiency of GMLO under the CPU environment.
- A robust and accurate ground extraction method (PR-GPF) is proposed and implemented in the proposed GMLO method.
- To process both the ground and non-ground parts in the point cloud, a joint scan-matching optimization objective is proposed, which contains the joint

optimization problem of GICP and ground-to-ground alignment to reduce drift in the vertical direction.
- To optimize the estimation result and memory cost, a lightweight Scan-to-Mapping method is proposed and applied in the GMLO.

The paper is organized as follows: in Sect. 2, we review the related works on point cloud registration, LiDAR Odometry and ground segmentation; in Sect. 3, we present the details of the proposed LiDAR Odometry; in Sect. 4, the experimental resuls are shown and in Sect. 5 the conclusion and future works are discussed.

2 Related Works

The fundamental work in LiDAR Odometry research is Scan-Matching, which addresses the problem of finding the relative pose (or transform) between the two robot positions at which laser scans are taken. The most classical method for Scan-Matching is Iterative Closest Point (ICP) [7] proposed in 1992, which is a method that iteratively computes the SE(3) transform between two 3D point sets by associating the closest neighbors in different sets for each individual data point. In the past decades, ICP-based methods have been extensively investigated with various types of improvements [8–13], such as 'point-to-plane' ICP [8] with a modified optimization objective. Generalized ICP (GICP) is a variant of 'plane to plane' ICP [9] that considers point data with probability density, making it one of the most popular ICP-based methods with good accuracy and robustness. Normal ICP (NICP) [10] is a powerful extension of GICP, this method extends the point data to $\mathbb{R}^6$, where the first three dimensions of the data are point locations in the 3D Euclidean space and the last three dimensions are normal vectors of local surfaces. With the extended features, NICP is able to outperform GICP on dense point cloud data, especially in small-scale indoor environments. Despite its robustness and accuracy in real-world problems, ICP-based methods that directly estimate transforms between two frames are often considered time-consuming and computationally expensive, making the algorithm not efficient for real-time robotics localization. IMLS-SLAM [14] is one such example with accurate estimation but over 1.2 s per frame processing time, which is far from a real-time localization solution.

Feature-based methods of LiDAR Odometry are complementary to ICP-based methods, one of the typical examples of feature-based methods is LOAM [15]. LOAM conducts a feature extractor based on the local curvature values of the points and performs transformation estimation between feature points instead of the full set of point cloud data. In the pose estimation of LOAM, different cost functions are defined for the edge, planar, and corner parts. In the meanwhile, a historical point cloud map is maintained in the system for loop closure and backend optimization in order to reduce the accumulating error from the Scan-Matching of the consecutive laser scans. Several variants of LOAM-based methods have been investigated in the past decade, most of them follow LOAM's idea of feature-based scan-matching method. For example, LeGO-LOAM [16] optimized the implementation of LOAM to make it lightweight enough to support the application on the robotics platform, F-LOAM [22] optimized the computational speed of LOAM, T-LOAM [17] proposed the cost functions based on the theory of truncated least squares, etc. However, feature-based methods are not as robust as direct methods in textureless environments because the feature extractor may not be able to extract enough accurate feature points, leading to failure for LiDAR Odometry. In addition, these hand-crafted feature extractors are often computationally expensive. Moreover, in the typical LOAM-based LiDAR Odometry methods, the memory cost of the historical map is not considered, which can lead to memory overfloating with the time increases.

To address the problem of vertical direction drifting in LiDAR Odometry, one of the popular method is to extract ground part from the point cloud data and define an enhanced constraint in pose estimation. The simplest method for ground extraction is to fit a monocular plane model by RANSAC with the sensor height as prior knowledge [24]. Unfortunately, fitting ground with a plane model cannot represent sophisticated cases that exist in the real-world, such as uneven ground, bumpy curbs, and steep slopes. To solve this problem, a number of methods based on multiple plane fitting have benn proposed. For example, Ground Plane Fitting (GPF) [25] divides the point cloud into three parts by sorting the points by x-values, and applies Principal Component Analysis (PCA) based method to efficiently fit plane models in different parts. Cascaded-Seg [26] is a method that uses successive LiDAR ring patterns and multi-region RANSAC plane fitting. LineFit [27] divides the point cloud into segments and bins based on uniform polar grid, reduces the dimension of point cloud data to 2D, and fits different line models for a bin. As a classical method, LeGO-LOAM extracts the ground part from the point cloud in the data pre-processing with a method based on projecting LiDAR point cloud onto the range image [21]. Apparently, as the part of the pre-processing of the point cloud data, the ground segmentation process needs to be computationally efficient enough, so that the total computation of the LiDAR Odometry will still support real-time applications.

Methods based on sophisticated mathematical theories like Gaussian Mixture Model [29] or Markov Random Field [28] are often considered time-consuming and computationally expensive, which makes them not suitable for real-time applications. There are also many existing ground segmentation methods based on Deep Learning (DL) [30–33], but the performance of DL-based methods are highly relying on the training data quality, which makes them not robust in various working scenarios. In addition, DL-based methods often requires the GPU acceleration, which also increases the cost of hardwares of robots.

3 Proposed Method

In this section, Ground and Memory optimized LiDAR Odometry (GMLO) is presented. Starting from the original idea of Generalized ICP (GICP), GMLO is introduced in detail. The working process of the proposed LiDAR Odometry is shown in Fig. 1, in which point cloud data in the i-th timestamp is denoted

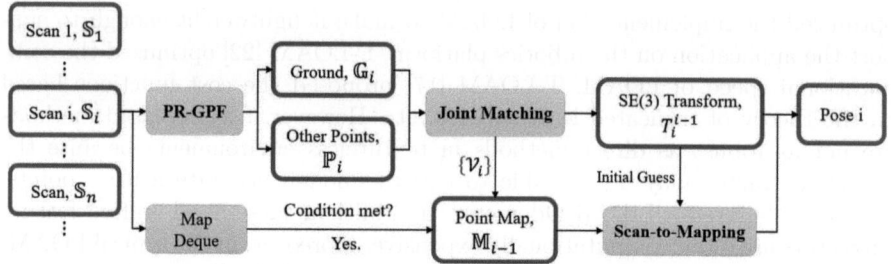

Fig. 1. Ground and Memory optimized LiDAR Odometry (GMLO) Framework. Our proposed LiDAR Odometry firstly computes the relative transformation between adjacent LiDAR frames (scan-to-scan), if current frame meets the conditions, scan-to-mapping will be activated to eliminate accumulated errors. The output is the SE(3) pose of current LiDAR frame from scan-to-scan or synchronized from scan-to-mapping.

as Scan i $\mathbb{S}_i$, point cloud map generated at the moment is denoted as $\mathbb{M}_{i-1}$, the relative SE(3) transformation from frame $i-1$ to frame i is denoted as T_i^{i-1}. In the LiDAR Odometry, point cloud is segmented into ground part $\mathbb{G}_i$ and non-ground part $\mathbb{P}_i$.

3.1 Generalized ICP (GICP)

In point cloud registration problems, a transformation $T \in \text{SE}(3)$ is estimated by aligning two finite size point sets, target point set $A = \{a_0, \cdots a_n\}$ and source point set $B = \{b_0, \cdots b_m\}$. Iterative Closest Point (ICP) algorithm is widely used in point cloud registration problems to properly align source point set with target point set.

In the classic ICP algorithm, the correspondences between point pairs from A to B are determined by closest neighbor searching, and the error term between a pair of corresponded points is given by (1), in which b_i is a single point in the source point set, T is the spatial transformation estimated, the operator $\odot$ represents the SE(3) transform of a point or a point cloud, and m_i is the point in A which has the closest distance to b_i. Then the transformation is estimated by the ICP algorithm by minimizing the sum of errors of every correspondence as in (2), in which, **T** is the optimal solution of the objective function.

$$d_i = m_i - T \odot b_i \tag{1}$$

$$\mathbf{T} = \underset{T \in \text{SE}(3)}{\operatorname{argmin}} \sum_i d_i = \underset{T \in \text{SE}(3)}{\operatorname{argmin}} \sum_i \|m_i - T \odot b_i\|_2^2 \tag{2}$$

Generalized ICP (GICP) is an enhanced modification of ICP, instead of treating points in both sets as fixed data, GICP considers points as samples from Gaussian distributions on surfaces, which are defined as: $a_i \sim \mathcal{N}(\mu_a^i, C_a^i)$, $b_i \sim \mathcal{N}(\mu_b^i, C_b^i)$. In the mean time, the optimization objective (2) has been attached with a probabilistic model to minimize the Mahalanobis distance between different Gaussian distributions as in (3), in which, R is the rotation matrix taken from T to transform source point's covariance into target point cloud's local coordinate frame.

$$\mathbf{T} = \underset{T \in SE(3)}{\mathrm{argmin}} \sum_i ||m_i - T \odot b_i||^2_{(C_i^A + RC_i^B R^T)^{-1}} \tag{3}$$

3.2 Voxel-to-Voxel GICP

In this paper, Voxel-to-Voxel GICP is proposed to balance the efficiency and accuracy of GICP's estimation. Comparing with original GICP's implementation, the proposed method contains an essential step of voxelization that transforms point cloud into a set of voxels, defined as (4).

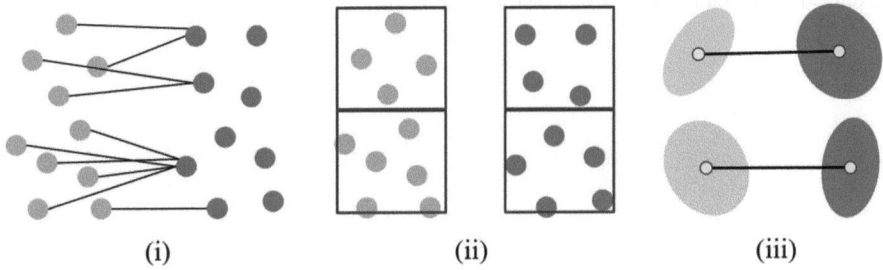

Fig. 2. 2D Example of Voxelization. (i) Original point cloud data and nearest neighbor matching. (ii) Voxelization for point clouds. (iii) Voxel-to-voxel matching with surface covariance.

$$\mathbb{P}_i = \{\cdots, \mathcal{V}_i, \cdots\}, \; \mathcal{V}_i = \{\mathcal{C}_i, p_i\} \tag{4}$$

In which, $\mathcal{V}_i$ is the i-th voxel in the point cloud data. $\mathcal{V}_i$ contains the local surface covariance $\mathcal{C}_i$, the coordinate of the central point of the voxel p_i selected by Approximate Voxel Grid Filter, and $\mathcal{C}_i$ calculated by neighboring points inside the voxel. A 2D case voxelization process is visualized in Fig. 2, where the target and source point cloud are colored in blue and yellow respectively. In (i), the process of the closest neighbor searching for correspondences is shown. In (ii), sets of voxels are assigned on the point clouds for $\mathcal{V}_i = \{\mathcal{C}_i, p_i\}$ calculation. Finally, (iii) visualizes the $\mathcal{C}_i$ covariance ellipse and voxel correspondences in 2D space.

To better illustrate the process of voxelization, Fig. 3 is plotted. In Fig. 3, the left plot shows the raw point cloud data, and the right plot shows the information after the process of voxelization, in which the white ellipsoids are used to visualize covariances of the point data. From Fig. 3, we can see that the point cloud becomes sparser after voxelization, but the covariance information are reserved.

Point pairs correspondences are simplified as voxel pairs correspondences after voxelization of the proposed method, while the original spatial information

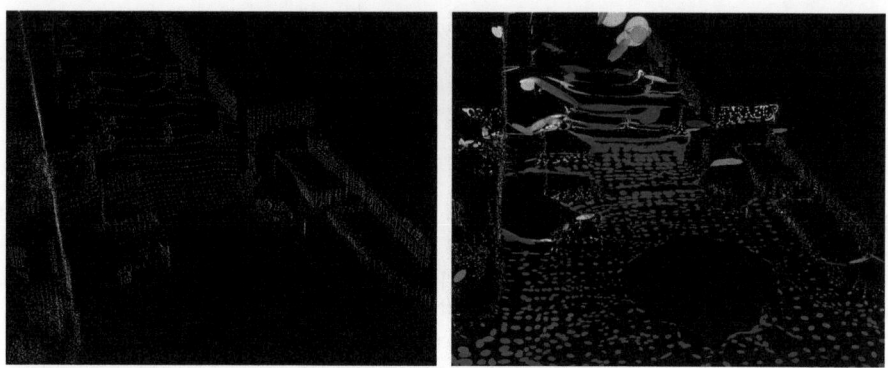

Fig. 3. Point Cloud Voxelization. Left: Raw data from KITTI Dataset. Right: Voxelized point cloud and covariance information.

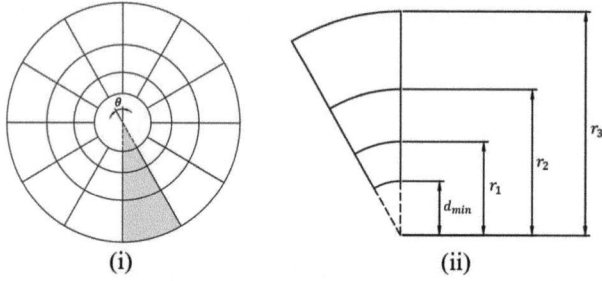

Fig. 4. Polar Grid. (i) Dividing point cloud into different segments by polar grid in the x-y plane, θ denotes segment's azimuth angle. (ii) In one of the segments, colored with cyan in (i), Polar Regions are segmented based on point distances.

is preserved for registration. The GICP's cost function in (3) is modified to (5), in which, $\mathbb{F}(\cdot,\cdot)$ is the cost function taking two voxels as inputs, $\mathcal{V}_i^S$ is the i-th voxel in the source point cloud and $\mathcal{V}_i^M$ is the closest neighboring voxel in the target frame, while p_i^S and p_i^M are the coordinates. Σ is the voxel-to-voxel covariance defined in (6), in which $\mathcal{C}_i^M$ and $\mathcal{C}_i^S$ are local surface covariances of voxels $\mathcal{V}_i^M$ and $\mathcal{V}_i^S$ respectively.

$$\mathbf{T} = \underset{T\in SE(3)}{\operatorname{argmin}} \sum_i \mathbb{F}(\mathcal{V}_i^M, \mathcal{V}_i^S) = \underset{T\in SE(3)}{\operatorname{argmin}} \sum_i ||p_i^M - T \odot p_i^S||_{\Sigma^{-1}}^2 \qquad (5)$$

$$\Sigma = \mathcal{C}_i^M + R\mathcal{C}_i^S R^T \qquad (6)$$

3.3 Polar Region Ground Plane Fitting (PR-GPF)

In the original Ground Plane Fitting (GPF) algorithm [25], points are sorted and divided into different segments by the x-value, then points with the lowest z-value are picked to generate plane models for these segments. However, this method performs poorly in boundary cases where the lowest points are off-road and not close enough to include road parts. Moreover, GPF follows the assumption that the vehicle is always taking the direction of the x-axis, which does not consider the vehicle's rotation movements. These problems limit the application of GPF, since incorrect ground constraints will reduce the performance of LiDAR Odometry.

To accurately and robustly extract ground points, Polar Region Ground Plane Fitting (PR-GPF) shown in Algorithm 1 is proposed and presented in this section. Instead of segmenting based on the direction of x-axis, a dividing method based on polar coordinate is applied, which is suitable for LiDAR's rotational range sensing method. The polar grid example is shown in Fig. 4.

As shown in Fig. 4. (i), the point cloud is firstly divided into segments by the azimuth angle, and $\theta = \pi/m$. Then a range list $\mathcal{R}_{1:n}$ is given for polar region division in one segment as in (7). After that, every point in the segments will be classfied into different polar regions based on the distances to the LiDAR's location as shown in Fig. 4. (ii). In $\mathcal{R}_{1:n}$, d_{min} is determined by LiDAR's height h and FOV angle η by $d_{min} = h/sin(\eta)$. It should be noted that in the example shown in Fig. 4, $n = 3$ and $m = 12$.

$$\mathcal{R}_{1:n} = \{(d_{min}, r_1), (r_1, r_2), \cdots, (r_{n-1}, r_n)\} \tag{7}$$

After points are divided into polar regions $PR_{m \times n}$, point seeds are selected in every polar region as the point with the least z-value to extract a plane model defined as in (8).

$$\begin{aligned} ax + by + cz + d = \vec{n} \cdot p + d = 0, \\ \vec{n} = [a, b, c]^T, \ p = [x, y, z]^T \end{aligned} \tag{8}$$

The covariance matrix C of one set of points P is defined as in (9). To estimate the plane model defined as in (8), Singular Value Decomposition (SVD) is applied to C, and $\vec{n}$ is the singular vector corresponding to the least singular value.

$$C = \sum_i (p_i - \bar{p}) \cdot (p_i - \bar{p}), \ \forall p_i \in P \tag{9}$$

The performance comparison of PR-GPF and GPF on several point cloud data is shown in Fig. 5, in which GPF is not able to achieve satisfying performance. As shown in the figure, PR-GPF can get more accurate in ground segmentation, while GPF has a lot of ground points missing. The quantitative comparison is shown in Sect. 4.

Algorithm 1: Polar Region Ground Plane Fitting

Input: point cloud $\mathbb{S}$, number of iteration N, number of segments m, distance threshold δ, range list $\mathcal{R}_{1:n}$

1 $PR_{m \times n} = $ **PolarRegionDivision**($\mathbb{S}$, m, $\mathcal{R}_{1:n}$);
2 **for** pr in $PR_{m \times n}$ **do**
3 　$P_g = $ **ExtractSeed**(pr, δ);
4 　**for** i = 1:N **do**
5 　　model = **EstimatePlane**(P_g);
6 　　**if** $model(p_i \in P_g) < \delta$ **then**
7 　　　$\mathbb{G} \leftarrow p_i$
8 　　**else**
9 　　　$\mathbb{P} \leftarrow p_i$
10 　　**end**
11 　**end**
12 **end**

Output: ground points $\mathbb{G}$, non-ground points $\mathbb{P}$

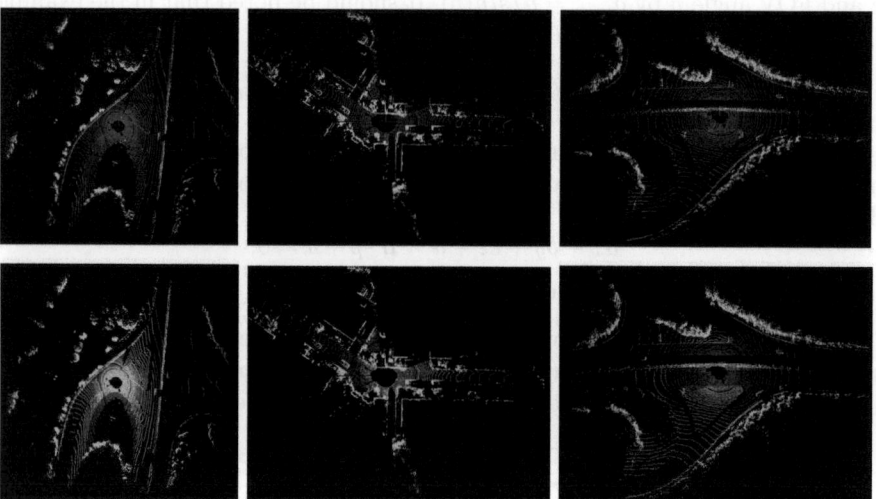

Fig. 5. Performance of PR-GPF vs GPF. The upper row shows the performance of PR-GPF, while the lower row shows GPF. In this figure, ground points extracted from the algorithms are plotted in red color, and non-ground points are plotted in green color.

3.4 Joint Matching

As shown in Fig. 1, PR-GPF is segmenting $\mathbb{S}_i$ into $\mathbb{G}_i$ and $\mathbb{P}_i$. Then the point cloud has the mathematical definition as (10), in which N_{voxels} is the number of voxels after voxelization step mentioned in Sect. 3.2, N_{ground} is the number of points in $\mathbb{G}_i$, and $(p_k^g)^{(i)}$ is a point in $\mathbb{G}_i$.

$$\mathbb{S}_i = \mathbb{P}_i \cup \mathbb{G}_i = (\bigcup_{j=0}^{N_{voxels}} \mathcal{V}_j^{(i)}) \cup (\bigcup_{k=0}^{N_{ground}} (p_k^g)^{(i)}) \qquad (10)$$

After ground segmentation, Joint Matching is applied to consecutive point cloud pairs, $\mathbb{S}_{i-1}$ and $\mathbb{S}_i$, to minimize vertical estimation error. For $\mathbb{P}_{i-1}$ and $\mathbb{P}_i$, Voxel-to-Voxel GICP is applied and the objective function is defined by (5). Correspondence pairs are generated by closest neighbor searching with KD-Tree, and nano-FLANN is applied for KD-Tree's implementation to improve the efficiency.

For $\mathbb{G}_{i-1}$ and $\mathbb{G}_i$, point-to-plane residual is applied, which is defined in (11), in which $(\vec{n}, d)$ is the local plane model that is refined by five nearest neighboring points in $\mathbb{G}_{i-1}$.

$$\mathbb{L}((p_k^g)^{(i)}, \mathbb{G}_{i-1}) = \vec{n} \cdot (T \odot (p_k^g)^{(i)}) + d \qquad (11)$$

The optimization problem of joint matching is defined in (12) and the Gauss-Newton algorithm is applied to solve the problem. In (12), the first error term is different than the term defined as in (5), because the target frame and the source frame are $\mathbb{S}_{i-1}$ and $\mathbb{S}_i$ respectively for the Joint Matching.

$$\begin{aligned} \mathbf{T} &= \underset{T \in SE(3)}{\operatorname{argmin}} (\sum_j \mathbb{F}(\mathcal{V}_j^{(i-1)}, \mathcal{V}_j^{(i)}) + \sum_k \mathbb{L}((p_k^g)^{(i)}, \mathbb{G}_{i-1})) \\ &= \underset{T \in SE(3)}{\operatorname{argmin}} (\sum_j ||p_j^{(i-1)} - T \odot p_j^{(i)}||_{\Sigma^{-1}}^2 + \\ & \quad \sum_k \vec{n} \cdot (T \odot (p_k^g)^{(i)}) + d) \end{aligned} \qquad (12)$$

3.5 Scan-to-Mapping Method

In our proposed LiDAR Odometry, a point cloud deque of size five is maintained while relative transforms are being computed on consecutive frames, only the recent frames are stored in memory for the Scan-to-Mapping process. It is worth noting that $\mathbb{S}_n$ is merely able to be matched with point clouds inside a range of distance, since farther point cloud does not contain enough overlapping area with $\mathbb{S}_n$. We denote pose change as the relative transform between two non-consecutive frames, $\Delta T = T_u^w$, u and w are frame numbers, ΔR and Δt are the rotation part and translation part in ΔT respectively.

$$||\Delta t||_2 >= 10\,\mathrm{m} \ \text{ or } \ \deg(\Delta R) >= 10° \qquad (13)$$

When the pose change meets condition (13) at frame $\mathbb{S}_i$, the point clouds in the deque is concatenated to generate the point cloud map, defined as (14), in which the most recent five frames are translated to the coordinate frame of $\mathbb{S}_{i-1}$. Voxel-to-Voxel GICP is applied on $\mathbb{M}_{i-1}$ and $\mathbb{S}_i$ with the initial guess from Joint Matching to refine the Pose T_i with historical LiDAR mapping. While generating the point maps, pre-computed voxel information are maintained from the Joint Matching process.

$$
\begin{aligned}
\mathbb{M}_{i-1} &= \bigcup_{k=0}^{4} ((T_{i-1})^{-1} \cdot T_{i-1-k}) \odot \mathbb{S}_{i-1-k} \\
&= \bigcup_{k=0}^{4} T_{i-1-k}^{i-1} \odot \mathbb{S}_{i-1-k}
\end{aligned}
\quad (14)
$$

In (14), the operator $\odot$ for $T \in SE(3)$ and $\mathbb{S}$ is defined in (15), R and t are the rotation and translation part in T respectively.

$$
\begin{aligned}
T \odot \mathbb{S} &= (\bigcup_{j=0}^{N_{voxels}} T \odot \mathcal{V}_j) \bigcup (\bigcup_{k=0}^{N_{ground}} T \odot p_k^g) \\
&= (\bigcup_{j=0}^{N_{voxels}} \{T \odot p_j, RC_j R^T\}) \bigcup (\bigcup_{k=0}^{N_{ground}} T \odot p_k^g)
\end{aligned}
\quad (15)
$$

Unlike existing LiDAR Odometry methods, all LiDAR mapping results are stored without management, which will lead to the rapid growth of the memory cost, while our proposed method is keeping the recent frames instead of all mapping results. This modification does not only utilize historical data to improve the estimation accuracy but also significantly improve the memory efficiency.

4 Experiments

4.1 Ablation Study of Voxel-to-Voxel GICP

In the existing research works of point cloud registration, the general method is to apply a voxel grid filter to downsample the point cloud to reduce the noise and improve the computing speed. However, the voxel grid filter downsampling is a compromise method, as the downsampling of points increases the computation speed, the original information is lost in the meantime. The advantage of the proposed Voxel-to-Voxel GICP is to improve the efficiency while preserving the information in the original data. The comparison between traditional GICP and the proposed method is tested on the KITTI dataset to verify this point.

We compared the performance of Voxel-to-Voxel GICP, Fast-GICP [38], and GICP implementation in Point Cloud Library (PCL-GICP) [35] by applying different downsampling resolutions to the raw point cloud data. For the three chosen registration methods, only scan-to-scan matching is considered. The experiments are performed on 2000 consecutive point cloud pairs from the KITTI dataset [34] in the different sequences. The covariance voxelization resolutions mentioned in 3.2 are set as two times of point cloud downsample resolutions. Note that the Voxel-to-Voxel GICP is applied to the full set of point clouds without the process of ground extraction, joint matching, and scan-to-mapping registration.

The average relative pose error (RPE) [37] and the average computation time are shown in Fig. 6. In the plots, we can see that the average error increases and the average computation time decreases, as the downsample resolution increases. In Fig. 6(a), the accuracy of the proposed Voxel-to-Voxel GICP and Fast-GICP [38] remain the same, while the efficiency of the proposed method is better than Fast-GICP at every downsample resolution of the input data. From this, we can see that the proposed Voxel-to-Voxel GICP method is able to improve the computational efficiency while maintaining the registration accuracy.

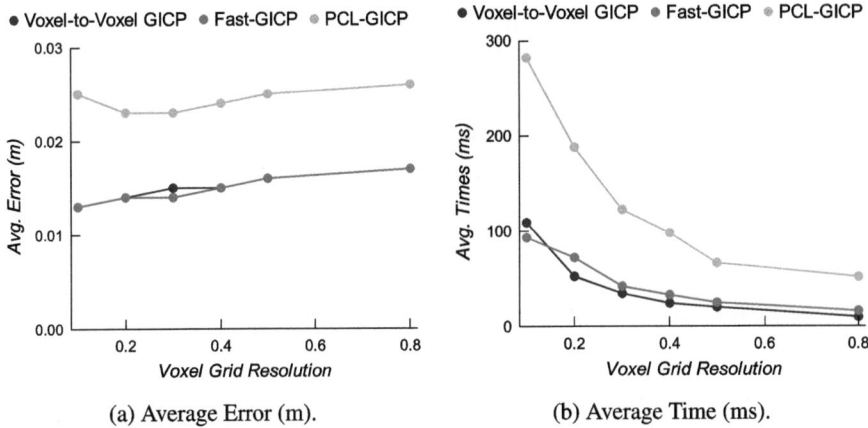

(a) Average Error (m).   (b) Average Time (ms).

Fig. 6. Different Voxel Resolutions Comparison. The plot shows the comparison result of average computing errors and times by applying different downsample resolutions on raw data.

4.2 Ablation Study of PR-GPF

To evaluate the performance of ground extraction, experiments are conducted based on the SemanticKITTI dataset [36], and the points with annotation of road, parking, sidewalks, other-ground, lane-marking, and terrain labels are considered as ground truth ground points. The accuracy metric as defined in (16) is chosen to quantitatively evaluate the accuracy and robustness of PR-GPF. In (16), N_{TP} and N_{TN} are the number of points correctly classified as ground and non-ground respectively, N_{FP} and N_{FN} are the number of points incorrectly classified as ground and non-ground, respectively. For comparison, the GPF and LineFit methods are selected. The result is shown in Table 1, where μ and σ are the mean and standard deviation of the accuracy on different semantic KITTI sequences. As shown in Table 1, PR-GPF shows more accurate and robust results on most of the sequences in SemanticKITTI [36].

$$accuracy = \frac{N_{TP} + N_{TN}}{N_{TP} + N_{TN} + N_{FP} + N_{FN}} \quad (16)$$

Table 1. Accuracy Result of PR-GPF on SemanticKITTI.

	PR-GPF μ (%)	PR-GPF σ (%)	GPF μ (%)	GPF σ (%)	LineFit μ (%)	LineFit σ (%)
00	**95.32**	**1.56**	94.15	6.09	94.61	3.74
01	**90.80**	4.96	84.17	13.64	89.29	**3.48**
02	**92.76**	4.30	90.37	8.11	91.09	**4.13**
03	85.92	**7.59**	**86.22**	8.46	82.35	9.06
04	**92.43**	2.34	90.44	3.60	92.40	**2.29**
05	93.80	**1.66**	93.08	4.02	**94.34**	1.98
06	**94.98**	**1.33**	85.95	6.27	89.41	2.16
07	95.48	**1.14**	95.66	2.93	**95.94**	2.61
08	**94.26**	**2.54**	89.06	9.41	92.15	4.81
09	**91.45**	**3.90**	86.63	12.22	91.36	5.32
10	**91.42**	4.28	89.01	6.99	90.85	**3.96**

4.3 Ablation Study of Ground Optimization

In the LiDAR Odometry problem, the pose of six Degrees of Freedom (DoF) is estimated, which is often represented by SE(3) Lie groups. The SE(3) poses can be converted into six DoF variables of Euler angles and translation vector in the Euclidean space ($[\theta_{roll}, \theta_{pitch}, \theta_{yaw}, \Delta x, \Delta y, \Delta z]$), which is shown in Fig. 7.

To evaluate the performance of GMLO in reducing the drifting error of the vertical direction, the estimation error for the three DoFs which are related to the vertical direction (roll angle, pitch angle, and Δz) is analyzed, and the Relative Pose Error (RPE) [37] is applied as the error metric. The test results of LeGO-LOAM [16] and GMLO are compared because LeGO-LOAM also uses a similar joint scan-matching method by associating ground point costs with non-ground point costs. For the test data, three of the sequences from the KITTI dataset [34] are selected, which consist of rich uphill and downhill scenarios. The

Table 2. Average Relative Pose Error (RPE) of Vertical Direction Degree of Freedom (DoF)

Sequence	Method	Roll (°)	Pitch (°)	Δ Z (m)
02	GMLO	0.067	0.037	0.061
	LeGO-LOAM	0.170	0.165	0.119
05	GMLO	0.049	0.035	0.017
	LeGO-LOAM	0.126	0.129	0.025
10	GMLO	0.062	0.037	0.013
	LeGO-LOAM	0.166	0.184	0.056

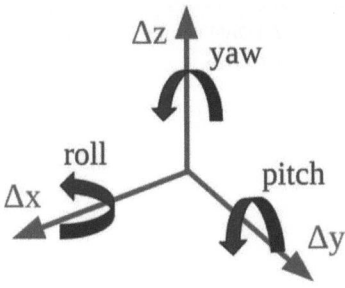

Fig. 7. SE(3) poses represented in Euclidean space. The estimation result of $[\theta_{roll}, \theta_{pitch}, \Delta z]$ are used for ablation study since these DoFs are more related with the ground optimization of GMLO.

results are shown in Table 2. From this, we can know that the proposed GMLO is effective in reducing the drifting error of vertical direction estimation, and the performance of GMLO in this aspect is better than LeGO-LOAM.

4.4 Ablation Study of Memory Optimization

To analyze GMLO's performance on memory saving, the point number of historical LiDAR mapping of GMLO is measured and compared with A-LOAM on KITTI sequence 00, which is shown in Fig. 8. From the figure, the memory cost of A-LOAM grows with time linearly, which will cause overflow in life-long applications. In contrast, GMLO is able to discard old historical data by Map Deque and the number of points storage is not growing with time.

4.5 KITTI Odometry Evaluation

The performance of GMLO is evaluated based on the KITTI Odometry Benchmark [34] through comparing with Fast-GICP [38], A-LOAM [15], and LeGO-LOAM [16]. The percentage error metric considered is defined by the KITTI Odometry Benchmark with translational errors for all possible subsequences of length (100, ..., 800) meters.

Table 3 shows the evaluation results, the best results among the considered methods for each sequence are bolded. The results indicate that our method is able to achieve the best localization performance among the benchmarks on 8 out of 11 sequences.

The localization result of KITTI sequence 00 is shown in Fig. 9. As shown in the figure, GMLO can significantly reduce the vertical estimation error comparing with existing state-of-the-art LiDAR Odometry methods. The trajectory plots of KITTI sequences 01-10 are shown in Fig. 10 from left to right.

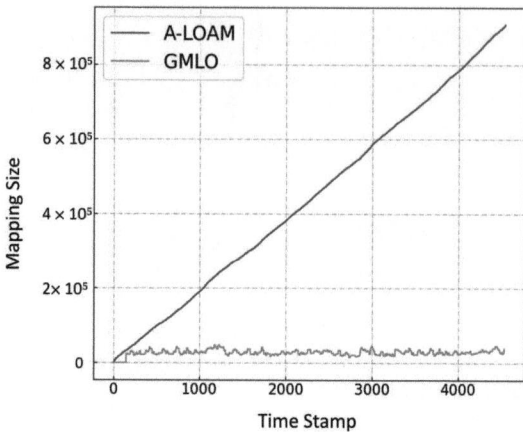

Fig. 8. Point number in storage comparison with A-LOAM. LiDAR Odometry methods often contains Scan-to-Mapping procedure which requires storage of historical mapping data. To evaluate the memory optimization of GMLO, the number of points in storage measured on KITTI sequence 00 is shown with the comparison of A-LOAM. The x-axis is the time stamp number, the y-axis is the number of points in storage.

4.6 Computational Efficiency

The average time of GMLO's procedures is measured with an Intel i5-12400F CPU, including the voxelization described in Sect. 3.2, PR-GPF described in Sect. 3.3, Joint Matching described in Sect. 3.4, and Scan-to-Mapping described in Sect. 3.5. Time cost measured in millisecond of GMLO on KITTI Sequence 00

Table 3. Absolute Trajectory Error (ATE) Evaluation based on the KITTI Dataset (%)

	GMLO (Proposed)	Fast GICP	A-LOAM	LeGO-LOAM
00	**1.01**	1.03	1.32	1.38
01	2.35	7.76	**1.88**	28.03
02	**1.20**	1.63	4.99	2.14
03	1.46	**1.24**	1.35	1.21
04	**0.82**	1.23	1.05	1.27
05	**0.59**	0.83	0.77	0.91
06	**0.58**	0.62	0.66	0.80
07	**0.51**	0.54	0.74	0.74
08	1.12	**1.03**	1.05	1.40
09	**0.93**	1.03	1.26	1.25
10	**0.89**	1.24	1.31	1.70

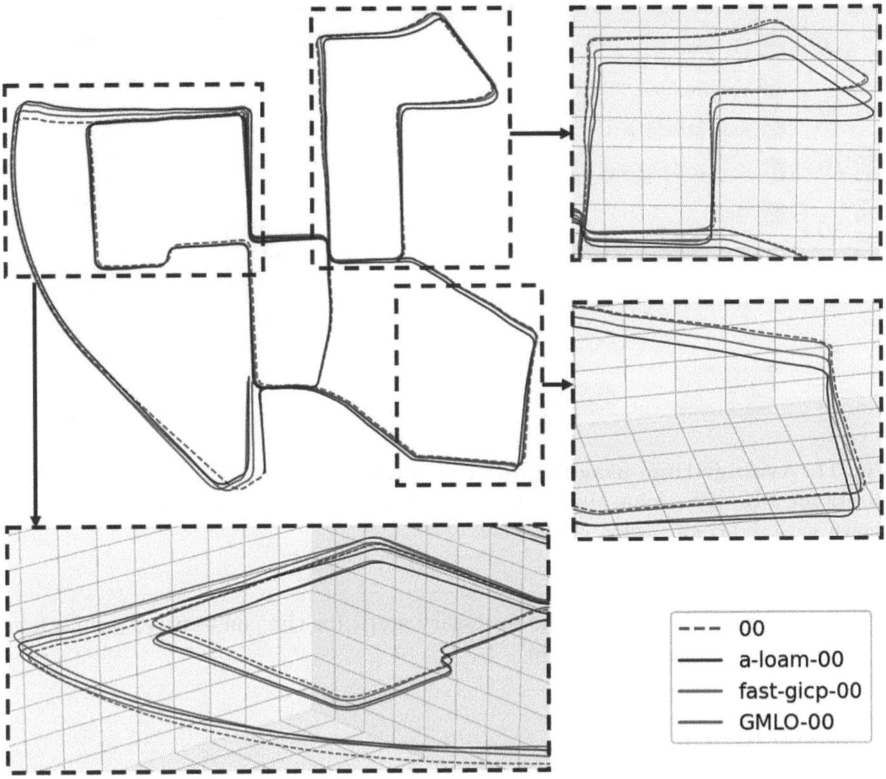

Fig. 9. Result comparison of GMLO, Fast-GICP and A-LOAM on KITTI 00. In the figure, several areas are zoomed and switched viewing angle in order to fully demonstrate the performance of GMLO.

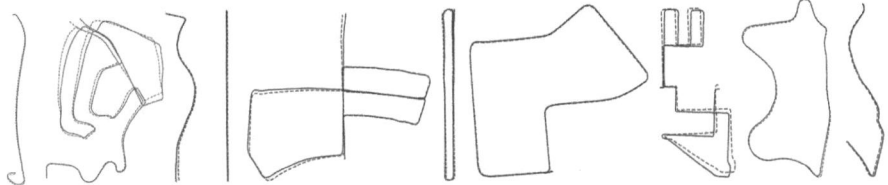

Fig. 10. Evaluation results of GMLO on KITTI Dataset 01-10. Ground truths are plotted in gray dotted line.

is shown in Fig. 11 with different colors, the total time per frame is also plotted in the figure. Since the typical mechanical LiDAR has a data frequency of 10 Hz, a processing time that less than 100 ms will guarantee the LiDAR Odometry to operate in real-time. The result of time statistics shows that GMLO is able to achieve real-time performance on CPU environment. Noted that the time-consuming part Scan-to-Mapping will not be activated for most of the point

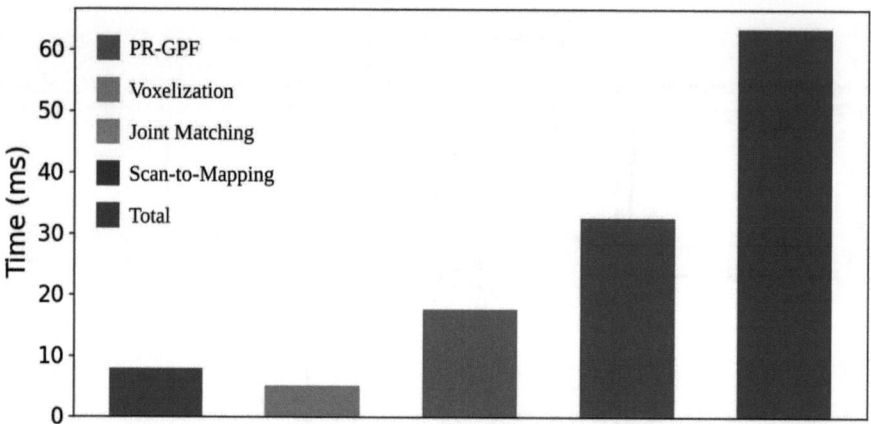

Fig. 11. Average time usage of different procedures in GMLO. Including Voxelizationn, PR-GPF, Joint-Matching and Scan-to-Mapping. Average total time cost is shown with red color, which is 63.47 ms.

cloud data, the total time of the necessary steps for the consecutive point cloud pairs matching is less than 40 ms.

5 Conclusion

This paper proposed a Ground and Memory Optimized LiDAR Odometry (GMLO) method, which is a novel, accurate, and lightweight registration-based approach. This approach takes advantage of ground information which is extracted and incorporated via the PR-GPF and joint scan-matching method. Additionally, a scan-to-mapping method is proposed to reduce the memory cost of GMLO. Evaluation of the proposed GMLO demonstrates that it provides state-of-the-art localization for autonomous vehicles with real-time performance, verifying the effectiveness of PR-GPF, the ground and memory optimization. For future works, GMLO can be applied to additional sensor inputs, such as IMU and camera, to implement a multiple sensor fusion SLAM framework.

References

1. Visvizi, A., Lytras, M.D., Damiani, E., Mathkour, H.: Policy making for smart cities: innovation and social inclusive economic growth for sustainability. J. Sci. Technol. Policy Manage. **9**(2), 126–133 (2018). https://doi.org/10.1108/jstpm-07-2018-079
2. Lv, B., et al.: Lidar-enhanced connected infrastructures sensing and broadcasting high-resolution traffic information serving Smart Cities. IEEE Access **7**, 79895–79907 (2019). https://doi.org/10.1109/access.2019.2923421

3. Syamal, S., Huang, C., Petrunin, I.: Enhancing object detection and localization through multi-sensor fusion for Smart City Infrastructure. In: 2024 IEEE International Workshop on Metrology for Automotive (MetroAutomotive), vol. 32, pp. 41–46 (2024). https://doi.org/10.1109/metroautomotive61329.2024.10615661
4. Bresson, G., et al.: Simultaneous localization and mapping: a survey of current trends in autonomous driving. IEEE Trans. Intell. Veh. **2**(3), 194–220 (2017). https://doi.org/10.1109/tiv.2017.2749181
5. Kazerouni, I.A., Fitzgerald, L., Dooly, G., Toal, D.: A survey of state-of-the-art on visual SLAM. Expert Syst. Appl. **205**, 117734 (2022). https://doi.org/10.1016/j.eswa.2022.117734
6. Chen, X., et al.: Range image-based lidar localization for autonomous vehicles. In: 2021 IEEE International Conference on Robotics and Automation (ICRA) [Preprint] (2021). https://doi.org/10.1109/icra48506.2021.9561335
7. Besl, P.J., McKay, N.D.: A method for registration of 3-D shapes. IEEE Trans. Pattern Anal. Mach. Intell. **14**(2), 239–256 (1992). https://doi.org/10.1109/34.121791
8. Chen, Y., Medioni, G.: Object modeling by registration of multiple range images. In: Proceedings of the 1991 IEEE International Conference on Robotics and Automation [Preprint] (1991). https://doi.org/10.1109/robot.1991.132043
9. Segal, A., Haehnel, D., Thrun, S.: Generalized-ICP. In: Robotics: Science and Systems V [Preprint] (2009). https://doi.org/10.15607/rss.2009.v.021
10. Serafin, J., Grisetti, G.: NICP: dense normal based point cloud registration. In: 2015 IEEE/RSJ International Conference on Intelligent Robots and Systems (IROS) [Preprint] (2015). https://doi.org/10.1109/iros.2015.7353455
11. Ramalingam, S., Taguchi, Y.: A theory of minimal 3D point to 3D plane registration and its generalization. Int. J. Comput. Vision **102**(1–3), 73–90 (2012). https://doi.org/10.1007/s11263-012-0576-x
12. Billings, S.D., Boctor, E.M., Taylor, R.H.: Iterative most-likely point registration (IMLP): a robust algorithm for computing optimal shape alignment. PLOS ONE **10**(3) (2015). https://doi.org/10.1371/journal.pone.0117688
13. Fitzgibbon, A.W.: Robust registration of 2D and 3D point sets. Image Vis. Comput. **21**(13–14), 1145–1153 (2003). https://doi.org/10.1016/j.imavis.2003.09.004
14. Deschaud, J.-E.: IMLS-slam: Scan-to-model matching based on 3D data. In: 2018 IEEE International Conference on Robotics and Automation (ICRA) [Preprint] (2018). https://doi.org/10.1109/icra.2018.8460653
15. Zhang, J., Singh, S.: Low-drift and real-time lidar odometry and mapping. Auton. Robot. **41**(2), 401–416 (2016). https://doi.org/10.1007/s10514-016-9548-2
16. Shan, T., Englot, B.: Lego-loam: lightweight and ground-optimized lidar odometry and mapping on variable terrain. In: 2018 IEEE/RSJ International Conference on Intelligent Robots and Systems (IROS) [Preprint] (2018). https://doi.org/10.1109/iros.2018.8594299
17. Zhou, P., et al.: T-loam: truncated least squares lidar-only odometry and mapping in Real time. IEEE Trans. Geosci. Remote Sens. **60**, 1–13 (2022). https://doi.org/10.1109/tgrs.2021.3083606
18. Zheng, F., Liu, Y.-H.: Visual-odometric localization and mapping for ground vehicles using SE(2)-XYZ constraints. In: 2019 International Conference on Robotics and Automation (ICRA) [Preprint] (2019). https://doi.org/10.1109/icra.2019.8793928
19. Su, Y., et al.: GR-LOAM: LIDAR-based sensor fusion slam for ground robots on complex terrain. Robot. Auton. Syst. **140**, 103759 (2021). https://doi.org/10.1016/j.robot.2021.103759

20. Zheng, F., Tang, H., Liu, Y.-H.: Odometry-vision-based ground vehicle motion estimation with SE(2)-constrained SE(3) poses. IEEE Trans. Cybern. **49**(7), 2652–2663 (2019). https://doi.org/10.1109/tcyb.2018.2831900
21. Bogoslavskyi, I., Stachniss, C.: Fast range image-based segmentation of sparse 3D laser scans for online operation. In: 2016 IEEE/RSJ International Conference on Intelligent Robots and Systems (IROS) [Preprint] (2016). https://doi.org/10.1109/iros.2016.7759050
22. Wang, H., et al.: F-LOAM: fast lidar odometry and mapping. In: 2021 IEEE/RSJ International Conference on Intelligent Robots and Systems (IROS) [Preprint] (2021). https://doi.org/10.1109/iros51168.2021.9636655
23. Chen, K., et al.: Direct LIDAR ODOMETRY: fast localization with dense point clouds. IEEE Robot. Autom. Lett. **7**(2), 2000–2007 (2022). https://doi.org/10.1109/lra.2022.3142739
24. Fischler, M.A., Bolles, R.C.: Random sample consensus: a paradigm for model fitting with applications to image analysis and automated cartography. Read. Comput. Vision 726–740 (1987). https://doi.org/10.1016/b978-0-08-051581-6.50070-2
25. Zermas, D., Izzat, I., Papanikolopoulos, N.: Fast segmentation of 3D point clouds: a paradigm on LIDAR data for Autonomous Vehicle Applications. In: 2017 IEEE International Conference on Robotics and Automation (ICRA) [Preprint] (2017). https://doi.org/10.1109/icra.2017.7989591
26. Narksri, P., et al.: A slope-robust cascaded ground segmentation in 3D point cloud for autonomous vehicles. In: 2018 21st International Conference on Intelligent Transportation Systems (ITSC) [Preprint] (2018). https://doi.org/10.1109/itsc.2018.8569534
27. Himmelsbach, M., Hundelshausen, F.V., Wuensche, H.-J.: Fast segmentation of 3D point clouds for ground vehicles. In: 2010 IEEE Intelligent Vehicles Symposium [Preprint] (2010). https://doi.org/10.1109/ivs.2010.5548059
28. Byun, J., Na, K., Seo, B., Roh, M.: Drivable road detection with 3D point clouds based on the MRF for intelligent vehicle. In: Mejias, L., Corke, P., Roberts, J. (eds.) Field and Service Robotics. STAR, vol. 105, pp. 49–60. Springer, Cham (2015). https://doi.org/10.1007/978-3-319-07488-7_4
29. Chen, T., et al.: Gaussian-process-based real-time ground segmentation for Autonomous Land Vehicles. J. Intell. Robot. Syst. **76**(3–4), 563–582 (2013). https://doi.org/10.1007/s10846-013-9889-4
30. Velas, M., et al.: CNN for very fast ground segmentation in velodyne LIDAR data. In: 2018 IEEE International Conference on Autonomous Robot Systems and Competitions (ICARSC) [Preprint] (2018). https://doi.org/10.1109/icarsc.2018.8374167
31. He, D., et al.: SectorGSnet: sector learning for efficient ground segmentation of outdoor lidar point clouds. IEEE Access **10**, 11938–11946 (2022). https://doi.org/10.1109/access.2022.3146317
32. Zhang, M., Morris, D.D., Fu, R.: Ground segmentation based on loopy belief propagation for sparse 3D point clouds. In: 2015 International Conference on 3D Vision [Preprint] (2015). https://doi.org/10.1109/3dv.2015.76
33. Paigwar, A., et al.: GndNet: fast ground plane estimation and point cloud segmentation for autonomous vehicles. In: 2020 IEEE/RSJ International Conference on Intelligent Robots and Systems (IROS) [Preprint] (2020). https://doi.org/10.1109/iros45743.2020.9340979
34. Geiger, A., Lenz, P., Urtasun, R.: Are we ready for autonomous driving? The KITTI vision benchmark suite. In: 2012 IEEE Conference on Computer Vision and Pattern Recognition [Preprint] (2012). https://doi.org/10.1109/cvpr.2012.6248074

35. Rusu, R.B., Cousins, S.: 3D is here: point cloud library (PCL). In: 2011 IEEE International Conference on Robotics and Automation [Preprint] (2011). https://doi.org/10.1109/icra.2011.5980567
36. Behley, J., et al.: SemanticKITTI: a dataset for semantic scene understanding of Lidar sequences. In: 2019 IEEE/CVF International Conference on Computer Vision (ICCV) [Preprint] (2019). https://doi.org/10.1109/iccv.2019.00939
37. MichaelGrupp. MichaelGrupp/Evo: Python package for the evaluation of odometry and SLAM, GitHub (2024). https://github.com/MichaelGrupp/evo. Accessed 18 Aug 2024
38. Koide, K., et al.: Voxelized GICP for fast and accurate 3D point cloud registration. In: 2021 IEEE International Conference on Robotics and Automation (ICRA) [Preprint] (2021). https://doi.org/10.1109/icra48506.2021.9560835

Author Index

B
Bi, Jingyun 299

C
Chaini, Sai Sambhab 229
Chen, Menglin L. N. 324
Chen, Taiming 20
Chen, Xiaofeng 60
Chen, Yanfeng 258
Cheng, Zhimin 240
Cheng, Zhiming 175, 330
Chong, Peter Han Joo 73, 131, 229
Chu, Kai-Fung 361
Cui, Haixia 271
Cui, Xiangyu 240

D
Dai, Hong-Ning 47
Dematawaarachchi, Hasini Prabodhika 73
Deng, Zengjie 271
Ding, Cao 90
Ding, Haili 385
Dissanayake, Manoj Bandara 73
Duan, Xuting 117

F
Fang, Kaiduo 414

G
Gong, Yongsheng 161
Guo, Audrey Christine 147
Guo, Cai 47
Guo, Xuanzhi 175

H
He, Jianhua 161, 310, 345
He, Qinwei 34

Hei, Yuekun 117
Ho, Ivan Wang-Hei 90
Hota, Lopamudra 131, 229
Hou, Lanxiang 330
Hu, Haibo 215
Hu, Ting 385
Huang, Chao 373

I
Iida, Fumiya 361
Indrasiri, Shamika Lakshan 73

J
Jia, Yanmei 147, 310

K
Kong, Chun Ho 215
Kumar, Arun 131, 229

L
Lam, Albert Y. S. 361
Lan, Tian 34
Lau, Francis C. M. 187
Lei, Tao 271
Li, Anping 60
Li, Hongmei 60
Li, Jinze 3
Li, Menghan 161
Li, Peiya 258
Li, Peng 34
Li, Shilei 60
Li, Sijie 324
Li, Yang 117
Li, Yueyao 324
Liang, Haoqi 330
Liang, Jing 258
Lin, Wei 200

Liu, Junwei 20
Liu, Mengda 310
Liu, Tong 200
Lu, Lu 147, 161, 310, 345

M
Ma, Deen 282
Ma, Xianping 240
Mao, Liang 175, 330
Mei, Xutao 108
Meng, Xiangjuan 60
Mu, Feng 60

N
Nakano, Kimihiko 108
Ngai, Edith C. H. 3
Niu, Guanchong 175, 330

P
Peng, Fei 385
Priyadarshini, Prangya 131
Pun, Man-On 175, 240, 330

R
Ren, Ruiqi 402

S
Shen, Defan 310
Shu, Wake 175
Song, Rui 414
Sudheera, Kalupahana Liyanage Kushan 73
Sun, Jiayi 330

T
Tao, Bishenghui 47
Tian, Hewei 345

V
van den Bos, Chris 34
Visee, Richard 34

W
Wang, Taotao 282
Wang, Wanshu 108
Wang, Yixin 20
Wang, Zheng 108

X
Xie, Xinyan 310
Xie, Yue 361
Xiong, Jian 345
Xu, Jinfeng 3
Xu, Wenjie 20
Xu, Wenzheng 20

Y
Yan, Shaokui 385
Yang, Bo 108
Yang, Jingyao 60
Yang, Liguo 60
Yang, Qing 282
Yang, Shuo 3
Yang, Xiaolong 117
Ye, Xiao 60
Yu, Zhitao 175

Z
Zhang, Hangfei 147
Zhang, Runxin 161, 345
Zhang, Shengli 282
Zhang, Xinyu 324
Zhang, Yuheng 161
Zhang, Zheng 402
Zhao, Chonghe 282
Zhou, Xinyu 299
Zhou, Yangyang 373
Zhou, Yuanfeng 385
Zhu, Jiajun 187

MIX
Papier aus verantwortungsvollen Quellen
Paper from responsible sources
FSC® C105338

If you have any concerns about our products,
you can contact us on
ProductSafety@springernature.com

In case Publisher is established outside the EU,
the EU authorized representative is:
**Springer Nature Customer Service Center GmbH
Europaplatz 3, 69115 Heidelberg, Germany**

Printed by Libri Plureos GmbH
in Hamburg, Germany